CONRAD EMIL LINDBERG

Christian Dogmatics and Notes on the History of Dogma

First published by Just and Sinner 2021

Just and Sinner

Ithaca, NY 14850

www.JSPublishing.org

First edition

ISBN: 978-1-952295-54-6

This book was professionally typeset on Reedsy.
Find out more at reedsy.com

Contents

Introduction

The Science of Theology is generally divided into four main divisions: Exegetical, Historical, Systematic, and Practical Theology. Exegetical Theology constitutes the foundation; Historical Theology gathers and supplies the material for the doctrinal edifice; Systematic Theology is the edifice itself; while Practical Theology constitutes the adornment of the building and indicates the purposes for which it is to be used. Among the disciplines of Systematic Theology, Dogmatics occupies the chief place.

Dogmatics is that science which systematically develops and defines the Christian dogmas mediated by faith in conformity with the teaching of the Bible and the Church.

This science includes the following seven divisions: 1) Theology; 2) Anthropology; 3) Christology; 4) Soteriology; 5) Pneumatology; 6) Ecclesiology; 7) Eschatology.

The study of Dogmatics should include also the most important parts of the history of dogma.

The History of Dogma is that part of historical theology which sets forth the gradual development and formulation of the Christian doctrines as to their genesis, growth, more precise definition and final form during the various periods of Church History.

The principal periods are the following:

I. *The Apologetical Period* from 70 to 254 A. D. (Death of Origen).

II. *The Polemical Period* from Origen to John of Damascus (254—754 A. D.).

III. *The Catholic Scholastic Period* from John of Damascus to the Reformation (754—1517).

IV. *The Reformation Or Protestant Scholastic Period* from the beginning of the Reformation to Leibnitz and Wolff (1517—1716 or 1754).

V. *The Speculative And Modern Critical Period.*

1

Theology

Theology constitutes that part of Dogmatics which treats of the doctrine of God and includes the following main subjects: The Existence of God, Natural Revelation, Supernatural Revelation, God as the Absolute Personality, the Divine Attributes, the Doctrine of the Trinity, Election, Creation, Providence, the Good Angels and the Evil Angels.

Opinions differ as to whether the proofs for the existence of God together with the doctrines of natural and supernatural revelation should be included in Dogmatics. Strictly speaking, these should be treated in Prolegomena or Apologetics. Different opinions have also been expressed concerning the place of Angelology in the dogmatic system.

§1. Concerning the Existence of God.

Christian Dogmatics presupposes God's existence. If God did not exist, no theology could be written. Every man is certain of his own existence and is likewise convinced that other men exist. Whatever certain philosophical systems may present concerning the reality of the world, but few doubt its existence. Inasmuch as it cannot be proved that man and the world are eternal, they must have had a beginning, and in such case, necessarily a cause. The concept of causality has therefore great weight in proving God's existence. This concept is also of the greatest importance in relation to the proof of God's existence which is based on our idea concerning a higher being. It may likewise be stated as a generally acknowledged fact that religion is the basic element in human personality. The existence of God belongs to the content of religion and is therefore as certain as the existence of man himself. In accordance with the concept of causality as a proof of God's existence we consider God as a cause by reason of the fact that we know ourselves as causes. We know ourselves as causes because we are conscious of our will. To will is to cause. Furthermore, by virtue of the exercise of the powers of our understanding we reach the conclusion that God is not only the first cause but that He is likewise the greatest intellect. The clearly revealed purpose in the world in things great and small has also great weight in the proof of God's existence. We may also state that our knowledge of God is acquired in the same manner as the knowledge of our fellow men. This latter knowledge is no more *a priori* and intuitive than our knowledge of God. Our heavenly Father becomes known in very much the same way as an earthly father and mother. Real character cannot be discerned with the physical eye nor comprehended by the senses. The child, however, soon learns to know its parents and the spirit that dwells in them. The children of men are likewise so constituted that they may know the Father of spirits through His works.

There are some who consider that the existence of God cannot be proved. Jacobi said: "A God that can be proved is no God." Kant denies that we can know anything of God through theoretical reasoning. Fichte made light of the proofs and stated that the Supreme Being was equivalent to the moral government of the world. Hegel, who proclaimed the identity of thought and being, simply stated that man's knowledge of God was the same as God's knowledge of Himself. Others have expressed opinions along the same or similar lines.

Even if objections may be raised against the common proofs for the existence of God, they nevertheless possess relative value, particularly from the viewpoint of Apologetics. Generally speaking, a Christian needs no such proofs, but in the hour of doubt and spiritual assault they become of great value and help.

In presenting arguments to prove the existence of God the following methods must be rejected: 1) When men essay to prove God's existence as they would that of a material object; 2) when proofs are asserted to be based on direct or intuitive experience; 3) *argumentum a tuto,* which implies that it is doubtful whether or not God exists, but that it is safer to assume His existence and does no harm, while it may be dangerous to deny His existence, if He does exist; 4) *argumentum ab utili,* which sets forth the great benefit of faith in a personal God.

The ordinary proofs of God's existence are the following:

1. *The Psychological Philosophical Proof*.

Human personality is made up of a union of receptivity, which finds expression in the emotions, and spontaneity, expressed in thought and will. From these three viewpoints the proof is divided as follows:

a. *The Eudaimonistic Proof*.

The human emotions find no rest in themselves nor in man. The world with all that is finitely good in it cannot satisfy the soul. Man feels that there must be something higher, something absolutely good, yea, an absolutely good personality. This absolute personality is God.

Augustine in his *Confessiones,* I. 1, says: *"Fecisti nos ad Te, et inquietum est cor nostrum, donec requiescat in Te."*

Kant presents a eudaimonistic proof, but confuses it with the moral proof. He says that harmony between the internal and external is not found on earth, for which reason there must be an absolute being who at least in another world must abolish discord between the desire for happiness and the requirements of the moral law.

b. *The Ontological Proof*.

The expression is derived from ἐκ τῶν ὄντων = from the essence of things. This is an *a priori* argument, but not in the sense that we should find in it a cause of God's existence. The argument proves His existence to us, but His existence is not dependent on the argument.

Man is so constituted that in all his reasoning he concludes that there must be an absolute being. He possesses an innate idea of an absolute personality or a supreme being. When through education he learns to know of God, his understanding apprehends the reality of this truth and his heart says yea and amen thereto. Man thinks of himself as real, and since God constitutes his highest thought, he conceives of God as the most real and the most perfect being (*ens realissimum et perfectissimum*). The most real and the most perfect being must exist not only in our thought but in reality. The proof has been presented in many ways. There are certain indications of it in Plato and Kleanthes. Some even assert that Plato suggested the proof, while Anselm merely perfected the syllogistic form. Augustine presents a proof that is analogous to the ontological proof. He said: "Nothing higher than truth can be thought, because it embraces all true being." He also declared that God as the highest truth must exist, because truth is sought at all times and by all men as something that is certain and unchangeable.

Anselm's Proof sets forth that man has an idea of a most perfect being, but perfection implies real existence. All men have an idea concerning God, even those who deny it, because it is impossible to deny something concerning which men have no idea. The thought of God is the idea of a being who is absolutely perfect, a personality than whom there is none higher. When we realize that we are imperfect and yet exist, it is self-evident that the most perfect being must exist; otherwise the most perfect being would be less perfect than we are. The idea of a most perfect being proves the existence of such a being. Existence is thus proven, otherwise we might imagine that a still higher being existed.

Descartes presents the second main form of the proof. He considered that all other ideas except the idea of God contain only the characteristics of possibility and contingency (*contingentia*), but the idea of God implies *necessaria et aeterna existentia*. Because we have ideas that possess no corresponding reality, therefore we are uncertain as to whether or not the idea of God may not be simply a product of our thought. But he endeavors to prove that the idea of God is innate, that this idea is not *adventicia*, because it could not possibly come wholly from without, nor yet *facticia* by abstraction, since it is only by abstraction from the finite that we reach the infinite. He considered that existence was inherent in the essence of God. Existence as a mark of perfection could not be thought of as an attribute. He taught that inasmuch as the idea of God was innate, therefore the cause could not be less real than the effect. The Cartesian Proof is twofold: 1) We have an idea concerning an absolutely perfect being and in this idea itself lies the proof of the existence of such a being. 2) We are imperfect, but nevertheless have an innate idea concerning a perfect being. Only a perfect being could give us this idea. The saying of Descartes: "I think, therefore I am," also proves the existence of God, as all human beings have not only self-consciousness, but also God-consciousness. We think God and cannot get rid of this thought; therefore, God exists just as surely as we exist.

Of course, the ontological proof has been criticised. The monk Gaunilo says that thinking a thing does not necessarily make it real. He uses the following figure: If someone in speaking of an island declared it to be more perfect than all other known islands, intending thereby to draw the conclusion that it existed, that it would not be the best and most perfect if it did not exist, then one would not know who was the more foolish, the one who presented the proof or the one who believed it. The existence of the island must be proved first. Anselm defended himself against Gaunilo.[1] It is evident that Gaunilo and Anselm argue from different viewpoints. Anselm said, if the island was necessary, he would find it. God is a necessary thought.

Kant enters an objection and declares that existence is not perfection and that an idea is just as perfect whether the corresponding reality exists or not. It is only through the processes of reason that man can know how he understands God. Hegel confuses human thought with the divine essence and denies a personal God. In accordance with the Hegelian philosophy the ontological proof is a true, speculative proof when the assertion: God is thought, therefore He exists, is changed to: God thinks,

---

1 *Hagenbach's History of Dogma*, §163.

that is, He exists.

The ontological proof is, however, not a mixture of thought and being, nor yet the result of a subjective thought. Rather man possesses an innate idea of God and in all his thinking proceeds from and returns to God, whose existence is just as certain as his own self-consciousness.

c. *The Ethico-Theological Proof.*

The will of man cannot be ethically determined by any human will, nor in the last instance can it be determined by impersonal nature. The human will points to a personal God by whom it is materially determined so that the formal freedom receives its proper content. This proof has two forms or names: 1) *Argumentum a conscientia recti* or *the proof of conscience*, which implies that conscience is aware of the moral law and that man perceives an inner voice which convinces him of the existence of a higher being. 2) *Argumentum morale* or *the moral proof* by which man, conscious of the union of virtue and blessedness, draws the conclusion that a higher being must exist who shall reward the virtuous and punish the unrighteous.

This proof was presented by Cicero and Seneca. Later also by Abelard and Raimund of Sabunde. It was further developed by Kant.

2. THE HISTORICAL PROOF OR *ARGUMENTUM E CONSENSU GENTIUM.*

This proof stands in close relationship with the preceding one. It may, however, be counted one of the chief proofs, inasmuch as it sets forth the thought, not of individuals, but of whole peoples. The idea of God is found among all peoples. Every people has some form of worship. Objections have also been made against this proof, but the historical truth of the universality of the idea of God cannot be gainsaid.

This proof was set forth by Cicero and was often used by the Church Fathers, such as Clement of Alexandria, Cyprian and others.

3. THE COSMOLOGICAL PROOF OR *ARGUMENTUM A CONTINGENTIA MUNDI.*

The world is not self-caused. An absolute personality must exist who has caused it. We cannot go back interminably from cause to cause without finally reaching the first, from which all things proceed and which in itself is uncaused by anyone or anything. The first cause could not have been a primitive cell, since the first organism could not have been self-produced. The world must therefore be an *ens contingens* and created by God.

This proof was suggested by Plato and Aristotle. Augustine says in his *Confessiones*, X, Chapter VI, 9: "And what is this? I asked the earth and it answered, I am not he, and all that is therein gave the same answer. I asked the sea and the deep and all creeping things, and they answered, We are not thy God; look higher than us. I asked the sun, the moon and the stars. Neither are we the God whom thou seekest. And then I made answer to all these things round about me: Ye have told me concerning my God that ye are not He. Tell me something about Him! and with a loud voice they answered: He made us."

Thomas Aquinas presented the proof in three forms: a) According to Aristotle, from the motion in the world to a primary cause which is not moved by anything, *causa efficiens prima*; b) according to Diodorus of Tarsus and John of Damascus, from the unchangeableness of the world to the unchangeable being who is the cause of all change; c) according to Richard of St. Victor, from the accidental nature of the world to a necessary being who is *per se necessarium*.

Among the objections that have been raised against this proof we mention those of Kant. He says that man sees the world as it appears and not as it really is. The accidental nature of the world cannot be proved. Against this it may be urged that Kant misunderstood the relationship between spirit and nature. He should have proved first that the world appears different from what it is. Hume states that there is no analogy to the assertion that all things are caused by a cause outside the world. Hegel, who changes the causal relationship between God and the world into a state of substantiality, says that that which is temporal is mere appearance, simply external changing forms, but the substance of the world is unchangeable in all change.

This pantheistic objection is contradicted by the consciousness of man, which declares that the world is not determined by a world soul or by impersonal substance.

4. THE TELEOLOGICAL PROOF.

Design or purpose in the world points to an absolutely wise personality. This is an *a posteriori* argument. Purpose is *causa finalis.* Compare Janet's splendid work on Final Causes. Every effect must have an adequate cause, and where purpose is evident this cause must likewise be intelligent. We cannot describe or comprehend a piece of machinery save as we know its use and purpose. The teleological proof is one of the oldest, best and most convincing proofs of the existence of God.

The argument is presented in two forms: a) The *physicotheological,* when design in nature is considered; b) the *historical theological,* when plan and purpose in the history of the world are considered.

Among those who have presented this proof in one form or another the following may be mentioned. Anaxagoras stated that the guiding hand in the world was *νοῦς*. Socrates asked if this world could be kept in order by something which lacked understanding. Aristotle said that neither the Divine Being nor nature did anything in vain. Theophilus of Antioch set forth the figure of a ship and a helmsman. When we see the ship sailing along we conclude that there is a helmsman aboard. Minucius Felix pointed to the heavens and said that a being with the highest understanding must have set all in order. Athanasius remarks concerning the statues of Phidias that by viewing their form one could recognize the sculptor, and adds, "How much more certain must one not be, in viewing the heavens, that all these wonders have not arranged themselves, but are the work of a Creator." This proof occurs in one form or another in many other writers down to the time of Melanchthon, after which it was abandoned for a considerable period until the representatives of the Wolffian philosophy and the advocates of natural theology exerted their influence.

Many objections have been raised against this proof. Bacon of Verulam rejected *causa finalis* and set forth instead *causae efficientes* or the genetic method. Hume and Kant say that we know the world in very small part. We cannot have faith in an absolutely perfect being because the creator cannot be more perfect than his work. It is not certain that there is design in the world, however much it may so appear. Hegel says that this proof leads to the idea of a world soul. The Materialists say that the world is not a finished piece of work, but a workshop which produces its own tools. Moleschott says that the will is conditioned by external influences and that the thinking man is the sum of his sensual experience, or the sum of parents, time, space, atmosphere, sound, light, food and clothes. However, the Materialists have not proved their assertions. They have not proved that the principle of life is a modification of matter and as such the formative principle. Neither have they proved that the soul is a product of matter, nor that ideas are inductively derived from the same source. Even if the Darwinians could prove their doctrine of the original cell, this would still not be a proof that God does not exist. Rightly considered, evolution implies a wonderful teleology that points to an intelligent cause. The teleological proof is incontestably one of the best natural proofs of the existence of God.

§2. Natural Revelation.

The question of revelation and therefore also natural revelation is closely connected with the proofs of God's existence. If a God exists, He must reveal Himself in some way. Revelation means *to be revealed* and *to reveal*. God has actively revealed Himself in a general and special sense. In that way His existence has been proved. This reasoning may indeed be in a circle, but it is nevertheless true. Tholuck says: "Reasoning in a circle is not forbidden in the realm of truth. Is not every logical proof to a certain extent based on this reasoning? If the final conclusions were not found in the premises, how could it ever be derived therefrom?"

Revelatio Generalis, or General Revelation, is *that natural revelation of God through which He reveals Himself in the conscience of man, in the kingdom of nature, and in history.*

The invisible God reveals Himself in His works which reflect His attributes. But we could not know this, did He not reveal Himself in us. But God is also a living God who rules and therefore reveals Himself in the events of history. Someone has said that creation and history both conceal and reveal God. Creation and history are books written with consonants as the Hebrew Bible, while man in hearkening to the voice of conscience and reason supplies the vowel signs.

There is therefore a natural knowledge of God, *cognitio Dei naturalis,* which is partly *insita,* partly *acquisita.*

a. *Cognitio Insita* or *Innata,* which is also called constitutional or subjective, is the general conception of God which is found in the heart of every man as a remnant of the divine image.

To this so-called *scintillula notitiae* belongs the conscience, which in the first place is the voice of God in man, but also the voice of our deepest nature. The concept of conscience is expressed in the very name. Compare the expressions for conscience used in different languages. From the legislative point of view conscience is called *conscientia antecedens*; as a witness of special acts, *conscientia concomitans*; from the critical viewpoint, *conscientia subsequens.*

Quenstedt presents the following proofs of the existence of this *cognitio insita*: 1) The inherited distinction between good and evil; 2) the fear of the Supreme Divinity which is natural to all men; 3) terror of an evil conscience and the security of a good conscience; 4) the anguish of conscience when a crime has been committed; 5) the common testimony of all peoples; 6) the natural inclination to some form of religion; 7) moral laws produced by natural religion.

In the early days of the Church natural religion and the knowledge of God derived therefrom were also set forth. Compare the doctrine of *λογός σπερματικός* Justin Martyr says in *Apol.*, II: "Every man spoke in accordance with the measure of the *λογός σπερματικός* (the word planted among men), which he had received. Clement of Alexandria expresses himself as follows in *Stromata,* I, Chapter VII: "The husbandman among men is only one, viz., He who causes the rain to fall at all times, the Lord, the Word. The times and the places, which were the recipients, brought about the differences that occur." Tertullian in his XVII Apol. says: "Although burdened under the slavery of the body, although led astray by harmful habits, although weakened by passion, although under the dominion of false gods, yet whenever the soul comes to itself out of a condition of debauchery, or of sleep, or of sickness, and regains something of its natural health, it speaks of God, using no other expression, because this is the name of the only true God. 'God is great and good; may God grant it,' are expressions upon every tongue. It also bears witness that God is the judge. God sees! O beautiful testimony of the soul, which is naturally Christian! And when it makes use of these words it looks not up to the Capitoline Hill, but to heaven." Arnobius, C. Gent. 33: "Is there a human being that has not begun the first day of his life with the thought (as idea) of the great head? In whom has it not been implanted by nature, imprinted and impressed almost from the mother's womb, in whom is it not an inherited instinct, that He is King, Lord and Regent of all that exists?"

b. *Cognitio Acquisita*, which is also called objective, *is gained by considering the works and activity of God in the kingdom of nature and in history.*

Gerhard sets forth the following points among others: 1) The variety, beauty and order of nature; 2) the maintenance and government of creation; 3) the rich gifts that satisfy the wants of all creatures; 4) the divine retribution; 5) the miracles; 6) the prophecies; 7) the periodical destruction of earthly kingdoms; 8) the series of *causae efficientes* and *causae finales*.

This cognition, although imperfect and weak, is nevertheless true, since Paul calls it truth. Cf. Rom. 1:18ff. However, we must distinguish between this knowledge before and after the Fall. After the Fall it has been falsified and made imperfect, containing only a partial knowledge of God, His power, wisdom and providence. This knowledge is insufficient for salvation.

The natural revelation of God has, however, a threefold usefulness, as pointed out by Calovius: 1) *Utilitas paedagogica*, so that man seeks true knowledge; 2) *utilitas paedeutica*, which leads to moral and general education both within and without the Church; 3) *utilitas didactica,* because natural revelation can shed light upon the supernatural revelation.

§3. Supernatural Revelation.

Revelatio Specialis, or the Special Revelation, is *that external act of God by which He reveals Himself to man through the Logos, the personal Word, and through the Holy Scriptures, so that all men may receive saving knowledge of Him.*

This revelation is divided as follows: a. *immediata* or direct, b. mediata or indirect.

Hollazius presents the following *modi* for the direct revelation: 1) By the hearing of an articulated voice, 2) through sleep, 3) through ecstasy, 4) through urim and thummim, 5) through an inspiration, 6) through the Son.

1. THE POSSIBILITY OF A SPECIAL REVELATION.

Although it is evident since God exists that He can also reveal Himself, still the following points may be considered: 1) On the divine side there can be no obstacles, since God is able to do what He wills; 2) there is nothing to hinder such a revelation in the laws of nature, since God is the ruler of these laws; 3) on the human side there are no obstacles, because man is able to receive, know and examine such a revelation; 4) it cannot be proved that the truths of reason are violated by the special revelation.

The objections to the possibility of the supernatural revelation come principally from the Deists and the Pantheists.

The *Deists* object: a. That God after creation has withdrawn Himself from the world and left it to develop according to the laws of nature. A special revelation would disturb this order. While the Deists have not proved their contention, still it may be said that God never ceases to work. All nature is permeated by spiritual power and God is ever active in sustaining the universe in never-ceasing creational activity. The laws of nature do not develop from blind necessity, but are God's way of working.

b. The special revelation, if actual, would be a *post factum* activity and designed to improve the perfect creation of God, which would be unworthy of Him. In dealing with these and other objections we must consider the freedom of man and the disturbing influence of sin.

The *Pantheists* object: a. That a special revelation would militate against the immutability of God. But this immutability must not be considered as a cold and petrified immobility.

b. God and the world are one. Therefore if anything intervenes in nature that would militate against the laws of nature there arises a conflict with the divine essence. Clearly a world substance of this sort is no God. Pantheism cannot accept any other revelation than the manifestation of the absolute substance in nature and man.

2. THE NECESSITY OF A SUPERNATURAL REVELATION.

The necessity of a special revelation was recognized even by the heathens, such as Plato. The history of religion clearly demonstrates this necessity. The founder of every religion has claimed a special revelation. The history of philosophy itself reveals the need of a special revelation when we consider the contradictions and conflicts that have arisen on all the most important subjects.

The necessity of a special revelation is grounded in the need of salvation, the occasion for it being the Fall into sin. This revelation was accidental on the ground of sin as a presupposition, but it was not accidental in the sense that it could have been inhibited after sin had entered the world. Revelation was necessary from the divine viewpoint in order that the design and purpose of creation and salvation might be realized. Revelation was necessary for man because he was powerless to save himself from the power and condemnation of sin.

3. THE REALITY OF REVELATION.

The Christian Church is now in the world and Christianity is the dominating religion. The historical reality of Christ, His words and deeds, the testimony of the Apostles, the miracles, the fulfilment of prophecy, the content of the Holy Scriptures and the fruits of Christianity prove incontrovertibly the reality of revelation.

4. THE RELATION BETWEEN REASON AND REVELATION.

Reason has been defined in many ways, but we may say that reason consists in our power to comprehend necessary truths, while understanding is the ability to judge and draw conclusions. We may also say that reason sets forth the principles that are revealed by the light of nature and the conclusions that are based on these principles. They are divided as follows: 1) Organic, which belong to the mediating disciplines, such as grammar, logic, etc.; 2) philosophical: a. absolutely and unrestrictedly universal, which cannot be controverted by any argument, not even by Scripture, e. g., it is impossible for a thing to be and not to be at the same time; b. restrictedly universal, which are true to a certain extent, i. e., as far as human knowledge goes, but they are limited and may be invalidated through proof, e, g., the number of essences is the same as the number of persons. This assertion does not hold in the doctrine of the Trinity.

Concerning the use of the reason Hollazius says: "Reason is not the leader but the follower of theology. Hagar acts as the handmaid of her mistress, but does not command; when she seeks to command, she is driven from the sanctuary of the home." In theology reason is acknowledged as possessing organic and instrumental power, *usus organicus et instrumentalis,* but not a normal or material influence, *non usus principiorum philosophicorum normalis.*

Concerning the function of reason in theology the following division may be observed: 1) *usus organicus,* which sets forth the assistance rendered by grammar, logic, etc. in the work of exegesis; 2) *usus catascevasticus* or *edificativus,* which is the power of the sanctified reason to set forth the content of faith for edification. There is a natural knowledge of God, but it must always be subordinated to the revealed knowledge. When these two forms of knowledge do not appear to agree, the former must yield to the latter; when, however, they do agree, the latter strengthens the former; 3) *usus anascevasticus* or *destructivus* is the power of the reason to defeat error. In the first place Holy Scripture must supply the arguments, but in the second place philosophical arguments may be employed.

Of course we must distinguish between reason *per se* before the Fall and reason such as it is now, as well as between unregenerated and regenerated reason. The doctrines of faith are *supra rationem* and in reality *contra rationem corruptam*. We must likewise distinguish between the diverse character of the fields of the natural and the supernatural. In this manner an apparent contradiction will be avoided. For example, Gerhard and with him others set forth the following: When the philosopher says *ex nihilo nihil fieri,* sc. *per modum generationis,* he does not contradict the theologian who teaches *per modum creationis aliquid fieri ex nihilo.* In the same manner when the philosopher says that the virgin Mary could not give birth to a child and still remain a virgin, he does not contradict the theologian who says that it took place in a supernatural manner. A Christian and true philosophy does not conflict with theology, because their fields are different.

§4. Concerning the Being of God.

1. The Definition Or Conception Of God

A true theological knowledge cannot be obtained except through special revelation. Theology must be studied in the light of Christology. For this reason our Lord says in His high-priestly intercessory prayer: "This is life eternal, that they should know thee the only true God, and him whom thou didst send, even Jesus Christ." In Matt. 11:27 He says: "No one knoweth the Son, save the Father; neither doth any know the Father, save the Son, and he to whomsoever the Son willeth to reveal him." God cannot be defined in an adequate manner. We can only obtain an *aliqua descriptio, a definitio Dei nominalis.* In Isa. 40:18 we read: "To whom then will ye liken God? or what likeness will ye compare unto him?"

Gerhard says: "We are certainly able to know God, but not to comprehend Him, i. e., we cannot know Him completely, for He is infinite." Quenstedt defines God as *essentia spiritualis infinita* and Hollazius as *spiritus independens*. Some of the modern theologians define God as the absolutely harmonious life. Granfelt says, God is personal, holy love. The more recent orthodox theologians in Germany and Björling in Sweden emphasize the conception of absolute personality. There is no doubt that the best definition is to be obtained by considering God as the absolute personality. God is not an absolute undetermined substance, according to Spinoza, rather He is a personality who in Himself lives the life of everlasting love.

2. The Divine Being Defined And The Conception Of The Absolute Personality.

We may say that the being of God consists of two parts: a) *the formal*, or that God is self-conscious and self-determining; b) *the material*, or that God is love. The parts are therefore being, self-consciousness or thought, and self-determination or will, united in love, which is the qualitative factor. These parts abide in and through each other and are therefore equally primitive. The being cannot precede the knowing and the willing, for that would result in substance that is without consciousness or will. The knowing could not precede the being and the willing, for then God would become an empty form or idea without any corresponding reality. The willing could not precede the being and the knowing, for this would result in blind power. As an absolute personality God is therefore a unity, a union in love of being, thought and will. God is therefore one, for which reason we can say that true Theism is Monotheism. But Monotheism in no wise conflicts with the doctrine of the Trinity, but is rather explained by it, because as triune God is absolute personality both from the formal and the material point of view.

The unity of God comprises two parts: a) the *intensive*, by which God in His position of eternal independence is the union of all attributes of His being, which is called the *qualitative* unity; b) the *exclusive*, in accordance with which God is all that He is only by and through Himself, which is called the *numerical* unity. In accordance with the first part God is *perfect* by reason of the harmony between the being, the knowing and the willing. The will agrees with the being so that God is power; the thought agrees with the being so that God is truth; the will agrees with the absolute good so that God is the Holy One; the thought agrees with the absolute good so that God is wisdom. By reason of the second part God is *self-sufficient,* which constitutes His autarchy.

The harmony of the divine attributes in the unity of love from the internal point of view constitutes His *blessedness* and from the external point of view His *majesty.*

The conception of the absolute personality which expresses His being is set forth by Dogmaticians in the following manner: *God is a unity in love of being, knowing and willing, and by reason of this unity He is the perfect, self-sufficient and blessed majesty.*

In the Holy Scriptures the names of God express His being. The word "countenance" is also used to express God's being, as in the following passage: "I shall behold thy face in righteousness; I shall be satisfied, when I awake, with beholding thy form." The attributes of God's essence are set forth in their relation to the world, but in this connection the following passages may be quoted: "God is one" (Romans 3:30) ; "There is no God but one" (1 Cor. 8:4); "One God and Father of all" (Eph. 4:6); "For there is one God" (1 Tim. 2:5); "Your Father which is in heaven is perfect" (Matt. 5:48); "Neither is he served by men's hands, as though he needed anything" (Acts 17:25); "For as the Father hath life in himself, even so gave he to the Son also to have life in himself" (John 5:26). In 1 Tim. 6:15 God is called the blessed and only Potentate. In addition many passages could be quoted that describe the being, knowing and willing of God, and also that He is love.

John 4:24 "*πνεῦμα ὁ θεός*" is a most wonderful and remarkable definition of God. The omission of the article does not make the expression indefinite, but is the most definite and emphatic way of saying that God is the Spirit in the absolute sense. Spirit stands first in the original, and, therefore, occupies the most emphatic place, literally translated: "Spirit is God." He is not a spirit, but spirit in the fullest and highest sense. The only corresponding dogmatic expression is, God is the Absolute Personality. We human beings, although created in the image of God, cannot comprehend the infinite Spirit. Man knows partly his own spirit through his self-consciousness, but the Spirit of God man knows only by analogy. A divine self-consciousness is necessary to know the essence of God. Compare Matt. 11:27, where it is stated that only the Father knows the Son and the Son the Father. And when the Son revealeth the Father to the believers, the knowledge imparted is only relative.

When God is defined as absolute spirit and incorporeal, we should not look upon the divine Spirit as unreal. The spiritual essence of God is the most real substance. God as Spirit is more real than any phenomenon. The Spirit of God is more real than the soul or spirit of man, and the soul of man is more real than his body. The soul is not exposed to changes like the body, and at death the soul remains a spiritual entity just as real as before death. It is easier to think of the soul as intact after death than the body, because we know how the body dissolves. The reason, will and feeling occupy no space, but are nevertheless real. The soul, although naturally penetrating every part of the body, as an entity occupies no space. The forces or laws of nature, such as gravity, are invisible. The fact that a thing is invisible does not make it unreal. We do not see the soul, but we feel that the spiritual in us is our real being. God is just as real without a body as if He had one. God has no eyes and ears as we have, but it is self-evident that He sees and hears. Compare Ps. 94:9. God makes an impression on the human soul as really as matter does upon the human body. Compare Ps. 77:3: "I remember God and am disquieted." Although God has no body nor bodily organs, He still can manifest Himself. And the Son of God as incarnated has a body and will appear as the God-man with a glorified body in all eternity. Philip wanted to see the Father. He said to the Lord Jesus Christ: "Lord, show us the Father, and it sufficeth us. Jesus saith unto him, Have I been so long time with you, and dost thou not know me, Philip? he that hath seen me hath seen the Father." Philip desired to see a bodily manifestation just as he saw the Lord Jesus. The disciples did not understand that in knowing the character of Jesus Christ they also knew the character of the Father. They did not then realize that the divine essence is one that exists in three relative persons. Christ did not at that time explain that the hypostasis of the Father, as it is in reality, could not be seen with bodily eyes. We do not even see one another except in the picture form. The outward appearance is not the most important; the soul and character are essential. The Father has revealed Himself by means of many manifestations. Some of the disciples had heard His voice, as on the mount of transfiguration. The Holy Spirit also had revealed Himself.

God as absolute Spirit in the highest sense is also the absolute Personality. Personality implies self-consciousness and self-determination. Self-consciousness is the power which a rational being possesses of making itself the object of its own thought and of knowing that it has done so, and, therefore, it also knows the identity of subject and object. We must clearly discriminate between consciousness and self-consciousness. In consciousness the object is something different from the subject. An animal is conscious of another object, but never duplicates its own unity and contemplates itself. The animal has many experiences, but cannot refer them back to itself as a person can. There is no self-knowledge in an animal. Man is both conscious and self-conscious. But God is not first conscious and then self-conscious. God is eternally self-conscious. In the doctrine of the Trinity it is self-evident that the divine self-consciousness is trinal. But there are not three independent self-conscious persons. God is one, and there can be but one divine essence. Three separate and independent divine essences would be an axiomatic contradiction, because none of them would be absolute, and as a consequence none could be God or Absolute Personality. The doctrine of the divine unity was as important to the Israelites and Jews of old as the doctrines of the resurrection of Christ and justification by faith to the Christians. When the Old Testament people emigrated from Egypt their motto was: "Hear, O Israel: Jehovah our God is one Jehovah." If they did not fully understand the trinal unity, they were ready to die for the doctrine that God is one. God is one God and the only God. The unity of God is unique. God is not a unit, but a unity implying distinctions. God is blessed forever independently of the universe. His majesty is manifested to the rational beings. God was blessed before creation, being eternally blessed. As the material element of the conception of God as the absolute personality is His love within Himself independent of creation, it is plain that His blessedness belongs to His very nature, but on account of His love He created rational angels and man and also created for them a universe suitable to their condition.

But God is not a part of the universe and the universe is not a part of God. The All is not the infinite God. The Infinite and the universe are wholly diverse. God as infinite cannot be finite, and He is not limited by the finite world which He created according to His wisdom. The simplicity, spirituality and immutability of God also preclude the thought that God in His immanence is extended. When we say that God is the Absolute as a real person, we also reject such views as the following: God is an absolute idea, a universal mind, a world-soul, a moral order of the universe, etc.

3. Anti-Theistic Theories.

a. Pantheism. By this is meant the view that God and nature or that God and the entire universe are one and the same substance. All things temporal are considered as modifications or parts of the one substance. Pantheism therefore implies Monism and cannot be separated from Determinism. In considering the question of God's relation to the world, Pantheism is the opposite of Deism. Pantheism is said to be twofold: 1) *Acosmism*, or the Oriental Pantheism, according to which the world has been entirely merged in God. In this class are counted the Eleatics, such as Xenophanes, Parmenides and Zeno. Parmenides taught that being is not an abstract unity, but the only reality, an absolute unity and the only one. Being is likewise indivisible and unchangeable with neither beginning nor end. He also stated that being is identical with thought, for thought must be being; non-being is nothing. According to Parmenides the world has entirely entered into God or what he calls being. The world of phenomena is non-being and exists only in the thought of man; 2) *Atheism*, or the Occidental Pantheism, by which God is merged in the world. According to this view becoming is set forth, but not being.

Modern Pantheism began with Bruno, who was a forerunner of the most noted of all Pantheists, Spinoza. His system contained the ideas substance, attribute and mode. There exists only one substance. This substance he calls God. All separate existences are merely modifications of the substance. He considers the world as an accident of the divine substance. The substance has attributes, each of which gives expression in its way to the essence of the substance. These are thought and extension. God is thinking substance when considered from that point of view; He is extended substance when so considered. But the extension of the divine substance does not imply length or depth or shape. The attributes do not belong to the substance, for the substance excludes all determination. *Res cogitans* and *res extensa* are the same thing. The infinite substance appears in finite forms or *modi* which are like the waves of the sea. Therefore all that we see, yea, the entire universe, is nothing more than the modes of the attributes or of the substance.

Among idealistic Pantheists may be mentioned Fichte, Schelling and Hegel. Fichte represents Subjective Idealism, the identity of thought and being, of the subjective and the objective in the ego. Things as to their substance are not found outside the ego. Schelling represents the Objective Idealism, the identity of thought and being even independent of the ego. What Fichte calls the highest principle or the ego, Schelling calls the world soul. While Fichte sets forth the subjective ego as the principle of all being and knowing, Schelling endeavors to show that the objective non-ego or nature could just as well be set forth as the principle of being and knowing. Hegel is the representative of the Absolute Idealism; thought is the source of the indwelling concept and is the only reality and truth. The absolute ego realizes itself in the non-ego. Hegel's Pantheism is logical. He said that reason is the organ of philosophy. The absolute is the result which the reason reaches through the exercise of dialectical thinking from undetermined being. According to Hegel all that exists is simply the revelation of God in 'the exercise of thought. God is everything and nothing. He is all because He is the only substance that sustains all consciousness and every existing thing. He is nothing because He is conscious of Himself only through man. Clearly such systems conflict with Christianity.

b. *Materialism.* Materialism says that matter is the only substance, from which everything is derived. There is therefore no spiritual essence either in the universe or in man. The anti-theistic theory appears in so many variations that it is difficult to give a precise definition. Materialism may be divided into two main divisions: 1) *The ancient,* which is represented by Democritus and Epicurus; 2) *the modern,* which is represented by Hobbes, whose materialism, however, was not complete, La Mettrie, von Holbach, Darwin, Herbert Spencer, Huxley and others. The last named do not desire to be classed as Materialists, but they are clearly materialistic philosophers and their positions are anti-theistic.

c. *Positivism.* This designation was originated by Auguste Comte who may be said to be the foremost champion of Positivism. The main principles of Positivism are not new, for they were set forth in ancient times by Protagoras and in modern times by Hume and Kant. Comte has, however, formulated into a system the ideas that are characteristic of Positivism. It is not easy to define Positivism, for skeptical, materialistic and general atheistic tendencies bear the name of Positivism. Positivism forms a link between Skepticism and Materialism. Comte says that we know nothing but physical phenomena and their laws. He rejects both *causa efficiens* and *causa finalis.* The world phenomena has not been produced by any supernatural cause. Religion in the ordinary sense was not needed and is considered as a weakness. The religion of Positivism presented as objects of worship the earth, the universe and humanity. This is enough to show the anti-Theism of Positivism.

4. Notes On The History Of Dogma.

A. *Concerning the Comprehensibility and Nature of God.*

When we consider the development of the dogma during the different periods we find that most thinkers take the position that God cannot be understood or defined in an adequate manner. Among those who took another view were Arius and especially Eunomius. Duns Scotus held the view that man could attain essential knowledge. Dionysius the Areopagite and John Scotus Erigena were both influenced by Pantheism, as were also Bohme, Servetus and others later on. There were some that held anthropomorphic views. The Alexandrian school and Origen fought against them. Tertullian laid emphasis upon the substantiality of God without ascribing to Him a material body.

Justin Martyr says that there is no name for the Father of all, who is unborn. For by what name He might be called, the person who gave Him the name would be the older. The words Father, God, Creator, Lord and Master are not names but designations derived from His good works. Clement Of Alexandria says that we can tell, not what God is, but what He is not, and he removes from God all finite characteristics. God is neither genus nor species, substance nor accident. Even after giving ourselves to Christ our consciousness of Him is more negative than positive. His views were not anthropomorphic. Tertullian ascribed to God a body, not an ordinary human body, but a form of existence. He maintained that nothing could be without bodily form except that which did not exist. However, we cannot count him among the anthropomorphists. Origen said that God was incomprehensible and past finding out. As the brilliance of the sun exceeds the light of a lantern, so the glory of God exceeds our conception of Him.

The *Audians*, so-called from their founder, Audius of Mesopotamia, held anthropomorphic views of God. Athanasisus holds that only a pure and sinless being can see God. God cannot be seen nor comprehended. His essence cannot be discovered by man and He is above all substance. Gregory of Nazianzus calls God the sea of being. Eunomius declared that God did not know more of His own being than we do, and that we can comprehend Him. Augustine would not call God a substance, for that would imply the conception of accident. Our language cannot define the essence of God. John of Damascus said that God is above all knowledge.

John Scotus Erigena held the view that God did not know Himself. He is nothing, and therefore knows not what He is. He divides nature, which includes God, as follows: 1) That which creates and is not created (God); 2) that which is created and creates (Logos 1); 3) that which is created, but does not create (the world); 4) that which is neither created nor creates (God as the goal). Anselm taught that God indeed knows Himself, but we cannot obtain adequate knowledge of Him. Thomas Aquinas declared that man cannot have a quidditative (essential) knowledge of God, but may know Him in His relation to the created world. Albert the Great distinguishes between *Deum intellectu attlngere et comprehendere* and ascribes the first-named to man. Duns Scotus maintained that man could have a quidditative knowledge of God. The controversy was settled as follows: That man can obtain knowledge of God's being, *cognitio quidditatis Dei,* but not a knowledge complete in every detail, *cognitio quidditativa.*

The fathers of the Reformation and the old Dogmaticians in general consider that the human conceptions of God are inadequate. Thomasius considered that our knowledge of God contains elements that objectively represent the nature of God. Phillippi said that our knowledge of God, while true and well-founded, does not objectively express the essence of God.

B. *Concerning the Unity of God and the Primitive Characteristics of His Being.*

Because Christianity acknowledged Monotheism, as explained in the doctrine of the Trinity, it became necessary to combat Polytheism, Dualism and Gnosticism. A variety of natural and mathematical figures of speech were used to prove the oneness of God. Through the subsequent controversies within the Church itself the doctrine of Christian Monotheism was established. Different opinions concerning that which is primitive in the essence of God have been set forth during the different periods and in our own church there has likewise been a diversity of views.

Justin Martyr said that the unity of God is an innate idea, and that God is the perfect intellect. Minucius Felix and Cyprian say that as there is one ruler in a kingdom, one queen in a bee-hive, and one leader in a flock, so there can be only one God. Julius Africanus said the will was the primitive characteristic of God's essence. Origen said that God is intelligence and intellect.

Gregory of Nyssa sets forth the unity of God from the concept of God's perfection. If there were many gods, then all must be perfect; still in such case they must either be alike or unlike; in the latter case they would each lack the perfection of the others, in the former case there would be only one God. Augustine set forth the divine self-consciousness as the primitive characteristic of God's essence. John of Damascus endeavored to conceive of the unity of God by considering His immensity, for if there were many gods, the one could find no room because the other filled all space. Anselm says that self-consciousness is the primitive characteristic of God's essence. Thomas Aquinas sets forth being, while Duns Scotus sets forth the will as the primitive characteristic of the essence of God.

Luther lays stress on love as the primitive characteristic, and in his work *De Servo Arbitrio* he makes mention of the absolute power. Gerhard emphasizes essence, but he also says: *in Deo idem est esse et intelligere et velle.* Calovius also emphasizes essence, but speaks of God as the absolute Spirit and mentions *intellectus* and *voluntas.* Thomasius, Jul. Müller and Delitzsch set forth the will as the primitive characteristic. Phillippi presents God in the first place as the absolute substance, but then also as the absolute subject and as love He also mentions, 1) self-consciousness and 2) self-determination. Björling and Granfelt set forth being, intellect and will as equally primitive. The latter says that in every part and at all points they must come in contact with, measure up to and determine one another.

§5. Concerning the Divine Attributes.

1. The Conception Of The Attributes.

In the theological terminology the attributes are called *attributa. Proprietates* set forth the trinitarian relationship and *praedicata* special acts, such as creation, etc. But in speaking of the attributes and the predicates we must not consider the former as inactive, for God is an *actus purissimus.*

The attributes are based upon the essential characteristics of God's essence. The attributes set forth the relationship of God's essence to the world. His essential characteristics are therefore both transcendent and immanent. They have two sides, one inward toward God Himself, the other outward toward the world. In the latter case the essential characteristics become the same as the attributes. The attributes are not supplements to the essence of God which can be laid aside without detriment to the divine being. The attributes are therefore unchangeable and permanent. Gerhard says that the attributes, considered *per se*, are really one with the divine essence. God is not, therefore, a combination of essence and attributes.

With regard to the subjectivity of the attributes it may be remarked that they are not the subjective products of our thought, but are grounded in the essence of God and are objectively true, although they are not to be considered as disintegrated parts. Their relation is such that they subsist in and through each other. Each attribute expresses the whole of the divine essence, otherwise the essence would be divided. However, this does not nullify the distinction above mentioned. Each attribute gives expression to the divine essence in a special manner.

Various opinions have appeared from time to time concerning the objectivity and the subjectivity of the divine attributes. According to Augustine they are distinguished subjectively only in our own thought. In De Trin., VI, 7, he says: "His greatness is the same as His wisdom, for He is not great by bulk but by power; His goodness is the same as His wisdom and His greatness, and His truth is the same as all these things, and in Him it is not one thing to be blessed and another thing to be great or wise, true, good, or in a word, to be Himself." Thomas Aquinas said that the conceptual distinctions on the part of man were well grounded objectively (*fundamentum aliquid in re*), and distinguished between *distinctio rationis ratiocinantis*, a subjective distinction, and *distinctio rationis ratiocinatae*, which is grounded in the object. Quenstedt follows Thomas Aquinas and uses his terms, but says, nevertheless, that strictly and correctly speaking, God has no attributes, but is the most simple essence, which cannot be resolved into parts and is without all composition. By reason of the fact that we cannot comprehend the divine essence in an adequate manner, therefore we endeavor to apprehend it by means of distinct and inadequate conceptions which imperfectly represent the divine essence, and these conceptions are called attributes. Hollazius says: "The divine attributes are distinguished from the divine essence and from each other *not nominally, nor really*, but *formally*, according to our mode of conceiving, not without a certain foundation of distinction." Schleiermacher says that the attributes do not represent anything in the essence of God, nor in His relation to the world, but are the relationships inherent in the idea of God as found in the Christian consciousness. Thomasius considers that the attributes are found not only in our reason, but also in God Himself. Phillippi takes the view that they are not objective and distinct attributes in the essence of God, but that they are nevertheless true and grounded in the revelation of God.

2. How We Gain Knowledge Of The Divine Attributes.

The Church Fathers in general taught that we gain knowledge of the attributes in three ways. Dogmaticians, such as Gerhard and Hollazius, used the same method and likewise taught that we gain knowledge of the attributes *via negationis, via causalitatis* and *via eminentiae*.

Via negationis sets out from the principle: *quod summe perfectum est, ei nullus inest defectus*, or that there is no imperfection in that which in the highest sense is perfect. We remove from God whatever implies imperfection in creatures, and ascribe to Him an opposite perfection, so that we say that He is perfect, independent, immeasurable, immortal, etc.

Via causalitatis is based upon the following principle: *effectus testatur de causa eiusque perfectione,* or that an effect testifies of the cause and its perfection. We ascribe to God as the cause the good attributes which are revealed in His works.

Via eminentiae is derived from the principle: *quidquid exstat in effectu praeexistit in causa,* or whatever exists in the effect, pre-exists in the cause; so that we ascribe to God in the highest degree those attributes which we find in a lower degree in ourselves.

Through *via negationis* we learn of God's transcendence and through the other methods we learn of His immanence. It is necessary to unite these three ways and not to separate them, in order to derive a perfect idea of God's attributes.

3. Division Of The Attributes.

Dogmaticians have divided the attributes in many ways. Baier, Schmid and others have divided them into *negative* attributes, such as unity, simplicity, eternity, immensity and immutability; and *positive,* such as life, wisdom, justice, truth, power, goodness and perfection. Others, such as Björling, divide them into the attributes of being, knowing and willing. The attributes of absolute being are, eternity, omnipresence, immutability, and immensity; the attributes of the absolute intellect are, omniscience, omnisapience; the attributes of the absolute will are, power, holiness, righteousness, truthfulness and love. Phillippi: The attributes of the absolute substance are eternity and omnipresence; of the absolute subject, power and omniscience; of the absolute love, wisdom, righteousness and goodness. Thomasius divides the attributes into immanent and relative. Among the former are eternity, immensity, etc., and among the latter power, omniscience, omnipresence, etc. It is our purpose to follow this division in the section of Christology.

Luthardt in his dogmatics makes use of a combination of Schleiermacher and Nitzsch: 1) *Essential* characteristics according to the conception of the absolute personality or according to the Scriptures: *Life, light and love.* 2) Those attributes that express the relationship of the absolute personality to the world: A. God's relationship to the natural world: a) Distinct from the world (eternity, infinity and immutability); b) Contact with the world (omnipresence, power, omniscience and wisdom); B. God's relationship to the moral world: a) Separated from but active in the moral world (holiness, righteousness and truthfulness; b) Contact (love as expressed in goodness, mercy, longsuffering, patience, meekness, faithfulness, etc.).[2]

4. Essential Characteristics.

In accordance with the conception of the absolute personality we might say that the essential characteristics or the transcendental attributes are the following: Perfection or the harmony between being, intellect and will, self-sufficiency and love. In this connection, however, we wish to consider the essential characteristics according to Biblical expressions, as life, light and love.

a. *Vita* or life. God is the absolute life, the absolutely harmonious life. He possesses the principle of His own existence in Himself. Quenstedt says: "The life of God is that attribute by which His essence ever manifests its activity." Cf. Ezekiel, chap 1, concerning the living creatures and the wheels, etc.; "A living God" (Acts 14: 15); "The Father hath life in himself" (John 5: 26) ; "Neither is he served by men's hands, as though he needed anything, seeing he himself giveth to all life, and breath, and all things" (Acts 17: 25); "Who only hath immortality" (1 Tim. 6: 16).

b. *Lux* or light. God is the absolute light. Of all things light is the purest. God is therefore the absolute truth, wisdom and holiness. Compare how the divine majesty is described in Ezekiel 1 and in Daniel 7. "Every good gift and every perfect gift is from above, coming down from the Father of lights" (James 1: 17) ; "And this is the message which we have heard from Him an announce to you, that God is the light, and in him is no darkness at all" (1 John 1:5), etc.

c. *Amor* or love. God lives within Himself the life of everlasting love. In God are found both the subject and object of love and also the union

---

[2] Luthardt's *Compendium*, §29, p. 99.

between them. "He that loveth not knoweth not God; for God is love" (1 John 4:8); "The Father loveth the Son" (John 3: 35) ; "Thou lovedst me before the foundation of the world" (John 17: 24). Compare vv. 23, 26.

In regard to these three essential characteristics or attributes of the divine essence we add to what is above stated: *Vita* is the essential attribute which corresponds to His perfection as an expression of the divine intensive or qualitative unity. No one can define life, and God is the essence of life. All life depends on God, spiritual, physical, angelic, human, animal and vegetable. In regard to Logos John says: "In him was life." The incarnated Logos, or Christ, says: "I am the life." Christ defines eternal life as knowledge of God and Himself. Cf. John 17:3: "And this is life eternal, that they should know thee the only true God, and him whom thou didst send, even Jesus Christ." *Lux*, the second great essential attribute, corresponds to the self-sufficiency of God as expressed by the exclusive or numerical unity of the divine essence. According to the numerical unity God is *unicus* and none is like Him, and He is the only one who is self-sufficient. He is, therefore, the absolute light and has all light within Himself. And all light in the world has its source in Him. The incarnated Logos is the light of the world. In John 1: 9 we read: "There was the true light, even the light which lighteth every man, coming into the world." In James 1: 17 God is called the Father of lights. *Amor* is the third attribute which is characteristic of the divine essence. God is love, which is the material element of the Absolute Personality. The diversification of external attributes was not necessary for God Himself. He lived eternally and lives eternally in love. When God created angels and man the love of God flowed out in the universe. What would the world be without the life, light and love of God!

5. The Special Attributes.

A. In Relation to the Natural World.

a. Immanent Attributes, Distinct from the Natural World.

AETERNITAS, or eternity, *is that attribute of God which expresses His possession of the fulness of infinite life and that in an absolute sense He is independent of time by which all finite existences are conditioned.*

We cannot comprehend the idea of eternity because we view it from the standpoint of time and because we lack suitable analogies. Someone has compared eternity to a circle and time to a line passing off from the periphery of the circle. It might still better be said that the line is within the periphery. In the nature of the case God must be eternal also from the point of view that He is without beginning, for who or what could have existed if God had not been? We cannot conceive of anything existing before God. And if there was nothing, neither could there be the concept "nothing." We cannot comprehend the eternity of God because of the limitations of our thought, but it would be just as incomprehensible that God should not be eternal.

Among Scripture passages the following may be here noted: "Before the mountains were brought forth, or ever thou hadst formed the earth and the world, even from everlasting to everlasting, thou art God" (Ps. 90:2); "Thou art the same, and thy years shall have no end" (Ps. 102: 27); "With thee is the fountain of life" (Ps. 36:9); "His everlasting power and divinity" (Rom. 1:20); "And he is before all things" (Col. 1:17); "And sware by him that liveth for ever and ever" (Rev. 10:6), etc.

Augustine understood eternity to be never-ceasing being, Boethius defines eternity thus: *Quod sit interminabilis vitae tota simul et perfecta possessio*. Anselm declares that concerning God it can only be said that He is. Thomas Aquinas said that eternity is the same as *tota simul*. Gerhard[3] says that the Scholastics define eternity as follows: *Quod sit duratio interminabilis, indivisibilis et independens. Interminabilis, quia excludit terminum a quo et ad quem; indivisibilis, quia excludit omnem successionem temporis; independens, quia excludit omnem imperfectionem ac mutationem.*

Hase defines: "That attribute by which God, Himself independent of all time, is the creator of time, by which all finite existences are conditioned." Martensen: "God is eternal as that essence which possesses life and fulness

---

[3] Gerhard, *Loci Theologici*, Tomus I, Cap. VIII, Sectio IV, pp. 307, 137.

in itself, a living eternity which ever blossoms forth in unfading youth." Luthardt[4]: "Super-time, which is not quantitatively but qualitatively separated from that which exists in time, that which is purely present, and which therefore comprises the background which sustains time and which at every moment can dwell within the same."

Immensitas, immensity, Baier defines: "The immensity of God consists in this, that the divine essence cannot be measured by, or included within, any local limits."[5] Immensity is the infinity of God or His absolute transcendence above spatial relations. We must understand God's immensity not extensively but intensively.

"Do not I fill heaven and earth? saith Jehovah" (Jer. 23: 24); "But will God in very deed dwell on earth? behold, heaven and the heaven of heavens cannot contain thee; how much less this house that I have builded!" (1 Kings 8: 27).

Immutabilitas or immutability, according to Börling, is that attribute by which God, independent of time, is also independent of all those changes that continually take place in time. Baier: "*Immutabilitas consistit in eo, quod Deus nulli mutationi, neque secundum esse, neque secundum accidentia, neque secundum locum, neque secundum voluntatem aut propositum est obnoxius.*"[6] According to this definition the immutability of God consists in this, that God cannot be subject to any change: 1) in regard to essence, because He is eternal, 2) in regard to accidental attributes, because all in God is essential, 3) in regard to space, because He is omnipresent, 4) in regard to will, because He can do what He wills, 5) in regard to purpose or resolution, because He is omniscient and all-wise. But the immutability of God *ad extra* and *ad intra* does not imply a monotonous sameness, a barren, petrified existence, or such like. When, therefore, we read of God's repentance, and that He does not punish men when they repent, as in Nineveh, although He had threatened to punish, this does not militate

---

4 Kompendium, Fifth Ed., Trans, by Neander, p. 100.

5 Baieri Comp. Pars. I, Cap. 1, §XII.

6 Baieri Comp. Theol. Pos., Caput. I, §X.

against His immutability, but rather emphasizes it, because God thereby corresponds to His own nature. God's seeming change is in fact a change of relation on the part of man. When sinners, like the people of Nineveh, are wicked and do not repent, they are exposed to the justice of God, but when they repent, they enter into a new relation and receive God's grace and mercy. As an analogy we may use the sun and our relation to it. We may place ourselves in such a relation to the sun that we are healed and live, but we may also expose ourselves in such a way that we are hurt and killed by sunstroke. God is not only love, but also a consuming fire. Each attribute of God works immutably according to its nature. How God's love and justice work immutably and do not conflict is evident in the great work of reconciliation. In love God sends His Son and in justice He sacrifices Him for the expiation of the sins of the world. The immutability of God is an earnest that in a living way He answers to all His attributes. Prayer, for instance, would be worthless, if God were mutable *ad intra* or ad *extra.* But because He is immutable, therefore prayer has a sure foundation. God appears in history and enters into the life of individuals and of nations and follows the history of mankind with great sympathy. The following Scripture passages may be quoted: "I, Jehovah, change not" (Mai. 3:6); "Every good gift and every perfect gift is from above, coming down from the Father of lights, with whom can be no variation, neither shadow that is cast by turning" (James 1:17).

b. Relative Attributes or Attributes of Contact.

OMNIPRAESENTIA, or omnipresence, Hase defines as follows: *"That attribute by which God, Himself independent of all space, is the creator of space, by which all material substances are conditioned."* God's transcendence as well as His immanence are united in His omnipresence. Of course we are unable to understand completely how God can be omnipresent, but we can understand it in part by presenting certain qualifying characteristics.

Negative characteristics are such as the following: 1) *non circumscriptive,* because God is not limited as to space; 2) *non definitive,* as pneumatic bodies and angels are present somewhere; 3) *non extensive,* by extension as the ether or the universe; 4) *non per rarefactionem,* because God is not present through rarefaction or diminution; 5) *non per multiplicationem* or through multiplication; 6) *non per divisionem* or through the division of His essence. Positive characteristics of His *praesentia* are the following: 1) *illocalis,* because, although His throne is in heaven, He is intensively present everywhere but not limited to any certain place; 2) *intensiva*[7] or that His essence is of such a nature that He can be present everywhere without extension; 3) *repletiva,* or that God, Himself contained within no bounds, contains or enfolds all things as in a little point (Gerhard: *omnia instar minutissimi puncti continens*); 4) *indivisibilis,* because *ubicunque est, totus est,* for God cannot be divided, so that a part of His essence should be at one place and a part at another; 5) *incomprehensibilis* or incomprehensible, for there is no analogy that can represent the substantial presence, but we can understand that a being can be constituted in such a manner when that being is an absolute personality or God. The thought of man can be at many places. While this is not an analogy, still we may learn from it that God who is an absolute spirit can intensively be present everywhere; 6) *operativa,* so that God is actively present everywhere. Our soul is operatively present in the body. A speaker in an auditorium is operatively present everywhere in the whole room, although not locally through extension. A king is present in an operative sense throughout his whole kingdom. There is, however, this difference with God, that He is

---

[7] When we say that God is everywhere present in an intensive sense, this implies in the first place the opposite of an extensive omnipresence. The theological expression implies more than intensity in the ordinary sense. Although God cannot be or rather is not extended everywhere in a local sense, yet He is everywhere by reason of the inward power and nature of His essence. There is no analogy. Our thought can be present at many places without extension. In a real sense God can be everywhere. Our spirit or soul can without extension be present throughout the body, and still the soul has its seat somewhere. God is everywhere present throughout the universe, but He reveals Himself specially in heaven, from whence He is intensively and repletively present everywhere. It is not unthinkable, although it is inexplicable, that an absolute essence can be so constituted that it can be present everywhere in an illocal sense, and yet reveal itself somewhere. If we think of Christ, the matter becomes clearer.

both substantially and operatively present everywhere.

The Scriptures clearly teach the omnipresence of God: "Know therefore this day, and lay it to thy heart, that Jehovah he is God in heaven above and upon earth beneath" (Deut. 4:39) ; "Do not I fill heaven and earth? saith Jehovah" (Jer. 23:24); "Thou hast beset me behind and before, and laid thy hand upon me. If I ascend up into heaven thou art there: if I make my bed in Sheol, behold, thou art there" (Ps. 139:5, 8); "Jehovah is nigh unto all them that call upon him" (Ps. 145:18); "Christ says: "I am with you always, even unto the end of the world" (Matt. 28: 20); Paul says concerning God: "In him we live, and move, and have our being" (Acts 17: 28), etc.

Hermes Trismegistus said that God is an intellectual sphere whose center is everywhere and whose periphery is nowhere. Augustine said that it would be more suitable to say that all things are in God than that God is in all things. Thomas Aquinas said that the essential presence of God gives reality to space and its affections. Gerhard says among many other things on this subject: *"Deus est totus in omnibus, totus in singulis, totus in se ipso."* The old Dogmaticians call God's substantial presence in things *immediatio suppositi,* and His activity they call *immediatio virtutis.* The former term implies that there is no intermediary subject, the second that there is no intermediary power beside God's own. God's presence has also been considered as revealing His power, grace and glory. The *Giessen* and *Saxon theologians* taught *a specialis approximatio essentiae divinae ad substantiam credentium.* The *Tübingen theologians,* however, and especially Gerhard and Musaeus in Jena, spoke of a *gratiosa operatio.* In general it is taught that the presence of God is both *substantialis* and *operativa.* Some have taught a *modified* omnipresence which implies merely an operative presence, while others have taught a *relative* presence, i. e., God is present wherever He wills to be. But the Scriptures set forth an omnipresence that is more general than those implied in *omnipraesentia modificata* and *relativa,* so that we may say that it is an *omnipraesentia absoluta* which also implies the *operativa.* The omnipresence of God is absolute, both substantial and operative. Just as the soul in its entirety is everywhere in the body, God as the absolute spirit is totally in every place of the universe. But His presence may not be recognized. As a figure or analogy we may use electricity. There must be an induction. Think of the induction of electricity by Franklin's kite and how it led to the great electrical inventions! God has given us the means of grace, and we should use those means. And there may be so-called spiritual induction by prayer, when we realize the presence of God. A Christian feels daily the presence of the Lord in the mystical union. There are many promises as to the presence of the Lord. But God is present independent of our feeling.

OMNIPOTENTIA or power. On the basis of the intensive unity, God is the perfect essence. He is also the absolute power because His will harmonizes with His essence. *Omnipotence is therefore that attribute of God by which He can do all things that are not contrary to His will.* Omnipotentia is called *absoluta* when we consider the divine power as active at the creation and in the miracles; *relativa* or *ordinata*, when we consider it as mediated through the laws of nature.

The divine will is named and divided as follows: *Voluntas necessaria* or *naturalis*, by which God wills and determines Himself, and *voluntas libera*, by which God determines the whole universe and all definite things. *Voluntas libera* is divided as follows: 1) with regard to the relation of the will to outside objects, a) *prima, absoluta* or *antecedens,* and b) *secunda, conditionata* or *consequens.* The former refers to a disposition of God without reference to any conditions; the latter to one in which conditions and circumstances are considered; 2) with regard to the imparting of the content of the divine will, a) *beneplaciti* or *abscondita*, the secret will, and b) *signi* (on account of certain signs) or *revelata*, the revealed will. These divisions have mostly arisen through the controversy on election.

The Scriptures present the power or omnipotence of God in the form of figures or in direct statements: "The arm of thy strength" (Ps. 89:10); "The right hand of the Lord doeth valiantly" (Ps. 118:16); "or he spake, and it was done: he commanded, and it stood fast" (Ps. 33:9); "With God all things are possible" (Matt. 19:26); "The Lord almighty" (2 Cor. 6:18; Rev. 1:8), etc.

Chrysostom and John of Damascus spoke of an antecedent and subsequent will. Prosper Aquitanus distinguished between a secret and a revealed will of God. The former was *seria* or *efficax* and the latter was *non seria,* for the secret will had reference to those chosen for salvation, but the revealed will had reference to the universal call which was not serious. Clearly the secret and the revealed will cannot conflict with each other, for then the veracity of God would be annulled. Abelard said that God cannot do anything except what He does. We may say that God can do all that He wills, but He does not do all that He can. Duns Scotus declared that God could determine what is good, and therefore conceived God's will to be arbitrary. Luther sanctioned the division of the will as secret and revealed. Calvin misinterpreted the division in the same manner as Prosper Aquitanus. But the misinterpretation does not hinder the use of terms which, when correctly employed, serve to explain this attribute, as in the relation between the determined order of God and His daily providence.

OMNISCIENTIA or omniscience. By this attribute is meant that God in an immediate and perfect manner knows all that which under certain conditions can happen and be. To God are ascribed memory, vision and foreknowledge. There is, however, no distinction as to the formal part of God's knowledge, but only as to the objects. With regard to *praescientia* it may be remarked that there is no determinism implied in it, inasmuch as the acts do not take place by reason of God's foreknowledge, but God foresees that they shall occur. With regard to the character of God's knowledge it may be pointed out that it is called *intuitiva,* in contradistinction to demonstrative and discursive knowledge, for in the thought of God all things are immediately present; *simultanea,* to distinguish it from that which is successive, for God knows and sees all things simultaneously; *distinctissima,* or perfectly clear, and *verissima,* or perfectly true.

Scientia is divided as follows: 1) *Scientia necessaria* or *naturalis,* by which is meant that God knows His own absolute essence and all possible things. This knowledge is called *scientia simplicis intelligentiae,* when the knowledge embraces those possible things that are the objects of thought only. As examples we call attention to the fact that God knows evil ideally or theoretically, but not by personal experience. There are many things we know ideally and are able to present concretely in our minds. The Supreme Mind can understand fully everything and picture it correctly in His own thought. If man had not fallen, evil would have been known to him according to the method of *scientia simplicis intelligentiae.* 2) *Scientia libera* or God's knowledge of all that exists. This knowledge is also called *scientia visionis* or God's penetrating vision or perception of real beings and things, *coram intuendo.* 3) *Scientia media* or *conditionata,* by which is meant God's knowledge of those things that could have happened or can now happen under certain conditions.

There are many Scripture passages that set forth the omniscience of God, among which the following may be quoted: "Known unto God are all his works from the beginning of the world" (Acts 15:18); "And there is no creature that is not manifest in his sight: but all things are naked and laid open before his eyes" (Heb. 4: 13); "God kneweth all things" (1 John 3:20); "Thou knowest the hearts of all the children of men" (1 Kings 8: 39); "Thou understandest my thought afar off; There is not a word in my tongue, but, lo, O Jehovah, thou knowest it altogether" (Ps. 139: 2-4), etc.

Origen said that God's foreknowledge is not the same as His predetermination, for the free acts do not happen by reason of God's foreknowledge, but God foresees that they shall happen. However, Origen limited the knowledge of God when he endeavored to prove the finiteness of the world by the argument that God could not understand the world if it were infinite. The term *scientia media* originated with the Jesuits Fonseca and Molina in the sixteenth century during the controversy concerning election. The Socinians declared that the acts of man could not be free by reason of God's foresight. Rothe and Martensen both sought to defend the Socinian view asserting that God arranged a schedule of the world plan and that the free acts of man as they occur constitute the filling in of this schedule. However, this view militates against the perfection of God and is not a satisfactory explanation. We must distinguish between the foreknowledge and the predetermination of God. The knowledge of God and His will do not always agree, inasmuch as God knows much that He does not will.

Omnisapientia or wisdom. God's wisdom is the perfect correspondence of His thought with the absolute good. God is all-wise because He infallibly knows the best means to be used to accomplish purposed ends. God's omnisapience implies, therefore, teleology or *causa finalis*.

The Word of God teaches the omnisapience of God, as in the following passages: "Whence then cometh wisdom? And where is the place of understanding? God understandeth the way thereof, and knoweth the place thereof. He made a weight for the wind: yea, He meteth out the waters by measure. When He made a decree for the rain, and a way for the lightning of the thunder; then did he see it, and declare it" (Job 28:20, 23, 25-27); "O the depth of the riches both of the wisdom and the knowledge of God" (Rom. 11: 33); "The only wise God" (Rom. 16: 26); "Christ, in whom are all the treasures of wisdom and knowledge hidden" (Col. 2:3), etc.

B. In Relation to the Moral World.

a. Immanent Attributes, Distinct from the Moral World.

SANCTITAS, Justitia Interna, or God's holiness is the correspondence of the will of God with the absolute good or perfection. God's holiness contains a negative element, inasmuch as God is separated from all that is unclean and sinful, and also a positive element, because God as the absolutely Holy One wills that all creatures should be holy.

Baier defines God's holiness as the rectitude of His will, wherefore He wills all things that are right and good in accordance with His eternal law.[8] But Baier adds that God is Himself the law.

JUSTITIA EXTERNA is the term that is used to express the righteousness of God in its narrow and specific sense. Righteousness in a broader sense is understood to include all the moral perfections of God. In the narrow sense the righteousness of God is the same as His holiness in an external

[8] Part. I, Cap. I, §XXIII.

sense, which makes laws. *Justitia externa* is divided in the following way: 1) *Legislativa* or *antecedens,* by which is meant God's legislative righteousness, 2) *judicialis, consequens* or *distributiva,* i. e., His retributive righteousness. This latter is divided as follows: a) remtmeratoria, or the remunerative righteousness, b) *punitiva,* or the punitive righteousness, for which reason God is said to become angry, which implies the righteous reaction of God's holiness against sin.

The following Scripture passages may be quoted: "Ye shall be holy, for I am holy" (Lev. 11:45); "The Holy One in Israel" (Ezek. 39:7); "And provoked the Holy One of Israel" (Ps. 78:41); "As your heavenly Father is perfect" (Matt. 5:48); "Each shall receive his own reward according to his labor" (1 Cor. 3:8); "After thy hardness and impenitent heart thou treasurest up for thyself wrath in the day of wrath and revelation of the righteous judgment of God; who will render to every man according to his works" (Rom. 2: 5, 6). Other passages could be cited.

Many objections have been raised against the righteousness of God, against His righteous government, against His righteous judgment, and some have desired to deny the wrath of God towards sinners. For this reason they have also attacked the doctrine of substitutional atonement. They emphasize the love of God at the cost of His holiness and righteousness and forget that God is holy love, that He loves Himself as the Holy One. God has been compared to a sinful father, who forgives His children. The argument is that God must be more merciful than an earthly father. Indeed, He is more merciful, but He is not sinful, for which reason He is more just. The love of God does not encroach upon His righteousness, nor does His righteousness limit His love. Both attributes function according to their own nature and characteristics. We must remember that when God is forced to manifest His wrath He is not cruel. Even the punishments of hell conform to an infallible justice, and men shall some day acknowledge the righteousness of God as they now acknowledge His love and mercy.

VERACITAS or truthfulness. Baier defines veracity as that attribute by which God is ever constant in the telling of the truth and in the keeping of His promises.[9] *The veracity of God is the correspondence of His thought with His essence,* so that God is the absolute truth, which is another acknowledged definition.

The following passages may be quoted: "For Thy loving kindness is great unto the heavens, and thy truth unto the skies" (Ps. 57:10); "All thy commandments are faithful" (Ps. 119:86); "Loving kindness and truth go before thy face" (Ps. 89:15); "He that hath received his witness hath set his seal to this that God is true" (John 3:33); "In hope of eternal life, which God, who cannot lie, promised before times eternal" (Titus 1:2), etc.

b. Attributes of Contact or Relative Attributes.

AMOR or love. Hollazius defines love in the following manner: *"Amare significat velle alicui bonum."* Love may be understood in many ways. Granfelt[10] combines God's intra-essential love and His love manifested to the world and defines as follows: "That attribute by which God eternally imparts Himself ad intra and ad extra."

The Scholastics divide love as follows: 1) *complacentia,* or that God loves all creatures, in other words, God's general good-will, 2) *benevolentia* or His love to man, 3) *amicitia* or His love for the faithful.

Scripture passages: "God so loved the world" (John 3:16). This is the cardinal passage by which to prove God's general love to men. "Jehovah loveth the righteous" (Ps. 146:8); of Jesus we read: "Having loved his own that were in the world, he loved them unto the end" (John 13:1); "He that loveth me shall be loved of my Father, and I will love him, and will manifest myself unto him" (John 14:21). The expressions which the Lord uses concerning the faithful manifest the special love (*amicitia*) which He has for them, such as betrothed, bride, flock, fold, a beautiful crown, a kingly diadem, etc. We might also speak of an *amicitia specialis,* such as was manifested in relation to such as Enoch, Abraham, Moses, Samuel, David, Peter, James, John, Lazarus, etc.

---

[9] Part. I, Cap. I, §XXIV.

[10] Kristlig dogmatik, Third Ed., p. 91.

Love manifests itself as *bonitas* or goodness toward all creatures; *gratia* or grace toward sinners; *misericordia*, or mercy towards sinners in their wretchedness; *dementia*, or meekness, mildness; l*onganimitas*, or long-suffering, in which love manifests itself in the deferring of punishment, and *patientia*, or patience, which bears with many faults. We should always use the expressions correctly. *Bonitas* or goodness refers to the love of God as in providence, when the sun shines on all and the rain waters the fields of both good and wicked. Grace should be used in relation to sinners and criminals. Only sinners and criminals before the law of God need grace in the sense of pardon. Mercy is needed on account of the consequences of sins in suffering, sickness and all kinds of misery. God is long-suffering towards the wicked and delays punishment in order to give them an opportunity to repent and reform. God exercises patience towards the pious or His own children in education and correction of faults.

Among the Scripture passages that set forth love from these various points of view are the following: "Jehovah is good to all" (Ps. 145:9); "Where sin abounded, grace did abound more exceedingly" (Rom. 5:20); "Jehovah is merciful and gracious" (Ps. 103:8); "The Father of mercies" (2 Cor. 1:3); "Endured with much longsuffering vessels of wrath fitted unto destruction" (Rom. 9:22); "Slow to anger, and abundant in lovingkindness" (Ps. 103: 8); "For he is kind toward the unthankful and evil" (Luke 6: 35) ; "The riches of his goodness and forbearance and longsuffering" (Rom. 2:4).

Fidelitas, or fidelity, is that attribute by which God continues to manifest His love and grace until the object has been won. This attribute constitutes the external side, an *opus ad extra*, of God's veracity. "He is faithful that promised" (Heb. 10:23). "But the Lord is faithful, who shall establish you" (2 Thess. 3:3).

§6. The Trinity.

By reason of the conception of the absolute personality, which also includes the qualitative characteristic that God is love, we must come to the conclusion that God is triune. Besides, we are led through the revelation of God's economy to the conception of His intra-essential trinity. The following propositions have therefore generally been accepted in the Christian Church: *Deus est trinus, h. e. in essentia unus, tres habet subsistendi modos,* or God is triune, i. e., one in essence with three modes of subsistence; *una divina essentia in tribus personis subsistis,* or a divine essence subsists in three persons. There are therefore three in one and one in three or a trinity in the unity and a unity in the trinity. Apart from the clear presentation of the Trinity in the Bible, it lies in the intensive and exclusive nature of the matter that God cannot be *one* person in the ordinary sense, inasmuch as love demands an object. According to the two parts of the unity of God He is absolutely perfect and also self-sufficient. The world could not be the object of God's love, for this would conflict with His perfection and also with His self-sufficiency. These essential characteristics do not imply that there are only two persons in the divine essence, but that God, who is one, subsists in three persons or three persons in one essence or three persons in one absolute personality, otherwise there would be lacking the common object of love, which at the same time unites and distinguishes.

The human reason cannot comprehend the mystery of the Trinity, and the inadequate terms of human language cannot express the content of this mystery, wherefore reason must give way to the obedience of faith, forasmuch as the doctrine of the Trinity has a firm basis in the Word of God and finds an empirical response in the Christian consciousness. But faith contains knowledge, and the Church correctly maintains that it is her duty to set forth what can be learned concerning this important doctrine.

1. The Ordinary Methods Of Explanation.

a. Through the conception of the absolute personality. Man is an ego which reaches self-consciousness and self-determination in opposition to a thou. Without this relationship of duality we could not speak of personality. But the ego is not merely a relationship of duality, i. e., in opposition to a thou, there is a unity likewise, a union of the ego and the non-ego. The union is not found, however, in a person, but in the human organizations of the family, state and church.

We may also speak of a threefold ego: the substantial ego, which places itself before itself as an object, the objective ego, in which we contemplate ourselves as an object, the subjective ego, which looks upon the other as identical with itself.

Man is made in the image of God; his personality is relative and determined by something outside of himself. God is absolute and infinite, for which reason the dual relationship is found in His own essence, as well as the union which is mediated by the Spirit.

b. Through the conception of love. Love implies self-impartation between persons. Since God is a unity and absolute love, He must therefore include within Himself three persons. God must be the subject and the object of love. Between the Father and the Son there arises a reciprocal activity of divine love. The moving power or force in this reciprocal activity is common to both, the third person, contemplated and loved by both, who constitutes the uniting bond between both and saves them from losing each other, that is, each in Himself. The third person is the Spirit. As triune God is therefore an absolute personality, who in Himself lives the life of everlasting love, for which reason the characteristics of His essence are likewise trinitarian, and we may say that they are of the Father, through the Son, and in the Spirit. It follows that one of the persons does not possess the whole fulness of the divine essence independent of the others, but only in relation to one another does each possess the divine essence. The whole essence is in each person undivided, and this essence is the one God or the absolute personality subsisting in three relative persons. Each one of them is the absolute personality only in a special relational form. This does not imply, however, that the absolute personality is a combination of three separate persons in the ordinary sense, for the persons in the Trinity are not absolute *per se*, but relatively, and subsist in and through one another. From the conception of the absolute personality and also of love it is seen that the position of the Spirit in the Trinity implies an *element* of union and also one of separation or distinction. Emphasis must be laid on both sides of this relationship, for if the emphasis is laid on the former, then the Spirit becomes more than the Father and the Son, not to say the whole essence; if the latter is emphasized, then the position of the Spirit becomes simply a relation between the Father and the Son.

c. Through the conception of the atonement. In the experience of the atonement there is a difference between God, who is atoned, God, who atones, and God, through whom the atonement is applied.

d. By the use of analogy. Hereby are meant the general analogies that have been presented at different times. However, they do not possess any scientific value as proofs of the Trinity, and many objections could be raised against them. Among analogies of this sort may be mentioned, the root, the tree and the fruit; the sun, rays of light, and heat; length, breadth and depth in space; the past, present and future of time; the triangle with its three sides; the personal pronouns, I, thou and he; the subject, the predicate and the copula of a sentence; the noun with its three genders; the adjective with its three degrees of comparison. In the realm of man there are better analogies which still are inadequate: the family, consisting of man, wife and children; the body, soul and spirit of man; the intellect, will and emotions of the mind. These analogies simply prove that the ideas of unity and trinity are not foreign to our thought, but they cannot explain the Trinity. The analogy of man as a unit of intellect, will and emotion is probably the best, especially as we remember that we are created in the image of God, but the analogy does not explain a divine essence and the three persons.

e. Through the teaching of the Word of God. The presentation of the Trinity in the Bible does not aim to solve the problem for the human reason, but every one who believes that the Scriptures are the Word of

God can become convinced that the doctrine of the Trinity is true. The declarations and words of the Bible are incontrovertible proofs of the divine Trinity, if it can be shown that the Scriptures clearly teach this doctrine. In the history of creation God appears as more than one person. *Elohim* created. When we compare this expression with John 1, where we learn that the Son of God created, then it is evident that *Elohim* includes both the Father and the Son. But when we also read the following passages: "By the word of Jehovah were the heavens made, and all the host of them by the breath of his mouth" (Ps. 33:6), and also, "The spirit of God moved upon the face of the waters" (Gen. 1:2), then the proof is clear that *Elohim* in Gen. 1:1 must imply the Father, Son and Spirit. In Gen. 1:26 we read: "And God said, Let us make man." This cannot be explained to mean that God spoke to angels, for this conflicts with the story of creation. It proves that the Father, Son and Spirit spoke together. The Messiah is represented as the Son of God, the servant of God: "Jehovah said unto me, Thou art my son; this day have I begotten thee" (Ps. 2:7); "Behold, my servant" (Isa. 42:1). In this connection servant is used in a higher sense, and the life-work of the Son of God is considered. In Isa. 9:6 He is called God; also in Ps. 47:7. The three persons of the Godhead are mentioned in Isa. 63. In Isa. 48:16 we read: "And now the Lord Jehovah hath sent me, and his spirit." The following passages may be cited from the New Testament: "Into the name of the Father and of the Son and of the Holy Spirit" (Matt. 28:19); "And the Word was with God, and the Word was God" (John 1:1); "The grace of the Lord Jesus Christ, and the love of God, and the communion of the Holy Spirit, be with you all" (2 Cor. 13:14). In addition there could be cited many passages that clearly contain the doctrine of the divinity of Christ. The personality of the Holy Spirit is set forth in many places. Among these we will limit ourselves to the quotation of only one passage, where the Holy Spirit speaks and uses the first person of the pronoun: "And as they ministered to the Lord, and fasted, the Holy Spirit said, Separate me Barnabas and Saul for the work whereunto I have called them" (Acts 13:2). Besides many other passages, the above quotations show clearly that the Bible contains the doctrine of the Trinity.

2. Remarks On Terminology.

Since the time of Athanasius and the Gregorians the expression *οὐσία* has meant the divine essence common to all three persons of the Godhead. Prior to that time the use of the word was uncertain and the definition of Aristotle was accepted that an essence or being was an individual thing or an ordinary person. But the Church does not understand by essence either a general essence or *substantia secunda* according to Aristotle, for God is represented as an absolute personality and in the sense of a *substantia prima.* However, since the Church employs the expression *οὐσία,* or essence, it possesses a meaning, which, as John of Damascus says, is far above the ordinary conception of essence.

The expression *ὑπόστασις*, or person, was first used in the same sense as essence is now used, but when *οὐσία* came to be used to designate the divine essence, then *ὑπόστασις* came into general use as designating the persons in the divine essence. The expression cannot be understood in the ordinary empirical sense, so that the Father, the Son and the Spirit should be like three distinct persons.

The unity in the divine essence is numerical and not one of its kind, as in man. In man the essence in three persons is not one in number but in species. Concerning men it cannot be said that one is in the other, but Jesus says in John 14:10: "I am in the Father." Furthermore, it cannot be said concerning men that where one is, there the other is also, because they are locally distinct; but the Lord says in John 8:29: "He that hath sent me is with me; he hath not left me alone." God is not divided into three persons, but the three persons share the divine essence indivisibly, so that each one possesses the divine essence without multiplication or division. It is therefore not a *pluralitas essentialis,* nor a *pluralitas accidentalis,* for personality is not something that is temporarily added to the divine essence, but it is a *pluralitas hypostatica seu personarum.* There is therefore a real distinction, but not in a human way. Philippi says that above all things it is necessary to understand in what sense the

Church interprets the expression person. He says in his Glaubenslehre II, pp. 145—147: "Personality is found only where self-consciousness and freedom are found, for where there is personality it manifests itself in self-consciousness and self-determination or freedom. But in itself we may say that personality is something deeper, that forms the foundation of self-consciousness and self-determination, the real inner essence which is reflected in the two forms in which it is revealed. In man, and especially when he has reached perfect spiritual development, the essence and manifestation of personality cannot be separated from each other. But what cannot be separated in reality can be distinguished in thought. The ecclesiastical terminology has been based upon the possibility of this conceptual distinction and has applied the one factor, the inner essence of the personality, the ego, or the independent form of subsistence, to mean the true, immanent distinction in the Godhead, while, on the other hand, the second factor, the revealed form of the personality, the self-consciousness and the freedom are conceived of as the predicate of the one divine essence. Therefore the three persons in the Godhead are self-conscious and free subjects, by reason of their communion in the one, self-conscious, free divine essence, which reveals itself in the three persons in distinct and independent forms of subsistence." Therefore when on the one hand we emphasize the absolute personality, we express our antagonism in the first place to Pantheism, and in the second place to Sabellianism and Arianism together with other related theories.

Ὁμοουσία constitutes the predicate of all three persons. Therefore the Son and the Spirit are of the same essence as the Father. Wherefore we confess in the Athanasian Creed: "The Godhead of the Father, of the Son, and of the Holy Ghost, is all one: the glory equal, the majesty co-eternal. Such as the Father is, such is the Son, and such is the Holy Ghost. And in the Trinity none is afore, or after the other; none is greater, or less than another. But the whole three persons are co-eternal together, and coequal."

Although we cannot apprehend God or attempt to do it, we have the right to present what the Bible teaches. To those who believe in the

Biblical statements and meditate on them, the being of God becomes more concrete. It is plain that the Bible teaches the unity of the essence of God and yet speaks of three distinctions. It is Biblically evident, therefore, that essence and persons are differently understood. The oneness of God is not the same as the unity of man, and the different persons in the Godhead are not three separate persons like three human persons. And they are not confused or mixed, because each relative person has His own consciousness by which He knows that He is not the other relative person, but He is Himself. The Father is not the Son, the Son is not the Father, neither of these two is the Holy Spirit, and the Holy Spirit is Himself and not the Father or the Son, but all three know that they are one, having the same undivided essence and consequently one self-consciousness and one self-determination. Notice again what we quoted from Philippi: "The ego, or the independent form of subsistence, means the real, immanent distinction in the Godhead, while on the other hand the second factor, the revealed form of the personality, the self-consciousness and freedom (self-determination) are conceived of as the predicate of the one divine essence." The three relative 'egos' or relative persons, who have a consciousness of their own, constitute one and are one self-consciousness and one self-determination, which is the same as one God or one Absolute Personality. Apparently or superficially considered it looks as if man had an advantage in possessing his own self-consciousness, but a closer view reveals the plenitude of God as trinal unity. The unity of God eternally exists as trinality, three in one and one in three. But the three persons do not exist within the one essence as the fourth. Neither does the trinitarian person exist as a part of the one essence. The three persons possess simultaneously the whole divine essence. The divine essence subsists eternally and permanently in three modes, but not successively, as the Sabellians taught. Paul speaks of "the form of God" (μορφῆ). The divine essence subsists in three forms, each form or relative person being the essence or substance of the others, both numerically and identically. But two or three human persons, like Peter, John and James, although having the same kind of nature, have not the same nature or substance numerically and identically, because each human person is a fractional part of the human nature. The personality of God is therefore richer than an ordinary person. God was self-sufficient before other persons were created and blessed in Himself. There is no adequate analogy to make the Trinity concrete to our vision. If a triplex mirror would produce three images of one personality containing all in each and each having its own peculiarity, this would be a mental analogy. Or if three persons could be conceived of as having the same undivided soul, it would also give an idea. In His manifestation God does not appear as one person, as we can deduce from the manifestations related in the Bible. At the Baptism of Christ there were three personal manifestations, although only the voice of the Father was heard and the Holy Ghost appeared in the form of a dove, but the Second Person of the Godhead in His incarnation was visible to all. In heaven we will see the incarnated Son of God in a glorified body. It is then evident that God the Father and God the Holy Spirit will also appear as persons in manifestation. The omnipresence of God is not affected by these manifestations, as the omnipresence of the divine essence is not local or circumscribed. From revelation or the Bible we learn that the three divine persons are objective to each other. The manifestation of God is not like a mathematical unit. There are many actions of the relative divine persons which prove their relative objectivity to each other. One divine person loves another, addresses another, is the way to another, suffers from another, sends another, glorifies another, etc. But on the other hand, on account of the unity, there are not three almighty, but one almighty, etc. If we pray to one, we pray to all the persons in the Trinity. In the Lord's Prayer our Father is not the first person only, but the triune God, our providential Father. We cannot speak to one of the persons to the exclusion of the others. They dwell in one another and work together according to the order stated in the Economical Trinity.

Περιχώρησις implies a common and peculiar indwelling, so that the one is in the other, by which we can understand that the three persons do not subsist separately or by the side of each other. Also they are alike, so that the Father is not God in a higher sense than the Son and the Holy Ghost.

As is already mentioned, the persons are absolute only in a relative sense and together constitute the absolute personality. The Son of God says: "I and the Father are one" (John 10:30); "Believe me that I am in the Father, and the Father in me" (John 14:11); "As thou, Father, art in me, and I in thee" (John 17:21).

But as the persons are relatively distinct, so there exists a certain order in their internal relationship and in their manifestation; for which reason they have their distinct characteristics and work.

The term incommunicabilis is therefore used to explain that that by which the one divine person is distinguished from the others cannot be transferred from the one to the other. The common name given to the characteristics that separate one person from the other is *character hypostaticus*.

3. Divisions.

I. The Ontological Trinity.

By this is meant the Trinity when considered from the intra-essential viewpoint. Here belong the inner characteristics or *notae internae*, which constitute the *modus subsistendi* or *τρόπός ὑπάρξεως*, by which the persons are distinguished from one another in their ontological relationship.

A. *Actus personales* or the personal acts. These are also called *opera ad intra*, which are *divisa*, divided or *incommunia*. They are: a) *generatio* (*opus Patris*), that the Father from eternity begets the Son. "This is therefore the Father's *opus ad intra*; b) *spiratio activa* (*opus Patris et Filii*) is the *opus ad intra* by which the Father and the Son simultaneously as an eternal principle send forth the Holy Spirit.

Generatio and also *spiratio* are described especially by the following negative and positive terms: 1) *non metaphorica et accidentalis et impropria, sed vera, substantialis et propria*, for the generation is not metaphorical, neither is it accidental or improper, but true and substantial. The Son is the substantial image of the Father; 2) *non physica, sed hyperphysica*, because the natural birth of man is not a real analogy, although the expression birth is the only relatively adequate human expression that can be used to set forth the activity of the Father in producing the Son; 3) *non voluntaria, sed necessaria,* since the generation is not dependent upon a preceding act of the Father's will, but was necessary and conformed to the nature of God; 4) *non temporalis, sed aeterna.* If the generation were not eternal, then it would have had a beginning and an end and in such case the Son would not be eternal. Quenstedt says therefore, that the Father from eternity begat, and always begets, and never will cease to beget His Son. Nevertheless, this generation cannot be said for this reason to be imperfect and successive, for the act of generation in the Father of the Son is considered perfect in work and constant in operation. We must divest ourselves of all thoughts of human analogies concerning conception, birth and time. Both the Father and the Son are eternal, and the Holy Spirit is eternal. There is an eternal communication of one and the same essence. The Father could not exist without the Son, nor without the Holy Spirit. However, a relative order exists among the persons, so that the Father, who has life in Himself, is named first, the Son, whom the Father begets from eternity, is the second person in the Godhead, and the Holy Spirit, who is sent forth both by the Father and the Son, is the third person. By reason of the idea of eternity, however, there is no priority, which would imply the existence of one person before the other. There is no perfect analogy to explain this primitive simultaneous existence. Quenstedt presents the analogy of the sun and its rays; 5) *non externa, sed intima,* since it is a generation that occurs within the essence of the Godhead and a perichoresis. The Son is in the bosom of the Father, according to John 1:18.

That the Father and the Son send forth the Holy Spirit, or that the Holy Spirit proceeds from the Father and the Son, is presented in the symbols of the Church in complete harmony with the teachings of the Word of God. If the Son did not send forth the Spirit as does the Father, then He would be less than the Father.

The internal activities in the ontological Trinity are eternal and unceasing. The personal acts as stated are two. They are the eternal generation and spiration, and when viewed in respect to the result these activities are called filiation and procession. These acts are not creative, because all the three persons are eternal and equal. The acts do not add anything to the divine essence, but modify eternally the existing eternal essence. The eternal begetting, not being like a physical conception and birth, is like a communication of the whole undivided divine essence by the Father to the Son. Some Trinitarians use the term "emanation" which may be an analogy *in opera ad intra,* but not *in opera ad extra.* When God created the world, He made a new substance from nothing and it was not an emanation of the divine essence in a gnostic sense. But the internal and eternal generation of the Son may be like an emanation of the divine essence by the activity of the Father. The Nicene Trinitarians, like Athanasius, use figures such as these: The community of the Father and the Son is like light and brightness, fountain and stream, the solar substance and the rays; and yet the sun and the brightness are not the same. The Father in begetting the Son did not exist before, because then the Son would not be eternal. The Father and Son coexisted. The same is the case in spiration. The spiration is eternal. The Father as unbegotten is not superior or older, but in the Trinitarian process of eternal existence the Father is the first in the order of process, but not in time. The eternal and internal life-movement necessarily required an originating process. In John we read: "For as the Father hath life in himself, even so gave he to the Son also to have life in himself" (John 5:26). When God in His all-wisdom decided to use the terms Father and Son, it is self-evident that the Father must be first in order. A subordination of person is not a subordination of essence. The Arian and Semi-Arian subordination concerns the essence and also the person. Neither should we confound the subordination of Christ in His state of humiliation with the order of persons in the Trinity. Here the question is only one of order in the Trinity. The Father must be first, the Son the second, and the Holy Spirit the third. It relates to characteristics of paternity, filiation and procession. Compare the Athanasian symbol. The three relative persons all have the same eternal essence in common, without division and with equal majesty.

In regard to the Third Person or Hypostasis He is not more spirit than the Father and the Son. The Holy Spirit is called Spirit on account of the mode in which the divine essence is communicated to Him. He is denominated Holy, because in the application of salvation He works holiness in men. He is not begotten, as in the divine eternal wisdom there should be only one Son. The difference between generation, spiration and procession is ineffable. The Father and Son spirate the Spirit and the Spirit proceeds from the Father and Son. By this internal process the one undivided essence is modified as the Third Hypostasis. The Spirit is called the Spirit of the Son just as of the Father. "God sent forth the Spirit of his Son" (Gal. 4:6); "The Spirit of Jesus Christ" (Phil. 1: 19). In the application of salvation we experience the Spirit in the first place and through the Spirit we know Christ and through the Son, Jesus Christ, we know the Father. In our spiritual experience the name Holy Spirit becomes clearer in the knowledge of the Father and the Son from whom the Spirit is spirated.

Among the Scripture passages that set forth the generation of the Son and the sending forth of the Spirit by the Father and Son, the following may be cited: "Thou art my son; this day have I begotten thee" (Ps. 2:7; Heb. 1:5; 5:5); compare other passages where the eternity of the Son is set forth: Isa. 9:6 (everlasting Father, literally, Father of eternity); Heb. 7:3; John 8:58; 17:5. "And the witness is this, that God gave unto us eternal life, and this life is in his Son" (1 John 5:11), etc. "But when the Comforter is come, whom I will send unto you from the Father, he shall bear witness of me" (John 15:26); "He shall take of mine, and shall declare it unto you" (John 16:14); "Spirit of Christ" (Rom. 8:9); "And because ye are sons, God sent forth the Spirit of his Son" (Gal. 4:6).

B. *Proprietates personales* or the personal attributes. These attributes are based upon *actus personales*, but are called personal attributes because they describe the inner distinction that characterizes each person. They are the following: *paternitas* or *generans* (generating), in relation to the Father, *filiatio* or *genitus* (generated), in relation to the Son, and *processio* or *procedens* (going forth) in relation to the Spirit.

C. *Notiones personales*, or the personal characteristics. These are abstracted from the personal acts and attributes and express in the form of concepts the inner characteristics, by which the divine persons are distinguished from one another. The following are the characteristics: 1) with regard to the Father: innascibilitas (ἀγεννεσία), *paternitas et spiratio activa*; 2) with regard to the Son: *filiatio* (*generatio passiva*) *et spiratio activa*; 3) with regard to the Holy Spirit: *processio et spiratio passiva*.

II. The Economical Trinity.

Under this head are discussed the external characteristics or *notae externae*, which constitute the *τρόπός* ἀποκαλύψεως of the persons, and by which they are distinguished from each other in their relation to the world, or *in opera ad extra*, which are *indivisa* or *communia* (common). These *opera ad extra* belong to each person of the Godhead, but in the order that is peculiar to each. Although it may be said concerning God that all things are of Him, and through Him, and unto Him, yet the following *particulae discriticae* are used, ἐκ of the Father, *διά* of the Son, and ἐν of the Holy Spirit. *Opera ad extra* are divided as follows:

A. *Opera oeconomica* or the economical acts. These are *personalia* and *minus communia* or *minus indivisa*.

a. The Father determined upon the redemption, which therefore includes election, and He gave the Son. "And we have beheld and bear witness that the Father hath sent the Son to be the Saviour of the world" (1 John 4:14); "Fear not, little flock; for it is your Father's good pleasure to give you the kingdom" (Luke 12:32); "He spared not his own Son, but delivered him up for us all" (Rom. 8: 32).

b. The Son has performed the work of redemption, which therefore presupposes the incarnation. "Even as the Son of man came not to be ministered unto, but to minister, and to give his life a ransom for many" (Matt. 20:28); "And the Word became flesh" (John 1:14), etc.

c. The Holy Spirit applies reconciliation or redemption. "No man can say, Jesus is Lord, but in the Holy Spirit" (1 Cor. 12:3); "God chose you from the beginning unto salvation in sanctification of the Spirit" (2 Thess. 2:13), etc.

B. *Opera attributiva* or the attributive acts. They are *communia* or *indivisa*, and yet different acts are ascribed to each person, by which they are distinguished.

a. To the Father are ascribed creation and providence. "Have we not all one father? hath not one God created us?" (Mai. 2:10); "Yet to us there is one God, the Father, of whom are all things" (1 Cor. 8:6); "He careth for you" (1 Peter 5:7).

b. To the Son are ascribed the raising of the dead and the judgment. "The dead shall hear the voice of the Son of God; and they that hear shall live. And he gave him authority to execute judgment, because he is the son of man. Marvel not at this: for the hour cometh, in which all that are in the tombs shall hear his voice" (John 5:25-28).

c. To the Holy Spirit is ascribed inspiration: "For no prophecy ever came by the will of man: but men spake from God, being moved by the Holy Spirit" (2 Peter 1:21).

4. Notes On The History Of Dogma.

The primitive Church accepted the doctrine of the Trinity, but the doctrine underwent development a little at a time and became more precisely defined by reason of the controversies that arose concerning it. During the Apologetical period the words *τριάς* and *trinitas* were used for the first time, the former by Theophilus and the latter by Tertullian. Origen taught the eternal generation of the Son. The doctrine of the Trinity was given relatively final definition during the Polemical period through the Councils of Nicaea and Constantinople on account of the Arian, Macedonian and related controversies. During this time the expressions *ὁμοουσία* and *περιχώρησις* came into permanent use. The expression *filioque* was added to the Constantinopolitan Creed. The speculative development of the doctrine of the Trinity began at this time and continued during the Scholastic period. The controversy concerning the Holy Spirit was also continued, without resulting, however, in any special dogmatic definition. At the time of the Reformation the Trinity was deduced from the religious experience of the atonement, and there was no tendency toward speculative treatment, at any rate not so much in the Lutheran Church. During the Reformation and Protestant Scholastic period the true doctrine was established through the controversies with the Anti-Trinitarians of the time. The dogmatic terms were increased in number and more carefully defined. The modern critical period is not distinguished by the production of any dogmas, although speculative and philosophical expositions have not been wanting. Orthodox dogmatics has been compelled to combat philosophical Anti-Trinitarianism and Unitarianism in various forms. We wish now to present some special quotations and notes, which set forth the history of the dogma during the various periods.

Clement of Rome speaks of the Father, Christ and the Spirit and also sets forth the unity in the economical activity. He presents the divinity and pre-existence of Christ. Ignatius confesses the Father, Son and Holy Spirit and calls Christ God. The *Ebionites* did not acknowledge the Trinity and denied the supernatural birth of Christ. At His baptism He received divine powers. Some Ebionites also taught that God immediately brought forth the man, who received the Messianic spirit. They likewise taught that this spirit had been present in others, such as Abraham and Moses. The *Nazarenes* did not deny the supernatural birth, but did not acknowledge the hypostatical preexistence of Christ's divine nature, holding that at baptism God, the source of all holy spirit, united Himself with the human personality of Jesus.

Justin Martyr is the first to emphasize the word generation with regard to the relationship between the Father and Son. The generation of the Son was an act of the will. It was to the Son, who was born before all creatures, that the Father said: Let us make man. He also speaks of the Spirit. Theophilus of Antioch was the first to use the expression *τριάς* of the Trinity. He speaks of *λόγος ενδιάθετος* and *προφορικός* and calls the Spirit *σοφία*. Before we continue we must mention the three different kinds of Monarchians: the Dynamists, the Patripassians and the Modalists. The dynamistic Monarchians regarded the Father as a divine person, but considered the Son and the Spirit as divine powers. The founder of the so-called Dynamists was Theodotus the Tanner, who said that Jesus was a mere man who had been endued with special divine power. Theodotus the Money-Changer belonged to the same school and taught that Jesus at His birth was the recipient of special power from *Logos* or God. To this school also belonged Artemon. The most distinguished representative was Paul of Samosata. He speaks of *logos endiathetos* and *prophorikos*, but the latter was merely an impersonal power. The power of the *Logos* was united with Jesus, a mere man, who nevertheless was supernaturally conceived and born of a virgin. The personality of Jesus was not determined by the Logos, but by His human nature. The Patripassians taught that the Father had become man and suffered. The most prominent representatives of this school of thought were Praxeas, Noetus and Beryllus of Bostra. Beryllus of Bostra, in Arabia, held that Christ did not pre-exist as distinct from the Father, but became a separate person by incarnation. He inclined to the views of Modalism and Sabellianism. Eusebius presents his view in the following way: "Beryl attempted to introduce certain new articles of faith, daring to say that our Saviour and Lord did not pre-exist according to His own form of being before His coming among men, and that He did not possess a divinity of His own, but only that of the Father committed to Him." — The modalistic Monarchianism was completely developed by Sabellius. According to his view the eternal divine unity, which admits of no distinctions, had appeared in three modes or phases of development. These were the Father, Son and Spirit. They were not persons, but personifications. First God appeared as Father, and when His work was finished He withdrew, and then appeared as Son and finally as Holy Spirit. Tertullian defended the hypostatical pre-existence of the Logos and used the word Son. He also set forth the personality of the Spirit. He said, however, that the Spirit was subordinated to the Son and the Son to the Father, although he thought especially of the order and the gradation (*tres non statu, sed gradu*). He taught a threefold *filiatio*: 1) the eternal one in the mind of God, 2) the appearance at creation, and 3) the incarnation of the Son. He sought to explain the Trinity by the process of self-consciousness and also used the analogy of the root, trunk and fruit of the tree. Origen taught the eternal generation of the Son, but took the position that the

Son was subordinate to 'the Father. The Father was God in Himself, but the source of the Son's divinity was in the Father.

Dionysius of Alexandria was led astray in the beginning and gave utterance to expressions that implied that the Father was as much a stranger to the Son as a shipbuilder to the ship, or that the Son was absolutely distinct from the Father. Dionysius Of Rome opposed the former and used the term *homousios* to express the essential relationship between the Father and the Son. This expression was afterwards used as adequately setting forth that relationship. Arius said that inasmuch as the Son was born, there was a time when He was not. He was careful, however, not to use the word time; his expression was literally: There was, when the Son was not. Afterwards he said that the Son was created out of nothing, and that therefore He was not of like essence with the Father. He seems also to have considered the Spirit as less than the Son. Aetius and Eunomius developed Arianism and taught that the Son was of a different essence from the Father, and the term *ἑτερύσιος* came into use. The Semi-Arians, such as Basil of Ancyra and George of Laodicea, said that the Son was born of the Father and used the term *ὁμοιούσις*, wherefore they were called *Homoiousians*. Eusebius of Cesarea taught that the Father preceded the Son as a cause, for which reason the Son is not eternal in an absolute sense. He is not God in the highest and primary sense, but in a secondary sense. He denies the eternally unceasing generation of the Son, and looks upon the generation as having been completed in one act. The Holy Spirit was subordinate to the Father and the Son. Marcellus of Ancyra denied the hypostatical pre-existence of the Son. The man Jesus became the Son of God in this wise, that the *Logos* united Himself with Him. *Logos* was not born and was just as eternal as the Father. Before the creation of the world God was silent, but at the creation *Logos* appeared as drastic power, but was not personal. Athanasius, who defended the divinity of Christ, taught likewise that the Spirit was of the same essence as the Father. The Father, the Son, and the Spirit are three distinct modes of existence in God. Basil the Great said that the Father, Son and Spirit, although alike in essence, are nevertheless so distinct that the one is not the other. They are considered in and with each other. Cyril of Jerusalem taught the eternal generation of the Son and the personality of the Spirit. Both Gregory of Nazianzus and Gregory of Nyssa taught the divinity of the three persons. The latter set forth that the idea of plurality does not belong to the essence but to the hypostases, since the essence is not divided into persons. The persons stand in the most intimate relationship to each other and constitute a unity. From this time the terms *οὐσία* and *ὑπόστασις* came to be used to designate essence and person respectively. Augustine developed the essential unity of the Son and the Spirit with the Father. He placed the divine monad not in the person of the Father, but in the divine essence. He compared the three persons to the memory, the intellect and the will. He likewise represented the Trinity as *amans, quod amatur and mutuus amor*. He also uses the figure of cause, means and end. Concerning the Holy Spirit, he taught that the Spirit proceeds both from the Father and the Son. By reason of the authority of Augustine the expression *filioque* was added to the Constantinopolitan Creed at Toledo, 589. (At Constantinople in 381 the heresy of Macedonius was rejected. Macedonius taught that the Spirit was created by the Father through the Son. His disciples said that the Spirit must either be born or unborn. If He were born, then He would be either the son or the grandson of the Father; if He were unborn, then there would be two primitive essences. At the second Ecumenical Council in 381 it was decided that the Holy Spirit proceeds from the Father, should be worshiped as the Father and the Son, and that He is like unto them in glory.) But as the Council at Toledo did not represent the Eastern Church, therefore the addition of *filioque* to the creed gave rise to the schism between the Eastern and the Western Catholic Church. John Askusnagus and John Philoponus were guilty of a heresy that has been called Tritheism. The former taught that Christ had but one nature and he ascribed to each of the persons of the Trinity a distinct nature, so that there resulted three essences and three divinities. The latter considered essence as a basic concept, the persons being three individuals under this genus. Damianus was accused of supporting Tetratheism, but the accusation cannot be proved. By Tetratheism is meant the subordination of the Father, Son and

Spirit under the divine essence, which becomes God. Maximus Confessor, who prepared the way for the introduction of the writings of Dionysius the Areopagite to the Western Church, by which NeoPlatonism exerted great influence, stated that God is incomprehensible, but a personal spirit, who is the cause and goal of the world. He says that *Logos* occupies a central position, and that the Spirit proceeds from the Father and the Son. The three persons exist in and through each other and therefore he speaks of a *perichoresis*.

John of Damascus came under the influence of Maximus and taught as did the latter that the persons exist in and through each other and expressed this relationship by the term *περιχώρησις*. He ascribed unity to the Father, in whom dwelt the *Logos*. The Spirit proceeds from the Father and is mediated by the Son. He explained this relationship by the analogy of the sun, the rays and the light. The rays and the light proceed from the sun, but the light is mediated by the rays. The controversy concerning the Holy Spirit continued during the Scholastic period. Alcuin defended the position of Augustine. Photius of Constantinople accused the Roman Church of heresy, because, he asserted, it introduced two primitive causes in the Trinity. Ratramnus defended the position of the Roman Church. At the eighth Ecumenical Greek Council, held at Constantinople in 879, every one was condemned who made any additions to the Nicaeno-Constantinopolitan Creed. Some of the Greeks made the concession that the Spirit proceeded from the Father through the Son. John Scotus Erigena said that God is the absolute essence without determination, and taught therefore that there was no real Trinity, but that the distinctions were mere subjective conceptions. The Father is *essentia*, the Son is the world of ideas or *sapientia*, and the Holy Spirit is *vita* or the realization of the ideas. He uses the analogy of the fire, rays and light. Anselm thought of God as eternally realizing Himself through the process of self-consciousness in accordance with thesis, antithesis and synthesis. God is self-conscious Spirit as subject-object. The Father is *memoria*, the Son *intelligentia*, and the Holy Spirit is *amor*. He defended the view that the Spirit proceeds from both the Father and the Son. He also sought to show that there is in the

Trinity neither past nor future, this by analogy with the simultaneity of the sun, its light and its heat. Roscellinus said that the persons of the Godhead were *tres res per se*, for otherwise they would be only nominal distinctions. They were identical only in will and power. He therefore supported Tritheism. Abelard leaned somewhat toward Sabellianism, but taught, nevertheless, that the distinctions belong not only to the development in time, but that they were found in eternity before time. The Trinity consists of power, wisdom and goodness. He originated the grammatical analogy, representing the Father as the first, the Son as the second, and the Holy Spirit as the third person of the personal pronouns; also the analogy of the seal, the material and the inscription. Richard of St. Victor says that power and wisdom are the essential characteristics in the essence of God, and that the Trinity is explained through the concept of love. Love also demands a *condilectum*. Alexander of Hales speaks of a *diffusio per modum dilectionis*, which expresses the procession of the Holy Spirit. Thomas Aquinas reaches the conception of the Trinity by reasoning from the essence of man. God thinks Himself in the Son, and in the exercise of His will He loves Himself in the Spirit. The Holy Spirit proceeds from the Father and the Son, because He is loved by both. John Duns Scotus teaches that there is distinction in the essence of God, i. e., through the persons of the Trinity. But he does not have a clear conception of the Trinity. The Father is conceived of as *memoria*. The generation of the Son was an act of the free will, but nevertheless dependent upon thought. The Father generates the Son when in memory He realizes Himself as thinking. The procession of the Spirit as to its principle is in the will. He explains the procession of the Spirit from the Father and the Son by comparison with the light and the rays that proceed from the sun as one with it. Raymond of Sabunde compares the Father to *verbum activum*, the Son to *verbum passivum* and the Holy Spirit to *verbum impersonale*. Master Eckhart does not set forth the Christian doctrine of the Trinity, but represents the mystical pantheism. God is the eternal All. God is the eternal object of His thought. The thinking of God or the self-revealing of God as the object of His thought, constitutes the eternal generation of the

Son. "God speaks is equivalent to God begets." When God contemplates Himself as an object in the *Logos*, His thought is all-inclusive. But all things would return into God, into unity, and this process is likewise eternal. In this process love, which is the Spirit, is the mediator. This procedure out of God and return into God is, as it were, a game which God plays with Himself.

Luther, who had no taste for scholastic distinctions, said that we should believe that there were three persons in the Godhead, that the persons were not to be confused, that the essence should not be divided. From the economical Trinity revealed in the Word of God he inferred the truth or reality of the ontological Trinity. He makes use of a variety of figures, such as, word, image and reflection. Melanchthon explained the Trinity in the first place on the basis of the religious and practical needs of man, subsequently following Augustine and others in reasoning from the nature and character of the human spirit to the divine. After the Reformation there were three anti-Trinitarian tendencies: 1) Anabaptists, such as Hetzer, Denk, and others; 2) theosophical natural philosophers, headed by Servetus; 3) Socinians, such as Faustus Socinus. Michael Servetus accepted only an economical Trinity. God revealed Himself in a double form of revelation, the objective in the Word and the subjective in the Spirit. The three persons are *diversae facies et species deitatis*. The Word is the ideal world, the archetype of the world, *Logos endiathetos*. Through a supernatural generation this pre-existent Christ became *Logos prophorikos*. He is not an eternal son, inasmuch as he was only typified before. When a word is spoken there takes place an exhalation. In like manner the Holy Spirit proceeded from the word of creation, the second mode of revelation. This is the spirit of life which reaches self-consciousness in the spirit of man. Faustus Socinus said that there is no distinction in God. Christ was a mere man. He was received into heaven before He had begun the work of His office. After the resurrection He received divine power and might. The Holy Spirit was merely a divine force. Among pantheistic mystics may be counted Jacob Böhme, who taught that the Father was all, the Son was the heart of the powers of the Father, and the Holy Spirit the principle of motion. The Father is nature, the Son the intellect of nature, and the Spirit the bond of union between the two. The Trinity has significance within the sphere of natural life, but otherwise God is all. The *Arminians* hold the doctrine of subordination, for which reason their conception of the Trinity is faulty.

Among the philosophers who have exercised either direct or indirect influence on the development of the dogma of the Trinity may be mentioned Leibnitz, Kant and Hegel. Leibnitz explained the Trinity through the process of thought. The Father is the thinking subject, the Son is the object, and the Spirit is the thought process itself. Kant sets forth the Trinity merely as a practical idea, and therefore teaches no Trinity at all. From the moral viewpoint God is considered as the law-giver, the ruler and the judge. According to the idea of the law, God must be love. The Father is therefore conceived of as the one who loves. The Son is man made morally perfect. God is Holy Spirit because love is dependent upon the agreement of man with the holy good-will of God. Hegel said that God is a process which proceeds from one stage of development to another, but the distinctions are lost. The Son of God is the world, but the world returns to its source. As the Spirit God returns from *non ego* to Himself. This takes place in the spirit of man, through which God becomes conscious of Himself. The unity of God and man has been revealed in Christ. Schleiermacher criticizes the church doctrine, because he considers that it gives the Father more power and glory than the Son and the Spirit. He says that we have no knowledge of God outside the world. Christ had no pre-existence, but was the man in whom the consciousness of God had been clearly and perfectly developed. Sanctification does not have its source in the Holy Spirit, as the Church's doctrine declares, but in the spirit of communion in the Christian Church. During the 18th and especially the 19th century Arianism, Socinianism and related tendencies have sprung up in a new form under the name of Unitarianism. Among the representatives may be mentioned James Priestly, James Freeman, James Freeman Clarke, W. E. Channing and James Martineau. These men and the Unitarians in general are the most ardent anti-Trinitarians in modern times. Within the Lutheran Church during recent times more or less confessional theologians have expressed themselves concerning the Trinity, but there has been no special development of the dogma. Among the least confessional theologians we may mention Kahnis, and among the confessional or near confessional we would mention only Thomasius, Philippi, Martensen and Granfelt. Kahnis says that the Son and the Spirit are divine personalities, who came into being from the Father before time and mediate the relationship of God to the world. The Father is God in the highest sense, but the Son and the Spirit are only called divine. Thomasius says that the threefoldness of the atonement is experienced as being combined in one because it is the expression of the same gracious will. In the economical Trinity there are both distinction and union, and likewise in the ontological Trinity. The absolute personality subsists in three distinctions or persons. Philippi explained the Trinity through the atonement. He speaks of God, by whom, through whom and in whom we are reconciled. Like others he reaches the ontological Trinity through the economical. Compare what has been previously quoted from Philippi's Dogmatics. Martensen proceeds from the concept of love. He seeks an analogy in the being of man, but says that the threefoldness in man, thought, will and emotion, while not corresponding, is ideal, inasmuch as man develops in relation to the world. What the world is to man, that the Son is to the Father. The Spirit mediates this relationship of love. Granfelt holds that the Trinity cannot be explained by means of the process of self-consciousness. He speaks of the threefold ego, the substantial, the objective and the subjective. Nor can the Trinity be explained through the principle of love alone. The two methods must be combined. God, who is absolute love, is the subject and object of love. In both there is the same loving will, which, loved by both, becomes a third personality. The Father is the original and eternal principle, the Son is the original and eternal intellect, and the Holy Spirit is the original and eternal will.

§7. THE ETERNAL PURPOSE OF GOD.

It is customary to speak of two eternal decrees of God, viz., the decree to create the world and the decree to redeem fallen man. Although both of these decrees are eternal, still in our thought we distinguish between them and place the creational decree first. In this decree God conceived of the rational creatures as being blessed in Him, and, in communion with Him in the bonds of holy love and with each other, constituting a blessed organism, the Kingdom of God. For this reason man was made in the image of God through the Son and unto Him. But sin prevented the realization of the original plan. Wherefore the decree concerning salvation became necessary, which in an objective sense was carried out through the Son and unto Him, inasmuch as He is the eternal archetype as well as the goal of man. The determination to save man was by grace alone and included all men, in like manner as the creational decree contemplated the salvation of all in God through the Son. We speak first therefore of the universal benevolence of God.

1. The General Benevolence Of God.

Benevolentia Dei universalis or *praedestinatio late dicta,* which is conditioned by or refers to *voluntas antecedens, is that act of the gracious will of God which implies that God in eternity has willed to save all men through Christ and through the Spirit to offer to all men this acquired salvation.*

This general decree of salvation, which, strictly speaking, is not election, contains three specifications: a) God did not desire the death of any sinner, but had mercy upon the fallen human race; b) God determined to send the Son to perform the work of atonement and the Spirit to apply salvation; c) God determined the order in which men should be made partakers of salvation.

The following passages may be quoted: “This is good and acceptable in the sight of God our Saviour; who would have all men to be saved, and come to the knowledge of the truth” (1 Tim. 2:3,4); “For God so loved the world, that he gave his only begotten Son, that whosoever believeth on him should not perish, but have eternal life” (John 3:16); “But when the Comforter is come, whom I will send unto you from the Father, even the

Spirit of truth, which proceedeth from the Father, he shall bear witness of me" (John 15:26); "Except one be born of the water and the Spirit, he cannot enter into the kingdom of God" (John 3:5).

The following attributes are used concerning the universal will of God: 1) *gratuita* or gratuitous: "By grace have ye been saved" (Eph. 2:8); 2) *liberalis* or free: "But all things are of God" (2 Cor. 5:19); 3) *aequalis* or equal: "God was in Christ reconciling the world unto himself" (2 Cor. 5:19); 4) *seria* or serious: "Have I any pleasure in the death of the wicked, saith the Lord" (Ezek.18:23); 5) *efficax* or efficacious: "But when the fullness of time came, God sent forth his Son, born of a woman, born under the law, that he might redeem them that were under the law, that we might receive the adoption of sons" (Gal. 4:4,5); and since God thought of men as saved in Christ and that without Him there is no salvation, we may add: 6) *conditionata* or conditioned: "Him who knew no sin he made to be sin on our behalf; that we might become the righteousness of God in him" (2 Cor. 5:21).

2. The Special Will Or Benevolence Of God.

Benevolentia Dei specialis, which refers to *voluntas consequens,* constitutes *praedestinatio stricte dicta* or *electio* (election). On account of the relation of men to the condition, the opposite of *electio* must also be treated, viz., *reprobatio* or reprobation. We desire at this juncture to remark that *praedestinatio* is not a genus with *electio* and *reprobatio* as subordinated species. *Praedestinatio* and *electio,* therefore, art not logical synonyms, but they are grammatical synonyms. They are to be distinguished formally, not materially. *Praedestinatio,* as can be seen by the prefix *prae,* has reference to priority, the order and the means. *Electio,* as seen by the prefix *e,* has reference to the objects for election, those taken out of the mass for election. In Ephesians 1:4, 5, the corresponding verbal forms are used, from which it is clear that there is no material distinction.

Electio, or predestination, *is the eternal and conditioned decree of God to save all who believe in Christ and who persevere in this faith to the end of their earthly life.*

Causa impulsiva interna is equivalent to the free grace of God alone. *Causa impulsiva externa* is equivalent to the merit of Christ, considered in relation to the foreknown final application. The Calvinists, on the other hand, say that the expression is equivalent to God's unconditioned will. They also say that according to *voluntas signi* God wills to save all men, but not according to *voluntas beneplaciti*. But we say that the revealed and the secret will of God agree. *Electio* comprises the following three terms: a) *πρόθεσις*, or the decree of God to save those that believe in Christ; b) *πρόγνωσις*, or God's foreknowledge of those that would believe in Christ; c) *προορισμός*, or God's predetermination or foreordination to save those whom He foresaw would believe.

The following attributes are ascribed to *electio*: *non absoluta*, because election depends upon the attitude of man, *sed ordinata et conditionata*, since God has determined a certain order of salvation and necessary conditions. Although the foreknowledge of God does not imply any compulsion, yet by virtue of His omniscience God cannot make any mistake in His foreknowledge, wherefore dogmaticians generally say from this point of view that *electio* is also *categorica*, or determined and clear, immutable and irrevocable. In this sense *electio* is *non conditionata*, but this is something entirely different from the Calvinistic doctrine of predestination.

Hollazius presents therefore the following syllogism concerning predestination: "Every one who will perseveringly believe in Christ to the end of life, will certainly be saved, and, therefore, shall be elected and be written in the Book of Life. But Abraham, Peter, Paul, etc., will perseveringly believe in Christ to the end of life. Therefore, Abraham, Peter, Paul, etc., will certainly be saved, and, therefore, shall be elected and written in the Book of Life." This syllogism contains the three terms or the major and minor premises as well as predestination itself. God does not predetermine that any one shall believe, but He foresees those who will be moved by the grace of God, and who will believe, whom He also elects to eternal salvation. This does not imply any contradiction between the General and Special Will of God, for, although God would that all men should be saved, still He cannot force anyone in a predeterministic way to believe, and without faith no one can be elected and saved. The foreknowledge of God does not imply any determinism, so that this foreknowledge should be the cause of faith, but God foresees that this or that person will believe. Although God works faith in a manner to exclude all Pelagianism, Semi-Pelagianism and Synergism, still this divine work of grace does not imply that God predetermines in whom He will work faith, for although He would that all men should be saved, yet man is able to hinder the gracious work of God's Spirit. The responsibility of man must not be overlooked. God knows in advance whether or not the sinner will oppose the work of the Spirit, whether he will be moved by the Spirit to believe, and whether he will endure unto the end. If this were not the case, then predestination would be unconditional. Human Reason balks at this because it cannot comprehend how God can seriously call those concerning whom He foreknows that they will not believe. But it is clear that the call of God must be the same to all, since His predetermination depends upon His foreknowledge of the attitude of man to the proffered grace of God. The individual man could not enter into any relationship with God in this sense, if Christ had not died for him, and if the work of the Holy Spirit were not performed in his heart. Neither can we believe in God and limit His omniscience, for then He would cease to be the absolute personality. His omniscience does not encroach upon His love, His righteousness, and His faithfulness. As God is omniscient He necessarily foreknows. He must, therefore, foreknow persons who will have faith in Christ. If it is claimed that faith is antecedent to election, we must consider that from the divine viewpoint there is no antecedence, because God is eternal and omniscient. He does not reason in regard to election as we do. When He foresees who will believe, He does not think of faith as a cause of election. No one is saved on account of faith, but faith is necessary to salvation. If God in His omniscience has made such a condition, His knowledge in regard to believers does not mean that their faith is a merit or cause of election. The believers themselves know by their experience that the Holy Spirit effects faith. The phrase "election in view of faith" does not necessarily imply Synergism and cannot mean that, as no one can believe by his own powers. The cause of salvation is *sola gratia*, but only believers will be saved. If God wills that all should be saved by grace, through faith, would not God save every one, if it were possible? As the Holy Spirit works faith, why do not all men believe? Should we say that the reason is a mystery? We know that men resist the Holy Spirit, but why do some give up resistance? Is the grace of God irresistible? But such a belief would be Calvinism. Should we again exclaim: It is a mystery! The Scriptures demand faith or repentance and faith; where shall we place the responsibility? The Holy Spirit works on the hearts of men by calling, illuminating, convincing, convicting, etc. According to the Bible, He calls all seriously. If the Holy Spirit awakens sinners and illumines them by the Law to experience contrition and by the Gospel to become believers, the failure of conversion with its attendant responsibility must be due to the resistance of the sinner. But if the awakened sinner ceases to resist and becomes passive through the illumination of the Spirit, this passivity cannot be called Synergism, Pelagianism, etc. The psychological moment and reason when and why some become passive and do not resist may look mysterious, but the fact that a person becomes passive and does not hinder the Spirit from continuing the good work to effect conversion cannot be called Synergism. Man cannot convert himself. But if a sick person becomes convinced that a certain physician can cure him and then yields to his treatment, this yielding or passivity is not a self-cure. Transferring the case to the spiritual domain of conversion, such an instance would not be Pelagianism, Semi-Pelagianism and Synergism. When resistance ceases, the Spirit effects conversion. If God elects in view of such work of the Spirit as leads the sinner to faith and preserves him in Christ unto death, such an election is not a causal antecedent of election to be styled Synergism. No one is elected on account of faith, but God elects believers who have faith at death, and the cause is *sola gratia* and the merit of Christ applied by the Holy Spirit through faith. As God is omniscient and not limited by the past, present or future, He knows His own elect also by foreknowledge, which expression is used in relation to us, since omniscience covers all relations of God.

As the Bible is the Word of God and a revelation to us who live in time, the Holy Spirit uses the words suitable to our condition. In Rom. 8:29, 30 we find the order of God as to election expressed in a way which will permit the use of the word foreknowledge in regard to the justified and we are justified by faith. We read: "For whom he foreknew, he also foreordained." The Greek word for *foreknow* cannot in English be rendered by *foreordain*. God foreknew certain persons from eternity, whom He also foreordained or predestined to be saved, and He began to realize this decree in time by calling, justifying and glorifying. These persons were not foreknown, because they were predestinated, but their predestination to salvation or election was dependent upon foreknowledge, since God is omniscient. Who are the persons whom God elects? Christ died for all, but only believers are elected to salvation. It is not an unconditional predestination to faith. No one is excluded from salvation by an absolute decree; every one is privileged to become a Believer. If we are justified by faith, we are also elected by being in Christ at the end of life. God knows beforehand from eternity who are His elect. Gerhard says: "Justification, which occurred in time, is a mirror of the election which occurred before time." The expression "elected in view of faith" has been differently explained. *Bene docet qui bene distinguit.* The larger part of the Lutheran Church uses this expression while denying that it implies Pelagianism. If a phrase is not recognized by all, but the definition is correct as to the meaning, there should be no dispute. If the rejection of the words "in view of faith" would be looked upon by a large part of the Church as a Calvinistic tendency and the retaining of the words would appear to the rest as Synergism, we should keep in mind that God elected the believers who are in Christ at the close of their life, and He elected them from eternity, as He is omniscient. If the expression "elected to faith" may be defended according to *Praedestinatio latae dicta*, the wording "elected through faith" may be just as correct according to *Praedestinatio stricte dicta* or *Electio*. We have already discussed faith as the work of the Spirit. But the Spirit does not compel men to believe. Man is responsible, if he does reject the proffered grace.

If the elect are those who die as believers, it may be that not all believers at present are elect, because they may fall from grace and die in unbelief. On the other hand there may be unbelievers at present who are elect and, therefore, will be regenerated. Though they fall, they will be restored to faith and will die as believers. God is infallible in His foreknowledge or omniscience. Faithfulness unto death is not the consequence of predestination or election, but the condition of election. An elect person remains in Christ, not by his own power, but by the grace of God. The only cause of election to salvation is the sole grace (*sola gratia*) of God as effective in the merit of Christ, but the condition of election is faith in Christ. Whatever the mystery in the election, it is revealed that "God so loved the world, that he gave his only begotten Son, that whosoever believeth on him should not perish, but have eternal life." The new birth or regeneration is a necessary condition for entering heaven. Christ said to Nicodemus: "Except one be born of water and the Spirit, he cannot enter into the kingdom of God." The Lutheran Church believes that children at their Baptism are regenerated and, therefore, have faith. If children die without falling from baptismal grace, there is no Christian who doubts their salvation. Only a Calvinist might ascribe absolute or unconditional rejection to such children in case they were not unconditionally elected or predestinated. Why do not all grown persons become regenerated at Baptism? The answer is, because of resistance in unbelief. When they come to believe, Baptismal grace is fully applied and effective. Why does Baptismal grace apply immediately to a child? The answer is, that such a child does not self-consciously resist the Spirit at Baptism. As omniscient, God must have foreknown the circumstances and have from eternity elected those children who die without having fallen from grace. In the Christian Church, except for some sects, all children are baptized, but many fall from Baptismal grace. As the Spirit calls them to return to God by prevenient grace and by so-called preparatory grace and continues to work through illumination, when does the Spirit work faith? The answer is, when resistance ceases. The Spirit of God works upon the spirit of man, illumines his mind and appeals to his feelings. In the impelling, not compelling, work of the Holy Spirit man may yield and faith be effected. If such a person remains in Christ or dies in faith, he is elected from eternity. But we must not ignore the work of the Spirit in Baptism and on account of Baptism. The decree of election has no *proviso* in itself. God is omniscient and knows His own from eternity. From the viewpoint of God their names are irrevocably written in the Book of Life. Our own certainty is not absolute, but relative, but we are ordinarily certain of our justification and regeneration, and we know; that God will spare no effort to preserve us. The Lord says: "No one shall snatch them out of my hand." We should use the means of grace, accordingly and trust the Lord. Compare also the following passages: Rom. 8:38, 39; 1 Cor. 9:27; 2 Tim. 4:7, 8; Rev. 3:5.

The following Scripture passages may especially be noted: "Even as he chose us in him (Christ) before the foundation of the world, that we should be holy and without blemish before him in love: having foreordained us unto adoption as sons through Jesus Christ unto himself, according to the good pleasure of his will" (Eph. 1:4, 5). There are some who would refer this passage to the general or universal will of God, maintaining that the general decree of salvation in Christ is here expressed. But since the letter is written to the saints and the faithful, it is clear that the special will of God is referred to. However, the special will of God is connected with and grounded in the general will. This is important for the reason that some say that all are elected. To be sure, everything depends upon a good interpretation, and if we add—in Christ, then it would be correct. Nevertheless, it is better to express oneself in such manner that no misunderstanding may arise. The faithful are the elect, as expressed in the special decree or will of God. It is one thing that God would that all men should be saved, and another, to be elected, since in the latter case the relationship of man to the proffered salvation is taken into consideration. The cited passage also shows that election is *eternal*. Cf. 2 Tim. 1:9: "Before times eternal." The *particularity* of election is expressed in Matt. 22:14: "Many are called, but few chosen." Its *immutability* is expressed in

2 Tim. 2: 19: "Howbeit the firm foundation of God standeth, having this seal, The Lord knoweth them that are his," and also in 1 Peter 1:5: "Who by the power of God are guarded." Cf. Rom. 8: 29, 30. Its *certainty* is expressed in the following passages: "Rejoice that your names are written in heaven" (Luke 10: 20); "For I am persuaded, that neither death, nor life, nor angels, nor principalities, nor things present, nor things to come, nor powers, nor height, nor depth, nor any other creature, shall be able to separate us from the love of God, which is in Christ Jesus our Lord" (Rom. 8:38, 39). That the elect can fall and have fallen is referred to in such passages as the following: "Restore unto me the joy of thy salvation, and uphold me with a willing spirit" (Ps. 51:12) ; "When once thou hast turned again, establish thy brethren" (Luke 22:32); "Wherefore let him that thinketh he standeth take heed lest he fall" (1 Cor. 10:12). When the elect fall, God foreknows their return to faith and that they will die in faith. Otherwise they would not be elect. Concerning perseverance in faith unto the end the following passages may be quoted: "He that endureth to the end, the same shall be saved" (Matt. 10:22). "Be thou faithful unto death, and I will give thee the crown of life" (Rev. 2:10). One of the most important passages that throw light upon the doctrine of election is Rom. 8:29, 30: "For whom he foreknew, he also ordained to be conformed to the image of his Son, that he might be the firstborn among many brethren: and whom he foreordained, them he also called: and whom he called, them he also justified: and whom he justified, them he also glorified." Cf. Acts 13:48. The verb for ordain is *τάσσω* and not as in Rom. 8:30. The expression does not support the Calvinistic view. Finally we must direct attention to the 9th chapter of Romans, which, the Calvinists claim, militates against the Lutheran position. Verses 11, 12, 13, 18, 22 and 23 treat specifically of the question: "That the purpose of God according to election might stand—Jacob I loved, Esau I hated.—So then he hath mercy upon whom he will, and whom he will be hardeneth." —Vessels of wrath fitted unto destruction—vessels of mercy, which he afore prepared unto glory." Hollazius says that these passages speak of God's *voluntas consequens*. The hardening is judicial. Quenstedt says that

the text speaks of Jacob and Esau from the temporal point of view, and not concerning their election in a spiritual sense. If the Calvinists were right in their interpretation, then this passage would mean that the descendants of Jacob would be saved and the descendants of Esau damned. We must likewise bear in mind the object of Paul's arguments in the 9th chapter, inasmuch as he does not treat directly of the doctrine of election, but speaks of the position of the Jews and the heathens. Besides we should not forget the analogy of faith. In the preceding chapter Paul clearly expounds the doctrine of election. The clear passages explain the doubtful.

3. Concerning Reprobation.

Reprobatio, or reprobation, is the eternal and conditional decree of God by which He leaves to eternal condemnation those that are unfaithful to the end of life and who therefore die in unbelief.

Causa Impulsiva Interna is equivalent to the punitive righteousness of God, *justitia punitiva. Causa Impulsiva Externa* is equivalent to the rejection of the merit of Christ by the unbelievers, i. e., the foreseen *incredulitas finalis.*

The terms that are used in describing *reprobatio* are the following: a) *πρόθεσις,* or the decree of God that all men who continue in unbelief shall be condemned for their sins; b) *πρόγνωσις,* or God's foreseeing who they are; c) *ἀποδοχιμασία,* or the application of the decree that those whom God has thus foreseen shall, by reason of their rejection of the grace of God, be left to eternal condemnation.

Reprobation does not imply determinism, but is *conditionata,* i. e., dependent upon the attitude of man in rejecting the proffered grace of salvation, and *immutabilis,* because God correctly foresees who will die in unbelief and bases His decree to leave them to eternal condemnation upon that foreknowledge. The knowledge and the will of God do not correspond. The free acts of man do not take place because God foresees them, rather God foresees that they will take place. God is therefore not the cause of the rejection of any man, and is not active in the same manner in reprobation as in election.

The following passages may be quoted: "But after thy hardness and impenitent heart treasurest up for thyself wrath in the day of wrath and revelation of the righteous judgment of God" (Rom. 2:5); "He that obeyeth not the Son shall not see life, but the wrath of God abideth on him" (John 3: 36); "Depart from me, ye cursed, into the eternal fire which is prepared for the devil and his angels" (Matt. 25:41); "A stone of stumbling, and a rock of offence; for they stumble at thy word, being disobedient: whereunto also they were appointed" (1 Peter 2:8). This latter implies no other predetermination than that contained in the definition. God has foreseen their unbelief and He has determined that all unbelievers shall be rejected.

4. Notes on the History of Dogma.

During the first or Apologetical period it was generally taught that Christ "had suffered and died for all, that the call is general, and that God has predetermined men only on the ground of His foreknowledge of their belief or unbelief. In the following period the struggle between Augustine and Pelagianism, etc., took place, when it may be said that the foundation of the doctrine of predestination was laid, which was developed with all its implications by Gottschalk during the Scholastic period and by Calvin during the period of the Reformation. Within the Catholic Church the controversy concerning predestination again waxed warm at the close of the sixteenth century, and through the Jansenistic struggle during the first half of the seventeenth century. In the Lutheran Church at the same time a struggle arose on account of Huber, who had come over to the Lutheran Church. Concerning election he taught a limitless universalism. Aegidius Hunnius combated Huberts heretical view. Within the Reformed Church there arose at the same time a tendency that has been called Amyraldism, and still another called Pajonism. In modern times Schleiermacher sought to nullify the dualism of the doctrine of predestination and was thereby led to a solution of the problem that would imply the final salvation of all men. Within the Lutheran Church during recent times there has been no important controversy concerning predestination with the exception of a bitter struggle within a part of the Lutheran Church in North America. The controversy arose on account of the expression *intuitu fidei*, whose content in the doctrine of predestination the Missouri Synod did not approve. This synod sets forth a view that partly may imply Calvinism and Amyraldism in the actual result. But the Missourians protest that they do not teach Calvinism in any sense, because they accept the General Benevolence of God and reject double predestination. We herewith append some special notes.

Origen was first to present clearly the relationship between the foreknowledge of God and the acts of man. The acts of man do not take place by virtue of God's foreknowledge, but God foresees how men will act.

During the Polemical period Basil the Great, Cyril of Jerusalem and Gregory of Nyssa took similar positions on the doctrine. Chrysostom says that predestination to salvation depends both upon the love of God and the virtue of man. According to the first will of God He would that all men should be saved, and in accordance with His second will He would that those who obey His will should be saved, and that the others should perish. Jerome taught that grace was offered to all, but that predestination was dependent upon God's foreknowledge and that therefore election was conditional. In the beginning Augustustine taught that grace was conditioned by the free will of man, and that predestination was dependent upon God's foreknowledge of man's faith. But when he later began to emphasize man's inability, maintaining that only that grace could save which was not conditioned by the relation of man, he was led on to the doctrine of *gratia irresistibilis*. From this point he reached the position that God through a decretum absolutum had chosen out of the fallen mass of humanity a certain number of vessels of mercy upon whom He conferred faith and *donum perseverantiae*. The other He left to everlasting condemnation. Nor was any injustice done, because they had deserved the perdition of hell. He said that the fall into sin depended upon the freedom of Adam. Augustine held the *Infralapsarlan* view. The *Infralapsarians* taught that God had made His unconditional decree to save some and leave the others to condemnation, because of the fact that through the fall into sin man had made himself guilty of condemnation. The *Supralapsarians* taught that God had made His unconditional decree prior to and independent of the fall into sin, which He nevertheless foreknew, so that the fall itself was a result of this decree. The *Pelagians* rejected the unconditional theory of predestination. Their position was dependent upon their conception of human freedom. The *Semi-Pelagians*, such as Cassianus, Faustus and others, taught the universality of grace and rejected the unconditional theory of predestination. Naturally this depended upon their doctrine of man's assistance in his conversion. The *Semi-Pelagians* were victorious at Aries in 472 and at Lyons in 475. Prosper Aquitanus, who defended Augustine, taught that God's foreknowledge and predetermination coincide merely with regard to the elect. He spoke of a concealed will of God, according to which only the elect were considered, and of a revealed will, in accordance with which God would that all men should be saved. During the second half of the fifth century a book appeared that bore the title, *De Vocatione Gentium*, which is supposed to have been written by Leo the Great. This book rejects Semi-Pelagianism and unconditional predestination, but speaks of universal grace and also of special grace with reference to the elect. Fulgentius of Ruspe and Caesarius of Arles did much to accomplish the defeat of Semi-Pelagianism at Orange in 529. The question of predestination was not touched, but the theory that God had predestined certain persons to sin was rejected. Gregory the Great supported a moderate Augustinian view. He based his theory of predestination on the foreknowledge of God and rejected the doctrine of *decretum absolutum*. Although he taught that grace could be lost, still he seems to have supported the theory of *gratia irresistibilis*.

John of Damascus followed Chrysostom, but said: "It behooves us that God knows all things beforehand, but that He does not determine all things. With relation to us He foresees all, but does not determine it." Alcuin supported the views of Augustine, but rejected predestination to perdition. Gottschalk was the first to present clearly the doctrine of a double predestination. He did not teach that God had predetermined sin, but that He had predetermined the reprobate to eternal perdition.

Therefore he also taught that God did not desire that all should be saved, and that Christ had not died for all. His doctrine was condemned at the Synod of Quiercy in 849, chiefly through the efforts of Rabanus and Hincmar. Rabanus Maurus rejected the doctrine of double predestination. He said that predestination was unconditional in relation to the elect, but in relation, to the damned it was conditioned on their attitude, which God had foreseen. Like Prosper Aquitanus he distinguished between *voluntas beneplaciti* and *voluntas signi*. Hincmar, Florus and John Scotus Erigena fought against the doctrine of Gottschalk, but Prudentius and Ratramnus supported the doctrine of double predestination. Anselm considered that that which was necessary from the viewpoint of eternity may appear in its temporal development to be dependent upon the will, and that the foreknowledge and predetermination of God are united in relation to the good. Peter the Lombard set forth that predestination and foreknowledge were united only in relation to the good. He said that God rejected those He knew would sin and thereby deserve eternal death. Like Anselm, Lombard tried to follow Augustine without accepting Augustinianism in all its severity. Thomas Aquinas considered that both *electio* and *reprobatio* belonged to God's predetermination, but that God did not predetermine the evil, only the punishment of evil. Antecedenter God would that all should be saved, but not consequenter. The will of God was therefore twofold. He predetermined to salvation certain ones upon whom He would show His mercy, and others upon whom His goodness would reveal itself in the form of punitive righteousness. Duns Scotus held the Semi-Pelagian view. Thomas Bradwardine was an Augustinian, yea, a new Gottschalk. He complained that nearly the whole world had fallen into the Pelagian error. Wickliffe and Huss approached closely the view of Augustine.

Luther at first supported the stern doctrine of predestination, as may be seen in his book *De Servo Arbitrio* against Erasmus. He held that he could not be certain of his salvation, if it were dependent upon human freedom. By his doctrine of the total inability of man, he considered himself compelled to accept the stern doctrine of predestination. Afterwards, however, he liberated himself from the Augustinian doctrine of predestination, when he succeeded in harmonizing his new viewpoint with the doctrine of all by grace. Zwingli supported the doctrine of predestination as it had been developed after Augustine, and said also that sin had been predetermined. Calvin set forth that God, in order to tear down all human righteousness and in accordance with His own will, independent of any foreknowledge of the belief or unbelief of man, had decided to elect certain persons to salvation in order to glorify His mercy, and to elect others to condemnation to glorify His righteousness. Predestination was therefore unconditional, and based upon the absolute will of God without reference to the death of Christ. Christ died only for the elect. Calvin was a Supralapsarian, i. e., according to his view, the fall itself was predetermined. Regeneration and predestination become almost identical, and the elect cannot fall.

The *Formula of Concord* treats of the doctrine of predestination principally in a broad sense and from the practical standpoint. Predestination is referred to election and therefore has reference to those that believe. The condemnation of the unbelievers is not an object of predestination. For this reason rejection is called *reprobatio* and not *praedestinatio*. In relation to the evil there is only *praesciens*. Christ died for all. The evangelical promises of grace belong to all. There is no secret decree concerning which we need feel disturbed. There is no twofold call. It also sets forth how we become certain of our election. We are directed to the call of God and to the means of grace. We must look away from ourselves. Those that believe and follow the Word are the elect, etc. The following are the eight points in the *Formula of Concord*: 1. That the human race is truly redeemed and reconciled with God through Christ, who, by His faultless obedience, suffering and death, has merited for us righteousness which avails before God, and eternal life. 2. That such merit and benefits of Christ is offered, presented and distributed to us through His Word and Sacraments. 3. That He is efficacious and active in us by the Holy Ghost through the Word when it is preached, heard and pondered, to convert hearts to true repentance and preserve them in the true faith. 4. That all those who in true repentance receive Christ by a true faith justifies and receives unto grace, adoption and inheritance of eternal life. 5. That those who are thus justified He also sanctifies in love, as St. Paul (Eph. 1:4) says. 6. That, in their great weakness, He also defends them against the devil, the world, and the flesh, and rules and leads them in His ways, and when they stumble raises them again (places His hand beneath them), and under the cross and in temptation comforts and preserves them (for life). 7. That the good work which He has begun in them He strengthens, increases, and supports to the end, if they observe God's Word, pray diligently, abide in God's goodness (grace) and faithfully use the gifts received. 8. That those whom He has elected, called and justified, He eternally saves and glorifies in life eternal.[11]

Gerhard says: "Election is the eternal decree of God to justify and save men. Therefore also He decreed from eternity to justify and save only those who will believe (credituros), and consequently He elected those only whom He foresaw as remaining in Christ through faith. — As Paul accordingly declares, Eph. 1:4, that God elected us in Christ, so he declares, 2 Thess. 2:13, that God elected us in faith, since we could not be elected in Christ except in view of faith which embraces Christ."[12] Baier defines election: "Predestination or election can be defined in the stricter sense to be the eternal decree of God by which God in His infinite mercy determined to give eternal salvation to all those, and only to those, of whom He foresaw that they would believe in Christ till the end, and this for the sake of Christ's merits, which must be apprehended by persevering faith, and foreseen as such,—for the sake of their salvation and of His glory."[13]

The *Socinians* adopted the view of the Pelagians and rejected Calvinism for the same reason that the Pelagians rejected Augustinianism. At the end of the sixteenth century a controversy arose between the Thomists and

---

[11] See Jacobs, *Book of Concord*, pp. 652, 653. Miiller, Symb. B. , II Pars, pp. 707, 708.

[12] Gerhard, *Loci Theol. II*, 86. 87.

[13] *Baieri Comp.* Part. Cap. 12, §20.

Dominicans on the one hand and the Scotists, Franciscans and Jesuits on the other. The former held Augustinian views. Michael Baius expressed himself in favor of strict Augustinian views as against Semi-Pelagianism, for which reason Pope Pius V condemned 76 propositions in his writings. The Jesuit Louis Molina referred salvation to the self-determination of man. God elects those of whom He foresees that they will fulfill the conditions. In his presentation he introduced into dogmatic terminology the expression *scientia media*. The controversy had no result.

During the seventeenth century controversies concerning predestination occurred within the Catholic, Lutheran and Reformed Churches, The Jansenist controversy was fought out in the Catholic Church. Cornelius Jansen defended the strict Augustinian system of doctrine in his work on Augustine. He accepted a double predestination and took the view that absolute predetermination was founded in the will of God. Like Augustine he was an Infralapsarian. Blaise Pascal, Arnauld and Quesnel held Augustinian views. The latter wrote an exposition on the New Testament. Clement XI in his Bull *Unigenitus* condemned 101 propositions in Quesnel's book, yet Jansenism extended its influence into the eighteenth century. In the Lutheran Church, Samuel Huber, who had come from the Reformed Church, fought against the Reformed Particularism to such a degree that he lapsed into a species of Universalism. Huber rejected the doctrine of the Lutheran theologians, that God elects only those of whom He foresees that they will believe. But Huber was not consistent, for he said that not all would be saved, but only those who accept election. Aegidius Hunnius combated the universal doctrine of predestination that Huber championed.

In the Reformed Church there arose the controversy between the *Arminians*, who developed Semi-Pelagian tendencies, and the *Gomarists*, who supported Calvinism. The *Arminians*, or the *Remonstrants*, taught concerning predestination that God through an eternal and inscrutable decree before the foundation of the world had arranged in Christ, on account of Christ, and through Christ, to save all those who through the grace of the Holy Spirit believe in Christ and persevere in this faith unto the end of life. Besides, the controversy on predestination continued in the Reformed Church through Amyraldism and Pajonism. Amyraldus essayed to modify the strict Calvinism of the Synod of Dort. His doctrine, which has been called *universalismus hypotheticus*, contained a real Particularism and an ideal Universalism. God would save all, but faith was the condition. Man himself cannot fulfill the condition. He speaks therefore of a particularistic will, in accordance with which God from eternity has determined to save a certain number, to whom He grants the gift of faith. The objective grace offers salvation to all on condition of repentance and faith. The subjective grace is particularistic. Pajon accepted the doctrine of objective grace, but rejected the subjective, according to which the Holy Spirit acts immediately upon some. He supported Reformed determinism in the form that conversion and election depend on external circumstances, such as the environment in which the individual is placed.

Schleiermacher presented religion as the feeling of absolute dependence. He conceived of God as causality. There was no distinction between God's foreknowledge and His predetermination. God had predetermined both sin and redemption from sin. But he translated the Calvinistic doctrine of predestination into another form that led to universalism, if not in this life, then in eternity. He essayed to nullify the dualism in God's being and in His acts, which had clung to the doctrine of predestination. He therefore declared that sooner or later men would be saved. God has from eternity determined upon the redemption of the human race, and He carries out His decree, albeit through a temporal election, so that the one sooner, the other later, becomes the object of the practical application. Those that cannot be reached in this world become objects of the same work of salvation in another world. Martensen considered that predestination was an eternal act and election a temporal act. He rejected the expressions ex praevisa fide and ex praevisa incredulitate. Thomasius, did not approve of the division of the will into *voluntas antecedens* and *voluntas consequens*. Because the notion *ex prasvisa fide* does not enter into the universal election, therefore it should not be used, but he approves of the doctrine of God's foreknowledge. Philippi considers that in the foreknowledge of God in election is included the passivity of man in relation to the proffered grace.

As has been stated before, a controversy concerning predestination has occurred in the Lutheran Church in the United States. The main question at issue concerned the expression *ex praevisa fide* or *intuitu fidei* and its significance. The *Missouri Synod's* leading theologians did not approve of the expression, while on the other hand the theologians of the *Iowa Synod* maintained strongly that the content of this expression agreed with the Lutheran confession and the development of orthodox theology. The *Ohio* and *Iowa Synods* accused the *Missouri Synod* of Calvinism. However, the *Missouri Synod* taught the universality of the atonement, as well as the universality and the seriousness of the call. The *Missouri Synod* set forth with reference to the merit of Christ that men are predestined to faith in order to be saved.[14] The *Iowa Synod* and the others laid the emphasis on the fact that by virtue of or in view of faith in the merit of Christ men are predestined to salvation. H. E. Jacobs, having discussed the relation

[14] In this note we follow statements presented in *The Error of Modern Missouri* by Stellhorn and Schmidt. The sum and substance of the doctrines of Walther and Modern Missouri would be the following: "Election is the unalterable and eternal decree of God, by which, from the entire human race, according to the free purpose of His will, out of pure grace and mercy. He ordained unto salvation a certain number of persons, neither better or worthier than others, lying together with them in the same universal destruction." In regard to the will of God: "The will of God, however, is also itself not determined by any other will. Therefore, because it is already certain through election that a person is to reach heaven, God foreknows it." As a judge's foreknowledge of the execution of a criminal is conditioned by his foreordaining the act, so also God's foreknowledge is 'dependent' upon His foreordination, and not vice versa. "All regard to man's conduct must be excluded, also all regard to faith. Election is conditioned only in so far as God has regarded Christ's merit, obtained for all, and faith, in so far as He has determined to give it to the elect." Concerning the relation of faith and election: "Election is the cause of all that takes place for the salvation of the elect; it is the cause that any one comes to repentance." Missouri teaches that predestination is dependent only on the will of God and prescient faith has no bearing. Faith is the result of election. "God has predestined us unto faith." Grace overcomes all opposition. An unconditional election is rejected, but it is maintained that the conditions are expressed in this that God predestines on account of the merit of Christ, and that He works saving faith. The expression '*ex praevisa fide*' is rejected as implying Synergism. But the Lutheran Church has never taught that any one is saved *propter fidem*, but *per fidem propter Christum*. In regard to the eight points in the *Formula of Concord*, Modern Missouri holds that they refer to election in the narrow sense (*praedestinatio stricte dicta*). Most Lutherans or nearly all except Modern Missouri hold that the eight points refer to the *praedestinatio late dicta*.

In order to know the position of Missouri we also call attention to a booklet by Dr. Pieper which bears the title, *Conversion and Election*. In this book man's inability to convert himself is correctly emphasized and Calvinism is rejected. But the author gives no explanation why the Spirit works faith in some except as God has elected them. He holds that the election of the finally saved is a mystery and no explanation should be attempted. As election and salvation are accomplished by grace alone, we should not use the expressions *ex praevisa fide* or *intuitu fidei*, because they are presumptuous in prying into the mysteries of the divine decree. All men are in the same depravity and equally guilty. Although universal and serious grace is recognized, it will always be a mystery in this life why some should be converted and saved rather than others. "When studying the cause why men are saved we never get beyond *sola gratia Dei*; when studying the cause why men are lost, we never pass beyond *sola culpa hominum*."

of justification and election or predestination, reduces this relation to a tabular form, using Paul as the personal example: Paul was justified and elected in view of the merits of Christ accepted by faith; or, of faith accepting the merits of Christ. The formula of justification and that of election are one and the same. Nothing dare be admitted with respect to justification which is rejected with respect to election. We also quote Dr. Jacobs definition of election: "It is the eternal decree, purpose or decision of God, according to which, out of pure grace, He determined to save out of the fallen, condemned and helpless human race each individual, who from eternity He foresaw would, by His grace, be in Christ unto the end of life."[15]

§8. The Creation.

Cosmology contains the doctrine of the universe and Cosmogony the doctrine of the origin of the world. When we consider God as the absolute personality, we find the explanation of the truth of the Christian cosmogony. The Triune God is active not only internally, but also externally.

The latter activity is not necessary in the same sense as the former. The external activity is connected, however, with the internal. *Opera ad extra,* of which creation is a part, have their starting point in the *opera ad intra.*

Quenstedt defines the act of creation as follows: "*Creation is an external act of the Triune God, whereby, to the praise of His name and the benefit of man, in the space of six days, by the power alone of His most free will, He omnipotently and wisely produced from nothing all things visible and invisible.*"

The Triune God is *causa efficiens principalis.* In accordance with *opera attributiva* in the economical Trinity creation is indeed ascribed to the Father especially, but *opera attributiva* are *communia* or *indivisa,* for which reason both the Son and the Holy Spirit participate. Dogmaticians

[15] Compare *A Summary of the Christian Faith* by Jacobs, Chap. 41.

generally say therefore that the world was created *by* the Father, *through* the Son, and *in* the Holy Spirit. Because the Son from eternity is the image of the Father, therefore the thoughts of the Father are reflected in the Son. Some Dogmaticians say therefore that the Son is *κόσμος νοητός*. He is the principle of the world through whom all is made. The world idea or archetype in the Son is reflected in time as an image or unfolding portraiture of the divine world plan. In creation as well as in the Trinity the Holy Spirit occupies a position which both unites and separates. Through the activity of the Spirit in creation and also in providence the world is transfigured and consecrated to God, but at the same time is separated from Him, so that God, while immanent in the world, is nevertheless transcendent, and the world does not, in accordance with the acosmism of the Pantheists, become immanent in God. Because God has Himself created the world and is the principal active cause, there is no *causa instrumentalis*. The goodness of God alone is the *causa impulsiva creationis*. Before we proceed we would cite the following passages: "Of him, and through him, and unto him, are all things" (Rom. 11:36); "To us there is one God, the Father, of whom are all things" (1 Cor. 8:6); "All things were made through him" (John 1:10); "For in him were all things created, in the heavens and upon the earth, things visible and things invisible, whether thrones or dominions or principalities or powers; all things have been created through and unto him" (Col. 1:16); "Who worketh all things after the council of his will" (Eph. 1:11); "Thou didst create all things, and because of thy will they were, and were created" (Rev. 4:11). Cf. Rom. 1:19, 20 and Acts 17:26, 27.

1. The Modus of Creation.

Forma Creationis consists in the external act, through which God partly from nothing and partly out of the created material brought forth all things. For this reason creation is divided into *creatio prima* or *immediata* and *creatio secunda* or *mediata*.

The scholastics of the Middle Ages distinguished between *nihilum privativum*, the chaotic material, and *nihilum negativum*, which even excludes the former, and taught therefore that God had created the world *ex nihilo negativo*. In the Lutheran scholastic period Quenstedt changed *ex* to *post*. In explanation of the expression "from" or "out of nothing" the following may be cited: "By faith we understand that the worlds have been framed by the word of God so that what is seen hath not been made out of things which appear" (Heb. 11:3). There was, therefore, no *prima materia*, which God used in *creatio prima*. But God did not create the world out of nothing in the ordinary sense, for it is stated that the worlds have been framed by the Word of God. Viewed from this angle, theology does not conflict with the expression: *ex nihilo nihil fit*. We may therefore say, *ex aliquo aliquid fit*. Of course those that continually urge the principle *ex nihilo nihil fit* deny that the world was created by the Word of God. Against such we must emphasize the fact that the world was created from nothing. On the other hand, when we set forth that the world was created by the Word of God, we must beware of theosophical speculations, which assert that in God there is a real *φύσις* with potentialities which constitutes the material of creation. Against such we must maintain that God created the world from nothing by His Word.

To be sure, we cannot explain the mystery of creation, for we know only in part. Through experience we find, however, that the spiritual forces are the most powerful. The spirit of man, although finite and dependent, is nevertheless a great power in the world of nature. We can therefore without difficulty understand how God, the infinite and independent Spirit, can be almighty.

The world is, therefore, not eternal, either as cosmos or as *αἰών*. This we learn in the first sentence on the first page of the Bible through the word *bereshith*. The same truth is expressed in other places, such as Eph. 1:4, where we read: before the foundation of the world. With regard to the time and the creation of the world the old Dogmaticians taught that God created the world with time. Hollazius says: *in tempore non praeexistente, sed coexistente*."

We find two accounts of the creation in Genesis. The object of the first account is to present the order of creation, for which reason man, who was created when all was ready, is mentioned last, because he was the crown of creation. In the second account the creation of man is presented more in detail, while we are told how the garden of Eden was planted for his sake. No mention is made in this account of the creation of flora and fauna. We are told that the animals that had been created were brought before man that he might name them, etc. With regard to the Biblical accounts of the creation and the scientific presentations on the subject, there have been many attempts to harmonize the two. Although the Bible is not a textbook in the natural sciences, still it ought to be considered normative. It has often happened that science has been compelled to acknowledge the truth of the declarations of the Word of God, although the Bible does not express the truths in the same terms as science employs, but makes use of the language of the common man. Among the explanations that have been advanced, three may be mentioned. There are some who consider that the days of creation were extended periods of time, by which theory it has been sought to harmonize the teachings of the Bible with geological science. According to this theory a day might be a thousand years or thousands of years. Others say that the first three days were long periods, but that the last three were ordinary days. Still others present the view that the demands of science might be met by placing the period of the geological formations before the first day of creation as set forth in Genesis. The first thing that is presented in Genesis before the days of creation are mentioned is that in the beginning God created the heavens and the earth, and that the earth was waste and void. It is not impossible that an extended period of time may have intervened before the first day of creation when light was made. According to this view the remaining days of creation were ordinary days. The first of these theories is probably the most popular, while the third contains the suggestion of a harmony that is the most satisfactory to the Christian thinker. It is set forth and defended by Kurtz in a most admirable way. However, the last and deciding word has not been uttered in this question. The different harmonies that have been attempted have considerable importance in the service of Apologetics. When geology and astronomy have reached a greater degree of exactitude and perfection, then we shall find that the facts of science will not conflict with the Biblical account.

In regard to the first of these theories we would be just in calling attention to the fact that "*yom*," the Hebrew word for day, transliterated to English, has several meanings. In Gen. 1:5 it means an ordinary day and also day and night. In Gen. 2:4 day means all the six days. The day of salvation is not an ordinary day. It may be questioned, if the seventh day was an ordinary day of twelve hours. We should also pay attention to 2 Peter 3:8, "But forget not this one thing, beloved, that one day is with the Lord as a thousand years, and a thousand years as one day." In regard to the words "in the beginning" or "to begin with God created heaven and earth," we should not forget that not only heaven, but also earth has various meanings. In the first verse "earth" is a chaotic matter or mass and in the second verse "earth" means evidently not only the planet earth, but also the beginning of the formation of the solar and stellar systems. On the fourth day of creation the sun, moon and stars were made visible. But light existed also in itself from the first day. At first vegetation did not depend upon sunlight, but upon the original created light or a phase of it. The contents of the second verse are also corroborated by 2 Peter 3:5, "There were heavens from of old, and an earth compacted out of water and amidst water." In that time or period the Spirit of God was brooding (according to the Hebrew) on the waters. Then the implanting took place which explains the repeated "after their kind" during the days of creation. But the expression is not used in relation to man, because he was created directly. There are consequently no data in Genesis to support pseudoevolution. The Biblical narrative of creation only contains an outline, but will stand the test of true science.[16]

The record of creation was given to man by revelation, either directly or by vision, just as John received the revelation of the end of the world and the genesis of the new heaven and the new earth.

Concerning the *modus* of creation many different theories have been

[16] Compare Lindberg's Apologetics, p. 41.

presented in the world of science. Many scientists accept the theory of Laplace, according to which our solar system is supposed to have developed out of a greatly attenuated gaseous mass. He considered that this mass was like star clusters. Many of these nebulae are supposed by astronomers to be fixed stars. Laplace said that in the motions of the heavenly bodies the nebulous rings that encircled the planets were thrown off into space and afterwards formed separate bodies. The ring of Saturn is considered a proof of this theory. The gaseous mass, once at white heat, afterwards cooled and became solid.

It is probably not within the province of Dogmatics to account for theories of this sort, but it is nevertheless permissible to state them, particularly as they do not decidedly conflict with the clear expressions of the Bible. It is also necessary at least to point out such theories as plainly conflict with the Scriptures. Among theories of this sort, which must be rejected, may be mentioned: 1) The *theory of emanation*, in accordance with which all creation has emanated from God as the stream from its source or the rays from the sun. In this way God Himself becomes material and imperfect. 2) *Hylozoism*, which acknowledges a formative principle, but ascribes it to matter. God is simply a force or world-soul. This theory has made its appearance in many forms. Straton of Lampsacus, the Stoics, the disciples of Plotinus, Spinoza and others have presented this theory which implies either Pantheism or Atheism. 3) *Materialism*, which declares that only matter exists. Matter is eternal and all things are explained through mutations of matter, hence the theory does not acknowledge any real creation. 4) *The Evolutionary Theory*, or Darwin's doctrine of *transmutation*, according to which the universe has resulted from a gradual development of natural forces which has continued through countless ages.

There is a true evolution which implies a development within the homogeneous domain, but pseudo-evolution means the transmutation of the homogeneous into the heterogeneous. The extreme pseudo-evolution as presented by such men as Haeckel denies a Creator. But the theory of pseudo-evolution has not been proved. No naturalist has been able to discover an actual transmutation of species. Agazziz says: "Darwinism is an *a priori* conception and a burlesque of facts." Virchow says: "I am of the opinion that, before we designate such hypotheses as the voice of science, we should first have to conduct a long series of elaborate investigations. We must therefore say to teachers in schools, 'Do not teach it.'... Of spontaneous generation we do not possess any actual proof." If the doctrine be true, it should be supported by a multitude of sure facts like the law of gravitation.

2. The *Effectus* of Creation.

Effectus Creationis is all that has been created, both the visible world and the invisible. The earth itself reveals to us the great works of God, and with the growth of human knowledge the wonders of creation become more and more marvelous. But the eye of man pierces through the firmament and views and contemplates the thousands of worlds in the wide universe. Concerning the heavens Dogmaticians make use of the following division: 1) *coelum physicum,* which includes *serum et aethereum;* 2) *coelum angelorum et beatorum,* the home of the angels and the saints, where the Lord reveals Himself, which is also called Paradise and constitutes one of the many mansions; 3) *coelum Dei majestaticum,* where God is enthroned in everlasting glory and light. The Scriptures also mention *terra nova et coelum novum,* which implies a new creation or at least a transformation.'

The following passages may be quoted: "For in him were all things created, in the heavens and upon the earth, things *visible* and things *invisible*" (Col. 1:16) ; "And God called the firmament Heaven" (Gen. 1:8); "Behold the heaven and the heaven of heavens" (Deut. 10:14); "In my Father's house are many mansions" (John 14:1) ; "Caught up even to the third heaven, caught up into Paradise" (2 Cor. 12: 2-4); "But ye are come unto the city of the living God, the heavenly Jerusalem, and to innumerable hosts of angels, to the general assembly and church of the firstborn" (Heb. 12:22, 23) ; "Dwelling in light unapproachable" (1 Tim. 6:16); "The city which hath the foundations, whose builder and maker is God" (Heb. 11:10); "He that sitteth on the throne said, Behold, I make all things new" (Rev. 21:5).

3. The Objects of Creation.

Finis Creationis is twofold and the two objects must not be separated from each other. The objects are: 1) *finis intermedius,* which has reference to the blessedness and welfare of man. When the decree concerning creation and therefore *finis intermedius* by reason of sin could not be realized in accordance with the original plan, then God nevertheless carries out His purpose according to the decree of salvation and realizes *finis intermedius* in relation to all those that have been made new creatures through faith in Christ; 2) *finis ultimus,* which is the glory of God.

The following passages set forth *finis intermedius* and *ultimus*: "He made of one every nation of men to dwell on the face of the earth" (Acts 17:26); compare Rom. 1:25; "The heavens declare the glory of God and the firmament showeth his handiwork" (Ps. 19:1); "Jehovah hath made everything for its own end" (Proverbs 16:4); compare Rev. 4:11.

4. Notes On The History of Dogma.

The earliest Christian Church in general accepted with childlike faith the Mosaic account of creation and rejected the teachings of the Gnostics concerning a creator of the world as distinguished from the highest God. They also rejected their doctrine of an eternal creation. The Alexandrian school was more speculative. The allegorical method came into use with Origen, whose views in general on this subject were contested by Methodius and rejected by Athanasius. Augustine's views were characterized by spiritualistic tendencies. During the Scholastic period a pantheistic tendency began to make itself felt through Scotus Erigena, but did not gain many followers. The orthodox faith prevailed. If some of the mystics were in danger of being led astray by their speculations, they were generally strengthened in their faith by the consideration of the marvelous wonders of God in creation. Through the Reformation and the subsequent development of orthodox dogmatic theology faith in the teachings of the Bible concerning creation was confirmed. The Socinians do not seem to have held the view of a *creatio ex nihilo,* while the modern mystics occupied themselves more or less with theosophical and pantheistic speculations.

The Wolffian school sought indeed to harmonize the Mosaic account with natural philosophy, but the old struggle still continues, which is not to be wondered at, when we consider the influence of Pantheism and Materialism in the modern critical period. Schleiermacher became a new Origen. The number of those, however, that maintain and vigorously struggle for the conservative faith is very large.

Heathenism does not seem able to reach a clear conception of the creation of the world. The great heathen philosopher Plato held the view that creation was merely the activity of the eternal Idea in relation to matter. The Creator was the Demiurge or architect who plastically wrought His ideas into the formless eternal mass.

Justin Martyr says in his first Apology, X, that God created the world from formless material. He does not declare with sufficient clearness that God also created the *hyle*. Hermogenes taught that God created the world out of pre-existing material, which is tantamount to an external world-creation. The hyle is as eternal as God Himself. Tertullian opposed his views. Origen said that other worlds had existed before this one. God could not remain inactive. He denied the eternity of matter in the heathen sense, but taught, nevertheless, an eternal world-creation.

The Neo-Platonists, like Plotinus, taught that the world of ideas, the divine intellect, was the mediating principle in the formation of the world. The higher powers of nature give form and life to the lifeless material. Athanasius rejected the doctrine of eternal matter, and said that the result of such a doctrine would be to make God powerless and merely an artist. Augustine rejected the doctrine of an eternal world-creation. In answer to those who asked what God did before He created the heavens and the earth he says in his Conf., XI: 12: "I do not answer, as a certain person is said to have done, dodging the question: He was busy preparing hell for those that delved too deep in mysteries, for I should rather have answered: I do not know," etc. He says that God could have created all things at one time, but because of our limitations He extended the creation over several days. He explained the history of creation itself in an allegorical way.

John Scotus Erigena conceived of God both as *natura creans, sed non creata,* and as *natura non creata et non creans.* And yet he says that the nothing from which God created the world was His superessential glory. God is in all things, which is equivalent to saying that God has made all. Thomas Aquinas said that the creation of the world was an article of faith. He seems to have inclined to the theory of emanation. God's object in creating the world was to impart His being. The power of God was *causa efficiens,* His wisdom *causa exemplaris,* and His goodness *causa finalis.*

Mystics like Sebastian Frank and Bohme taught that the essence of God develops itself in creation. Böhme said that the nature of God was the substance from which all things were created. Spinoza set forth that the substance was never without its *modi, natura naturans* never without *natura naturata.* It is not necessary in this connection to present anything further on Pantheism.

It is self-evident that Schelling, Fichte and Hegel held anti-Christian views on creation. Darwin set forth that the floral and animal kingdoms resulted from an evolution out of a few primitive types. SchleierMacher rejected the doctrine of a creation. Martensen follows Böhme in the doctrine of a *φύσις* in the being of God, an impersonal essence, not dead matter, but something real, a *πλήρωμα,* which made creation possible. The Finnish theologian Granfelt says that the creation proceeded out of the free love of God. The conception of the world creation implies that God through His almighty mandate called the world into being, whose foundation is in Him, and to which He ultimately imparts Himself. There has been no real development in the formulation of dogmas in recent times. The leading theologians of the Church have defended the conservative faith, and in the interest of peace some have endeavored to harmonize the Biblical doctrine with the so-called facts of science.

§9. Providence.

Providence stands in the most intimate connection with creation. It lies in the nature of the case that the One who created the world also should exercise care over His creation so as to sustain it and to direct it to the end that was purposed. For this reason the Creator may work concurrently with the laws of nature or He may intervene immediately. Providence implies God's immanence, which is emphasized against the Deists, and God's transcendence, which is emphasized against the Pantheists. The presence of God is an *adessentia ad creaturas substantialis* or *immediatio suppositi* and *presentia operativa* or *immediatio virtutis*. With regard to the mode of activity Providence may be divided into two main divisions: *providentia ordinaria* and *providentia extraordinaria*. In general by Providence is meant only *providentia ordinaria*.

I. *Providentia Ordinaria* or *Mediata*.

1. The Definition of Providence.

Providentia is that act of God, by which He cares for the world, so that He preserves, co-operates with and governs all things for the welfare of all. Quenstedt defines *providentia* as follows: "Providence is the external action of the entire Trinity, whereby God most efficaciously upholds the things created, both as an entirety and singly, both in species and in individuals; concurs in their actions and results; and freely and wisely governs all things to His own glory and the welfare and safety of the universe, and especially of the godly."[17]

Providence includes the following determining factors: a) *πρόγνωσις*, or that God foreknows what is beneficial for His creatures; b) *πρόθεσις*, or the decree by which He wills to realize the things which He foresees to be best; c) *διοίκησις*, or Providence proper, which implies the carrying out of

[17] Quenstedt: *"Providentia est actio externa totius Trinitatis, qua res a se conditas universas ac singulas tam quoad speciem quam quoad individua potentissime conservat inque eorum actiones et effectus coinfluit et libere ac sapienter omnia gubernat ad sui gloriam et universi huius atque imprimis piorum utilitatem ac salutem."*

the decree.

Apart from the clear expressions of the Scriptures concerning the Providence of God the following arguments have been used to prove that God cares for His creation: 1) the *theological or metaphysical,* which implies that God by reason of His goodness, wisdom and immutability must care for all things and direct all to the end for which they were created; 2) the *teleological or physical,* by which we reach the conclusion that God cares for His creation on account of the adaptability of means to ends in the world, in world development and in history; 3) the *moral,* based upon the holiness and righteousness of God, making it imperative for Him to rule in accordance with these attributes, so that the virtuous are rewarded and the wicked punished; 4) the *religious experimental proof,* which in a certain sense may be called the Christian historical proof. All Christians have, to a smaller or greater extent, experienced the Providence of God.

The following theories must be rejected: 1) *Fatalism,* which sets forth that all things happen by blind necessity, so that the world is not governed by an intelligent and loving being. 2) *Mechanism,* presented by the Deists, which implies that all things are governed by the laws of nature, so that God never acts directly. 3) *Casualism,* which declares that all is governed by chance or accident. 4) *Occasionalism,* presented by Descartes, Melbranche and others, in accordance with which God is the immediate and only cause of all that happens, so that the creatures merely afford God the opportunity to act, while they themselves are powerless to concur.

The expression Providence does not occur in the canonical books of the Bible, but what is implied in the expression is a universal teaching of the Scriptures. Cf. Wis. 14:3. The expression is based upon Gen. 22:8, 14: "God will provide himself the lamb...Abraham called the name of that place Jehovah-jireh: as it is said to this day, In the mount of Jehovah it shall be provided." Providence is really ascribed to the Father, but is the common *opus ad extra* of the Trinity. For this reason the three persons are mentioned as working: "Jesus answered them, My Father worketh even until now, and I work" (John 5:17) ; "In him all things consist" (Col. 1:17);

"Upholding all things by the word of his power" (Heb. 1:3); "Thou sendest forth thy Spirit, they are created" (Ps. 104:30).

2. The Object of Providence.

All creation and especially man is the object of God's providential care. The object therefore includes all things, both great and small, the whole complex of creation as well as the individual. Someone has said that God is *maximus in minimo.* "Who is like unto Jehovah our God, that hath set his seat on high, that humbleth himself to behold the things that are in heaven and in the earth? He raiseth up the poor out of the dust, and lifteth up the needy from the dunghill" (Ps. 113: 5-7). Cf. Ps. 104. "Are not two sparrows sold for a penny? and not one of them shall fall on the ground without your Father" (Matt. 10:29). Although the Providence of God is manifested to all, still it differs with regard to the objects, hence the following division: a) *providentia generalis,* where the object is all creation. "Jehovah is good to all; and his tender mercies are over all his works" (Ps. 145:9); "He giveth to the beast his food, and to the young ravens which cry" (Ps. 147:9). Cf. Acts 14:17; Col. 1:17, etc. b) *providentia specialis,* or God's special care of man. "He maketh his sun to rise on the evil and the good, and sendeth rain on the just and the unjust" (Matt. 5:45); "In him we live, and move, and have our being" (Acts 17:28); c) *providentia specialissima,* or the special care of the faithful. "But the very hairs of your head are all numbered" (Matt. 10:30); "To them that love God all things work together for good" (Rom. 8:28); "Specially of them that believe" (1 Tim. 4:10); "For the sake of them that shall inherit salvation" (Heb. 1:14), etc.

3. The Special Acts of Providence.

Forma Providentia is divided into three acts: *conservatio, concursus* and *gubernatio.*

A. Conservatio or Preservation.

Quenstedt defines as follows: "Preservation is that act of divine providence by which God, as He wills, preserves all things created by Him in their natural essence and with the natural attributes and powers that they received at their first production."[18] This act of God is not to be considered negatively only, so that in His preservation of the world He should merely have bestowed the powers necessary for their unobstructed activity, but preservation is also positive and direct, so that God in a real sense is present and works. Preservation consists of two parts: a) *conservatio materiae* or the preservation of the original matter, and b) *conservatio formae* or the preservation of the form in order that cosmos may not return to chaos.

The following passages may be observed: "These wait all for thee, that thou mayest give them their food in due season" (Ps. 104:27); "Thou hast established the earth, and it abideth" (Ps. 119:90); "Upholding all things by the word of his power" (Heb. 1:3).

B. Concursus or Concurrence.

The co-operation of God enters into both preservation and government, but Dogmaticians have considered that concurrence should especially be emphasized in order to counteract, on the one hand, the false doctrine of transcendence of the Deists, and on the other, the misleading doctrine of immanence of the Pantheists. Concursus *is the action of the Triune God in providence, by which He, as the primary cause, concurs with the secondary causes in accordance with their nature.* The definition of Quenstedt is as follows: "Concurrence is the act of the divine Providence by which God exercises a general influence on the actions and effects of the secondary causes, through which He quietly influences such immediately by Himself and at the same time with them, according to the need and requirement

[18] Quenstedt: "Conservatio est actus divinse providentiae, quo Deus res omnes a se creatas in suo esse natura et naturalibus proprietatibus et viribus, quos in prima sui productione acceperunt, conservat quousque vult."

of each."[19]

The action is produced not by God alone, nor yet by the secondary cause, but by both at the same time. By way of illustration it may be mentioned how in writing the hand and the pen are active at the same time. The co-operation of God is accommodated to the nature of the active objects. For this reason Hollazius says: "With necessary agents God concurs uniformly, e. g., with fire, in order for it to burn, with the sun, in order for it to shine. With free agents God concurs variously, leaving to them their free decision and the free power to choose this or that; for the order that God has once established He does not easily change."[20] Toletus says that God co-operates with the free in a free way, necessarily with the necessary, feebly with the feeble and vigorously with the vigorous.

In substance Hollazius sets forth the following: That God co-operates with creation by the immediacy of His being and power. He concurs by reason of *immediatio suppositi* and *immediatio virtutis*. A person is said to act immediately, either exclusively or inclusively. Exclusively, when he acts alone; inclusively, when he concurs or cooperates. God's immediate influence upon creation is not exclusive, but inclusive.

Among the Biblical passages that set forth God's concurrence may be quoted: "Am I a God at hand, saith Jehovah, and not a God afar off?" (Jer. 23:23); "In him we live, and move, and have our being" (Acts 17:28); "The same God worketh all things in all" (1 Cor. 12:6); "For it is God who worketh in you both to will and to work, for his good pleasure" (Phil. 2:13).

The most difficult problem for Dogmatics to solve in relation to this question is to exhibit the method of divine concurrence in the evil actions of men. God can, of course, do no evil. In order to determine the relationship between the concurrence of God and the evil

---

[19] Quenstedt: "Concursus est actus providentiae divinae, quo Deus influxu generali in actiones et effectus causarum secundarum, qua tales, se ipso immediate et simul cum iis et juxta indigentiam et exigentiam uniuscujusque suaviter influit."

[20] Hollazii *Exam. Theol. Acre*, Ed. V, Part I, Cap. VI, 483.

the Dogmaticians have made use of the following terms: *concurrit Deus ad materiale, non ad formale* or *ad effectum, non ad defectum.* Quenstedt also sets forth that God concurs with respect to the entity and the natural form of the actions or *species naturae,* and not with respect to their moral form or *species moris.* God concurs therefore in the sense that He supplies the power by which the action might have been good, but man misused the power. Hollazius says that God concurs with the remote, not with the proximate material of actions morally evil. The former is an indeterminate act, the latter is a determinate act and applied to a prohibited thing. He illustrates this by the fall of Eve. When she extended her hand to receive the forbidden fruit, two acts were present: 1) the extension of the hand, and 2) the extension applied to the forbidden fruit. The former act is said to be the remote material; the latter, the proximate material. God concurred therefore because He did not inhibit the power of nature, but He did not participate in the sinful action. Many other examples could be presented.

C. Gubernatio or Government.

Gubernatio is the action of the Triune God by which He in a righteous, wise and loving manner governs all things and realizes His purposed plan. Calovius defines as follows: "Government is the action of the divine Providence, by which God in the best way arranges, limits and directs the conditions and actions of His creatures in accordance with His own wisdom, justice and goodness to the glory of His name and the welfare of men."[21]

Government implies that God rules in creation so that He is not an indifferent onlooker or that He is passive. He directs all and governs all things, both the small and the great. He is King not only in the invisible, but also in the visible world. History, both that of the world and of the Church, the general and the particular, has a spiritual background. Inasmuch as

---

[21] Calovius: *"Gubernatio est actus divinae providentiae, quo Deus optime res et actiones creaturarum ordinat, moderatur et ad fines suos dirigit secundum sapientiam, justitiam et bonitatem suam ad nominis sui gloriam et nominis salutem."*

the divine government has especial reference to the rational creatures and man in the first place, who is the crown of creation, therefore we cannot understand the government of God without taking into consideration the factor of freedom. But even if we could take all the factors into consideration, we should still be unable to solve the problem of the divine government, because we lack the higher understanding and the necessary breadth of view.

Many attempts have been made to vindicate the government of God with reference to His wisdom and goodness by reason of the existence of evil and the discordant and inexplicable contrasts in life. Theodicy is the scientific term applied to such theories as attempt the justification of the government of God, a term that was originated and used by Leibnitz. Portions of the Bible contain such theodicies, as the Book of Job, Ps. 37 and Romans 9-11. Some of the scientific attempts also have a certain value. But we can be absolutely certain that the righteous God shall finally prove that He was both loving and just.

Among Scripture passages the following may be noted: "He will judge the world in righteousness, he will minister judgment to the peoples in righteousness" (Ps. 9:8); "Thou wilt judge the peoples with equity, and govern the nations upon earth" (Ps. 67:4). Cf. Ps. 91. "For he must reign, till he hath put all his enemies under his feet" (1 Cor. 15:25); "Righteous and true are thy ways, thou King of the ages" (Rev. 15:3).

Gubernatio is divided into: *permissio, impeditio, directio* and *determinatio.*

a. *Permissio.* Quenstedt defines: "*Permission is an act of governing Providence, by which God does not employ hindrances which no finite agent can overcome, in order to restrain rational creatures, inclining of their own accord to sin, from an evil forbidden by the law, but for just reasons permits them to rush into sins.*"[22] Concerning *permissio* Hollazius sets forth that it does not imply: 1) kind indulgence on the part of God, 2) a mitigation of the law,

---

[22] Quenstedt: "*Permissio est actus providentiae gubernatricis, quo Deus creaturas rationales ad peccandum sua sponte sese inclinantes per impedimenta, quibus agens finitum resistere nequit, vel quibus non resisturum novit, a malo lege vetito non retrahit, sed justis de causis in peccata ruere sinit.*"

3) weakness in God as to His emotions, intellect or power, 4) indifference. It is a negative act. God does not will that which He permits.

We quote the following passages: "But my people hearkened not to my voice; and Israel would none of me" (Ps. 81:12); "Wherefore God gave them up in the lusts," etc. (Rom. 1: 24-28).

b. *Impeditio.* Quenstedt defines: "*Hindrance is an act of governing providence, by which God limits the action of creatures according to His judgment, so that they do not produce the result which otherwise they would effect, either by a natural or a free power to act.*"[23]

Biblical examples: Abimelech, Gen. 20:6; Laban, Gen. 31:24; Balaam, Num. 22:12.

c. *Directio.* Quenstedt defines: "*Direction is an act of governing Providence, by which God so regulates the good actions of creatures, that they tend and are led to the object intended by God, but directs the evil actions to a certain end prescribed by Himself, yet not considered by those who sin, and frequently contrary to their intention.*"[24]

Among the Scripture passages that illustrate this point we quote: "Ye meant evil against me; but God meant it for good" (Gen. 50:20); "But Jehovah said unto Samuel, Look not on his countenance, or on the height of his stature; because I have rejected him: for Jehovah seeth not as man seeth; for man looketh on the outward appearance, but Jehovah looketh on the heart" (1 Sam. 16:7); "To do whatsoever thy hand and thy counsel foreordained to come to pass" (Acts 4:28); "We know that to them that love God all things work together for good, even to them that are called according to his purpose" (Rom. 8: 28).

d. *Determinatio.* Quenstedt defines: "*Determination is an act of governing Providence, by which God has appointed to the strength, actions, and sufferings*

---

[23] Quenstedt: "*Impeditio est actus providentiae gubernatricis, quo Deus actionem creaturarum pro arbitrio suo constringit, ne effectum dent, quod vel naturali vel libera agendi vi alias efficerent.*"

[24] Quenstedt: "*Directio est actus providentiae gubernatricis, quo Deus creaturarum actiones bonas ita moderatur, ut tendant et ferantur in objectum a Deo intentum, actiones vero malas ad certum finem a se praestitum, sed a peccantibus non spectatum et saepe ipsorum intentioni contrarium dirigit.*"

of creatures certain limits within which they are restrained, with respect both to time and to greatness and degree."[25]

The following Scripture passages may be quoted: "Jehovah said unto Satan, Behold, all that he hath is in thy power; only upon himself put not forth thy hand" (Job 1:12); "Let not the rebellious exalt themselves" (Ps. 66:7). Cf. Job 38:11 and Jer. 5:22.

4. The Objective

Finis Providentiae is divided into: 1) *finis intermedius* or *proximus*, which is the welfare of the children of men, and especially the godly; 2) *finis primarius* or *ultimus*, which is the glory of the divine power, wisdom and goodness.

II. *Providentia Extraordinaria* or *Immediata*.

1. The Conception of Miracles.

Luthardt defines: "*The miracle is the act of the immediate divine activity in intervening in the life of the world, which is possible by reason of the freedom of God, and which became necessary and real in the history of salvation.*"[26] We may say that the miracle consists of two elements: a) the negative, or that the miracle cannot be explained by the powers of nature, b) the positive, or that the miracle must be referred to the immediate activity of God in revelation. The old Scholastics accepted an antecedent and a consequent in relation to the miracle, viz., miraculum *suspensionis legum naturae* and *miraculum restitionis legum naturae*. However, it is not necessary so to conceive of the matter, for God is Lord of nature's laws.

Concerning miracles or the direct intervention of God it may be remarked that we are not familiar with all the laws of nature, and even if in every case these laws are counteracted by the miracle, still they are

---

[25] Quenstedt: "*Determinatio est actum providentiae gubernatricis quo Deus creaturarum viribus, actionibus et passionibus certos termlnos, intra quos se contineant, tum ratione temporis, tum ratione magnitudinis et gradus constituit.*"

[26] Luthardt, *Dogmatics*, §35, page 141.

not thereby abrogated. They are no more abrogated than the laws of gravitation are abrogated when the arm is lifted. The harmony of nature is not destroyed in the miracle, rather the divine life which is the foundation of and manifests itself in the harmony of nature thereby reveals its activity.

We would point out three Biblical expressions that are used for miracles. They are: i-tpas or the miracle as causing astonishment, indicating its effect upon the onlooker; Swo/i« or the miracle as revealing the divine or supernatural power and effect; o-^ttov or the miracle as a sign with the end in view of testifying to a divine revelation.

2. The Possibility of Miracles.

The discussion of this subject belongs, strictly, to Apologetics, but a few remarks may here be appended. Objections to the miracles have been made by the Deists and the Pantheists. The former declare that God cannot intervene in nature because He has subjected the world to the rule of the laws of nature. The negative aspect of the miracles destroys the continuity of the present world order, while the positive aspect establishes a new order. — This conception deprives God of His freedom, forgetting that God works by and through Himself. The continuity of the world order is not destroyed. The Pantheists declare that God and Nature are one. The laws of Nature are therefore identical with the will of God. God would not interfere with His own laws. It would be unworthy of a god to improve upon his own work. It is the ignorance of man that speaks of miracles. The belief in miracles is to a certain extent dependent upon a misinterpretation of the Hebrew mode of expression, which referred everything to the primary cause. — Inasmuch as Pantheism does not accept the belief in a personal God, therefore the objections that it raises can be met by Theism and the proofs of a supernatural revelation.

Hegelianism, while not acknowledging the possibility of miracles, has a method of presenting the matter which can be turned into a proof for miracles by transforming the expressions of that philosophy into Christian form. RosenKrantz says: "The miracle is the determination of nature through the spirit, so that nature cannot withstand the will of the spirit. The ground of nature is not in itself; its principle is the spirit, for which reason nature possesses no power to set limitations for the spirit. This power of the spirit was fully concentrated in Christ." But Strauss objects in the interest of Pantheism: "To be sure the spirit possesses power over nature, but not the spirit that takes notions to fly, or walk upon the water, or change water into wine, but the spirit that works quietly as law and formative power in nature, and which in man by strenuous effort through intellect and will works itself up to a position of lordship over nature." However, we must not forget what Pantheism means by spirit. It is not a spirit separated from the world, but rather the world spirit which finds itself in man.

3. The Truth of Miracles.—Their Division.

This truth is set forth clearly in the divine-human nature of our Lord and in His resurrection. The historical personality of Jesus Christ cannot be denied. His divinity and resurrection can be so clearly and convincingly demonstrated that no doubt need be entertained. The historical proofs of the truth of the miracles are overwhelming. The proofs of the testimony of Christ Himself and of the Apostles possess great value, especially when we consider carefully the character of these persons. To every Christian the miracles are true by reason of his own regeneration. Regeneration is in itself a miracle.

The miracles are divided as follows: a) *Miracula naturae et potentiae* or miracles in the ordinary sense; b) *Miracula praescientiae* or the prophecies and their wonderful fulfilment; c) *Miracula gratiae* or miracles in the kingdom of grace, which Luther considered the most important.

4. The Object Of Miracles.

The miracles belong to the history of revelation and served to set the seal of approval upon the messengers of God, the Lord Jesus Christ and the Apostles, as also to establish the divine origin of the Church. For this reason no miracles are necessary during the period of the Church's activity. But the Church itself is a constant miracle, and in the latter days.

5. Notes on the History of Dogma.

The doctrine of Providence has always occupied a prominent place in the Christian Church, although in the beginning it was treated more from the apologetic than the dogmatic standpoint. The oldest Church Fathers defended the doctrine of Providence against Stoicism and Agnosticism on the one hand and epicurean Deism on the other. In the discussion great weight was laid on the question of purpose. During the Polemical period several works on Providence appeared, which aimed at a clearer definition of the subject. Julius Africanus spoke of a general and a special Providence. In relation to *providentia extraordinaria,* Augustine was the first to define more clearly the concept of Providence. During the Middle Ages it was taught that the presence of God in the world was an *adessentia ad creaturas substantialis* which was termed *immediatio suppositi* and *immediatio virtutis.* Thomas Aquinas gave more definite form to the concept of the miracle and distinguished between the miracles as ordinary and relative, which Augustine did not. The Reformers did not speculate concerning Providence. The dogmatic formulation of the doctrine was accomplished by the old Lutheran Dogmaticians. Pantheism and Deism endeavored to refute the doctrine of Providence, while the theory of Occasionalism arose through the philosophy of Descartes. Leibnitz explained the miracle on the theory of pre-established harmony. Since then many controversies have arisen concerning Providence and the miracles by reason especially of the attacks of modern Materialism, but there has been no particular development of the dogma.

Justin Martyr based his view of the Providence of God on the order that he found everywhere prevalent in nature. God ruled the whole, while the details were entrusted to the angels. Clement of Alexandria was the first to distinguish between the will of God as positively active and as permissive, the latter in relation to the evil. He also taught a concursus divinus. Tertullian said that physical evil or *malum poenae* was the punishment for the moral evil or *malum culpae*. Cyprian taught that the cause of evil was the age of the world. Origen considered that God employed the physical evil as a means for the improvement of man. Concerning miracles Origen said that they proved the truth of the teachings of Christ, while he also stated that the moral effects of Christianity were greater works than the ordinary miracles.

Lactantius attempted to defend God on the ground of the existence of evil. He maintained that good must have its opposite in evil, but God could not Himself create evil. For this reason two beings were created, one the Son, the right hand of God, the other Satan, the left hand, who is the cause of all evil.' Augustine taught that God has not forsaken the world which He created, but continues His unceasing activity through preservation. He did not consider miracles in a narrow sense but included miracles in general. The miracles conflict with the laws of nature as far as we know them. He placed great value upon all miracles, yet held spiritual miracles the greatest. John of Damascus set forth that the *voluntas antecedens* of God was directed toward the good, and that the *voluntas consequens* permitted the evil.

Thomas Aquinas called Providence *creatio continuata*. As the primary cause God exerts influence upon the secondary causes in a peculiar manner. He considered that evil was necessary for the perfection of the whole.

Leibnitz says that evil is partly metaphysical, the imperfection of the finite, which evil is willed directly, partly physical and moral, which God indirectly wills. Physical evil is a means and moral evil a condition without which that which is best cannot be attained. He explained miracles by the theory of pre-established harmony, which implies that God has set certain limitations in the ordinary processes of nature, which occur at predetermined times.

Kant declared that theoretically it is impossible to prove or deny the possibility of miracles but held the doctrine of miracles pernicious inasmuch as it sets forth improper moral motives. Schleiermacher speaks of the absolute causality of God and includes both creation and providence under the head of preservation. Confessional theology has retained the old dogmatic definitions and terms, while rejecting such explanations of the miracles as the theory of pre-established harmony.

§10. The Angels.

The word angel, meaning messenger, occurs in the Word of God in at least a threefold significance. Used in the broadest sense the word angel may apply to the powers of nature and natural phenomena. "Who maketh winds his messengers: Flames of fire his ministers" (Ps. 104:4). In a broad sense it may apply to human beings, such as priests, prophets and pastors. In the narrow sense, however, the word angel has reference to those personal spirits who are specifically called angels.

Angels are finite, incorporeal beings, endowed with personal form and attributes, and a high order of intelligence, created to serve God and glorify Him.

Like the world and all living creatures the angels were created before man. Cf. Job 38:7. They were not created before the original substance of the world, for only God existed before the foundation of the world. They were created in connection with the creation of the world. "Who laid the corner-stone thereof, when the morning stars sang together, and the sons of God shouted for joy?" Compare Col. 1:16 for an account of their creation. Of their existence as real beings and not personifications we are absolutely certain on the basis of the Word of God.

However, attempts have been made to prove that angels exist. Among such attempts may be mentioned that of Godet. He says: "We know of three kinds of living beings: plants, animals and man. Our thought requires a fourth series. Among plants there exists only the species, for which reason we speak of specimens. Among the animals the species are indeed essential, but the individual appears. The animals are governed by instinct. The individual lives but as if bound by the fetters of the species. In man the species is found because we speak of the human race. Instinct is found, but it is not dominant. Man bursts open the prison doors of species and instinct, because he is a distinct person. Should there not be found a fourth series of living beings to complete the system? In a mathematical proportion the fourth term can be ascertained when the three are known. May it not be that the angels must be the living beings that complete the system of creation?"[27]

The original estate of the angels is described as *habitus concreatus bonus.* They possessed a *propensio ad bonum*. Their *justitia* or righteousness was *perfecta,* but *amissibilis*. They possessed freedom of choice, the form in which created freedom is realized. The concept of freedom implies self-determination and an ultimately determinate will. In God these elements are eternally and indissolubly united, because God is absolutely free, but in the creatures freedom must be realized. Many of the angels used their freedom of choice in a right manner and remained good; others abused this freedom and became evil.

I. The Good Angels.

The good angels are those who remained in their original goodness, righteousness and holiness, in which estate God confirmed them as a reward for their obedience, wherefore they can no more fall into sin. From *status gratiae* they entered forever into *status gloriae*. In this manner all their good attributes were confirmed and increased.

1. Their Attributes.

The following attributes are ascribed to the good angels: 1) *spiritualitas* or spirituality. Angels are called *spiritus completi,* because they have no need of ordinary bodies, although they have form. Men are called *spiritus incompleti*; 2) *invisibilitas* or invisibility, that is, they are ordinarily invisible to us; 3) *indivisibilitas* or indivisibility; 4) *immutabilitas relativa* or relative immutability. This includes also *incorruptibilitas ab intra et ab extra*; 5) *immortalitas relativa* or relative immortality in contradistinction to God, who is immortal in the absolute sense; 6) *aeternitas relativa* or relative eternity. The word *aevum* is also used for this attribute, which implies an intermediate state which is neither *aeternitas* or *tempus*; 7) *illocalitas,* i.e., they are not present anywhere *in ubi circumscriptive,* because they do not have material bodies, which are defined by limits; 8) *ubeitas definitiva,*

---

[27] Godet, *Bibl. Studier*, pp. 2-4.

i.e., they are somewhere and not everywhere present. Their substance at a given moment is definitely somewhere, which Dogmaticians express with *πού* or *ubi*, for which reason it is said of the angels that they are in *ubi definitive*; 9) *agilitas* or that they move with great celerity, which nevertheless, according to human calculations, requires time, inasmuch as they are finite beings, unable instantaneously to traverse the universe. Cf. Dan. 9:23; 10:12-14; 10) *bonitas* or goodness; 11) *cognitio naturalis, relativa et beatifica*, inasmuch as they possess great knowledge, but are not omniscient. They know God *a posteriori* and also the thoughts of man *a posteriori*. Their knowledge is great by reason of their natural gifts, but they grow in knowledge mediated through revelation. As confirmed in the good their knowledge is also blessed; 12) *potentia magna, sed limitata ac finita*, because their power is great, but they are not almighty; 13) *libertas voluntatis* or the freedom of the will.

We would call attention to the following passages: "Thousands of thousands ministered unto him, and ten thousand times ten thousand stood before him" (Dan. 7:10) ; "Twelve legions of angels" (Matt. 26:53); "Things invisible, whether thrones," etc. (Col. 1:16); "For neither can they die any more: for they are equal to the angels" (Luke 20:36); "All the holy angels" (Matt. 25:31); "The elect angels" (1 Tim. 5:21); "According to the wisdom of an angel of God" (2 Sam. 14:20); "Knoweth no one, not even the angels in heaven" (Mark 13:32); "Which things angels desire to look into" (1 Peter 1:12); "Angels, mighty in strength" (Ps. 103:20); "The angel of Jehovah went forth, and smote in the camp of the Assyrians a hundred fourscore and five thousand" (2 Kings 19:35); "The prince of the kingdom of Persia withstood me one and twenty days; but, lo, Michael, one of the chief princes, came to help me" (Dan. 10:13).

2. Their Abode and Degrees.

Although we do not know for certain, still it may not be considered altogether illusory to assume that the abode of the angels is to be found in the shining world of the starry universe. Compare Job 38:7. However, this passage cannot be considered conclusive proof, inasmuch as the stars did not appear before the fourth day. Still it is not impossible that angels inhabit the universe of the stars. We do know that their special abode is in heaven, and in the heavenly places (Eph. 3:10), although they are also on earth, where as ministers of the Lord they do His pleasure. In Matthew 18:10 we read: "Their angels do always behold the face of my Father who is in heaven."

In reference to a spiritual world and abode of angels reason endorses what analogy suggests, that there is not only a world of spirits, but there must also be starry worlds suitable for homes, where these rational spiritual beings dwell. When we know from revelation the countless ascending orders of angelic beings and we see the innumerable stars it is very reasonable to hold the opinion that the great universe of solar systems and stellar worlds are inhabited by angels. Many students of the Bible and also scientists claim that the all-wise Creator would not have created such a vast universe to be an empty void. And it is very clear that human beings do not inhabit the other planets or stars. Human beings are found only on earth, in Hades and in Paradise. It is a mystery why God prepared this comparatively small globe as a habitation for humanity, but it is sufficiently large, when we consider that our abode here, if we are God's children, serves as a school to prepare the heavenly citizens for the eternal life-work in the world to come. It is, therefore, reasonable to think that the habitable planets and stars in the great universe are inhabited by orders of angels. We must not forget that the angelic hosts are of many kinds, such as thrones, dominions, principalities and powers. Lucifer, so called, had his principality before he fell. Order reigns in the kingdom of God. There may be angelic orders who have no direct relation to this earth, but still have the greatest interest in what takes place here. Eph. 3:10. Notice also in the same verse "heavenly places." In the angelic worlds distances do not prevent communication. Compare Dan. 9:21. In this verse we find the expression, "being caused to fly swiftly." But countless numbers of angels minister to the Church, just as Gabriel ministered to Daniel and to Mary at the time of the incarnation of the Son of God. And we may be sure that Gabriel ministers continually in the kingdom of God.

Without seeing these angels we stand in near relation to them. Compare Heb. 12:22.

There is rank in the angelic world. Equality is found neither among the angels in heaven nor among men on earth, yet in heaven superiority causes no envy, the angels being holy and governed entirely by God's will. The Bible speaks of archangels. Among these are mentioned Michael and Gabriel. Michael means: *Who is like God?* Although elevated to such a lofty eminence, he is nevertheless the humblest in spirit and knows full well the immeasurable distance that separates him from the Creator. Gabriel means: *Hero of God.* He made known to Daniel the deliverance of Judah out of the Babylonian captivity. He is the heavenly evangelist who revealed to Mary that she would give birth to the Saviour of the world. Paul speaks of thrones, dominions, principalities and powers. We read of *cherubim* and *seraphim.* The occupation of the angels seems also to be graded. In Daniel we read of "one of the chief princes." In Zechariah we find mentioned the "angel of the Lord," also a leader of a group who brings reports to the angel of the Lord, and also an interpreter.

3. The Occupation of the Angels and Their Relation to Men.

The angels praise and serve the Lord. Angels were present at most of the acts of creation, revealed themselves to the Patriarchs, were present at the giving of the Law, defended Israel, punished the enemies, etc. They were present at the birth of the Lord Jesus and at various other times during the life of Christ. We also find that they assisted individual persons, and on the last day they will participate in the judgment. It lies in the nature of the case that the angels are not unoccupied. In most cases God acts indirectly. On the earth He uses human means, but back of the visible world lies the spiritual background. In reading Daniel and Zechariah we find this truth set forth in a living and realistic way. Furthermore, the Word of God tells us that the angels are active not only in heaven, but also on earth, in the family and in the Church. For this reason Dogmaticians speak of *status oeconomicus, ecclesiasticus* and *politicus,* in which the angels are active.

Concerning the activity of the angels in *status oeconomicus* the following examples and passages may be cited: The visit of angels to Abraham and Lot (Gen. 18, 19); the angels of God met Jacob and he called the place Mahanaim; "The angel of Jehovah encampeth round about them that fear him" (Ps. 34:7); "He will give his angels charge over thee, to keep thee in all thy ways" (Ps. 91:11) ; "God hath sent his angel, and hath shut the lions' mouths" (Dan. 6:22); an angel of the Lord revealed himself to Joseph in a dream; cf. Matt. 2:13; Lazarus was carried by angels into Abraham's bosom; cf. Luke 16:22; an angel came to Cornelius; cf. Acts 10:3; the angel of the Lord liberated Peter out of prison; cf. Acts 12: 7-11; "Ministering spirits, sent forth to do service for the sake of them that shall inherit salvation" (Heb. 1:14); "Entertained angels" (Heb. 13:2).

As examples of their co-operation in *status ecclesiasticus* the following may be observed: The Law ordained through angels by the hand of a mediator (Gal. 3:19); Gabriel made known to Mary that she would give birth to Christ (Luke 1:26); the appearance of the angels to the shepherds (Luke 2: 9-13); the revelation of the angel to Paul (Acts 27:23); "For this cause ought the woman to have a sign of authority on her head, because of the angels" (1 Cor. 11:10); "To the intent that now unto the principalities and the powers in the heavenly places might be made known through the church the manifold wisdom of God" (Eph. 3:10); I charge thee in the sight of God, and Christ Jesus, and the elect angels" (1 Tim 5:21); "Compassed about with so great a cloud of witnesses" (Heb. 12:1); "I am a fellow-servant with thee" (Rev. 19:10).

The following Bible passages may be cited to set forth their activity in *status politicus*: An angel slew the Assyrians (2 Kings 19:35); an angel fights with the prince of Persia, etc. (cf. Dan.10); "Then the angel of Jehovah answered and said, O Jehovah of hosts, how long wilt thou not have mercy on Jerusalem and on the cities of Judah?" (Zech. 1:12). Compare the activity of the angels in the last days in accordance with Rev. 15, 16, 17, 18, 19, etc.

4. The Objects of the Activities of the Angels.

These are first and foremost, *finis primarius*, that they shall glorify God and serve Him. *Finis secundarius* implies that they shall serve the faithful. For this reason they come in the closest contact with the true members of the Church of Christ. Although the redeemed stand closer to God than the angels, the latter shall nevertheless belong to the kingdom of Christ. As Jews and heathens were united in the Church of Christ, so men and angels shall be united so as to form a common organism or the kingdom of God. In Eph. 1:10 we read: "To sum up all things in Christ, the things in the heavens, and the things upon the earth."

5. Notes on the History of Dogma.

In the Apostolic Church it was generally taught that the angels were personal beings and not personifications, as Philo taught. The worship of angels was disapproved. The Council of Laodicaea in 363 expressed such disapproval. This proves that the worship of angels took place at that time, viz., during the fourth century. Constantine the Great had built and consecrated a church to Michael. Others did the same. In this manner the people were influenced to worship angels. Gregory the Great disapproved of the worship of angels. At the Council of Nicaea in 787 angels were accorded what Augustine had called *δουλεία*. Dionysius the Areopagite divides the angels into three hierarchies with three subdivisions under each. John of Damascus retained the same division. The Lateran Council in 1215 declared that the angels were spiritual beings and that they were created good. At the time of the Reformation there was no dispute between Catholics and Protestants with regard to angels except as related to the subject of worship, which the latter rejected. The Council of Trent confirmed the doctrine of the worship of angels. The doctrine concerning angels has not been the subject of any extensive dogmatic development. During the modern critical period the theory of personification has been presented by many, but the orthodox Dogmaticians maintain correctly that angels are persons who are highly endowed and serve the Lord both in heaven and on earth.

Justin Martyr rejected the personification theory of Philo. He also speaks of guardian angels. Origen said that the angels were created before the world. He speaks likewise of guardian angels, maintaining that they pray for us and instill good thoughts.

Lactantius said that living spirits proceeded from God; that one of these was the Son who emerged from the mouth, while Satan on the other hand came forth from the nostrils. Augustine taught that the angels were created, on the first day, for which reason he interpreted the light in an allegorical manner. He said that their knowledge was twofold: 1) *matutina,* because they viewed objects in their original images; 2) *vespertina,* because they viewed objects in themselves. With regard to worship Augustine distinguished between *λατρεία,* which is accorded to God, and *δουλεία,* which is accorded to the angels. John of Damascus ascribed to the angels pure spirituality.

At the meeting at Nicaea in 787 it was taught that the angels were possessed of a refined corporeality. The Lateran Council in 1215 taught that the angels were pure spiritual essences. Thomas Aquinas maintained that there were not two angels belonging to the same species. He also said that more than one angel could not occupy the same point, as Occam taught.

Luther believed that the angels were graded and that there were guardian angels. The Confessions concede that the angels pray for us, but the doctrine of their adoration and supplication is rejected. Compare the Apology, Art. 9, which also speaks of the supplication of the saints.

Swedenborg denies the existence of the angels and declares that they are the spirits of the glorified dead. Fichte says that the angels are the *πλήρωμα* of God and the types of the world-creation and the essence of things. Schieiermacher declared that faith in angels had arisen through the imagination, inasmuch as it was thought that there were other rational creatures besides men. De Wette asserted that faith in angels was based on pious presentiments. Martensen speaks of the world of ideas, but he also declares the angels to be personal beings. Delitzsch says that angels have rarified pneumatic bodies, while Philippi says that they are pure spiritual essences.

II. The Evil Angels.

The evil angels are those that failed in the test and did not therefore remain in their concreated or original wisdom and holiness, but became the enemies of God and men, for which reason they shall be punished with everlasting torment.

1. The Existence of Satan and the Evil Angels.

Satan is spoken of in the form of a serpent in Gen. 3. Undoubtedly he is also referred to in Lev. 16 under the name of Azazel. The doctrine did not therefore originate among the Persians, the Jews being supposed to have brought it with them from the Babylonian captivity. Satan is represented in the New Testament as a personality. The Lord's Prayer may also be considered as containing an argument for the personality of Satan, inasmuch as the expression *τοῦ πονεροῦ* need not necessarily be translated in the abstract sense. The existence of evil angels is clearly taught in the Word of God. Without the existence of the evil spirits it would be much harder to explain man's fall into sin. Christian experience in relation to temptation also presents an indubitable proof of the existence of the powers of evil.

Among the theories that in one form or another deny the teachings of the Scriptures on this point may be mentioned: a) Dualism as it is represented in Hylism and Parseism. The former regards matter as an eternal principle of evil, for which reason the conception of personality is eliminated. The latter speaks of a concrete personality who is the creator of evil, b) The modern theory of personification. According to this theory the evil spirits are merely the symbolic expressions of evil principles and desires.

2. The Original and Present Condition of the Evil Angels.

The original condition of the evil angels is termed *status gratiae.* It was necessary that they be tried and tested in order that they might become self-determined. When they should realize this self-determination, which is the content of real and material freedom, then the moment of test presented itself. In fact the very presence of God as the Absolute demanded a decision. They had to decide for or against the Supreme Being. Such a necessity meant that they had to go through a trial or probation. In such a trial they could not escape a decision by deliberate volition. If the formal freedom or power of choice together with the determinate result should mean anything as a test, there could not be a determinism on the part of God. All the angels were created relatively good, but in order to be perfectly good they must make a free choice. God was not satisfied to be surrounded by mere animals; He desired rational beings with character. The finest specimens of animals, the most beautiful vegetation and precious stones as costly as Kohinoor would mean nothing to God, if there were no persons who of their own free will had chosen to love and obey Him. There would be no real power of choice, if rational beings could not decide one way or the other. If all the angels had determined to be good, there would be no criticism on the conception of freedom as implying two possibilities. The creation of free beings meant a risk. Should God have desisted from creating them on account of the implied risk? Some say that God should not have created the angels of whom He must have foreseen that they would make a wrong choice. But God foreknew only actualities. When God had conceived the creation of angels, He could not but complete their actual creation, because His thoughts are not vain and empty speculations. Though almighty, He did not, for wise and just reasons, annihilate the beings He foreknew would abuse their freedom. The angel afterwards called Satan, together with the others who fell, determined in the test of their own free will upon an existence of self-will and utter selfishness. In this way their condition was changed into *status miseriae*, in which they now and ever shall remain because their very essence is evil. Their fall occurred before the creation of man and possibly before the six days of creation. The Scriptures make no mention of the time, hence nothing certain can be said about it. Christ says concerning Satan that he was a murderer from the beginning. Cf. John 8:44. In 1 John 3:8 we read: "The devil sinneth from the beginning." However, this expression is not to be construed to mean that the devil fell immediately after his creation, but that he remained for some time, even if but a short time, in his original state before he became puffed up with pride. Cf. 1 Tim. 3:6. The evil angels had a principality, but abused their freedom of choice and of their own free will abandoned the path of right. "And the angels which kept not their own principality, but left their proper habitation, he hath kept in everlasting bonds under darkness unto the judgment of the great day" (Jude 6).

3. Their Attributes.

In part they have the same attributes as the good angels. Among these may be mentioned: spirituality, indivisibility, relative eternity, illocality, having a definite habitation and the power of moving with great swiftness from place to place. The evil angels possess great knowledge, although it is perverted. Their power is also great, though limited.

The following Scripture passages may be cited: "Evil spirits" (Luke 7:21); "The spiritual hosts of wickedness" (Eph. 6:12) ; "What have I to do with thee, Jesus, thou Son of the Most High God?" (Mark 5:7); "The demons also believe, and shudder" (James 2:19); "The devil is gone down unto you, having great wrath, knowing that he hath but a short time" (Rev. 12:12); "They worshipped the dragon, because he gave his authority unto the beast" (Rev. 13:4) ; "Whose coming is according to the working of Satan with all power and signs and lying wonders" (2 Thess. 2:9).

4. Their Habitation and Gradation

The present habitation of the evil angels, that is, before the judgment, is partly ἄβυσσος or the abyss. Tartarus is probably the same place. They are not consigned to Gehenna or the everlasting hell until after the judgment. In 2 Peter 2:4 we read: "For if God spared not angels when they sinned, but cast them down to hell (Gr. Tartaros), and committed them to pits of darkness, to be reserved to judgment." Whether or not they are also in Hades, the Scriptures do not say, but it is possible. However, all the evil spirits are not confined to the abyss, for in Luke 8:31 we read: "They entreated him that he would not command them to depart into the abyss." In this connection we would also call attention to the following passages: "The unclean spirit when he is gone out of the man, passeth through waterless places, seeking rest" (Luke 11:24); "The world-rulers of this darkness" (Eph. 6:12); "The devil, as a roaring lion, walketh about, seeking whom he may devour" (1 Peter 5:8).

The evil angels are also classified. Satan is the prince of darkness. The Scriptures speak of principalities and powers. "For our wrestling is not against flesh and blood, but against the principalities, against the powers, against the world-rulers of this darkness, against the spiritual hosts of wickedness in the heavenly places" (Eph. 6:12; cf. Col. 2:15).

5. Their Occupation

In every way they seek to dishonor God and fight against the good angels. In relation to man their desire is only to do injury to man as an individual, to the family, the Church and the State.

The following examples and passages may be cited in regard to their activity in *status oeconomicus*: Satan led astray Saul and David, while he tormented Job. He seduced Judas. Scripture says that Satan entered into him. Cf. John 13:27. In Luke 22:31 we read: "Simon, Simon, behold, Satan asked to have you, that he might sift you as wheat." Satan led Ananias and Sapphira astray so that they lied. A messenger of Satan buffeted Paul. Other examples could be cited.

The Bible plainly teaches that Satan is a person and not a personification. The demons are likewise real persons. Satan himself tempted Eve. A devil or Satan also tempted the Lord. Judas Iscariot was at the time of his treason possessed by Satan. At the climax of anti-Christianity the last personal Antichrist will be possessed by the devil. Satan is not omnipresent but as ruler in the kingdom of darkness he directs the demons and the evil agencies. There are also princes in Satan's kingdom. Compare Rev. 9:11, where the angel of the abyss is called Apollyon.

Special attention must be paid to those possessed by evil spirits. The Dogmaticians speak of *possessio corporalis* and *possessio spiritualis.*

Quenstedt says that even the pious may, by way of trial, suffer from an *obsessio corporalis,* but not *spiritualis.* Only the wicked can become the objects of spiritual possession by evil spirits, but this *possessio spiritualis* also implies *possessio corporalis.* There are some who have maintained that those possessed by evil spirits have merely been insane, but such an assertion is contrary to Scripture. There is no ground for the view that Christ accommodated Himself to the current thought and manner of speaking concerning those possessed. The whole attitude of our Lord in casting out devils proves clearly that He not only cured a disease of the mind, but that He cast out evil spirits. Among the many examples that could be cited we would refer only to the occasion when He cast out demons from the man in the land of the Gerasenes. Cf. Luke 8: 26-33. Christ speaks to the demon and makes a clear distinction between the demons and the man. At that time there were also insane people who were not possessed, and many that were possessed who were not insane, although they appeared to be. Many were sick because of evil spirits and were healed when Christ cast out the evil or unclean spirits, but the Lord also healed many that were not tormented by demons. Wherefore there is a clear distinction which would not exist if all diseases were supposed to be caused by the obsession of evil spirits. Christ, who is the personal Truth, could not have said that He cast out demons, if that were not true. At the present time there would seem to be few cases of obsession, but there have been instances when no other explanation would seem possible. It is not strange that there were so many instances of demoniacal possession at the time of our Lord, inasmuch as He had come for the express purpose of casting down the works of the devil, for which reason Satan was more than ordinarily active in combating the Lord.

Concerning the attempt of the evil spirits to injure the *status ecclesiasticus* and the Church of Christ we would cite the following: "While men slept, his enemy came and sowed tares" (Matt. 13: 25); "Then cometh the evil one, and snatcheth away that which hath been sown in his heart" (Matt. 13:19); "Because we would fain have come unto you, I Paul once and again; and Satan hindered us" (1 Thess. 2:18); "And the dragon waxed wroth with the woman, and went away to make war with the rest of her seed, that keep the commandments of God, and hold the testimony of Jesus" (Rev. 12:17).

The evil spirits are also active in *status politicus*. Compare 1 Kings 22:21; also compare Daniel 10:13, where it is stated that the prince of the kingdom of Persia withstood the Angel of the Lord twenty-one days. "And they worshipped the dragon, because he gave his authority unto the beast" (Rev. 13:4).

The old Dogmaticians also speak of the evil spirits appearing as ghosts. In Isa. 13:21 and also 34:14 we read of doleful creatures and night-monsters. According to Matt. 14:26 and Luke 24:37 the disciples were troubled and affrighted because of the appearance of ghosts and spirits. In proof of the fact that the dead do not as a rule reveal themselves Luke 16:31 may be cited: "If they hear not Moses and the prophets, neither will they be persuaded, if one rise from the dead."

Noises that are ascribed to ghosts may often be caused by natural causes, but voices and momentary appearances are often caused by telepathy. When it is impossible to explain such voices and appearances by natural causes, we may be safe in assuming that it is a work of demons. Some ridicule Luther on account of his belief in noises and disturbances as sometimes caused by demons, but Luther, if melancholy sometimes, was not superstitious and fearful. The courageous monk at Worms could not have seen ghosts in daylight.

6. The Punishment of the Fallen Angels.

Their punishment may be said to be twofold: a. *poena privatum,* or that they have been cast out and suffered the loss of God's favor and all that is implied in the glory of everlasting life; b. *poena sensus seu positiva,* implying all their suffering in this present state and in Gehenna after the judgment.

7. Notes on the History of Dogma.

During the first and second periods the opinion was general that Satan and the evil angels were personal beings and not merely personifications.

The opinions were divided, however, with regard to the cause of their fall. There was no special dogmatic development during the Scholastic period. Luther had realistic conceptions with regard to the spiritual background of evil. Influenced by Pantheism, Rationalism and other tendencies, the modern critical period has embraced the theories of accommodation and personification. This denial of the clear teaching of the Word of God has, however, brought about a reaction in the form of Spiritualism which has won many adherents. The Church has nevertheless been strengthened in her faith and is more than ever conscious of the fact that she has to struggle not only against evil men, but also against personal evil spirits.

Justin Martyr, Athenagoras, Clement of Alexandria and others taught that the fall of the angels was caused by their marriage with the daughters of men, whence came the giants and intermediate creatures which were neither angels nor men. Athenagoras also stated that the fall of the angels was caused by their lust after material things. Tatian taught that the bodies of the angels consisted of air and fire. Irenaeus, Tertullian and Cyprian said that envy was the cause of their fall. Origen ascribed their fall to pride. With regard to their bodies he taught that they were more gross than those of the good angels, while they needed sustenance and inhaled the incense that arose from heathen altars.

Lactantius said that the fall was caused by envy toward the Son. Augustine believed that the bodies of the angels became more gross in substance through the fall. He says that the cause of the fall was probably pride, although it cannot be explained. Boethius taught that God created man in order to fill the gap that had arisen through the fall of the angels.

Anselm likewise taught that pride was the cause of the fall, and that it was God's purpose that man should fill the place that had been voided by the fall of the angels.

Luther considered that each person was tormented by an evil spirit, that Satan was closer to a person than the skin of the body, that he was the cause of many bodily ailments, etc.

Semler said that *possessio diabolica* was merely insanity. The Rationalists declared that the doctrine of the evil spirits was only an accommodation to Jewish ideas. Schelling taught that evil is the motive power in history and therefore necessary. Schleiermacher denied the personality of Satan. Concerning the fall he said that pride could not have been the cause, inasmuch as that would have implied an antecedent fall. He could not understand why all the angels did not fall. Daub acknowledges the existence of Satan and sets forth Judas Iscariot as an incarnation of evil. Strauss held that at the most Satan was a personification of evil as set forth in the imagination. Martensen considers the demons as impersonal spirits or principles. Personality is reached in the instrumentality of the evil. Satan is an angel who occupies the center of the kingdom of evil.

From the rise of modern Spiritualism in the year 1848, the belief in possible communication with the spirits of the dead has had many adherents and the Spiritualists grow in number and have been confirmed in their religious tenets, when prominent men and some scientists have professed faith in mediumship. In these short notes on the History of Dogmas we cannot discuss spiritualistic phenomena, but in the study of evil angels we have come to the conclusion that the so-called mediums are not of God, and the so-called spirits, in such cases when they evidently are spirits and not deceiving mediums, are demons and not the souls of men. In 1 Kings 22: 21-23 we read how God allowed a lying spirit to enter into the prophets of Ahab. We can be assured that God does not give a medium the key to Hades or Paradise to call forth the souls of the departed to appear at a spiritualistic gathering. The so-called appearances of dead persons, if they occur, are demons or lying spirits who imitate the dead in speech and manner, and the information received is incoherent and of no value. The rich man in Hades could not visit his brethren, and Abraham did not permit Lazarus to reveal himself in the house of Dives. When God has allowed visits from Paradise, like Samuel, Moses, Elijah and the raised dead after the resurrection of Christ, the appearances have been clear and the messages plain. In the appearances and revelations of Christ after His resurrection everything was manifest, convincing and of a continued nature. — In the stances of mediums everything is gloomy, uncertain and ghostly. And to seek what God has forbidden is sin. Paul warns against seducing spirits and doctrines of demons. 1 Tim. 4:1, 2.

2

Anthropology

Anthropology is that section of Dogmatics which treats of the subject of man and comprises the following main divisions: man in general, his original state, the doctrine of sin, or hamartology, and moral freedom, or freedom of the will.

§11. Man.

Man is a being made up of body and spirit. On his spiritual side he is a unit of spontaneity and receptivity or a personal unity of thought, will and feeling. As an intellectual-corporeal organic entity he is capable of self-contemplation and self-determination. In reaching the state of self-consciousness man looks upon himself as distinct from the world and yet as standing in relation to it. But he also feels that he is determined by something higher. This feeling is inborn. He is determined by an absolute being, while he himself is a relative being.

1. The Creation Of Man.

Concerning the creation of man in general it may be said that he was not created like the irrational creation by the simple mandate of God's almighty power; rather a decision was reached in the Godhead when the Lord said: "Let us make man."

Concerning the corporeal part of man the following ought to be observed: 1) That it was created, as to time, before the soul, for which reason the theory that the soul pre-exists and produces its own body must be rejected; 2) the body was made of the dust of the ground, out of *aphar* or damp earth, and *adama* or red soil. From this we learn that the component parts of the human body are made up of earth and water. Man is the highest expression of nature and the crown of creation. Man was intended to be and still remains a *microcosm* or a world in himself; 3) the body was fashioned by God, but not in a mechanical way as a sculptor produces a statue.

The spiritual nature of man was produced when *Jehovah Elohim* directly breathed into the corporeal formation the breath of life and man became a living soul. This inbreathing is not to be thought of as though God had produced some spiration outside of Himself, but He breathed out of the fulness of His being and gave to man a relative spirit. It was not a gnostic emanation. Neither did the creative spirit become immanent in the human spirit. God is a spirit, but man has a spirit, wherefore there is a difference between the Spirit of God and the spirit of man. The race of men are, however, the offspring of God. We must also reject the theory of the Theosophists that the soul is a potency in the body which came to life through the inbreathing of the Creator. The soul and the spirit are identical in substance, but set forth two different aspects of man's spiritual being. As already stated, man became a living soul when God breathed into his nostrils the breath of life. According to Gen. 1:27 this act of creation implied that man was made in the image of God, so that God was imaged forth in man. We may, for this reason, say that man became a *microtheos*.

2. The Unity of the Human Race and Divergent Theories of Creation.

The unity of the human race must be manifest, inasmuch as it cannot be proved that God created more than one man and one woman as the progenitors of the race. The unity is evident when we consider that God took a rib from the man and made or built woman.

Among divergent theories concerning the creation of man may be mentioned: 1) The theory of the Preadamites, or that men were in existence before Adam, spoken of in Genesis 1, while the creation of Adam is first spoken of expressly in the second chapter of Genesis.[28] 2) The theory of the Coadamites, or that many pairs were created at different places, which argument is designed to explain the origin of the different races. 3) The theory of the Autochthones, or that many thousands of men have been produced out of the ground at one time, so that man has come into being without creation, produced from earth and moisture, or from the earth as heated by the electricity of the air (*generatio aequivoca* or *simultanea*). 4) The Transmutation theory of Darwin. The main argument in this theory is not that species of a lower degree can develop into species of a higher, but concerns the factors by which these transmutations can take place. Darwin and his followers say: a) that in accordance with physico-chemical laws in a purely mechanical way a living primitive cell can be formed and develop out of inorganic bodies without the presence of any previous life; b) that in the course of numberless generations

[28] The words of Paul in Acts 17:26 are literally true when he declares that God made of one every nation of men to dwell on all the face of the earth. The Athenians and the Greeks in general boasted of springing from the soil on which they lived. They therefore called themselves autochthones. The doctrine of Preadamites has been presented by Lanini of Solcia, 1459, by Isaac la Peyrere, 1655, by Schelling, and some others. But many distinguished scientists, such as Linne, Blumenbach, Prichard, Buffon, John Müller, Rudolph Wagner, Max Müller, and others, set forth the possibility and the probability of the unity of the human race. The following reasons are adduced: 1) The races do not lose their power of procreation through mixed marriages; 2) from the physiological standpoint they have much in common; 3) climate, diet and occupation explain the differences in color etc.; 4) the differences in language can be easily understood, inasmuch as examples may be cited where different peoples have changed their language, such as the Phoenicians, the Longobards, the Berbers in Morocco, and others; 5) ethical and religious similarities also constitute an argument; 6) the different forms of religion may be satisfactorily explained; 7) the more recent scientific research establishes the teaching of the Bible concerning the unity of the race.

higher organisms had developed out of the lower organisms without the intervention of any outside cause, the developments taking place through blind causality without any purpose.

3. The Component Parts of Man's Being or Nature.

Man possesses body and soul or spirit.[29] There are many that consider that man's nature consists of three parts, viz., body, soul and spirit. Compare 1 Thess. 5:23 and Heb. 4:12. However, on the basis of other passages (Matt. 16:26; Acts 20:10; 2 Cor. 12:15; Heb. 13:17; Rev. 6:9, etc.), where the soul includes the spirit and the spirit the soul, we may say that the spiritual part of man has two sides, the spirit, which is turned toward

---

[29] Theological anthropology does not contain an extended treatment of somatology or psychology, but views man from the theologico-ethical viewpoint. Although the spiritual side of man is emphasized more than the corporeal, still the significance of the body is not to be underestimated, for the body is the dwelling-place of the spirit, and it is called the temple of the Holy Ghost. Furthermore, the body has great significance because of the resurrection. But the spiritual part of man is comparatively of the greatest importance, inasmuch as the spirit in man functions through the body and exerts its influence upon it. The spiritual part of man, the soul or the spirit, is the expression of the personality, which is characterized by self-consciousness and self-determination. Many attempts have been made to define the soul or the spirit, but no entirely satisfactory definition has been made. The activity of the soul can be more readily described than its essence. The substance of the soul is not material, yet real. Although the soul or the spirit in this life is dependent upon a material nervous system for its contact with and its activity in the material world about us, nevertheless this does not prove that the soul does not possess its own spiritual powers and faculties. The soul is conscious of many things that are not material. It knows that it is a thing apart from the senses that it uses. The human soul is capable of knowing itself. It knows of its own existence, because it thinks in a self-conscious and self-determinative way. It has been proved that the soul thinks even when every part of the brain has been injured. The spirit, which is, so to speak, the soul of the soul, is conscious of its relationship with the Father of Spirits. The purely spiritual thinking may be perfectly clear, even when the mind functions abnormally with regard to material things. It has been conclusively proven that the soul or the spirit belongs not only to this world, but also to the invisible world of the spirit. The soul is everywhere present in the whole human organism, with which it stands in the closest possible union. The Scriptures speak of an inward as well as an outward man. Cf. Rom. 7:22; 2 Cor. 4:16; Eph. 3:16. In 1 Peter 3:4 the inward man is called ὁ *κρυπτὸς τῆς καρδίας* ἄ*νθρωπος*.

God, and the soul, which is turned toward the body and the material world. The soul is the form of the spirit and mediates the connection of the spirit with the body. The dichotomic theory is thus acknowledged to be the correct one, but the trichotomic theory is accorded a certain degree of recognition.

The dichotomic view being the correct one and different expressions being used for the spiritual part of man, we must investigate how unity in teaching may be attained. In a dogmatic textbook we cannot study the exegetical expressions in the various forms in which they occur. But there must be some usage which makes the distinction clear. It is evident that spirit is used to express the animating principle, and soul, the animated result. If spirit expresses the life principle directly inbreathed by God, it is clear why "spirit" is used in John 19:30, "And gave up his spirit." And in John 10:11 soul (transl. from the Greek, *psyche*) is used, although the translators have rendered the Greek to mean 'life.' The *psyche* or soul means here the entire being as the human life. Compare Rev. 20:4, where souls are mentioned. But in fact spirit and soul is the same entity looked upon from different viewpoints. The soul-spirit or spirit-soul is the same spiritual nature in man. The soul is of one nature with the spirit.

In Biblical psychology the expression *heart* is prominent. The Bible phrase "the life (or soul) is in the blood" called attention to the organ of the distribution of the blood. The heart came to be looked upon as the collective focus of the personal energies. Just as Harvey's famous discovery of the circulation of the blood showed the importance of the heart as the center of the going and returning of the blood, the heart was looked upon from olden times at least metaphorically as the central seat of the circulation of the mental and moral activities. But Ecclesiastes 12:6 proves that the wise Solomon had discovered the circulation of the blood and also claimed that there is nothing new under the sun. But whatever the reason there are many Bible references to the heart in regard to man's mental and moral life. Among the many references we quote the following: Deut. 11:13: "And to serve him (Jehovah) with all your heart and with all your soul," Ps. 90:12: "Get us a heart of wisdom," Matt. 6:21:

"There will thy heart be," Matt. 15:19: "For out of the heart come forth evil thoughts." According to philosophical psychology thoughts come forth from the brain. In the Bible conscience takes its place beside the heart as the legislative and critical function of the inner man. When the spirit represents the principle of life, the soul stands for the personality and the heart is the organ of life. Mind in philosophy and general usage would correspond to soul in Biblical phraseology. Many psychologists deny the existence of the soul and, therefore, reject the doctrine of immortality. According to these scientists mind is identical with the brain. From the Christian viewpoint the brain is the instrument used by the soul.

4. The Propagation of the Soul.

There are three theories that have been presented and are still being defended by prominent theologians and thinkers on this subject, viz.: 1) *The Pre-existence Theory,* which teaches that all souls came into being before time was, or before they were united with men. 2) *Creationism,* which teaches that every soul is brought forth by an immediate act of creation. 3) *Traducianism,* which teaches that the soul of each individual person is propagated with the body. This last-named theory is the correct one. Some Dogmaticians have accorded to the Creationist theory a" certain degree of recognition, acknowledging that God acts immediately in the matter of the soul's endowment. The following Scripture passages may be observed in relation to Traducianism: "Adam begat a son in his own likeness, after his own image" (Gen. 5:3). Compare Gen. 1:28; 9:1; 46:26; Ps. 51:7; Acts 17: 24-26.

The Pre-existence theory confines the idea of species to the body, as the soul existed before the creation of Adam. According to this theory the Fall occurred before the sixth day or in a timeless condition. Some hold that it happened in an ante-mundane state and others, in a supra-temporal; the latter view was held by Julius Müller, which was in fact the doctrine of Kant, who held the conception of sin as a noumenon which always is both timeless and spaceless. Creationism is like the theory of Pre-existence except in regard to the time when the soul was created. In both views the body was propagated and the soul was individual and had no race-existence in Adam. According to Creationism the soul was a new creation and united with the human body about the 40th day after the conception. This theory teaches a continued creation which is in conflict with the Word of God. Traducianism or the theory of mediate creationism teaches that both body and soul are derived from the parents, which is the best explanation of original and hereditary sin. Inherited sin and guilt cannot be explained by *imputatio immediata* or the theory of representative or forensic union with Adam, as such immediate imputation would not be just, when we consider that the posterity had not chosen Adam as a representative, not existing at the time of Adam and his test. But according to Traducianism and mediate imputation the problem may be more easily solved, although it belongs to the mysteries of Providence. In the scheme of the theory of Pre-existence the problem why all human souls fell in the pre-existing state remains unsolved. And if the idea of Creationism is accepted, the sinful condition would be in the body, and the pure soul would be contaminated after its creation without any probation in the union with the body.

Traducianism is plainly taught in the Scriptures. We cannot investigate exegetically all the passages. In Rom. 5:12 the original rendering *ἥμαρτον* proves or at least strongly supports the Traducian view. It is an active form. Therefore, if all sinned in Adam, they must have existed in him. In 1 Cor. 15:22 we read: "In Adam all die." Notice in the Greek the article before "Adam." As in Gen. 1:27 "man" denotes Adam and Eve and includes the whole species. To die in Adam implies existence in him. The whole human race was in Adam and sinned in him. Posterity was not present at the Fall as individual persons with self-consciousness and self-determination, but the race was there invisibly and yet really, which explains why all sinned in and with Adam. Some argue that this works injustice to posterity, individuals of which might not have failed in the test. But if Adam had not included the race, if man had been created like the angels, the outcome might not have been better but rather worse, as the fallen angels cannot be saved. All human beings have the opportunity to return to God and be saved. God has sent the second Adam, the Second Person in the Trinity, Jesus Christ, that all who believe in Him shall be saved. God has provided the means both objectively and subjectively. If many reject the simple test and resist the operations of the Holy Spirit, it is their own fault. The condition in the test for returning is in fact easier than the test of Adam and Eve, although no one can complain that the probationary test of man was unreasonable. Man was created good and was only requested to obey a certain commandment, which was comparatively easy.

We desire to add an explanation of the meaning of numerical and specific unity, which makes it easier to understand Traducianism. A numerical unity may both be and not be a specific unity. In the Trinity there is a numerical unity of nature, as there is only one essence, but there is no specific unity, because the one nature in God cannot be divided, as each hypostasis in the Trinity possesses the whole essence and there is no division of the divine nature, only modification in mode of subsistence in the internal relation. But if we consider man, the unity is both numerical and specific. In Adam the human nature was specifically and numerically one at the same time, but by propagation the one human nature has become a multitude of persons, who are still specifically one. — In regard to the presence of the race in Adam the following observations may make it plainer. The species contain all the individuals. The first acorn cell implanted in creation by God contained all the oaks. The great oak tree was once a mere acorn. One cell divides indefinitely and produces the same kind. The product is as old as the parent cell. Sexual propagation illustrates the same principle. Man has two existences, one kind in Adam as an invisible principle, another as individualized nature in persons. The one human nature in Adam was an entity; the multitude of men propagated from Adam is likewise an entity. The invisible principles to be individualized in the posterity were not atoms, nor were they only ideas. A specific nature constituted to continue by propagation has a real existence. Human reason cannot comprehend the laws of the spiritual world, hence the invisible existence made visible by propagation in conception is a mystery. But the Word of God has revealed the fact that there is such a mystery. Besides the passages referred to, notice Heb. 7:10, "For he was yet in the loins of his father," and compare Ps. 13:15, 16; Jer. 1:5. Note also the invisibles mentioned in Col. 1:16 and the "things not seen" in Heb. 11: 1-3. Agazziz and other scientists speak of the real invisibles behind the first appearance. The entire substance, both physical and psychical or spiritual, was propagated and existed both as physical and psychical, as things not seen, from the creation of Adam. And by the laws of propagation, conception and birth they become visible as individualized human beings. The doctrine of Traducianism throws a clear light on the conception of original sin and its imputation.

5. Notes On The History Of Dogma.

The teachers in the Orient in general accepted the Trichotomistic theory. The theory of Dichotomy gained headway on the ground of the teaching of Apollinaris. Even in the primitive Church the three different theories of the propagation of the soul were current. Tertullian held the Traducian view, Origen the theory of Pre-existence, while Lactantius adopted the Creationist theory. As early as the middle of the sixth century the theory of Pre-existence was condemned as a heresy. During the Middle Ages and within the Catholic Church the theory of Creationism was generally advocated. The theologians of the Lutheran Church have as a rule advocated Dichotomy and Traducianism. The theory of Pre-existence has gained many distinguished adherents in recent times. However, Traducianism is the view held by all orthodox and conservative theologians, because according to this theory the transmission of original sin can best be explained.

Plato taught that man had a two-fold soul, an intellectual and a sensual one. He, and later Philo, advocated the theory of Pre-existence. Aristotle was a Creationist. Justin Martyr held the Trlchotomic view. Tatian taught that before the fall man possessed body, soul, which was material, and spirit. The latter was lost in the Fall, but could be regained. Good men had a body, soul and spirit, but evil men had only body and soul. Clement Of Alexandria was a Creationist. Tertullian taught Dichotomy and Traducianism. Concerning the soul he said that it possesses form and members like the body, that it increases in size with the growth of the body. Origen taught Trichotomy and the theory of Pre-existence. The souls were consigned to bodies because of the sins that they had committed in the ante-temporal state.

Arnobius said that the souls were not created by God, but by lesser spirits, and that the soul was material. Gregory of Nazianzus advocated Dichotomy. Gregory of Nyssa taught Trichotomy and Traducianism. He said that there was no sexual relationship before the Fall. Jerome taught Dichotomy. Augustine taught the same together with the immateriality of the soul. The doctrine of Pre-existence was pronounced heretical at the meeting of Constantinople in 543. John of Damascus taught Dichotomy.

Anselm, Peter Lombard and Thomas Aquinas advocated Creationism. The last named made a distinction between *anima sensitiva* and *intellectiva*. The former was propagated in a physical way, but not the latter. He taught, in common with the majority of the Scholastics of the Middle Ages, the theory of Dichotomy.

Luther taught Dichotomy and Traducianism. Melanchthon advocated Creationism. Luther acknowledged that there was some truth in Creationism. The old Lutheran Dogmaticians taught Traducianism. Calixtus and Musaeus advocated Creationism.

The modern Arminians, following the ancient Semi-Pelagians, hold the view of representative union only. Posterity is not guilty of Adam's first sin either as to culpability or liability to punishment, but suffers from it as in spiritual weakness, bodily sickness and death. The real guilt and consequences depend upon actual sin.

Kant taught the theory of Pre-existence and explained the radical evil in man on the basis of deeds done in the ante-temporal state. Julius Müller also advocated the theory of Pre-existence or rather an extra-temporal state. Harless, Nitzsch, Beck, Kahnis and Thomasius were Dichotomists, while Olshausen, Neander, Meyer, Lange and Delitzsch, to a greater or less extent, were Trichotomists.

In his psychology, Delitzsch accords as much recognition as possible to Trichotomy. In like manner as the Triune God possesses a sevenfold *δόξα* through the Spirit, so the spirit of man also possesses a sevenfold *δόξα*, which reveals itself first in the soul and through the soul in the body. The soul is the image of the spirit, and the body is the image of the soul. The human ego is called näphäsh or soul, because the soul is the medium or form of the human personality. But the soul itself is personal only because of the immanence of the spirit. Delitzsch explains the beginning of the soul's existence in the following way: The first step in the process is *contractio*, thereafter *expansio* or reaching out, then *rotatio*, or the process of becoming, thereafter comes life and then reflection, followed by the sixth power or *manifestatio* (*λόγος ενδιάθετος* becomes *λόγος προφορικός*); the seventh power includes all the others and constitutes the substantiality of the soul as the image of the spirit. All this expresses the internal relationship between the soul and the spirit, but the spirit through the medium of the soul must enter into relationship with the body. The soul possesses, therefore, a sevenfold *δόξα* and, as Luther says, constitutes the seven-armed candlestick in the sanctuary. When the soul reveals its seven forms of life, it appears in the first place as an embryo; the second form is breathing; the third is the blood, for which reason it is said that the soul is in the blood; the fourth form is the heart, which is the drive-wheel of life; the fifth form is the nervous system, including the brain, through which medium thought becomes possible, and by which the soul, and through the soul the spirit, may enter into relationship with the external world; the sixth form is the productive form or the power of speech, which reveals the inward man, while the seventh form is the outward form or the *μορφή* of the soul.[30]

---

[30] Delitzsch, *Biblical Psychology*, IV, §VI.

§12. The Original State

Status integritatis vel innocentiae is the original condition of man as created in the image of God, which implied especially wisdom in understanding, holiness in will, and purity in feeling.

In defining the image of God we confine ourselves especially to the spiritual nature of man, although the corporeal nature must also be considered. Man is made up of soul or spirit and body, but inasmuch as he became a living soul through the spirit, we hold forth man as a unit of intellect, will and emotion. Inasmuch as religion was and in a certain sense still remains basic in man's nature, so the formal aspect of religion will likewise appear as a unit of the three basic concepts that constitute human personality, for which reason we must conceive of the image of God, not only in a general sense, referring to man as a person, but take into consideration the qualitative distinction. The thought of man could not be content with derivative knowledge, but sought God directly and found rest in Him, who also became the light of his reason. Furthermore his will was determined by the will of God, while his emotional nature found peace and happiness in God.

God is absolutely free, while man possesses only relative freedom. However, man was not to render obedience by reason of any arbitrary law. In human freedom two factors must be taken into consideration, viz., self-determination and determination. If we consider the determining activity of God to the exclusion of human self-determination, the result would be determinism; contrariwise, the result would be arbitrariness. Created freedom was to be realized by way of choice. For this reason man could either sin or refrain from sinning. He could not remain neutral. The will of God became a factor as the source or motive of his actions, but he was conscious of the fact that he could act contrary to this motive. Augustine said that man's original nature was *posse non peccare*, which was to become *non posse peccare*.

In Gen. 1: 27 the Hebrew expressions *tzelem* and *demuth* are used to set forth the image of God. The latter is an exegetical expression of the former. The Latin expressions are *imago* and *similitudo*. Hollazius says that *imago* is not the same as *vestigium*, inasmuch as *imago* clearly portrays the original of which it is an image, while *vestigium* is only a dim portrayal. The image of God was clear and not dim.

1. Divisions And Attributes.

The image of God is divided into the formal and material images.

A. The Formal Image.—By the formal image is meant the human personality as consisting of the faculties of intellect, will and emotion. The content of these faculties is not taken into consideration, the question concerns merely the concept of personality. If the formal image were lost, the essence of man would be destroyed. The formal image, therefore, cannot be lost, for which reason it is called essential. The old writers called it *imago Dei.* The formal image of God is *imago Dei late dicta, generaliter et abusive spectata* or *αχύρως*. In considering the formal image *per se*, or the image of God as both formal and material, we must bear in mind that the image of God is not man in the sense that he is a portrait of God, but that the image is in man. Man is a relative personality.

B. The Material Image.—By this is meant the original endowment or the qualitative content of the formal image of God. This is the image of God in a special sense. For this reason it is also called *imago Dei stricte dicta* or *κυρίως*. It is also called *primaria* or accidental. The old writers called it *similitudo Dei*. As embodying all these attributes it is called ὁλικῶς; as embodying only the essential it is called *μερικῶς*.

The material image of God is divided as follows: a) *perfectiones principales* or the essential perfections, also expressed by *justitia originalis* or the original righteousness, meaning enlightenment in the understanding, holiness in the will, and purity in the emotions. In his original state man was perfect, yet undeveloped. However, it was not the helpless condition of a child. Neither were the wisdom in the understanding, the holiness of will and the blessedness in feeling possessed only *in nuce*. Man was created in the mature state; b) *perfectiones minus principales* or the less essential perfections were: 1) *impassibilitas* or that man was not subject to suffering.

Originally the body was a pure and faultless organ or instrument of a pure and holy spirit. There was perfect harmony between the sensuous appetites and the higher life of man. This harmony the Apology calls *sequale temperamentum qualitatum corporis*; 2) *immortalitas* or immortality. In case man had remained *in status integritatis,* he would have undergone a transformation without the intervention of death and would have been translated with a pneumatic body into the world of glory; 3) *dominium in creaturas,* or that man was lord of creation. He stood in perfect harmony with nature and was the crown of creation.

2. The Attributes of the Image of God.

The attributes (*affectiones*) that are ascribed to the image of God are: a) *concreata* or concreated, so that the image was in no sense increased after creation. The Roman Catholic Church teaches that man was created in a purely natural condition (*status purorum naturalium*). He possessed intellect and free will, but was without character. He was neither good nor bad. In addition God had bestowed upon him a *donum superadditum,* which was a gift of grace, and which did not belong to his nature, through which his development in the right direction would be rendered more easy. Hollazius has compared this gift with the bit that directs the horse. Some Catholic Dogmaticians have taught that this gift was bestowed after creation; b) *naturalis* or natural. According to Quenstedt this attribute has five specific significations: 1) *constitutive,* or that which constitutes nature itself or an essential part of it, such as soul and body, 2) *consecutive,* or that which is derived from nature, such as the faculties of the soul, 3) *subjective,* or that which adheres to nature as a natural property, 4) *perfective,* or that which perfects and adorns it internally, 5) *transitive,* or that which is transplanted. We conceive of *naturalis* according to the last three significations; c) *propagabilis ad posteros,* or the propagation to posterity; d) *accidentalis* or accidental, inasmuch as it was not the essence of man, but a qualification in his essence. This was taught against Flacius, who maintained that the image of God was essential. This term has also been employed in order to distinguish between the image of God in man and the substantial image of God or the Son. In the Son the image is original, uncreated, and in relation to man, prototypical (Hollazius: "He exhibits in Himself the entire essence of the Father, being distinguished from Him by the mode of His subsistence"); e) *amissibilis,* or that the image can be lost.

With regard to the image of God in general the following passages may be observed: "God created man in his own image" (Gen. 1:27); "God saw everything that he had made, and, behold, it was very good" (Gen. 1:31); cf. Gen. 9:6; "And put on the new man, that after God hath been created in righteousness and holiness of truth" (Eph. 4:24); "And have put on the new man, that is being renewed unto knowledge after the image of him that created him" (Col. 3:10); "Men, who are made after the likeness of God" (James 3:9).

3. The Purpose or the Object of the Image of God.

Finis is conceived of either *specialiter* or *generaliter.* In the first sense, or *specialiter,* the object is thought of as: 1) *proximus,* or the immediate object, which implies that man may live a godly life, well-pleasing unto the Lord; 2) *remotior,* or the more remote object, which consists in everlasting salvation. *Generaliter.* In this sense the object is the glory of the divine wisdom, power and goodness.

4. Notes On the History of Dogma.

During the first period it was generally acknowledged that the Mosaical story of Paradise and man was real history. Origen departed from this view. The image of God was thought to consist in intellect and freedom, while stress was also laid on the formal content. It was also argued that the material image could be lost. The same views were current during the period that followed. The Roman Catholic conception, developed during the Scholastic period, made a sharp distinction between *imago Dei* and *similitudo Dei,* the latter being conceived of as implying an extra gift of grace. Both set forth a concreated and special gift of grace. The power to overcome the sensual in man's nature was not a natural gift, but was added by God as a special gift. Luther rejected this Scholastic teaching. Our confessional writings clearly set forth the formal and material concepts of the image of God. The old Dogmaticians taught as did Luther and said that *justitia originalis* was not a *bonum superadditum*, but a concreated perfection. The Socinians and the Arminians did not acknowledge the doctrine of the Church on the original state. The Rationalists declare that the original state consisted simply in good traits. In general the philosophers reject the truth of the account in Genesis. Among theologians Schleiermacher and those most closely associated with him in thought took a position nearly akin to Rationalism in relation to the historical content of Genesis. They limited the original perfection to a consciousness of God. Many of the leading Dogmaticians in modern times, however, favor the old orthodox view.

Justin Martyr and many of the older Church Fathers taught that the image of God consisted in intellect and freedom. Justin also stressed the ethical content. The similitude was also extended to the body. The Encratites and the Severians denied that women were made in the image of God. Irenaeus and Tertullian extended the likeness unto God even to the body. The former stated that Adam possessed the garment of righteousness, but that his state was not that of the matured man, but must be developed. Origen said that the story of Paradise was an allegory. Together with Clement of Alexandria he taught that death was natural even in the original state of integrity.

The Audians limited the image of God to the body. Augustine said that the prototype of the creation of man was the Trinity. It had previously been taught that it was the Logos. He not only sets forth the image of God as *memoria, intelligentia* and *voluntas*, but also the positive inclination of the spirit to that which is good. In regard to death he used the same terms as with relation to sin. Before the Fall man possessed *posse non mori*, which was to be transformed into *non posse mori*. Cyril of Alexandria taught that a positive inclination toward good was implanted in the first man. Man was righteous and good. He says, however, that man received the Spirit of God, basing his assertion on Gen. 2:7.

Thomas Aquinas conceived of the image of God from three points of view. In the first place man possesses *aptitudo moralis* to know and love God; in the second place he knows and loves God, although imperfectly, which is *imago per conformitatem gratiae*; in the third place man loves God perfectly, and this is *imago secundem similitudinem gratiae*. In the first place the image is natural, in the other instances it is a supernatural gift of grace. He says that *donum superadditum* was bestowed upon man at his creation and designed to serve as a rein on nature. Alexander of Hales, Bonaventura, Duns Scotus, and others maintained that *donum superadditum* was given after creation. Bellarmine also asserts that this gift did not belong to the nature of man, but was bestowed upon him later.

Luther taught that the image of God consisted in a pure will, true knowledge, and peace in God. He distinguished between *imago Dei* and *similitudo Dei*, but rejected the teaching of the Scholastics. The tree of life bestowed health and the strength of youth on Adam, who would be transformed without the intervention of death. Calovius, Quenstedt, and Hollazius look upon immortality as a natural attribute. Buddeus derives it from the tree of life. The *Socinians* conceive of the image of God principally as dominion over nature and the animal creation. Woman is excluded from participation in this dominion. The *Arminians* also state that the image consisted in the dominion over the animal creation. Men were like good children and their goodness came from natural instinct.

The *Rationalists* declared that the image of God consisted in inclination toward good and that the difference between now and then is simply relative. Schleiermacher said that the original perfection consisted in the possibility of uninterrupted consciousness of God in the soul. He rejects the expression "image of God," because, he declared, there existed no perfect correspondence. Neither did he consider "*justitia originalis*" a proper expression, Inasmuch as man has not reached independence through development. Thomasius and Philippi advocated the orthodox view, but stressed the principle of development.

§13. The Fall and Original Sin.

We begin herewith the study of hamartology or the doctrine of sin. The existence of sin presupposes the Fall, inasmuch as man was originally in a state of relative perfection or status integritatis. Now he finds himself in *status corruptionis*. By this is meant that state of corruption into which man was plunged when of his own free will he became disobedient toward God and transgressed the law of Paradise. The possibility of the first sin becomes evident when we consider the implications in the concept of freedom. No real reason has been presented to prove the historical recital of the Fall, as found in Gen. 3, an allegory. We may be sure that the story of the Fall is a literal recital of the actual historical truth.

1. The Origin of Sin.

God is not the author of sin. Quenstedt says: "God is not the cause of sin: 1) in a physical sense, because in such a sense sin or evil has no cause; 2) in a moral sense, by commanding, persuading, or approving, because He does not desire sin, but hates it; 3) by way of accident, inasmuch as nothing can happen to God by chance or fortuitously." The causes were as follows: a) *causa externa et principalis remotior* was Satan; b) *causa instrumentalis* was the serpent, possessed by Satan; c) *causa interna, directa et propinqua* was man's abuse of the understanding and the free will.

We can formulate a conception of the origin of sin by the consideration of the principle of freedom. There are many that have asked the question why God, who is omniscient, should have created man such that he could fall into sin. Those who propound such a question, however, forget that man would not have been a man, but an irrational animal, if he had been created without self-consciousness, self-determination, or freedom. According to the principle of freedom a mechanical determinism could not be brought into play. The freedom of man as to its content must needs be realized by way of choice. A test was therefore necessary. The will of God was therein revealed in a manner that cannot be considered too stern, inasmuch as the test that ensued is expressed in the following words of the Lord: "Of the tree of the knowledge of good and evil, thou shalt not eat of it." This was a reasonable demand, but a strong enough challenge to bring into play the principle of self-determination on the part of man, so that he could determine for himself what he would do. It may be considered at once a piece of good and evil fortune, if we may so express ourselves, that the temptation to sin came from Satan, i. e., from without, because if man had fallen into sin without an external temptation, then his fall would have been like unto that of the evil angels. To be sure, it was a great misfortune that Satan tempted men, but there is no excuse for man on that ground, inasmuch as man possessed power to overcome temptation. He had an enlightened understanding, so that the temptation should have been perfectly transparent. Of his own free will the egoism of man became dominant, so that his own will instead of the will of God became the decisive element of his self-determination. The essence of sin, therefore, is selfishness. Man would become like unto God. He was made in the image of God, but became perverted through the assertion of rebellious independence. Viewed from the standpoint of man, the Lord said after the Fall: "Behold, the man is become as one of us, to know good and evil." There was holy irony or at least a terrifying truth expressed in this assertion of the Lord, inasmuch as man had gotten knowledge of evil in a wrong way that led to eternal death. If man in his self-determination had chosen the will of God he would have learned to know of evil in a detached way. while now by reason of the Fall he knew what was good only in a detached way as a reminiscence of the period when he stood in blessed communion with God.

Various theories have been propounded to explain the origin of sin. The following must be rejected: 1) *The theory of privation* or *imperfection,* according to which the source of sin is to be found in finiteness and sin is considered only an imperfection, just as a person loses a limb or suffers from some defect, physical or moral. The positive element of sin is ignored in this theory; 2) *the Sensualistic theory,* according to which the source of evil is to be found in the body. This theory is related to the Manichaean Dualism. In recent times a modification of this theory has been presented to the effect that inasmuch as the sensuous in man is first to be developed, therefore sin arises as the sensuous outbalances the influence of the spiritual; 3) the *Pantheistic theory*, which declares that the evil is necessary as a process in the development of the spirit. The good stands in need of the evil, since all life is developed through contraries; 4) the *Calvinistic theory*, which asserts that God has predetermined sin and therefore also decided upon the Fall; 5) the *Rationalistic theory*, which denies the Fall. Man still possesses his original freedom, and sin arises through the exercise of his free will. Sin is general by reason of bad example and habits; 6) the old and modern *Negative theory*, which teaches that sin does not exist and is only an imagination of the mind. The so-called "Christian Science" holds this view.

2. Concerning Original Sin and Its Definition.

Hollazius defines original sin as follows: *"original (or Hereditary) Sin is that corruption of human nature by evil desire which deprived man of his original righteousness through the Fall of our first parents and which is transplanted in all men by natural generation, rendering them indisposed to spiritual good and inclined to evil and making them subject to the wrath of God and eternal damnation."*[31] Original sin may therefore be said to consist of two and to imply three elements: 1) the negative, or the loss of the material image of God, 2) the positive, or the evil desire, *concupiscentia prava*, which is real sin, 3) *imputatio ad reatum et poenam*, or, as it is also expressed, *reatus culpae* and *reatus poenae*.

In the confessional writings the following metaphorical terms are used: 1) *vitium*, corresponding to the negative element, the word meaning fault or deformity, such as blindness or lameness, and therefore a permanent defect; 2) *morbus*, corresponding to the positive element, meaning a sickness that extends throughout the whole body, a contagious disease,

---

[31] Hollazius: *"Peccatum originale est privatio justitiae originalis cum prava inclinatione conjuncta, totam humanam naturam corrumpens, ex lapsu primorum parentum derivata et per carnalem generationem in omnes homines propagata, ipsos ineptos ad bona spiritualia, ad mala vero propensos reddens reosque faciens irse divinae et aeternae damnationis."*

such as fever; or, changing the figure, sin is said to permeate man's nature as the heat penetrates the iron in the crucible; 3) *seuche* (Latin, *lues*), which is different from both *vitium* and *morbus*. The relation between this word and sickness and pest is the same as the relation between genus and species.

Original sin is also designated by the following terms: 1) *peccatum originale originans,* or the first sin of our race; 2) *peccatum originale originatum,* or the depravity that is transplanted to the whole race in consequence of the first sin.

Sin is called *peccatum originale,* in the first place, because it originated with Adam, in the second place, because every man is born with it, in the third, because it is the root of all sins.

Concerning the sinfulness of original sin Dr. C. P. Krauth in *The Conservative Reformation* (pp. 398-406) argues that it is truly sin, because: 1) it has the relations and connections of sin; 2) it has the names and synonyms of sin; 3) it has the essence of sin; 4) it has the attributes of sin; 5) it does the acts of sin; 6) it incurs the penalties of sin; 7) it needs the remedies of sin.

The following Scripture passages may be cited: "Behold, I was brought forth in iniquity and in sin did my mother conceive me" (Ps. 51:5); "As through one man sin entered the world" (Rom. 5:12); "That which is born of the flesh is flesh" (John 3:6); "He begat a son in his own likeness, after his image" (Gen. 5:3); "Every imagination of the thoughts of his heart was only evil continually" (Gen. 6:5); "By nature children of wrath" (Eph. 2:3). The selfishness of sin is set forth both directly and indirectly, as in the following passage: "That they that live should no longer live unto themselves" (2 Cor. 5:15); compare also Gal. 2:20; Phil. 2:4; Luke 14:26; John 12:25. With regard to the attributes, the acts and the consequences of sin the following passages may be observed: "What is man, that he should be righteous?" (Job 15:14); "For out of the heart come forth evil thoughts," etc. (Matt. 15:14); cf. Gal. 5:19-21; "Sin which dwelleth in me" (Rom. 7:20); "I see a different law in my members" (Rom. 7:23); "The judgment came of one unto condemnation" (Rom. 5:16); "Create in me a clean heart, O God" (Ps. 51:12); "In the putting off of the body of the flesh, in the circumcision of Christ" (Col. 2:11); "Who shall deliver me out of the body of this death?" (Rom. 7:24); "Except one be born of water and the Spirit, he cannot enter into the kingdom of God" (John 3:5).

3. Characteristics or *Affectiones*.

These are: 1) *naturalis inhaerentia,* because original sin belongs to the depraved nature of man. In the original state of man sin was unnatural. Against Flacius, who declared that original sin constituted the essence of man, the following terms are used, *non essentiale, sed accidentale,* because original sin is a quality in the essence of man; 2) *naturalis propagabilitas,* because original sin is propagated through natural birth; 3) *generale,* or general, a term used against the Roman Catholic Church, which teaches the immaculate conception of Mary. Therefore all men are *subjectum quod;* 4) *duratio per omnem vitam,* because original sin is never rooted out in this life. The *reatus* or the imputation of sin ceases in regeneration whose Sacrament is Baptism, but the *materiale* remains. The domination of sin is done away with through sanctification, and in death, finally, so far as the children of God are concerned, sin itself is totally obliterated in a manner past finding out; 5) *damnabile* or damnable. This is true because peccatum originale originatum is *vere peccatum.* Original sin condemns all that are not regenerated through Baptism and the Holy Ghost.

4. *Imputatio* or Imputation.

Imputation is presented in a threefold manner: 1) *imputatio immediata,* or immediate imputation. Adam is regarded as the representative and the moral head (*caput morale*) of the human race. Therefore all men sinned in him. The children of men, who constitute one race, cannot be separated from each other; 2) *imputatio mediata,* or the mediate imputation, which is based upon the fact that Adam is the natural head of the race or *caput naturale.* Compare Traducianism, Section II, 4; 3) *imputatio individualis,* or the individual imputation, because with the development of self-consciousness each person appropriates original sin as his own through actual sin.

Original sin is something that is imputed, not only because of the transgression of another, which view tends toward Pelagianism, but because original sin implies the corruption of our nature. The sinful state stands in relation to the sin of Adam because he is the *principium naturale et morale* of the whole race. Original sin is therefore guilt or *reatus propter inobedientiam Adae et Hevae*. For this reason the confessional writings state that on account of this corruption and the disobedience of our first parents the nature of man is accused and judged by the law of God.

Inasmuch, therefore, as not only grown persons, but also small children who have not committed actual sins, come under the judgment of the sin of our first parents, it would seem as though the small children, not to speak of grown persons, would thereby suffer unjustly and without cause. However, we must not forget that Adam was the representative of the race and as such must be tested for the race. Inasmuch as he failed in the test, therefore all must suffer by reason of the solidarity of the race. If men had not constituted a racial solidarity, they would have been like unto the angels and each would have stood his own test, but in His wisdom God created man to form an organism. Despite the fact that sin has come into the world through one man, still men are not compelled to remain in the state of sin. The compensation which has been gained through the Second Adam is greater than the original loss sustained, and through another test man may become finally liberated from original sin, provided he make use of the means of salvation. Thus Paul writes in Romans 5:14,15: "Nevertheless death reigned from Adam until Moses, even over them that had not sinned after the likeness of Adam's transgression, who is a figure of him that was to come. But not as the trespass, so also is the free gift. For if by the trespass of the one the many died, much more did the grace of God, and the gift by the grace of the one man, Jesus Christ, abound unto many." The act of the second Adam is meant for the whole race of men without merit and without distinction. Therefore the way to Paradise is open to all, although a test is necessary for all, since God does not force anyone to return.

5. The Effects of Original Sin or *Effectus*.

The effects of sin are the following: 1) The loss of the free will; 2) actual sins; 3) spiritual death; 4) sickness and suffering; 5) bodily death; 6) eternal or the second death.

The loss of the free will is naturally included in the negative element of sin, inasmuch as man lost *perfectiones principales* or *justitia originalis*. Spiritual death or separation from God is also included under this head. Although original sin in a special sense destroyed the spiritual powers of man, still the effects necessarily also were extended to his physical nature so that *perfectiones minus principales* were likewise lost. Bodily death became the necessary result of spiritual death. Death did not belong to the nature of man and even now is something unnatural. Provided man had remained in the state of integrity, he would have escaped death and when fully developed for the higher life would have been transformed in nature and translated to heaven. But by reason of sin, not only did physical death as a king of terror enter into the world, but what is still worse, eternal death or the second death also entered.

The following Scripture passages may be cited to show the effects of original sin: "I am carnal, sold under sin" (Rom. 7:14); "Then the lust, when it hath conceived, beareth sin: and the sin, when it is full grown, bringeth forth death" (James 1:15); "Dead through your trespasses and sins" (Eph. 2:1); "The wages of sin is death" (Rom. 6:23); "In the day that thou eatest thereof thou shalt surely die" (Gen. 2:17); "This is the second death, even the lake of fire" (Rev. 20:15).

6. Notes on the History of Dogma.

The older teachers of the Church considered that the depravity of sin was general, but their opinions did not agree on the heredity of sin through natural propagation. This in turn was dependent on the distinctive opinions with regard to the propagation of the soul. The Oriental fathers seemed to identify the natural imperfections with sensuality. The Occidental theologians took a deeper view of sin. Stress was laid on *imputatio immediata*. Augustine regarded sin as *reatus*, and the principal seat of sin he places in the sensual nature of man. The teaching of the Roman Catholic Church was developed during the Scholastic period. According to this doctrine original sin is something negative, a loss of the original righteousness, which, however, was only a *bonum superadditum*, through the loss of which man merely fell back into the state of *puris naturalibus*. The golden rein was lost and to that extent man was weakened. Original sin was regarded indeed as lust, which had its seat in the flesh, but it was not real sin. Baptism does away with the *reatus* of the Fall and therefore also with the evil of hereditary sin. Luther and the Church that bears his name teach clearly that all men are born in sin, without religion, without trust in God, and with evil desires. Original sin is real sin and condemns all that are not regenerated through Baptism and the Holy Ghost. On the other hand, Zwingli leaned toward the Roman view, while the teaching of Calvin stood in alignment with his doctrine of predestination. The Formula of Concord emphasized the doctrine that had been expressed in the Augsburg Confession. During the modern critical period the theories of privation and sensualism have been advocated besides that of Rationalism. The idealistic philosophy naturally rejects the Church's doctrine of original sin. In accordance with the tenets of this philosophy sin was necessary and beneficial. Schleiermacher and Julius Müller speak of an original sinfulness. But the orthodox Lutheran Theologians have firmly set forth the teachings of the Church. In recent times Ritschlianism has sought to undermine the orthodox doctrine of sin, but many voices have been raised against this destructive theology.

Justin Martyr considered that the Fall consisted in disobedience and superstitious credulity, but he does not clearly present the doctrine of original sin. Every man deserves death that chooses to do evil and walk in the footsteps of Adam. Tatian said that before the Fall man possessed a material soul and a spirit, but that the spirit was lost in the Fall and in consequence man became mortal. Irenaeus taught that the human race had sinned in Adam and become guilty before God, while it fell into the power of Satan. Clement of Alexandria taught that sin is the free act of man and not an evil inherited from Adam. Tertillian said that the essence of sin was selfishness. The soul is transplanted with the body and sin through heredity. He was the first to set forth clearly the doctrine of original sin and used the expression *vitium originis*. In children sin is found as to its material content, but not in a formal sense, that is, there is no guilt. On the other hand, Cyprian said that children have inherited guilt from Adam. Origen did not believe in original sin, but said that all men were born in sin, basing his assertion on the supposition that a fall into sin had taken place in the ante-temporal state, for which reason every man brought sin with him into the world.

Lactantius taught that sin had arisen through the infirmities of the body, but that we had inherited death from Adam. Athanasius ascribes sin to *inertia* or slothfulness. He did not consider the sin of Adam as really being the cause of human corruption. Small children are guiltless. There were sinless men before Christ. Cf. Oratio III, 26, 33. Basil taught that freedom was the root of sin. It was dependent on man himself as to whether he would sin or not. Cyril of Jerusalem ascribed sin to the free will of man and said that Satan leads such men astray as would be led astray. Gregory of Nazianzus and Gregory of Nyssa conceived of sin negatively. Small children are guiltless. Ambrose taught that we all sinned in Adam and that we are born in sin. Pelagius maintained that man was indifferent. Adam brought injury only upon himself through the Fall and only through his example has he brought injury upon his descendants. There is no original sin. Lust is not sin, but can give rise to it. Augustine taught that in Adam all men sinned. He conceived of sin as implying a negation or *privatio boni* in contradistinction to the Manichaeans who set forth the substantiality of sin in man. He presented the negative and positive elements in sin, but *concupiscentia* was not sin *per se*. According to his view original sin was *reatus* or the imputation of the sin of Adam, for which reason he did not consider it so much our sin as rather a punishment for sin. The real seat of sin is to be found in the sensuous nature of man. Gregory the Great set forth spiritual death as the punishment for sin, because Adam did not die the same day that he fell into sin. John of Damascus viewed sin more from the negative than the positive standpoint.

John Scotus Erigena rejected the doctrine of original sin and accepted the teaching of ante-temporal sin. As a Pantheist he considered sin as *μή ὸν* and necessary for development. Anselm considered that the essence of sin was selfishness. He expressed the relationship between Adam and his posterity in the following language: *in Adamo fecit persona peccatricem naturam, in posteris facit natura personas peccatrices.* Hugo of St. Victor taught that sin had arisen through a disparity between *appetitus justi* and *commodi,* both of which are concreated in man. Man passed beyond or exceeded moderation in the Fall, and as a consequence he also lost moderation in seeking the lower good. He lost *appetitus justi* and *justitia.* Original sin was principally *privatio boni.* Abelard detracted from the significance of the Fall, making sin dependent on intention. Strictly speaking, therefore, small children have no sin. He laid stress on the punishment of sin. Peter Lombard said that sin, *fomes peccati,* was mediated through lust at the time of conception. The souls were then created immediately by God, but contaminated by contact with the body. He taught, however, that all men sinned in Adam, but viewed sin principally from the negative standpoint or the loss of the primitive goodness. Thomas Aquinas declared that the b*onum superadditum* was lost in the Fall, by which there resulted a disorder in the powers of the soul, a *vulneratio naturae Materialiter,* sin consisted in *concupiscentia,* which in itself was not sinful. He viewed the human race as a living body and held that original sin brings guilt to all. The souls of men are created by God as included in the Fall of Adam. Duns Scotus did not consider that any great damage had been wrought through the Fall, because it was only the *bonum superadditum* that had been lost, which had been given after creation. Still, *concupiscentia,* which in itself was no sin, thereby lost its rein. He advocated the doctrine of the immaculate conception of the Virgin Mary Durandus of St. Pourcain said that guilt was inherited from Adam, but not sinful corruption. Bellarmine taught that there is no other difference between man before and after the Fall than that man has lost the supernatural gift of grace and now is in a state of *puris naturalibus.* The guilt of Adam, however, is imputed to all men.

Luther experienced a deep sense of sin and laid stress on both the positive and negative elements in sin. He compares original sin to the leaven of Satan which has poisoned the whole of our nature. On the other hand, Zwingli had a superficial sense of sin, considering it simply as a sickness. The hereditary damage is neither sin nor guilt. He does not acknowledge the imputation expressed in the term *imputatio mediata*. Flacius taught that original sin constitutes the nature and essence of man. Striegel, on the other hand, in his argument against the term "substance," lays stress in an ambiguous way on the accidental element in sin. Flacius declared against him that if sin be accidental, original sin would simply be an external thing. At least, Striegel used a very peculiar expression, although neither he nor Flacius understood the effects of their terminology and explanations. Striegel made use of the figure of the juice of garlic, which, when spread on a magnet, nullifies the magnetism. According to this figure sin would become an external and accidental thing merely, a *privatio* or imperfection. *The Formula of Concord* uses still stronger expressions than the preceding Lutheran symbols. Original sin is set forth as *peccatum* and worthy of condemnation, even though no actual sin had followed. Emphasis is laid on the fact that the sinful state is man's very own. It is, however, connected with the sin of Adam, because he is *principium naturale et morale. Imputatio mediata* is set forth. The *formale* of original sin is guilt. The *materiale* of sin in the negative sense is the loss of man's original righteousness, so that in a material sense he lacks the image of God; in a positive sense the *materiale* of sin is set forth as *concupiscentia* with its seat especially in the spiritual nature of man. In the antithetical portion Pelagianism and related theories are condemned. *The Formula* further condemns the theory that original sin is merely a spot or stain in human nature and not a corruption. The contention of Striegel is rejected, in which he declared that through original sin nature was deprived of the use of its powers as the magnet is demagnetized by the application of garlic juice. The teachings of Flacius were also rejected. The *Socinians* reject the doctrine of original sin and its imputation. The sin of Adam was the cause of physical death. Man was, indeed, mortal by nature, but God had granted unto him immortality. Men are indeed weak, but this is to be ascribed to the influence, the evil habits and examples of their ancestors. The *Arminians* also reject original sin and call it merely a weakness. *Justitia originalis* was lost, so that the grace of God is necessary for salvation. They also teach that physical death came as a result of the sin of Adam. The lusts of men are not sinful, provided they are natural and have not arisen through some evil habit.

Leibnitz says that sin is a lesser degree of good, as the cold is a lesser degree of heat. The Rationalists, such as Wegscheider, reject the doctrine of original sin, stating that it does not accord with the attributes of God that He should permit the whole of human nature to be corrupted through the sin of one man. He says, furthermore, that the doctrine is inexplicable. Kant stated that the Fall consisted in man's liberation from the domination of instinct and transition to that of the intellect. Adam was man in general. The root of sin was to be found in the evil tendency which he called the radical evil. This arose in the ante-temporal period. He is the author of the rationalistic theory of sensualism. Man arranged the determining factors of the practical reason in accordance with the sensuous appetites. Hegel considered the paradisaical state the same as the animal state, but through the Fall man became true man. Evil is necessary for progress. The Hegelian theologians considered that sin was necessary. The Supranaturalists teach that man participates in the guilt and punishment of Adam, but no one is condemned because of original sin. Man is condemned, if, in self-determination, he sins as Adam sinned. Schleiermacher acknowledges the universality of sin, but denies its heredity from Adam. Human nature was sinful from the beginning. Sin is an element in progress. In relation to God sin possesses no objective reality; it exists in our subjective consciousness. With his Pantheism he combines the theories of privation and the sensual. Julius Müller believes that every man has had an ante-temporal existence, when his will was turned against the will of God. Martensen considered original sin as an evil fate. Only on becoming personal does racial sin imply guilt. Ritschl denies that original sin is evil desire (concupiscence). He considers original sin simply as the fateful influence which evil continually exerts upon man.

§14. Actual Sin.

Original sin, *peccatum originale* or *prava concupiscentia,* is the ground and source of *peccata actualia* or actual sins. As man progresses morally there are to be found in his development two conditions, one called *habitus,* or the settled state, the other, actus, or the free-will action. *Habitus* is dependent on natural character and repeated acts of the will, while *actus* implies a distinct act of the will in each separate action. Both of these elements must be emphasized, because if the former alone is emphasized, the result will be determinism, while if the latter is emphasized to the exclusion of the former, the result will be a rationalistic interpretation of the origin of sin.

Man is therefore in a state of corruption to which he conforms more and more through sinful actions which are fostered in this state. *Status corruptionis* is characterized by various states, dependent on the moral development of man. These states are the following: 1) *status securitatis,* or the state of sinful security; 2) *status servitutis,* or the state of bondage; 3) *status hypocriseos et phariseismi,* or the state of hypocrisy or Pharisaism; 4) *status indurationis,* or the obdurate state.

1. The Characterization of Actual Sin.

The essence of sin is selfishness or self-will. It must be borne in mind, however, that although sin is a matter of the will and therefore *voluntarium subjective,* still it cannot be said that sin is *voluntarium effective,* inasmuch as sin does not originate in the free assent of the will, as the Roman Catholics, the Socinians and others teach. We must always bear in mind the sinful nature of original sin or the state of man.

The most general definition of sin is the following: *Sin is every departure, in thought, word and deed, from the Law of God.* But what distinction is there between actual and habitual sins? Some say that actual sin is an act of the will and stands under the domination of the will, while habitual sin dominates the will. Against this it may be urged that Christians may commit actual sins that are *involuntaria*. Actual sin is momentary, while habitual sin is dependent on the permanent bent of the will.

The cause of sin is naturally the person who sins, tempted by his own flesh, the world and the devil. God is in no sense the cause of actual sin, just as He was not the cause of original sin. Some have declared that He is the cause of the sin of obduracy. This view is based on the following passage: "Whom he will he hardeneth" (Rom. 9:18). This passage implies only an act of divine judgment upon an already existent state of sin. God punishes sin with sin. Hollazius defines the sin of obduracy as follows: "God does not harden men causally or actively, by producing hardness of heart, but judicially (*judicialiter*), permissively (*permissive*), and by forsaking them (*desertive*). For the act of hardening is a judicial act by which, on account of antecedent, voluntary, and inevitable wickedness, God justly permits a man, habitually wicked, to rush into greater crimes, and withdraws His grace from him, and finally delivers him up to the power of Satan, by whom he is afterwards driven into greater sins, until He finally cuts him off from the right of the heavenly inheritance."

Concerning *subjectum quo* it may be observed: 1) that *primaria sedes* is the spirit of man with his attributes, faculties or endowments, intellect, will, and emotion; 2) *secundaria sedes* is the body or the physical nature of man.

In the Word of God sin is regarded from different points of view. When sin is looked upon as a failing to hit the mark, or to reach the right goal, the word *ἁμαρτία* is used. Concupiscence, or the positive side of sin, is called *ἐπιθυμία*. The difference between *ἁμαρτήμα* and *ἁμαρτία* is that the latter term sets forth sin in both the abstract and concrete sense, while the former has reference to the specific deed as disobedience toward the Law of God. Compare Mark 3:28; Rom. 3:25; 1 Cor. 6:18. Considered as ungodliness sin is called *ἀσέβεια*. The expression παρακοή means unwillingness to hear, with disobedience as a result. Lawlessness and transgression of the Law are expressed by *ἀνομία* and *παράβασις*. When sin is considered as a fault, an insufficient ability to judge, a deviation from truth or higher moral standpoint, then *παράπτομα* is used. As implying ignorance sin is called *ἀγνόημα*. When forgetfulness of duty or imperfection is implied, ἥττημα is used. Cf. 1 Cor. 6:7. *Πλημμέλεια* is often used in the Old Testament to express discord. The word *σάρξ* is used with a variety of meanings, but most generally with a strongly ethical significance.

2. Classification Of Actual Sins.

Actual sin has been classified in the following way: 1) *ratione causae* or *culpae*, or in respect of the defective cause: a) *voluntaria* or intentional; b) *involuntaria* or unintentional, to which are counted *peccata ignorantiae, praecipitantiae et infirmitatis*, or sins committed through ignorance, rashness and infirmity. "And that servant, who knew his Lord's will, and made not ready, nor did according to his will, shall be beaten with many stripes; but he that knew not, and did things worthy of stripes, shall be beaten with few stripes" (Luke 12:47,48); the denial of Peter (Matt. 26:70); "And there arose a sharp contention, so that they parted asunder" (Acts 15:39); "The good which I would I do not" (Rom. 7:19); "But when they came, he drew back and separated himself, fearing them that were of the circumcision" (Gal. 2:12); 2) *ratione subjecti totalis*, or in respect of the person sinning in general: a) *mortalia et venalia*, or mortal and remissible sins; the former imply spiritual death, the latter may be found in Christians, i. e., unintentional sins that are repented of and forgiven. Concerning *venalia* compare 1 John 2:1,2; b) *nostra et aliena*, our own and others. We may become partakers in the sins of others by internal or external assent. "Be not ye therefore partakers with them" (Eph. 5:7; 5:11); compare the admonition in 1 Tim. 5:22; "He that giveth him greeting partaketh in his evil works" (2 John 11) ; 3) *ratione subjecti partialis* or in respect of the individual mode of sinning: a) *peccata cordis seu interna* or the sins of the heart; b) *peccata oris et operis seu externa* or the sins of the mouth and deeds. "For from within, out of the heart of men, evil thoughts proceed," etc. (Mark 7:21, 22); "The tongue is a fire: the world of iniquity among our members is the tongue" (James 3:6) ; 4) *ratione actus* or in respect of the deed itself against the Law of God: a) *peccata commissionis* or sins of commission; b) *peccata omissionis* or the sins of omission. "To him therefore that knoweth to do good, and doeth it not, to him it is sin" (James 4:17); 5) *ratione objecti* or in respect of the object: a) *peccata in Deum,* sins against God; b) *peccata in proximum,* or sins against our neighbor; c) *in ipsum peccantem,* or sins against ourselves; 6) *ratione effectus* or in respect of the effect: a) *clamantia,* or sins which cry out for punishment; b) *non clamantia,* or sins which do not so cry out. With reference to the former compare the sin of Cain, the sins of the Sodomites, the oppression of the Israelites in Egypt and the hire of the laborers. With regard to the last named we quote the following: "Behold, the hire of the laborers who mowed your fields, which is of you kept by fraud, crieth out: and the cries of them that reaped have entered into the ears of the Lord of Sabaoth" (James 5:4) ; 7) *ratione adjunctorum* or in respect of their adjuncts: a) *graviora et leviora,* sins more or less grievous (as to degree), because a Christian in certain cases sins more grievously than a heathen. He that commits adultery with another man's wife sins more grievously than the man who steals when he is hungry. A person who kills his mother sins more than the man who kills an enemy, etc. "Therefore he that delivered me unto thee hath greater sin" (John 19:11); b) *occulta et manifesta,* secret and manifest. A secret sin is one that may be little known to the sinner himself or that may be known only by him and others who endeavor to keep it secret. A manifest sin may grow into a great scandal which may not only cause public offense, but also become a snare to others. "For the things which are done by them in secret it is a shame even to speak of" (Eph. 5:12); "I know how manifold are your transgressions, and how mighty are your sins—ye that afflict the just, that take a bribe, and that turn aside the needy in the gate from their right" (Amos 5:12); c) *mortua et viventia,* dead and living sins. Dead sins are such as are not known as sins, or which are not considered as great as they really are, or else such as have been partially or wholly overcome. They are therefore no longer dominant. "But sin, finding occasion, wrought in me through the commandment all manner of coveting: for apart from the law sin is dead" (Rom. 7:8); "Wherein ye also once walked, when ye lived in these things" (Col. 3:5-7); d) *manentia*, which still oppress by their guilt, and *remissa* or forgiven; e) *conjuncta cum induratione et ab ea sejuncta*, i.e., some sins that are connected with hardness of heart and others not. Compare 2 Cor. 4:4; Acts 5:3; 1 Sam. 6:6; "Hardened by the deceitfulness of sin" (Heb. 3:13); f) *remissibilia et irremissibilia* or remissible and irremissible sins. To the latter belongs the sin against the Holy Ghost. Hollazius defines this sin as follows: "*Sin against the Holy Ghost consists in a malicious denial of, a hostile attack upon, and a horrid blasphemy of divine truth, clearly known and approved by conscience, together with an obstinate and finally persevering rejection of all the means of salvation.*"[32] All of these characteristics ought to be emphasized and combined. This sin can be committed by persons who in a Christian sense have not been converted, as well as by Christians who have fallen from grace. In the former sense this sin was committed by the Pharisees. Compare Luke 11:15 and Mark 3: 28-30. The last-named passage reads as follows: "All their sins shall be forgiven unto the sons of men, and their blasphemies wherewith soever they shall blaspheme: but whosoever shall blaspheme against the Holy Spirit hath never forgiveness, but is guilty of an eternal sin: because they said, He hath an unclean spirit." With regard to sin against the Holy Ghost in the latter sense we quote Heb. 6: 4-6: "For as touching those who were once enlightened and tasted of the heavenly gift, and were made partakers of the Holy Spirit, and tasted the good word of God, and the powers of the age to come, and then fell away, it is impossible to renew them again unto repentance; seeing they crucify to themselves the Son of God afresh, and put him to an open shame." Cf. 1 John 5:16: "There is a sin unto death: not concerning this do I say that ye should make request." Sin against the Holy Ghost is a decided and absolute evil, an absolute hardness of heart which

---

[32] Hollazius: *"Peccatum in Spiritum Sanctum est veritatis divinae evidenter agnitas et in conscientia approbate malitiosa abnegatio, hostilis impugnatio horrenda blasphematio et omnium mediorum salutis obstinata et finaliter perseverans rejectio." Dogmatics*, 7.

already in this life has identified itself with satanic egoism and blasphemy. Therefore those that have committed this sin cannot be forgiven, because they will not repent. There is a relative hardness of heart from which men may be saved, but when a person has become definitely and absolutely hardened in heart, there is no longer any hope. It is an abysmal defection which merits the judgment of hell. Such persons are ripe for hell before they die, i.e., the time of their visitation is at an end before the period of grace is finished. The sin against the Holy Ghost in this sense is to be distinguished from sins against the Holy Ghost in ordinary cases where sinners withstand the Holy Spirit and where even Christians grieve the Holy Spirit of God. The irremissible sin must also be distinguished from a special form of sin against Christ. Men may blaspheme Christ and by means of true repentance receive the forgiveness of their sin. Such blasphemy is relatively superficial and is brought about by ignorance, infirmity and the fear of man. Compare Luke 12:10 together with the context. "And every one who shall speak a word against the Son of man, it shall be forgiven him: but unto him that blasphemeth against the Holy Spirit it shall not be forgiven." In Matt. 12:31 we read: "Every sin and blasphemy shall be forgiven unto men; but the blasphemy against the Spirit shall not be forgiven." Cf. the following verse.

3. The Effects Of Actual Sin.

The consequences of actual sin are: a) the confirmation of the will in sin; b) accumulated guilt; c) temporal punishment, for sin often punishes itself; God punishes here and now; d) eternal punishment in hell. God shall measure the punishment in the judgment when He shall judge every man according to his deeds.

§15. The Freedom of the Will and Moral Bondage.

As a person man possesses a will or the power of self-determination and cannot be influenced irresistibly from within or without by instinct. Human freedom consists of two elements: 1) the formal or self-determination; 2) the material or determination by which the will of God becomes the determining ground for the will of man. By reason of the Fall the will of God ceased to determine the will of man. Man's power of self-determination became dominated by selfishness. The form of freedom was filled with a false content. After the Fall man indeed possesses a will, but he has lost the free will as determined by God. He has therefore lost the freedom of the will in relation to that which is good and determines upon that which is evil, if not influenced from above. The Augsburg Confession declares that the natural man lacks all freedom and power in spiritual things, that he possesses freedom, although curtailed through sin, in the realm of the intellect, and that in some measure he is able to abstain from the commission of gross sins.

1. Definition of the Subject.

The principal question is, What is the relation of the will to spiritual things after the Fall? The Formula of Concord states the subject as follows: What unregenerated man, by his own powers of intellect and will, can accomplish toward his conversion and regeneration. The answer is summed up in the terms: *defectus liberi arbitrii in rebus spiritualibus*, or the loss of free will in spiritual things. Additional points are comprised under two heads: 1) *liberum arbitrium in malis*, or free will in evil things; 2) *liberum arbitrium in rebus externis*, or free will in external things.

2. The Loss of the Free Will In Spiritual Things.

This *defectus* or loss consists of two elements: 1) the negative, or the absolute want of all power; 2) the positive, or that the intellect and the will are hostile toward God, which is expressed in the formula *liberum arbitrium in malis*. By nature, therefore, man withstands the grace of God.

The Formula of Concord says that even in the regenerate the natural man in himself is constituted in the same way as these points express. Strong expressions are used with regard to the unregenerate. In his natural state man is represented as a stock and a stone. This expression does not mean that man has become a stock and a stone, nor that in all things he resembles a stock and a stone. Man has not lost his own personal nature. But as the stock and the stone are unyielding and withstand external influences, so the natural man possesses no power in himself in spiritual things save to obstruct and withstand the power of God. The question concerns the power that man possesses in himself and then he is like a stock and a stone. But he is not unimpressionable like a stock and a stone.

3. The Two Hemispheres.

Some Dogmaticians, in denning the natural power and want of power in man, make use of the following terms: *hemisphaerium inferius* and *hemisphaerium superius*.

Hollazius refers the following to *hemisphaerium inferius*: "All things and actions, physical, ethical,apolitical, domestic, artificial, pedagogic, and divine, as far as they can be known by the light of the intellect and can be produced by the powers of nature, aided by the general concurrence of God."[33] To this belongs liberum arbitrium in externis. To this hemisphere belong the reading and hearing of the Word of God, civic righteousness, etc. Still the natural ability that belongs to this lower hemisphere of the powers of the will is weak and infirm. There are internal and external impediments. Among the internal impediments may be mentioned blindness of the intellect, obstinacy of the will, vehemence of the affections and perverseness of the natural appetites of man. Among the external impediments may be counted the influence of Satan, the fascinating blandishments of the world, the fear of men, unforeseen happenings and misfortunes. In *hemisphaerium superius* man is totally helpless and possesses no power in purely spiritual conditions. In this

[33] Holl. *Exam. Theol. Acroam.* Pars II, Cap. V, 623.

sphere is also counted the reading and hearing of the Word of God in such manner as to be of profit and blessing. Man has indeed the natural ability to read and hear, but by his own power he cannot be influenced thereby to salvation.

4. Human Freedom and the Grace of God.

The human will can be liberated through grace, but not by force and coercion. All determinism must be excluded in order that the responsibility of man may be maintained. Man is incapable of his own power to do anything toward his own spiritual welfare (indeed, in his natural state he counteracts that welfare); still he must be brought into a state or condition where his sense of responsibility can be aroused. He cannot bring himself into such a state, but the Lord has arranged a way of escape and made it possible for man to be influenced from above. The Holy Spirit approaches man especially through the means of grace and through these alone exerts His saving influence and activity. Through the means of grace man becomes the object of the work of grace. It is not the work of man, but from beginning to end all is by grace. In this incipient activity the grace of God is called prevenient grace or *gratia praeveniens*. By this means man is put in a position where he can determine for himself whether he will cease or continue to withstand the activity of the Holy Spirit. Left to himself, man would continue in a state of sin and hostility. It is possible for prevenient grace to operate in the heart of man, inasmuch as the image of God in a formal sense still remains, thereby providing a ground of religious life. Although man is permeated by sin and totally incapacitated in spiritual things, still the essence of man is not sinful. The image of God in the formal sense as found in man does not denote that man possesses ability in spiritual things, it simply provides a point of contact. In its activity prevenient grace comes in touch with this point of contact, the ground of the religious life in man. To illustrate by a figure what takes place, let us say that it is like a man listening to a familiar note from the homeland, the Paradise that is lost. In his original state in Paradise man was put to the test, but failed in that test. Through prevenient grace man is again put to the test, and the question is whether or not he will return to Paradise. In coming in contact with the means of grace man cannot escape the activity of prevenient grace. For this reason *gratia praeveniens* has been called *inevitabilis* or inevitable, and *irresistibilis* or irresistible, in the sense that man cannot escape the distinctive influence of this activity. At this juncture the self-determination of man comes into play, otherwise man would not be responsible. The Holy Spirit exerts His activity, but He cannot force a man. Luther and the Formula of Concord state that man possesses (*δύναμις παθητική*) or *capacitas, non activa, sed passiva,* by which is meant that man can become, although he cannot make himself, a partaker of the grace of God. There is no activity through the freedom of the will toward that which is good, but by grace man may become passive. If he remain in quietness, then the redeeming power of grace will continue, and he will become active through the powers bestowed by the Holy Spirit in conversion. But if he withstands the work of the Spirit, then the result will not only be *resistentia naturalis,* but *resistentia malitiosa* or *nolle positivum.* In this way a higher state of corruption is reached.

Some have thought that the Lutheran Church is not consistent in this doctrine, teaching as she does that man is incapable of doing anything toward his salvation and still is responsible, but when we understand the question as dealt with in the Augsburg Confession, and which the Formula of Concord emphasizes, then it is evident that there is no inconsistency. This subject has already been discussed; we would merely add that man has power to use the Word of God, even if by his own power he cannot read and hear in such manner as to receive a blessing. In this way man first becomes responsible, inasmuch as God works through the means of grace. But as soon as a man reads and hears the Word of God, then the Holy Spirit is present with prevenient grace. In this connection attention ought to be called to the fact that there is a great difference between the unbaptized heathen and a baptized Christian, even though the latter has fallen from the grace of Baptism. He that has been baptized has at one time possessed an *arbitrium liberatum* or liberated will and is therefore continuously an object of special grace. The strong expressions in the Formula of Concord concern the natural man and tell what the unregenerated man is able to accomplish by his own power, and the answer is that he can do nothing of his own power, indeed, he only resists the work of the Holy Spirit. He that has been regenerated once in Baptism is therefore more responsible than the heathen, who has never, as has the Christian, possessed a liberated will.

Therefore of his own natural power man can do nothing, but grace does all. Although there is no real co-operation before conversion, it is nevertheless taught that man cooperates after conversion. This co-operation is, however, not a natural product, but is the activity of the regenerated man through the powers and endowments which the Holy Spirit began to bestow in conversion.

The following passages of Scripture may be quoted as being of importance in the solution of this question: "For ye were once darkness" (Eph. 5:8); "The natural man receiveth not the things of the Spirit of God: for they are foolishness unto him; and he cannot know them, because they are spiritually judged" (1 Cor. 2:14); "Not that we are sufficient of ourselves, to account anything as from ourselves" (2 Cor. 3:5); "The mind of the flesh is enmity against God" (Rom. 8:7); "Every one that committeth sin is the bondservant of sin" (John 8:34); "When Gentiles that have not the law do by nature the things of the law" (Rom. 2:14) ; "As touching the righteousness which is in the law, found blameless" (Phil. 3:6); "But without thy mind I would do nothing; that thy goodness should not be of necessity, but of free will" (Philemon 14); "But hath power as touching his own will" (1 Cor. 7:37); "Now when they heard this, they were pricked in their heart... .and Peter said unto them, Repent ye" (Acts 2:37, 38); "Repent ye therefore, and turn again" (Acts 3:19); "So belief cometh of hearing, and hearing by the word of Christ" (Rom. 10:17); "I said therefore unto you, that ye shall die in your sins: for except ye believe that I am he, ye shall die in your sins" (John 8:24); "If therefore the Son shall make you free, ye shall be free indeed" (John 8:36); "For by grace have ye been saved through faith; and that not of yourselves, it is the gift of God" (Eph. 2:8); "For the law of the Spirit of life in Christ made me free from the law of sin and death" (Rom. 8:2); "For as many of you as were baptized into Christ did put on Christ" (Gal. 3:27); "Look therefore carefully how ye walk, not as unwise, but as wise" (Eph. 5:15); "Give the more diligence to make your calling and election sure" (2 Peter 1:10); "I can do all things in him that strengthened me" (Phil. 4:13); "If by the Spirit ye put to death the deeds of the body" (Rom. 8:13).

5. Notes on the History of Dogma.

The Greek Fathers laid stress in general on human freedom and self-determination. Still they speak of the assistance of grace and the work of enlightenment. The Occidental or Latin Fathers, indeed, lay greater stress on grace, but they also set forth the ability of man. The real controversy on the relationship between grace and freedom began with Pelagianism and has continued ever since in one form or another. Pelagius teaches that man is practically sound and can do whatever he wills to do, for which reason grace is superfluous or else possesses little significance. Augustine said that man is bound and in a spiritual sense dead. He rejected the formal element in freedom and ended in Determinism, just as Pelagius, who went to the opposite extreme, ended in Indifferentism. Semi-Pelagianism set forth the spiritual sickness and weakness of man, who nevertheless possessed the power to begin his conversion. During the Middle Ages a synergistic tendency began to appear. The Thomists represented this tendency, although neither Semi-Pelagianism nor Synergism are found fully developed in Thomas Aquinas. The Scotists represented Semi-Pelagianism and Indifferentism. For this reason the Roman Catholic conception became synergistic in theory and Semi-Pelagian in practice. The Protestant Churches taught that man does not possess *liberum arbitrium in spiritualibus* and Calvin was led into the doctrine of unconditional predestination. The Lutheran Church was fortunate in avoiding extremes in setting forth the grace of God and still maintaining, and emphasizing the responsibility of man. However, during the period of the Reformation a controversy broke out concerning the freedom of the will. The Synergists declared that the will constituted a third factor in conversion, that man was indeed unable to begin his conversion, but that he had the power in himself to co-operate with the grace of God. The Socinians and Arminians adopted Pelagian and Semi-Pelagian views. The Kantian School, the Rationalists, the mediating theologians in general together with the Ritschlians advocate more or less strongly developed Pelagian and synergistic views.

Justin Martyr presented the power of self-determination on the part of man in the choice between good and evil. Clement of Alexandria says that power for good is found in every man. Irenaeus stresses human freedom, but says that man is like a withered tree that cannot bear fruit unless watered from above. Tertullian set forth the necessity of grace, not only as an aid in spiritual things, but also as a creative principle. Man, however, can will to accept grace and thus begin repentance. Origen says that man can decide for the good, although the co-operation of God is necessary. Cyprian declared that our strength was lost, but that faith is ours and upon its quantum depends how much we receive. Cyril of Jerusalem teaches that God grants His grace to those that are worthy and that faith is our own possession. Gregory of Nazianzus says that penitence depends both on us and God. Gregory of Nyssa says the human will and the grace of God must co-operate. Chrysostom teaches that we must first begin, then God comes to our assistance. Ambrose says that the grace of God is needed to begin repentance, and he speaks of a *gratia praeparans interna*. However, he makes a distinction between *praecepta* and *concilia*, stating that the latter have special merit. Pelagius ascribes to man power to choose. There is a natural capability (*posse*) which is the gift of God, but to will and to do (*velle et facere*) belong to human freedom. There is special grace for the Christians, which confers the forgiveness of sins for actual sins and renders assistance in that which is good or enlightenment through the teaching and example of Christ. The conferring of this grace makes easy what man of himself is otherwise able to accomplish. Augustine says that the human will is incapable, that it tends toward sin. There is no real good outside of grace. The grace of God is a creative principle and is bestowed without merit. He speaks of *gratia irresistibilis, praeveniens, operans et cooperans* and of *donum perseverantiae.* The Semi-Pelagians taught that nature had simply become infirm through sin. By his own power man is capable of co-operating in his own conversion when supported by grace. Man begins and then the grace of God enters in to assist. Pelagianism was rejected in 418 and 431, while Semi-Pelagianism was rejected in 529. John of Damascus declared that the moral power of man was only weakened through the Fall. Man is now just as free as Adam. Reason and freedom have not been lost.

John Scotus Erigena taught that man possesses freedom, but that it does not become active except through grace. Man is capable of seeing even in darkness, but the objects of vision do not become visible before the light appears. Anselm rejected the view of Augustine that man is free to choose only the evil and considered that the power of the will to choose and do the right was indispensable. We must distinguish between the faculty and its use. Adam failed in its use, but the faculty remains. Hugo of St. Victor has the following to say concerning human freedom: 1) In the state of integrity man possessed the power to sin or not to sin (*posse peccare et posse non peccare*); 2) after the Fall, before the restoration, freedom is infirm, so that man possesses the power to sin and is incapable of not sinning (*posse peccare et non posse non peccare*); 3) after the restoration, but prior to confirmation in that which is good, there is power to do the good and infirmity in relation to evil, so that man is capable of sinning, but has the ability also of not sinning (*posse peccare et posse non peccare*; 4) in the more perfect state there is the possibility of not sinning and the impossibility of sinning, the latter dependent on the confirming grace of God (*posse non peccare et non posse peccare*). Peter Lombard like Augustine speaks of *gratia operans et cooperans*. However, while Augustine says that the natural will is dead in relation to the good, Lombard considers that it is merely weak and infirm. He also makes use of the following classification of grace: *gratia gratis dans,* who is God Himself, *gratia gratis data,* which is the same as *gratia praeveniens et operans,* and *gratia gratum faciens,* which is the same as *gratia cooperans,* which is meritorious. Alexander of Hales advocated the Semi-Pelagian view and says that after the Fall there is to be found a receptivity for grace. Thomas of Aquinas said that God works that which is good in us without our assistance, but not without our consent. Man is capable of inclining himself to receive the grace of God and thus win for himself *meritum de congruo*. This merit of fitness has, however, not come about except through the presence of the grace of God. Through *meritum congrui gratia habltualls* is received, by means of which man gains for himself the merit of worthiness or *meritum ex condigno*. Even in the converted soul he distinguishes between *meritum congrui* and *meritum condigni*. In his doctrine of *meritum congrui* there is a Semi-Pelagian tendency and in the doctrine of *meritum condigni* a synergistic tendency, but in general Thomas Aquinas represents the synergistic view. Duns Scotus, who advocated Pelagianism, says that after the Fall man still possesses the use of his free will, which is arbitrary, and that he can incline himself to receive the grace of God. Gabriel Biel taught that even after the Fall man is capable of producing *bonum morale* and of his own power to love God above all things, but *bonum morale* becomes *bonum meritorium* through *gratia gratum faciens*, which man lost on account of original sin. The Council of Trent taught that *liberum arbitrium* was not extinct through the Fall, but only made infirm. The grace of God begins conversion, but man is afterwards capable of cooperating. In theory the Council supported the synergistic view. Bellarmin sets forth human freedom and the grace of God as coordinated and makes use of the following illustration: It is the same as when two persons are engaged in the act of carrying a huge stone which neither of the two was able to carry; neither increases the power of the other nor does he urge him on; each is perfectly at liberty to leave the burden, but if one of the two no longer desires to cooperate, then nothing will come of their labors.

In the beginning Luther indeed advocated Determinism, but the reason for this is easily understood, and he afterwards abandoned this position. His explanation of the Third Article shows clearly what he thought about the ability of man. Melanchthon departed from the position of Luther, which he first advocated. He taught that to a certain extent man possesses a free will in spiritual things. In his revision of the Loci which he published in 1535 he set forth that there are three factors that co-operate in conversion, viz., the Word, the Holy Spirit, and the human will. In the edition of 1548 he ascribes to the will of man *facultas applicandi se ad gratiam*. Man was at least capable of saying "yes" to the grace of God. His doctrine gave rise to the synergistic controversy. In 1555 Pfeffinger published a work on the free will in which he set forth the co-operation of the free will or Synergism. Striegel taught that the Holy Spirit must begin the work of conversion, showing in this respect the inability of man, but he nevertheless possesses *modus agendi et aptitudo moralis*. This contained a positive power toward the good. The human will is not dead, but infirm. Aroused by the Spirit, the will becomes synergistic. The power to do good is therefore not the work of the Spirit, but a natural capacity. The ability of man was therefore a factor in conversion. *The Formula of Concord* naturally rejected Synergism as well as Pelagianism and Semi-Pelagianism and recognized only two factors in conversion, viz., the Word and the Holy Spirit. Selnecker spoke of the natural man as possessing *carnalis conatus* in relation to the Word of God. Aegidius Hunnius ascribed to man a general longing for salvation. The Socinians taught that in his natural state man possesses freedom both with regard to good and evil. The Armenians said that man possesses power to incline himself to obey the will of God. Hornejus declared that between *actiones spirituales*, which can be wrought only by special grace, and *opera civilia*, which can be done by natural man, there ought to be placed *opera moralia*. The latter can be produced by general divine grace. Musaeus ascribes to man certain *actus pedagogici* in regard to knowledge and will which may develop into a high regard for salvation. Buddaeus taught that the grace of God was to be found in a general way even outside of the pale of salvation.

Although Kant set forth the doctrine of radical evil, still he took the position that man could convert himself, basing it on the teaching of the so-called categorical imperative, thou shalt, because thou canst. Schleiermacher, Hase, Nitzsch, J. Müller and others advocated to a greater or less extent synergistic views. Martensen speaks of grace that is inborn, of essential freedom, and that man has ability to open his heart to receive the grace of God. Such theologians as Thomasius and Frank, of course, reject Synergism, but require that emphasis be placed not only on the active relationship during conversion on the ground of the liberating activity of salvation, but also on the possibility of a state of preparation on the basis of the general divine activity through the conscience.

3

Christology

Christology is that part of Dogmatics which treats of the doctrine of Christ's person, under which the following main subjects are discussed: The Necessity of the God-man, the Incarnation, Jesus Christ as True God and True Man, the Personal Union and the Communion of Natures, *Communicatio Idiomatum*, and the States of Christ.

Christology, which stands in the closest union with Soteriology, constitutes the central theme in Dogmatics. Theology cannot be properly understood except in the light of Christology. Moreover, so far as the remaining parts of Dogmatics are concerned, Christology is the sun that illumines them and about which they all revolve in harmony and order.

The Christology of the Lutheran Church is the foundation of her doctrine of Justification, and therefore when we consider the importance of this doctrine as the material principle of our Church, we can readily appreciate why Christology should be accorded the important position it occupies. Faith justifies because it accepts Christ, who is the Saviour. The Saviour must be true God and true man. Luther, for whom our Church was named, was certain of his justification, because in faith he had accepted Christ. The theology of Luther did not depend on scientific investigations and research, but was grounded in his religious experiences. The experience of faith is also the argument for the Christology of the

Lutheran Church.

The Lutheran Christology reaches its culmination in the doctrine of *communicatio idiomatum*. The doctrinal development concerning the communication of the attributes and the communion of the actions or concerning the idiomatic or personal propositions is characteristic of our Church. This doctrinal presentation in turn provides a sure foundation, according to the Word of God, for other important doctrines of our Church. Among these may be mentioned the atonement, justification and the Lord's Supper. In considering especially the Lord's Supper it is true that Luther did not in the final analysis base his conception of it on his doctrine of Christology, but upon the sure words of Christ at the institution of the Holy Supper; still *communicatio idiomatum* throws a clear light on this subject and explains the Lutheran standpoint. From one point of view we may say that the doctrine of Christology is based on the doctrine of the Lord's Supper, while from another we may say that the latter is grounded in the former.

§16. The Necessity and Reality of the God-man

God-man is a word that expresses a heaven-born and eternal thought which was realized in the fulness of time. No man could have attained unto so exalted a thought. There must be a special reason why God became man. He who was eternally self-sufficient could not feel the need of assuming manhood. We remember what the creative will of God implied. When this could not be realized because of sin, then there followed another divine decree. It is always in such connection that the Scriptures speak of the incarnation of the Son of God. The Word of God does not tell us whether or not the Son of God would have become man in case sin had not come into the world. But since the Scriptures always present the incarnation as a necessity for the salvation of man, this fact itself forms a sure basis for the opinion that the Son of God would not have assumed human flesh had not the decree of salvation required it. The possibility of the incarnation cannot be denied, inasmuch as it is a fact that the Son of God has become man. In any other case Jesus Christ would be the riddle and unsolved problem of human history.

1. The Necessity of the God-man.

The necessity for the Son of God to assume our human nature is therefore based on sin and the human need of salvation through a Saviour and Mediator that belonged to both sides, i. e., was both God and man.

There are many theologians who declare that the incarnation lay within the scope of creation itself. Such theologians consider the idea absurd that man should have come into closer relationship with God through sin than would have been the case had he remained in the state of integrity. If so, they argue, sin would have brought about such a great effect, that a foreign element, viz., human nature, would forever have entered into the Trinity. Their real argument for the incarnation independent of sin is that the Son of God is considered as the head and center of humanity. The head must be a part of the organism.

With regard to these views the following answers may be given: It is impossible to prove that the incarnation was a part of the plan of creation. It may be said, indeed, that in a way man as saved through Jesus Christ has come nearer to God by reason of the incarnation which took place on account of sin, and yet God was very near to man and man near to God in the state of innocence, Besides, man was created in the image of God, so that the race of men was the offspring of God. The question of a foreign element entering into the Trinity is not disconcerting, inasmuch as this was foreseen and determined upon in eternity. The Son of God could have been the head of humanity without being a part of the organism. We must be careful not to lay too much stress on the relationship between the body and the head in the figure and thereby lose sight of the main idea, viz., that the Son of God was the eternal prototype of humanity, indeed the ideal man. The doctrine of incarnation independent of sin has no clear support in Scripture. It is based on vague speculation and mere guesswork, having no sure foundation.

2. The Possibility of the God-man.

The necessity of the God-man would seem to presuppose His possibility. To the superficial thinker it appears altogether impossible for the Son of God to assume human nature and become true man. Neither is there any analogy. We might refer to *unio mystica* in the experience of the Christian, but this is no adequate comparison. Although no analogy can be found to illustrate the possibility of the God-man, still no true Christian doubts this possibility, having experienced the reality of it through faith. Of course, there are always nominal Christians who raise objections.

These objections are of the same character as those of the Deists and the Rationalists. They declare that He who is infinite, immeasurable and omnipresent could not possibly unite Himself with that which is finite and limited to time and space. Their misconception arises from the fact that they consider God as infinite and man as finite in an extensive sense. But God is infinite and immeasurable in an intensive sense. True, man is finite, being only a relative personality, but from the religious aspect man realizes that he is created in the image of God and for this reason he is in a certain sense partaker in the infinity of God. The fact that man was created in the image of God and destined for eternal life explains the fact of the incarnation. This miracle could take place because God willed it. A king can assume the position of a servant. Why should not the Son of God be able to become man and still remain supramundane? There was no hindrance. The imperfection of the human intellect and our inability to explain the great miracle prove nothing, for many things are possible which we do not comprehend, while to God nothing is impossible save that which militates against His holy will.

3. Concerning the Incarnation.

Hollazius gives the following definition: "*incarnatio* or *unitio is the divine act through which the Son of God assumed in the unity of His person a human nature in the womb of the Virgin Mary.*" In this connection we quote the following from Björling's Dogmatics: "In the act of the incarnation the divine self-consciousness takes up the human into communion with itself, and the divine self-determination takes up the human into communion with itself. In this manner there arises a person who is conscious of the fact that He is both God and man."[34]

When the Son actively assumed the nature of man, while at the same time the other persons were active in the incarnation, it is important to define more closely in what the other persons participated. When the question concerns the cause of the act of incarnation, then it is an *opus ad extra* and is ascribed to the Trinity. On the other hand when the question concerns the accomplishment of the act, then it is an *opus ad intra* and is ascribed to the Son. The activity of the three persons is divided in the following way:

1) The Father sends the Son. The following passages may be cited: "For God so loved the world, that he gave his only begotten Son" (John 3:16). "That spared not his own Son, but delivered him up for us all" (Rom. 8:32). "When the fullness of time came, God sent forth his Son" (Gal. 4:4).

2) The Son assumed human nature and became man. In Luke 1:35 we read: "The power of the Most High shall overshadow thee." This refers to the Son. Hollazius says: "Overshadowing denotes the mysterious and wonderful filling of the temple of the body, formed by the Holy Ghost, for the Son indeed overshadowed the Virgin Mary and by a peculiar assimilation filled and united to Himself a part of the Virgin's blood, influenced by the Holy Ghost, so that He dwelt in it bodily as in His own temple."[35]

3) The work of the Holy Ghost is presented in a threefold way: a) *δημιοργική* or *formativa*, by which is meant that the Holy Ghost influenced Mary, so that without male seed she could conceive. The Holy Ghost formed in the womb of Mary the substance which became the human nature of Christ; b) *ἁγιαστική* or *sanctificativa*, for the Holy Ghost cleansed from sin and sanctified the substance of which the body of the Son of God was formed; c) *τελειωτική* or *conjunctiva*, which denotes the mysterious

[34] Björlings *Dogmatik*, Part II, sec. in, p. 56.

[35] *Exam. Theol. Acroam.*, Pars III, Qu. 14, p. 87.

union by which the eternal Logos was indissolubly united with the nature formed and sanctified by the Holy Ghost. And yet, although Christ was conceived by the Holy Ghost, still we cannot say that the Holy Ghost is the Father of Christ. It was not an *ἐπέλουσις σπερματική*, so that the Holy Ghost was a spermatic cause. The cleansing of the natural substance from sin is furthermore explained through the activity of the divine nature.[36] The following passages may be quoted concerning the activity of the Spirit and the incarnation of the Son: "And the angel answered and said unto her.

---

[36] In the Creeds of the Church we confess that Christ was conceived by the Holy Ghost. This was not an ordinary, but an extraordinary and absolutely miraculous conception. We also confess Him "born of the Virgin Mary," which emphasizes the supernatural in the event. The correct translation of Luke 1:35 in rendering it *the Holy Spirit* supports the Confession. Spirit (compare the original) has the emphatic position which makes it more definite without the article. The indefinite translation 'Holy Spirit' only serves the exegesis of Nestorians, Kenotics and Dorner. While it is impossible to explain the supernatural conception, it is evident that the Holy Spirit was active in a supernatural manner to segregate the cell, purify it from inherited sin in the physico-psychical propagation and at the very same instant conjoin the human and divine nature, the latter as Logos at the same moment assuming human nature actively and not passively. The Son of God did not assume human nature as entire, but a human nature as separated by the Holy Spirit and possessing all that belongs to human nature except sin. The personalization took place in the same act, the result being the God-man and not a man-God. Compare the following passages: "God, sending his own Son in the likeness of sinful flesh," Rom. 8:3; "The Holy Spirit shall come upon thee (conception), and the power of the Most High shall overshadow thee (Logos)," Luke 1:35; "And the Word became flesh," John 1:14. —The Roman Catholic Church attempted to establish the sinlessness of Christ by the doctrine of the Immaculate Conception of the Virgin Mary. Pope Pius IX. (infallible *ex cathedra,* as officially decreed in 1870) declared at a Convention in 1854 that the Virgin Mary was, in the first instant of her conception, preserved free from every stain of original sin. — It is idle to discuss whether or not Jesus was born *clauso utero Virginis,* which would be a miracle. No Lutheran would deny the possibility, while a Calvinist, rejecting the *Communicatio idiomatum,* would be forced to teach *aperto utero,* but it is not based on Scripture passages. The Scriptures teach plainly that Jesus was born of a virgin, and her virginity was destroyed neither morally nor physically by the changes connected with pregnancy and the natural birth. — Another question, perhaps also idle, or at least curious, is discussed by theologians, namely, why the Second Person in the Trinity became man, and not the First or the Third. The following answers may be adequate: The First Person, being the Father, it was most fitting that the Father should send the Son and not the Son the Father; it was most suitable that in the incarnation the relation of the three should remain as before; it was also proper that He by whom all things were made was to be the Mediator to bring the lost back to God; and it was also fitting that the Spirit was not incarnated, but that He, proceeding from the Father and the Son in the ontological relation, was sent by the Father, and the Son to apply salvation. It was wonderful love that prompted the Son to become man to suffer and die for the salvation and redemption of man.

The Holy Spirit shall come upon thee, and the power of the Most High shall overshadow thee: wherefore also the holy thing which is begotten shall be called the Son of God" (Luke 1:35); "When his mother Mary had been betrothed to Joseph, before they came together she was found with child of the Holy Spirit" (Matt. 1:18); "And without controversy great is the mystery of godliness; he who was manifested in the flesh, justified in the spirit" (1 Tim. 3:16); "Since then the children are sharers in flesh and blood, he also himself in like manner partook of the same" (Heb. 2:14); "Yet without sin" (Heb. 4:15).

4. Concerning the Divinity of Jesus.

The incarnation being necessary, the gracious will of God required that it also should be realized. All the proofs indicate and make clear that the incarnation of the Son of God or His assumption of human nature was carried into effect through the appearance of Jesus Christ. The incarnation is therefore an historical fact.

The ordinary proofs for the divinity of Jesus are the following: 1) *argumentum ὀνομαστικόν* or that divine names are ascribed to Him; "This (Jesus Christ) is the true God and eternal life" (1 John 5:20); 2) *argumentum ἰδιωματικόν* or that divine attributes are ascribed to Him; "Jesus came to them and spake unto them, saying, All authority hath been given unto me in heaven and on earth" (Matt. 28:18); cf. John 17:3; 17:24, etc.; 3) *argumentum ἐνεργητικόν* or that divine deeds are ascribed to Him; "All things have been created through him, and in him all things consist" (Col. 1:16, 17); cf. John 1:3; John 5:20, 21; Matt. 9:6, etc.; 4) *argumentum λατρευτικόν* or that divine worship is ascribed unto Him; "That all may honor the Son, even as they honor the Father" (John 5: 23); cf. Phil. 2:10, 11; 5) *argumentum αὐτομαρτυρητικόν Χριστοῦ* or the testimony of Jesus Christ Himself concerning His divinity. Note the following passages: "The Father loveth the Son, and hath given all things into his hand" (John 3:35); "I that speak unto thee am he" (John 4:26); "Before Abraham was born I am" (John 8:58); cf. John 17, etc.; "And they all said, Art thou then the Son of God? And he said unto them, Ye say that I am" (Luke 22:70).

Many other passages bear directly or indirectly upon the same subject. The testimonies of Christ Himself possess great significance, inasmuch as He was an intellectual, truthful, unselfish, meek and holy man, even when considered from the merely human point of view. Even His enemies have acknowledged that His character was spotless, that He was the ideal man, and that He was elevated far above all selfish aspirations. A good man would not have borne such testimony of himself, had it not been true. It is plainly evident that a sinful man never would have spoken as He did. He presented the truth boldly and uncompromisingly. He never sought popular favor and played no political role. His words and manner never indicate any mental aberration. His words always convey thoughts of profound wisdom. However critically considered, He was perfectly normal. In His appearance and speech there was something supernatural, but nothing abnormal. Every unprejudiced thinker who loves the truth must therefore acknowledge the testimonies of Christ concerning His divinity as the best proofs of His divine origin.

5. Concerning the Humanity of Jesus Christ.

Jesus Christ was not only true God, but also true man. Proofs for the true humanity of Jesus have been presented against the advocates of Docetism and other related theories, definitions have been formulated in order to forestall misleading conceptions, while the special prerogatives of the human nature of Christ have been set forth in order to counteract Nestorian and rationalistic tendencies as well as for the purpose of making clear the pure and harmonious character of Christ as Mediator. We would herewith present more precisely the content of these considerations which have such great bearing on the development of the doctrine of the humanity of Jesus.

1) The ordinary proofs for the true humanity of Jesus are the following: a) *argumentum ex nominibus humanis,* or the proof on the ground of the human names of Jesus; "A man that hath told you the truth" (John 8:40); "Man, Jesus Christ" (1 Tim. 2:5); "Is not this the carpenter's son? is not his mother called Mary? and his brethren, James, and Joseph, and Simon,

and Judas?" (Matt. 13:55); b) *argumentum ex partibus hominis essentialibus*, or proofs gathered from such passages as mention that He possessed body, soul, spirit, emotion, knowledge, will, etc.; "The temple of his body" (John 2:21); "My soul is exceedingly sorrowful" (Matt. 26:38); "Yielded up his spirit" (Matt. 27:50); cf. also Luke 2:52; John 11:35; Matt. 26:39, etc.; c) *argumentum ex operationibus humanis*, or proofs on the ground of His human deeds, such as that He taught, conversed, journeyed, etc.; d) *argumentum ex attributis vero homini propriis*, such as hunger, thirst, fatigue, sleep, etc.: e) argumentum ex genealogia Christi according to Matt. 1 and Luke 3.

2) Designations ascribed to the humanity of Jesus are: a) *vera*, or true, which term is used against Docetism and other related theories; b) *completa*, or perfect, which term is used against Apollinaris and others, and against Monoteletism; c) h*omousia*, or of the same essence with us in accordance with His humanity, which is used against Gnosticism and against Schwenkfeld.

3) Concerning the natural and personal human infirmities it is taught that Christ assumed *infirmitas naturales*, such as hunger, thirst, fatigue, trials, etc., but He did not assume *infirmitates personales*, because these latter denote imperfection in formation, from which are derived deformities and hereditary sicknesses. The assumption of these would not have served any purpose, and at the same time would have detracted from His human dignity.

4) *Praerogativa humanae Christi naturae*, or the special prerogatives of the human nature of Christ, are: a) *ἀνυποστασία*, By this is meant that the human nature did not exist *per se* as a special personality which was assumed in the act of incarnation, since in that case there would have been two persons and two mediators and not two natures in one person. The human nature, therefore, lacked personality, but became personal by being made partaker in the personality of the Son of God, which is called *ἐνυποστασία*. There was no separation in time so that the human nature of Christ should have lacked the elements of personality even for a moment. At exactly the same moment that the human nature through the divine

activity came into existence, it was made partaker in the most real and perfect way in the personality of the Son of God; b) *ἀναμαρτησία*, or that the assumed nature was sinless; c) *singularis animae et corporis excellentia*, denoting a singular measure of understanding, will and emotion. Cf. Luke 2:47; John 7:46. His body constituted a harmonious organism. He was immortal and died therefore of His own free will, for which reason He did not see corruption. His form and appearance were perfect and beautiful. Cf. Ps. 45:3: "Thou art fairer than the children of men." Isa. 53 refers to Christ in the garb of His suffering. Christ was normal in all things. Even in His appearance He was the ideal man. It is not necessary to think of Him as wearing a heavenly halo. His appearance was that of men in general, although His external features undoubtedly expressed something of the inward purity of His spirit. Even Pilate was captivated by His personality.

In regard to the second point touching upon the impeccability and temptability of Christ we must consider that the divine nature by itself could not be tempted, but when the divine and human natures are by the incarnation united in one theanthropic person, temptation is possible. But His sinlessness does not lessen the reality of His temptation by Satan. The good angels were tempted and our first parents were tempted in their state of innocence. But it was impossible for Christ to fall a prey to Satan's wiles, and yet He could suffer the anguish of soul and the internal struggle of temptation to the utmost. This experience belonged to His suffering. We must consider that He was in the state of exinanition and, therefore, the experience of temptation was real. Being sinless, He was endowed with enlightenment in the understanding, purity in the feeling and holiness in the will and therefore felt the attack of Satan all the more keenly. If an enemy attacks a strong fortress, like Gibraltar, the bombardment will be correspondingly heavy. The temptation of Christ was evidently the severest that Satan was able to plan and execute. The reason that Christ could not fall depends upon the fact that the divine nature would not leave the human nature to itself in moments of special danger. In the state of exinanition the divine nature ordinarily withdrew from the human nature the use of omniscience and other relative attributes and the God-man was left to suffer desertion by God in His experience of hell, but would never have been left to fall. He" had been sent to suffer and die vicariously to save men. According to Heb. 5:8, He learned obedience by the things which He suffered, and He was the more able to help those who experience temptation. The fact that the Second Person in the Trinity has Himself passed through all kinds of trials and the hardest sufferings and death possesses great consolation for every Christian.

6. Notes on the History of Dogma.

In the earliest period the doctrine of the Christian Church was in danger through influences both from Judaism and heathenism. There were two kinds of heresy that arose from Judaism. We refer to those of the Ebionites and the Nazareans. The former considered Christ only a man who had been consecrated as Messiah at His baptism. The latter acknowledged the supernatural birth of Christ, but denied His hypostatical pre-existence. They considered that at the baptism of Christ God united Himself with the human personality as it had been fashioned by the Spirit of God. There was also a Greek Ebionitism which was pantheistic in character. According to this theory the human nature of Christ was considered divine, which from the practical point of view simply meant that He was a great genius. Gnosticism arose through the influence of heathenism. Among its representatives we would mention Basilides, Valentinus and Marcion. Gnosticism also implied Docetism. The Church was also compelled to fight against the Monarchians, Apollinarism, and other tendencies. While Origen was heretical in many things, he nevertheless advocated the eternal generation of the Son. Among the many doctrinal controversies we would make mention of the struggle against Arius and the different forms of Arianism. During the second period there arose the controversy between the Nestorians and the School of Alexandria, of which Cyril was the representative. The Alexandrian School emphasized the union of the natures of Christ, while the Nestorians, on the other hand, separated them, resulting in two persons. Eutyches laid such emphasis on the union of the natures as to result in only one nature. At the Council of Chalcedon in 451 it was decided that the two natures were united inconfusedly (ἀσυγχύτως), unchangeably (ἀτρέπτως), indivisibly (ἀδιαιρέτως) and inseparably (ἀχωρίστως). At the same Council the following was adopted: "We confess that He is truly God and truly Man, of a reasonable soul and body; consubstantial with the Father, according to the Godhead, and consubstantial with us, according to the Manhood; in all things like unto us, except sin." Several attempts were made to unite the Monophysites with the Church. Among such attempts may be mentioned the one made by Emperor Heraclius together with the patriarchs Sergius in Constantinople and Cyrus in Alexandria. Through this attempt there arose the heresy of Monotheletism, which was condemned at Rome in 649 and at Constantinople in 680. In the West there arose a doctrinal tendency known as Adoptionism, which set forth a double sonship. Peter Lombard developed a new doctrine which has become known as Nihilism. The Roman Catholic Church sought to effect a compromise between the different tendencies. The doctrines of this Church overshadow the humanity of Christ not only by laying special emphasis on the divine, but also through the worship of the saints, the mass and the exaltation of the Virgin Mary, who through her intercession represents the divine love in human form. During the following period, or the period of the Reformation, the Lutheran Church devoted itself to the most thoroughgoing study and treatment of the Christological question, which reached its culmination in the logical doctrine of *communicatio idiomatum*. The Reformed Church laid emphasis on the expression, "*finitum non est capax infiniti*," in accordance with which the union of the two natures is not real, except in the sense that it is the same person that is active at times through the one and at other times through the other nature. Such a position is related to Nestorianism. The Reformed view is often expressed in the same language as the Lutheran, but the content is not the same. The Reformed doctrine of *communicatio idiomatum* makes this clear. During the Protestant Scholastic period there arose many Docetic tendencies, as in Schwenkfeld and Weigel, while other tendencies set forth only the human nature of Christ, such as Socinianism. Servetus rejected the doctrine of the two natures of Christ as well as the eternal existence of a personal Son of God. This period was also characterized by a still more profound development of the Lutheran Christology. During the following period, which includes the modern critical development, there arose as a result of Deism and the philosophical schools of the day the modern development of Rationalism, which considers Jesus as simply a man. Kant laid stress on Christ from the practical and moral point of view, while it became more and more customary to look upon Christ as the ideal man. Schleiermacher presents the doctrine of the ideal man and really rejects the doctrine of the divinity of Christ, although in a pantheistic way he recognizes Christ as divine. Christ was the God-man as the highest development of humanity. And yet, although the school of Schleiermacher and Hegel have undermined the faith in the true divinity of Christ, still the orthodox doctrines have had many powerful defenders. The iconoclastic theology of Ritschl has won many adherents in our modern day. This theology robs Christ of essential union with the Father. The expression "Son of God" is used, but not in the sense that the Church teaches. In reality Ritschlianism denies the divinity of Christ. But while this destructive theology has exerted great influence, still it bears within its own heart the seeds of self-destruction. The old truth shall conquer. We would herewith as before give a more detailed resume of the ideas and conceptions that have characterized different tendencies as well as the views of the leading men during the various periods of development.

Clement of Rome calls Christ the effulgence of the Father, while he calls the suffering of Christ the suffering of God. Barnabas taught the pre-existence of Christ. Ignatius says that Christ is God who became man. He calls His blood the blood of God. Cerinthus, whom John, according to Polycarp, considered a heretic, taught the opposite, declaring that Jesus was a man who had received the aeon Christ at his baptism. This Christ left Jesus before His suffering.

Justin Martyr taught that the Logos was a potency that had existed eternally in the Father, but appeared as a hypostasis at the creation of the world and was then born out of the essence of the Father. He therefore taught the birth of the Son. This Son of God assumed manhood. Justin therefore did not teach that the Son was born of eternity, but that the birth of the Son was dependent upon the will of the Father. Athenagoras partly followed the conception of Justin, but nevertheless considered that the Son was an eternal hypostasis in the Father. Among the Monarchians may be mentioned first the *Alogians,* who rejected the doctrine of the *Logos* as contained in John's Gospel and taught that the *Logos* was not a divine hypostasis as distinct from the Father. We would further mention the *dynamic Monarchians,* such as Theodotus the Tanner, Theodotus The Money-changer, and Artemon, who taught that it was only a divine power that was imparted to Jesus, who had been brought forth by the Holy Ghost and the Virgin Mary. Later on Paul of Samosata further developed the teachings of the Monarchians. There were other Monarchians, the so-called Patripassians, who taught that the only person in the Godhead, or the Father Himself, had become man and suffered for the sins of the world. Among these may be mentioned Praxeas, Noëtus and Beryllus. The third form of Monarchianism was the so-called *Modalistic Monarchianism,* which in developed form is called Sabellianism. Sabellius taught that *per se* God was a unity that was impersonal and admitted of no distinctions. In the course of the world's development this unity appeared in three different modes or forms, each constituting, however, the whole monad. The Godhead, which is fixed and stable, reveals itself in three different phases of development, so that the Father, the Son and the Holy Spirit exist successively in the concrete, but it is the same God. — *Gnosticism* flourished during the second century and was represented by Basilides. Valentinus and Marcion. The system of Basilides contained among other things the following: The nameless God through His creative word first produces a world embryo or chaos, from which the world develops. In this embryo there are found three sons, the pneumatic, the psychic and the hylic. The first of these liberates himself instantly from the embryo and arises with lightning rapidity to God and remains there as the blessed world of the spirit or *πλήρωμα,* which constitutes the seven highest aeons, and together with the primitive being forms the first Ogdoad. The emanations continued and there arose 365 spiritual worlds. The second Son with the help of the Holy Spirit, whom He has produced, endeavors to follow the pneumatic son, but reaches no further than the border-line of the ir\rjpaifia or the firmament. The third son is caught in the embryo and stands in need of redemption. Two *ἄρχοντες* or *δημιουργοί* are created which proceed from the world substance. The first *ἄρχων* creates the firmament, the second creates and rules the planetary heavens. Both the *archontes* bear sons who arise and bring unto their father knowledge mediated through the Holy Spirit, leading him to repentance. This is the beginning of the process of redemption by which the children of God or the pneumatics are to be brought back to the supramundane God. Christianity is the means. Christ is threefold. He is the son of the first *ἄρχων*, also of the second, as well as the son of Mary. It is the same principle. The body of Christ returned to formlessness at death. His soul arose and ascended, but stopped in the planetary heavens. His spirit ascended to the first son and the primitive being. The threefold pneumatic principle attracts all spiritual beings by which redemption is accomplished. The system of Valentinus contains briefly the following main points: The primary substance is *βυθός* which is inscrutable and throughout limitless ages lives in silent contemplation of his own perfection. This silence or ἡ *σιγή* is the spouse of Bythos and constitutes the feminine principle. After the silence begins the evolution. The first to be born are *νοῦς* and *ἀλήθεια*, which in turn bear *λόγος* and *ζωή*, and these in their turn bear *ἄνθρωπος* and *ἐκκλησία*. The first pair bring forth ten aeons and the second pair twelve. The last or the 28th aeon is called *σοφία*. Thereafter the first pair also brought forth the heavenly Christ and the feminine Holy Spirit. *Σοφία* forms the transition to the lower world. The thirty aeons together constitute *πλήρωμα*, for which a boundary is fixed when *βυθός* gives birth to *ὅρος*. *Σοφία* longs for the primitive being and at once plunges into the *βυθός* and then chaos arises. *Ὅρος* prevents her destruction, bringing her back and releasing from her *πάθος*, who sinks down in *κένομα* and constitutes the lower *σοφία* or Akamoth. The whole world of aeons sympathized with this aeon who belonged nevertheless to the *πλήρωμα*, For this reason the aeons were brought forth that were to accomplish redemption, viz., the heavenly Christ and the Holy Spirit. The thirty aeons together brought forth *σωτήρ* or Jesus as a spouse to *σοφία*. The Demiurge, who had created the sensuous, also brought forth a lower Christ with whom *σωτήρ* was united at His baptism. This lower Christ had passed through the womb of Mary like water through a pipe, but had no real body. He was crucified, but did not suffer. After many sufferings *σοφία* is purified and as the bride of *σωτήρ* is brought to *πλήρωμα* and brings all the pneumatic spirits with her. Marcion accepted two principles, viz., the highest God and the Demiurge, the God of the Jews. The former was the good God, the latter was the angry God which was connected with the material. The Son of God without any preparation had suddenly come in a phantom body and without having come in contact with the body of Mary. He revealed the good God. Irenaeus taught that the Son had co-existed with the Father from eternity. He believed that there was an intimate union between the two natures. He further believed that *Logos* would have become man, even if sin had not come into the world. He said that *Logos* rested when Jesus suffered. Tertullian set forth a threefold sonship or *filiatio*. He wavered somewhat in his expressions concerning the humanity of Christ, but he was a powerful opponent of Docetism. Against Marcion he declared that Christ could not have appeared suddenly and without preparation. Origen taught the eternal generation of the Son. He called Christ the God-man or at least he conceived of Him as a divine-human person. He said that Christ had a human soul, but on the ground of his theory of the pre-existence of souls he declared that the *Logos* had united Himself to the soul of Jesus before time was. For this reason he believed that the Son of God had received from Mary a human body, but not a complete human nature. He also taught subordination. Concerning the body of Jesus after His resurrection Origen taught that the human nature of Christ was lost in the essence of God, so that Christ is not now a man.

Arnobius taught also that the human nature of Christ consisted only of His body. He calls Christ *Deus sublimus*. Arius presented the same idea, viz., that at His incarnation the Son had assumed a human body without a soul. He taught that there was a time when the Son did not exist. It was not necessary for the Son to be born. God is an absolute causality. The Son was created out of nothing and is not of the same essence with the Father. The logical sequence of Arianism was developed by the Heterusians. The Semi-arians were represented by Basil of Ancyra and George of Laodicea, who used the term ὁμοιούσιος. Eusebius of Caesarea said that the Father was before the Son as to cause and that the generation did not take place in one act and therefore it was not from eternity. The Son was God in a secondary sense. Marcellus denied the hypostatical pre-existence of the Son. Only through the incarnation did the *Logos* become personal and the Son of God. Hilary of Poitiers taught that the human soul of Christ was like ours, although it was created directly by God; also that His human nature, formed by the flesh of Mary, was like unto ours. He set forth three acts of generation, the first was the eternal generation of the Father, the second was the incarnation, and the third was the resurrection. The human nature of Christ was made divine after the resurrection. Athanasius laid emphasis on the intimate relationship between the two natures of Christ. He not only fought Arianism, but also Apollinarism, stressing against the latter the true human nature of Christ. Gregory of Nazianzus and Gregory of Nyssa emphasized the union of the natures and used the term *σύγκρασις*. The Alexandrian School set forth the union, but the Antiochian School distinguished between the natures of Christ. Apollinaris did not accept the views of the latter, for he said that there was only one nature in Christ, which had a divine and a human side. He taught further that God and a complete man could not be united in one person, for which reason he declared that Christ lacked the human spirit. This was necessary, inasmuch as the seat of sin was in the spirit. Diodorus of Tarsus said that the union between the two natures was not substantial but moral. Toward the close of the fourth century the *Priscillianists* appeared in Spain. They declared that the devil was an independent ruler. The souls of men were brought forth by the good eternal being. They descended in order to conquer Satan. But he imprisoned them in the material body.

When the Redeemer came to deliver them, He came with a heavenly body. This sect advocated Docetism. Augustine rejected all Docetic tendencies and clearly set forth the teaching that Christ was God and man in one person. He makes use of the analogy of the union of the soul with the body. The Christological controversy between the schools of Antioch and Alexandria reached its culmination when Nestorius presented his doctrine which has become known as Nestorianism. He taught that the incarnation did not consist in the Son of, God assuming manhood in the womb of the Virgin Mary, but through the mediation of the Holy Ghost Mary had given birth to a man as an organ for the divinity, in which man the *Logos* had taken His abode as in a temple. The union of the natures was therefore only moral. The union was considered as a *συνάφεια*. Mary was a *χριστοτόκος*, but not a *θεοτόκος*. Cyril of Alexandria rejected the doctrine of the communion of the natures and taught instead an *ἕνωσις*. He used the illustration of the union of the soul with the body. *Logos* united Himself with an impersonal human nature. He called Mary *θεοτόκος*. Cyril presented partly the doctrine of *communicatio idiomatum*. The doctrine of Nestorius was rejected at the third Ecumenical Council in Ephesus in 431. Eutyches was a spirited opponent of Nestorianism, but went to the opposite extreme, and his position has been termed Eutychianism. He stressed the union to such a degree that it resulted in only one nature. The human nature of Christ was not like ours, but was wholly merged in the divine. The doctrine of Eutyches was rejected in Ephesus in 448, but was acknowledged at the so-called Robber Council at Ephesus in 449. His doctrine was condemned at Chalcedon in 451. Nestorianism was rejected at this same Council. The letter of Leo the Great to Flavius exerted a great influence on the decisions of this meeting. The Council of Chalcedon confessed that Christ is truly God and truly man, of a reasonable soul and body; consubstantial with the Father, according to the Godhead, and consubstantial with us, according to the manhood; in all things, except sin, like unto us. It was also stated that He was born of the Virgin Mary, the mother of God, according to the manhood; that He was one person with two natures which were united inconfusedly, unchangeably, indivisibly and inseparably. Through the attempt to reconcile the Monophysites there arose a new doctrinal development known as Monotheletism, which declared that Christ was indeed possessed of two natures, but that there was only one Will and one divine mode of activity. Monotheletism was condemned at Constantinople in 680 when it was decided that in Christ there were two wills and modes of activity. The human will, however, must be thought of as being subject to the divine will. Docetism was revived in the East through the Paulicians, who taught that the Demiurge kept the souls imprisoned, but that the good God sent the Redeemer, who brought with Him from heaven a phantom body, which passed through Mary as though through a pipe without receiving anything. John of Damascus taught that the *Logos* did not assume a human nature that was an individual (*individium*), which would imply Nestorianism. Neither did he conceive of the human nature generically, which would lead to Monophysitism. Through the incarnation the human nature of Christ was made the recipient of real subsistence. The human nature did not exist independently either before or after the union; it was an *ἀνυποστασία* that became an *ἐνυποστασία*. He also speaks of a *περιχώρησις*, which is active on the side of the divine nature. The basic lines of the doctrine of *communicatio idiomatum* are also to be found in this Church father.

During the following period there arose a tendency that has been termed *Adoptionism*. in accordance with which there was a double sonship in Christ. In accordance with His divine nature He was, strictly speaking, the Son of God, but in accordance with His human nature He was adopted. In the former sense He was the Only Begotten, in the latter sense He was the First Born. Elipandus of Toledo and Felix of Urgellis were the leading representatives of this doctrine. Felix of Urgellis also taught that *Logos* was united with an unsanctified human nature, but Christ never committed any actual sin. Adoptionism was rejected at Regensburg in 792, in Frankfort in 794, and in Aachen in 799. John Scotus Erigena taught that the *Logos* assumed human nature in general, so that the whole of humanity became deified. Anselm presented the Son as the prototype and in general taught the same as John of Damascus. The incarnation was effected because sin had come through *one*, and therefore salvation must come through *one* who could make satisfaction. Peter Lombard taught that the human nature of Christ did not possess personality and then drew the conclusion that the Son of God did not become anything when He became man, because God is unchangeable. He conceived of the incarnation as an *indumentum* or that the Son of God was invested with human nature without becoming man in a real sense. This view, denominated Nihilism, was condemned in 1179. Thomas Aquinas denied that the Logos had become united with the whole race or with all individuals, because it served no purpose to effect through many what could be accomplished through one. Christ was Mediator in accordance with His human nature. Duns Scotus taught that the Son of God would have become man irrespective of sin, because the will of God must be fulfilled. John Wessel likewise taught that the Son of God would have assumed manhood independent of the Fall in order to complete humanity as an organism. In such case *Logos* would have become King in the kingdom of God, which reaches its goal in the world of men.

Luther clearly presented the true Christological position and emphasized the true manhood and divinity of Christ as well as the union of the two natures in one person. He taught communicatio idiomatum. An important utterance in the Christology of Luther is the following: Where Christ is, there He is entire. Zwingli considered the communication of the attributes in accordance with the doctrine of *communicatio idiomatum* simply as a figure of speech. Each nature has its own attributes and functions in its own way. According to His human nature Christ is limited by space and is therefore not omnipresent; only the divine nature can be omnipresent. The Reformed Church adopted the saying: *finitum non est capax infiniti*. On the other hand, Luther declared that *natura humana capax est divinae*. Calvin stood closer to Luther than to Zwingli. He had a deeper conception of *communicatio idiomatum* than Zwingli. Although he fought against the Christology of Servetus and also that of Osiander, still he did not show any great desire to delve too deeply into the mysteries of Christology. However, he laid emphasis on the significance of *genus apotelesmaticum.* Schwenkfeld asserted that the body of Christ was not taken from the material world, but that it came from the essence of God, for which reason Jesus was the natural Son of God. The body which He received from Mary was simply the external form. Weigel also spoke of an invisible and a visible body; the latter had been received from Mary. The Formula of Concord presents clearly the doctrine of the person of Christ without swerving either to the right or to the left. The doctrine of *communicatio idiomatum* is given profound treatment in a religious sense in relation to the doctrine of the Lord's Supper, while the doctrine of the union of the persons together with its effects is also included in the same discussion. The Socinians declared that Jesus was merely a man, but that He was conceived by the Holy Ghost, and before He entered upon His office, He was taken up to heaven and instructed. As a reward for His obedience He was accorded divine attributes and worship. The *Arminians* taught subordination and presented a view which approached Nestorianism.

According to Reimarus and Lessing Christ was a wise and prudent man, indeed, they considered Him a demagogue, who endeavored to establish an earthly kingdom. This also to a certain extent expresses the attitude of the Deists, who at the most considered Jesus Christ as a moral teacher, comparing Him to Apollonius of Tyana. Kant asserted that Christ possessed significance merely as the founder of a church in which the religion of the intellect finally would conquer. He considered Christ as an example and as the ideal of moral perfection. The principal thing is faith in the ideal, not in the historical Christ. Fichte said that Christ possessed the most highly developed knowledge possible to man, viz., the knowledge of the absolute union of being as revealed in the unity of man and the divine essence. Christ does not now possess any other historical significance than that He was the person who imparted the knowledge of this union. Hegel, together with the representatives of modern Pantheism in general, teaches that the incarnation is not to be considered empirically, in the sense that God should have assumed human nature at a certain time. Jesus was not, strictly speaking, the God-man.

The question does not concern the union of God with a particular man, but with the whole of humanity. The self-consciousness of God is reached through the spirit of man. Some of Hegel's disciples have endeavored to harmonize Hegellanism with the Christian doctrine of an historical divine-human person, but Strauss has proved that this is impossible from the Hegelian point of view. Strauss said that ideas are not ordinarily realized in such manner that all the wealth of their content is poured out in one individual representative, but in the many. Humanity is the divine form of revelation. Schleiermacheb considered Christ as the greatest fruit of humanity. The consciousness of the divine appeared in Him as in no other. Christ was the ideal man, but He was not the real Son of God. Schlelermacher leaned toward Sabellianism. De Wette taught that we transfer our religious emotion to Christ and imagine that He forms the connecting link between the infinite and the finite. But divinity has not become united with humanity in an individual. Toward the close of his life, however, he gave stronger recognition to the historical realization of the religious ideas in the person of Christ. Ritschl sought to eliminate from the Christological question all metaphysical consideration. He stated that knowledge was not the principal thing, but the will. Ethical considerations were of prime importance. He endeavored furthermore to forestall any collision with the natural sciences and the higher criticism. He therefore attacked the doctrine of the pre-existence of Christ, while avoiding all dogmatic considerations of the person of Christ. The work of Christ was of prime importance, considered from the ethical standpoint. It is evident that Ritschl denies the teachings of Christianity concerning Christ. The more recent confessional Dogmaticians combat Ritschlianism with all their power. The confessional Dogmaticians agree with the old Lutheran orthodoxy and lay all stress on the divinity as well as the humanity of Christ, although all are not agreed on the question of kenosis. Some of the most recent theologians set forth that Christ could have come into the world independent of sin. The Scandinavian Dogmaticians Martensen and Granfelt hold such views.

§17. Unio Personalis and Its Immediate Results.

The result of the incarnation or *unitio* was the intimate union of the divine and the human nature, considered as a *conditio,* which union is called *unio personalis seu hypostatica.* But this personal union must imply the communion of the natures or their real communion and communication. This communion of the natures is generally expressed in what are termed Personal Propositions.

1. The Personal Union.

Hollazius defines the personal union as follows: "unio Personalis *is the union of the two natures, the divine and the human, subsisting in the one hypostasis of the Son of God, implying a mutual, indissoluble communion of the two natures.*"[37] Christ is therefore a personal σύνθετος. The hypostasis is called complex, because it is a hypostasis of two natures, while before the *unitio* it was an hypostasis of the divine nature only. Therefore the two natures are inseparable. Gerhard says in this connection that neither has a part been united to a part, but the entire Logos to the entire flesh and the entire flesh to the entire Logos; wherefore it follows that because of the identity of the person and the pervasion of the natures by each other, the Logos is so present to the flesh and the flesh is so present to the Logos, that neither the Logos is without the flesh, nor the flesh without the Logos, but wherever the Logos is, there is the flesh, and wherever the flesh is, there is the Logos.[38] The following negative and positive terms are employed to define more closely the personal union: 1) *negativa*: a) *non verbalis,* inasmuch as the God-man is not a title; b)*non notionalis seu rationis,* i. e., it is not a conceptual union; c) *non habitualis seu respectiva,* such as a union between husband and wife or between friends; d) *non accidentalis,*

---

[37] Hollazius: *"Unio personalis est duarum naturarum, divinae et humanae in una filii Dei hypostasi subsistentium, conjunctio, mutuam eamque indissolubilem utriusque naturae communionem inferens."*

[38] Gerhard, *Loci Theol.* Tomus I, Loc. 4, pp. 501, 502, or 3, 427, 428.

inasmuch as it is not a union such as that of substance and quality in a learned man or whiteness and sweetness in milk or like two beams joined together; e) *non essentialis,* so that the two natures become one, which term was used against the Eutychians; f) *non naturalis,* like the soul in the body. It is not that sort of a natural union. 2) *Positiva*: a) *realis,* or real; b) *personalis,* or personal, but not a union of two persons; c) *perichoristica,* inasmuch as the divine nature of the Logos entirely penetrates the human nature and imparts itself in the totality and perfection of its essence; d) *perpetuo durans,* because it is an eternal union.

2. The Communion of the Natures.

Communio naturarum is a necessary consequence of the *unio personalis.* Hollazius defines as follows: "communio naturarum *is the mutual participation of the divine and human natures of Christ, through which the divine nature of the Logos, having be.en made partaker of the human nature, permeates, perfects, inhabits and appropriates it unto Himself, while the human nature, having been made partaker of the divine nature, is permeated, perfected and inhabited by it.*"[39] The divine nature is therefore active in this permeation which is more clearly defined by the old Dogmaticians, such as Hollazius, in the following terms: 1) *intima et perfectissima,* by which is meant that the union or the communion is not an external one, such as when angels have been revealed in human form, or like the clothes on a body; 2) *mutua* in the sense that the divine nature in actual essence or in the most absolute act (*ἐντελέχεια*) permeates and perfects the assumed human nature, which is permeated and perfected. This is therefore a *περιχώρησις*, which, however, is neither local nor quantitative, but permeates indivisibly and simultaneously every part of the human nature. In this connection we may quote Col. 2:9: "In him dwelleth all the fulness of the Godhead bodily." The old Dogmaticians made use of various analogies, such as *permeatio* in the

---

[39] Hollazius: "*Communio naturarum est mutua divinae et humanae Christi naturae participatio, per quam natura divina τοῦ Λόγου, particeps facta humanae naturae, hanc permeat, perficit, inhabitat, sibique appropriat; humana vero, particeps facta divinae naturae ab hac permeatur, perficitur et inhabitur.*"

Trinity, the permeation and the indwelling of the soul in the body and the permeation of the iron by the fire; 3) *inseparabilis*, i. e., after the incarnation the divine nature was never separated from the human nature, not even when the soul was separated from the body in the grave. The divine nature of the Logos was in the highest degree present in the assumed human nature; 4) *sine confusione, mixtione et transmutatione* (ἀσύγχυτος, ἄμικτος, και ἄτρεπτος), i. e., without confusion, mixture or change, as the soul is not commingled or changed in the body; 5) ἀδιάστατον, or that both natures are so intimately united in a permanent sense and so present in and through each other that the one nature is never outside of nor apart from the other. We find analogies in the Trinity, and in more comprehensible form in the normal relationship between the soul and the body.

The third term, *inseparabilis,* means that the two natures could never be separated, not even at the death and burial of Christ. When Christ died His soul was separated from the body just as every person experiences death. The body of Christ was placed in the tomb and His spirit-soul was transferred to Paradise, where the spirit of Christ remained until vivification on the resurrection morning. The dead body of Christ was not exposed to decomposition, as He was sinless and had completed the reconciliation in its two objective parts, namely, satisfaction and expiation or atonement. His state of exinanition ended with His burial. Cf. Acts 2: 31; 13: 35, 37. The brief separation of His soul and body made no break in the continued personal union of the two natures. The unsevered union of body and soul with the divine nature or *Logos* was necessary for the verity of the uninterrupted personal union and communion of natures. The personality of the God-man depends actively upon the divine nature, as the Son of God or *Logos* was personal or a person before He assumed the human nature. A human soul is the active factor in the personality of man. In Paradise the divine nature or *Logos* was united with the soul of Christ and also with the body. This becomes clearer, when we consider that the divine omnipresence is intensive and not extensive. Besides we should remember the communication of attributes according to *genus majestaticum* which concerns the entire nature and not a part of it as the soul. The old theologians spoke of *praesentia intima* and *praesentia extima*, the former term meaning the presence of the natures to one another and the second term denoting the presence to created things. Even in the state of exinanition, when *praesentia extima* was an extraordinary exception, the *praesentia intima*, which is independent of space and time, could not cease on account of the personal union.

The fifth term under our heading, *communio naturarum*, is connected with the preceding. One nature cannot be without or outside of the other. The divine nature cannot be locally encircling in space and the human nature circumscribed in a place as in heaven. Where the God-man is, He is entire. There are two modes of presence, depending upon the natures. The God-man has one definite presence on account of the human nature and one omnipresent mode according to the divine nature. But in both modes He is entire and undivided. According to the mode of His manifestation in heaven, He is entire, and according to His presence with us here on earth as He has promised, He is entire in both natures by a divine mode. This presence of Christ in both natures as one person is explained by the action of the divine nature upon the human in the communication of attributes. Cf. *genus majestaticum.*

3. The Personal Propositions.

Propositiones Personales. — *In these propositions or designations the concrete expressed concerning one nature is the predicate of the concrete of the other nature, and still in a way that is pecidiar and unusual, in order to express the union of the two natures and their communion in the one person.*

It is important to note that the question concerns the concrete of the natures; the concrete of the divine nature when the designation is derived from the divine nature, and the concrete of the human nature when the designation is derived from the human nature. The question cannot concern the concrete of the person, the concrete being the designation of the person that consists of the two natures. The abstract designation of the natures is also excluded, inasmuch as we cannot say that *divinitas est humanitas.* Concrete designations for the divine nature are such as

God, and the Son of God. The designations of the human nature are such as man, the Son of man, and Son of Mary. The concrete of the person is expressed in such designations as Messiah, Immanuel, and Christ. According to *propositiones personales* with reference to the concrete names of the natures we can therefore say, God is man, Jesus is God, etc. These personal propositions are true because of the personal union. The following Bible passages may be quoted: "Unto us a child is born, unto us a son is given, and his name shall be called Mighty God" (Isa. 9:6); "Who do men say that the Son of man is? Simon Peter answered and said, Thou art the Christ, the Son of the living God" (Matt. 16: 13—16); "The holy thing which is begotten shall be called the Son of God" (Luke 1:35); "The second man is of heaven" (1 Cor. 15:47); "The Son of God is come; we are in him that is true, even in his Son Jesus Christ. This is the true God, and eternal life" (1 John 5:20).

The personal propositions are further defined by the following terms: 1) *negative*: a) *non mere verbales*. The propositions are not to be understood as if only the name, but not the nature thereby designated, were predicated of the subject, as Nestorius does, when he says that the Son of Mary was the Son of God, ascribing to the subject merely a title, but positively refusing to acknowledge that He who was the Son of Mary was also true Son of God; b) *neque impropriae aut tropicae*, such as a painting or a statue, which may represent a person, so that we may say, this is such and such a person. Christ was not the Son of God in only an ideal sense or in any unreal or figurative sense; c) *neque identicae*, i. e., the predicates that are ascribed to the subject art not to be so explained as if they applied to it only in so far as the predicate precisely corresponds to that nature from which the designation of the subject is derived. For example, the proposition, The Son of God is the Son of Mary, cannot be interpreted as follows, The man who is united with the Son of God is the son of Mary; consequently the concrete of the predicate ascribed to the concrete of the subject should not be of the identical nature; we should not say: Jesus is the son of Mary; d) *neque essentiales*, as if the subject, in its essential nature, were that which the predicate ascribes to it. God is man, would then mean,

The nature of God is this, that it is the nature of man; 2) *positive*: a) *reales*, or in the real sense; b) *inusitatae*, or unusual; c) sine exemplo, or without any analogical or real examples. In accordance with these propositions therefore Nestorianism, Eutychianism and Adoptionism together with other related theories are rejected.

§18. Communicatio Idiomatum.

As a necessary result of *unio personalis* and *communio naturarum* the doctrine of *communicatio idiomatum* and *communis operatio* occupies a central and important place in the Lutheran Christology. The communication of the attributes is defined by Hollazius as follows: "communicatio idiomatum *is the true and real participation of the properties of the divine and human natures, resulting from the personal union in Christ, the God-man, designated by either nature or by both natures.*"[40]

By *idiomata* we understand the properties and the distinguishing characteristics of the natures, through which the two natures are distinguished, and by which they are known. Gerhard points out that the divine properties belong to the essence of the *Logos*, while the human properties do not belong to the essence of the human nature, but are derived from it. There is a communication of the *idiomata* between the natures and the person and also between the natures reciprocally.

Dogmaticians use the following terms more clearly to define *communicatio idiomatum*: 1) *negative*: a) *non verbalis et titularis*. This term is used against the Calvinists or the Reformed in general, who say that the *communicatio idiomatum* is real in regard to the person, designated either in accordance with the divine or human nature, but that in regard to the natures themselves *communicatio* is simply verbal, so that it is a

[40] Hollazius: "*Communicatio idiomatum est vera et realis propriorum divina? et humanae et naturae in Christo θεανθρώπω ab alterutra vel utraque natura denominato, participatio ex unione personali resultans.*"

communicatio verborum and not *idiomatum*; b) *non intellectualis,* because it is not a bare concept without concrete content; c) *non exaequativa,* inasmuch as the distinction of the natures remains; d) *non multiplicativa,* so as to imply a multiplication and therefore different subjects; e) *non transfusiva,* since the divine nature does not pour out over or impart to the human nature something which it would not afterwards possess; f) *non accidentalis,* or accidental; g) *non commixtiva,* not through commingling; h) *non essentialis,* inasmuch as the properties of the one nature cannot become the essential possession of the other nature; 2) *positive*: a) *realis,* or a real communication; b) *personalis,* i. e., a communication *κατά συνδύασιν* or such a communion of the natures, through which the two natures are so intimately united with each other, that, their essence remaining distinct, the one nature without mixture really receives and participates in the peculiar power, work and property of the other on the ground of the communion of the natures in the one person; c) *supernaturalis,* because it takes place in a supernatural way.

Communicatio idiomatum is divided into three classes: *genus idiomaticum, genus majestaticum* and *genus apotelesmaticum.* Some would also add *ταπεινοτικόν* or *κενοτικόν.*

I. Genus Idiomaticum. *Genus idiomaticum* is *that genus by which the attributes that are peculiar or belong to the divine or to the human nature are truly and really ascribed to the entire person of Christ, designated by either one of the natures or both.*

Genus idiomaticum is divided into three species: 1) *ἰδιοποίησις* or *appropriatio* is the species in accordance with which human *idiomata* are predicated concerning Christ, designated by the concrete of the divine nature. The following may serve as examples: "Crucified the Lord of glory" (1 Cor. 2:8); "The Son of God gave himself up for me" (Gal. 2:20); 2) *κοινωνία τῶν θείων* (*participation of the divine*) is that species by which divine *idiomata* are predicated concerning Christ, designated by the concrete names of the human nature. "The Son of man ascending where he was before" (John 6:62); "Before Abraham was born, I am" (John 8:58); 3) *ἀντίδοσις, alternatio* or *reciprocatio* is that genus by which both the divine and the human *idiomata* are predicated concerning the concrete of the person, designated from both natures. The following may serve as examples: "Christ as concerning the flesh, who is over all, God blessed for ever" (Rom. 9:5); "Jesus Christ is the same yesterday and today, yea and forever" (Heb. 13:8); "Christ also suffered for sins once, the righteous for the unrighteous; being put to death in the flesh" (1 Peter 3:18).

It follows from this that the subject in *genus idiomaticum* may be either the concrete of the natures or the concrete name of the person, but neither the one nor the other nature in the abstract sense. We can say that God is dead or that the Son of God is dead. We can also say that Jesus is dead or that Christ is dead, but we cannot say that the divine nature is dead. In order to show which nature is immediately concerned in the predicate, although both natures are included by reason of *unio personalis*, the following *particulae discriticae* are used, viz., *ἐν*, *ἐξ*, *διά*, and *κατά*. The use of these particles does not, however, mean that it is only the designated nature that is active. In the third genus on that account there is presented *communicatio operationum*, by which the concept of *ἰδιοποίησις* in *genus idiomaticum* is made complete.

II. Genus Majestaticum. *Genus majestaticum seu auchematicum* is *that genus by which the Church declares that the Son of God really communicates the properties of the divine nature to the human nature.*

This genus is like unto the second species in *genus idiomaticum* with this difference, which is principally formal, that in the latter the real subject is the entire person of Christ, while in genus majestaticum the real subject (*subjectum cui*) is the assumed human nature.

The subject (*subjectum cui*) therefore is really the concrete of the human nature, but the concrete names of the person may also be used and sometimes also the abstract designations of the human nature. The following examples may be quoted: "There was given him (Son of man) dominion, and glory, and a kingdom" (Daniel 7:14); "And he gave him authority to execute judgment, because he is the Son of man" (John 5:27);

"The Son of man hath authority on earth to forgive sins" (Matt. 9:6); "And Jesus came to them and spake to them, saying, All authority hath been given unto me in heaven and on earth" (Matt. 28:18); "Where two or three are gathered together in my name, there am I in the midst of them" (Matt. 18:20); "Christ, in whom are all the treasures of wisdom and knowledge hidden" (Col. 2:3); "My flesh is meat indeed" (John 6:55).

These Scripture passages prove clearly that *genus majestaticum* possess a Biblical foundation. And still the Reformed Church rejects this genus, saying that all expressions in this direction are figurative. When anything is ascribed to the divine nature of Christ which is a property of the human nature, as well as the reverse, this Zwingli calls alloeosis. Luther condemned the Zwinglian doctrine of alloeosis in the strongest terms. The opponents of this genus argue that the divine *idiomata* cannot be imparted to the human nature except as the divine essence is also imparted, because the properties cannot be separated from the nature of God. However, the properties referred to, while founded in the divine essence, must nevertheless be considered as attributes *ad extra*. For this reason they can be imparted, although not in such manner as to become the essential possession of the human nature. Another objection has been made to this genus which asserts that it is one-sided and that consistency demands a reciprocity to be expressed by a genus *ταπεινοτικόν* or *κενοτικόν*. In answer it may be said that only the divine nature is active. A genus *ταπεινοτικόν* would militate against the unchangeableness of God, not to speak of the reflex action which such a genus would exercise on the doctrine of the human nature and in consequence also in relation to the validity of the atonement.

In the discussion of the doctrine of *genus majestaticum* we must not confuse the imparted *idiomata* of the divine nature with the special prerogatives of the human nature. These prerogatives surpass the most excellent gifts of men and angels, and still they are created gifts, while, on the other hand, the divine majesty which is imparted is infinite and not to be counted among finite attributes.

1. Concerning Modus Communicandi.

Concerning the manner of communication the Dogmaticians use the following terms: 1) Negative: a) non per geminationem or through duplication, so that the divine nature should possess properties and in addition to this that the human nature should come into possession of the same or similar properties; b) non transiens, so that the one nature would pass over into the other; c) non transfusiens, so that the divine properties would be poured out over the human nature in such' manner as to become the real possession of this nature; d) non acbequativus, or that the nature became alike; e) non destructivus, so that the human nature would be destroyed and only the divine nature remain thereafter. 2) Positive: a) entelechialis et perichoristicus, i. e., in an active permeating way; b) ad possessionem (with reference to possession) in regard to all the attributes, and c) ad nsurpationem (with reference to use) in regard to the relative attributes.

2. Division and Communication of the Attributes

As we recall, the Dogmaticians divide the divine attributes in many ways. We here use the division into immanent and relative attributes.

1) *Ἀνενέργητα* or the immanent are such attributes as eternity and infinity. These are imparted to the human nature of Christ mediately through the relative or operative attributes as to denomination (*ad denominationem*), as to indwelling (*ad inhabitationem*) and as to possession (*ad possessionem*), but not as to use (*ad usurpationem*), or, briefly stated, as to *κτῆσις* or possession, but not as to *χρῆσις* or use, which depends on the nature of the attributes. It is self-evident that the human nature could not become eternal, as it had a beginning from the time of conception, wherefore this attribute was imparted for possession only.

2) *Ἐνεργητικά* or the relative and operative attributes, such as power, omniscience, omnipresence, etc., were immediately imparted as to name, indwelling, possession and use or both as to *κτῆσις* and *χρῆσις*. It was because of His humiliation that the Lord used them only partly. All the attributes, both the immanent and the relative, were imparted to the

human nature of Christ at the incarnation.

As examples we would especially present the divine power, omniscience, and particularly omnipresence, although others, such as the active principle of life, could be referred to.

a) Omnipotence.—According to this genus omnipotence is imparted to the human nature of Christ both as to possession and use. The Reformed teach that only the divine nature is omnipotent. Christ used almighty power in performing miracles. We have already quoted Daniel 7:13 and Matt. 28:18. We would add: "Even as thou gavest him authority over all flesh" (John 17:2); "When the multitude saw it, they were afraid, and glorified God, who had given such authority unto men" (Matt. 9:8); "All things have been delivered unto me of my Father" (Matt. 11:27).

b) Omniscience.—The human nature of Christ also became endowed with omniscience through the divine nature. The following passages may be quoted: "Now know we that thou knowest all things, and needest not that any man should ask thee: by this we believe that thou camest forth from God" (John 16:30); "But Jesus did not trust himself unto them, for that he knew all men" (John 2:24); "When thou wast under the fig tree, I saw thee" (John 1:48); "In whom are all the treasures of wisdom and knowledge hidden" (Col. 2:3). Mark 11:32 as well as Luke 2:52 are to be explained by the doctrine of humiliation.

c) Omnipresence.—Christ received this attribute as well as the others at His incarnation. A limitation of its use naturally took place through the voluntary humiliation of Christ. The following passages throw light on the omnipresence of Christ: "Where two or three are gathered together in my name, there am I in the midst of them" (Matt. 18:20); "And lo, I am with you always, even unto the end of the world" (Matt. 28:20); "The Son of man, who is in heaven" (John 3:13); "The fulness of him that filleth all in all" (Eph. 1:23); "He that is the same also that ascended far above all the heavens, that he might fill all things" (Eph. 4:10). In case the reading, "The Son of man, who is in heaven" (John 3:13) is correct, then Christ even during the period of His humiliation was in a certain sense in heaven, but this expression is lacking in certain manuscripts. Still the same question is made clear especially in the light of *unio personalis* and *communio naturarum*. However, His human nature remained in possession of its own natural attributes, for which reason during His earthly existence He was present somewhere *circumscriptive*, and between His resurrection and ascension He was present somewhere *definitive*. His presence during the latter period, although real, was nevertheless different from His presence before His death, as may be gathered from the words: "While I was yet with you" (Luke 24:44).

Between His resurrection and ascension Christ was in one sense *definitive* present on the earth, but in another sense He was really present everywhere and therefore also in heaven. After the ascension in accordance with His human nature and on the basis of *unio personalis* in one sense or in a certain mode Christ is present *definitive* as to His whole person in heaven, but in another and just as real sense He is present *repletive* everywhere as to His whole person and therefore also according to His human nature through the divine nature. He is omnipresent as God is intensively and illocally omnipresent. God is not omnipresent in an *extensive* sense. As an absolute person His essence is such that He is omnipresent in an *intensive* and *repletive* sense, otherwise God would become a world-soul or the All. But as we must reject Pantheism and believe in a personal God, therefore we must conceive of His omnipresence in the light of the concept of His absolute personality. What is applicable to the one person in the Godhead, is likewise applicable to the other. By reason of the incarnation and on the ground of *unio personalis* we cannot exclude the human nature of Christ. Luther correctly emphasized the fact that wherever Christ is, there He is entire. His divine nature must be where His human nature is, and His human nature must be where His divine nature is, because this is a necessary consequence of the union of both natures in one person.

The old Dogmaticians had different conceptions of the omnipresence of Christ. We will again present the three different terms and explanations: 1) *omnipraesentia modificata*, by which those that held that view understood, with reference to *praesentia extima*, a powerful dominion or an operative omnipresence in the affairs of the world. In this connection they did not take into consideration *nuda adessentia,* or else they ignored it; 2) *omniprsesentia relativa seu respectiva,* by which is meant that Christ as to His human nature with reference to *praesentia extima* was present wherever He willed to be (*multivolipraesens*), or wherever He had promised to be, as in the Church or the Lord's Supper; 3) *omniprsesentia absoluta,* by which is meant a real omnipresence in a substantial and operative sense. This view is really the only one that logically agrees with the doctrine of *unio personalis.* The divine nature must necessarily possess *omnipraesentia absoluta,* whence it follows that the human nature through the divine nature must likewise be omnipresent in a substantial and operative sense. The human nature, however, has not lost its own attributes or properties and must for this reason be *definitive* present in heaven. In this sense, so far as we know, Christ has not been present on the earth since the ascension and shall not be so present until the last day. But, as stated, this does not prevent Him in another mode and as to His whole person, and therefore also as to His manhood, from being present on the earth as well as in heaven, yea, everywhere. And this presence is just as true and real as the other. The divine is not outside of the human, as the Reformed teach. They limit the human nature in a local way to heaven. But in this manner Christ is divided and the personal union is not true. Christ is present, in a definite and repletive manner. The natures are not made into one substance through mixture, nor is the one nature changed into the other, but each nature retains its own essential attributes or properties, so that they cannot become the attributes of the other. For this reason Christ must have a definitive presence as well as a divine omnipresence. This will be more easily understood when we remember that this is not a local extensive omnipresence, but as the personal God is omnipresent.

We should always keep in mind the statement of Luther that, where Christ is, there He is entire. But there are two modes, because there are two natures and yet the presence according to each mode is real. The Lutheran Church holds that the attributes of one nature of Christ do not become essentially the attributes of the other, but on account of *genus majestaticum* in accordance with the Word of God the divine nature communicates to the human nature the possession and use of omnipresence. But this does not mean a local ubiquity or expansion of the human nature. It is a presence of the human nature with the divine, being one person, according to the divine mode. Even matter may have different modes, for instance, water may be turned into ice or steam, but it is the same water. A human body may change and be the same. In the resurrection the human body will exist in a different mode, but the identity is not lost. Paul speaks of the resurrection body as a "spiritual body." When Christ rose from the dead in His spiritual and glorified body, He entered into the state of exaltation and used constantly the relative attributes imparted by the divine nature.

By the divine power the human nature and, therefore, the whole person, could be omnipresent. He is omnipresent in such a mode that belongs to the divine nature. We should not be confused by the existence and form of an ordinary human body which has had many modes in growing or developing from a tiny cell and an invisible principle. And the human soul, although penetrating and limited to the human body, is entire in every point and less dependent upon space than the body. We do not need to refer to the attributes of the resurrection body. The omnipotence of God solves the whole problem. The Triune God, who in creation made the visibles to appear from the invisibles, is also able to cause the human nature of Christ through the divine to be omnipresent in both natures or as the God-man. But on account of the attributes of the human nature Christ has also a definite presence in heaven, from whence He returns at the second Advent. Both presences are equally real.

For this reason the Formula of Concord rejects among others the following doctrines:

"That the human nature of Christ has become equal to, and like the divine nature, in its substance and essence, or in its essential properties. That the human nature of Christ is locally extended in all places of heaven and earth, which would not be ascribed even to the divine nature. That because of the property of His human nature, it is impossible for Christ to be able to be at the same time in more than one place, much less to be everywhere with his body. That Christ is present with us on earth in the Word, the sacraments and all our troubles, only according to His divinity, and this presence does not at all pertain to His human nature, according to which He has also nothing

more whatever to do with us even upon earth, since He redeemed us by His suffering and death. That the Son of God, who assumed human nature, since He has laid aside the form of a servant does not perforjn all the works of His omnipotence in, through and with His human nature, but only some, and those too only in the place where His human nature is locally."[41]

III. Genus Apotelesmaticum.

Genus Apotelesmaticum, or *communicatio operationum,* is that genus by which, in official acts, each nature does that which is peculiar to itself, the other nature participating. In accordance with this genus, therefore, every act of Christ which has reference to redemption is referred not only to the one nature to the exclusion of the other, but to the entire person of Christ or to one of the natures, the other participating. The subject, therefore, is either the concrete of the person or the concrete of the divine nature or of the human nature and sometimes also an abstract name. *Ἀποτέλεσμα* means a common work. The following examples from the Scriptures may be cited: "Christ died for our sins" (1 Cor. 15:3); cf. also Gal. 1:4; Eph. 5:2; "To this end was the Son of God manifested, that he might destroy the works of the devil" (1 John 3:8); "For the Son of man is come to save that which was lost" (Matt. 18:11); "The blood of Jesus his Son cleanseth us from all sin" (1 John 1:7).

We can therefore say that God or the Son of God suffers, although the divine nature cannot suffer, but only the human nature. The suffering of the human nature could not per se make atonement, neither could

---

[41] *The Formula of Concord,* Nos. 9, 10. 11, 13, 14. *Müller's Symb. Bücher,* p. 548, 549. *The Book of Concord,* Dr. Jacobs' English edition, p. 520.

the divine nature per se make atonement. The divine nature wills this atoning suffering, permits it, assists and strengthens the human nature. If a person is wounded, as for instance Paul, it is indeed his flesh that has been wounded, and yet, although the soul cannot be wounded in the ordinary or natural sense, we nevertheless say that Paul, or the person of Paul, has been wounded. For this reason we cannot agree to the explanation of Zwingli, who says: "The man, Jesus Christ, who at the same time is God, has suffered." The Calvinists say that *genus apotelesmaticum* cannot be counted with *communicatio idiomatum* and that both natures function each by itself without the participation of the other. On this point Luther writes the following against Zwingli: "Zwingli names it an alloeosis when anything is ascribed to the divine nature of Christ, which, nevertheless, is a property of the human nature, and the reverse. For example, where it is said in Scripture, 'Behooved it not the Christ to suffer these things, and to enter into his glory?' On this passage Zwingli triflingly comments that the term Christ refers to his human nature. Beware! beware! I say of this alloeosis, for it is a mockery of Satan, who in the end would set up a Christ whom I as a Christian would not follow, inasmuch as this alloeosis would introduce a Christ that could accomplish no more than any other saint with his suffering and his life. For if I believe that the human nature alone has suffered for me, then Christ will not be to me a Saviour of great worth."[42] Then the *Formula of Concord*, which contains many quotations from Luther, makes this observation: "From all this it is evident now that man errs who either writes or says that the expressions quoted: God suffers, God is dead, are merely *verbales praedicationes*, i. e., simply words without reality or foundation. Our simple Christian faith teaches that the Son of God, who has become man, has suffered and died for us and redeemed us with His blood."[43]

This genus and *διοποίησις* are related, but genus *apotelesmaticum* is necessary, because it emphasizes the communion of activity especially with

---

[42] Müller's *Symb. Bücher*, p. 682, 39, 40.

[43] Müller's *Symb. Bücher*, p. 684, 45.

regard to the work of salvation. *Communicatio operationum* constitutes a refutation of the positions of both Osiander and Stancarus. The former taught that Christ was our Saviour only in accordance with His divine nature, while the latter declared that it was only in accordance with His human nature. We find, therefore, that this genus has profound significance in relation to one of the cardinal doctrines of Christianity, viz., the atonement.

§19. The Two States of Christ.

By reason of the necessity of the atonement for the salvation of man and by reason of the impossibility for an ordinary man to reconcile God, therefore the Son of God must needs become man and as the God-man reconcile the world unto God. But the accomplishment of this reconciliation demanded self-renunciation or humiliation. In this connection we must note especially that the incarnation and the self-renunciation are not identical concepts, inasmuch as the divine nature was not humiliated, and the Son of God continues to be a man in His state of exaltation. The manner of the incarnation belongs to Christ's humiliation, but the self-renunciation must be more deeply conceived and is best understood when we consider what in accordance with *genus majestaticum* is imparted to the human nature. Inasmuch as the divine nature is unchangeable, therefore the self-renunciation must have reference to the human nature, which is also the case with the exaltation, although considered in the light of the union of the person. On this ground the states of Christ are two in number, viz., the state of humiliation (*status exinanitionis*) and the state of exaltation (*status exaltationis*).

I. The State of Exinanition or Humiliation.

1. The Definition of Humiliation.

Status exinanitionis is *the state of Christ in which He, as to His human nature, abstained from the continual use of the divine attributes imparted to this nature.*

König gives the following definition: "Self-renunciation is that state of the God-man in which He really but voluntarily renounced as to His human nature the plenary and uninterrupted exercise of His divine majesty, in order that He might satisfy the justice of God for the robbery committed upon our first parents in depriving them of the divine likeness.[44] Hollazius describes the state of humiliation as consisting of the following four requisites: 1) *κένωσις* or the "withholding and restraining of the full activity of the divine majesty, really imparted to Christ as a man"; 2) *λῆψις μορφῆς δούλου*, or that He took upon Himself the form of a servant; 3) *ὁμοίωσις ἀνθρώπων*, or His likeness to the poorer classes of men in birth, education, work, walk and conversation among men; 4)*ταπείνωσις ὑποστατική*, or the most humble, active and passive obedience.[45]

Before we proceed with the development of this doctrine we would consider its Scriptural foundation and direct attention especially to Phil. 2: 6, 7: "Who, existing in the form of God," or "*ὃς ἐν μορφῇ θεοῦ ὑπάρχων*." The form of God does not refer to the essence of God itself, but to the condition of glory, inasmuch as *μορφῆ* refers to the endowment or adornment of a nature. Still He was the Son of God, and when He took the form of a servant (*μορφή δούλου*), He did not lay aside the form of God, although it was only at times that He used divine attributes. He therefore continued to remain divine and in the form of God. We read further: "Counted not the being on an equality with God a thing to be grasped," Or "*ὀυχ ἁρπαγμὸν ἡγήσατο τὸ εἶναι ἴσα θεῷ*."

By this is meant that it would not have been robbery if Christ according to His human nature had made use of the divine attributes, but He voluntarily abstained from the full exercise of the attributes, as expressed in the words: "But emptied (*ἐκένωσεν*) himself, taking the form of a servant *μορφὴν δούλου*." He took the *conditio* of a servant, for *μορφή* does not refer to

---

[44] König: *"Exinanitio est status θεανθρώπου, quo secundum humanam naturam majestatis divinae uso plenario et incessante realiter, libere tamen se abdicavit, ut pro commisso in protoplastis deiformitatis raptu justitiae Dei satisfaceret."*

[45] Hollazius *Exam. Theol. Acroam.* Part III, pp. 198, 199.

the nature itself. Jesus had assumed and possessed manhood, but even in His exaltation He still possesses the human nature and shall never cease to be the God-man.

Humiliation or self-renunciation did not therefore consist in the incarnation. The subject in *incarnatio* is *λόγος ἄσαρχος*, but the subject in *exinanitio* is *λόγος ἔνσαρχος*. *Subjectum quod* is Christ; *subjectum quo* is the human nature. Self-renunciation did not consist in a complete renunciation of divinity, for in that case the personal union would have ceased, and Christ would have existed as an ordinary man. Neither can the self-renunciation imply the hidden use of the divine attributes or a *κρύψις χρήσεως* Furthermore, we cannot say that He entirely renounced the use of these attributes, inasmuch as He used them on certain occasions, as in the performance of miracles and in the institution of the Lord's Supper, when the disciples for he first time ate and drank His body and blood. Dogmaticians have adopted the following terms: *κρύψις κρήσεως* or the concealment of the possession and partly *κένωσις χρήσεως* or the self-renunciation in regard to exercise.

As already stated, the subject of exinanition is not the divine nature. The states of exinanition and exaltation do not refer to the divine nature. *Logos* is immutable inasmuch as He is God. Logos as incarnated is called Jesus Christ. Christ suffered humiliation or exinanition according to His human nature. When we consider the contents of Phil. 2:6-8, we find it stated that Christ Jesus (not *Logos*), being in the form of God, emptied Himself and took the form of a servant. As *Logos* He did not exist in the form of God, because He was essentially or by nature God. The incarnated Logos was in the form of God from the very moment of conception or incarnation and at the same instant the state of exinanition began. Christ was in the form of God throughout the whole period that He was in the form of a servant, in the likeness of men in their experiences, and was found in fashion as a man, being hungry, thirsty, sleepy, tired, etc. He had a perfect right to use the divine attributes communicated to His human nature and in such use there would have been no infringement of any divine prerogative, or a grasping after a victor's prize or loot for Himself;

but instead of doing this He emptied Himself and abstained from the full use of the divine attributes. We have already stated that He used the attributes occasionally, as in the miracles, in knowing of the death of Lazarus and at the institution of the Sacramental Supper, etc. The "form of a servant" does not mean the human nature which is exalted, inasmuch as the form of a servant has ceased. Christ will continue to be divine-human for ever and ever.

Concerning the personal union and the imparting of the majesty to the human nature the *Formula of Concord* presents the following with regard to the states of Christ: "This majesty, according to the personal union, He (Christ) always had, and yet, in the state of humiliation He abstained from it, and, on this account, truly grew in all wisdom and favor with God and men; therefore He exercised this majesty, not always, but as often as it pleased Him. Compare Epitome VIII: 11. Further in the *Solida Declaratio* VIII, 65: "At the time of the humiliation this majesty which was imparted to the human nature was concealed and withheld for the greater part."[46] In another place: "Because of this He also wrought all His miracles and manifested His divine majesty according to His pleasure, when and as He willed, and therefore not only after His resurrection and ascension, but also in the state of humiliation."[47] According to Epitome VIII: 20, we find that the *Formula of Concord* emphasizes that only the human nature was humiliated or emptied: "We reject and condemn also that the saying of Christ (Matt. 28:18), "All power is given unto me in heaven and earth" is thus interpreted and blasphemously perverted, viz., that to Christ, according to His divine nature, at the resurrection and ascension to. heaven, was restored, i. e., delivered again all power in heaven and on earth, as though, in His state of humiliation, He had also, according to His divinity, divested Himself of this and abandoned it."

The Confessions have not treated the question of self-renunciation in an exhaustive manner, indeed, the most important points have only

46 Müller's *Symb. Bücher*, VIII, p. 688, 65.

47 Müller's *Symb. Bücher,* VIII, p. 679, 25. Müller's *Symb. Bücher,* VIII, p. 550, 20.

been touched upon, but from the passages quoted above it is evident that the old conservative Dogmaticians' development of the doctrine was in accord with the tendency manifested in the Confession. The last quotation sets forth clearly that Christ according to His divine nature did not renounce any power during the period of His humiliation. Self-renunciation has reference only to the human nature. We must therefore draw the conclusion that in accordance with His divine nature He exercised the prerogatives of the divine majesty during the period of His self-renunciation. The conception of the absolute personality, which implies that God is triune, makes it clearly manifest that two of the persons could not perform the divine works independent of the third. To be sure, this is a peculiar condition, especially when we consider the implications of *unio personalis*, viz., that Christ as one person in accordance with the one nature (divine) participated in the divine activity, while in accordance with the other nature He did not so participate. On the other hand, it certainly would be an inexplicable situation if one of the persons in the divine being would for a considerable period renounce the exercise or even the possession of the divine attributes, inasmuch as such a change would create a disturbance in the life and activity of the divine being. In such case there would have been a period when God would have ceased to be triune, or as two persons would have exercised the internal and external activity of the Godhead, especially the latter. Such a position militates just as much against the doctrine of the divine essence as the Lutheran doctrine of self-renunciation seems to conflict with the doctrine of *unio personalis*, and that wherever Christ is, there He is entire. In a choice between different views from the point of view of the Christian reason, it is evident that the Lutheran doctrine of self-renunciation is the most acceptable, for it does not encounter as many difficulties as a theory that extends the self-renunciation of Christ much further. The objection has been made to the general Lutheran position that it implies a duality in His person, in so far that in accordance with the one side of His person He is omniscient, while in accordance with the other side He has renounced the exercise of this attribute. He is both omniscient and

He is not omniscient. Even if it cannot be satisfactorily explained, the assertion that the divine nature has renounced omniscience and the other attributes is just as inexplicable, if not more so. We must therefore assume that Christ, according to His divine nature, knew all things, but as He, according to His human nature, became conscious of the possession of the divine attributes, so He also according to the same nature renounced the exercise of omniscience, etc.

In order to get some idea of how Jesus Christ could be omniscient according to His divine nature and according to His human nature know only as a man, we may use some analogies or illustrations. The human mind of Christ during exinanition stood somewhat in the same relation to *Logos* or the divine nature as a prophet to the Holy Spirit, except that the divine and human natures of Christ constituted one person. The prophet would not know more of the future than the Spirit revealed. If the divine nature had continually allowed the human nature to use omniscience and all-wisdom, Jesus could not have developed as a child and grown in knowledge and wisdom. Sometimes we cannot recall things we know, but in another minute we may remember them. In the same way our subconscious mind knows things which our conscious mind is ignorant of. Sometimes in awakening from sleep the subconscious mind has the connection and we know things that we otherwise would never know. In Christ the divine nature or *Logos* was always present, but did not always become manifest and work through the human nature. The sun is often dimmed by the clouds. When Christ said that concerning the time of the last day no one knew except the Father, He still knew it according to the divine nature, but could not disclose through the human nature by the ordinary channels why it was as if unknown according to the human consciousness. But now, in the state of exaltation He knows it also according to the human nature.

Objection has likewise been made to our doctrine concerning omnipresence, since, it is said, the *Logos* as omnipresent would be distinct from the human nature, which had renounced omnipresence. Such a distinction comes in conflict with *unio personalis.* The following answer may be given:

The omnipresence of the Son of God is neither extensive nor local, the union of the human nature with the divine nature is not dependent on space, for which reason, as united with the human nature, He could be everywhere present, as God is omnipresent, without being locally, outside of the human nature and without the human nature being omnipresent during the period of humiliation through the divine nature. Indeed, the self-renunciation of Christ consisted in renouncing according to His human nature the exercise of such attributes. His *praesentia intima* of the two natures would be the same during the state of exinanition. Krauth in discussing Christ's presence answers a Reformed theologian in the following way: "He (the Reformed theologian) says: 'Before the Ascension the human nature was located on earth.' With this proposition as a positive one, we agree; but if it means that even when on earth the human nature of our Lord had no capacity of a higher presence through the divine in the one person, our Church would deny it. Our Lord speaks of Himself to Nicodemus as 'He that came down from heaven, even the Son of man which is in heaven.' The difference between our Lord on earth and in glory was not in what He had intrinsically, nor in what He had the ability to do, but in what He voluntarily exercised, or chose to forego. His humiliation consisted in the ordinary abnegation of the use of the powers which abode in Him intrinsically; but at times He chose, even on earth, to reveal that glory. He allowed the form of God to manifest itself in His transfiguration, and in His miracles, but His equality with God was none the more positive then than when His sweat, mingling with His blood, fell to the ground in Gethsemane. He moved on earth in the ordinary voluntary suspension of the exercise of His great prerogatives. While our Church, therefore, holds most firmly that His human nature was on earth locally, she denies that it had no other power of presence than the local, and that in every sense, necessarily and unchangeably, it was on earth only."[48]

We would direct attention to some Scripture passages which prove both that He was conscious of His eternal divinity during His humiliation, and

---

[48] *The Conservative Reformation and Its Theology*, p. 483.

that He was not humiliated as to His divine nature: "Know ye not that I must be in my Father's house?" (Luke 2:49); "No one hath ascended into heaven, but he that descended out of heaven, even the, Son of man, who is in heaven... For God so loved the world, that he gave his only begotten Son" (John 3: 13-16); "Jesus answered them, My Father worketh even until now, and I work" (John 5:17); "The Father loveth the Son and showeth him all things that himself doeth" (John 5:20); "I came forth and am come from God" (John 8:42); "Before Abraham was born, I am" John 8:58); "He was transfigured before them; and his face did shine as the sun" (Matt. 17:2, etc.); "We beheld his glory, glory as of the only begotten from the Father" (John 1:14); "He that hath seen me hath seen the Father" (John 14:9); "Who, existing in the form of God, counted not the being on an equality with God a thing to be grasped" (Phil. 2:6). These passages together with others clearly prove that He did not renounce the divine nature at the incarnation; nor is there any intimation that He was humiliated as to His divine nature.

That the self-renunciation is referred to the human nature is evident from the following examples: That He did not use His power, for instance, at the time of His suffering, although He revealed that power (John 18:6; 13:3); that He did not know of the location of Lazarus' grave (John 11:34), nor of the barrenness of the fig tree (Matt. 21:19), nor of the judgment day (Matt. 24:36). He renounced His operative omnipresence: "Lord, if thou hadst been here, my brother had not died" (John 11:21). He renounced divine worship according to Heb. 2:7, where it is stated that for a little while He was lower than the angels.

At times, however, He used, in accordance with the will of the Father, the divine attributes, as for instance in the miracles. Compare the following passages: Concerning Nathanael (John 1:48); concerning the life of the Samaritan woman (John 4:17, 18); concerning the death of Lazarus (John 11:11); concerning the institution of the Lord's Supper (Matt. 26: 26-28), etc.

2. The Grades of Exinanition or the State of Humiliation.

The humiliation or self-renunciation of Christ, which consisted chiefly in abstaining from the exercise of the divine majesty in regard to the human nature, is made manifest in a variety of ways by reason of His development and experiences during His earthly life, for Christ had a human history after His assumption of the form of a servant, being made in the likeness of men, and being found in fashion as a man. The various stages or grades of Christ's humiliation are the following: 1) *Conception.* The humiliation consisted in the assumption of a human nature that was conceived, because He could have become man in some other way. Neither Adam nor Eve came into being through conception. Eve belonged to the offspring of Adam, although she was not brought forth in the ordinary way; 2) *birth.* The humiliation consisted in the manner of His birth and in the humiliating external circumstances that surrounded it; 3) *circumcision.* Although He was the Master of the Law, still He subjected Himself also to the demands of the ceremonial law and fulfilled all righteousness: 4) *education,* according to which He subjected Himself to the laws of domestic life and rendered obedience; 5) *intercourse with all sorts and conditions of men,* by which He must needs bear with many things and suffer much because of the ignorance and cruel judgments of men; 6) *His great suffering,* which, particularly with regard to the manner of it, implied many insults and deep humiliation, yea, the self-renunciation in dereliction; 7) *His death,* the manner of which was also degrading; 8) *burial.* This also brought a new humiliation upon Christ, who, while sinless, must needs experience the wages of sin.

3. The New Development of the Kenosis Doctrine.

Inasmuch as the Christological question is one of the most important in Dogmatics, and inasmuch, furthermore, as the doctrine of Kenosis has been one of the burning questions in our Church, therefore it is necessary to dwell on the modern development of this doctrine. Modern Kenotism sets forth that the human nature of Christ together with the true human development is greatly denuded of its significance through the old Dogmatic doctrine of self-renunciation, which stresses the hypostatic unity, while nevertheless teaching the partial renunciation of only one nature. The Kenosis is conceived of in a more profound way, making the self-renunciation more complete, the *Logos* being humbled even according to His divine nature. To be sure, the Second Person of the Trinity did not abstain from anything essentially divine, but did renounce the divine form of being for the human mode of existence. He was still God, but His divine nature was modified as to its mode of existence and activity in order to conform to the requirements of human life. The divine attributes were present in Christ from the beginning in partial and involved form, from which a development afterwards took place. The Kenotists hold that when the *Logos* out of His free will and love withdrew to a condition of potentiality or to His innermost centrum in accordance with the will and love of the Father and the Holy Ghost, this did not act as a disturbing element in the immanent Trinity. The participation of the Son in the government of the world is not considered to be thereby disturbed in any essential, since He participates in a special way, viz., in the redemption of the world. The Kenotic view has been presented from time to time in more or less radical form, but it always implies that the divine nature, in addition to the human, renounced the use and exercise of the divine attributes, at least the relative. According to this view Christ renounced at His incarnation, even as to His divine nature, such attributes as power, omniscience and omnipresence. In answer to the question as to whether Christ would then be God, the Kenotists say that if He could not renounce such attributes, then His incarnation was an appearance merely, or else there was a contradictory duality in His mode of being. In His essence God is self-determinative and also He is absolute love. His love demanded the incarnation. In such case the other attributes could not stand in the way of love. If, in His love, He willed to become a true man, then His unchangeableness could not hinder Him from so doing, for this attribute also implied active love. Hence He could also, as to His divine nature, renounce the relative attributes during the period of His humiliation. To the objection that in such case the divine love of the *Logos* would cease in His state of humiliation, the Kenotists answer that the divine attributes were not nullified, but were preserved and reduced to such a form as would fit into the human development.

Although the modern development of the doctrine of the Kenosis from certain points of view would seem to be more natural and rational than the position of the old Lutheran Dogmaticians, still the objections to Kenotism are more powerful than those against the older orthodox view. We have already pointed out the disturbing element in the activity of the immanent Trinity, which is a consequence of the Kenotic position. Since (God is an absolute personality, who exists in three relative persons, not as three men, but self-conscious and self-determinative subjects by reason of their participation in the one self-conscious and self-determinative divine essence, so that there are not three that are separately self-conscious, nor three that are separately all-powerful, nor three that are omniscient, but one self-conscious, all-powerful and omniscient, how would it be possible for one of the persons in the Godhead in His divine capacity to renounce the divine power or any other attribute? According to the more radical Kenotists Jesus Christ becomes a mere man, according to the less radical He becomes almost exclusively a man during the period of His humiliation. Even if this would imply a transformation as to the mode of being, still the divinity has been withdrawn so far into the background that there is ample reason for the question: How could Christ perform the work of atonement with the emphasis placed so much more strongly on the human than on the divine nature, and with the latter reduced to a mere potency?

II. The State of Exaltation.

1. The Definition of Exaltation.

Status Exaltationis is *that state of Christ in which He laid aside the form of a servant and resumed, also according to His human nature, the full, general and uninterrupted exercise of the divine attributes, which He received according to His human nature at the incarnation and which He had possessed during the state of humiliation. Subjectum quod* is Christ, because on the ground of *unio personalis* we can say that Christ was exalted, but *subjectum quo* is the human nature, inasmuch as the divine nature cannot per se be exalted.

Among Scripture passages that refer to the doctrine of exaltation the following may be cited: "Thou hast made him but little lower than God, and crownest him with glory and honor. Thou makest him to have dominion over the works of thy hands; Thou hast put all things under his feet" (Ps. 8: 5, 6); "Even as thou gavest him authority over all flesh" (John 17:2); "Him did God exalt with his right hand to be a Prince and a Saviour" (Acts 5:31); "Wherefore also God highly exalted him, and gave unto him the name which is above every name" (Phil. 2: 9-11; cf. Heb. 2:7, 8).

2. The Grades of Exaltation.

The exaltation of Christ, beginning with the quickening of Christ (1 Pet. 3:18), consists of the following grades: the descent into Hades, the resurrection, the ascension and the sitting at the right hand of God.

The Lutheran Church regards 1 Peter 3:18 as the leading *sedes doctrinae* in determining the descent into Hades as the first degree in the state of exaltation, and the Reformed Church bases her view on Acts 2:27 and looks upon the descent into Hades as belonging to the state of humiliation. Note the translation in A. R. V. of Acts 2: 27, "unto Hades." It does not speak of descent.

Resurrectio interna or *ζωοποίησις* is the quickening of Christ, which denotes liberation from death and therefore the union of soul and body. The communion of the natures did not cease when Christ died. The divine nature was in communion with both soul and body, but Christ was in Paradise as to His soul or spirit, while His body rested in the grave. Compare the words of Jesus to the thief on the cross: "Today shalt thou be with me in Paradise" (Luke 23:43). Paradise was the place of the blessed in the world of the spirits or the blessed intermediate state. In that sense Christ was in Paradise until the resurrection morn. Early on Sunday morning, i. e., on the third day after His death, the quickening, or *resurrectio interna,* took place. Between death and the quickening our Lord was not in Hades or the kingdom of the dead, which in the New Testament means the place of the unbelievers in the world of the spirit or during the intermediate state. Between death and the quickening He was in the kingdom of the dead only in the sense that Paradise was the place of the blessed in that kingdom. In this connection we quote the following passage: "Neither was he left unto Hades, nor did his flesh see corruption" (Acts 2:31). Inasmuch as Christ was sinless, and the work of atonement was finished, therefore, it was not necessary that His body should see corruption. After He had been restored to life He descended to the world of unbelievers or the real kingdom of the dead.

1) *Descensus ad inferos*, or the descent to the Lower World.—The place to which He descended is called in Eph. 4:9 the lower parts of the earth or *κιτώτερα*, and in 1 Peter 3:19 prison or *φυλακή*. In His entire person Christ descended to the lower world after the quickening. The entire God-man or divine person descended into Hades according to the human nature which from the time of the quickening had spiritual properties, and, therefore, *πνέυματι*. The expression *πνέυματι* does not conflict with this, rather it strengthens the view that He descended in His entire person, for He was alive in the spirit in Paradise also. The words "made alive in the spirit" (1 Peter 3:18) have reference to the *resurrectio interna*. Through His divine power and in a divine way He betook Himself with His pneumatic body to Hades. His descent was *verus et realis*, but did not take place in a local way, humanly speaking, but *supernaturalis*. We ought, however, to observe that He descended (Eph. 4:9) to the lower parts of the earth, or as in 1 Peter 3:19, *πορευθείς*. But expressions like lower parts of the earth, prison or Hades do not explain the exact locality.

Concerning the object of the descent the Confessions declare that He overcame the devil and all his power. We quote the following from *Solida Declaratio* 9: "We simply believe that the entire person, God and man, after the burial descended into hell (*ad inferos*), conquered the devil, destroyed the power of hell (*potestam inferorum everterit*) and deprived the devil of all his might."[49] It was therefore a triumph and not a suffering of the pangs of hell. These He had suffered before His death, which is evident from

---

[49] Miiller's *Symb. Bücher*, p. 696, 697.

His words on the cross: "It is finished." In Col. 2:15 we read: "Having despoiled the principalities and the powers, he made a show of them openly, triumphing over them in it." In Rev. 1:18 Christ says: "I have the keys of death and of Hades.

With regard to the preaching spoken of in 1 Peter 3:18-20, the old Dogmaticians say that it was *verbalis* and *realis*. They furthermore characterize it as *non evangelica* but *legalis, elenchtica* and *terribilis*. To the question, "Why did Christ preach in Hades to those alone who were unbelieving at the time of Noah?" the reply is given: a) Others are not excluded, but these are presented as special examples; b) these are named in order to teach that the people before the flood should have believed in Christ according to the testimonies from the time of Adam and Enoch and especially by the preaching of Noah; c) the apostle Peter in his discussion of Baptism wished to refer to the time of Noah when the ark was built, wherein eight souls were saved through water.

Many of the more modern theologians, as well as some of the older Church Fathers, have declared that Christ also preached to those who were in the place of the blessed in the kingdom of the dead. They consider that before Christ preached in Hades it consisted of two divisions, one for the damned and the other for the blessed, the latter place called Abraham's bosom or Paradise. Christ preached first in the place of the damned and afterwards in Paradise. Those that support this view refer to 1 Peter 3:18-20 as having reference to the preaching in the place of the damned, and 1 Peter 4:6 to the preaching in Paradise. The object of the preaching in Paradise was to declare to the believers of the Old Covenant the completion of the work of salvation, liberate them from the kingdom of the dead and transfer them together with Paradise to heaven, which took place at the ascension of Christ. The proofs presented by the proponents of this theory are that in 1 Peter 4:6 the verb *ἐυανγγελίζω* used, while in 1 Peter 3:19 the verb *κηρύσσω* is used. The latter verb may include either legal or evangelical preaching, while the former means to preach the Gospel. The conclusion is therefore drawn that 1 Peter 3:19 has reference to legal preaching directed to the evil spirits and the damned, while 1 Peter

4:6 refers to the blessed declaration to the old fathers who had awaited the fulfillment of the promise. They were indeed comforted as being in the place of the blessed, but they were still in the kingdom of the dead and could not be liberated therefrom before Christ had finished the work of atonement. In further proof Eph. 4:8 is quoted, where it is stated, "When he ascended on high, he led captivity captive." In the context Paul speaks of the descent into the lower parts of the earth. The assertion is made that where these expressions are used in the Old Testament the reference is to the taking captive of friends. Compare Judges 5:12. Barak took his friends captive. Therefore the conclusion is drawn that Christ took captive His friends. He brought them with Him to heaven. This explains, it is said, why in the Old Testament the faithful believed that they went down in death, while in the New Covenant the thought is prevalent that Paradise is up in heaven. This theory, which has been briefly described, is still an open question. The Confessions do not refer to this matter. They only present the practical significance of the descent into Hades.

2) *Resurrectio externa*, or resurrection in the ordinary sense.—Hollazius defines the resurrection in the following way: "*The resurrection is the act of glorious victory by which Christ, the God-man, through the same power as that of the Father and the Holy Spirit, brought forth His body from the tomb, reunited with the soul and glorified, and by various proofs showed it alive to His disciples, for the confirmation of our peace, fellowship, joy, and hope in our own future resurrection.*"[50] The activity of Christ in the act of resurrection does not conflict with those passages which state that the Father raised up the Son from the dead, inasmuch as the doctrine of the Trinity implies that the Son was also active. The divine nature gave power to the human nature to arise. Per se the divine nature did not need to arise, but by reason of the personal union the entire person arose. *Subjectum quod* is Christ. *Subjectum quo* is the human nature, and *subjectum proximum* is the body of Christ.

The body with which Christ arose was the same body which He

[50] Hol. *Examin. Theol. Acroam.* Pars III, §1, Cap. III, p. 214.

possessed in His state of humiliation, but it was transformed, and in Phil. 3:21 it is called "the body of his glory." It was a pneumatic body with all the attributes that characterize a body of that kind. Apart from the fact that His body was not to be subject to corruption, the identity is clearly set forth in such passages as the following: Matt. 28:9; Luke 24:37-43; John 20:27; Acts 1:3. The many manifestations during the forty days clearly prove that His body was real, although pneumatic.

The proofs for the resurrection of Christ are incontrovertible and satisfying to every reasonable thinker both from the Biblical and rational standpoint.[51] There is no historical fact better attested than the resurrection of Christ. This is a comforting truth, especially when we consider the great significance of the resurrection. This significance is pointed out in such Scripture passages as the following: "If Christ hath not been raised, your faith is vain; ye are yet in your sins" (1 Cor. 15:17); "Who was delivered up for our trespasses, and was raised for our justification" (Rom. 4:25); "Begat us again unto a living hope by the resurrection of Jesus Christ from the dead" (1 Peter 1:3); "I live, ye shall live also" (John 14:19); "Knowing that he that raised up the Lord Jesus shall raise up us also with Jesus" (2 Cor. 4:14; cf. 1 Cor. 15); "As Christ was raised from the dead through the glory of the Father, so we also might walk in the newness of life" (Rom. 6:4). The resurrection, therefore, has a fundamental significance for Christianity.

3) *Ascensus in coelum.*—Hollazius defines the ascension as follows: "The ascension is the glorious act of Christ by which, after having been resuscitated, He betook Himself, according to His human nature, by a real, true and local motion, according to His voluntary determination (*per liberam oeconomian*), and in a visible manner unto the clouds, and thence in an invisible manner into the common heaven of the blessed, and to the very throne of God; so that, having triumphed over His enemies, He might occupy the kingdom of God, and reopen the closed Paradise, and

---

[51] Compare *Apologetics* by Lindberg, p. 117.

prepare a permanent inheritance for us in heaven."[52] Compare Acts 1:2, 9-11; 3:21; Eph. 4:10; Heb. 4:14. We do not interpret *δέξασθαι* in Acts 3:21 passively, as the Calvinists do, but actively, since the verb is deponent and the construction requires it, for we read *οὐρανὸν* and not *ὑπ᾽ οὐρανοῦ*. The ascension of Christ was not an *ἀφανισμός* or a disappearing, but a real ascension; neither after He had disappeared in the sky were there, humanly speaking, successive steps in a journey through all the planetary heavens till He had reached the *coelum empyreum*.

4) *Sessio ad dextram Dei.*—Hollazius defines as follows: "The sitting at the right hand of God is the highest degree of glory, in which Christ, the God-man, having been exalted, as to His human nature, to the throne of divine majesty, most powerfully and by His immediate presence governs all things which are in the kingdom of power, grace and glory, for the glory of His own name, and for the solace and safety of the afflicted Church."[53] The right hand of God is not to be construed locally, as the Reformed do, for it implies infinite dominion and therefore also omnipresence. The old Dogmaticians held various opinions concerning this *omnipraesentia*. But when we say that Christ in His state of exaltation also in accordance with His human nature possessed and exercised absolute omnipresence, this does not imply the ubiquity of the body of Christ in the sense that the Reformed misinterpret the Lutheran doctrine. Our Church teaches that in one sense the body of Christ is definitive in heaven, and that in another and just as real a sense He is omnipresent even as to His body through the divine nature, since it is impossible to divide the person of Christ. The Reformed Church teaches that Christ is omnipresent only in accordance with His divine nature. Among Bible passages that refer to Christ's sitting at the right hand of the Father we may quote the following: "So then the Lord Jesus, after he had spoken unto them, was received up into heaven, and sat down at the right hand of God" (Mark 16:19); "That he might fill all things" (Eph. 4:10); "But of which of the angels hath he said at any time,

---

[52] *Examin. Theol.* Pars III, §1, Cap. III, p. 218.

[53] *Exam. Theol.* Pars III, §1, Cap. III, p. 221.

sit thou on my right hand, till I make thine enemies the footstool of thy feet?" (Heb. 1:13); "Who is on the right hand of God, having gone into heaven; angels and authorities and powers being made subject unto him" (1 Peter 3:22).

III. Notes on the History of Dogma.

There were no real controversies concerning the states of Christ and therefore there was no dogmatic development before the period of the Reformation. The Lutheran and the Reformed Churches held divergent views also on the renunciation. The representatives of the Reformed Church did not consider that the subject of the renunciation could be the Son of God as incarnated, but the *Logos* as preexisting, since the God-man as such was not in the form of God according to the Reformed view. In a certain sense the Reformed Church considered that the renunciation referred to both natures, although the incarnation and the renunciation were almost identical. The human nature was humiliated in comparison with the subsequent exaltation. When the Lutheran Church emphasized *communicatio idiomatum*, the Reformed Church set forth the activity of the Holy Spirit on the incarnated Son. In the Lutheran Church there arose different tendencies owing to the divergent views presented by Brentz and Chemnitz. To a certain extent this explains the controversy between the Giessen and Tübingen schools. These schools both acknowledged that Christ possessed the divine attributes during the state of humiliation; the question in controversy was as to their use. The Tübingen theologians advocated a cryptic view that was related to gnostic Docetism, while the Giessen theologians supported a Kenotic conception in line with Chemnitz. But the real controversy on Kenotism belongs to more recent times, and the modern doctrine of Kenosis does not agree with the view of Chemnitz. The modern Kenotism teaches that the Son of God at His incarnation depotentiated and emptied Himself not only with regard to the divine glory, but also with regard to the mode of existence. Among advocates of the Kenotic theory may be mentioned Thomasius, Giess, Liebner, Lange, Kahnis, J. Miiller, Ebrard and Godet. Dorner criticised the Kenotic theory and presented a view of his own which implied a contradiction and stated that the incarnation was not completed before the resurrection of Jesus. This view of Dorner has not won many adherents. Many divergent theories continually make their appearance. We subjoin detailed notes on the history of dogma concerning the states of Christ and especially the renunciation.

Justin Martyr, Irenaeus, Clement of Alexandria, Origen and others taught that Jesus after His death had preached to the spirits in the spiritual world and that He had liberated the faithful of the Old Testament dispensation from the place of the blessed in the kingdom of the dead and taken them to heaven. Tertullian stated that a change had taken place through His birth, but the Son had not ceased to be what He was. Origen taught that the Son humbled Himself when He became a man, but the divine in Christ was unchanged. As *Logos* He could neither be humiliated nor exalted.

Hilary of Poitiers set forth that the *Logos* humbled Himself at the incarnation in such manner that He held back the fulness of His glory, which he calls *evacuatio*. The divine nature was not in any sense destroyed, but remained unchanged. Epiphanius and Jerome taught that Christ had descended to the lower regions of Hades only in the soul. Augutine, in presenting the doctrine of the descent into hell in his 164th letter, says that only unbelievers deny this doctrine.

Thomas Aquinas said that the descent of Christ into hell was not personal, but only the work of His spirit. Duns Scotus did not consider the doctrine of the descent into hell as Biblical.

Aepin taught that the descent into hell was the suffering of Christ. He suffered the anguish of hell. When the body of Christ lay in the grave, His soul was in Hades. Calvin set forth that the descent into hell consisted in the sufferings of Christ. Parsimonius denied that hell was a place, stating that it was merely a condition. For this reason Christ did not descend in reality, it was merely a change in condition. Beza, like Bucer before him, said that the descent was equivalent to the burial. Later on Lütkeman taught that Christ ceased to be a man when He lay in the grave.

This view conflicted with the Lutheran doctrine of *communio naturarum* as a result of *unio personalis*. With regard to the communication of the divine attributes to the human nature of Christ and also with regard to the states of Christ the Reformed Church did not sanction the Lutheran doctrine of *communicatio idiomatum* and referred the renunciation and exaltation to the two natures of Christ. The divine nature was humiliated by concealing itself under Christ's assumed form of a servant (*occultatio*). Brentz differed from Chemnitz in the doctrine of the communication of the attributes and in the use and exercise of the divine attributes in the state of humiliation. Brentz conceived of the divine attributes as having been poured out over the human nature of Christ, becoming its real possession. For this reason he spoke of an original and a derived divinity. He considered that Christ, even during the period of His humiliation, not only possessed the divine attributes, but that He also used them, such as power, omnipresence, etc , although secretly and under concealment. The Schwabian and Würtembergian theologians followed this tendency. Because of the *praesentio intima* of the human nature in the *Logos* they adopted as a necessary consequence a *praesentia extima*, although it was merely a *nuda adessentia* without a manifest and operative activity as in the state of exaltation. This view introduces a duality in the human nature of Christ and throws a Docetic glimmer on the humanity of Christ. The Saxon theologians avoided this difficulty by distinguishing between possession and exercise. Chemnitz taught that the divine attributes permeated the human nature and functioned through it as its organ. The human nature of Christ possessed the divine attributes, but it was a *retractatio*, a withdrawal of the effulgence of glory, a resting or a voluntary renunciation. Christ used the divine attributes only partially in relation to His human nature. The question of omnipresence was based on the indissoluble unity between the *Logos* and the human nature (*praesentia intima*). In accordance with His human nature Christ could be present wherever He willed to be (*multivolipraesens*). The *Formula of Concord*, which clearly sets forth the doctrine of *unio personalis* and its consequences, does not speak decisively on the question of renunciation. Undoubtedly this was dependent on the divergent views of Brentz and Chemnitz. However, the development of the doctrine takes place generally along the lines laid down in the position of Chemnitz. Kenosis has reference to the human nature of Christ. The divine nature remains in possession of and uses the divine attributes, while the human nature possesses them without using them to their full extent. This partial abstention in the use of them constitutes the renunciation or humiliation. About 1619 there arose a controversy in the Lutheran Church between the Giessen and the Tübingen schools of Theology. Thummius, Lucas Osiander and Nikolai in Tübingen taught that the possession of the attributes implied the use of them. When they spoke of *praesentia,* they declared that *extima* was a necessary result of *intima.* The communication of the attributes was reciprocal. The humiliation or renunciation of Christ consisted in His keeping secret the exercise of the attributes, which they expressed by the term *κρύψις τῆς χχρήσεως,* for which reason Christ even during the period of His humiliation and in accordance with His human nature exercised the operative attributes. Even in the manger in accordance with His human nature He was seated, although secretly, on the right hand of God. From the beginning He was omnipresent and all-powerful, etc. Later on, however, they acknowledged that there ensued a *retractatio* or withdrawal of the exercise of His divine power during the period of suffering under the High Priest. The difference between the states of humiliation and exaltation was in the mode, i. e., the one was hidden, the other open. The Giessen theologians Mentzer, Feuerhorn and Winkelmann denied this secret exercise of the attributes and rejected therefore the cryptic theory. They adopted the old Kenotic position (*κένωσις τῆς χχρήσεως*). They rejected an absolute omnipresence during the state of humiliation, but the divine nature was omnipresent. The *Logos* was active in, but not always through the human nature. They distinguished between the supernatural and illocal presence of God and His *omnipraesentia operativa.* This latter depended on the will of God. The union of the *Logos* was a *paesentia intima,* but not *extima.* The human nature possessed only the possibility of operative omnipresence. The humiliation consisted in the partial renunciation of the exercise of the attributes which depended on the will of God. But that which was a real potency during the period of renunciation manifested itself in complete activity in the state of exaltation. The *Decisio Saxonica,* pronounced by the Saxon theologians in 1624, was in the main favorable to the Giessen theologians, but the question was not treated with the necessary profundity, nor was it finally settled. Calovius and Hollazius taught that even during the state of humiliation there was a *realis adessentia ad creaturas,* but distinct from the present *operatio.*

The controversy that waxed so warm in the beginning of the 17th century has during the modern critical period again made its appearance in a new form, furnished with the scientific equipment of today. The modern Kenotic development goes beyond the views of the Giessen theologians and teaches a real abandonment of the divine attributes. The Kenotists do not indeed have the same conceptions concerning the theory, but in the main the distinction is as to the degree of renunciation. Their point of departure is the assertion, *infinitum capax est finiti.* The Kenotists pull down the infinite to the finite. The humiliation is a question of the renunciation not only of the divine glory, but also of the divine mode of existence. Among the Kenotists we name Thomasius first. He advocated a more profound conception of Kenosis than the ordinary. Humiliation did not indeed imply a renunciation of any essential elements in the divinity, but rather a renunciation of the divine mode of existence in favor of the human form of existence and eo ipso a renunciation of the divine glory. He distinguishes between the immanent and relative attributes of God and says that Christ on earth both possessed and exercised the former, but renounced both the possession and the exercise of the latter. The Kenotists like Thomasius contradict themselves in saying that Christ used the immanent attributes. But how could He use eternity in the proper sense according to His human nature? And how could He fully abstain from the relative attributes according to both natures and remain divine? The divine attributes of the *Logos* are not conceived of as made of none effect, but as it were condensed into such form as to harmonize with the true human nature. Gess was more radical in his conception. He said that before His earthly life the Son was God, but during the earthly life He was a man. Jesus was not conceived of as having a human soul besides being *Logos,* but *Logos* had become a human soul. At the incarnation the Son renounced the immanent as well as the relative attributes, i. e., His divine being. Liebner considered that the divine fulness which the Father from eternity had imparted to the Son returned to the Father at the incarnation by reason of the self-renunciation, wherefore in the beginning this fulness was outside the Son, but afterwards it returned as a gift to be appropriated by Christ during the period of His humiliation. Lange emphasized in his conception of Kenosis not so much the renunciation of the possession as of the exercise of the divine attributes. Some of the Kenotists, not to say the majority, consider that the divine attributes were present in Christ first in potential or undeveloped form, from which state they gradually developed. Julius Müller points out that Paul presents the contrast between the earthly life of Christ and His ante-temporal existence under the figure of poverty and wealth. The incarnation marked a real self-renunciation not only of the exercise, but also of the possession of the divine attributes. In Christ there was indeed a real union of a divine and a human nature, but in the beginning it was merely potential and hidden, while its full development belongs to the state of exaltation. Martensen taught a relative, yet real Kenosis. He speaks of the revelation of the *Logos* and the revelation of Christ. Kenosis belongs to the latter. The divinity was clothed in humanity. The external infinity of the divine attributes was transformed into an internal infinity in order that they might be contained within the limits of human nature. In the measure that the human nature grew, the divine nature also grew. At the same time that Christ realized the significance of His historical position, He became more and more conscious of His pre-existence and of His going forth from the Father. Dorner emphasized the opposition between the two natures to such an extent that there resulted a duality of related persons, *Logos* and Jesus, who, during the earthly life of the latter, gradually grew into each other. The incarnation was therefore a successive process. In the beginning the activity of the *Logos* had for its object the foundation of a divine-human nature (*unio naturarum*) as a basis for the personality (*unio personalis*). There was a continual development and a successive union. As the generation of the Son is eternal, so the incarnation is not momentary, but continues until its consummation in the state of exaltation, being complete at the resurrection and perfect at the ascension. Granfelt was a Kenotist. He says: "If we have been lifted up to a more living conception of the self-renunciation of the Logos as the ground of the incarnation, then it will be perfectly clear that we must refer the humiliation of Christ to His divine nature, which will then appear evident in the self-sacrificing love with which the Trinitarian Son renounced His external divine glory to become man. On the other hand, we refer the exaltation of Christ to His human nature, which through the incarnation passes successively from glory to glory until the divine nature is merely a restitution." Luthardt is also a Kenotist, and considers that the modern doctrine of Kenosis makes the earthly and historical existence of the God-man more real and comprehensible through a more profound conception of the renunciation. Philippi, however, and many others have combatted the modern theories of Kenotism and have presented the old orthodox doctrine of Kenosis.

4

Soteriology

Soteriology is that part of Dogmatics which treats of the work of Christ or the objective work of salvation. Hollazius defines *officium Christi mediatorium* as follows: "*The mediatorial office of Christ* is that function by which Christ performs the work of mediation between the aggrieved God and sinful man, in that through His blood and His death He sanctified the covenant of grace between the two, which He has ratified by declaring and offering His Gospel to sinners, while He confirms and preserves that which He has promised through His all-powerful dominion."[54] His office is therefore threefold, inasmuch as He is a prophet, priest and king. These three offices offer three different viewpoints from which to consider His work of salvation. Being distinct in the Old Testament, the three offices are united in Christ, who is the way, the truth, and the life. In such case the way signifies His priestly office, the truth His prophetic office, and the life His regal office. Christ was all in all. He is the *wisdom*, i. e., He is righteousness, implying that which is fundamental, or the priestly office; sanctification, or the prophetic office; and redemption, or the regal office. Cf. 1 Cor. 1:30. Although the high-priestly office occupies the central position among the offices of Christ, still we must exercise care lest we emphasize the one office to the

[54] *Exam. Theol. Acroam.* Pars III, §1, Cap. III, p. 182.

detriment of the others. When the prophetic office is over-emphasized it leads to Rationalism, when the priestly office is over-emphasized it leads to Mysticism, and when the regal office is over-emphasized it leads to Chiliasm. The tripartite distinction between the offices of Christ was introduced into Dogmatics by Calvin and has been used in the Lutheran Dogmatics from the time of Hafenreffer and Gerhard. To be sure, there was a time when objections were made to this division and only two offices, the sacerdotal and the regal, were named, but the threefold division is now more generally used.

§20. The Prophetic Office of Christ.

Quenstedt defines *officium* or *munus propheticum* thus: "*The prophetic office is the function of Christ, the God-man, by which He, in accordance with the purpose of the holy Trinity, fully revealed to us the divine will concerning the salvation and redemption of men, with the earnest intention that the whole world should come to the knowledge of the heavenly truth.*"[55] The prophets of the Old Testament taught, foretold future events, and performed miracles or did wonderful things. Such a prophet was Moses. In Deut. 18:15 we read that Moses said: "Jehovah thy God will raise up unto thee a prophet from the midst of thee, of thy brethren, like unto me; unto him shall ye hearken." Christ was the promised prophet. No one taught as He, since He is the Son of God. Both He Himself and His words were a divine revelation. He was the end both of the Law and the Prophets. A third great prophet after Moses and Christ cannot appear. "For the law was given through Moses; grace and truth came through Jesus Christ" (John 1:17). But Christ was in the highest sense the perfect prophet in teaching, prophecy and miracle. He also was a greater mediator. Cf. Heb. 8:6: "The

[55] Quenstedt: "*Officium propheticum est functio Christi θεανθρώπου, qua is sacrosanctae trinitatis concilio divinam de redemtione et salute hominum voluntatem sufficientissime nobis revelavit, ea seria intentione, ut in universum omnes ad agnitionem veritatis coelestis perveniant.*"

mediator of a better covenant."

The following attributes are ascribed to Christ as a prophet: 1) *the greatest prophet*; "A great prophet" (Luke 7:16); 2) *most enlightened*; "For he whom God hath sent speaketh the words of God: for he giveth not the Spirit by measure" (John 3:34); "In whom are all the treasures of wisdom and knowledge hidden" (Col. 2:3); 3) *the most authenticated*; "For him the Father, even God, hath sealed" (John 6:27). Cf Matt. 3:17; John 12:28 and other passages; 4) *the most powerful*; "A prophet in deed and word" (Luke 24:19); 5) *the most universal*; "The light which lighteth every man" (John 1:9), etc.

Christ performed and still performs the work of His prophetic office both immediately and mediately. In the former manner He labored during His earthly life. He is now no longer present in a visible manner and therefore His work is carried on immediately only through His Word in the Holy Scriptures. But He works mediately through His servants, so that the office of the ministry is the continuation of His prophetic office. We read, therefore, concerning His first disciples: "And they went forth, and preached everywhere, the Lord working with them" (Mark 16:20). Cf. Matt. 28:20; "Neither for these only do I pray, but for them also that believe on me through their word" (John 17:20); "Ye shall be my witnesses" (Acts 1:8); "We are ambassadors on behalf of Christ" (2 Cor. 5:20). The object of this prophetic activity is to impart to men the saving knowledge of Christ.

1. Christ as Teacher.

We may say that Christ was dedicated to His prophetic office as a teacher at His baptism. There are diverse opinions concerning the length of His public ministry. Some say that He labored in this office for three years or more, while others seek to prove that it lasted only one year, the gracious and acceptable year of the Lord.

As in all things, Jesus stood alone also as a teacher. Others cannot be compared to Him. During His three years as a teacher He did more than all other teachers in all time taken together. He Himself did not write a single book, and yet what He said and did was of such vast import and content that John cries out, saying: "And there are also many other things which Jesus did, the which if they should be written every one, I suppose that even the world itself would not contain the books that should be written" (John 21:25). He was not a new Moses, i.e., He was not strictly a lawgiver, but He fulfilled the Law and explained it in such a manner as to clearly prove Him a master as a teacher. Besides, whether He interpreted the Law or preached the Gospel, His words were spirit and life, principles that created a new world, truths that no human genius could have thought.

2. The Prophecies of Christ.

Many of the Old Testament prophecies concerning the Messiah were fulfilled in Christ, while the others are being fulfilled or will be fulfilled at His second coming. But Christ Himself gave utterance to prophecies that threw a clear light on the prophecies of the old prophets, that pictured briefly the history of the Church during the New Testament dispensation, and that finally set forth the future that shall take its beginning with His second advent. The eschatological addresses of our Lord are not shrouded in mystic clouds of darkness, but are clearly and plainly spoken. We feel as we read them that it is the Son of God that speaks. Many of His prophecies have already been fulfilled, such as that of the destruction of Jerusalem, the experiences of the disciples and the development of the Church. The Book of Revelation contains the revelation of Jesus Christ. In that book we hear again the prophetic voice of Jesus. He sends letters also to the churches, in which we may read briefly the history of the Church in all the world and in all time. The prophecies of Jesus Christ prove conclusively that in the foretelling of coming events He was the greatest prophet.

3. Christ as a Worker of Miracles.

Christ was Himself the greatest miracle. For this reason He performed miracles with the same ease that we perform our ordinary duties. The Scriptures make mention of only some of His miracles. We know from the testimony of the evangelists that He performed more than are related. About thirty-five miracles are described with greater or less detail. Among these are nine nature miracles, twenty-three miracles of healing, while in three the dead are raised. At the same time that the miracles bore testimony of the divine mission of Christ, they also constituted a counteraction to the destructive power of sin. If sin had not entered into the world, then man, created in the image of God, would have had dominion over the earth, while internal as well as external harmony would have prevailed. Nature was created for man, and not man for creation. Christ was the second Adam and through His miracles He made manifest the normal relationship between man and nature. The God-man set forth in the miracles what will be made manifest in the restoration. His work exerted an influence not only in the spiritual, but also in the natural world. He was the Saviour of the entire man, both body and soul, and Paul tells us that the earnest expectation of the creation waiteth for the revealing of the sons of God and the restitution of Paradise lost. Christ was indeed the greatest miracle worker both in a spiritual and an earthly sense. His miracles continue in the kingdom of grace and exert their influence in an external way, since the influence of Christianity implies the working of many miracles, so that in that way also the prophetic office of Christ is continued.

4. The Object of the Prophetic Office of Christ.

The Son of God performed the work of the prophetic office on earth and afterwards continues the same through the office of the ministry, hence the object of such activity must be very great. This object is twofold: 1) *finis proximus* or the impartation of the knowledge of the saving truth, so that all men may personally be made partakers of the content of the truth, as we read in Acts 26:18: "To open their eyes, that they may turn from darkness to light and from the power of Satan unto God"; 2) *finis ultimus* or the glory of God and the realization of His divine will that all men should be saved. In 1 Tim. 2:4 we read: "Who would have all men saved." Cf. 2 Peter 3:9.

§21. The Sacerdotal Office of Christ

The sacerdotal office of Christ or *munus sacerdotale* is *the work of Christ through which in our stead He satisfies the righteous demands of God, intercedes for us as our eternal High Priest and advocate with the Father and blesses us.*

When we compare the office of the High Priest in the Old Testament as a type with Christ as an antitype we find many similarities, but we also discover one dissimilarity of very special importance, viz., that Christ was both the High Priest and the Sacrifice. Christ was the Lamb that was led forth to the slaughter, but also the officiating Priest in the sense that He voluntarily offered Himself. Aaron must needs make sacrifices for himself, but Christ did not need to do this, because He was sinless. The priestly office of Christ was therefore wholly vicarious. The first priestly service of Aaron was performed at the altar situated at the entrance to the tabernacle. There the sacrifice was made. Then Aaron blessed the people and entered into the sanctuary. Christ also did the same after His sacrificial sufferings when He, after His resurrection, blessed His disciples before His ascension on high to enter the Holy of Holies. Concerning the entrance of Christ into the Holy of Holies the author of the letter to the Hebrews writes: "But Christ having come a high priest of the good things to come, through the greater and more perfect tabernacle, not made with hands, that is to say, not of this creation, nor yet through the blood of goats and calves, but through his own blood, entered in once for all into the holy place, having obtained eternal redemption" (Heb. 9: 11, 12). Our High Priest is there now and intercedes for us. But as Aaron came forth and blessed the people, so Christ shall come again and bless His own and shall punish the ungodly with fire. Cf. Lev. 9. Concerning the type of the great deed of Christ and His suffering on the great day of atonement or Good Friday, compare Leviticus 16. But not only Aaron and the priests of the Old Testament, or the priesthood, are types of Christ, the antitype; Melchizedek, who blessed Abraham, is also a type. Cf. Heb. 6:20-7:4. And yet, although the blessing is a part of the functions of the high priest, still the sacrificial suffering or the atonement and the intercessory prayer occupy the chief places. The blessing is poured out upon us in the kingdom of grace and will be imparted to the Church of Christ in complete measure when Christ shall come again. We shall therefore deal first with the doctrine of atonement and afterwards with the high-priestly intercessory prayer of Christ.

I. The Reconciliation or the Atonement in the General Sense.

1. The Necessity Of The Atonement.

There are some who have considered that the atonement would not be necessary in case God were the object, but such a view fails to grasp the meaning of the atonement, at the same time involving a misconception of the nature of God and man. The love of God is misinterpreted at the cost of His holiness, while the depth of human sinful corruption is overlooked. The main conception in every religion is reconciliation or atonement. Man himself feels the need of atonement. On this account all religions speak of sacrifice, and the Christian religion has realized what the other religions have sought for. Christianity is the religion of reconciliation or atonement. The special revelation of God in Christ makes clearly manifest the necessity of the atonement. Concerning this necessity the following points may be considered:

1) Man is conscious of his guilt as a sinner (both in harboring and doing sin), *reatus culpae*, and of his liability to punishment, *reatus poenae*. The fact is incontrovertible that all men, to a greater or less extent, feel that they are not what they ought to be, and for this reason fear a future retribution. The consciousness of guilt remains, although the special sin that has been committed may have been forgotten. But as man sins day by day, so the guilt increases, and even if he does not always consider, but rather forgets, that he is a debtor, still he cannot always turn a deaf ear to the warning voice of conscience. 2) The voice of conscience denotes that the will of one person has violated the will of another, which in this case can be no other than the will of God, whose Law man has transgressed. Man realizes in every sinful act that he has not only transgressed, it may be, some human law, but that he has sinned against a higher power, or God. Even the

heathen are conscious of this to a greater or less extent. Cf. Rom. 2:15: "They show the work of the law written in their hearts, their conscience bearing witness therewith, and their thoughts one with another accusing or else excusing them." 3) Inasmuch as the evil conflicts with the essence of God, therefore He reacts against it, since He is absolutely holy. Sin arouses the hatred and the wrath of God, and because the sinner and sin cannot in reality be distinguished, therefore the sinner becomes the object of the wrath of God. The following passages may be quoted: "Why doth thine anger smoke against the sheep of thy pasture?" (Ps. 74:1); "The wrath of God abideth on him" (John 3:36; cf. Rom. 2:5); "Children of wrath" (Eph. 2:3; 5:6). 4) Love does not prevent such a reaction as this, inasmuch as the character of love in the divine essence is such that He loves Himself as the Holy One. God's love cannot be separated from His holiness. God is holy love. For this reason we cannot compare the love of God with the indulgent love of sinful men, which very often is not real love, but the opposite. God is perfect in His love and just as perfect in His holiness. The one attribute cannot abrogate the other. 5) The reaction of God against sin and the sinner implies punishment, which denotes exclusion from the communion with God, or death, which has a negative side, or the loss of life, and a positive side, or damnation. The word *death* includes therefore both bodily and eternal death. 6) The sinner cannot again be received into communion with God if the demands of God's justice are not satisfied. Inasmuch as God is unchangeable not only in His love, but also in His righteousness, therefore He cannot act arbitrarily. The demands of the Law must be fulfilled, since otherwise God would not be the absolutely Holy One. There can be no compromise, for if there be any diminution of the holiness of God, which is made manifest in His punitive justice, then the love of God might be subject to diminution at the cost of some other attribute. The attributes stand in the closest relationship to each other, but in this relationship each attribute is unchangeable as to its nature and activity. 7) Man cannot satisfy the demands of God's righteousness; hence there would be no salvation, if God had not in His great love prepared the way of salvation. This inability of man is clearly presented in the

Word of God and is confirmed in the personal experience of man. The love of God, revealed in the sending of His Son, is presented in many places, as in John 3:16; Rom. 8:3, 32; 1 John 4:10, etc. This proves the evident necessity of the atonement. 8) The sending of the Son was the only way in which God could combine His love and righteousness in relation to man. If God had not been absolutely holy, then salvation could have been accomplished without the atoning work of Christ. In that case God could in His goodness like an indulgent father have granted to men the privileges that they had forfeited through sin. But the love of God was an absolutely holy love, and for this reason an atonement became necessary. The atonement was needed, and in His goodness God willed the salvation of men. Inasmuch as man could not make atonement, God sent His Son. There was no other way. In this manner both the love of God and His righteousness as justice were satisfied in relation to man.

2. The Subject of the Reconciliation or Atonement.

The subject of the atonement is God. It may seem strange that God is both the subject and the object, but inasmuch as man could not make satisfaction, and furthermore, since the atonement was absolutely necessary, therefore God Himself in His great love brought about the work of reconciliation between Himself and mankind. Although the sending of the Son is specially ascribed to the Father, still the Son was willing to be sent. *Opera oeconomica* are indeed *minus indivisa* in comparison with *opera attributiva,* which are *indivisa,* but all *opera ad extra* are still in a sense *indivisa* or *communia.* Therefore God is the subject as a Trinity, although the Father is especially named as the subject when we consider the content of John 3:16, where it is stated that God as the Father gave His only begotten Son. Compare Rom. 8:32, where we read: "He that spared not his own Son." Compare also the high priestly intercessory prayer of Christ in John 17, where He prays to His Father. In 2 Cor. 5:17, 19, we read that God reconciled.

3. The Concept of the Reconciliation or Atonement.

Reconciliatio (καταλαγγή,[56] Versöhnung, forsöning), which comprises and constitutes the result of *satisfactio* and *expiatio*, denotes the objective restoration of the original relationship between God and the human race that had been disturbed and nullified through sin. Atonement means the relationship of peace, since the reaction of the justice of God against sin or the wrath of God has been appeased, so that it is possible for God without violating His justice to be gracious toward sinners. For this reason the following assertion is true: Christ has reconciled God to the world and the world has through Christ been reconciled to God.[57] The atonement is also called redemption (ἀπολύτρωσις), but in that case the satisfaction of Christ is considered more especially in relation to man, as to how he was redeemed from the power of sin and Satan to God. The two elements that enter into reconciliation are *satisfactio* and *expiatio*. These terms seem indeed to express the same thing, so that *satisfactio* denotes *expiatio* and vice versa, but *expiatio* implies more than *satisfactio*. The definition of reconciliation would not be complete with *satisfactio*. The two terms complement each other, rendering the conception more perfect.

1) *Satisfactio* (satisfaction, Genugthuung, tillfyllestgörelse) *is that part of the high-priestly work of salvation of Jesus Christ through which in our stead He fulfilled the demands of the divine righteousness by means of His active and passive obedience.* The two terms that are employed to characterize *satisfactio* are therefore the following: a) *obedientia activa*, which consisted in the most perfect fulfillment of the Law in our stead, with the result that those who believe in Christ are liberated from the guilt of sin; b) *obedientia passiva*, which is *satisfactio* in the sense that Christ suffered the punishment of sin in our stead, so that the believers are liberated from the punitive suffering on account of sin. His satisfaction or vicarious obedience was

---

56 "*καταλαγγή*; (reconciliation), the exchange effected, then the reconciliation. Agreeably to the use of *καταλάσσειν*, it denotes the result of the divine act of salvation, to wit, the new molding of the relation in which the world stands to God as far as it no longer remains the object of this wrath, and He no longer stands to it as an ἀντίδος." Cremer's Lexicon (4th Engl. Ed.), p. 93.

57 Compare Thomasius, *Christi Person und Werk*, Dritte Auflage, §57, p. 79.

sufficient for all, but application by faith in Him was necessary. Among Scripture passages that refer to the obedience of Christ the following may be noted: "For as through the one man's disobedience the many were made sinners, even so through the obedience of the one shall the many be made righteous" (Rom. 5:19); "One died for all" (2 Cor. 5:14); "Who his own self bare our sins in his body upon the tree" (1 Peter 2:24; cf. Isa. 53:5); "Christ also suffered for our sins once, the righteous for the unrighteous" (1 Peter 3:18). The whole life of Christ was one of active and passive obedience, although His suffering culminated toward the end. He not only suffered for our sins, that we might be liberated from punishment; through His active obedience He procured a righteousness which He Himself did not need, and which therefore redounded to the benefit of mankind in the determined way. This righteousness was the fruit of His active and passive obedience. The wages of sin was eternal death. The death of Christ was therefore a vicarious death as a punishment for the sin of man. In Heb. 2:9 we read: "By the grace of God he should taste of death for every man." This could not have been done, had He not borne the sins of the world. It is not necessary to cite the many passages which present this matter. However, compare *χωρίς ἁμαρτίας* in Heb. 9:28 and 4:15. From this it is plainly evident that He Himself was sinless, and still had sin, the sin of others. Therefore He suffered for our sins and was obedient unto death, the death of the cross. Jesus Christ was made to be both *ἁμαρτία* and *κατάρα* for us. Compare 2 Cor. 5:21; Gal. 3:13. Being sinless Himself He could satisfy the divine demands. His satisfaction as to its active and passive obedience possessed valid power, so that He was our *λύτρον* or *kopher*. According to the Hebrew idiom it is he that pays, or he for whom the ransom is paid, that is covered with the price. Inasmuch as Christ Himself was sinless, but bore our guilt, therefore He became our Redeemer, and inasmuch as He was covered through His satisfaction, therefore it was really we that were covered. This means that God considers the whole transaction objectively as if the satisfaction had been performed by man. By reason of this *kopher* the state of guilt was annulled and the punishment inhibited. Christ blotted out the bond

(Col. 2:14) that was against us, which implied both guilt and punishment. With regard to the two terms used to describe *satisfactio*, they must not be separated, since they stand in the closest possible relation to each other, so that the *obedientia passiva* was also active (*obedientia activa*) and the *obedientia activa* was also passive (*obedientia passiva*).

2) *Expiatio* (*kippurim*, *ἱλασμός*, Sühnung, atonement, expiation) is *not only satisfaction but propitiation and expresses the modus of the atonement as the voluntary self sacrifice of Christ throughout the whole of His life as an atoning sacrifice, implying the voluntary suffering of the wrath of God by reason of sin, causing indescribable and intensive anguish or passion, which at the same time constituted the greatest deed*. As will be observed, the ethical element enters here, so that Christ not only suffered the punishment of sin and fulfilled the demands of the Law, but of His own volition He performed the work of reconciliation with the right spirit, the spirit of an absolutely righteous person, who offers Himself as a sacrifice to reconcile the sins of humanity. For this reason the sacrifice of Christ became not only a satisfaction, but also a satisfying atonement and an atoning satisfaction. This is expressed in the Hebrew *kippurim*, which comes from the verb *kipper*, to cover. That which is covered is sin and therefore also the sinner. In this manner the guilt is blotted out or paid. The atoning sacrifice of Christ explains therefore how God can be both *δίκαιος* and *δικαιῶν*, So that He is able without nullifying His righteousness or justice to love and save the sinner in the determined way. Some one has said that *satisfactio et expiatio vicaria* is the "*ἕυρηκα*" of the great and holy love of God.

The sufferings of Christ were not of a calamitous nature, as the reason for this suffering was not secret, neither were they disciplinary, as He had done no wrong. His sufferings were vicariously retributive. If He also suffered as a martyr, that was not the real reason why He suffered and died His suffering was a punishment for our sins. He suffered both physically and mentally. The physical pain He endured was extraordinary, but His mental suffering in the soul is inexplicable, having no parallel in human consciousness.

When Christ as the atoning sacrifice suffered the punishment of sin, He endured in His soul the anguish of hell, which the Dogmaticians express in Latin terms as follows: *poenae infernales, poenae damnatorum, mors seterna cum doloribus, angoribus et cruciatibus infernalibus.* This He suffered in the Garden of Gethsemane and especially on the cross, where His sufferings reached their culmination in the *derelictio.* This suffering is not to be considered extensive as to time, but intensive. Christ bore in death the punishment which our sins had deserved, so that He suffered the eternal punishment in our stead. He suffered the eternal punishment in an eternally intensive way. The *derelictio,* or the consciousness of being forsaken by God, expresses the culmination as well as the nature of the eternal suffering. The strong crying of Jesus as being forsaken by God was not a sentimental outcry by reason of great bodily pain or soul anguish; it was caused by the realizing sense of being actually forsaken, although not in the absolute sense. The dereliction went as far as it was possible without really severing the ties that bound the Father and Son together. The Son experienced the judgment on sin in all its terrible reality. Philippi endeavors to explain the suffering as intensive in such manner that men sinned against an infinite God and were therefore in accordance with the retributive justice of God adjudged guilty of an intensive and infinite punishment.[58] But as finite creatures they could not endure such a punishment, and its infliction would have annihilated them. For this reason God changed the intensive and infinite punishment to an extensive and infinite. But Christ as divine was capable of suffering the originally decreed intensive punishment, for which reason He did not need to suffer extensively as to time. Björling criticised partly the explanation of Philippi in the following way: "This view overlooks the fact that the spirit of man, while created and individual, and in this sense finite, is nevertheless a partaker of the infinity of God, because he is created in the image of God. Sin is in itself intensively infinite and the punishment of sin has therefore also the same property. Nothing can be taken from this intensive infinity of the punishment to be replaced by an extensive infinity, and since Christ

---

[58] *Glaubenslehre,* 2 Aufl., IV, 2, pp. 30-33.

in love to us took upon Himself in our stead the guilt and punishment of sin in order to satisfy the holiness and justice of God, He took this upon Himself in the same manner as it must be experienced by sinful men, both in an intensive and extensive way."[59] But the solution is to be found in the fact that the question concerns states or conditions that partake of eternity, and mathematical calculations are not necessary. The infinite worth of the person of Jesus, eternal in His essence, implies a character who made perfect satisfaction. The fall into sin and our disobedience are in reality finite, but infinite in guilt, because the transgression is committed against an infinite absolute personality. The active and the passive obedience of Christ together with His death were momentary as to time or *finitae*, but as to merit they are *infinitae*.

The Socinians claim that Christ could not suffer the eternal punishments, nor was it necessary, as God did not require a vicarious atonement. They evidently had a wrong conception of eternity as it would affect the God-man, for they denied His real divinity and only ascribed to Him a titular divinity. According to the Socinian view Christ only suffered as a martyr. There are others who hold that Christ should have suffered as the damned, extensively, and since this was not the case, they claim that He did not suffer eternal punishments. These persons think that God is reconciled by the endless punishments. The condemned cannot reconcile God's justice by their punishments. They rejected the vicarious atonement of Christ and are in a condition where conversion is not possible. Only Christ was able to reconcile God. His intensive and complete satisfaction and expiation or propitiation satisfied the demands of the holiness, righteousness and justice of God. We should not speculate in regard to the mode as to how Christ experienced hell's torments, but be assured from the Scriptures that He fulfilled the Law in our stead and that He suffered fully what was required to appease the justice and wrath of God. If the sufferings were not identical, they were equivalent and of greater value intrinsically. If a person receives a loan in ragged paper

[59] Björlings dogmatik, second part, third div., p. 178.

money and pays it back in shining gold, it is at least fully equivalent. When Christ, who could experience a timeless existence, offered Himself as a ransom and suffered intensely, we should not discuss identical modes of punishment. When God was satisfied, we should not make mathematical calculations. What Christ did can never be estimated.

We would call attention to the following Scripture passages: "Take thy censer, and put fire therein from off the altar, and lay incense thereon, and carry it quickly unto the congregation, and make atonement for them" (Numbers 16:46). The means of atonement steps between the wrath of God and the people. Compare Lev. 16 concerning the atonement on the great day of atonement. "The life of the flesh is in the blood; and I have given it to you upon the altar to make atonement for your souls: for it is the blood that maketh atonement by reason of the life" (Lev. 17:11). In like manner Christ was offered on the altar of the cross, and His blood became an atonement. Christ became the perfect antitype of the principal sacrifices: the sin-offering implied *expiatio,* the trespass-offering *indemnificatio,* the burnt-offering *oblatio,* the peace-offering *conciliatio.* The same holds with regard to the offering of the covenant in Ex. 24, the offering of consecration in Lev. 8, and the offering of the Passover, since Christ is our Passover (1 Cor. 5:7). He suffered in silence and willingly. Cf. Isa. 53. Christ foretold His own suffering and did not spare Himself, as He could have done. In Phil. 2:8 we read that He was "obedient even unto death, yea, the death of the cross." *Expiatio* or *ἱλασμός* is used for atonement in 1 John 2:2: "He is the propitiation for our sins." Compare also Heb. 5:7, 8, which speaks of His suffering and obedience, implying as a prerequisite a voluntary sacrifice of Himself. "Christ suffered for sins once" (1 Peter 3:18). That the one sacrifice was sufficient, so that Christ did not need to suffer extensively as to time, is evident in the light of Heb. 9:25, 26: "Nor yet that he should offer himself often, as the high priest entereth into the holy place year by year with blood not his own; else must he often have suffered since the foundation of the world: but now once at the end of the ages hath he been manifested to put away sin by the sacrifice of himself."

4. The Attributes of the Reconciliation or Atonement.

We ascribe to satisfaction and the atonement or expiation the following attributes: 1) *vicaria* or vicarious. If it be formally regarded there is required: a) a surrogation by which some one else is substituted for a debtor, with the understanding that the debt is charged to the surrogate or substitute; b) a payment of the debt or penalties. The Socinians objected to the vicarious atonement and stated that the act of one man cannot be the act of another. But an act may be considered from a physical and a moral standpoint. From the latter point of view an imputation may take place. The question must not be considered from the mathematical standpoint, but in a dynamic way. The idea of substitution is not a foreign one in the conditions of human life. A father, a mother, and others, often act vicariously. The one person often does that which another ought to do. The opponents of the doctrine of *satisfactio et expiatio vicaria* argue that if Christ has died in the stead of all, then no one should be damned by God, or if Christ has paid the debt, then God cannot enforce repayment. But this objection embodies a misinterpretation of the conditions that obtain in the moral world and in the realm of freedom. While an objective atonement has been accomplished, still God cannot arbitrarily force anyone to become subjectively reconciled to Him. The debt is not a monetary one, although the terms used are mercenary. Furthermore, with regard to the objection that no one ought to die, since Christ has died for us all, real death is not the bodily death, but the spiritual and the eternal death. The believers themselves, who have been reconciled in the subjective sense, are subject to bodily death, provided Christ does not in the meantime return, when the Christians will not be unclothed, but clothed upon, that what is mortal may be swallowed up of life (2 Cor. 5:4). But those who will not obey the laws in the moral world must suffer eternal death, in spite of the vicarious death of Christ, because they have not fulfilled the conditions of subjective salvation. Under such conditions God deals with perfect justice, inasmuch as such persons have rejected the reconciliation of Christ and have themselves chosen death. Furthermore, the objection has been raised that God could not impute our debts to Christ, who was guiltless. But Christ voluntarily assumed the guilt of our sin. The Scriptures declare most plainly that the death of Christ was vicarious. In Matt. 20:28 we read that "the Son of man came to minister, and to give his life a ransom for many (*λύτρον αντὶ πολλών*)." The expression reads therefore, ransom instead of many. Cf. 1 Tim. 2:6: "Ransom for all (*ἀντίλυτρον ὑπὲρ παντῶν*)." The idea of substitution is also seen in the translation of the Hebrew *kopher* by *λύτρον* in the Septuagint. Therefore the Lord gave His life in the stead of the many. Cf. John 6:51; 10:11. *Ὑπὲρ* does not nullify the meaning of *αντὶ*, rather it strengthens it and complements the sense, so that while it was done "instead of," it also was done "in favor of." Doctrines are fortified and explained through the analogy of faith. In 2 Cor. 5:19 we read: "Not reckoning unto them their trespasses," having imputed them to Christ, in accordance with verse 21, "Him who knew no sin he made to be sin on our behalf." Could the substitution be more clearly expressed? Compare Gal. 3:13; Eph. 1:7; Col. 2:14. In 1 Peter 2:24 we read: "Who his own self bare our sins in his body upon the tree." The expression *ἀνήνεγκεν* corresponds to the same verb used in the translation of Isa. 53 in the Septuagint. Cf. Heb. 9:28. We ought also to remember that Christ is the head of the race, that He is the second Adam, the Son of man, and therefore by reason of His organic relationship with humanity He can act in the stead of men. Compare Rom. 5:12-19; 3:25 (*ἱλαστήριον*). The Greek word corresponds to the Hebrew (transliterated into English) *kapporeth*, from *kaphar*, to cover. We will quote the following passages: "Whom God set forth to be a propitiation, through faith, in his blood, to show his righteousness because of the passing over of the sins done aforetime, in the forbearance of God" (Rom. 3:25); "Having a golden altar of incense, and the ark of the covenant overlaid round about with gold, wherein was...the tables of the covenant, and above it the cherubim of glory overshadowing the mercy seat" (Heb. 9:4, 5). Notice propitiation and mercy seat! The *kapporeth* became the propitiation and mercy seat covering the tablets of the Law as the Law accuses the sinner. The blood of the atonement was sprinkled upon the *kapporeth* which, therefore, was called the mercy seat. The sins of which the sinner was accused were covered by the blood in order that God should not see the sins and the sinner. This means that God was propitiated or reconciled. 2) *Universalis,* i. e., that it was an atonement for all. This term is used against the Calvinists, who teach that Christ died only for the elect. 3) *Sufficientissima et consummatissima,* because the atonement was in the complete sense of the word sufficient and perfect.

5. The Object of Reconciliation.

The object of the reconciliation may be presented from three points of view: a) *objectum proprium* is God, the Triune, but by reason of *opera oeconomica* in the doctrine of the Trinity, the *objectum proprium* is especially the Father; b) *objectum personale* is humanity or the world; c) *objectum reale* is sin, both *peccatum originale* and *peccata actualia.* However, the last two conceptions include the first, so that, strictly speaking, God is the object of the objective reconciliation.

There have been and still are Socinian tendencies that deny that God is the object of the reconciliation. Among other reasons advanced in defense of the Socinian position, it is stated that nowhere in Scripture is it said that God is reconciled. Of course they say that God is love and did not need to be reconciled. Either they ignore the justice of God or else they confuse His justice with His love. But even if the expression is not found in the Bible, still the substance is there. The word justice cannot be translated by love or any of its synonyms. In this connection we would call attention to the content of Heb. 2:17, where we read ἱλάσκεσθαι τὰς ἁμαρτίας. In the classical Greek the verb is used only with the gods as an object, but is not so used either in the Septuagint or the New Testament. The reason is evident when we consider the meaning of the corresponding Hebrew word *kipper,* which means *tegere* or *abstergere,* since it cannot properly be said that God is covered, but that the atonement covers the sinner before God. But if the atoning sacrifice intervenes between the wrath of God and the sinner, so that the sinner is covered, then in reality it is equivalent to the reconciliation of God. Since Christ has become the propitiation for our sins, therefore a sinner may cry out in supplication: "God, be thou merciful to me, a sinner!" Christ is also called our Advocate with the Father. The sacrifices in the Old Testament were offered before the Lord as a sweet savor. Cf. Lev. 1:9. Also cf. Eph. 5:2: "Christ also loved you, and gave himself up for us, an offering and a sacrifice to God for an odor of a sweet smell." Also Heb. 8:12: "I will be merciful to their iniquities." In comparing such passages as those quoted with Rom. 5:9, 10; 2 Cor. 5:18, 19, etc., it becomes clearly evident to every conscientious reader of the Bible that God is the object of the atonement, and not only the world or the sins of men.

The Socinians and other advocates of the Moral Theory claim that there was no need of propitiating God, as He loved mankind and was desirous of convincing every human being of this fact, and that no atonement was necessary. According to them Christ was only a man. Our doctrine of the atonement rests upon the fact that Christ was both human and divine. If Christ had been a sinless man only, God, being just, would not have punished the innocent instead of the guilty, and if He had done so, no redemption would have resulted. No human could have removed the guilt of the world. If a creature had suffered for the sins of the world in an atoning sense, God would not have made any sacrifice, but we remember the statement in Rom. 8:32, "He that spared not his own Son, but delivered him up for us all," which proves the great sacrifice of God. Some imagine that God has no feeling, because emotions would interfere with His blessedness. His love, justice and other attributes prove that He has feelings, but His intrinsic blessedness is not disturbed by the various emotions. Vicarious atonement is supreme proof of the most intense love and justice. The offended God sends His own Son to be incarnated to atone for the sins of the world. God does not only demand atonement, but offers the atonement Himself. "Herein is love, not that we loved God, but that he loved us, and sent his Son to be the propitiation for our sins." This proves the absolute requirement of reconciling God. It is evident that atonement was necessary and that God was the object of propitiation.

6. The Effects of the Reconciliation or the Atonement.

Briefly stated, it may be said that the *effectus* of the reconciliation is the merit of Christ with all that is implied therein, which He has gained for our benefit, inasmuch as He did not need it for His own sake. In Eph. 1:7 we therefore read: "In whom we have our redemption through his blood, the forgiveness of our trespasses, according to the riches of his grace." In an objective sense the debt has been paid, and redemption as a reconciliation has been completed. In this sense we have been redeemed from sin, death and the devil. This Christ has done and can therefore bestow His merit which has been secured for all men. Cf. Rom. 5: 8-18. We may also say that in principle the power of sin has been broken. Cf. Rom. 7:4: "Ye were made dead to the law through the body of Christ"; Titus 2:14: "Who gave himself for us, that he might redeem us from all iniquity, and purify unto himself a people for his own possession." In principle death is also conquered. Cf. Heb. 2:15: "And might deliver all them who through fear of death were all their lifetime subject to bondage." In the same sense He also overcame the devil. Cf. Heb. 2:14, etc. But the great significance of the merit of Christ shall appear more clearly when redemption in a practical sense is completed. The Lamb, who purchased unto God with His blood men of every tribe, and tongue, and people and nation, shall alone be worthy to open the book with the seven seals. Cf. Rev. 5.

The great vicarious work of Christ was finished on Calvary, when He cried: "It is finished," John 19:30. The objective reconciliation, including satisfaction and atonement, was then completed. But the same Christ will also be the Redeemer in the practical sense, and the word will go forth: It is done! Compare Rev. 16:17. The transactions leading up to this event are depicted in the seven seals, the seven trumpets and the seven bowls. In Rev. 5 the Saviour is called the Lamb on account of His work on Calvary and He is called the Lion in reference to His final redemptive work at the Second Advent. The book with seven seals and the events connected in the symbolism transfer us to the life of the Old Testament, when properties were lost and mortgage deeds were given in the form of book-rolls. One of these books or mortgages (as there were two copies) was closed by seals and contained specifications and conditions of redemption. Opening the seals was a symbol of buying back. A relative who would buy back or redeem such a mortgage roll was called *Goel* or redeemer.[60] When we transfer the figurative language in this case, the lost property is Paradise and Christ is the *Goel* or Redeemer who can change Paradise lost to Paradise regained. The opening of the seals means many conflicts and troubles to dispossess the princes of the evil world and the Prince of darkness, who have taken unlawful possession of the property of God and His people. Besides, there is a constant appeal to individuals to take interest in the kingdom of God. The objective reconciliation has as its aim the subjective. In 2 Cor. 5:20 we read: "We beseech you on behalf of Christ, be ye reconciled to God." In God's own time the final redemption will be realized. Rev. 10 describes one of the grand scenes in taking final possession. And in the seventh verse we read: "In the days of the voice of the seventh angel, when he is about to sound, then is finished the mystery of God.

II. Concerning the High-Priestly Intercessory Prayer of Christ.

Hollazius defines intercession as follows: "*Intercession is the second act in the sacerdotal office of Christ, through which Christ the God-man, on the ground of His infinite merit, really and properly intercedes for all men and especially for His elect, without in the least diminishing His majesty, to the end that He might obtain for them whatsoever things He knows to be salutary for them in a temporal and especially in a spiritual sense.*"[61]

The nature of intercession is more particularly defined by the following negative and positive terms: a) *negative*: 1) *non nuda interpretativa,* as though Christ interceded for us not by real prayers, but by His merit alone; 2) *non σαρκικῶς seu δουλικῶς,* so that He as a suppliant upon His knees and with outstretched hands should make a vocal outcry for mercy, inasmuch as this would conflict with His exalted and glorified state; b)

[60] Compare Seiss, *The Apocalypse,* Chap. 5, Lecture 10.

[61] *Exam. Theol. Acroam.* Pars III, §1, Cap. III, p. 182.

positive: 1) *realis,* inasmuch as He really prays for us; 2) *vocalis,* since He intercedes audibly or with words; 3) *θεοπρεπῶς*, or in a manner befitting the Son of God; 4) *specialis,* since He prays especially for the elect; 5) *generalis,* since He prays for all that still are in the kingdom of Grace.

The following passages may be observed: "It is Jesus Christ that died, yea rather, that was raised from the dead, who is at the right hand of God, who also maketh intercession' for us" (Rom. 8:34); "He ever liveth to make intercession for them" (Heb. 7:25); "A priest for ever" (Heb. 7:17); "I will pray the Father for you" (John 16:26; cf. John 17; also John 14:16); "An Advocate with the Father" (1 John 2:1). There is a temple of God in heaven. Cf. Rev. 11:19; Heb. 8:1-5. Dogmaticians differ as to whether the intercession of Christ shall continue through eternity or cease at the last judgment when Christ shall deliver up the kingdom of God. Quenstedt believes that the intercession will continue through eternity, because Christ is a Priest for ever. On the other hand, Luther said that intercession would continue until the end of the world. The Lord Jesus Christ is indeed a Priest and a King for ever, so that even after the consummation He is considered as the eternal High Priest, but intercession in the real sense will no longer be needed after the words of 1 Cor. 15:24 have been fulfilled. The work will then have been finished both in a juridical and an actual sense, and the blessed will forever have inherited all the results of the reconciliation.

Dogmaticians have also directed attention to Rom. 8:26: "The Spirit himself maketh intercession for us with groanings which cannot be uttered." Cf. verse 27. On the basis of these passages some have considered that the Holy Ghost also intercedes for us, but Quenstedt interprets these words to mean that the Holy Ghost merely urges us to pray, teaches us to pray, and assists us, as it were, dynamically, to formulate our prayers. Quenstedt does not use the word dynamically, but the sense is the same. He also says: "The one intercession, i. e., that of Christ, is *θεανθρωπική*, the other is merely *θεική*. The one is mediatorial; the other is not. The intercession of Christ is founded upon His suffering and death, which cannot be said of the intercession of the Holy Ghost."

Notes on the History of Dogma.

In the earliest period there was no formulation of the doctrine of reconciliation, and yet reconciliation occupied the central position in the teaching of the Church. The frequently recurring celebrations of the Lord's Supper prove that the majority of the Christians emphasized the atonement. In the Apologetic period and partly in the Polemic period it was asserted that the ransom was paid to Satan. The significance of the death of Christ was set forth from three points of view: as a redemption from death and the devil, as a reconciliation with God through sacrifice, and as a means to reach everlasting life. Irenaeus presented the so-called theory of "recapitulation." Gregory of Nazianzus rejected the theory that the ransom was paid to Satan and declared that it was paid to God. Even during the Scholastic period the old theory was still advocated that the ransom was paid to Satan. But during this period the following theories of reconciliation appeared: The theory of Anselm, the moral theory of Abelard, the doctrine of "*satisfactio superabundans*" of Thomas Aquinas together with the "acceptation theory" of Duns Scotus. Among these theories that of Anselm, in spite of its defects, occupies the most prominent place. Abelard and Duns Scotus were forerunners of Calvinism, teaching, as they did, that Christ died only for the elect. Among the mystics the teachings of Gerson, Tauler and John Wessel approached the doctrines of the Church, while others, such as Weigel, Böhme and Denk departed from and rejected the orthodox doctrine of satisfaction. During the period of the Reformation the doctrine of the atonement was presented especially by the Lutheran Reformers in a very complete way. The Scriptural immediacy of the Apostolic period again makes its appearance, while the internal experience of the infinite guilt of sin and the wrath of God upon the sinner prepares the way for a more profound conception of the objective reconciliation and redemption from the power of sin, death and the devil. The relationship between the love and justice of God is clearly set forth. Christ bore all our sins and the wrath of God. The two natures of Christ participated in the atonement. The active and passive obedience of Christ are presented. God was reconciled through the vicarious satisfaction of Christ. The doctrine of the Reformed Church suffers from the influence of the doctrine of predestination. After the Reformation had sown the seeds of life-giving truth, Socinianism began to sow tares. They rejected all the essential points in the Church's doctrine of satisfaction. The Arminians followed partly in their footsteps and advocated the "acceptation theory." Hugo Grotius set forth the so-called "government theory," in accordance with which God as a regent inflicted the punishment of our sin on the Son as a warning example. The Supranaturalists presented the atonement in a heretical way and considered that satisfaction was the most suitable way. Philosophical Rationalism advocated the theory of self-atonement. The vulgar Rationalists, of course, rejected the doctrine of the Church. Hegelianism presents the self-atonement of God in accordance with the tenets of Pantheism. Schleiermacher rejected the orthodox doctrine of atonement and emphasized a subjective redemption, which he placed before the atonement. The atonement becomes a subjective state in man. Von Hofmann set forth the so-called "mystical theory," which presents the organic union of Christ with the human race, so that we were reconciled to God, not through Christ, but in Him. He therefore denies the vicarious suffering of Christ. Maurice and Bushnell resurrected the old moral theory. The Hofmann theory has been refuted by Thomasius, Delitzsch and others. Ritschlianism places justification before reconciliation and rejects the orthodox theory of atonement altogether. There have been many, however, who have powerfully refuted the empty doctrine of atonement that Ritschlianism set forth and have presented the juridical doctrine of reconciliation. Many of the recent theologians would substitute the ethical theory of atonement for the juridical conception of punishment, but the conservative Lutheran theologians have indeed presented Sühne and consequently the ethical element, but not at the cost of the conception of the suffering and punishment from the juridical standpoint, rather they have harmonized the two conceptions. We now pass to the more detailed consideration of the development of the doctrine through the various periods.

Clement of Rome says that Christ gave His blood for us, and in accordance with his presentation it is evident that he taught that the death of Christ was vicarious. Ignatius says that Christ was a sacrifice offered to God in our stead.

Justin Martyr sets forth, somewhat obscurely, perhaps, the vicarious death of Jesus. He says that Satan was overcome through the death of Jesus. Christ took upon himself the condemnation of all. Irenaeus taught that the incarnated Son of God must conquer sin in all the grades of human existence. He was to pass through all the ages of man in order to sanctify them, and in such wise he recapitulated the whole history of man. With regard to the redemption he taught that since man had given his consent at the temptation, Satan rightfully possessed him in his power. Christ conquered the devil in a perfectly legitimate way. Irenaeus does not state expressly, however, that the ransom was paid to Satan. Christ has reconciled us to God, making God gracious, and thereby procuring the forgiveness of sins and immortality. Tertiullian beheld in the death of Christ a sacrifice. He used the word *satisfactio,* although not in the current theological sense, but as the sinner's own satisfaction. Cyprian says that Christ conquered death through the victorious sign of the cross, reconciled us to God and procured for us forgiveness for the sins that were found or were committed before Baptism. Origen taught that Satan had obtained power over man through the Fall. When man was to be liberated a ransom was necessary. Satan demanded the soul or the blood of Jesus, and he turned Him over to the Jews to be crucified. But he was deceived when he thought that he would secure the higher nature of Jesus together with His manhood. He could not retain the soul of Jesus permeated by the Logos, because this caused him great pain. The cross of Jesus became a net that took Satan captive. Origen speaks, however, of the reconciliation of God. He also taught that the redemption reached into the whole world of spirits.

Athanasius considered the death of Christ as vicarious. Christ set man free from the guilt of death through His death. Gregory of Nazianzus said that the ransom was paid to God. Although he taught that the death of Christ was vicarious, still he declared that God neither needed nor desired the atonement, but that it was of significance because men were sanctified through the manhood of Jesus. Gregory of Nyzza considered the redemption as a redemption from Satan. Satan demanded Christ because he liked Him best. God gave him Jesus and therefore arranged an exchange, but God had also made such arrangements that the human nature of Jesus became a bait for Satan. In the human nature of Jesus there was hidden the divine hook by which Satan was captured. The act of God was just, because Satan had deceived man. At the same time it was an evidence of love, since the connection with Jesus may at last save even the devil. Ambrose uses the expression *satisfactio* in the right sense. Hs speaks of the beguiling of the devil as a *pia fraus*. Chrysostom says that Christ died for us and thereby won the favor of the Father, whose wrath was aroused because of sin. The work of Christ was superabundant, like the ocean as compared with a drop of water. Jerome believed that Jesus offered Himself to Satan, who could not retain Him. Augustine said that God had dealt legitimately with Satan and therefore the ransom was paid to Him. But he also speaks of a redemption from the wrath of God. Christ assumed our guilt and atoned for it, and His merit is more than sufficient. Cyril of Alexandria stated that the world-atoning power of the death of Christ was dependent on the fact that His blood was the blood of the Son of God. The Father gave the Son as a vicarious ransom. Cyril also says that the *Logos* offered Himself to God the Father. He speaks of *satisfactio vicaria*. Gregory the Great developed the theory of the deceiving of Satan, who is likened unto leviathan that is caught by Christ like a fish on a hook. He would not state that Satan had justly ruled over men, but only *quasi juste*. John of Damascus declared that the ransom was paid to God, but also taught, however, that Satan had been deceived when he swallowed the bait, which was the body of Christ, and was caught by the hook of divinity.

Anselm presented his views in *Cur Deus Homo*. His starting point is the conception of guilt, and he rejects the juridical pretensions of the devil. Redemption from the devil presupposes redemption from sin and guilt. Sin is an insult to the honor of God and implies infinite guilt. God must demand a restitution. Such a restitution can take place through punishment and satisfaction. But the punishment would annihilate man. The other method or satisfaction implies a voluntary payment of that which was stolen, but more must be given, viz., something infinite, which man was not bound to pay. God could not forgive sins by His mercy alone, since that would overrule His justice. Man cannot make satisfaction. For this reason the Son of Man came. As man He could represent all men, but as God His life possessed unutterable value. His active obedience did not possess atoning value, because He was obligated to fulfill all righteousness for His own sake, but He was not obliged to give His life in death. When, therefore, Christ voluntarily sacrificed His life, it became a satisfaction of infinite worth. And because it was more than enough, it became necessary for God to repay, and this repayment redounded to the benefit of the children of men. He also taught that the salvation of men was intended by God to fill the void that had arisen through the fall of the angels. The weaknesses in Anselm's theory consist chiefly in the following points: That he sets forth the glory of God "at the cost of the divine holiness; that the work of Christ is considered from the quantitative standpoint; that the active obedience is excluded, and that the mathematical limitation disturbs the Christians' assurance of salvation. Abelard combatted the Anselm theory and set forth the so-called "moral theory," in accordance with which the atonement became subjective, the love of Christ nullifying the enmity of man and arousing in his heart love to God. He says, however, that Christ was a ransom that was paid to the Father. Redemption was intended only for the elect. Hugo of St. Victor set forth the necessity of the divine assistance in order that man might be liberated from the power of Satan. Through the reconciliation God became willing to help man against the devil. He also taught that God could have carried out the redemption in some other way, but the way determined upon was the most serviceable. BernHard of Clairvaux conceived of the atonement objectively. God redeemed us through the blood of His Son. But the ransom was paid to the devil. In the doctrine of reconciliation he set forth the ethical element and that Christ as the head made satisfaction for the members. Peter Lombard stated that Christ had set His cross as a trap for Satan. Alexander of Hales said that Christ as the head made satisfaction for the members. But he confuses the objective and subjective conceptions of the atonement. Thomas Aquinas denied the absolute necessity of satisfaction. God could have forgiven the guilt without setting His justice aside, but the sufferings of Christ constituted the most suitable way. He presented the doctrine of "*satisfactio superabundans*" by reason of the great value of the life of the God-man and also because of the ethical element in the atonement. The sufferings of Christ, however, were limited to His human nature, He did not suffer the anguish of hell. The transfer of the merit of Christ to the children of men was made possible through the mystical union between Christ as the head and the congregation as the members. Duns Scotus rejected the doctrine of "*satisfactio superabundans*" and stated that God had accepted the atonement of His own free pleasure. He therefore advocated the so-called "acceptation theory." The merit of Christ was intended only for the elect. With regard to the sufferings of Christ he taught that it was only the human nature that suffered. He did not place high value on the sufferings of Christ and did not consider that they were necessary in an absolute sense, since every man could have made satisfaction for himself. But the atonement of Christ was nevertheless the best because through it we are influenced to love God. Gabriel Biel, on the other hand, placed the highest value on the atonement of Christ. One drop of the blood of Christ would have been sufficient for our redemption. He speaks of the vicarious death of Christ and sets forth the significance of the justice and love of God in redemption.

Luther considered the atonement from two points of view. In the first place he set forth the concept of atonement, clearly presenting its vicarious character, that Christ fulfilled the Law in our stead, thereby appeasing the wrath of God. The vicariousness of the atonement is looked upon as an exchange, the Lord Christ taking upon Himself our sins and suffering our punishment. He also set forth the redemption, implying a victorious fight against the evil powers, a redemption from the power of sin, death and the devil. Melanchthon agreed with Luther and took as his point of departure the justice of God which was satisfied with the punishment. A mediation was necessary between the divine righteousness and love. Christ became the Mediator who suffered the punishment of sin, the eternal damnation, and therefore bore the wrath of God. Melanchthon also set forth the ethical element in the atonement. Brenz stated that the wrath of God had been reconciled. Calvin and the Reformed theologians on the whole taught about the same as the Lutheran theologians, except that their doctrine of predestination made necessary the concomitant doctrine of *satisfactio limitata*. Their standpoint in the Christological question also exerted its influence so that their doctrine of the atonement was not as complete as Luther's. The theologians of the Catholic Church held the doctrine of *satisfactio superabundans*, which is controlled by the Church. Despite this fact they taught that the satisfaction of Christ was sufficient from the practical point of view for original sin, but for other sins other satisfactions were necessary, although these must stand related to the merit of Christ. The satisfactions have reference especially to earthly punishments and the pains of purgatory. Out of the theory of Anselm the Lutheran Church retained such points as the following: Not only man needed reconciliation, but God also demanded a reconciliation; reconciliation implied a removal of the guilt of sin, while the atoning sacrifice must be the equivalent of the burden of sin to be removed. Of course, the weaknesses of Anselm's theory were rejected. But in addition the Lutherans set forth: That God was interested in the reconciliation for man's sake also; it was not so much the honor of God that demanded reconciliation as His righteousness and love; Christ bore the wrath of God and therefore suffered the punishment of sin, and this voluntarily; both the active and passive obedience of Christ possess significance as satisfactions, wherefore the reconciliation is the presupposition of the forgiveness of sins and justification; finally, it may be stated that the Lutherans taught that the atonement of Christ was intended for all. The Socinians reject the doctrine of the vicarious death of Christ. The principal points in their doctrine are the following: No satisfaction is necessary, since God can forgive without it. Guilt, punishment and merit cannot be transferred from one person to another. It would be unjust if the innocent were to suffer for the guilty. If God were to demand both punishment for sin and also the fulfillment of the Law. He would be requiring pay twice over. If Christ has fulfilled the Law in our stead, then God can demand nothing of us. So far as sufferings were concerned Christ could not suffer the eternal punishment of hell. Moreover, Christ was Himself as a man obligated to fulfill the Law (*obedientia activa*), and His suffering was merely that of a martyr. If He died in the stead of all men, then no man ought to die. His death was merely a confirmation of His teaching and a test of love. They reject the high-priestly office of Christ and mostly emphasize His calling as a teacher and the moral example of His life. God was not reconciled through the active and passive obedience of Christ, but revealed Himself as reconciled in all that Jesus did. Since Christ in recompense for His service was glorified and received divine glory and regal honor, therefore He is able to serve us continually and to liberate the faithful from their sins. Parsimonius and Piscator (especially the latter) advocated the view that *obedientia activa* was the personal obligation of Christ and had therefore no significance for us. The Arminians like the Socinians rejected the doctrine that Christ had suffered our punishment. But they say that the work of Christ was a sacrifice that procures for us forgiveness. Still the sacrifice was not an adequate satisfaction, but God accepted it as valid. Hugo Grottos set forth the so-called "government theory." He denied the ground of satisfaction in the punitive righteousness of God. God is not considered as being personally offended, but as a regent. As a regent He must maintain the majesty of the Law and punish transgression. The Son of God was delivered unto death for us and the punishment of sin was visited on Him in order that He might become a warning example. By reason of the suffering of the Son, God could exercise *commutatio* and forgive sins. It is not necessary to set forth in detail the views of our old orthodox Dogmaticians. We would simply call attention to Quenstedt's doctrine of *derelictio*. He teaches that a separation took place between the Logos and Jesus during *derelictio*. Of course, this view is misleading.

Kant presents Christ as the ideal man from the moral point of view. The doctrine of the Son of God as a vicarious mediator is merely symbolic and implies that the new man in us is to suffer the punishment for the sins of the old man. Man must reconcile himself. In this reconciliation he ought to suffer in the same spirit as Christ. The Rationalists, such as Wegscheider, rejected the high-priestly office of Christ and merely set forth His prophetic office. The death of Christ was the death of a martyr. The Supranaturalists said that the sufferings and death of Christ constituted a warning example. *Satisfactio* was the most suitable way and the best means of deterring men from sin and urging them to repentance. While Kant taught the self-reconciliation of man, Schelling and Hegel, on the other hand, taught the reconciliation of God with Himself. Hegel said that the death of the Son implied that the negative element had entered into the divine self-development, and that His resurrection constituted a negation of the negation. The objective reconciliation is the realization of the self-consciousness of God in man, while the subjective atonement is the realization of the unity of the finite spirit with the absolute. Goschel belonged to the right wing of Hegel's disciples. He teaches that the divine righteousness and love are one, and that the wrath of God's righteousness is merely the zeal of love. He denies the absolute necessity of satisfaction. In a certain sense Christ is a vicarious mediator, but He did not suffer vicariously. The object of punishment is *restitutio in integrum*. The guilty person must enter into relationship with the mediator, or, figuratively, the sick portion of the body must be united with the sound organism, which suffers for the ailing part. Schleiermacher could not accept the Church doctrine of satisfaction because he did not have a right conception of the Trinity or of sin. The suffering of Christ was vicarious only in the sense that He shared with man the consciousness of sin, but it was not a *satisfactio,* since we all must share the sufferings of Christ. The death of Christ was the death of a martyr. Through the redemption that was procured through Christ there was implanted in the human race a new power of life, which is mediated through the Church. Christ possessed the consciousness of God in its fulness. In the Church is found the principle of redemption through which the divine consciousness is strengthened in us. Our redemption consists in our translation into the strong consciousness of the divine as it is in Christ, while our atonement consists in participating in the blessedness of Christ. The atonement, therefore, is merely a subjective state. Menken emphasized the love of God, which did not require any vicarious satisfaction. The reconciliation is conceived of in a subjective sense and consists in man's reconciliation with God. He made violent attacks on the orthodox doctrine of atonement. The sufferings of Christ had no connection with guilt and punishment, but only with sin, which was to be annihilated. Christ was exposed to all kinds of temptations and sufferings, but He stood the test and presented a human nature without sin. Christ became the principle of purification for the salvation of men from sin. Sartorius presented the ethical element in the vicarious suffering of Christ. He says that the punishment does not atone, but the sacrifice. Nor is the suffering sufficient, the punishment must be endured with self-renunciation end with complete consecration to the will of God. Von Hofmann presented the so-called "compensative theory." The sacrifices were intended to teach men that God does not forgive sins without further consideration; that man must make satisfaction through sacrifice. Like others, who in thought approach the position of Schleiermacher, he was a representative of the so-called "mystical theory." We are reconciled in Christ by reason of the mystical union with Christ. The new humanity, well-pleasing to God, was presented in the person of Christ. Christ realized His calling as a Saviour, not as a mediator who suffered our punishment, but as the representative of the race, who endured the sufferings of humanity and stood the test perfectly. His sufferings came from beneath rather than from above. But this suffering did not imply an appeasing of the wrath of God. He therefore rejects the Church doctrine of the theory of satisfaction. Maurice advocated the "moral theory." He stated that the suffering and death of Christ constituted a perfectly consecrated sacrifice before God and then cites many examples to show the self-sacrifice which every man is obligated to make before God. Bushnell, was also an advocate of the moral theory of atonement. He stated that Christ suffered out of sympathy for us and because of the consciousness of solidarity with us, through all of which He acquired moral power over us. Thomasius together with other theologians opposed the theory of Hofmann and other related theories. He represents the Church doctrine of atonement and presents the doctrine from three aspects, viz., as satisfaction or Genugthuung, atoning or Sühnung, and reconciliation or Versöhnung. In the second of these aspects he presents the ethical element of the atonement, but does not sufficiently emphasize the significance of *obedientia activa*. Philippi in general adheres closely to the symbols and the older dogmatic development. He lays equal emphasis on *obedientia activa* and *passiva*. In relation to the sacrifice Bähr presented a "symbolic theory" and stated that as the sacrificial animals gave their life and blood to God, so man must submit himself to God, which takes its beginning in contrition and through justification is made complete in sanctification. Keil said that the slaying of the animal did not per se imply any satisfaction, although the sinner must know that sin implied punishment. The reconciliation consisted in the blood, which is the symbol of life. By reason of the shedding of blood the sinner was received into fellowship with the God of love. Kurz sets forth the *juridical* doctrine of reconciliation and views the slaying of the sacrifice as a punishment, while its suffering was considered as a *satisfactio vicaria*. Therefore the antitype must also suffer our punishment in our stead, so that His suffering might become a *satisfactio vicaria*. Ritschl was a disciple of Weisse and Lotze. Herein lies partly the explanation of Ritschlianism. Ritschl considers God only as love. The justice of God is merely the sequence through which the divine love cares for the welfare of those that belong to His kingdom. He rejects the doctrine of *justitia punitiva*. Christ has revealed the love of the Father. He was one with the Father only through His ethical obedience and subordination to the Father, while His redemption consisted in teaching men to will to do the Father's will. Then we feel blessed and independent of all that happens. We must believe that the Father is not subject to wrath. Our atonement does not take place through satisfaction and expiation, but through our faith in God as unchangeable love. When we are liberated from fear and approach God, then we are reconciled. Martensen acknowledges that the atonement has significance before God and that the opposition between the love and righteousness of God was solved in the objective reconciliation. However, his presentation of the objective reconciliation is not completely clear. Granfelt takes the conception of love as his point of departure and emphasizes the solidarity between Christ and the children of men. He calls his conception of the atonement the "ethical organic theory." But he rejects the juridical conception. He makes comparisons between Von Hofmann and Thomasius, stating that he must needs side with the Church doctrine against Von Hofmann and with Von Hofmann against the Church doctrine. He criticizes Von Hofmann because of the latter's position that Christ came in contact with sin only as an evil, which indeed caused Him great anguish, but that this suffering was not endured as a punishment in the place of all men. On the other hand, he criticizes Thomasius because he taught that Christ bore the guilt and punishment of sin. The theory of Granfelt is related to that of Waldenstrom, and he acknowledges that they have a common starting point, but he criticizes the latter's position for one reason, among others, because he does not set forth the solidarity between Christ and the children of men.[62] Granfelt denies that the death of Christ is to be looked upon as being demanded by the punitive righteousness of God. Christ suffered as the head of the human race in such manner that He experienced in concentrated form the suffering which God had determined upon as an unavoidable consequence of sin, but God was not directly active in the Son's passion. Many of the theologians of the Church of Sweden have strongly opposed the modern theories, which to a greater or less degree reject the orthodox theory of reconciliation. Among these may be mentioned A. F. Beckman and M. Johansson.

Luthardt states, on the one hand, that the Son, who united in Himself the human race, had to the uttermost experienced the wrath of God and suffered the punishment of human sin; on the other hand, the love of Christ, manifested in the willingness with which He obediently suffered and in His continuance in holiness in the face of all assaults, has constituted His sufferings as an act which in ethical import corresponds to the divine and as a sacrifice that was well pleasing to God. Christ satisfied the holiness and love of God, or the holy will of His love, offered an atoning sacrifice for sin through the union of corresponding suffering and activity,

---

[62] Waldenstrom rejects the doctrine of the reconciliation of God and sets forth the reconciliation of man. Concerning the necessity of reconciliation he states that an atonement that appeased God was not necessary, but only one that took away the sins of man. The atonement did not depend on the demands of the injured righteousness of God for restitution. In His suffering Christ was not our mediator to remove the wrath of God, but the mediator of God to take away our sins. Christ did not die in our stead, but only for our benefit. His active and passive obedience does not constitute any satisfaction before God for our sins. His suffering was, therefore, not a vicarious punitive punishment for our sins. As a mediator Christ is viewed as a middle person. With regard to the doctrine of redemption and the ransom he states that the Scriptures do not mention to whom it was paid, but if the figure were carried through to its logical sequence, then, he thought, the old teachers were right in their contention that it was paid to Satan. But he says that the figure merely means that salvation is generally considered as a liberation. In the doctrine of reconciliation there is a marked similarity between Waldenstrom and Socinus. Compare Dr. O. Olsson on the Reformation and Socinianism. Samlade skrifter, III.

through which in Himself He reconciled the human race unto God and redeemed it from sin and its effects.

§22. The Regal Office of Christ.

Munus Regium is that office through which Christ as to His entire person rules over the whole universe and especially His Church until He shall have delivered up the conquered and perfected kingdom to God (1 Cor. 15: 24-28), after which He shall as the God-man and the Second Person in the Trinity rule, although in a different way, together with the Father and the Holy Ghost in the eternal kingdom of glory.

The regal office of Christ is thus defined by Quenstedt: "*Munus regium* is *that function of Christ, the God-man, through which He divinely controls and governs, in accordance with both natures, the divine and the human, and the latter as exalted to the Right Hand of Majesty, all creatures in their totality in the kingdom of power, grace and glory, by infinite majesty and power, as to the divinity by virtue of the eternal generation, and as to His assumed human nature, by virtue of the personal union belonging to Him.*"[63] The human nature of Christ was made the recipient of regal glory at the incarnation, but, save in exceptional cases, He did not exercise His divine power during the period of His humiliation. The state of exaltation, however, implied that, also in accordance with His human nature, He again exercised in full the prerogatives of His divine glory. Even in the greatest depth of His humiliation Christ confessed that He was a King. Compare John 18:37: "Pilate therefore said unto him, Art thou a king then? Jesus answered, Thou sayest that I am a king." In John 13:3 we read: "Jesus, knowing that the Father had given all things into his hands." This power Christ

[63] Quenstedt: *"Officium regium est functio Christi θεανθρώπου, qua is secundum utramque naturam, divinam et humanam et hanc quidem ad dextram majestatis exaltam, omnes omnino creaturas in regno potentiae, gratiae et gloriae majestate et virtute infinita, quoad divinitatem ex generatione aeterna, quoad assumtam humanitatem ex personali unione ipsi competente, modo divino, moderatur et gubernat."*

began to exercise in accordance with His entire person, and therefore also as to His human nature, at the time of His quickening. The first stages of His exaltation included His ascending the throne, which was completed at the ascension. Seated at the right hand of the Father, He reigns in the kingdom of power and grace in heaven. His dominion in the kingdom of grace is called Christocratic under a pneumatocratic form. At His second coming or in the judgment period this dominion will become more directly Christocratic, and when the kingdom, in accordance with 1 Cor. 15:24, is delivered up to God and the Father, then His dominion together with the Father and the Holy Ghost will be a theocratic dominion throughout eternity.

1. Christ As King.

Jesus Christ was born to be a King. Compare John 18:37. In a way He was also acknowledged as a King on the cross. Through the cross He gained the victory. In three of the leading languages of the world it was stated that He was the King of the Jews. But He was not merely the King of the Jews, He was the King of the whole world. After the quickening He descended into Hades and declared His victory, whereupon His resurrection (*resurrectio externa*) took place, through which He was sealed in His threefold office, and hence also a King. His ascension constituted His coronation. He now shares the divine power with the Father and the Holy Ghost, but in a special sense He is King and is called the King of kings and Lord of lords, and as such He shall return in His second advent.

The following negative and positive attributes are ascribed to His dominion or characterizes Him as King: 1) *Non nominalis, sed realis,* which term is used against the Socinians, who said that before His death Christ was not a real King, but simply *rex designatus.* It is also used against the Rationalists, who deny both His divinity and His kingdom. 2) *Non metaphoricus, sed naturalis,* inasmuch as the Rationalists judge of Him as the Stoics in calling a wise man a king, but it was natural for Christ to be King, since to this end was He born. He was truly a King. 3) *Non mere moralis, sed personalis,* since Christ is not merely a King through His moral influence, but in a personal sense. Although the dominion of Christ is in a sense mediated through the work of the Holy Ghost, still Christ reigns in a personal way. Many Scripture passages set forth this truth. Shortly before His ascension, or on the occasion of the institution of Baptism, which took place in Galilee at the great gathering of the disciples, He said: "Lo, I am with you always, even unto the end of the world" (Matt. 28:20). Compare Acts 9: 4-19 and 1 Cor. 15:25: "For he must reign, till he hath put all his enemies under his feet."

2. The Kingdom of Christ or the Kingdom of God.

Since Christ is a King in a real sense, He must also have a kingdom. The kingdom is called in the Scriptures the kingdom of God, the kingdom of the Father, the kingdom, the kingdom of Christ," and the kingdom of heaven. This kingdom was also found in the Old Testament and for a time took form in the Jewish theocracy. When the Son of God became incarnate in the flesh, then the kingdom came in a higher sense. For this reason the forerunner of Christ preached on the text or the theme: "The kingdom of heaven is at hand" (Matt. 3:2). Christ and His disciples also preached concerning the kingdom. However, the kingdom did not appear as the majority expected. The disciples on the way to Emmaus said: "But we hoped that it was he who should redeem Israel" (Luke 24:21). Just before the ascension the disciples asked the Lord: "Lord, dost thou at this time restore the kingdom to Israel?" (Acts 1:6). They did not receive any answer as to the revelation of the kingdom in glory, but Christ directed their attention to the development of the kingdom through the activity of the Holy Ghost. Immediately thereafter Christ ascended the throne of His glory. There were two angels who spoke on that occasion of the second advent of Christ. There are many passages that set forth the fact that at the second coming of Christ His kingdom shall appear as a kingdom of justice and glory. Although we lay stress on the spiritual kingdom of Christ and the kingdom of heaven, still we must not forget that He likewise reigns in the kingdom of power. He is King in the kingdom of power, of grace, of justice, and of glory.

1) *Regnum potentiae.* Christ's sitting at the right hand of power denotes His participation in the divine government of the world. The creation of the world was mediated through the Son, and *opera ad extra* as well as *opera attributa* are *indivisa.* The Son was the principle and foundation of the whole creation as well as its original prototype. He is the ground, the means, as well as the goal of creation. Compare Col. 1:16, 17. The latter passage states that all things consist in Him. In Heb. 1:3 we read: "And upholding all things by the word of his power." This expression also coincides with the words of Christ Himself: "All authority hath been given unto me in heaven and on earth" (Matt. 28:18). The God-man possesses not only spiritual but also temporal power. Christ not only reigns in the Church, but also in the world, as God rules. He is therefore King in the kingdom of power and can do whatsoever is in harmony with His holy, wise and benevolent will. As King in the kingdom of power He can also serve His Church and punish her enemies.

2) *Regnum gratiae.* The kingdom of grace is that kingdom of Christ where He reigns partly in a *pneumatocratic* way through the means of grace, and partly in more direct fashion, dynamically and personally, in order that men might be made partakers of His saving grace and become members of the kingdom of glory which constitutes the goal of the kingdom of grace.

Jesus presented, while on earth, many parables concerning the beginning, development and completion of His kingdom. Among such parables we find that those contained in Matthew 13 have special significance, inasmuch as they not only portray the kingdom of grace at all times, but seem to characterize special periods in the development of the kingdom of God. In this respect they are partly analogous to the letters of Jesus to the seven churches. The parable of the sower portrays the establishment of the kingdom of Christ through the great missionary activities that were carried on during the first Apostolic period and the immediately succeeding period down to 250. This period is also portrayed in Rev. 2:1-7. The second parable, that of the tares among the wheat, tells how heresies arose. The letter to the Church in Smyrna portrays to a certain extent the same period down to 313, i.e., the period of the persecutions. However, the parable runs further on in time. The third parable, that of the mustard seed, sets forth the small beginning of the kingdom, but also its wonderful growth into a great tree, so that the birds of the heaven came and lodged in its branches. Reference is here made to the historical fact of Christianity becoming the religion of the nations. The character of this period corresponds to the content of the letter to Pergamus and includes the period from 313 or 323 to the seventh century. The word Pergamus means both a tower and marriage. During this period the kingdom appeared as a tower and entered into marriage relations with the world. The fourth, the parable of the leaven, shows how the kingdom through its inward power permeates society and exercises its great influence, which was also portrayed in the letter to Thyatira. This period began in the seventh century and continued for some time. During this period Jezebel represents the Church of Rome. The fifth parable, that of the hidden treasure, depicts the kingdom of God during the Dark Ages and the early part of the Reformation period, when the treasure was found. This period is also characterized in the letter to Sardis. The sixth parable, concerning the pearl of great price, is descriptive of the period succeeding the Reformation down to the present time. The letter to Philadelphia portrays the same period. During the last few centuries missionary activities have flourished, the Gospel pearls of great price have been carried from shore to shore, from country to country, brotherly love has been made manifest in divers ways through Christian organizations and institutions of charity, while a powerful spiritual activity has been everywhere in evidence in the kingdom of Christ. The last or the seventh parable, that of the net that was cast into the sea, refers to the kingdom of Christ especially in the last days and at the time of the second advent. The letter to Laodicea depicts the conditions that will obtain during the period immediately preceding the judgment period. We may already have entered this period of democracy, mob rule and lukewarmness in religion. But the periods overlap one another. These parables and letters portray the kingdom of Christ during every period between the first and second advents of Christ, while special periods are specially characterized, as we have sought briefly to point out. Christ reigns during all of these periods, and although invisible, still we experience dynamically His presence and activity. Just as God through the Son led the Children of Israel through the wilderness to the promised land, so the Lord leads His children to the appointed goal.

The form or the character of the government in the kingdom of Christ on earth is grace and truth. Compare John 1:17. In accordance herewith Christ reigns pneumatocratically through the means of grace. The Holy Spirit proceeds from the Father and the Son and works through the means of grace. Through the means of grace men become citizens or subjects in the kingdom and through these the kingdom is built up and wins its victories. While the dominion of Christ is mediated in this way, still He has not withdrawn His presence from the kingdom. In the beginning He exerted His influence by His immediate presence, now He also intervenes in the development of His kingdom through His personal activity. Among Scripture passages may be cited the following: "When he, the Spirit of truth, is come, he shall guide you in all the truth. He shall glorify me: for he shall take of mine, and shall declare it unto you" (John 16:13, 14); "I shall not leave you desolate: I shall come unto you" (John 14:18); "And they went forth, and preached everywhere, the Lord working with them, and confirming the word by the signs that followed" (Mark 16:20); "Where two or three are gathered together in my name, there am I in the midst of them" (Matt. 18:20). Compare also concerning the conversion of Saul in Acts 9: 4-6; also Acts 18:9-11; 22:17-21; "And he is the head of the body, the church" (Col. 1:18); "For he must reign, till he hath put all his enemies under his feet" (1 Cor. 15:25).

The subjects in this kingdom are all true Christians, although nominal Christians are also counted. There are tares among the wheat, and branches in the vine that do not bear fruit. The kingdom is also built up inwardly, so that it often happens that nominal Christians become true subjects in the kingdom of Christ. The subjects are called a royal priesthood and constitute the kingdom of Christ. They shall reign with Him in His glory. Christ said to His disciples: "And I appoint unto you a kingdom, even as my Father appointed unto me" (Luke 22:29, 30; cf. Rev. 3:21).

The object of the kingdom of grace is the salvation of men, and that the elect congregation shall in the consummation constitute the eternal kingdom of glory, through which God shall be glorified and the original plan of salvation in regard to man carried through to fruition.

3) *Regnum justitiae*. The old Dogmaticians conceived of the significance of this kingdom in a narrow way and said that it was the dominion of Christ over the evil angels and men, or the damned (*in angelos malos et homines damnatos*). But we may conceive of this kingdom as a kingdom of justice in a more general sense and consider it as a part of the dominion of Christ that constitutes a mediation between the kingdom of grace and the kingdom of glory. Christ is not simply the King of grace, He is also the King of justice. He is not only the thorn-crowned King, He likewise wears a bejewelled crown of glory. According to Rev. 19:11-16 Christ shall judge and smite the nations with justice, He shall rule them with a rod of iron. The judgment shall begin at the house of God and then continue. According to Rev. 2:26, 27 and other passages the faithful shall also in some way participate in the reign of justice.

4) *Regnum gloriae*. By this is meant the dominion of Christ in the Church triumphant especially after the judgment of the world. The members of this kingdom are both the good angels and the glorified children of men. Christ shall reign in this kingdom as the Second Person in the Godhead in all eternity. Christ rules now in the kingdom of the heavens. But Christ shall come again; the dead in Christ shall rise first, and the living shall be changed. When the Son of man shall come in His glory, and shall sit upon the throne of His glory, and when the dead shall arise, then shall the kingdom of God be made fully manifest. Then the prophecies concerning the kingdom shall be fulfilled and in a divine way Christ shall reign as the King of glory over the eternally blessed inhabitants in the new creation.

As the King of glory the following attributes are ascribed to Christ: 1)

Universalis, which term does not conflict with the fact that the Father is also the King in this sense. The Triune God is King in the absolute sense, but special mention is here made of the Second Person in the Godhead. The Scriptures make this distinction, as we note in Rev. 11:15, 17: "The kingdom of the world has become the kingdom of our Lord and of his Christ: and he shall reign for ever and ever. We give thee thanks, O Lord God, the Almighty, who art and who wast; because thou hast taken thy great power, and didst reign." 2) *Fraternus*, since His dominion is fraternal in the sense that He who is the firstborn among many brethren does not reign alone, inasmuch as the Scriptures declare that the redeemed shall reign with Christ, as we read in Rev. 22:5: "They shall reign for ever and ever." 3) *Gloriosus*, inasmuch as His dominion shall be glorious and surpass all human expectation. Compare 1 Cor. 2:8, 9. The Lord is called "the King of glory" (Ps. 24: 7-10).

5

Pneumatology

Pneumatology constitutes that part of Dogmatics which treats of the application of the grace of salvation through the Holy Ghost together with the order of salvation, or *ordo salutis*. The connection between Soteriology and Pneumatology consists in this, that the former is the foundation of the latter, while the Holy Ghost applies the salvation in Christ upon the heart of the individual. The objective reconciliation becomes subjective when the individual through the grace of the Spirit hearkens unto the words of reconciliation: "Be ye reconciled to God."

The sending of the Holy Ghost was dependent on the death, the resurrection and the ascension of Christ. Easter was the *causa* that brought forth Pentecost as the *effectus*. Christ said: "Nevertheless I tell you the truth: It is expedient for you that I go away; for if I go not away, the' Comforter will not come unto you; but if I go, I will send him unto you" (John 16:7). The Holy Ghost is, therefore, the divine representative who mediates the work of salvation in the world. The pneumatological activity is therefore necessary as the soteriological work was necessary. The third article of the Creed follows in necessary sequence upon the second. Both of these articles must receive equal emphasis, indeed, all three articles of the Creed must receive equal emphasis, inasmuch as they constitute a unity in the threefold confession corresponding to the divine Trinity.

By the sending of the Holy Ghost we are not to understand that He had been inactive before in relation to men, because He was active during the Old Testament dispensation and in a sense also among all men. The question concerns the sending of the Holy Ghost in a special sense. In John 7:39 we read: "But this spake he of the Spirit, which they that believed on him were to receive: for the Spirit was not yet given; because Jesus was not yet glorified." In the Greek text it is stated that the Spirit was not yet, i. e. He had not as yet entered into His New Testament office. Before the glorification of Jesus He could not unite the children of men as constituting a mystical body with Christ as the head. Godet says: "Before Pentecost the Holy Spirit had influenced men both in the Old Testament and in the circle of His disciples, but as yet He was not present as their possession and their personal life." In the Old Testament the Spirit worked more from without, while in the New Testament He works from within. As the Son of God in the New Testament came very near to the children of men and became one of the race, so the Third Person of the Trinity has also come very near to men and dwells in the hearts of the faithful. Likewise the Father has entered into close communion with men, a mystery which is expressed in the mystical union.

Pentecost denotes a new period of creation. The Holy Ghost has always been active in creative epochs. When the world was created the Holy Ghost was active in a formative way. He was also active in a special way at the incarnation. Through the activity of the Spirit on the day of Pentecost the Church of Christ was established, so that Pentecost became the birthday of the Church, and in like manner wherever the Holy Ghost is permitted to perform His work in the heart of the individual, there the result will be a new creation. The Holy Ghost is active in the Church through the means of grace, through which the believers become the temples of the Holy Ghost. Irenaeus says: "Wheresoever the Church is, there is the Holy Ghost, and wheresoever the Holy Ghost is, there is the Church and every species of grace."[64]

---

[64] Irenaeus against Heresies, III, xxiv.

The Rationalists and others denied the existence of the Holy Ghost, at least His personal presence and activity. The same arguments are advanced as are used generally against the special divine revelation. They declare that there are no reliable proofs of the personal presence and activity of the Holy Ghost in the Church. J. D. Michaelis declared openly that he had never experienced the testimony of the Holy Spirit. But all true Christians can testify that the testimony of the Spirit is true and real. The words of the Lord in Rom. 8:16 are verified in the life of every Christian: "The Spirit himself beareth witness with our spirit, that we are the children of God."

Dogmaticians ascribe a fourfold office to the Holy Ghost, but care must be taken that the distinctions in these offices be not over-emphasized to such a degree that the unity be obscured, since the distinctions depend upon the varying subjective states of man. These offices are the following: 1) *officium elenchticum,* which is the office of the Holy Ghost through which the sinner is so influenced as to become conscious of sin; 2) *officium didascalicum* is the office through which knowledge of the way of salvation is imparted; 3) *officium paedeuticum,* or that activity of the Holy Ghost through which the converting grace of God works true penitence and living faith; 4) *officium paracleticum,* or the office through which the converted soul is guided, admonished and comforted in the varied experiences of life until the goal of glory is reached. Compare the following Scripture passages: John 16:8; 14:26; 16:13-15; 2 Tim. 3:16; Heb. 12:1-13; Rom. 8:16, 26. Also compare Luther's explanation of the third article of the Apostles' Creed.

§23. The Grace of the Holy Ghost and the Order of Salvation.

The special grace of the Holy Spirit, in like manner as the saving grace of God in general, denotes the good will of God toward man at the same time as it excludes entirely all human merit. The word *χάρις* originally meant that which affords joy, pleasure, delight, and was used by the Greeks to express beauty, charm, loveliness. The word is so used in the Septuagint. Later, however, the word was used to denote the thing as realized. Aristotle used the word to mean a free gift, the giver expecting nothing in return. In the New Testament the word has received its full and consecrated significance to express the lovingkindness, favor and good-will of God toward sinners. The expression *ἔλεος* has also undergone a change in meaning from what it had among the classical writers. It means that the mercy of God is made manifest toward the wretched. Bengel makes the following distinction between *gratia* and *misericordia*: "*Gratia tollit culpam, misericordia miseriam.*"

1. The Definition of the Grace of God and Its Division.

Hollazius defines *gratia Spiritus Sancti applicatrix* as follows: "*The applying grace of God is the source of those divine acts by which the Holy Ghost by means of the Word of God and the Sacraments dispenses, offers to us, confers and seals those favors that were designed for man through the great good-will of God the Father and procured by the fraternal redemption of Jesus Christ.*"[65]

Gratia has been defined in divers ways. Quenstedt makes use of the following division: a) *gratia assistens,* which acts exterior to man, corresponding to prevenient or preparatory grace; b) *gratia ingrediens,* corresponding to operating grace; c) *gratia inhabitans,* or indwelling grace,

---

[65] Hollazius: "*Gratia Spiritus sancti applicatrix est principium illorum actuum divinorum, qutbus Sp. s. per verbum Dei et sacramenta beneficia spiritualia et aeterna, benignissima Dei patris benevolentia humano generi destinata et fraterna J. Christi redemtione acquisita dispensat nobisque offert, confert et obsignat.*"

corresponding to co-operating grace. However, the ordinary division is as follows: *gratia praeveniens, praeparans, operans et co-operans,* while sometimes *gratia conservans* is added. Hollazius defines as follows: *gratia praeveniens,* or prevenient grace, is the act of grace by which the Holy Spirit through the Word of God offers to man, dead in trespasses and sins, the good-will of the Father and the merit of Christ, removes the natural inability, invites, arouses, urges and continues to urge him to repent; 2) *gratia praeparans,* or preparatory grace, is the act of grace through which the Holy Ghost removes the natural and actual opposition, makes the will penitent through the Law and pours into the heart the knowledge of the gospel teaching, so that the penitent may be prepared to accept the saving faith; 3) *gratia operans* is the act of grace through which the Holy Spirit imparts the powers of faith, when justifying faith is brought about. To this division belong justification, regeneration and the mystical union; 4) *gratia co-operans* is the act of grace through which the Holy Spirit co-operates with the justified man in order to promote sanctification and the doing of good works; 5) *gratia conservans* is the act of grace through which faith and holiness of life are sustained and illumined to the end that the faithful may persevere steadfastly even unto death.[66]

2. The Attributive Terms Applied To Grace.

The following distinguishing epithets or attributive terms are applied to grace: 1) *supernaturalis;* "The grace of the Lord Jesus Christ be with you" (1 Cor. 16:23; cf. Titus 2:11); 2) medicinalis; "Oh save me according to thy lovingkindness" (Ps. 109: 21-26; cf. 2 Cor. 12:9); 3) salutaris; "The grace of God hath appeared, bringing salvation to all men" (Titus 2:11); 4) *forensis;* "Justified by his grace" (Titus 3:7); 5) *seria;* "Receive not the grace of God in vain" (2 Cor. 6:1; cf. Isa. 55; 1 Tim. 1:15); 6) *sufficiens;* "Where sin abounded, grace did abound more exceedingly" (Rom. 5:20); 7) *generalis;* "For of his fulness have we all received, and grace for grace" (John 1:16); 8) *libera;* "By grace have ye been saved through faith; and that

---

[66] Holl. Exam. Theol. Acroam. Pars III, §1, Cap. IV, p. 230.

not of yourselves, it is the gift of God" (Eph. 2:8); 9) *resistibilis*; "And ye would not" (Matt. 23:37); "Looking carefully lest there be any man that falleth short of the grace of God" (Heb. 12:15; cf. 2 Cor. 6:1; Jude, verse 4). In a sense we may say that although grace is *resistibilis*, still it is *inevitabilis* or inevitable, since when man comes in contact with the means of grace, he cannot hinder its activity as an exterior power of God. Sometimes the term *amissibilis*, or that which may be lost, is used. The terms generates, *seria* and *resistibilis* are used against the Calvinists, who teach that grace is only for the elect, and as such is irresistible.

3. *Ordo Salutis* or the Order of Salvation.

Neither the old nor the more modern Dogmaticians follow a common order in the doctrine of *ordo salutis*, indeed, great differences prevail. H. Schmid, who in general follows the old Dogmaticians, presents the doctrine in the following order: Faith, Justification, Vocation, Illumination, Regeneration and Conversion, the Mystical Union, Renovation, Sanctification and Good Works. Baier places *de regeneratione et conversione* between *de fide* and *de justificatione*. Hollazius uses the following order: *De vocatione, de illuminatione, de conversione, de regeneratione, de justificatione, de unione mystica, de renovatione, de conservatione et de glorificatione*. The following order is used in Hase's Hutterus Redivivus: first *fides et justificatio*, then *vocatio, illuminatio, conversio, sanctificatio et unio mystica*. Luthardt makes use of the following order: Vocation, Illumination, Conversion, Penitence, Faith, Justification, Regeneration, the Mystical Union, Sanctification: *renovatio, sanctificatio et bona opera*. Some Dogmaticians treat justification first, before the order of salvation, strictly speaking, because it constitutes a judicial act on the part of God. Regeneration is placed before justification when the latter is arranged in the order of salvation, because regeneration is conceived of as the genesis of faith. As may also be observed from the examples cited concerning the order of salvation, some Dogmaticians treat regeneration before conversion. The reason of this is that regeneration is conceived of as standing in connection with Baptism, while conversion takes place subsequently, in case the baptized and regenerated person should fall from the grace of Baptism. This order is also followed on the ground that regeneration sets forth the divine side of the work of the appropriation of salvation, while conversion presents the human side. In such case regeneration corresponds to *conversio transitiva*.

In dealing with the order of salvation we must remember that the treatment will be different as we deal with it from the standpoint of infant Baptism or the Baptism of proselytes. Here the question concerns chiefly the order of salvation within the Church, where infant Baptism is mostly used. Since regeneration takes place in Baptism, and since Baptism is the sacrament of regeneration, therefore some have questioned the possibility of both conversion and regeneration in the adult who has fallen from the grace of Baptism and afterwards been restored. The observation has been made that analogous to the natural birth spiritual birth ought to take place but once, and that the return of the sinner to the grace of Baptism ought to be termed a reawakening and conversion. In this manner the presentation of the order of salvation would indeed be simplified, but it must be stated that the analogy of the natural birth is not an adequate one. If regeneration takes place but once, then we must consider the state of the backslider as a state of sleep and not one of spiritual death. The Scriptures do not solve this problem so far as the terminology is concerned, but the following passages, nevertheless, throw an indirect light on the question at issue: "This thy brother was dead, and is alive again" (Luke 15:32); "Having been begotten again, not of corruptible seed, but of incorruptible, through the word of God" (1 Peter 1:23) "He brought us forth by the word of truth" (James 1:18; cf. John 3:3-5). Some Dogmaticians speak therefore of an objective and principal regeneration in Baptism and afterwards of a subjective regeneration through the regenerating power of the Word, when man again receives the spiritual life which he first received in Baptism, and now experiences in a conscious and personal way. It ought also to be noted that the presentation of *ordo salutis* is dependent on the definition of regeneration, as to whether it is simply *donatio fidei* or the spiritual life itself and the adoption as the children of God. In the solution of this problem we must bear in mind that the doctrine of "justification by faith alone" occupies a dominating and regulative position in the doctrines of the Lutheran Church, that this doctrine constitutes the material principle and in the doctrinal system stands *primus et principalis articulus*. Therefore it would seem to accord most closely with conservative and historical Lutheranism to place justification before regeneration in the order of salvation, justification taking place in the mind of God as cause and regeneration in the heart of man as effect. It may indeed be said that justification and regeneration occur simultaneously, but in reality, and for the sake of the logical sequence, one or the other must be placed first.

All the different acts that enter into the order of salvation are set forth in the Word of God, and Dogmaticians usually refer to Acts 26:17, 18, because this passage seems to include the whole order. We quote this passage, indicating the act involved: "Unto whom I send thee (vocation), to open their eyes (illumination), that they may turn from darkness to light and from the power of Satan to God (conversion), that they may receive remission of sins (justification) and an inheritance (regeneration) among them that are sanctified (renovation and sanctification)." We shall present the different acts or grades in *ordo salutis* in the following order: *Vocatio (et excitatio), illuminatio, conversio (contritio et fides), justificatio, regeneratio, unio mystica, renovatio (renovatio, sanctificatio et bona opera) et conservatio.*

While the acts of grace in the order of salvation cannot always be definitely fixed as to time, although each has its own time, still they occur in order, and each act is experienced in its principal features. The applying grace is present from the beginning, but can only gradually accomplish that which corresponds to the state of the individual. No act of grace is ever entirely completed, since by reason of sin man always stands in need of all the acts of grace. However, there is a special time when man is called, enlightened, etc., so that the *ordo salutis* is a truth which is grounded in the Scriptures and which is demonstrated in the subjective experience. We may say that illumination occupies a peculiar position in *ordo salutis*, since it is an act of grace through which the other acts are mediated, because of the fact that it stands in immediate connection with the Word of God, through which the Holy Spirit works. For this reason we may say that illumination occupies a special place after vocation, but in general occupies a mediating position in the entire order of salvation.

§24. Vocation.

The Holy Ghost begins His work of applying the grace of salvation through vocation. The expression *vocatio,* or the call, may be understood in so broad a sense as to include the children at Baptism, who may be said to be the objects of the calling and regenerating grace of God, or to be influenced at once by *gratia praeveniens, praeparans et operans,* but, strictly speaking, those persons are the objects of the calling activity of the Holy Ghost who are conscious of the call through the Word of God. Therefore the calling grace of God is operative both within and outside the Church through the hearing and reading of the Word of God. Even those children who have remained faithful to the grace of Baptism must in a certain sense experience the call, since the demands of their personal self-consciousness and self-determination require that they in a self-conscious and self-determined way learn of their blessed state and abide in it. While it is true that the gracious work of the Spirit in relation to such persons belongs principally to the province of sanctification, still to a greater or less degree they also experience the leading acts in the order of salvation, since all Christians must live in daily penitence and must daily repair to the throne of grace. The definition of vocation, however, in relation to the members of the Church, has reference, strictly speaking, to such as have to a greater or less extent fallen from the grace of Baptism.

The following definition is taken partly from Hollazius: *vocatio* is *the act of grace whereby the Holy Spirit manifests to those without the Church of Christ or not true members of it through the Word of God His will to save, and offers them the gracious benefits of Christ's redemption, so that they may become vitally connected with the Church through Baptism or conversion and obtain eternal salvation.*

The causa *impulsiva interna* of the call is the goodness and mercy of God on the ground of the merit of Christ, and *causa externa* is the profound misery of man and the need of salvation.

1. The Division Of The Call.

The Call is divided as follows: 1) *generalis, indirecta seu paedagogica,* by which is meant the general call, mediated through the conscience, nature and the world dominion of God. This general call is made operative in three ways: a) *objective,* through the natural revelation in the manifestation of the divine beneficence toward all creatures and in the divine government of the world; b) *effective,* through the efficacious divine influence and impulse, by which, both from the theoretic and practical innate notions, and by reason of proofs of the divine benignity, practical conclusions are produced in the minds of unbelievers to inquire concerning the true worship of God; c) *cumulative,* through the report concerning the Church spread over the world. Compare Rom. 1:19, 20; 2:14, 15; Acts 17:25-28; 1 Thess. 1:8; Acts 14:17; 2) *specialis seu directa,* or the special call which is based on the special revelation and is mediated through the Word of God. This special call has the following subdivisions: a) *ordinaria seu mediata,* by which is meant that as a rule God calls mediately; b) *extraordinaria seu immediata,* by which is meant an extraordinary or immediate call, which sometimes occurred in the Old Testament dispensation and in the beginning of the New Testament; c) *solemnis et minus solemnis,*—in the former case when the call comes to a person during the preaching of the Word at a church service,—in the latter case when the call is received during private devotions; d) *externa et interna,* or the external and internal call. This distinction has arisen on account of the Calvinists. The Lutheran Church acknowledges that the distinction can be made in a formal sense, but it is not a relationship of logical contraries; in a material sense it is the same call. In accordance with their doctrine of predestination the Calvinists present the distinction in the following way: 1) *ratione principiorum,* or in reference to their origin,— *vocatio externa* being made through the ministry of the Word to the many,—*vocatio interna*, through the illuminating work of the Holy Spirit in the hearts of the elect; 2) *ratione subjectorum*, or in reference to their subjects, so that the former call is designed for all, the latter call only for the elect; 3) *ratione efficaciae*, or in reference to the efficacy, so that the latter only is efficacious and irresistible.

2. The Means and Mode of the Call.

The Holy Ghost calls regularly through the Word of God in the ordinary sense and also through the Word in the Sacraments. Hollazius says: "God calls poor sinners directly and savingly to the Church by the Gospel (2 Thess. 2:14), to which Baptism also pertains (John 3:5). Nevertheless the divine Law contributes something to the call of sinners, but only indirectly, negatively and accidentally."[67] The Gospel is not to be interpreted here in its narrow sense but in its entirety. The call is experienced as an invitation and at times as a warning and a rebuke in order to arouse sinners. It may be brought about by a special Scripture passage or word that has caught the ear in hearing or the eye in reading the Word, or it may be that such a word is recalled in memory in the hour of silent meditation. These are moments of visitation for man, and he is unable to hinder the prevenient grace from exercising its influence. Such times of visitation are indeed critical, since the question is as to whether man will oppose the grace of God, or whether he will enter into a passive state and permit the Holy Spirit to continue the work of grace. Such times of visitation may occur often. The experience of the call to repentance is in principle the same for all, but the external manner in which attention is directed to the significance of the call may vary with a variety of experiences and conditions. We might call to mind the instances of Paul, the jailor at Philippi, Augustine and Luther, noting that while different conditions surrounded them, the call was the same.

---

[67] *Exam. Theol. Acroam.* Pars III, §1, Cap. IV, p. 242.

3. *The Attributes of Vocation.*

The following attributes are ascribed to vocation: 1) *universalis*, or that the call is universal. This term is used against the Calvinists, who teach that the call, strictly speaking, is merely intended for the elect. But we teach that the call is intended for all. The special call reaches all within the Church and many outside of the Church through missionary activities. The old Dogmaticians endeavored to prove that the call had gone forth into the world three times, namely, at the time of Adam, of Enoch and Noah, and in the Apostolic period. This contention may be true with regard to the first two periods, but not with regard to the last named. Hutterus, Gerhard, Quenstedt and Hollazius declare that the nations themselves are to blame because they do not as yet belong to the Church of Christ, since they despise or are indifferent toward the Christian teaching which they must know by report. They neglect to seek knowledge concerning the worship of the true God, although the general natural call ought to prove a sufficient incentive to that end. It is also objected that the children ought not to suffer for the transgressions of their fathers, to which the old Dogmaticians answer that while the children are born outside the Church, which is a temporary punishment, still they are not on that account barred from entering into connection with the Church, which occupies a prominent place in the world and is not unknown. In this connection it may be remarked that the Church has not been as faithful as it should have been in relation to foreign mission work, for if the mission work had been carried on energetically, then it would seem that the whole world long ere this would be Christian, at least in a nominal sense. But even when all the nations shall have received the Gospel of Jesus Christ and thereby received the call, there will nevertheless be countless masses of men who died in the ages past without having received the special call. The Bible indeed states that they have received the general natural call, but it does not deal further with the question, wherefore every attempt to solve the problem carries us into the realm of abstract speculation. The love, righteousness and wisdom of God are a sufficient guarantee that the righteous dominion of God shall sometime be justified, although the secret councils of God are for the present inscrutable. It is not our duty to concern ourselves anxiously about the world dominion of God, but to see to it that we ourselves do not neglect the call of God, while at the same time we ought to labor for the propagation of the kingdom of God in all the world. Furthermore the call is: 2) *seria*, or serious, which term is used against Calvinism; 3) *efficax*, or efficacious, both the external and internal, while the Calvinists say, as before stated, that only the internal vocation is efficacious with regard to the elect; 4) *resistibilis*, or that man can resist the call.

4. The Object of the Call.

The object of the call is twofold: 1) *finis proximus*, which is *excitatio* or awakening; 2) *finis ultimus*, which is conversion and regeneration together with their effects.

The old Dogmaticians say that *excitatio* is *prima initia fidei et conversionis*. Man is aroused when he pays heed to the call and under the influence of the co-operating grace begins to seek the way of salvation. Awakened out of the death slumber of sin, he realizes in a measure the dangerous situation in which he has been and still continues to be. His eyes are directed toward the straight gate and the narrow way. The illuminating grace of God is active in connection with the call, as it has been from the moment of awakening. In some instances the emotions are very greatly aroused; indeed, these emotions may at times become peculiarly delightful, for which reason it may happen that this awakening may be mistaken for the completed conversion. At so-called "revival meetings," especially among the Reformed, great emotional excitation is often called conversion. But awakening is only the beginning of conversion. It is not sufficient that the emotions are aroused; the understanding must be illumined and the will transformed. The Scripture passage to which reference is made with regard to awakening is Eph. 5:14: "Awake, thou that sleepest, and arise from the dead, and Christ shall shine upon thee"; cf. Acts 2:37: "Now when they heard this, they were pricked in their heart"; Acts 16:29, 30: "And, trembling for fear, he fell down before Paul and Silas, and said, Sirs, what must I do to be saved?"

§25. Illumination.

Illumination, *illuminatio*, is *that act of grace whereby the Holy Ghost through the Law convicts man of sin and through the Gospel imparts to him knowledge of the way of salvation. This act of grace belongs especially to the converting activity of the Holy Ghost, but is nevertheless continued through the state of sanctification, since the life of a Christian is characterized by daily repentance.*

Hollazius has the following definition: "*Illuminatio* is that act of applying grace whereby the Holy Ghost, through the ministry of the Word, instructs the sinner who is called to the Church, and imparts to him more and more knowledge for the earnest purpose of removing the darkness of ignorance and error, imbuing him with the knowledge of the Word of God, and instilling in him through the Law the knowledge of sin, and through the Gospel the knowledge of divine mercy, founded upon the merit of Christ."[68]

1. The Division of Illumination.

The following division is common and in part necessary: 1) *Illuminatio imperfecta, literalis et paedagogica,* or the more literal and pedagogical illumination or instruction. *Gratia assistens* is active in this connection. The object of this external illumination is the preparation of the sinner for the spiritual illumination. As to its object this pedagogical illumination is *vere salutaris* and as to its character *supernaturalis.* We quote the following Scripture passages: "And we have the word of prophecy made more sure; whereunto ye do well that ye take heed, as unto a lamp shining in a

---

[68] Hollazius: "*Illuminatio est actus gratiae applicatricis, quo Spiritus sanctus hominem peccatorem ad ecclesiam vocatum per ministerium verbi docet et sincero studio magis magisque informat, ut depulsis ignorantiae et errorum tenebris ipsum verbi Deo notitia imbuat, atque ex lege agnitionem peccati, ex evangelio misericordiae divinae, in merito Christi fundatae, cognitionem eidem instillet.*"

dark place, until the day dawn, and the day-star arise in your hearts" (2 Peter 1:19); "Unto me, who am less than the least of all saints, was this grace given, to preach unto the Gentiles the unsearchable riches of Christ; and to make all men see what is the dispensation of the mystery which for ages hath been hid in God who created all things" (Eph. 3:8, 9). 2) *Perfecta, spiritualis et complete salutaris,* or the complete, spiritual and saving illumination, which implies not only the impartation of external knowledge, but by means of this a living knowledge, so that the Holy Ghost through *gratia ingrediens et operans* works conversion and regeneration and afterwards continues the work of illumination through *gratia inhabitans.* Among Scripture passages we quote the following: "That the God of our Lord Jesus Christ, the Father of glory, may give unto you a spirit of wisdom and revelation in the knowledge of him; having the eyes of your heart enlightened" (Eph. 1:17, 18); "Seeing it is God, that said, Light shall shine out of darkness, who shined in our hearts, to give the light of the knowledge of the glory of God in the face of Jesus Christ" (2 Cor. 4:6; cf. 1 Thess. 1:5; 2 Thess. 3:15, 16). 3) *Legalis,* or illumination through the Law. The word of the Law enlightens the conscience of man like the lightning, so that he becomes terrified because of sin and fears the wrath of God. Through the content of the Law he is given further instruction concerning sin. Many Scripture passages could be quoted, but we cite only one: "Howbeit, I had not known sin, except through the law: for I had not known coveting, except the law had said, Thou shalt not covet" (Rom. 7:7ff.). 4) *Evangelica,* or illumination through the Gospel, which is like unto the sun which dispels the darkness and illumines the Christ. Compare the following passages: "The light of the gospel of the glory of Christ" (2 Cor. 4: 4; 3: 6-11; Luke 1:77, 78; 4:18; 7:22).

2. The Means and the Mode of Illumination.

The ordinary means of illumination are the means of grace, especially the Word of God. In Luther's explanation of the third article of the Creed we read that the Holy Ghost enlightens us with His gifts. Opinions are divided with regard to the meaning of these words. Some say that these gifts are the Law and the Gospel. Von Zeschwitz does not consider that the Law can be implied, and scarcely the Gospel, since the Gospel is especially mentioned in connection with the call. On the other hand, he sets forth Baptism, the Holy Spirit and the gracious gifts of the Spirit. But inasmuch as the Holy Spirit bestows the gifts, we must necessarily distinguish between Him and the gifts through which He enlightens. Some have presented the effects, such as penitence and faith, but this constitutes an inconsistency. Gez. von Scheele says in this connection: "What these gifts are depends on the character of the particular means of grace through which they are imparted to us. Inasmuch as the Word, apart from Baptism, constitutes this means, and since the Word is divided as to its contents into the Law and the Gospel, therefore the term 'gifts' must denote more particularly the knowledge of sin brought about by the Law together with the knowledge of the grace of God in Christ Jesus imparted through the Gospel."[69]

Through the Law and the Gospel the awakened sinner receives the light that is necessary in order to reach the goal of salvation. Although this light is necessary for the whole life of the Christian, yet the effect of this illumination is especially striking during the states of awakening and conversion. In the case of the person who has been baptized in infancy and through the Sacrament has become a child of God, but afterwards has fallen from the baptismal grace, the Sacrament itself is a gift of grace that points the way back home. The old Church Fathers also called Baptism *φώτισμα*. And when a prodigal son, in returning to the Father's house, visits the temple of the Lord, where the congregation celebrates the Holy Supper, this Sacrament in turn becomes a light that bears witness of the true home. In the ears of the soul awakened out of the state of sin the words of the Sacraments become both a penitential sermon and an evangel. The Word of God, therefore, is the means through which the Holy Spirit enlightens. We have not received the promise of any immediate illumination, for which reason we reject the doctrines of the Mystics and others bearing

[69] *Den Kyrkliga Katekisationen*, p. 145.

on this matter. The Holy Spirit illumines mediately. Among Scripture passages the following may be cited: "So belief cometh of hearing, and hearing by the word of Christ" (Rom. 10:17).

Adminicula, or auxiliaries, are *oratio, meditatio et tentatio*. The Lord has especially promised to give the Holy Spirit to them that ask Him. Cf. Luke 11:13. Concerning the searching of the Scriptures, compare John 5:39. With regard to trials we read in Ps. 119:71: "It is good for me that I have been afflicted; that I may learn thy statutes." Cf. 1 Peter 1:6, 7. Periods of quiet and rest are necessary. Compare Mark 6:31: "He said unto them, Come ye yourselves apart into a desert place, and rest awhile." With regard to the doctrine of the Mystics concerning *silentium verborum, cogitationum et desideriorum* and concerning *internum animae sabbathum*, we approve of *silentium verborum* in the sense that silence and rest are necessary, inasmuch as they render more effectual the reading of the Word with its attendant effects. An internal Sabbath rest is useful in promoting earnest meditation and prayer. But we cannot accept the doctrine concerning *silentium cogitationum et desideriorum* through which man is supposed to receive a special divine revelation and illumination. God illumines us sufficiently through the Word of God, but quiet meditation is necessary. The same is true with regard to the hearing of the Word. Compare Eccles. 5:1: "Keep thy foot when thou goest to the house of God." Worldly conversation before or after the service often has a disturbing effect.

3. *The Activity and Object of Illumination.*

The point of departure in illumination is the naturally darkened understanding of man. Compare Eph. 4:18. The activity of illumination is first directed to the *intellectus* or the understanding, so that the seeker after salvation receives knowledge through which the activity is directed to the *voluntas* or will, since the object is such an influencing of the will as will lead to conversion. Compare Eph. 1:18; 2 Cor. 4:6 and Titus 2:11, 12.

Finis, or the object, is divided as follows: 1) *finis proximus* is conversion; 2) *finis ultimus* is the immediate illumination in heaven. The reaching of the goal takes place gradually. Beginning with the call the light of the

Word of God penetrates into the darkness of the sinner's heart so that he is aroused. In case there is no wilful opposition to the influence of the Word, then his eyes are opened more and more and the awakening becomes deeper and more thorough. The sinner then becomes conscious of a profound need of the spiritual light. He reads and hearkens to the Word of God. In this manner he learns to know himself and God. The experiences that he passes through are both bitter and delightful in character, and if the activity of the Holy Spirit is permitted to continue without hindrance, man turns more and more from darkness to light, and from the power of Satan to God. The illumination grows during conversion, but never becomes complete in this life, for here we know only in part. However, the degree of our illumination is dependent on the diligent and prayerful use of the Word of God.

§26. Conversion.

Conversion, *conversio*, is *that act through which the Holy Ghost converts the understanding, the emotions, and especially the will of the awakened sinner, resulting in a self-determination of the will, which takes the form of contrition and faith.* The definition of conversion is dependent upon whether it is considered in the broad sense, the special sense, or the most special sense. In the broad sense conversion embraces all the acts of grace, while in the most special sense it embraces only contrition. We here employ the expression conversion in the special sense, as embracing contrition and faith, or *poenitentia.* Instead of contrition repentance is mostly used.

I. The General Characteristics of Conversion.

Conversion has both a human and a divine side. As experienced in the heart of the sinner, conversion is instantaneous as to the ultimate act, but successive as to the preparatory acts in reaching its object, with certain factors active.

1. The Division of Conversion.

The following terms are used to distinguish between the different points of view from which conversion may be considered: 1) *Conversio transitiva*, because the converting activity passes from God to another subject. This transitive side is active as proceeding from the Holy Spirit, and passive by reason of the seat of excitation in the sinner, and because he is the object of the preparatory and operating grace. 2) *Conversio intransitiva, poenitentia* or repentance. By this is meant the changed condition of the heart as affecting the intellect, the emotions and the will. Many passages in Scripture, not to speak of the majority of instances bearing on the subject, present conversion from the intransitive standpoint as consisting in repentance. Compare Mal. 3:7; Matt. 13:14, 15; Acts 3:18; 2 Cor. 3:16. Also cf. Jer. 31:18: "Turn thou me, and I shall be turned." When reference is made to the human activity, it is not the natural power of man that is implied. The following Latin sentence of the Dogmaticians applies in this connection: *se convertit veribus non nativis, sed dativis.*

2. The Starting Point of Conversion.

Chemnitz says that conversion has its starting points, its progress or degrees of development, through which it is completed in great weakness. Baier uses the following division: 1) *terminus a quo formalis* is sin, both habitual and actual; 2) *terminus a quo objectivus* consists of those things that are the objects of actual sins, especially those toward which the sinner feels a peculiar inclination, such as secret or bosom sins. Conversion must therefore proceed from the root of evil and include the whole gamut of sin. Inasmuch as secret sins are especially vulnerable points, therefore conversion must also include an attack upon these.

3. The Factors in Conversion.

The factors in conversion are the Word and the Holy Ghost. There are not three factors, as the Synergists assert. The Holy Ghost works through the means of grace. Man must therefore make use of these means. He is able to read and to hear the Word of God, but will receive no blessing to be converted by his own power. For this reason the Formula of Concord rejects the opinions of the Enthusiasts and Epicureans, who belittle the means of grace and expect that God shall make forceful intervention and convert man against his will, thereby removing all human responsibility. In this connection we would present the heretical tendencies which the Formula of Concord rejects:[70] 1) The doctrine of the Stoics and the Manichaeans, which declares that everything happens through necessity, so that man possesses no freedom. 2) The Pelagian view, which says that man is capable of converting himself with his own power. 3) The Semi-Pelagian view, which teaches that man himself is capable of beginning the work of conversion, but by reason of human weakness the Holy Ghost must continue the work. 4) The position of the Synergists, which holds that God begins the work of conversion, but that man is thereafter capable in his own power, which is weak, to co-operate in and continue that work. 5) The heresy of the Flacians, which teaches that in conversion God entirely outroots the substance and essence of the old Adam. 6) The further doctrine of the Flacians, that man even after his conversion withstands the Holy Spirit, so that no co-operation takes place with the spiritual powers imparted by the Holy Ghost. 7) The teaching of the popes and monks, that the regenerated man is fully capable of completely fulfilling the Law of God, which also constitutes the righteousness of man, and through which he merits eternal life. Such expressions as those of Chrysostom and Basil here quoted are also rejected: "God draws but him who wills; if only you will, God will meet you beforehand."

The Lutheran Confession sets forth the means of grace and the activity of the Holy Ghost through these. Through grace therefore the will of man is made free, but inasmuch as man is incapable of doing anything in his own power, therefore the natural human will is not a factor in conversion. Man could not possess himself in a state of passivity, except as the Holy Ghost works through His prevenient grace. The responsibility of man arises when he does not permit the Holy Spirit to perform this work, but withstands the Spirit and neglects to use the Word of God. For this reason

---

[70] Müller's Symb. Bücher, Epitome II, pp. 524-563.

the Formula of Concord says:[71] "And in this respect it might well be said that man is not a stone or block. For a stone or block does not resist that which moves it, and does not understand and is not sensible of what is being done with it, as a man, as long as he is not converted, with his will resists God the Lord. And it is nevertheless true that a man before his conversion is still a rational creature, having an understanding and will, yet not an understanding with respect to divine things, or a will to will something good and salutary. Yet he can do nothing whatever for his conversion (as has also been said often above), and is in this respect much worse than a stone and block; for he resists the Word and will of God, until God awakens him from the death of sin, enlightens and renews him." The Formula of Concord therefore treats of the utter inability of the natural man. In considering the natural state of man, and realizing that it is only the grace of God that can set at liberty the will of man, we comprehend the reason why there are but two factors in conversion, as has been stated. Cf. §15, 4, and §7, 2.

4. The Object of Conversion.

Finis conversionis is twofold: 1) *finis formalis* is faith in Christ; 2) *finis objectivus* is God. Inasmuch as conversion consists in contrition and faith, therefore conversion is completed through faith. Through faith man has returned to God. The converted man lives in daily contrition and faith, which is the same as daily repentance. The following Scripture passages may be quoted: "Repent ye" (Acts 2:38); "Believe on the Lord Jesus" (Acts 16:31); "For he that cometh to God must believe that he is, and that he is a rewarder of them that seek after him" (Heb.11:6); "I will arise and go to my father, and say unto him, Father, I have sinned against heaven, and in thy sight" (Luke 15:18); "And he arose, and came to his father" (Luke 15:20).

II. Contrition.

---

[71] Müller's Symb. Bücher, p. 602, 59.

Contrition is the first element in *conversio intransitiva* or *poenitentia*. The first contrition is called the great contrition or *poenitentia magna*, the renewed contrition of a fallen Christian is called *poenitentia iterata*, while the daily contrition of a Christian is called *poenitentia stantium*. Strictly speaking, however, contrition is the first element in *poenitentia* or repentance. We define contrition as follows: Contrition is that change of mind or heart in man in relation to sin, made known through the illumination by the Law, which manifests itself in deep sorrow and fear of conscience because of sin together with a detestation of sin and a faithful endeavor to be rid of it.

The Greek word that has been rendered with "repentance" is *μετάνοια* and means really change of mind or heart. The same word seems also to be used in the sense of contrition. Compare Mark 1:15: "Repent ye, and believe in the gospel." In this passage *μετανοιεῖτε* might be translated "be contrite" or "be changed in mind," followed as it is by the admonition to believe, which is a component part of the concept repentance. Compare, for example, Acts 2:38 and 2 Cor. 7:10. The verb that is used for contrition is *μεταμέλομαι*, but the substantive *μεταμέλεια* does not occur in the New Testament. *Μετάνοια* is used to express both contrition and repentance. 2 Cor. 7:10 speaks of repentance which bringeth no regret.

1. The Requisites and Marks of Contrition.

According to Gerhard the *partes contritionis* are the following: 1) *vera peccati agnitio*, or a true knowledge of sin; 2) *sensus irae divinae. adversus peccata*, or the consciousness of the wrath of God against sin; 3) *conscientiae angores et pavores*, or the anguish and terror of the conscience; 4) *vera coram Deo humiliatio*, or true humility before God; 5) *ingenua peccati confessio*, or a candid confession of sin; 6) *serium peccati odium ac detestatio*, or an earnest hatred and detestation of sin.[72]

The Confessions and the old Dogmaticians emphasize *terrores conscientiae*. In the Augsburg Confession, Article XII, we read: "Now repentance

---

[72] Loci Theologici, Tomus III, p. 238, 63.

consists properly of two parts: One is contrition, that is, terrors smiting the conscience through the knowledge. The terror of the conscience through the knowledge of sin," etc. The terror of the conscience may vary in degree, but all contrite souls experience this terror on different occasions. The anguish of heart because of sin may vary in accordance with many circumstances, both internal and external, but every one must know the nature of sin and its effects. This internal sorrow may not always manifest itself in strong crying, or in a manner that may be observed by others, but is nevertheless intensive. The external manifestation varies with the personal temperament and other influences. He that loudly laments may suffer less than the contrite sinner who quietly experiences the sorrow that is of the godly sort. It may often prove true that loud crying and lamentation and violent gesticulation indicate merely aroused emotions but no profound contrition, as is often the case at pre-arranged "revival meetings." It may not be possible, indeed, to determine theoretically the decisive and unfailing characteristics by which to gauge the experience of the contrite sinner, but the above named parts make clear the principal features.

The marks of true contrition may also be presented as follows: 1) *Interna*: a) knowledge of sin and the consciousness of God's wrath on account of sin; b) sorrow and anguish of conscience; c) detestation of sin and therefore an internal resolution to forsake sin; d) yearning for redemption. 2) *Externa*: a) earnest confession of sin before, God and in certain cases before a minister of the Word or some other Christian; b) the diligent use of the Word; c) the continued works of grace; d) the fruits of contrition in the newness of life.

The following Scripture passages may be quoted: "For I know my transgressions; and my sin is ever before me" (Ps. 51:3); "There is no soundness in my flesh because of thine indignation; neither is there any health in my bones because of my sin" (Ps. 38:3) ; "Have mercy upon me, O Jehovah; for I am withered away: my soul is sore troubled" (Ps. 6:2, 3); "Humble yourselves in the sight of the Lord, and he shall exalt you" (James 4:10); "I will confess my transgressions unto Jehovah" (Ps. 32:5); "What I hate, that I do" (Rom. 7:15); "God, be thou merciful to me a sinner" (Luke 18:13). In proof of the fact that contrition implies a new relationship the following may be cited: "If I have wrongfully exacted aught of any man, I restore fourfold" (Luke 19:8). Such a restitution proves the genuineness of contrition, provided that other characteristics are present.

2. The Object of Contrition.

Objectum contritionis is sin. The objects of contrition are sins, both habitual and actual sins, especially secret or bosom sins. Certain sins may manifest themselves more than others, but the contrite sinner grieves over his entire sinful state. Contrition may often begin on account of one individual sin, but through the activity of the Spirit the knowledge of one sin leads to the knowledge of others, at first more grievous and palpable sins, afterwards less palpable; at first external sins, then internal, the conscience becoming more sensitive all the while. The sorrow becomes all the deeper as man realizes his own inability to deliver himself from sin, and that his contrition is not as profound as it ought to be, wherefore he laments because of his impenitence. In a measure his experience becomes like unto that described in Rom. 7:7-14. The object of contrition is therefore not the punishment of sin, so as to cause grief only on account of the effects of sin; the penitent grieves over sin itself as sin against God.

3. The Effects of Contrition.

Effectus contritionis comprises the following parts: 1) more profound knowledge of the demands of the Law; 2) a genuine consciousness of sin; 3) the experience of inability to save oneself; 4) the elimination of hindrances in the way of repentance.

The transition from contrition to faith is a critical period in the experience of the awakened and contrite soul, for he stands in danger either of reverting to the natural state or of entering into a state of bondage under the Law. But where the spiritual experience is normal, there the contrite sinner becomes poor in spirit. The storm clouds of the Law may threaten overhead, but through the knowledge of the Gospel the clouds are dispersed. Faith is already present as a real possibility. A sense of yearning possesses the soul. Faith reveals itself first in seeking and longing. We find a Biblical expression of the effect of contrition in the words of Paul in 2 Cor. 7:10: "For godly sorrow worketh repentance unto salvation."

III. Faith.

The immediate end of contrition or penitence is faith, which is the second part of conversion. Faith may be defined as follows: *Fides* is *that gracious act of the Holy Ghost whereby the contrite sinner, in process of conversion, in a living way knows, with his whole heart assents to, and with childlike trust apprehends the saving grace of God, in order that he may be justified and eternally saved for Christ's sake.*

The Greek word for faith is *πίστις*. In Heb. 11:1 faith is defined as follows: "Now faith is assurance of things hoped for, a conviction of things not seen." The word translated assurance is in the Greek *ὑπόστασις*, which means foundation, substratum, substance, the essence of a thing, and therefore denotes the unshakable reliance of the heart, the assurance of building on a sure foundation. Faith is assurance or confidence. Compare 2 Cor. 3:4 and Eph. 3:12. The latter passage also speaks of boldness in confidence. Faith is also a certain and unmovable conviction. Compare Rom. 4:21; Col. 2:2, and Heb. 10:22.

It is God that works faith through the means of grace. *Causa efficiens principalis* is the Triune God, *causa impulsiva interna* is the goodness of God, *causa impulsiva externa* is the merit of Christ, and *causa instrumentalis* is the Word, or Baptism, or the means of grace in general.

1. The Elements of Faith.

Partes fidei are: 1) *Notitia*, or knowledge. The knowledge of faith is not so much *implicita*, it is principally *explicita*. When faith is considered as a *fides implicita*, it denotes simply an historic faith, so that without examination man believes what the Church teaches. On the other hand, the knowledge which is characteristic of *fides explicita* denotes that which is believed, that which is known in a distinctive sense, so that it can be distinguished from other objects, even though it cannot be clearly or completely comprehended. Among Scripture passages may be cited: "And we have believed and know that thou art the Holy One of God" (John 6:69; cf. 17:3; Luke 1:77; John 14:10). 2) *Assensus*, or assent. This assensus is twofold: a) *generalis*, or a general assent, when the acknowledgment is made that the promises of God and the merit of Christ are true; b) *specialis*, or an assent that implies that the contrite person considers that these promises and this merit are true for him personally. This assent includes a conviction of things not seen. Compare Heb. 11:1; also 1 Tim. 1:15, which sets forth both *assensus generalis et specialis*. Cf. also John 14:11. 3) *Fiducia*, or confidence. *Fiducia* is the childlike trust of the will in Christ and therefore implies the personal application and appropriation of the Gospel promises and the merit of Christ. In a higher degree it is the yearning of the faith of repentance, indeed, it is the confident assurance of the heart. Among Scripture passages may be mentioned: "And being fully assured that what he had promised, he was able also to perform" (Rom. 4:21); "In fulness of faith" (Heb. 10:22); "Confidence" (2 Cor. 3:4; cf. Eph. 3:12, etc.). Of course, confidence has its varying degrees, so that some can believe with greater trustfulness than others. Compare John 14:12; 17:8; 1 John 3:21; Heb. 11:1, etc.

The three elements of faith are set forth in John 14:10-12. *Notitia* is presented in the tenth verse, *assensus* in the eleventh and *fiducia* in the twelfth verse. The three elements are also expressed in the following Latin phrases: *Credere Deum*, which means faith in the existence of God and the knowledge of God in general, *credere Deo*, which denotes faith in the Word and promises of God, *credere in Deum*, which signifies the inmost essence of faith or confidence. Only a Christian has faith in the last-named sense, but in adults this includes also the first and second.

2. The Attributes of Faith.

The character of faith is determined through divisions which at the same time constitute attributes. These attributes describe more clearly the essence and degree of faith. The following are the most common: 1) *fides generalis*, or a general faith in the truth of the Word of God; 2) *specialis*, or the personal confidence of the contrite sinner in the gracious promises of God; 3) *apprehensiva et justificans* is faith as apprehending the merit of Christ, thus appropriating the grace of forgiveness; 4) *reflexa et discursiva* is the faith of the converted sinner, who knows that he believes, so that with childlike fear he is enabled to say with Paul: "I know him whom I have believed"; 5) *fides directa* is a faith like the faith of small children, wrought at their Baptism; 6) *infirma*, or a weak faith, which is nevertheless a true faith; 7) *firma*, or a strong faith.

When repentance has been completed, i.e., the so-called great repentance, then yearning faith enters into the heart of the contrite sinner, resulting in the conviction of faith, the consecration of the will and the confident assurance of faith. But this special and reflexive faith is not always firm, but often infirm. The converted sinner, however, is always inclined toward the object of his faith. This experience is closely connected with the effect of faith.

In distinguishing between reflex or discursive and direct faith we must consider that the first kindling of faith is direct faith both in children and grown persons. The Holy Spirit works faith by the means of grace, in children by Baptism, as before stated. The instrumental cause of faith is the preaching of the Word and the Sacraments, but the children cannot understandingly hear the Word. Their faith also becomes discursive later on. The direct faith of a child is nevertheless a true faith, although it is embryonic in its character. The acorn contains the entire oak. Just as God created a cell, a seed or an acorn, the Holy Spirit works faith in a child by Baptism, and this faith saves just as does the discursive faith. The saving faith does not depend upon our understanding and our own power, but upon the power of God. — Among other attributes we mention implicit, explicit, and crude, (*fides informis*), and faith energized or determined by love. The implicit faith is the same as *notitia implicita* which implies an acceptance of what is known and many particulars which are not known. When a member of the Church accepts the authority of the Church, such a person believes what the Church has taught, teaches and will teach. The explicit faith is like *notitia explicita*. Compare above. The crude faith is an assent to the Church doctrine and is in fact the same as a historical faith. But the Augsburg Confession says: "Faith does not signify merely the knowledge of the history." The scholastic 'faith energized by love' is a Roman Catholic doctrine. This term implies that faith justifies by the virtue of love pervading it. But the correct doctrine is that we are justified not on account of our faith, nor on account of our love, but through faith on account of the merits of Christ. The good works follow faith as fruits of faith. Compare the following paragraph.

3. The Effect and Object of Faith.

Effectus fidei is righteousness and the new life, since faith implies both *vis receptiva* and *vis operativa*. It is *vis receptiva* as a justifying faith and *vis operativa* as a renewing and sanctifying faith. Faith is indeed the beginning of a new life, but the character of faith is receptive. Operative faith is therefore not conceived of as being determined by love, as the Catholic Church speaks of a *fides caritate formata*. Love is a fruit of faith; love is not operative through faith, but faith through love. Gez. Von Scheele says in this connection: "In accordance with the direction of the Word of God the Lutheran Church combines in indissoluble union true faith and true love, but instead of the *fides caritate formata* of the Catholic Church, she sets forth a *caritas fide formata* in the certain conviction that no true love can be brought about except through union with Christ by faith; only as love enters the heart through justifying faith is it enabled to take form in the deeds of Christian love."[73]

Finis fidei is in the first place justification and then new relationship as the children of God, followed by renovation and finally eternal salvation. The doctrine of faith stands in the most intimate relationship to the doctrine of justification.

---

[73] Symbolik, page 224.

Notes on the History of Dogma.

The Apostolic Church set forth the great importance of contrition as the first element in conversion. Great emphasis was also laid on *contritio iterata,* especially in connection with church discipline. When a person had fallen into sin and become the object of church discipline it was not sufficient for his reinstatement that he manifested a contrite spirit, his penance must include a certain graduated order of procedure before restoration could be accomplished. This order of procedure included the following four stages: *Fletus,* or standing at the church doors to make supplication for restoration; *auditio,* in which the penitents were admitted again to the reading of the Scriptures and the sermon; *genuflexio,* in which they were admitted into the nave of the church to kneel at prayer; *consistentia,* or in standing posture to take part with the congregation in the whole of the public services. The conception of faith was not so profound during the Apologetic and Polemical periods. The Roman Catholic Church's doctrine of contrition and faith was developed during the early Scholastic period. It took the position that *poenitentia* or repentance consisted of the following parts: 1) Penitence, which is either *attritio,* imperfect penitence, which arises through the fear of punishment, or *contritio,* perfect penitence; 2) private confession before the priest; 3) satisfactions. Faith was conceived of as *fides informis* and *formata.* The Lutheran Confessions set forth contrition as the first part of conversion. Contrition is the sorrow of the heart and the terror of the conscience brought about by the knowledge of sin. Faith is conceived of as being apprehensive, and one of its most important characteristics is said to be *fiducia in voluntate.* The Reformed Church does not have the profound conception of the knowledge of sin which is characteristic of the Lutheran Church. The condition of guilt before God is not sufficiently emphasized, hence the reconciliation is viewed first and foremost as a redemption. The doctrine of penitence is affected to some extent by this view, although the Reformed Church acknowledges the importance of true contrition. However, the state of the emotions often forms the gauge by which to judge the genuineness of contrition. The Lutheran Church lays the greatest stress on the sorrow of the heart and the fear of conscience as a result of the profound consciousness of sin. The knowledge of sin must be such that the ensuing contrition will affect the will. The conception of faith held by the Reformed Church is more nearly related to that of the Catholic Church than the Lutheran. The apprehensive character of faith is not sufficiently emphasized; rather faith is presented as a principle of life. In some manner faith is determined by something within man. The conception of faith occupies a more prominent position than the doctrine of justification. We pass on now to the presentation of more detailed remarks concerning the doctrine of repentance during the leading periods.

Clement of Rome emphasizes the justifying character of faith, but declares, however, that love is a means to the forgiveness of sins. Ignatius says that faith is the beginning of life and love the goal. Justin Martyr speaks of faith in connection with the blotting out of sin. Irenaeus presents faith and obedience as being necessary for salvation. Tertullian, Clement of Alexandria and Cyprian indeed present faith, but they especially emphasize the necessity of penance for sins committed after Baptism. Origen lays great stress on the degree of contrition and teaches that minor sins may be reconciled through penances. He expresses himself very vaguely concerning faith.

Augustine considered that it was not proper to distinguish between sins and emphasized penance in relation to God. He says that faith is active through love and is determined by love. His doctrine of faith was expressed in the terms *fides historica et formata*. Penance was necessary for the grosser sins committed after Baptism. John of Damascus speaks of a twofold faith, being in the first place an *assensus* and then *fiducia*.

Anselm regarded faith as the acceptation of the objective teachings of the Church. Peter Lombard defines faith as *fides informis* or faith in the teachings of the Church and fides formata, i. e.. as determined by love. He also speaks of *credere Deum* or faith in the existence of God, *credere Deo* or faith in the truth of the Word of God, and *credere in Deum*, meaning to love God in faith, which faith is meritorious as one of the Christian graces. Thomas Aquinas also says that *fides formata* is one of the Christian graces.

Luther conceived of faith as being the true assurance of the heart. Faith embraces Christ as the bridal ring encloses the precious jewel. With regard to contrition the Schmalkald Articles state that it is effected by the Law, that it is not *contritio activa,* but *passiva,* excluding all merit. Contrition consists in the broken and contrite heart, the pain of the awakened conscience, the anguish of soul together with the consciousness and fear of impending death. The fear of conscience is therefore emphasized. Repentance must be experienced by every man, while it must embrace everything in life and continue always. In the Confessions the apprehensive character of faith is set forth, while the doctrine of a faith determined by love is rejected. Conversion is said to consist of two parts, namely, contrition and faith. Melanchthon divided conversion into two parts, but in the Apology he states that he would interpose no objection if a third part were added, i.e., the fruit of repentance. However, the fruit of repentance is not a part of conversion, but a result. Agricola held a position different from that of the Lutheran Church concerning the place of contrition in the order of salvation. His arrangement of the *ordo salutis* is as follows: 1) Man experiences the love of God which leads to Christ and the bestowal of His grace; 2) he apprehends this grace and thanks God for it; 3) then follows contrition or repentance; 4) thereafter comes the heart's confidence toward God and a resolution to sin no more. The Catholics reject the Lutheran doctrine that *poenitentia* or conversion consists of contrition and faith. They rather consider faith as a presupposition to conversion, which consists of *contritio, confessio* and *satisfactio.* The Council of Trent condemns those who say that faith is *fiducia.* Bellarmin says that the Catholics differ in three things from the heretics: in the first place concerning the object of justifying faith, because the heretics limit themselves to the promise of a special mercy; in the second place with regard to the seat (*sedes*) of faith, inasmuch as the heretics say *fiducia in voluntate* and the Catholics say *in intellectu*; in the third place concerning the conception itself, since the Catholics say that *assensus* expresses the content of faith, while the heretics declare it is *fiducia*.

The Rationalists, such as Wegscheider, reject the order of salvation and set forth the power of man to save himself. It is necessary only for the ignorant to believe in a supernatural activity in conversion, since they are incapable of comprehending how God influences *causas secundas* in accordance with the laws of nature. They reject the Church doctrine of faith and present the so-called intellectual faith. In the main Kant held the same position. He emphasized the freedom of man and the intellectual faith. The Supranaturalists desired to defend the Church doctrine of conversion, but in many respects yielded to the Rationalists. Some said that the work of grace was simply a strengthening of the powers of nature. The mediating theologians did not conceive of faith in its purely receptive character. The modern theologians are divided into two camps, depending upon whether they follow the conservative doctrine of the Church or the mediating theology. Thomasius, Philippi and others present the doctrine of the Church, while Kahnis and others tend toward Synergism. Schartau in Sweden has especially emphasized the third article of the Creed and in a very detailed manner has developed the doctrine of *ordo salutis*. Norbeck defines conversion merely as contrition and says that this is conversion in the real sense (*strictissimi*). But he conceives of repentance as consisting of contrition and faith. — Other quotations could be presented to show how Dogmatlcians differ in their definitions of repentance, conversion and regeneration. Although the differences may be explained in a satisfactory manner, still it would be well if the terminology and definitions could be made more definite.

§27. Justification.

Many Dogmaticians treat the doctrine of justification before the order of salvation by reason of the fact that justification is an act of God that takes place outside of man, and, therefore, *stricte dicto*, does not belong to the *ordo salutis*, but we present this doctrine of justification in its logical connection with faith, since, as has been stated, *finis fidei* is justification. The presupposition and condition of justification is faith. Inasmuch as the doctrine of forgiveness of sins is treated in the third article of the Creed, therefore it cannot be out of place to treat justification in the order of salvation. If the Holy Ghost were not active in the genesis of faith, then no justification could take place. The effects of justification also belong to the order of salvation. Let it be understood that justification is not to be compared with or is like other acts in the *ordo salutis*; its position is more objective. As reconciliation occupies the central position in the objective work of salvation, so justification occupies the central and dominating position in the applying activity of salvation. Conversion, whose end and purpose is faith, precedes, and sanctification follows justification. But since justification takes place in the heart or mind of God when the contrite sinner believes, so it is the divine side of the activity of grace, the invisible forensic act and the objective ground, whose effects are realized in the experience of the believer. Justification is the keystone of the Lutheran doctrinal system and therefore also of her order of salvation. *Justificatio sola fide* or *propter Christum per fidem* is the sun in the solar system of Lutheran doctrine. For this reason it has also been said that justification is *articulus stantis et cadentis ecclesiae*.

1. The Definition of Justification.

Justification is *the judicial act of God by which He sets the believing sinner free, which act includes the forgiveness of sins and the imputation of the acquired righteousness of Christ with the result that man becomes a child of God.* The definition of Hollazius reads as follows: "*Justificatio* is that act of grace whereby God, the most just and merciful judge, forgives sinful man, subject to guilt and punishment, but converted and regenerated, out of mercy alone on account of the satisfaction and merit of Christ, apprehended in true faith, and imputes to him the righteousness of Christ, so that he becomes a child of God and an heir to life eternal."[74] From this definition it is evident that Hollazius considers regeneration a *prius* to justification and therefore as a *donatio fidei. Subjectum justificationis* according to this definition is the sinner as *conversus et renatus*. Inasmuch as conversion or repentance consists in contrition and faith, therefore we may say that the subject of justification is the converted sinner who is both justified and regenerated by faith.

It is God that justifies. Concerning *causae* the Dogmaticians say that *causa impulsiva interna* is the love of God and *causa impulsiva externa* is the merit of Christ alone. The fourth article of the Augsburg Confession clearly sets this forth: "Man cannot become righteous before God through his own strength, merits or deeds, but is declared righteous by grace through faith for Christ's sake." *Propter Christum* is further explained in these words: "On account of the merit of Christ, who by His death has made satisfaction for our sins."

The ground of justification is, therefore, only the merit of Christ. God could not have justified man without a ground or foundation. The will of God is revealed in His Law and this cannot be broken. Satisfaction had to be made and perfect obedience rendered. In Adam we all sinned and by being implanted in the second Adam or Christ we become righteous. A comparison is made in Rom. 5:18, 19: "So then as through one trespass the judgment came unto all men to condemnation; even so through one act of righteousness the free gift came unto all men to justification of life. For as through the one man's disobedience the many were made sinners, even so through the obedience of the one shall the many be made righteous." But we must be in the second Adam as in the first. We are not righteous outside of Christ, but, believing in Him, His acquired righteousness is imputed to us. Then there is no imputation of sin. Ps. 32:1, 2. The acquired righteousness of Christ, the second Adam, is sufficient to save or justify

---

[74] Hollazius: *"Justificatio est actus gratia, quo Deus, judex justissimus et misericordissimus, homini peccatori, culpae et poenae reo sed converso et renato, ex mera misericordia propter satisfactionem et meritum Christi, vera fide apprehensum, peccata remittit et justitiam Christi imputat, ut in filium Dei adoptatus, haeres sit vitae aeternae."*

all the children of the first Adam, but only by faith can justification take place. Faith justifies, not by itself, but by embracing the merits of Christ. Justification is the work of God. When a converted sinner is justified, it is as if the obedience of Christ had been rendered by the man himself. The act of justification is not, like regeneration, a work of God within man, but is an external work in the mind of God. The effect, however, is experienced in the heart of man. There is nothing in us, as, e. g., our love, etc., which justifies, but we are justified through faith for Christ's sake. The Bible verses in the next paragraph show the juridical character of justification and how God justifies the individual.

Justification is a judicial or forensic act. The following Scripture passages make this clear from different points of view. The "judge" is spoken of in John 5:27; Heb. 12:23; the "judgment-seat" in Rom. 14:10; Matt. 18:21-35; the "sinner" or "criminal" in Rom. 3:19; Matt. 18:24; the "accuser" in John 5:45; the "witness" in Rom. 2:15; the indictment or "bond written in ordinances against us" in Col. 2:14; the "debt" in Matt. 18:24; the "advocate" in 1 John 2:1; the "trial" in Isa. 1:18; Zech. 5; Matt. 18:24-35; the "acquittal" in Ps. 32:1; Isa. 1:18; Luke 18:14.

Some theologians who distinguish sharply between the general and individual acts of justification will not acknowledge that the so-called individual justification is a judicial act, only the so-called general justification is such an act. Many theologians who take a mediating position on the question consider the individual justification in a figurative sense and limit it to a *nova relatio mentis et voluntatis divinae.* Among their objections may be mentioned that a Christian cannot be certain of his justification if it is made contemporaneous with the genesis of faith. It is further objected that the attribute *iteranda* is improper if the individual justification is considered a forensic act. Justification is considered by these theologians in the following way: That at the death of Christ God pronounced the judgment of justification upon the whole race, and that the Holy Ghost makes this known through the Gospel and transfers or applies this judgment of acquittal upon the sinner at the time of the genesis of faith. In proof of the general justification the following passages are used: Rom. 5:18, 19; 2 Cor. 5:21, etc.

According to this view, however, justification and reconciliation are apt to be confused or identified. It is much better to keep them distinct and to use the expression justification exclusively in relation to the application of reconciliation upon the individual. The objection that God does not act in a judicial way in the case of each individual does not hold, inasmuch as the Word of God clearly sets forth the providence of God in relation to the individual in all things and therefore with all the greater emphasis in the matter of salvation. In the application of salvation men must be justified as individuals. Inasmuch as justification is a forensic act of acquittal, therefore God must perform this act in relation to every believer. The divine act need not be considered in a formal and human way, it being performed in a divine way which harmonizes with the activity of God. God enters into direct relationship with each individual believer, forgives all his sins and imputes to him the righteousness of Christ. There arises therefore a judicial relationship between God and the penitent sinner, who through faith for Christ's sake is adjudged righteous.

Terminus a quo in justification is the state of man as deserving of the wrath and punishment of God not only in time, but subject also to the eternal punishments, both the privative and positive, which in a forensic way are removed through justification. *Terminus ad quem* is *justitia imputativa*.

2. The Acts or Parts of Justification.

According to the definition of justification it involves two principal acts or parts: 1) The negative or the forgiveness of sins, which corresponds to or is based upon Christ's *obedientia passiva*. 2) The positive or the imputation of Christ's righteousness, which is based on *obedientia activa*. However, the forgiveness of sins and the imputation of Christ's righteousness are not fundamentally distinct, there is merely a logical difference between them. Cf. Rom. 4. Still while they imply the same thing, they are nevertheless of importance and together express the significance of justification. For this reason the one act without the other would not adequately express the content of justification. No one can receive the forgiveness of sins without the imputation of Christ's righteousness, while he that has been declared righteous for Christ's sake has likewise received the forgiveness of sins. These acts are therefore not exactly identical, but constitute two sides of the same thing. In one sense we may say that justification stands in a superior relationship to the forgiveness of sins, inasmuch as sins are forgiven *propter imputationem justitiae Christi.*

The two acts or parts are necessary because human guilt implies accountability and indebtedness and obligation to fulfill the Law. It is not sufficient that the punishment is remitted; man is also obliged to fulfill the Law. If he therefore received the forgiveness of his sins, he would nevertheless feel his obligation to fulfill the Law, while his inability to fulfill the Law would become a burden and the Law itself a yoke to cause him grief. But from this condition man is liberated when he is adjudged righteous through the imputed righteousness of Christ.

The righteousness that is imputed is not the essential righteousness of Christ, but that righteousness acquired or procured through His active and passive obedience. The term "imputed" must be emphasized in order that the word *justificatio* may be understood, according to its etymology, as the act of making righteous. *Justificatio* or *justificare* is compounded of *justus* and *facere,* but in Scripture it does not mean to make righteous or pious or to infuse an habitual righteousness. *Hitzdiq* and *δικαιοῦν* always have a forensic sense.

Among Scripture passages may be mentioned: "That justify the wicked" (Isa. 5:23); "Enter not into judgment with thy servant; for in thy sight no man living is righteous" (Ps. 143:2); "This man went down to his house justified" (Luke 18:14); "And by him every one that believeth is justified from all things, from that which ye could not be by the law of Moses" (Acts 13:39); "Shall be justified" or, "accounted righteous" (marginal reading) (Rom. 2:13); "Being justified freely by his grace through the redemption that is in Christ Jesus" (Rom. 3: 24); "Believeth on him that justifieth the ungodly, his faith is reckoned for righteousness" (Rom. 4:5; cf. 4:7; 5:18);

"It is God that justifieth" (Rom. 8:33; cf. 1 Cor. 4:4; Gal. 2:16; 3:8, 11, etc.). Concerning the two acts compare especially Rom. 4: 5-8; 2 Cor. 5: 19-21; Eph. 1:7. "God also in Christ forgave you" (Eph. 4:32; Col. 2:13; 3:13, etc.).

3. The Means of Justification.

Media justificationis are divided into *media δοτικά* and *medium ληπτικόν*. The former are the Gospel and the Sacraments; the latter is faith. *Fides* or faith is also called *causa impulsiva minus principalis.* With regard to faith the following expressions are also used: *Sola fide, per fidem, non propter fidem, sed propter Christum.*

On the divine side the means are the Word and the Sacraments, which are carriers or vehicles of the grace of justification. The objective foundation of justification is to be found in the satisfaction of Christ, but on the human side there is necessary a subjective condition which man must fulfill in order to become partaker of the grace of salvation. This condition is faith, which is a *medium receptivum.* But faith is the work of God. However, faith is engendered in such a way that human freedom suffers no infraction; it is man that believes. And yet there is no merit in man's faith which might be construed to mean that faith is also a foundation for justification in addition to the satisfaction of Christ. Faith is receptive like a mouth or a hand. It is therefore not a faith engendered according to the Catholic or the Reformed conception. Faith does not justify through itself, but on the ground of that which faith appropriates. It is therefore not the ethical content of faith that justifies. Faith is reckoned for righteousness because it embraces Christ, who was delivered up for our trespasses, and was raised for our justification. Compare Rom. 4:22-25. As a receptive means faith is therefore like a hand that receives bread. The figure of a glass containing a refreshing drink has also been used as an illustration. By metonymy we say that the glass assuages the thirst, while it is the contents of the glass that produce the effect. Still the glass possesses great significance as a means. In case the draught could not be obtained in any other way the figure would be still more apt. Faith as the only *medium receptivum* in justification is of the utmost significance, but it is the object of faith that constitutes the foundation of justification. We therefore say that we are justified *per fidem*, not *propter fidem*, but *propter Christum*. Compare Rom. 3:24, 25: "Being justified freely by his grace through the redemption that is in Christ Jesus: whom God set forth to be a propitiation through faith." Faith is therefore reckoned unto righteousness for Christ's sake. Also Rom. 10:4-10, where it is stated that Christ is the end of the law unto righteousness. It is not necessary to run hither and thither to find Christ, He is present in the Word which we preach. Whoever receives the Word in true faith also possesses the Lord Jesus Christ unto righteousness. This justifying faith may not always correspond to the ideal faith, indeed, in the majority of instances it may lack the heroic character of the faith of Abraham; but even if it be weak, it is nevertheless a justifying faith, provided only it be true faith. Justification is equal and without degrees. The greatest saints, such as Abraham, the Virgin Mary, Paul or Luther, are not more justified than the poorest sinner who trusts in the merits of Christ. We are equally justified, whether our faith be weak or strong.

The Lutheran Church defines the conditions of justification not only by the term *per fidem*, but also by *sola fide*. We are justified by faith alone, not by love which determines faith, nor by any deed. This does not mean that faith is inactive, for the newness of life follows upon faith, but this newness of life is not the cause of justification, it is one of its fruits. Faith alone justifies on the ground of the merit of Christ, which it apprehends. But faith is not barren, it is followed by deeds as the fruits of faith. The reason that the word "*sola*" is used instead of the *particulae exclusivae* of the Bible is that this word implies all that is contained in the others.

In this connection we would point out the apparent though unreal difference between the doctrines of Paul and James concerning faith and good works in their relation to the conception of justification. Compare James 2:14-26. By faith alone James means a *fides solitaria*, a dead faith, and therefore a faith that bears no fruit. He endeavors to establish that a living faith is necessary, as Paul also does when he says in Gal. 5:6: "Faith working through love." Cf. James 2:22: "By works was faith made perfect." By deeds James means the deeds of faith, the life or fruits of faith, while Paul speaks in this connection of the deeds of the Law. Paul argues against self-righteousness and presents the genesis of justification through faith alone, while James argues against laxity in the observance of the Law together with antinomism, at the same time stressing the fact that justification proves its genuineness in the Christian life. Compare 1 Cor. 6:9-11. Paul and James therefore had the same doctrinal position. In the determination and fixation of doctrinal presentations we must study Scripture in the light of the analogy of faith, so that the clear passages may shed light on the obscure passages and not vice versa.

4. The Attributes of Justification.

The attributes ascribed to justification are the following: 1) *gratuita,* since justification is by grace; 2) *sequalis,* or without degrees; 3) *perfecta,* or perfect; 4) *certa,* because justification is certain; 5) *iteranda et continuenda,* since justification is renewed and continued day by day. The Christian daily confesses his sins and receives absolution; 6) *amissibilis et restaurabilis,* because it is possible for man to fall, but he may also be restored and again made partaker of the grace of justification.

Justification is not a process that continues throughout life, it takes place all at once when the penitent sinner apprehends the merit of Christ. The terms *iteranda et continuenda* do not denote a continuous process of justification, but simply set forth that justification can be renewed and that the believer lives always in the enjoyment of the grace of justification. Justification, therefore, is a momentary and real forensic act whose power and influence continue as long as a person remains a true Christian. A true Christian lives in daily penitence, while God forgives him daily and abundantly all his sins and considers him as clothed in the righteousness of Christ. Thus Paul in Rom. 8:1: "There is therefore now no condemnation to them that are in Christ Jesus." Justification possesses no grades so that one Christian may be said to be more justified than another; neither does justification vary with the varying subjective states of the believer. Justification is always perfect.

5. *The Purpose and Effect of Justification.*

Finis justificationis in relation to the justified person is eternal salvation; in relation to God it is His eternal glory.

Effectus justificationis are: 1) Liberation from the sense of guilt and the fear of punishment, which means peace of conscience; "Being therefore justified by faith, we have peace with God through our Lord Jesus Christ" (Rom. 5:1); 2) sonship and communion with God; "But as many as received him, to them gave he the right to become children of God, even to them that believe on his name" (John 1:12); "That Christ may dwell in your hearts through faith" (Eph. 3:17); 3) the gift of the Holy Ghost; "The Spirit of God dwelleth in you" (1 Cor. 3:16); "The Spirit himself beareth witness with our spirit" (Rom. 8:16); 4) renewal; "Be ye renewed in the spirit of your mind" (Eph. 4:23); 5) assurance that God answers prayer and grants us all good things; "The supplication of a righteous man availeth much in its working" (James 5:16; cf. James 1:5); "If we know that he heareth us whatsoever we ask, we know that we have the petitions which we have asked of him" (1 John 5:15); "How shall he not also with him freely give us all things" (Rom. 8:32); 6) the hope of everlasting life; "That, being justified by his grace, we might be made heirs according to the hope of eternal life" (Titus 3:7).

6. *Notes on the History of Dogma.*

The doctrine of justification did not become fixed dogmatically either during the period of the Apostolic Fathers or during the Apologetic period. The formulation of the dogma, begun during the Polemical period, took a trend in opposition to the Biblical presentation. The doctrinal views of Augustine became the dominating force in the Church. His doctrine of faith as determined by love together with his conception of justification as a transforming process extending throughout the whole of life formed the basis of the theology of the Middle Ages. Thomas Aquinas adhered to the theological conceptions of Augustine, but differed from him in the doctrine of human freedom. His doctrine of *meritum* does not agree with Augustinianism. The Scotists fought the Thomists, but their decided Semi-

Pelagianism did not lead them into the right current and they continued in the same direction. With few exceptions the general opinion was that faith justifies on the ground of love. The next step was entirely natural, that man is justified through faith and works. The Council of Trent definitely formulated the Roman conception. Justification was defined by the Council as consisting not only in the forgiveness of sins, but also in sanctification and renovation, indeed as a *justitia infusa*. It was taught that this *justitia infusa* could be increased by obedience to the commandments of God and the Church. The good works of man are meritorious. Righteousness is maintained through daily growth and increase.

The doctrine of justification by faith alone in accordance with the Lutheran presentation indicated a return to the Pauline doctrine and became the principle of a Scriptural formulation of doctrine. The fourth article of the Augsburg Confession declares: "That men cannot be justified before God by their own strength, merits or works, but are freely justified for Christ's sake through faith, when they believe that they are forgiven for Christ's sake, who, by His death, hath made satisfaction for our sins. This faith God imputes for righteousness in His sight." The Reformed Church speaks of grace, the forgiveness of sins and justification, but their presentation lays stress on the words rather than the matter, as can be seen by comparing the Reformed views with the Lutheran doctrine. The doctrine of justification does not possess prime significance for the Reformed Church. She considers justification not so much a liberation from the guilt and punishment of sin or an imputation of the righteousness of Christ, as rather a salvation in general and the means of removing the misery of sin. In this manner she confuses justification with regeneration. She uses the same terminology as the Lutheran Church, but not with the same fixed meaning. There are some tendencies in the Reformed Church that approach more nearly the Catholic than the Lutheran position. The Arminians rejected the doctrine of the imputation of Christ's righteousness and held that justification consisted in the forgiveness of sins and the cancellation of the punishment.

The Rationalists, of course, rejected the doctrine of the Church and declared that justification consisted in the goodwill and favor of God, when satisfied with our change of heart and mind. Philosophical Rationalism and other related theories embraced similar views and laid emphasis on the ability of man. The mediating theologians presented principally a doctrine of subjective justification. They emphasized the proposition, Christ in us, rather than Christ for us. Beck and his disciples taught that justification was a process and therefore he did not accept the Church doctrine of the imputation of Christ's righteousness. Ritschlianism naturally rejects the orthodox doctrine, lays emphasis on sanctification rather than justification and denies individual justification in a real sense. The conservative Lutheran doctrine of justification has many powerful champions, but the formulation of the doctrine seems to be fixed, and the confessional theologians in their presentation pay more particular attention to the material content. We now pass to the more detailed consideration of the development of the doctrine together with the views of the leading thinkers during the various periods.

Clement of Rome taught that we are not justified through ourselves, but by faith. He also speaks, however, of the forgiveness of sins through love. Justin Martyr said that sins are blotted out through faith and not through the sacrifices of animals or meal offerings. Just as the blood of the Paschal Lamb saved the Israelites, so the blood of Christ saves us from death. Irenaeus compares our faith with that of Abraham and says that man is justified through the revelation of the Lord when he turns to the light of His countenance. Tertullian taught that man is justified through the freedom of faith and not through the bondage of the Law, since the just shall live by his faith. Clement of Alexandria taught that we become the children of God through faith. He said that the sins committed before Baptism are blotted out or forgiven through Baptism, but that after Baptism forgiveness is received through penances. From this it can be seen that such a view would prevent him from having a correct conception of justification. In certain places Origen states that justification takes place through faith without works, in other places he contradicts himself and seems to teach that justification begins with faith and is completed with good works.

Ambrose had a very clear conception of justification. He speaks of forgiveness, the non-imputation of sins and justification as being the same. He refers justification to faith alone and not to love. Augustine performed a great service in the development of the doctrine when he taught that all is by grace, but he obscured the meaning of these words in his definition of justification. He taught that grace works faith, which is the foundation of the moral change. Love is infused. Through it faith becomes an active principle and man becomes righteous. The absolute predestination of God is the ground of justification. Justification is *justum facere*. It is a process that extends to the whole life and activity of man. Faith is justifying as determined by the love that is infused.

Anselm had an evangelical conception of the doctrine and in his admonitions to the dying he set forth the death of Christ, to whom they were told to turn in faith. Thomas Aquinas taught that justification consisted of the following parts: 1) An infusion of the grace of God; 2) the inclination of the will to God in faith; 3) the turning away of the will from sin; 4) the forgiveness of sins. Justification is not a forensic act, it consists of an infusion of righteousness. In agreement with Augustine he considered that justification is a process that continues throughout life. Bonaventura indeed taught that justification is a *justitia infusa*, but he speaks of faith as a foundation for the whole of the Christian life and as a ladder that reaches to heaven. Bernhard of Clairvaux stated that justification consists in the forgiveness of sins. He speaks of justification by faith alone, although at times he seems to confuse the conceptions of justification and sanctification. The Catholic mystics, such as Suso, Gock, Wicliffe and others, to a greater or less degree advocated the doctrine of *justitia infusa* and regarded justification as subjective. Even John of Wesel speaks of *justitia infusa*, but Savonarola and John Wessel came closer to the evangelical conception.

Luther, the Paul of the Reformation period, clearly presents tha doctrine of justification by faith alone. Justification is an act of God outside of us and consists of the forgiveness of sins together with the imputation of the righteousness of Christ. The foundation of justification is the work and suffering of Christ in our stead. Faith justifies because it embraces Christ. He that embraces Christ in faith God considers as righteous, etc. The Lutheran position, as set forth in the Augsburg Confession, IV, V and XX, was attacked in the Roman Confutation. The *Confutation* states that the Lutheran doctrine of *sola fide* conflicts absolutely with the Word of God. The Apology in a masterly way defends the position of the Lutheran Church on the doctrine of justification. It confutes the Roman doctrine of good works and proves that justifying faith does not consist in fides historica and good works, but is a *fides apprehensiva*; also it presents faith as accepting the promise that God graciously forgives the sinner for Christ's sake. By reason of the powerful defense of the doctrine of justification set forth by the Reformers, the Catholics were compelled to accord very great attention to this doctrine at the Council of Trent.[75] This Council decided that justification is a process that develops and continues through three principal stages. The first stage in this process of development is the so-called preparation. This beginning of the process of justification is dependent on the prevenient grace of God. The synergistic tendency of the Council is here plainly evident, although in practice the Catholic Church is Semi-Pelagian. The preparation works an historical faith (*fides historica*) together with a fear because of sin, but coupled with a knowledge of grace. This results in love and the resolution to repent. Thereafter the second stage of the process begins, or justification proper, which does not consist merely in the forgiveness of sins, but also in sanctification and in the renewal of the inner man. Love is infused and is made secure. Justification is a *justitia infusa*. Hereafter follows the third stage in which righteousness is to be daily increased, and by which righteousness or justification is to be preserved. To this end there occurs the cooperation of good works. In Canon IX *de justificatione* all those are condemned who teach justification by faith alone and in Canon

---

[75] Sessio VI.

XXIV those are condemned that deny that justification is increased and preserved through good works.[76] The Reformed theologians, such as Zwingli, Calvin and Oecolampadius, were not able on account of their doctrine of predestination to conceive of justification as clearly as Luther did. The Reformed Church looks upon justification as a dogma alongside of other dogmas. Justification is the carrying out of the absolute decree of predestination. The declaration of justification which follows upon faith is the declaration to the individual that he is elect, becoming a sort of assurance and certainty. The expressions *propter Christum, per fidem* and *sola fide* are used by the Reformed theologians, but they do not have the same meaning as in the Lutheran theology. In accordance with the Reformed position it would seem that one could say: *justificamur propter fidem per Christum,* and also: *propter Christum per fidem.* This Church declares that all is by grace in the same sense as Augustine did. They emphasize *per fidem et sola fide* as over against the Catholic doctrine of good works. Faith justifies because it places us in a living relationship with Christ. The conceptions of regeneration and justification are confused. Justification possesses a subjective character. The Reformed conception of faith and their doctrine of justification are more nearly related to the Catholic position than the Lutheran. Their conception of faith is similar to *fides formata,* while justification occupies a subordinate position. However, there is this difference, that the Reformed Church does not accept the Catholic doctrine of justification *per fidem caritate formata.* They do not teach that man is justified by faith and good works, but present the grace of God in Christ Jesus. According to the Reformed view faith does not justify as a principle of good works, but by reason of the fact that faith embraces Christ as a principle of life. For this reason Christ is conceived of more as a redeemer and not so much as a propitiator. Man is justified because he stands in living relationship with Christ, and not so much because through faith he apprehends the merit of Christ. Osiander taught that Christ is our righteousness not through the righteousness which

---

[76] Sessio VI, Caput X.

He has procured for us, but by reason of the fact that as the Son of God He dwells in us through faith in His essential righteousness. Stancarus based his view of the righteousness of Christ on the obedience of Christ in accordance with the human nature only, while Osiander emphasized the divine nature. The *Formula of Concord* sets forth clearly the position of the Lutheran Church. In Epitome 3 there are many positive and negative points. We herewith present an extract of the positive points: 1) Christ is our righteousness in accordance with both natures; 2) our righteousness before God consists in the fact that God by grace alone without reference to past, present or future deeds forgives us all our sins and imputes to us the righteousness of Christ; 3) faith is the only means by which we apprehend Christ; 4) faith is not historical knowledge, but assent and confidence; 5) to justify is the same as to absolve and declare free from sin; 6) the righteousness that is imputed through faith is not to be doubted; 7) the *particulae exclusivae,* such as, without merit, by grace, without works, etc., are to be retained; 8) although the antecedent contrition and the consequent newness of life are not a part of justification, still the true and living faith is active through love, and good works always follow after the living faith. The *Mystics,* such as Weigel and Schwenkfeld, together with others presented a subjective doctrine of justification which made of the latter a continuous internal life process. The *Socinians* acknowledged that justification takes place through faith, but that it merely implies the remission of the punishment of sin and not the imputation of the righteousness of Christ. The *Arminians* took the same position and taught that justification consisted merely in the forgiveness of sins, especially the remission of punishment. They rejected the positive element.

Kant and the moral Rationalists, of course, did not accept the Church doctrine of justification. By justification they meant that what is effected here on earth to make us well pleasing to God is credited to our account in advance, so that we are now considered as already possessing it. However, all takes place in our own subjective consciousness. *Rationalism,* as set forth by Wegscheider, rejects faith in the historical facts of salvation and presents an intellectual faith. The doctrine of justification is the fruit of an uncultured age. The only truth that it contains is that God does not scrutinize our separate acts but only our state of mind and for this reason grants us His favor. In accordance with the views of Schleiermacher justification is identical with the living union with Christ. The negative element in justification is the forgiveness of sins; the positive element is the adoption of believers as the children of God. He rejected the doctrine of the imputation of Christ's merit. A powerful consciousness of God is infused in man, which is considered by God as being perfect, although here in time it is imperfect. J. T. Beck did not consider justification as a momentary forensic act, but as a process that continues throughout life. He resembled Osiander in this that he considered righteousness as essentially indwelling in man. In this process of justification God deals with man in a prophetic, regal and priestly way. The call belongs to the first stage. The kingly judgment consists in this that God declares the sinner righteous, not because he in faith accepts a valid external righteousness, but because through faith man reaches a condition that God requires for a proper reception of grace. Thereupon follows the priestly work which is purifying in its effect by reason of the indwelling righteousness. According to Beck's presentation justification includes the whole order of salvation. However, the forgiveness of sins and the adoption enter into justification as special elements. He states that the forgiveness of sins is not a forensic act, but an act of grace. Hengstenberg also conceived of justification as a gradually developing process. Many others could be cited. Martensen says that faith justifies like an ethical principle. He does not conceive of justification as being purely objective. He presents Christ in us just as strongly as Christ outside of us or for us. Ritschl places justification above reconciliation and sanctification above Justification. He denies Justification in the real individual sense. As the correlative of redemption and justification we are not to think of the individual man, but of the Christian Church in her entirety. W. Herrman, a prominent disciple of Ritschl, emphasized more than Ritschl the separation of religion from metaphysical questions. Although he connects closely the religious and moral, he does not look upon religion as a postulate of morality. In

Sweden Fr. Fehr was an influential disciple of Ritschl. Granfelt sets forth that through faith man is transplanted from sinful ground to become a branch in the vine of Christ's righteousness. The righteousness of Christ is imputed to the man who has experienced not only Christ for us, but Christ in us. This imputation takes place by way of anticipation and becomes a declaration of righteousness in advance.

Many citations could be made from the dogmatic works of the confessional theologians and other sources, but there are so many that it would be difficult to make a selection. Frank in Germany (and many with him) have powerfully opposed Ritschlianlsm. Many theologians in Sweden have refuted the same tendency. The doctrine of justification as set forth by Beck has also been the object of critical treatment and confutation. The controversies concerning this important doctrine have served to establish the old Lutheran position and the confessional dogmatic development.

§28. Regeneration.

Justification and regeneration stand in the closest relation to each other. The terminology has not always been the same, but has been changed from time to time, while the subject matter concerned has always been fixed. We have already called attention to the fact that different presentations have been made by different theologians of our Church, and opinions are still divided, but everything depends on a good interpreter, i. e., if we understand the definition correctly, clarity and order will ensue. The *Formula of Concord* speaks of different definitions of regeneration.[77] We quote the following: "The word regeneration is sometimes understood in the sense that it includes both the forgiveness of sins, which is experienced for Christ's sake alone, and renovation, which the Holy Spirit works in those that are justified by faith. At times it signifies the forgiveness of sins alone and the adoption as the sons of God. In the latter sense it

[77] Sol. Declaratio III, 686, 19, 20.

is very often found in the Apology. As for example when it is stated: 'Justification is regeneration.' But Paul also makes a distinction between these words when he says in Titus 3:5: 'According to his mercy he saved us through the washing of regeneration and renewing of the Holy Spirit.' The word 'vivifying' (*vivificatio*) is therefore sometimes used to signify the forgiveness of sins. For since man is justified through faith, which the Holy Spirit alone works, it certainly is a regeneration, because man is changed from a child of wrath to a child of God." From this it is evident that regeneration has been variously defined. Some have considered it *late dicta,* others *stricte dicta,* and still others *strictissime dicta.* By regeneration *late dicta* is understood all the acts of grace or regeneration in the broad sense; *stricte dicta* denotes regeneration in the sense of new life and sonship; while *strictissime dicta* is equivalent to the gift of faith or *donatio fidei.*

1. The Definition Of Regeneration.

Regeneration is *the act of grace through which the converted sinner at the time of, in, with and through justification receives the new spiritual life, becomes a child of God and is renewed in heart.*

The definition here given corresponds with the technical term *regeneratio stricte dicta.* The so-called *late dicta* is rarely used. The selection is, therefore, between *stricte* and *strictissime dicta.* According to both of these definitions regeneration is instantaneous like justification. Since conversion, as most generally defined, consists of contrition and faith, there is a difference in the conception of conversion and regeneration, the former being progressive and the latter instantaneous. A baptized child is regenerated, and an adult Christian may also be converted, depending upon whether or not he has fallen from grace and been restored. There has been a dispute among theologians as to whether such a converted and restored person is again regenerated. This question depends upon whether or not regeneration can be lost. If faith can be lost, it is self-evident that regeneration can be lost. This takes place when a fall occurs by self-conscious, premeditated and intentional sin. A real apostasy may not result, if repentance follows soon. Still it is a fall. It is not always easy, however, to distinguish between an intentional and an unintentional sin. It may be a case like the fall of Peter, where faith is not entirely extinguished. A righteous person may in a certain sense fall seven times and yet arise again. When a real fall occurs, man is in the same condition as the prodigal son. Before he returned, he was looked upon as dead, but when he returned and was restored, the father said: "This my son was dead and is alive again." It is clear that a person cannot be regenerated and at the same time be dead in sins. We must be careful in using the analogy of human birth so that we do not identify a birth into the natural life with the experience of being born again in the kingdom of God. A spiritually dead person, who once lived spiritually, may be reborn in the kingdom of grace.

For the sake of clearness it is also of some importance to investigate or decide which definition of regeneration is the most Biblical. There is very little hope, if any, that theologians will agree on this question. Many will follow the old dogmatic view according to the definition *regeneratio strictissime dicta* or regeneration to faith. Just as many prefer *regeneratio stricte dicta* or regeneration by or through faith. Regeneration cannot exist before faith, and a person cannot be justified without faith. We are justified by faith. "Being therefore justified by faith, we have peace with God through our Lord Jesus Christ; through whom also we have had our access by faith into this grace wherein we stand" (Rom. 5:1, 2) ; "The righteous shall live by faith" (Rom. 1:17). Faith is receptive and apprehensive and manifests itself in confidence or trust. When the Lutheran Church rejects *fides caritate formata* and emphasizes the purely receptive character of faith, it seems that regeneration by faith is a clearer expression than regeneration to faith, although the latter term also presents the life in faith. The Bible teaches plainly that we are justified by faith. If we are justified by faith, we are also regenerated. It is clearly evident that regeneration cannot be the cause of justification. Justification as the objective act and fact is the causative factor. When the Holy Spirit works faith in the repenting sinner, that very moment God justifies him, and the subjective effect is regeneration. All three acts occur at the same time. But in order to have a logical and clear conception we must place justification before regeneration. A sinner could not be regenerated in the strict sense, if he were not justified. Justification is the great cause in the heart of God in heaven, and regeneration is the great effect by the Holy Spirit in the heart of man on earth.

According to the old Dogmaticians regeneration is the same as *conversio transitiva* and especially *donatio fidei.* Hollazius defines as follows: "*Regeneratio* is the act of grace through which the Holy Spirit endows the sinner with saving faith, so that after his sins have been forgiven, he may become a child of God and an heir to eternal life."[78] In such case man is regenerated to faith and not through faith. In a measure regeneration is thought of as successive and not momentary in its operation, which seems to conflict with the concept of birth. Gisle Johnson defines regeneration as follows: "*Regeneration* is the act of grace through which God has created in the heart of the penitent sinner a certain and living assurance of the objective reality of justification and in this assurance implanted in him the fruitful seed of a new life, in perfect holiness and blessedness, embracing the whole of his personal natural organism."

The relationship between justification and regeneration is of great importance. It is evident that, although the Confessions define regeneration somewhat differently, as for instance the Apology in the definition, "*Justificatio* is *regeneratio*," they do not teach that justification is received through regeneration, but quite the contrary. In the explanation of the Apology's presentation of justification Gottfrid Billing says: "Inasmuch as faith is both justifying and regenerative at the same time, therefore the word 'justify' may signify both to declare righteous and to regenerate, but faith does not justify because it is regenerative, on the contrary, it is regenerative because it justifies. Furthermore, it justifies because it is apprehensive, because it receives the forgiveness of sins, which

---

[78] Hollazius: "Regeneratio est actus gratiae, quo Spiritus sanctus hominem peccatorem salvifica fide donat, ut remissis peccatis fllius Dei et haeres aeternae vitae e reddatur."

can be received in no other way save through faith alone."[79] The old Dogmaticians, who placed *regeneratio* before *justificatio*, did not thereby mean to express that *justificatio* comes about through *regeneratio*. On this account Quenstedt sought to establish the following: "*Regeneratio, justificatio, unio mystica et renovatio tempore simul sunt*." He considered *renovatio* in another sense than that which is common now. With regard to the relationship between *regeneratio* and *justificatio* it is true that they take place simultaneously, but the question is as to whether *justificatio* as the dominating act ought not to be placed before *regeneratio*. Faith is indeed apprehensive, and when man is justified by faith, the new life is created or is born in him. Roos presents the relation between justification and regeneration in the following manner: "A justified Christian is also a regenerated Christian, because at the moment he believes he is justified, but at the same moment he is also regenerated, inasmuch as faith is the most important activity of the spiritual life, and consequently at the time of justification he receives the new life."[80] Schartau places justification before regeneration, but says that the gift of faith can be considered the first part of regeneration.[81] Nohrborg in his doctrine of the order of salvation presents regeneration as the great change that takes place in man when he is translated from spiritual death to spiritual life in Christ through faith, but he also says that regeneration is the gift of faith.[82] Citations could be made from many of the newer writers who define regeneration as *donatio fidei*. References could also be made to many places in modern theological literature which present regeneration as the new life and place justification before regeneration. Representatives of the latter view are Thomasius, Luthardt, Gisle Johnson, Landgren and others.

We would simply add the following to what has already been stated.

---

[79] Billing, Lutherska Kyrkans Bekännelse, p. 426.

[80] Roos, Troslara, p. 178.

[81] Schartau, Bref, No. XXVIII.

[82] Nohrborg, Postilla, pp. 460, 461.

It would seem as if regeneration were not adequately described by the definition *donatio fidei*. The first stage of regeneration may indeed be called the kindling of faith as a preparatory act, since indications of life precede the real birth. Even excitation in an earlier stage of development is an indication of life. A birth, to use the natural birth as an analogy, is not the beginning of life, it is the real appearance of life. The child possesses life before it is born, but its real life begins with its advent into this world. So in the awakened sinner there are indications of spiritual life through the activity of grace, but he is regenerated when he is born into the spiritual world and made a child of God. But we cannot conceive of a person regenerated and possessing spiritual life with sins unforgiven. Justification must precede the spiritual life. No one can be a child of God that is not justified. But faith is a condition of justification and must therefore precede it, since faith is receptive like the mouth or the hand. Faith itself is not the spiritual life, but receives the spiritual life through justification. The gift of faith would therefore not seem to define regeneration adequately. We may indeed speak of a living faith as contrasted with a dead faith, as well as the life of faith on the basis of that life which faith apprehends and contains, but faith is nevertheless not the same as life, and the gift of faith is an incomplete definition of regeneration. Then, too, regeneration implies a new relationship in the sense that the regenerated person is a child of God, since he is born of God. Inasmuch as this new relationship must belong to regeneration, it is evident that man is regenerated through faith and not only to faith. Compare John 1:12, 13: "But as many as received him, to them gave he the right to become the children of God, even to them that believe on his name." Faith is mentioned as preceding regeneration. That which follows immediately upon faith is justification, if, for the sake of logical sequence, we would distinguish as to time between justification and regeneration. "Being therefore justified by faith, we have peace with God through our Lord Jesus Christ" (Rom. 5:1). In 1 John 5:1 faith is presented as a criterion of regeneration. Compare Gal. 3:26: "For ye are all sons of God, through faith, in Christ Jesus." Some have used Titus 3: 5-7 as an argument in favor of the position that regeneration precedes justification, but these might with as much reason assert that renovation also precedes. In this passage Paul does not discuss the order of sequence in the acts of grace, but presents salvation by grace and the means by which it may be attained. We therefore maintain that regeneration is more completely, logically and Scripturally comprehended if we adhere to the definition that is called *regeneratio stricte dicta*, since *late dicta* embraces too much, and *strictissime dicta* (*donatio fidei*) expresses too little.

2. The Causes of Regeneration.

Man, who stands in need of spiritual life, is *subjectum quod*, while his spiritual nature (*anima humana*) is *subjectum quo*, but he is not the active subject, since he cannot regenerate himself. *Causa efficiens principalis* is God and in a special sense the Holy Spirit, since the Spirit applies salvation. Therefore the Scriptures use the expressions, "born of God," "the children of God," etc. *Causa impulsiva interna* is the mercy of God. Compare Titus 3:5. *Causa impulsiva externa* is Christ the mediator, or His merit. *Causa efficiens minus principalis*, which is the same as the means of regeneration, are the Word of God and Baptism.

Regeneration can not be wrought by man, but God is active in this wonderful work of grace. Cf. John 1:13: "Who were born, not of blood, nor of the will of the flesh, nor of the will of man, but of God." But this divine activity does not repress the freedom of man, which subject has been treated before in the doctrine of conversion. In accordance with the divine revelation regeneration is wrought solely through Baptism and the Word. For this reason Jesus said to Nicodemus: "Except one be born of water and the Spirit, he cannot enter into the kingdom of God" (John 3:5). James writes: "Of his own will he brought us forth by the word of truth, that we should be a kind of firstfruits of his creatures" (James 1:18). Compare 1 Peter 1:23: "Having been begotten again, not of corruptible seed, but of incorruptible, through the word of God, which liveth and abideth." Baptism and the Word work together in an indissoluble union, hence they must both be used in accordance with the order of God. Where they are rightly used, and the necessary conditions are at hand, they work regeneration.

3. The Starting Point and End of Regeneration.

Terminus a quo is the want of spiritual life. The understanding is by nature incapable of correctly knowing the spiritual life. Compare John 1:5; 1 Cor. 2:14; Eph. 5:8. The natural will of man is not fitted to will that which is good nor to seek the good of the spiritual life. Compare Rom. 8:7. The emotions are not inclined toward that which is spiritual, but seek after the lusts of the flesh. Compare Rom. 7:5.

Terminus ad quem is the spiritual life and the spiritual powers. Compare 2 Cor. 5:17: "Wherefore if any man is in Christ, he is a new creature; the old things are passed away; behold, they are become new." Cf. Col. 3:10; 1 John 5:12, etc. This change of spiritual life, however, is not substantial, but accidental, since the personality of man is not destroyed, but made different, so as to result in a new man, although the old man is not dead nor destroyed. For this reason we reject the teaching of the Fanatics, who say that regeneration destroys the human body, while the soul remains and a new body is formed. The doctrine of the Flacians is likewise rejected, which states that a new heart is created in such fashion that the essence of the old Adam and especially the intelligent soul is destroyed and a new soul essence is created out of nothing. If the change were essential or substantial, no fall from grace could take place and the spiritual life would become mechanical.

Finis proximus is *unio mystica* and *renovatio,* and *finis ultimus* is the salvation of the regenerate person and the glory of God.

§29. The Mystical Union.

The new life, brought about by regeneration, is evidenced in the fact that God dwells in the regenerated man, while the regenerated man dwells in God. The regenerated man is born to the life of the spiritual world. He has returned to the original state of man when God in a special sense dwelt in man. With justification and regeneration the subjective restoration of man has begun to be realized, so that the image of God comes to be restored more and more. The Triune God is not far from His children, indeed He dwells in them. This indwelling in the hearts of the believers possesses greater significance than the general presence of God. The mystical union is a union with God that is more intimate and more peculiarly operative than the presence of God spoken of by Paul in Acts 17:27, 28, where he says: "Though he is not far from each one of us: for in him we live, and move, and have our being." Although it is not easy, indeed hardly possible, in anything like an adequate manner to describe the mystical union, still the doctrine is well founded in the Word of God and forms one of the most precious treasures of the Lutheran Church and a source of rich comfort to the believer.

1. The Definition of the Mystical Union.

Hollazius defines the mystical union as follows: "the Mystical Union is *the spiritual conjunction of the Triune God with justified man, by which He dwells in him as in a consecrated temple by His special presence, and this substantial, and operates in the same by His gracious influence.*"[83] *Unio mystica* may be considered both as *unitio* and *unio*. *Unitio* is the act of union which is momentary and takes place at the same time as justification and regeneration. *Unio* is the continuous state. Dogmaticians also speak of the means of the mystical union. On the divine side these are the Gospel, Baptism and the Lord's Supper. On the human side the means is faith. The union is called mystical because it is a great mystery, while its *modus* is not completely comprehensible.

Quenstedt presents both the mystical union with the Triune God and the special union with the God-man. He says that the latter implies that

[83] Hollazius: "*Unio mystica est conjunctio spiritualis Dei triunius cum homine justificato qua in hoc velut consecrato templo praesentia speciali eaque substantiali habitat et gratioso influxu in eodem operatur.*"

Christ constitutes the spiritual union with the regenerated man, works in and through him, so that what the believer experiences, suffers, and does as a Christian, is all dedicated to Christ. Compare Gal. 2:20: "Christ liveth in me." He says that through this union a Christian becomes anointed and furnished as a spiritual prophet, priest, and king. This union is likewise a marriage covenant with Christ, so that the Christians become the bride of Christ. Compare Eph. 5:31, 32.

Among other Scripture passages we would call attention to the following: "If a man love me, he will keep my word: and my Father will love him, and we will come unto him, and make our abode with him" (John 14:23); "I come unto you" (John 14:18; cf. 15:4, 5; 17:21-23; Rom. 8: 9-11); "Know ye not that ye are a temple of God, and that the Spirit of God dwelleth in you?" (1 Cor. 3:16; 6:19; cf. also 6:15, 17; Gal. 3:27); "A habitation of God in the Spirit" (Eph. 2:22); "Partakers of the divine nature" (2 Peter 1:4). The mystical union is presented in 1 John 4:16 as a mutual covenant of love: "We know and have believed the love which God hath in us. God is love; and he that abideth in love abideth in God, and God abideth in him." The mystical union, therefore, not only finds expression in reciprocal love to God, but also love to all who are united with Christ. Cf. Eph. 5:29, 30: "For no man ever hated his own flesh; but nourisheth and cherisheth it, even as Christ also the church; because we are members of his body." Compare Eph. 4: 2-6; 1 Cor. 12:26. "Now ye are the body of Christ, and severally members thereof" (1 Cor. 12:27).

2. Negative And Positive Characteristics.

Inasmuch as the mystical union cannot be comprehended and described in an adequate way, therefore negative and positive terms are employed in order to obviate misunderstandings and as nearly as possible present the content of this doctrine. The negative characteristics are the following: 1) *Non transsubstantialis*. The believer is indeed a child of God, but is not made divine. The believers partake of the nature of God, but are not changed to a divine nature. 2) *Non consubstantialis*, so that two substances become one substance. 3) *Non substantialis formaliter*, i. e., like a grafted branch forms a unit with the tree. God dwells in the Christian, but the abode is not changed to the Indweller, nor vice versa. God can take His departure from man and therefore His indwelling is not an incarnation. Through the mystical union we put on Christ, but that which is put on is not identical with the person upon whom it is put. The followers of Weigel and Schwenkfeld taught that the union was essential. When Hollazius employs the term substantial he simply means that the divine substance is united with the human substance in a real although a mystical manner. 4) *Non mere moralis,* as for instance the union between the souls of David and Jonathan, since the union, implies a great deal more. 5) *Non mere operatio gratiosa,* since it it not only a divine activity. It is God Himself that dwells in man, not only His gifts. The positive terms are the following: 1) *Vera et realis,* since it is a true and real union and not one that is metaphoric and ideal. 2) *Intima,* so that God approaches the believer and enters into a special relationship with him. In a repletive sense God is omnipresent and can therefore enter into a special mystical union with the believers. He fills them with all the fulness of God, operates in and through them with all wisdom and power. This is a *concursus* in a higher degree. 3) *Gratiosa* in the Church militant or the kingdom of grace. 4) *Gloriosa* in the Church triumphant.

3. Testimonium Spiritus Sancti Internum.

Since God in accordance with *unio mystica* dwells in man, and man becomes the temple of the Holy Spirit, therefore the Christian must in some way experience the mystical union and receive some testimony that he is a child of God. The life-relationship with the Lord is capable of revealing itself in a palpable way. There are many who at the beginning of the life of faith experience unusual joy and happiness, while the majority experience at least some moment of exalted glory when the assurance of faith is powerful and strong. But this experience is not the same in all men. It may happen in the case of some that quite some time will elapse before they come to know of the assurance of faith with its transport of heavenly joy. The emotions vary and the child of God soon learns that the Christian life ofttimes implies a struggle without the presence of any joyous emotions to comfort and cheer. On this account it is necessary that some guidance be afforded so that the Christian may know and be assured that he is a child of God. The method by which this is accomplished according to the Word of God is the testimony of the Holy Spirit or *testimonium Spiritus sancti internum*.

Paul writes in 1 Cor. 2:10-12: "But unto us God revealed them through the Spirit: for the Spirit searcheth all things, yea, the deep things of God. For who among men knoweth the things of man, save the spirit of man, which is in him? even so the things of God none knoweth save the Spirit of God. But we received, not the spirit of the world, but the spirit which is from God; that we might know the things that were freely given to us of God." And in Rom. 8:16 it is expressly stated: "The Spirit himself beareth witness with our spirit, that we are the children of God."

Before the operation of the Spirit, as stated in *Ordo Salutis*, and especially before the new birth man knows God the Father only as a providential Father and usually only as the almighty and just judge of earth and heaven; Christ is known historically and the knowledge of the Holy Ghost is vague and His personality is not clear. By the co-witnessing of the Spirit the personality of the Holy Spirit becomes more and more distinct. The Holy Spirit reveals Christ through the Word in a real way and Jesus Christ becomes like a friend, yea, as a brother, and through Christ the Father becomes a real Father. A Christian understands then the meaning of the resurrection greeting of Jesus Christ: "Go unto my brethren and say to them, I ascend unto my Father and your Father, and my God and your God." In the new birth or regeneration a believer enters the spiritual world of the kingdom of God in its first form of experience. The great Christian facts become clearer and clearer. The co-witnessing of the Spirit with our spirit becomes a strong testimony. The Bible as a textbook becomes a living guide and the Christian experience is clarified.[84]

The testimony of the Spirit has been described in various ways. The

---

[84] Compare Lindberg's *Apologetics*, §19, 3, p. 151.

most prominent theologians hold different views concerning the proofs of Christian experience and testimony. Among these theologians may be mentioned especially Frank, Philippi and Dorner. Frank bases the testimony of Christian experience on the great transformation through which the Christian passes in conversion and regeneration together with what he experiences in the daily conversion or sanctification.[85] Dorner opposes the viewpoint of Frank, which he characterizes as subjective, i.e., according to Dorner, Frank has presented a subjective and not an objective principle of knowledge.[86] Dorner declares that we may possess an immediate knowledge of God, not merely a secondary knowledge obtained through ratiocination which leads us back to the cause. He says that we do not become assured of God on the ground of our consciousness of regeneration and conversion, but because we know that God in Christ is for us, therefore we know that we are saved. Furthermore, faith possesses a spiritual intuition concerning God as our Father; it possesses knowledge not only concerning itself as redeemed, but also, and in a primary sense, concerning the God of our salvation. Dorner's doctrine in regard to an immediate intuition does not correspond to true mysticism, it tends toward the false. Philippi sets forth the objective reconciliation performed by Christ, as attested and offered in the Word of God, both as the starting point and the only foundation on which a Christian can base his assurance of salvation.[87] Nohrborg states that the testimonies of the Holy Spirit are twofold: internally in the heart and externally in the Word.[88] In accordance with the first class of testimonies the Spirit bears witness through all His gracious acts taken together and He bears witness with our spirit, not alone. The effects which belong to the testimonies of the Holy Spirit begin with the gift of faith and continue on down through daily sanctification. In accordance, therefore, with the continued acts of

---

[85] *System der Chr. Gewisshelt*, §§ 15, 16.

[86] *System of Chr. Doctrine*, Vol. I, pp. 31-184.

[87] *Glaubenslehre*, V. 2. Zweite aufl., p. 58.

[88] *Nohrborg, *Postilla*, 18th ed., p. 474.

the Spirit, we know that we are the children of God. Compare 1 John 3:24: "And hereby we know that he abideth in us, by the Spirit which he gave us." The Spirit bears witness with our spirit through the Word when we read and hear it, thereby learning to know the character of those that are the Lord's. It is, therefore, not a new revelation, but the Spirit, dwelling in the believers and bearing testimony through the Word, that is the ground of faith and grants the internal assurance through His works of grace. This testimony of the Spirit will at times become especially clear, giving rise to great joy in the Lord. The Christian is also admonished in the Scriptures to seek the assurance of faith and joy in the Lord. But even if these experiences of joy be infrequent, still he relies and rests in faith on the promise of God in the Word.

§30. Renovation.

The life of the regenerated Christian must grow and develop. It is not sufficient that a man has been born into the spiritual world, thereby coming into possession of spiritual life, but as a child of God he must grow and develop under the fostering care of the Spirit. Man begins his walk in the newness of life, clothed in the righteousness of Christ, with the power of sin broken in principle, but with the old Adam still alive. Through the act of regeneration the Christian has received new powers by which he willingly co-operates in the continued work of redemption through the grace of the Spirit. The development of Christian liberty is always conditioned by grace. This grace is called *gratia cooperans,* and although the Christian cooperates in the work of renovation, still he does not do so through his own natural powers, but through the powers granted by the Spirit, and in a direct sense grace always remains the principle of renovation and sanctification.

Renovation and sanctification have been considered in both a broad and a more restricted sense. Sanctification can be considered as a part of renovation. By sanctification some understand all the works of grace, and then it is called *sanctificatio late dicta. Sanctificatio stricte dicta* is equivalent to *renovatio negativa,* and *strictissime dicta* is equivalent to the positive side of *renovatio.*

While *regeneratio* is a momentary act, *renovatio,* on the other hand, is a progressive process, which continues through life. The Christian experiences anew the gracious acts of the Spirit, in general, not with the same limitations as during the period of conversion, but in a more intimate way with the acts of grace interlocking and overlapping.

1. The Definition of Renovation.

Renovation is *that act of grace by which the Holy Spirit through the means of grace with the co-operation of the regenerated person more and more overcomes the power of sin and restores the image of God, so that the old man is put off and the new man is put on.* Renovation consists of two acts, one the negative, and the other the positive.

Renovatio negativa or *sanctificatio stricte dicta* is that part of the grace of renovation by which the power of sin is ever increasingly overcome and the old Adam is put off or dies, although slowly.

Renovatio positiva or *sanctificatio strictissime dicta* is therefore the gracious act of the Spirit through which He renews in man the image of God, while man co-operates with the powers granted in regeneration. Renovation is therefore considered both from the transitive and intransitive point of view.

Causa efficiens principalis is the Triune God, but *terminative* the Holy Spirit. Compare 1 Thess. 5:23; Rom. 15:16; Gal. 5:22; Titus 3:5. The regenerated person is considered *causa efficiens* in a secondary sense. Compare Phil. 2: 12,13. *Terminus a quo* is the old Adam and unconquered sins. *Subjectum quo* is in a primary sense the spiritual nature of man, which sin has permeated and corrupted as to the intellect, will and emotions. In a *secondary sense* the *membra corporis* are also included. The *media* or means that are to be used are the means of grace, although the means employed in ascetic morality may at times prove useful as formal auxiliaries.

Among Scripture passages that present the negative and positive sides of renovation the following may be quoted: "Though our outward man is decaying, yet our inward man is renewed day by day" (2 Cor. 4:16); "Our old man was crucified with him, that the body of sin might be done away, that we should no longer be in bondage to sin" (Rom. 6:6); "Put ye on the Lord Jesus Christ" (Rom. 13:14; cf. 4: 22-24; Col. 3:9, 10).

2. The Degrees of Renovation or Sanctification.

Inasmuch as renovation is progressive and therefore continually developing, it must have degrees. The above-cited passage from 2 Cor. 4:16 as well as other passages indicate this. Sometimes a backsliding will take place on account of the weakness of man, but the normal state is one of progress. In this matter the emotions are not always a reliable gauge, and man himself is seldom able to measure the progress of his spiritual development. Under normal conditions the Christian passes through the various spiritual ages such as the age of spiritual childhood, youth, and manhood. Compare 1 Cor. 3:1; 1 John 2:12-14; Heb. 6:1; 1 Cor. 16:13. But although *terminus ad quem* is the new man, yet renovation never becomes complete in this life, which doctrine we stress against Methodists and others, who assert that man can become perfectly sinless on earth. Compare Rom. 7:19-22; Gal. 5:17; Phil. 3:12-16; Heb. 12:1; 1 John 1:810; 3:2.

3. The Proof of Renovation in Good Works.

Renovatio is demonstrated in good works. They are called good works, not because they are perfect in themselves, but because they proceed from faith. Only the regenerated are therefore capable of doing good works. By good works are meant not only external deeds, but also the emotions of the heart and the decisions of the will. Hollazius defines *bona opera* as follows: "*Bona opera are the free acts of justified persons which stand forth as good in the light of the preceding true faith in Christ and are performed through the renewing grace of the Holy Spirit, according to the prescription of the divine*

Law, to the honor of God and the edification of man."[89]

The Lutheran Church has never underestimated the significance of good works, and her doctrine of justification does not conflict with the Biblical doctrine of good works. But by reason of the teachings of the Catholic Church concerning good works and her false doctrine of justification it became necessary for the Protestant Church to emphasize the doctrine of justification by faith alone, without thereby denying the necessity of good works as the fruits of faith. The Catholics have intermingled good works in justification and have falsely conceived both justification and sanctification. The Church of the Middle Ages taught that the works that proceed from *gratia habitualis* merit everlasting life. The *consilia evangelica* were placed above the fulfilment of *praecepta,* such as abstention from the pleasures of the world, voluntary poverty, chastity and obedience. The Council of Trent decided that the justified man is able to fulfill the commandments of God, and the meeting condemned those that deny this.[90] In the confutation of the Augsburg Confession the Catholic Church states that the doctrine of *sola fide* conflicts absolutely with the Word of God, while the doctrine of good works is emphasized. The Apology presents clearly the relation between faith and good works. Major, Menius and Amsdorf especially gave rise to an investigation of the relationship between justification and good works. These theologians expressed themselves in a way that could be misunderstood. Major and Menius expressed themselves as follows: Good deeds are necessary to salvation. No one can be saved without good works. Good works are necessary in order to retain salvation or are necessary in order not to lose salvation. Amsdorf, on the contrary, stated that good works are injurious for salvation. The *Formula of Concord* sets forth the following points among others: That it is the will of God that the believers perform good

[89] Hollazius: *"Bona opera sunt actus hominum justificatorum liberi per gratiam Spiritus sancti renovantem ad praescriptum legis divinae praelucente vera in Christum fide praestiti in honorem Dei ad hominum aedificationem."*

[90] Sessio VI, Caput XI et Canon XIII.

works; that good works are not performed through the natural powers of man; that good works are well-pleasing to God for Christ's sake through faith; that good works are to be performed not by constraint (*coactio*), but by the free spirit, which freedom is not arbitrary.[91] Such modes of expression as those used by Major and Menius ought to be avoided, since they may be misunderstood, while they conflict with particulae exclusivae. The Epicurean doctrine that faith, justification, and salvation could not be lost through intentional sins was also rejected. But if salvation could be lost through intentional sins, still it could not be kept through good works. Faith is indeed the only organ for the reception of justification and salvation both in regard to the beginning, middle, and end. The expressions of Amsdorf were also criticized. Good works are injurious only when intermingled in justification so as to constitute the foundation for self-confidence. But when performed with the proper intention and for a proper end they are the characteristic marks of the Christian and are well-pleasing to God, who shall reward them both in this life and in that which is to come.

Affectiones operum bonorum are therefore: 1) *sponte fiunt,* or that they take place voluntarily; 2) *necessaria,* or that they are necessary as the fruits of faith; 3) *imperfecta,* inasmuch as they are imperfect.

Bona opera are divided into *interna* and *externa.* With regard to their so-called *forma* the old Dogmaticians say that when they are considered in the absolute sense, then *forma* is *conformitas cum lege,* but when considered in the relative sense, on the ground of the special favor of God, then *forma* is *fides in Christum,* since the works do not completely conform to the demands of the Law, but nevertheless are well-pleasing to God on account of faith which apprehends Christ.

There are different degrees of good works and all are not of the same quality. *Bona opera* have therefore been divided into different grades, as follows: 1) *interior obedientia cordis,* such as good intentions, the inclination of the will and the pure motives of the heart. To this class belong the

---

[91] Müller, Symb. Bücher, Sol. Decl. IV, p. 624.

invisible works of sanctification which God alone sees; 2) *opera moralia tabulae primae,* to which belong worship in an internal and external sense and therefore also love to God; 3) *opera moralia tabulae secundae,* to which belongs love to our neighbor, which manifests itself in a variety of ways. In every case God sees all of these deeds and in many cases they are seen and observed by our neighbors also.

The quality of the *bona opera* is set forth in the Scriptures in figures of speech, such as gold, silver, precious stones, etc. Compare 1 Cor. 3:12-15; 2 Tim. 2:19-21. Although the first passage on account of the context must be applied in a primary sense to the teachers of the Word as to how they build on the foundation, still there are lessons to be drawn in the interest of sanctification for Christians in general. All Christians build on the same foundation, but they do not all build alike. The works of some are like gold, silver, and costly stones, while the works of others are like wood, hay, and stubble. The quality of sanctification, therefore, is of great importance before God, and this not only for time, but also for eternity. This phase of the matter is clearly presented in vv. 14 and 15. There are, besides, so-called Christians who bear no fruit, an evidence of the fact that they have become withered branches. This condition denotes that they have lost their salvation. They withered because they did not abide in Christ. Compare John 15:2-6. But true Christians desire to bear fruit and to build in such a fashion on the true foundation that their works shall stand the test of the fiery trial. This does not always mean that they shall stand the test in their own estimation or in the estimation of others, but God judges a righteous judgment. The deep-seated desire of all true Christians, is to follow after sanctification, without which no man shall see the Lord. Cf. Heb. 12:14.

4. The Object of Renovation.

Finis proximus is the same as the term *terminus ad quem,* i. e., the new man. Renovation has its beginning, its continuance and its completion. The Holy Spirit is continually occupied with the gracious work of restoring man to the likeness of God, i.e., to the divine image in which he was originally created. If man had remained in the original state of integrity, he would have developed more and more until he had become prepared for entrance into the world of glory. In accordance with the divine plan of salvation the same work is now accomplished in another way. This work, however, is hid from the eyes of the world, and in certain cases also from the Christians themselves, since our life is hid with Christ in God. Compare Col. 3:1-10. The Christians, nevertheless, experience the activity of the Spirit of the Lord. If they remain faithful, the new man will in due season become complete. But renovation has also a final goal, *finis ultimus,* which is life eternal and the glory of God. This object possesses great significance, inasmuch as the glory belongs to God and He is glorified through the salvation of man.

§31. Conservation.

Since the object of the next preceding acts of grace is the salvation of the believers, therefore it is of importance that those persons who have been regenerated and are in a state of sanctification be preserved and that they endure in faith even unto the end. Someone has said that from a human point of view it is not an easy matter to become a Christian, but it is more difficult to remain a Christian. The gate is narrow on account of sin, although the grace of God is abundant, but the way is strait and in the case of some it may be too long. On this account *conservatio* is of vast importance as an act of grace. To this belongs *perseverantia fidelium*. It is true that *conservatio* can be subordinated under *renovatio,* but it can also be considered as a special act of grace. Hollazius does this when he treats of *gratia conservans* or the doctrine of God's preserving grace.

1. The Definition Of Conservation.

Conservation is that act of grace whereby the regenerated person is preserved in true faith especially through the right use of the means of grace so that he does not finally fall, but is at last redeemed and admitted into the kingdom of glory.

Hollazius defines as follows: "*Conservatio* is that act of grace whereby the Holy Spirit, who dwells in justified and renovated men, preserves them through supernatural powers from the temptations of the devil, the world and the flesh, through which they are tempted to sin and apostasy from God, confirms and increases their faith and the sanctity of their life, so that they do not fall from the state of grace, but are preserved in it and eternally saved."[92]

In a primary sense it is the Triune God and *instrumentaliter* the Holy Spirit that preserves the regenerated man, but in a secondary sense preservation takes place through the concursus that is active by reason of the spiritual powers granted to the regenerated man. *Gratia cooperans* is therefore active in conservation. Conservation does not therefore depend upon an arbitrary decision, and the grace of conservation is not a *gratia irresistibilis,* as many of the Reformed declare. The Calvinists and therefore many of the Reformed teach that the truly regenerated man, who is therefore elect in accordance with the doctrine of unconditional predestination, cannot fall. The Lutheran Church emphasizes the responsibility of the Christian in the exercise of his Christian freedom, but at the same time stresses the preserving grace of God, since without the grace of God no man can be preserved. But some Christians may fall. They may fall many times, and finally be lost. It may also happen that they fall from the grace of God and finally are restored and saved. The old Dogmaticians speak of *apostasia* as duplex: *dogmatica et moralis.* By *apostasia dogmatica* is meant such a departure from the true teaching as to extinguish the saving faith. *Apostasia moralis* is the intentional abandonment of the exercise of sanctification coupled with the practise of evil deeds as finally to result in the shipwreck of faith. Cf. 1 Tim. 4:1; 1 Tim. 1:19.

Among Scripture passages that present the preserving grace of God

---

[92] Hollazius: "*Conservatio est actus gratiae quo Spiritus sanctus habitans in hominibus justificatis et renovatis, hos adversus diaboli, mundi et carnis tentationes, quibus ad peccatum ac apostasiam a Deo solicitantur, supernaturalibus viribus praemunit, fidemque Ipsorum et vitae sanctitatem confirmat et auget, ne e statu gratiae excidant, sed in eodem perseverent, et aeternum salventur.*"

together with the responsible co-operation of the Christian the following may be quoted: "Being confident of this very thing, that he who began a good work in you will perfect it until the day of Jesus Christ" (Phil. 1:6); "Faithful is he that calleth you, who will also do it" (1 Thess. 5:24); "Who by the power of God are guarded" (1 Peter 1:5; cf. John 10:28, 29; 2 Tim. 4:17, 18); "If a man abide not in me, he is cast forth," etc. (John 15:6); "And in like manner the Spirit also helpeth our infirmity" (Rom. 8:26; 1 Cor. 1:4-9); "Perfecting holiness in the fear of God" (2 Cor. 7:1); "Stand fast therefore" (Gal. 5:1); "Let us run with patience the race" (Heb. 12:1); "Be thou faithful unto death" (Rev. 2:10).

2. The Means and Manner of Conservation.

The *primary* means are the means of grace. If we consider Baptism as the basis of the new life, then the means are the Word of God and the Lord's Supper. God works through these means, and the Christian must make diligent use of them. Co-operation takes place, but the means are divine and the powers of man are granted powers. No one can be preserved who does not use the Word of God in accordance with the directions of Scripture. God has not promised to preserve anyone in an immediate way. The means of grace are not primary in the sense that there are other means that could be employed to the neglect of the means of grace. The Word of God and the Sacraments are necessary for us in order to be preserved. The Lord's Supper is therefore also necessary as a means of grace for preservation in the faith, although not in the same sense as the Word. A wilful neglect of the Lord's Supper is deadening to faith.

There are, besides, *secondary* means, which, however, are dependent on the Word of God and set forth in the Scriptures as necessary. The secondary means are therefore in reality the putting into practice of the primary means under various conditions. These are: Prayer in the name of Jesus, watchfulness, and an earnest fight against all the internal and external enemies that may hinder preservation in the faith. It is often necessary for the Lord to chastise the Christians in order that they may more diligently use the means of grace together with the auxiliary means here set forth which are dependent on the primary means of grace. This chastisement may be either internal or external, general or special. The Christians are preserved in faith by bearing the cross of suffering.

Hollazius presents the formal statement in reference to the preservation of the faithful when he answers the question: *In quo formaliter consistit conservatio fidelium?*[93] He says that *conservatio* comprises three acts of grace: 1) *gratia praeservans seu praemuniens,* which means that God preserves the faithful in granting to them supernatural powers against temptations and all enemies. James 4:6, 7; 1 John 5:4, 5; Jude 24; 2) *gratia confirmans et consolans,* when God strengthens and consoles the faithful through the means of grace. 2 Cor. 1:21, 22; 1 Cor. 1:4-9; 1 Peter 1: 3-12; 3) *gratia locupletans,* or the grace by which the believers receive more and more of the riches of the divine grace, being thereby so strengthened as to be able to endure until the victory is won. Col. 1:9-11; 2 Peter 1:3-11; 3:18; Eph. 3:14-21.

3. The Goal Of Conservation.

Finis proximus is *perseverantia,* by which is meant that the believer is preserved and that he endures until the end. *Perseverantia* has, however, been characterized either as *temporaria* or as *finalis.* For examples of *temporaria* read Matt. 13:20, 21. Some endure for a long time, but finally succumb. *Perseverantia finalis* is either *continua* or *interrupta.* Some Christians fall because of the weakness of the flesh, but are restored again and endure to the end of life, wherefore their *perseverantia* is called *interrupta.*

The personal assurance of the Christians with regard to their endurance or their *certitudo* is *non absoluta, sed ordinata et conditionata.* In this conditional sense the Christians may be certain and happy by reason of the Word and promises of the Lord. God has promised His help (1 Cor. 1:8, 9); the Son intercedes for them (John 17); they are sealed with the

[93] Exam. Theol. Acroam. Pars III, §1, Cap. xi, p. 416.

Spirit until the day of redemption (Eph. 4:30). At times their assurance and confidence may rise to the heights of glorious triumph. Cf. Rom. 8:35-39.

Finis ultimus conservationis is naturally, as in the preceding acts of grace, the eternal salvation of the believers together with the glory of God. The goal is reached when the believers have been preserved until the end and they have been privileged to enter into the state of glory.

6

Ecclesiology

Ecclesiology is that part of Dogmatics which treats of the doctrine of the Church and the manner of her working. In the section on Pneumatology we dealt with the gracious work of the Holy Spirit, which is performed in the Church of Christ, so that the Church may be styled the "workshop" of the Holy Ghost. Ecclesiology defines in the first place the concept of the Church. But the Holy Spirit works through means, and for this reason the doctrine of the Word and the Sacraments constitutes the dominating subject in Ecclesiology. The Founder of the Church also established an office to administer the means of grace through which the Holy Spirit works, and for this reason Ecclesiology also sets forth the doctrine of the Christian Ministry.

§32. The Church.

The great day of Pentecost was the birthday of the Church when the Holy Spirit was poured out and His specific work begun. In a certain sense, to be sure, the Church had existed before, since the community life of religion did not originate on the day of Pentecost. In its essence religion is a unifying force uniting God and men with one another and the children of men with each other. On the day of Pentecost, the real birthday of the Church, religion appeared in its mature form. Christianity, which is the true essence of religion, then entered upon the stage of complete activity. Christianity is life and its present organism is the Church. The Church is God's creation, and within her fold are born the children that shall become members of the kingdom of eternal glory.

1. Definition.

Ecclesia, or the Church, *is the communion of saints, in which the Word of God is taught in its purity and the Sacraments are administered in accordance with the institution of Christ.* The concept of the Church therefore embodies two elements, each one of which must be given proper emphasis, since otherwise misconceptions may arise such as we find prevailing in the high-church and low-church groups of the Church. Historically speaking, these tendencies are to be found in the Roman Catholic Church and among the Reformed sects. The definition of the Church would not be complete if it were simply defined unqualifiedly as the communion of saints, since in that case the communion might be conceived of as being invisible, without any external form of appearance. On the other hand, it would not be sufficient to say simply that the Church is a communion where the means of grace are administered, since it is necessary to emphasize the fact that the Church is not merely a *politia externa*, as the Catholics teach, but that it is a *congregatio sanctorum*. The communion of saints on the earth cannot be found apart from the means of grace, but where the means of grace are found and used, there faith will be effected; there will also be found believers and saints, and as a result a communion of believers among whom the means of grace are administered. The one cannot be separated from the other. However, the expression *congregatio sanctorum* does not imply that the actual Church consists only of believers, since by reason of the historical development of the Church together with other circumstances it is practically impossible to prevent hypocrites and unbelievers from belonging to the visible church. However, the Church always strives to reach the ideal, although the militant Church on earth can never become a completely triumphant Church.

Ecclesia stricte dicta comprises therefore the believing members within the Church who use the means of grace, i. e., when we consider the Church in this world. *Ecclesia late dicta* is the term applied to the Church by the use of a common figure of speech, synecdoche, which puts a part for the whole, and by which that which belongs only to a part is ascribed to the entire communion consisting of both believers and unbelievers.

There are not, however, two churches, one a true and internal, the other a nominal and external, church, but the Church is one and the same, namely, the assembly of the called considered from two different aspects: ἔσωθεν and ἔξωθεν. Hutterus says: "Although it is "not sufficient for salvation that you are a member of the Church described in this general manner and only in relation to the external confession of the Christian faith, still it is true that salvation is not to be found outside of this communion. In this connection the comparison to Noah's ark is applicable, for inasmuch as no one was saved during the flood outside the ark, and yet not all who were in the ark were on that account saved unto everlasting life, so no one is saved outside the Church, and yet all are not saved that belong to the Church in the general sense." With regard to the Church considered *stricte dicta* the assertion is absolutely applicable: *extra ecclesiam nulla salus.*

Among the Scripture passages that set forth the real nature of the Church, *stricte dicta,* the following may be cited: "So we, who are many, are one body in Christ" (Rom. 12:5); "The church, which is his body, the fulness of him that filleth all in all" (Eph. 1:22, 23); "The house of God, which is the church of the living God" (1 Tim. 3:15). This latter passage may apply to the Church in its twofold character. The following passages present to a greater or less degree the Church considered *late dicta* or as it appears actually or in history: "Take heed unto yourselves, and to all the flock, in the which the Holy Ghost hath made you bishops, to feed the church of God" (Acts 20:28) ; "He that prophesieth edifieth the church" (1 Cor. 14:4); "The church of God which is at Corinth" (1 Cor. 1:2; compare the conditions as described in 1 Cor. 5:1, etc.). The congregations to which the apostolical letters as well as the letters of Christ are addressed present the Church in a real sense as a communion of saints where the means of grace are administered, but whose membership also includes hypocrites and unbelievers. The parables of Christ also present the Church in the same manner. But essentially the Church is not a communion of believers and unbelievers, but the communion of saints.

Inasmuch as the definition of the Church states that it is the communion of saints in which the Word of God is taught in its purity and the Sacraments are administered according to the institution of Christ, the question may arise as to whether a church exists in case the Word of God in its entirety is not taught in its purity and the Sacraments are not rightly understood and administered. The Augsburg Confession does not deal with this question, but seems to acknowledge that the Roman Church is a Church of God. Billing says in this connection: "One would surely not go far wrong in assuming that the Lutheran Church, with regard to the degree of purity required, would limit itself to the following, that the means of grace be so administered that faith may thereby be brought about."[94] The Lutheran Church does not claim that she alone is the Church of Christ on earth, but she does assert that the true Church ought to be such that within her the Word of God be purely preached and the Sacraments administered according to the institution of Christ. Otherwise the Church is not normal. When Christians unite to form a church but do not teach in accordance with the whole Word of God, then such a church is abnormal to that extent. In defining the Church it is necessary to set forth its true essence and character. The Lutheran Church lays great stress on true harmony between faith and doctrine. The Lutheran Church desires to be and confesses herself to be a church that faithfully abides by the Word of God. For this reason she could not set forth a different conception of the Church from that which is presented in the definition. She does not, however, assume an exclusive attitude and sit in judgment upon others, as does the Roman Catholic Church, not to speak of certain ultra-Protestant and separatistic sects.

---

[94] Luth. Kyrkans Bekännelse, p. 482.

2. The Founder and Head of the Church.

Causa efficiens ecclesiae is the Triune God and especially Christ the God-man. *Causa impulsiva interna* is the goodness or gracious favor of God. *Causa impulsiva externa* is Christ by reason of His mediatorial office. *Caput ecclesiae,* or the Head of the Church, is Christ. He occupies this position not only by reason of His superior eminence above the members, but also because of the moral and physical or real influence, which, according to both natures, He exerts over the members of His mystical body or the Church. *Influxus Christi,* or the influence of Christ, is twofold: 1) *moralis,* which consists in this, that Christ, by virtue of His merit, has acquired all spiritual blessings (Eph. 1:3); 2) *physicus sive realis,* which implies the operative activity of Christ in the Church in accordance with His promise to be with His disciples always, even unto the end of the world. He is the head of the Church in a real sense and directs all things for the welfare of the whole Church as well as the individual members.

We therefore reject the Roman Catholic doctrine that Peter became the head of the Church and the vicar of Christ, and that the pope is his successor. With regard to the interpretation of Matt. 16:18 the Protestant theologians understand the "rock" to mean the confession of Peter. Christ Himself is declared to be the foundation. Compare 1 Cor. 3:11. Note also the twentieth verse of the same chapter, which says, "Let no one glory in men." With regard to the keys it may be stated that they were entrusted not only to Peter, but to others as well. Compare Matt. 18:18: "What things soever ye shall bind on earth shall be bound in heaven: and what things soever ye shall loose on earth shall be loosed in heaven." Compare John 20:21-23. Not only Peter but also James and John are called pillars. Cf. Gal. 2:9.

Some theologians interpret the "rock" to mean not only the confession of Peter but also Peter as a confessor becoming thereby an ideal Christian confessor. In this special character he became the norm for all confessors, who also are living stones in the building. Compare Eph. 2: 20-22. For this reason *πέτρος* is also changed to *πέτρα* in Matt. 16:18. For further study compare the following passages: Matt. 16:18; Mark 8:27-30; Luke

9:18-21; John 1:41-43, where Simon for the first time is called Petros, but in Matt. 16:18 he has come to deserve the name; Rom. 15:20; 1 Cor. 3:4-11; Eph. 2:20-22. Some commentators have interpreted the expression "The foundation of the apostles and prophets" as a *genetivus appositivus* (Chrysostom, Olshausen, DeWette and others), others say that it is a *genitivus originis* (Calvin, Harless, Meyer, Ellicott and others), while still others say that it is a *genitivus possessivus* (Beza, Bucer, Alford, etc.). Some theologians accept all three interpretations. Compare Gal. 2:9; 1 Tim. 3:15; 1 Peter 2:4, 5 and Rev. 21:14.

3. *Materia Et Forma Ecclesiae.*

By *materia ecclesiae* the old Dogmaticians mean the believers or the saints. Some have used the expression "the elect," but to avoid misunderstandings the expression "the communion of saints" is used instead of "the communion of the elect." The Church is therefore the communion of saints, the assembly of believers and the household of God.

Forma ecclesiae comprises the assembly of the believers and saints, who as members of the Church are united with the head of the Church, even Christ, through a true and living faith, which is followed by the union and communion of the members in true love.

The Christians do not stand in isolation but in the closest union and communion with Christ and with one another. An intelligent Christian therefore can not support a one-sided individualism, be it religious or ecclesiastical. The individual Christian must not concentrate all his interests in himself, he must be ever ready in love to serve his Master and fellow saints in the kingdom on whose banner are inscribed the words, Faith, Love and Hope. There are many Scripture passages that speak of this loving relationship. "But he that is joined unto the Lord is one spirit" (1 Cor. 6:17); "One body and one spirit" (Eph. 4:4); "By this shall all men know that ye are my disciples, if ye have love one to another" (John 13:35). By reason of our earthly imperfections this love does not always manifest itself as it should; however, all true Christians love each other, although they cannot love all with the same degree of intensity, nor every trait or characteristic of the individual Christian.

4. The Attributes of the Church.

The attributes of the Church are of two kinds, some more general and symbolical, others more particular.

A. *Attributa ecclesiae vulgo*: 1) *Una*. The Church is one and undivided because the members of the Church are united in Christ as the head, which union implies not only love to God but also to our neighbor. Furthermore, we say that the Church is one and no more because it does not acknowledge a plurality of assemblies of the same nature and existing simultaneously, inasmuch as the Church catholic, is the communion of saints, in which sense there cannot be more than one such holy communion. The Church is also one because there cannot be a succeeding church. The Church has always existed and will ever continue to exist unto the end of the world. 2) *Sancta*. The Church is holy because Christ its head is holy in the absolute sense and because its members are justified and sanctified, ever striving after perfect holiness. It is also holy because the means of grace through which the Holy Ghost works in the hearts of men are holy; likewise because the whole purpose and aim of all its activity is spiritual and heavenly, so that it is not of the world, although in the world. 3) *Catholica*. The Church is catholic (*καϑ ὅλον*) both with respect to its orthodoxy, confessing the faith which was once for all delivered unto the saints, and with respect to its extent, being spread over the entire globe and among all people. 4) *Apostolica*. The Church is called apostolic because it was founded through the mediation of the apostles, confesses their teachings and is built up on the foundation laid by the prophets and the apostles.

B. *Attributa ecclesiae particularia*: 1) *Visibilis et invisibilis*, or visible and invisible. The Church is visible as an assembly of the called and baptized who are members of particular churches which use the means of grace and carry on religious work, but it is not visible in the sense that we know for a certainty who in each particular assembly are members of the *ecclesia stricte dicta*. We may, however, be certain of the fact that the true Church is found in the visible Church, inasmuch as the baptized infants and small children are members of the body of Christ, and where the means of grace are used they must always be efficacious. It is hardly possible that a Christian congregation can be found where true Christians would be altogether wanting. But the Church is invisible with respect to the believers or the elect and their hidden life with God and spiritual communion. The spiritual gifts are likewise invisible. We may also say that the Church is invisible because Christ, the mystical head, is not present in a visible manner, while many, nay most, of its members are no longer upon earth. But the invisible Church on the earth is found in the visible Church like the soul in the body. Some Christians would belong to the invisible Church, but not the visible, although it is the visible Church that administers the means of grace. This is certainly just as abnormal as if the soul were outside the body. All true and sensible Christians therefore desire to be members of the visible Church, i. e., to be recorded as members in some Christian congregation. 2) *Universalis et particularis*. The Church is universal both in place and time. With respect to place the Church is universal because its goal is to extend its activity into all the world. With respect to time it is universal inasmuch as it extends through all time, so that it has been in existence from the beginning of time, exists now and shall continue to exist. It might seem as though the two terms *universalis* and *catholica* were expressive of the same thing, which is indeed true to a certain extent, although the term *catholica* stresses particularly that which is general and common in doctrine. All particular churches, therefore, comprising as they do the different sections of the Church Universal acknowledge the ecumenical creeds, while the sectarian groups, although true Christians may be found among them nevertheless tear themselves away from the traditional trunk of the general ecclesiastical tree, reject all that which is ecumenical, including the fixed symbols of the Church Universal, and accept that which is individual and personally characteristic. The Church is *particularis,* not as a whole, but as divided. It is *particularis* with respect to time, e. g., the Church of the Old or of the New Testament. It is *particularis* with respect to place and location, e. g., in a country, in a city, etc. The Church is likewise *particularis* from the confessional viewpoint, such as the Greek Catholic, the Roman Catholic, the Lutheran, the Reformed Church. 3) *Pura et vera*. Pura is contrasted with *impura* and *vera* with *falsa*. The purpose in the use of these terms is to state that particular churches may be pure and true in varying degrees, while some may be the reverse. A pure Church is one in which the Word of God is taught in its purity and the Sacraments are rightly administered. But even if the Word of God is not preached purely in its entirety, still there is a Church, although relatively impure, provided that the Word of God is preached in such manner that souls may be saved. A man is a man even though certain parts of the body may be injured. However, certain organs are necessary, such as the head, the heart and the lungs. A Church may become so heretical in essential doctrines that it can no longer be counted as a Christian Church. But even with respect to relatively unessential members of the body it is desirable that we possess the perfect use of all of them in healthy condition. The same conditions obtain with regard to the churches. Even if men may be saved in an *ecclesia impura*, still every intelligent Christian understands that it is better to belong to an *ecclesia pura* where the Word of God is taught in its purity and the Sacraments are rightly administered. In speaking of true and false churches there is no thought of any oppositional relationship, as between the Christian Church and false religions, rather the question concerns the different churches in Christendom which either teach the Word of God correctly or falsify their teachings with heresies. There are some who have misunderstood the concept of a pure Church, declaring it to be a congregation of believers only. However, such a pure Church can never be realized on earth for any length of time. Even if such a congregation might be organized among a limited group of Christians, still there would soon appear backsliders and unbelievers. The parables of our Lord, the apostolical epistles, the letters of Jesus to the seven churches prove conclusively that a pure Church is beyond the limits of possibility on the earth. Some separatists have misinterpreted 2 Cor. 6:14-18 as an admonition to withdraw from a congregation in which the majority of the members would seem to be unregenerated. It is evident that Paul did not admonish the believers in the congregation at Corinth to leave the congregation, rather the admonition concerned the relationship of the Christians to unbelievers outside of the congregation. We do not mean to say that unbelievers are normal members of the Church, for only believers are true members. It is the duty of each congregation to exercise the power of church discipline in accordance with the Word of God. 4) *Synthetica sive collectiva et representativa.* By the former is meant the Church in its entirety, while by the latter is meant the Church in a representative capacity, such as in general councils, ecclesiastical assemblies, synods, etc. 5) *Militans et triumphans,* or the militant and triumphant Church. The Church is a militant Church on the earth, inasmuch as it combats the devil, the world and the flesh. In reality only the true believers participate in this struggle, and yet it may also be said that the whole Church takes part in the fight. The Church achieves many victories in this world of strife, but only in heaven will it become the Church triumphant when the goal is reached and the kingdom of God is made complete, or is perfectly consummated.

5. *Status Ecclesiae.*

Status ecclesiae are: 1) *status ecclesiasticus,* or the office of the Ministry established by Christ to preach the Word of God, make application of the power of the keys, and administer the Sacraments (See paragraph 39); 2) *status oeconomicus sive domesticus* is divided by the old Dogmatians into three parts: a) *societas conjugalis;* b) *societas paterna;* c) *societas herilis.* Hollazius defines marriage as follows: "*Conjugium* or marriage is in accordance with the divine institution the indissoluble union of one man and one woman by reason of the mutual consent of both for the begetting of offspring and mutual assistance in life."[95] In general the justifiable reason for divorce is represented as being adultery, but some Dogmaticians say that *causae justae divortii sunt adulterium et malitiosa desertio.* However, this is a moot question and the most conservative

[95] *Exam. Theol. Acroam.* Pars IV, Cap. iv, p. 900.

position is that only adultery is a *causa justa*. With respect to other questions of marriage compare Schmid's Dogmatics, paragraph 61, and also Church Polity. With regard to *societas paterna et herilis* consult the same author and textbooks in Catechetics; 3) *status politicus. Magistratus* is considered partly in the abstract or as the government and power per se, and partly in the concrete, i. e., those that govern. *Causa efficiens principalis* is the Triune God, who sometimes directly but generally indirectly establishes the government. *Potestas* or the power is divided as follows: a) *officium legislatorium*, b) *judiciarium*, c) *punitivum*. *Bonum publicum*, for which the civil magistrate has been ordained, is said to be fourfold: a) *ecclesiasticum*, b) *civile*, c) *morale*, d) *naturale*. The Christians are in duty bound to obey the government in all things that are not contrary to the Word of God, fulfill all their obligations and pray for those in authority. Finis proximus is the general good, while finis ultimus is the honor of God. Cf. Schmid's Dogmatics, paragraph 60.

6. The Aim and Purpose of the Church.

Finis proximus is the edification of the entire body of the Church as well as of the individual members. The Church grows inwardly as well as externally. It must care for the material as well as the spiritual welfare of its members, but especially the spiritual welfare. The Church must be vitally interested, not only in home missions and inner missions with all their diverse activities, but also in the external development of the local congregations as well as in the foreign mission of the Church in its entirety, so that in accordance with the command of our Lord in Matt. 28:19, 20, the Gospel may be preached to all the earth. This is the great mission of the Church, and even if at times the prospects of reaching the goal do not seem so bright, still the Church must be obedient to the Lord and prosecute the cause of missions with all vigor and power until the Lord shall come again to complete the victory. *Finis ultimus* is the eternal salvation of the members together with the establishment of the kingdom of God through which His name is glorified and the divine will and purpose concerning the salvation of men is accomplished.

7. Notes on the History of Dogma.

During the earliest period there was no real development of the doctrine of the Church. During the Apostolic period the congregations were not united in ecclesiastical groups; many of them, however, sustained certain relationships with each other. The unity of the Church was emphasized. The so-called mother churches were held in the highest regard, especially the churches that had been founded by the Apostles. When the Judaistic and Gnostic tendencies began to make their schismatic influence felt, then the congregations also began to feel the need of a closer union. It was considered to be of the utmost importance to possess the same doctrines as the apostolical churches. In this way the expression "apostolicity" came into vogue. After the second ecumenical council it became customary to speak of one holy, catholic, and apostolic Church. The controversy with the Donatists and other similar tendencies gave rise to a special development of the doctrine of the Church. Their position with regard to the purity of the Church was powerfully combatted by such men as Optatus of Mileve, Augustine, and others. High Church tendencies made their appearance through Cyprian, but Augustine was also one of the founders of the Roman hierarchical position. It became more and more common to set forth the external unity of the Church to the detriment of its true essence. The Roman Church laid pronounced emphasis on the external civil and political rights of the Church so that it became an *externa politia*, a *societas externarum rerum ac rituum*. It became customary to pay little or no heed to the spiritual character of the members. It was only the external connection with the Church that was emphasized, inasmuch as no salvation could be found outside of the Catholic Church. In accordance with the conception of the Church held by the ultra-Protestants as it arose especially in the Swiss Reformation, the exact opposite view was taken, so that personal faith became all in all, the Church was considered invisible, while only true believers were to belong to the external organization. The significance of the means of grace was disregarded, inasmuch as the Lord often dealt immediately with the children of men. The Lutheran Reformation took the true apostolical position and set forth a doctrine of the Church that was conservative as well as comprehensive. Proper emphasis was laid both on the inner essence and the external character of the Church. In its true being the Church comprises the communion of saints, but the explanation was made that the Church on earth cannot possibly be composed of believers alone. The Church was set forth as an institution in which the grace of God was freely dispensed, while the historical continuity of the Church was stressed by pointing out that no new Church was established, but the Church was the old apostolical and catholic Church which had been reformed in accordance with the Word of God; hence it was confessedly one, holy communion, which shall continue forever. The different views that obtained during the period of the Reformation are still to be found among the various church denominations. The Catholic Church never changes as to its doctrinal positions. The Lutheran Church is faithful to its confessions, although, by reason of the principle of formal freedom in Church polity, divergent tendencies have appeared. Among the Reformed groups we find both high-church and low-church tendencies, but, generally speaking, they hold to the original Reformed views in principle, although there are practically many differences owing to the influence of circumstances at the time of organization and during the period of subsequent development. We shall now proceed to present more detailed notes on the history of this dogma.

Clement of Rome presents the Church as the people of God gathered together from the whole earth, the true Israel which replaces the old. Ignatius makes use of the expression catholic Church in the sense that it comprises all the congregations in the world and that in its essence it is invisible. Justin Martyr says that the Church is a priestly people but that some of its members are only nominal Christians. Indeed it was a common opinion in those days that the Church consisted really of true believers, but that many members were Christians only in name. Irenaeus said that the Church was the paradise of salvation and that the activity of the Holy Spirit was limited to the Church so that only the members of the Church could enjoy its benefits. He set forth the following phrase: *ubi ecclesia ibi Spiritus Dei, et ubi Spiritus Dei ibi ecclesia*. In choosing as between divergent doctrinal positions regard must be had for the views held in the apostolical congregations. Tertullian calls the Church Noah's ark. He said that God was our Father and the Church our mother. He also laid stress on that which was taught in the apostolical churches and especially the church in Rome as being normative for all doctrinal development. When he became a Montanist he spoke of two churches, the one consisting of the Spirit and the spiritually minded, the other is the church of the bishops, the members of which are *ψυχικοί*. Clement of Alexandria declared that there was only one catholic Church, since there is but one God and the earthly Church is an image of the heavenly. Cyprian likens the Church to the house of Rahab and the seamless garment of Christ. The Church is one and the Trinity is the eternal image of its unity. The external expression of this unity is the episcopacy. The bishops are the representatives of the Church. Although he held that the Roman bishop was only *primus inter pares,* still he maintained that the cathedra Petri constituted the chief seat of the unity of the Church. No one could be saved that did not belong to the Church, and if anyone parted from the bishop he also separated himself from the saving Church. Origen also uses the figure of the house of Rahab and compares the Church to the light of the moon that streams forth from Christ as the sun.

The Donatists required that all the members of the Church should be true Christians, declaring that if the Church tolerated unworthy members it would lose the qualities of holiness and purity, thereby nullifying the effects of its sacramental acts. Optatus of Mileve defended the doctrine of the Roman Church and set forth that the universal Church could not be conceived of as limited to a small section of Africa. He also maintained that the purity of the Church could not consist in the holiness of its members and that the efficacy of the Sacraments did not depend on the character of those that administered them. Agustine also combatted the Donatist heresy, setting forth a defense of the state church. The chair of Peter was the center of the Church. However, by the rock in Matt. 16: 18 he did not understand Peter, but Christ, whom Peter confessed. He set forth the great authority of the Catholic Church and declared that he would not believe the Gospel, provided the great authority of the Church did not compel him to do so. Vincent of Lerins presented the phrase: *quod semper, quod ubique, quod ab omnibus creditum est.* This assertion was meant to constitute a gauge of the doctrine of the Catholic Church. Leo the Great and Gregory the Great were enthusiastic defenders of the teaching that the Roman bishop was the successor of Peter and that consequently the unity of the Church was dependent on the union with Rome. The Catholic conception of the Church was therefore fixed before the Scholastic period, although it was during this period that it was developed more into its logical sequence.

Gregory VII exerted a very powerful influence on the polity of the Roman Church, while Innocent III called the pope the vicar of God and Christ, extending his power and influence to all the world. Thomas Aquinas held the same view with regard to the Church and the power of the papacy. The pope, he declared, was like a king in his kingdom and the defender of the faith. Bellarmin said that the concept of the Church is comprised of three parts: *professio verae fidei,* by which Jews, heathens, heretics, and backsliders are excluded; *sacramentorum communio,* by which *catechumeni et excommunicati* are excluded, and finally *regimen unius Christi in terris vicarii,* by which all schismatics are excluded. The Church is just as visible and palpable as the Roman people or as Venice and Gaul.

The position of Luther was presented in the Augsburg Confession and also in his catechisms. Calvin looked upon the Church as having been founded by God. The Church is our mother, whose mission it is to rear us in the fear and admonition of the Lord, i. e., sanctification. Not only the means of grace, but also church discipline, were reckoned as distinguishing marks of the Church. His doctrine of Church polity was aristocratic and in principle implied the same as the present-day Presbyterianism. The Lutheran position is set forth in the Augsburg Confession, Art. VII and VIII, and further developed in the remaining symbols. With regard to the membership of unbelievers in the Church the Apology says: "We acknowledge that hypocrites and ungodly men may in this life be found together with others in the congregation and that they may be members of the congregation in an external way and stand in relation to the external signs of the Church, namely, the Word, the confessions and the sacraments, especially if they have not been excommunicated or otherwise excluded from the congregation."[96] But the Apology also stresses the fact that only the believers are the true members who really comprise the congregation. However, the unbelievers are the objects of the saving activity of the Holy Spirit through the means of grace and may therefore become true members. Although the Apology and the other symbols do not deal at great length with the pedagogical mission of the Church, still there are many expressions which at least in principle set forth the educational activity and influence of the Church. The old Dogmaticians developed the doctrine of the Church in accordance with the Confessions.

In recent times we would in the first place mention the name of Kant, who regarded the Church as an ethical communion only. The position that he took has exercised influence on such theologians as merely lay emphasis on the ethical element in Christianity. The *Rationalists*, such as Wegscheider, regarded the Church as an educational institution, but some considered that the Church was superfluous. The *Supernaturalists* also took a superficial view of the Church and merely considered it an assembly of the confessors of the Christian religion. Hegel considered the State as being self-sufficient, that the dualism of the Church and the State was an intermediate state which would cease to be when the State had realized its ethical ideas. For this reason Strauss considered that the State rendered the Church increasingly dispensable. *The mediating theologians* consider that the Church consists of such as have entered into life-communion with Christ, but their view of such life-communion is not the Lutheran view. Schleiermacher rejected the distinction between the visible and the invisible Church. The Church is not the assembly of all baptized and regenerated persons, rather it is the combination of all the activities of the Spirit or of that which has been accomplished through the effects of redemption in the world. Among the special characteristics of the Church

---

[96] Müller, Symb. Bücher, p. 152, 3.

he counts the Word and the ministry of the Word, which corresponds to the prophetic office of Christ, the Sacraments, which correspond to the high-priestly office of Christ, together with the power of the keys and prayer, through which the regal office of Christ is represented. In more recent times some theologians have presented the symbolic and old dogmatic conception of the Church, others have made departures to the *right* and to the *left*. Stahl defends the Episcopal system. He distinguishes between the terms congregation and Church. The congregation is the more temporary activity at a particular place, but the Church exists at all times. The congregation represents the activity of men as directed toward God; the Church comprises the divine activity in relation to men. Vilmar presents the Church as an objective institution. He says that the Church possesses great significance in carrying on its work through the means of grace, and also serves as a protector in preserving these same means of grace. Löhe declared that the Lutheran Church was the queen among the churches on earth. This is true with reference to the doctrine. With regard to the concept of the Church and other related matters Löhe represents the "right" or the conservative element. Münchmeyer sets forth the Church as the visible assembly of the baptized. Delitzsch holds a similar position. Kliefoth makes a distinction between the Church and the congregation, declaring that the latter is only a part of the Church. The Triune God is the living foundation of the Church, but the Triune God is also in the Church. The Jerusalem that is above together with the company of believers constitute the Church. The Church is a divine institution whose mission is to mediate the application of redemption. It is a living organism which consists of institutions, callings, offices and states of society. It is an institution for the salvation of men by means of which God gathers unto Himself a congregation of men. The assembly of God is a *coetus vocatorum* and is visible. Inasmuch as the Church contains within itself this *coetus vocatorum*, therefore it is not merely an assembly of believers. The believers comprise the communion of saints. Kliefoth had prominent adherents in Sweden, among whom may be mentioned E. G. Bring, W. Flensburg and A. N. Sundberg. The instruction at the university of Lund reflected the views of Kliefoth. The conception of the Church as invisible was more or less rejected and the visible Church emphasized. While in Germany the Sacraments were placed above the Word, the Swedish adherents of Kliefoth paid no special attention to the question of superiority of the different means of grace, but they stressed the importance of holding the view that the Church had its fundamental origin in the grace of God and the Means of Grace and not in the membership as the spiritual priesthood. The Personal Idealism of Böstrom and the religious idealistic views of Wikner exercised great influence at the university of Uppsala and throughout the Northern countries, but the Bostromian philosophy has not dominated Theology and doctrinal views as did Hegelianism in Germany. The Ritschlian theology has been counteracted by the Bostromian philosophy, because the disciples of Böstrom and Wikner could not be attracted by the Ritschlian standpoint as to Metaphysics. Among the theologians at Uppsala W. Rudin was influenced by the views of J. T. Beck. Rudin was a mystic in the best sense, and his views in regard to the Church, though inclining to low church tendencies, were not unchurchly. At the university of Christiania Gisle Johnson wielded an unequalled influence on the Church of Norway and gave the Pietistic movement inaugurated by Hauge a churchly direction. Kierkegaard in Denmark represented religious individualism, just as Vinet in Switzerland argued for churchly individualism. Kierkegaard became a strong opponent to Hegelianism and theoretical presentation of doctrine. The ethical side of Christianity appealed to him. He was opposed to the Church as an institution and what he called official Christianity. He describes infant baptism, confirmation and the marriage ritual with biting irony and takes no interest in common divine service for edification. He seems to have no clear idea of the meaning of church life. To him the Church belonged to the future, when the individuals, after their individual experiences and sufferings here, come together as a society in heaven. Grundtvig arrived at his standpoint concerning the ideal of the Church during his contentions with the Rationalists. He says that Orthodoxy looked upon the Scriptures as the foundation of the Church, but when orthodox theology interpreted the Bible according to subjective opinions, it was necessary to find a more firm ground. And this firmer foundation he found in the Sacrament of Baptism and in the Apostolical Confession of faith. He strangely held that the Apostles' Creed is the Word from the mouth of Jesus Himself, and that this Word is the living Word and above that of the Bible. Grundtvig's ideal of the Church was a free development of all the religious forces within the Church on the foundation of authority. He sought to satisfy Pietistic tendencies and at the same time Roman Catholic ideas by his doctrine of tradition and the living Word. On account of vacillation between two opposite tendencies he failed in attaining his ideal. In general, the leading Lutheran theologians support the ordinary Lutheran view. This is also the case in the United States, although the Missouri Synod in its concept of the Church, particularly in regard to Church polity, takes a position which most closely resembles that of the congregational and collegiate system.

§33. The Means of Grace in General.

The Church stands in need of the means of grace for the purpose of carrying on its work. The Lord has also given the Church such means. These means are the Word and the holy Sacraments, through which the Holy Spirit presents and applies the salvation that is in Christ. These means comprise both word and deed. The Word may be said to partake of the nature of deed in a certain sense, but the Sacraments are such in a very special sense. They constitute the visible bearers and means of the grace of God.

I. The Necessity of the Means of Grace.

Generally speaking, the Reformed denominations, in common with all religious visionaries, take the position that God through His grace deals directly with the children of men, at least as often directly as mediately, through the means of grace. On the other hand, the Lutheran Church emphasizes the necessity of the means of grace. Of course our Church does not take the position that God is thereby absolutely bound, but so far as we know God works solely through the means of grace, so that justifying faith is wrought through these means and man could not be saved without them. They constitute the necessary means for the salvation of man, the means by which God enters into relation with man and man with God. In the Schmalkald articles we read: "And in those things which concern the spoken, outward Word, we must finally hold that God grants His Spirit or grace to no one, except through or with the preceding outward Word. Thereby we are protected against enthusiasts, i.e., spirits who boast that they have the Spirit without and before the Word. —Therefore in regard to this we ought and must constantly maintain that God does not wish to deal with us otherwise than through the spoken Word and the sacraments," etc.[97]

2. God's Relation to the Means of Grace.

Although God in His spiritual activity is not absolutely bound by the means of grace or any other external means, still He has Himself instituted these means through which He works in the kingdom of grace, just as He has established the laws of nature through which as a rule He reigns in the kingdom of nature. The fifth article of the Augsburg Confession says of the relationship of God to the means of grace: "The Holy Ghost, who works faith wherever and whenever it pleases God, is given through the Word and the Sacraments as through instruments and means." The words in this quotation: *"ubi et quando visum est Deo,"* might be misunderstood, hence this explanation: they do not imply that God has withdrawn from His creation, as the Deists teach concerning God's relation to the laws of nature, nor that God only occasionally works through the means of grace as it pleases Him, rather God works in a free and personal way through the means of grace and is present in them in accordance with His promise. God desires to work in this manner and deals with the

---

[97] Müller, *Symb. Bücher*, p. 321, 3.

world and the children of men in accordance with His will, but not arbitrarily. It certainly was necessary for God in some manner to carry out His council and purpose of salvation both objectively, as through Christ, and by application, as through the Holy Ghost. In His eternal wisdom God determined upon the best way. The fact that God in His wisdom followed His own plan does not imply predestination in accordance with the Calvinistic view. If faith is brought about *quando visum est Deo*, this does not signify that God makes a choice of persons in whom to work while passing others by, since it is His will and purpose to work faith in the hearts of all that use the means of grace. If faith is not thus effected, then the responsibility rests with man himself. However, the expression would indicate that it is by His gracious good will that God works through the means of grace. Man has no right to make demands upon God, but he may rely absolutely upon the assurance of God that He will keep all His promises. The Lutheran doctrine of the means of grace is therefore a great and glorious treasure, a treasure meant for use and not to be hidden away. Inasmuch as the Catholic as well as the Reformed Churches do not possess this doctrine of the means of grace, therefore in their practical work they make use of all manner of human and earthly means to effect what God would bring about through the means of grace. But this is the mere work of man and strange fire on the altar of the Lord.

3. The Effect of the Means of Grace in General.

With regard to the effect of the means of grace the Augsburg Confession says in Art. V: "*Per verbum et sacramenta tamquam per instrumenta donatur Spiritus sanctus.*" Thus the means of grace not only declare the grace of God, they are also the bearers and means for its inspiration. It is said that the Spirit is given because He applies the grace of God. As an effect of the means of grace faith is especially mentioned because of its relation to justification. The means of grace are therefore objective and do not become means of grace through the faith of man. However, they do not work ex opere operato. The benefits of the means of grace are dependent on the subjective state of man; they do not operate mechanically and in a deterministic manner. The means of grace are presented to man and through them the Holy Ghost would bring about a receptive or passive attitude which afterwards becomes active, when man becomes a true believer. However, the believer stands in need of the means of grace increasingly throughout the period of sanctification. Holy Baptism always remains a basis for the new life in Christ, while the Word of God together with the Sacrament of the Lord's Supper furnish the spiritual food on the journey toward the final goal.

§34. The Inspiration and Authority of Holy Scripture.

Inasmuch as the Holy Scriptures are a means of grace, it is important that every thinking Christian should be assured concerning the complete inspiration of the Bible, that it is indeed the Word of God, not only that it contains the Word of God or divine thoughts. It does not lie within the province of Dogmatics to set forth the proofs of the inspiration of the Bible, and possibly it would be more proper to treat of the doctrine of the inspiration and authority of the Scriptures in the prolegomena to Dogmatics. For this reason we merely enumerate the ordinary proofs, which are the following:

The testimony of the books of the Old and New Testament themselves with regard to their inspiration; the content of the books of the Bible, the good character and trustworthiness of the writers; the miracles; the fulfillment of the prophecies; the effects of Christianity and the internal testimony of the Holy Spirit. These proofs are variously classified. The old Dogmaticians divide them into internal and external proofs. Others divide them into Biblical, historical and critical proofs, but all acknowledge that the internal testimony of the Holy Ghost is the best proof. The early Protestants and the old Dogmaticians presented *testimonium Spiritus Sancti internum* in a more limited sense than is now usual. They held that the same Spirit who inspired the Biblical authors also testifies to the believers that the Scriptures are the Word of God. The unregenerate do not receive such witness and do not come to such a conviction, at least not so convincing. In later and recent times the evidence of Christian experience has been fully developed in Apologetics. The proofs supplied by Christian experience are the best arguments for the inspiration of the Bible. The other proofs may serve as guides. The most convincing proofs for the majority are the fulfillment of prophecy and the effects of Christianity.

1. The Definition of Inspiration.

The expression *inspiratio* arose from the Vulgate translation of *γραφή θεόπνευστος* by *scriptura inspirata.* Compare 2 Tim. 3:16. Inspiration may be defined as follows: *Inspiratio was the dynamic influence of the Holy Ghost on the writers of the Scriptures through which their receptivity was enabled to understand correctly the truth and their spontaneity to render adequately, in a real and verbal sense, the revealed and historical truth.* There is no perfect analogy with which to compare inspiration, neither are we able in a completely satisfactory manner to comprehend the *modus* of inspiration. An imperfect analogy may be found in the general influence of the Holy Spirit on the believers in the enlightenment that is imparted to them in their Christian life. However, as stated, the analogy is not perfect, for we must bear in mind that the inspiration of the writers was perfect, so that the material content of faith was set forth both as to content and form in a faultless and perfect manner. Inspiration was effected directly through the creative activity of the Holy Spirit, while the enlightenment of the believers is mediated through the influence of the Word of God. In reality inspiration was a miracle and therefore supernatural. However, it is possible to think of a state in which the Holy Spirit dwelling dynamically in the heart of man co-operates with him without creating a state of ecstasy, the resultant activity being supernatural and natural at the same time. In this manner the mechanical conception of inspiration is avoided. The old Dogmaticians, who held to the mechanical theory of inspiration, were indeed on the right path to a proper conception of inspiration. Their mistake lay in over-emphasizing the divine influence with a corresponding repression of the human element, which resulted in a sort of monophysitism. A reaction followed, others going to the opposite extreme, imperiling and undermining faith in the Word of God. It is necessary to emphasize both the divine and the human factors in inspiration, yet, as between the two one-sided views, it is better to lay stress on the divine, at the expense of the human factor. In every case God is the *auctor primarius*. The orthodox dynamic theory holds the true middle ground, in the first place setting forth the divine activity but also placing proper emphasis on the human side. *Causa efficiens principalis* is the Triune God. Compare 2 Tim. 3:16: "Every scripture inspired of God"; with regard to the Father, compare Heb. 1:1; the Son, John 1:18; the Holy Spirit, 1 Peter 1:11: "The Spirit of Christ which was in them did point unto"; 2 Peter 1:21: "Being moved by the Holy Ghost." *Causa instrumentalis* were the holy men of God. Compare 2 Peter 1:21. God being the *auctor primarius,* we may say that inspiration comprises two elements, one a negative element, whereby God preserved the writers from falsity and error, the other a positive element, whereby the writers were inspired with the true message both as to content and words. Inasmuch as men were both *causa instrumentalis* and authors in a secondary sense, we understand why linguistic imperfections crept into their writings.

The human individuality was not suppressed in the act of inspiration. It was a condescension on the part of the Holy Spirit to the character of the human instrumentality, so that it may be said that the act of inspiration was a divine-human act. The holy writers were not merely mechanical instruments, such as pens or amanuenses, rather there was an auto-activity analogous to the new life that succeeds the new birth when the regenerated soul cooperates with the Holy Ghost. The human life of the Son of God may also be taken as an analogy of the divine-human character of the written Word. We acquire a false impression of the personal Word in overemphasizing either His divine or His human nature. The same holds true with regard to the Scriptures or the written Word, which is a divine-human Word. It is hardly necessary to point out the human element in the Word of God, but by way of example we may mention that Luke

(1:1-4) speaks of having made thorough investigations, from which the conclusion is drawn that if inspiration had been mechanical and the Holy Spirit had dictated the contents of the Gospel of Luke, he could have remained passive and received the message without any investigation. For further study, compare 1 Cor. 1:16; 2 Cor. 12:2, etc. We know of the human peculiarities in the Scriptures. The language is not always perfect and seldom reaches the classical standard. If the Holy Spirit had employed the writers as mechanical instruments, the Scriptures would have been faultless judged from the most critical standpoint. However, in spite of its human form, the divine content is everywhere apparent and in many instances in such an overpowering manner that it can easily be discerned how insufficient are these earthly means to convey the heights and the depths of the heavenly content.

The Pantheistic theologians, of course, set forth their usual objections. They argue the absolute opposition between the infinite and the finite and therefore the dictum: *finitum non est capax infiniti.* But they raise the same objection against the whole system of Christianity. However, Christianity is a fact. The divine-human character of Jesus Christ has been proven in a most satisfactory way by thinkers as great as or greater than the Pantheistic philosophers and theologians. If the great miracle could happen that the Son of God could assume human nature, then it was also possible for the Holy Spirit to dwell in the hearts of men and influence them in an extraordinary manner, inspiring them dynamically to put in writing the content of divine truth.

The question has arisen as to whether the inspirational state was momentary or permanent. Some of the old Dogmaticians said that it was *non habitus permanens, sed actus transiens.* This is certainly true of the production of a specially inspired word, whether in speech or written form. But, generally speaking, we must consider the holy writers to have been in an inspired state. Inspiration indeed consisted in a special act in every specific instance, and yet it was a vital factor in the life and activity of the writers and not an isolated occurrence. As to the Apostles it would hardly be proper to assert that their writings alone were inspired, although we would not thereby declare that all that they said was inspired; it is sufficient for us to know that the canonical writings are inspired. Paul made no distinction between his epistles and the spoken word which he preached. Compare 2 Thess. 2:15: "Stand fast, and hold the traditions which ye were taught, whether by word, or by epistle of ours." Cf. Gal. 1:6-12; John 20:30, 31; 1 John 1:3, 4; 2:7; 2 John 5, 6.

We should carefully distinguish between revelation and inspiration. All the canonical books of the Bible are inspired in a plenary sense, but there are parts of the Bible which are not revealed, such as historical facts. But in case an event, a happening, circumstances of personal life and civil conditions are known to the author, it does not preclude that the Holy Spirit may guide a writer in correct and apt description, in selection of the best material and in quotations. Daniel quoted from the narratives of Nebuchadnezzar and had access to the royal archives, but all the statements of Daniel were inspired, because the Holy Spirit influenced him in true selection, in correct rendering and in guarding him that no mistakes in narration were made. The Spirit co-worked with him and all the Biblical writers in their thinking, in the elaboration of the thoughts and their verbal expression, but there was no dictation in inspiration, no teaching of language in expression and no interference with the individual characteristics. We have referred to the investigation of Luke. It is interesting to notice his fine classical Greek in the opening verses of his Gospel and how he continues his narrative in the common dialect. The fact that he was a learned man, and that he carefully weighed the testimony, adds to the authority of his narrative. In writing to Theophilus he says: "It seemed good to me also, having traced the course of all things accurately from the first, to write to thee in order, most excellent Theophilus; that thou mightest know the certainty concerning the things wherein thou wast instructed." But the modern critics, not those who lived in the Apostolic and Apologetic periods, have attacked the historicity of the Gospel of Luke. Their criticism concerns Luke 2:1-7. One German critic calls verses 1-3 "*das Lukas-legende*," holding that Augustus never issued a decree ordering a census, and when a casual census was held, the presence of the wife was not required. The critics have claimed that Luke stood alone, unsupported by ancient authorities. But the statement by Luke has been confirmed by the most recent discoveries. The rubbish heaps of Egypt and also the excavations in Asia Minor cause the stones to cry aloud in support of the narrative of Luke! Ramsay in his archeological research has amply and clearly vindicated the historicity of Luke and his veracity.[98] By the investigation of Ramsay and others it has been proved that there was a periodical census system in the Roman empire. It has been shown that there were two enrollments, just as Luke holds. In Luke 2:2 the first enrollment is mentioned, and in Acts 5:37 Luke speaks of the great census A.D. 6 or 7, when Judea had just been incorporated as part of the Roman province of Syria. If the first census began 8-7 B.C., according to Ramsay, it was slow in materializing on account of the situation in Syria and Palestine. The new discoveries in regard to the Augustan cycle of census places the execution of the enrollment in 6—5 B. C.. the probable time of Christ's birth. Ramsay has also unravelled the problem of Quirinius. A series of inscriptions bearing on the career of Quirinius proves that he was governor of Syria in the first census and governor and procurator in the second. The modern findings in stones and papyri vindicate the accurateness of the Gospel of Luke. In regard to the question of Revelation and Inspiration the facts mentioned in regard to Luke as a truthful historian prove that Luke received no revelation in regard to circumstances surrounding the two enrollments, but as an inspired writer he was dynamically influenced by the Spirit in giving a correct record both as to *suggestio rerum* and *verborum*. When there is both revelation and inspiration, the narrative is not more true, but becomes more convincing to our feeling as inspired revelation. Read, for instance, Luke 1:26-37. Compare also 1 Cor. 7:10 and 40. Both utterances are the Word of God. The whole content of the Bible is the Word of God as inspired. If, for instance, the narrative relates what Satan said, the satanic words are in themselves not God's word, but the whole statement is the

---

[98] *Bearing of Recent Discovery*. Also: *Was Christ Born at Bethlehem?*

Word of God verbally as truthfully recorded by the concurrence of the Holy Spirit. Different parts of the Bible may be more or less interesting to different readers, but all are the Word of God. There may be parts of which we do not understand why they were inserted, but we can be assured that they have had some purpose or will be of the greatest importance. Seeming contradictions disappear by better understanding, and dark prophecies by intense studies, and if not, by plain fulfillment. There are many doctrines in the Bible which evidently are revelations, such as the creation, the propagation of sin from Adam, the vicarious atonement, the import of Baptism, the doctrine of the Lord's Supper, regeneration, the second advent, the resurrection, and so forth. It is self-evident that God would not reveal a fact and do nothing towards inspiring an accurate record of its content or import. And as many doctrines depend as to their meaning upon the words used, the verbal inspiration is necessary. A revelation would not be an apocalypse, but an apocrypha, if nothing were revealed, and there cannot be a revelation without words. If man did not think in words, there would be no thought, but chaos. When God revealed, it is stated that He spoke. "God, having of old time spoken unto the fathers in the prophets by divers portions and in divers manners, hath at the end of these days spoken unto us in his Son." When the Lord Jesus Christ delivered His last discourses, it was to a great extent a revelation. But when John recorded the wonderful sayings in the latter part of the first century, inspiration was necessary and also the fulfillment of the promise in 14:26, where the Lord refers to the coming of the Comforter and says: "He shall teach you all things and bring to your remembrance all that I said unto you." Inspiration and revelation are alike in the superhuman influence, but revelation discloses new truth, and in this instance we have a superhuman reminder of what Christ said many decenniums before. There is no book like the Book of books, the Word of God, or the Bible, with its revelations and plenary inspiration.

2. The Constituent Parts of Inspiration.

The constituent parts of inspiration are: 1) *Adspiratio* or *impulsus ad scribendum*, i.e., an admonition to write, which occurred partly through external command and partly through an internal impulse. Compare Ex. 17:14; Deut. 31:19; Isa. 8:1; Jer. 36:2; Hab. 2:2; Matt. 28:19; 2 Tim. 3:16; 2 Peter 1:21; Rev. 1:11, etc. The Catholics deny that there was any such divine command and teach that the holy writers wrote by chance as they happened to be influenced or urged by necessity or some accidental external circumstances. Gerhard remarks that these external circumstances do not nullify the special command of God, rather they strengthen the admonition and the urging. 2) *Suggestio rerum*, or material inspiration. This includes everything and not simply the principal things. Hollazius says in this connection that the Scriptures contain historical, chronological, genealogical, astronomical, natural-historical and political matters which are revealed by God because an acquaintance with them assists not a little in the interpretation of the Holy Scriptures and in illustrating the doctrines and moral precepts. If only the mysteries of the faith were inspired, then not all of the Scripture would be inspired. But Paul declares that the whole of Scripture is divinely inspired. The negative criticism, whether cultured or uncultured, of course, enters many objections, some of them apparently valid, to the doctrine that the whole of Scripture is inspired. We must remember, however, that that which does not seem to be of moment for a certain period or for certain nations has possessed peculiar significance for other periods and for other peoples and may come to possess great significance for the future. The Bible was not written for our time only, but for all time, and not for the educated alone, but for the uneducated as well. Of course, the holy writers do not use the language of science, but that of the common people. When we realize that science is continually undergoing development, that it makes assertions today which are retracted or controverted tomorrow, that therefore it is not exact, certainly it would have been a great misfortune if the writers of the Bible had made use of scientific language and terms. The all wise God directed the writers and inspired them in an intelligent way so that they used a common language suitable for all times and all people. Science often has had to yield to the Bible. Many apparent contradictions have been harmonized, and we may be assured that all its problems will be solved in another world, if not here. Some men possess greater understanding than others. Some, who reject the plenary inspiration of the Bible, have never attempted to investigate any contradiction, but nevertheless have greater demands on Scripture than on science itself, whose results they are ever ready to accept with childish simplicity, even though science is frequently compelled to change its dogmatic assertions. It does not lie within the province of a text-book on Dogmatics to take up the various objections and answer them. 3) *Suggestio verborum*, or verbal inspiration. By this is meant that every word in the original text is inspired, not in a mechanical way as in a dictation, but in a dynamic sense. Inasmuch as the Bible not only contains the Word of God, but really is the Word of God, therefore it is insufficient to acknowledge that the essential facts and basic thoughts are inspired. This would simply imply that the thoughts were divine, but the words human. If so, we would possess no certain ground for faith, as we would not surely know whether or not the writers had chosen the proper words. The situation would not be improved if verbal inspiration were confined to the truths of salvation and other important matters, since in that case a special revelation would be necessary to decide whether or not any particular Scripture passage were inspired. The seeker after salvation would then be compelled to build his hope on the sands of human opinion. Naturally the content of the Word of God must possess an adequate form. The form is not only an external garment, but a body as well. Just as the soul has its body, so the thought has its word. Thought and word stand in the closest relation to each other. A clear thought cannot be entertained except in the form of words. It is hardly possible that the Holy Spirit should have imparted a mass of thought material or a chaos of ideas which the writers afterwards worked out and crystallized into verbal form. In that case the Bible would have become a human message rather than the Word of God. It would have been very much more strange if the Holy Spirit had inspired the writers with chaotic thoughts than if He had inspired the words themselves in a mechanical way. If we believe that the thoughts were inspired we must also believe logically that the words were inspired as well. Some persons, who do not have a clear conception concerning inspiration and boast that they are liberal, say: We believe in the inspiration of the idea but not of the words. Even the best modern Psychology holds that there cannot be an idea without form or words. The suggestion of an idea implies some form of the words, not by dictation because dictation separates thought and words; verbal dynamic inspiration unites them. Man thinks in words. In dynamic inspiration the Spirit concurs with the writer all through in thought formation. In mechanical verbal inspiration the Holy Spirit is alone the thinker and dictates just as an author dictates to a stenographer. This shows the difference between mechanical and dynamic inspiration In the dynamic way the Spirit and the human author work together. The Holy Spirit filled the hearts of the writers and brought about a state in which they were enabled to receive the content of revelation and in cooperation with the Holy Spirit adequately to set down in writing all that God would have imparted to the Church. By means of an inspirational concurrence of this character we can easily comprehend how human peculiarities might appear even in the choice of words, for the Holy Spirit did not impart any new linguistic knowledge nor did He alter the literary ability of the writers, but cooperated with them just as they were constituted. Even where the writer was as gifted as Paul, the treasures were nevertheless contained in earthen vessels, as Paul himself acknowledges. The Holy Scriptures testify that the words themselves possess significance as the Word of God. The following proof passages may be quoted in favor of verbal inspiration: Ex. 20:1; 24:4; 32:16; "Till heaven and earth pass away, one jot or one tittle shall in no wise pass away from the law, till all things be accomplished" (Matt. 5:18); "The oracles (*λόγια*) of God" (Rom. 3:2); "Which things also we speak, not in words which man's wisdom teacheth, but which the Spirit teacheth; comparing spiritual things with spiritual" (1 Cor. 2:13); "Sacred writings (letters, *γράμματα*)" (2 Tim. 3:15, 16); compare Rev. 22:19. Some objections have been made to verbal inspiration with apparent support from the Bible, e.g., 1 Cor. 7:10, 12, 25. But this is not a proof, as a comparison of verses 25 and 40 in accordance with the analogy of faith will show that these words of Paul were likewise inspired. Paul only states that the Lord Jesus in His earthly ministry had expressed Himself directly in these matters and cites what Christ had uttered and places this beside what he himself says as inspired by the Holy Spirit. Both the expressions and the explanations are therefore the inspired Word of God. It has also been objected that the Apostles quoted arbitrarily from the Old Testament and that the majority of the quotations are taken from the Septuagint. However, the apostolic epistles show that the Apostles regarded the books of the Old Testament with the greatest piety. The translation of the original text which was in common use among converted heathens as well as among Jews was the Septuagint. It was but natural therefore, that the Apostles quoted from the Septuagint. They were guided by the Holy Spirit. Where the translation was correct they quoted verbatim, but otherwise they made the necessary correction in accordance with the original Hebrew text. Inasmuch as the Holy Spirit cooperated with them, free translation was also the inspired Word of God. In a special measure they possessed the Holy Spirit, who directed them in this as well as other matters. With regard to this concurrence, compare Acts 15:28: "For it seemed good to the Holy Ghost, and to us." Other objections might be cited, but it is unnecessary to do so. When we read that every Scripture inspired of God is profitable for teaching, then we draw the conclusion that the words must be inspired, since a scripture would not be a scripture without words, and it is the Scripture that is inspired.

3. The Attributes of Holy Scripture.

Affectiones seu attributa scripturae sacrae are the following: 1) *Auctoritas,* which contains two elements: a) *auctoritas causativa* depending on inspiration or that the Scriptures are the Word of God through which the assent of man to the saving truths is effected and confirmed. This *auctoritas* is proven by means of the criteria *interna et externa,* which are just about the same as the proofs for the inspiration of the Bible. The authority of the Scriptures is not dependent on the testimony of the Church, as the

Catholics teach. The Church bears testimony ministerially, but in the last instance the Scriptures must testify of themselves; b) *auctoritas normativa et judicialis*, through which the Scriptures are distinguished from other writings and through which also the true is distinguished from the false. The Scripture is *norma normans* and *judex controversiarum*. The Church is *judex inferior* and this especially through *ministerium ecclesiae*, which is *judex ministerialis publicus*. An enlightened Christian is called *judex ministerialis privatus*. The Confession is *normata*. 2) *Perfectio et sufficientia*, by which is meant that the Scriptures in a perfect and adequate way impart instruction in all things that are necessary for salvation, whether *κατὰ ῥητόν* or *κατὰ διάνοιαν*. The Scriptures are not only perfect in part or, as the Catholics teach, *implicite, veluti in radice*, etc., but in such a complete way as to be capable of leading the children of God all the way to their heavenly home, indeed they reveal very much more than what might be deemed absolutely necessary for salvation. The Catholics put the Church above the Scriptures. The Scriptures should have declared, *audite ecclesiam*, but in Matt. 17:5 we read, *hunc audite*. Christ speaks to us in the Scriptures and constantly refers to them. As a result of the position of the Catholic Church tradition was accorded as great prominence as the Word of God. Tradition was called *verbum Dei non scriptum*. Originally the Catholics divided tradition into divine, apostolic, and ecclesiastical tradition: divine, as having its source in Christ; apostolic, as coming from the Apostles, the main content of which was found in *Constitutiones et Canones Apostolici*; and ecclesiastical, in which were counted the decisions of ecumenical councils, the opinions of the Church Fathers and the decretals of the popes. However, all the traditions are really ecclesiastical, inasmuch as they receive their sanction through the authority of the Church. In respect to content the traditions are divided into ritualistic, historical, exegetical, moral, apologetic, and dogmatic traditions. Our Church does not reject tradition, but accords to it its proper value and place; only Scripture, however, is *norma normans*, the confessions based on Scripture being *norma normata*. 3) *Perspicuitas*. by which is meant that the Scriptures present everything connected with the way of salvation in so clear and simple a manner that all can acquire this knowledge. This clearness is *gradualis*, i. e., some passages are clearer than others. 4) *Efficacia*, setting forth the effect and activity of the Scriptures as a means of grace. The effects are made manifest by means of the preaching of the Word and in the private study of the Bible. Both ways are necessary; it is not sufficient to distribute Bibles, the Word of God must also be preached and the Sacraments administered.

4. Notes on the History of Dogma.

The concept of inspiration was not closely defined in the post-Apostolic period. During the first two historical periods the mantic or mystic theory was supported by many. In accordance with this theory the writers were taken absolute possession of by the Holy Spirit and transformed into a state of ecstasy, losing all power of volition. Others supported this theory in modified form, while still others entertained more liberal views. With few exceptions there prevailed during the Scholastic period a rigid conception of inspiration which was extended, however, to tradition and the decision of councils. Later on different views came into evidence. The Jesuits supported more liberal views in which inspiration was confined only to the doctrinal content. The Roman Church underestimates inspiration in a general sense because of the fact that it lays so much stress on tradition, for which reason inspiration is principally considered as an *assistentia et directio Spiritus sancti*. In the Lutheran Confessions verbal inspiration is reckoned as a presupposition. The Reformed Church leans toward a mechanical conception of inspiration and in general rejects tradition. The old Dogmaticians to a greater or less extent supported the strict mechanical theory. In more recent times the following theories have been supported: The mechanical, the naturalistic or latitudinarian. the modern theory of limitation and the dynamic theory. The mechanical theory, which prevailed during the Protestant Scholastic period, implied that the writers were the pens, hands, or amanuenses of the Holy Spirit, while it failed to attach proper significance to the personality of the writer. The naturalistic theory is of the lowest type and declares that the Bible is like other good books and that its inspiration simply consists in a lofty flight of poetic fancy. The modern theory of limitation implies that inspiration is to a greater or less extent limited. On the one hand, it is said to embrace only the thought; on the other hand, where verbal inspiration is accepted, it is said to be limited to the real material of revelation or the facts of salvation. The Bible contains the Word of God, but is not the Word of God. The dynamic theory, which is generally accepted by the orthodox theologians of today, declares inspiration to be the supernatural dynamic influence of the Holy Spirit on the human spirit, by which the holy writers without losing their independence were enabled adequately as to thought and expression to impart the divine truth, so that the inspiration was complete or plenary.

Clement of Rome and Ignatius do not present any special theory of inspiration, but merely make use of Biblical expressions in reference thereto. Justin Martyr speaks of the writers as the instruments of the Holy Spirit. As the bow produces tones in being drawn across the strings of a musical instrument, so God used the holy authors as instruments, but inspiration was limited to the religious content. Athenagoras makes use of the figure of a flute-player and the flute. Tertullian supported the mantic theory. Irenaeus believed in verbal inspiration, but laid stress on the human element and speaks of the faulty syntax in Paul's writing. Origen did not accept the mantic theory, but still he spoke of a passive state. The Holy Spirit increased the spiritual powers.

Eusebius of Caesarea adopted the strict theory of inspiration and taught that the writers were guided by the Holy Spirit in such a rigid manner that they could not substitute a single name or word for any other. Jerome said that the Scripture was perfectly inspired, but acknowledged the human element and stated that there were to be found solecisms and incomplete sentences in the writings of Paul. Augustine compared the Apostles to hands which wrote in accordance with dictation, but he says at one place that the Evangelists wrote as they remembered, either briefly or more at length. Gregory the Great, who stated that the Holy Ghost was the author of the Book of Job, nevertheless allowed the privilege of making investigations with regard to its human authorship. John of Damascus declared that it was through the Holy Spirit that the Law and the Gospel, Evangelists and Apostles, pastors and teachers had spoken. The Holy Scriptures were inspired throughout by God.

Agorard of Lyons entertained liberal views on inspiration and rejected the theory that the words had been dictated by God. He also said that the writers had violated grammatical rules. Fredrigis of Tours defended the strict theory of inspiration. Abelard did not regard the writers as faultless. He also pointed out contradictions in the traditions. Thomas of Aquinas presented varying degrees of inspiration, stating that David knew more than Moses, etc. *The Council of Trent* determined nothing concerning inspiration, but in referring to the purity of the Gospel as containing the saving truth and moral .discipline, the council expresses itself in the following manner with reference to tradition and the Scripture: "Seeing clearly that this truth and discipline are contained in the written books, and the unwritten traditions which, received by the Apostles themselves, the Holy Ghost dictating, have come down even unto us, transmitted as it were from hand to hand; (the Synod) following the examples of the orthodox Fathers, receives and venerates with an equal affection of piety, and reverence, all the books of the Old and of the New Testament— seeing that one God is the author of both—as also the said traditions, as well those pertaining to faith as to morals, as having been dictated, either by Christ's own word of mouth, or by the Holy Ghost, and preserved in the Catholic Church by a continuous succession."[99] Bellarmin divides tradition into *traditio divina, apostolica et ecclesiastica.* He says that tradition is necessary because of the incompleteness of the Scriptures. With regard to inspiration there were two tendencies that developed within the Catholic Church. The *Jansenists* defended the strictest sort of verbal inspiration, the *Jesuits* as well as others in the Catholic Church held a more liberal view.

Luther expressed himself differently at different periods in his life,

---

[99] *Sessio* IV.

especially with regard to certain books, but he entertained the deepest piety for the Word of God, which became the formal principle of the Lutheran Church. He set forth both the divine and human character of inspiration. Although at times his expressions were somewhat free, still at other times he declared that not a single jot of the Scriptures had been written in vain, neither were there to be found any contradictions in them. Zwingli acknowledges the perfection of the Scriptures, although he states that possibly some relative faults may be found, without, however, doing any harm to the real truth-content. Calvin supported a stricter theory of inspiration, but points out, nevertheless, the human element which appears in the divergent styles of the writers. *Formula Consensus Helvetica* says that the Hebrew vowal signs are inspired just as the words themselves. In this way the Scriptures become a law of the letter. In the practical interpretation of the Scriptures, however, the Reformed Church has assumed great freedom, which has borne fruit in a great number of sects detrimental to the unity of the Church. The *Socinians* held that inspiration was confined to that which was essential, but that mistakes could easily have been made in unessentials. The *Arminians* limited inspiration to the doctrines of faith and morals. It was not necessary to conceive that the historical sections of the Bible had been dictated by the Holy Ghost. Inspiration was an *assistentia divina*. The Bible contains much that has no significance for the Christian religion. As has already been mentioned, *the Lutheran theologians* from the time of Chemnitz supported a strict theory of inspiration. The theories established by Chemnitz and Gerhard were afterwards developed by Calovius, Quenstedt, and Dannhauer. The loose theories of the Socinians, Arminians and Syncretists were disproved. There were some Dogmaticians who carried the mechanical theory to the extreme, declaring that the vowel signs, etc., were inspired and that the words were dictated, the difference in the styles of the writers depending on the accommodation of the Holy Spirit. Quenstedt says, however, that the authors wrote cheerfully, willingly, and intelligently. The old Dogmaticians aimed to establish the truth that the Bible is the Word of God, but their method of explanation was somewhat one-sided and was probably misunderstood. Cailixtus held very liberal views, declaring inspiration to include only the essential objects of faith. That which could be comprehended by the material sense was not inspired. Musaeus hesitated about accepting verbal inspiration and took the position that the content of Scripture alone was inspired.

But *Rationalism* and the modern critical school soon started the work of undermining the Scriptures. *Deism* in England set forth its doubts relative to the divine origin of the Scriptures as well as with regard to the trustworthiness of the writers. Voltaire and the *Encyclopedists* in France in a degrading way attacked the historical contents of the Bible. In Germany the attacks on Christianity and the Word of God were clothed in a more scientific form. Pfaff supported a liberal theory, accepting a *suggestio divina* with regard to the truths of faith, a *directio* in relation to historical facts and denying inspiration in inessentials. Töllner reduced inspiration to divine influence in general. Semler set forth the human origin of the canon and advocated the theory of accommodation. Ernesti pointed out the individual characteristics in the language of the authors. The mediating theologians in general express themselves with uncertainty in regard to inspiration. Schleiermacher did not acknowledge any direct divine inspiration. He considered that it was the fellowship spirit in the Church that constituted the moving power in the so-called inspiration, but not the Holy Spirit. The spirit of inspiration was the spirit of the common consciousness of the Christian Church working through the deepest emotions and finding its loftiest expression in Christ. Following Kant and Fries, De Wette conceived of inspiration as an expression of the religious presentiment of man, that there was a divine-natural influence which was exerted not on the intellect but in relation to the faith and the emotions of the writers. According to the Hegelian philosophy, represented by Daub and others in theology, inspiration was merely an expression of the divine life which arises when God reaches the stage of self-consciousness and realizes Himself in the souls of men. Tholuck, Rothe, Kahnis and others supported the old theory of inspiration. Stier inclined to the so-called theory of limitation. Almost without exception those who reject the orthodox theory have adopted the theory of limitation in one form or another. It is unnecessary to enumerate the names of the leading representatives of the modern Bible critical movement. Of course, these men do not support the old theory of inspiration. Nevertheless, the conservative position will finally prevail. Grundtvig placed the Apostles' Creed as a living word even above the written Word and declared this symbol to be inspired. Philippi speaks of different forms of inspiration. The first is the historical form, in which the spirit of man and the objects of revelation stand in external relation to each other. The second form is prophetical, in which revelation and inspiration approach each other more closely. In this form inspiration renders the prophet capable of correctly transcribing what has been seen in the state of ecstasy and in vision. The highest form is the apostolical, in which inspiration proceeds from revelation independently appropriated. In this last form revelation and inspiration are intimately related. Philippi defends verbal inspiration, but makes a distinction between *Wortinspiration* and *Wörterinspiration** He adopts the former and declares the latter to be unnecessary.[100] In this way he endeavored to avoid the difficulties that the divergent readings and variants had thrown in the way. But what distinction can be made between "word" and "words" in the theory of inspiration? The way he seems to explain it is the following: The inspired writer originated a sequence of ideas that as a whole was inspired dynamically both in thought and language. But the words, taken one by one, were not separately suggested. Thomarius presents inspiration as an illumination of the Holy Spirit through which He imparted to the writers a correct understanding of the content of revelation and gave them power infallibly and adequately to write that which He revealed, having reference both to their spoken and their written words. All orthodox theologians advocate a plenary theory of inspiration, including both material content and verbal expression.

[100] Philippi, *Glaubenslehre*. Dritte auflage. I, p. 252.

§35. The Word of God as the Means of Grace.

The Lutheran Reformation restored the Word of God not only to its place as a *norma normans* but also as a means of grace. The Word of God is a means of grace in whatsoever form it may be used, whether it be read, heard or recalled in memory. Quenstedt remarks that we must distinguish between the Word of God as it is materially expressed and exhibited in the written characters, etc., and formally considered, as the divine conception and sense which we find expressed in these written letters and syllables and in the words of the preached Gospel.[101] In the former sense it is called the Word of God only figuratively (o^/wi-tKis) ; while in the latter sense («vpi’<«s) it is properly and strictly the Word of God, to which are ascribed divine power and efficacy. The preached Word is a means of grace insofar as it agrees with the Scriptures and presents the Biblical content of faith. “So belief cometh of hearing, and hearing by the word of Christ” (Rom. 10: 17).

1. The Power of the Word of God as a Means of Grace.

The Word of God is efficacious not only objectively as revealing the divine purpose of salvation, but also subjectively as possessing power unto regeneration and sanctification. The Word possesses this power because it is the living Word of God in which He speaks to us through His Spirit. The effects are produced *principaliter* through the Holy Spirit and *instrumentaliter* by means of the Word. God has not once for all given us His Word and then forsaken us; He is actively present whenever the Word of God, is read and preached. The Holy Ghost does not operate alongside of the Word, but in and through the Word, so that the Word of God is actually a vehicle or bearer of the grace of God. In this connection Hollazius says: “It possesses and retains its internal power and efficacy even when not used, just as the illuminating power of the sun continues, although, when the shadow of the moon intervenes, no person may see it;

---

[101] From H. Schmid, translated by Hay and Jacobs.

and just as an internal efficacy belongs to the seed, although it may not be sown in the field."[102] The Word of God retains its power even *extra usum*. With regard to the relation between the power and operation of the Word of God Quenstedt teaches that the Holy Ghost does not do something by Himself and the Word of God something else by itself, but they produce the one effect by one and the same action, just as the soul and the eye see, not by distinct actions, but by a single action. Relative to the power and efficacy of the Word of God, compare the following passages: John 6:63; Acts 7:38; 1 Cor. 2:4; 1 Thess. 2:13; 2 Tim. 3:15; Heb. 4:12; 1 Peter 1:23; 1 John 1:1; James 1:21.

2. Negative and Positive Terms.

In the presentation of the Word of God as a means of grace there are certain terms used to define more closely the content of this doctrine both from the negative and the positive point of view. The negative terms are the following: 1) *non efficacia physica,* inasmuch as the Word of God does not operate physically as when a person comes in contact with a material object. The Word of God is preached and heard, but the efficacy does not lie in the physical act, thereby producing regeneration; 2) *non mere naturalis,* so that the Word of God would be as efficacious as other good books and no more. Of course, the Word of God possesses natural power or *efficacia naturalis,* and in that sense the Bible is the Book of books, but the power of the Word of God exceeds the influence of the best books of man, inasmuch as the effects produced by the Scriptures are not only temporal but eternal and determine the true welfare of man; 3) *non mere significativa,* as, e.g., a monument or a sign-post. A sign-post may show the way, but imparts no strength for the journey. The *positive* terms are the following: 1) *moralis,* inasmuch as the Word of God enlightens the mind, moves the will and purifies the emotions, so that man is converted and sanctified, provided no opposition is made to the gracious work of the Spirit; 2) *supernaturalis,* as an effect of divine power, inasmuch as the

---

[102] *Exam. Theol. Acroam.* Pars III, §2, Cap. I. p. 455.

gracious work of regeneration unto life eternal cannot be performed by the mere word of man; 3) *effectiva,* since the Word of God does not merely possess its inward power, but operates in its divinely appointed way; 4) *essentialis,* inasmuch as this power is always resident in the Word by reason of the continued union of the Holy Spirit with the Word; 5) *ordinata,* by reason of the relation of men to the Word, which does not operate in a mechanical and compulsory manner, nor *ex opere operato,* wherefore the following term is also used; 6) *resistibilis,* or that the Word may be resisted.

3. The Contents of the Word, or the Law and the Gospel.

The Word of God is divided with regard to its contents into the Law and the Gospel. The term law is used in a variety of senses. In the most general sense it refers comprehensively to the teachings of the whole Scripture and therefore also includes the Gospel (Ps. 1:2). In the general sense law refers to the Old Testament (1 Cor. 14:21). In a restricted sense law is understood to comprise the Pentateuch as distinguished from the Psalms and the Prophets (Luke 24:44). In the most restricted sense law is that part of the Word of God which is contrasted with gospel. This is also the ordinary sense in which the two terms are used (Rom. 13:8-10).

Lex, or the Law, is divided in the following manner: 1) *moralis;* 2) *ceremonialis;* 3) *forensis. Lex moralis* is the Law in the ordinary sense and is still applicable in accordance with the doctrine of the use of the Law. *Lex ceremonialis* in the Old Testament set forth the regulations and ceremonies connected with the divine service of the chosen people, revealed the uncleanness of sin, admonished the people to lead holy lives and in a typical way set forth the blessing which would become real through the advent of Christ. *Lex forensis* had for its object the maintenance of external discipline in the civil life of the Jews and to preserve their national prerogatives and position in relation to other nations. Hollazius also speaks of *lex primordialis* or the law that was given to our first parents. He says, however, that this law does not differ from the Sinaitic Law in substance of doctrine, but in the mode of revelation.

Usus legis, or the use of the Law, is threefold: 1) *usus politicus,* which has reference to external discipline and is therefore a benefit accruing from the Law in which the unconverted also share, although they do not often acknowledge it; 2) *usus elenchticus seu paedagogicus,* by which the Law convicts man of his sinful and guilty state, admonishes him to seek salvation and thus becomes a tutor to bring men to Christ; 3) *usus didacticus,* which consists in the efficacy of the Law as a perpetual rule of life. The doctrine of the Christian's relation to the Law stands in connection with this use of the Law. In a certain sense the believers are free from the Law, having been liberated from the bondage and condemnation of the Law through their justification in Christ. Before God, therefore, they are no longer under the Law, but under grace. The Law does not exercise any compulsion over them. Compare the following passages: "Ye also were made dead to the law through the body of Christ; that ye should be joined to another" (Rom. 7:4): "There is therefore now no condemnation to them that are in Christ Jesus" (Rom. 8:1); "With freedom did Christ set us free" (Gal. 5:1); compare also Gal. 3:13, 25; 4:31. However, the believers are nevertheless bound by the Law in their daily walk and conversation. Yet this is not considered a burden, inasmuch as the Law is written in their hearts. They stand in need of the Law because their renovation is not complete,—the old man must be crucified day by day. They need the Law, moreover, as a means of education and to keep them in humility as they compare the progress they make in sanctification with the demands of the Law. In this comparison they are sensible of a judgment, but not as though they would again come under the condemnation of the Law; rather they are thereby impelled to repair daily to Christ and His saving grace and to pray for renewed strength to fight against sin and to walk in the way of sanctification. The believers are therefore in the Law, but not under the Law. Compare Rom. 7:6: "But now we have been discharged from the law, having died to that wherein we were holden; so that we serve in newness of spirit, and not in oldness of the letter." See also John 15:10; Gal. 5:18-24; 1 Tim. 1:8, 9; 1 John 2:3; 3:19-22; James 1:22-25.

Effectus legis, or the effects of the Law in a primary sense as contradistinguished from the Gospel, are *contritio, terrores conscientiae,* or contrition. The effect of the Law in this sense belongs to usus *elenchticus seu paedagogicus. Poenitentia* in a restricted sense is the same as *contritio* and when so regarded the Law may be said to be *concio poenitentiae.* It is also taught that the Law and not the Gospel reproves unbelief.

Like the term law, the word gospel is used in a variety of senses. In the most general sense gospel is understood to mean the teachings of the New Testament taken as a whole (Mark 16:15). In the general sense gospel refers to the account of salvation as contained in the four Gospels (Mark 1:1). In a restricted sense gospel signifies the gracious promises of God both in the Old and in the New Testament (Rom. 1:1, 2). In its most restricted and real sense gospel is the New Testament doctrine of salvation. This is the sense in which the term is generally understood (Mark 1:15).

The Gospel, therefore, presents the work of Christ, which has already been treated dogmatically in the sections on Christology and Soteriology. While there is a real distinction between the Law and the Gospel, still they are organically connected, inasmuch as they complement each other. Both are necessary. This can be seen in *poenitentia,* which consists in contrition and faith. The Law works contrition and the Gospel faith. The Law cannot save, and no man can fulfill the Law so as thereby to be saved, but the Gospel contains the saving grace of God. *Effectus evangelii* is therefore saving faith, inasmuch as the Gospel declares and imparts to us the forgiveness of sin, while the Holy Spirit operates through the Gospel to the end that by faith we may accept the grace of God and become justified. Faith could not be produced except through the Gospel. Compare Rom. 8:3; 1:16; 10:15-17; 1 Cor. 15:1, 2.

4. Notes on the History of Dogma.

The earliest Church Fathers set forth the great power of the Word of God, but there was no dogmatic formulation of doctrine. Although the influence of tradition began to be felt, still the Word of God as a means of grace occupied the dominating position until the Scholastic period. The high regard which the Scholastics entertained for tradition together with the supremacy of the Church in all things to a great extent eclipsed the significance of the Word, in consequence of which preaching was greatly neglected during the Middle Ages. There were of course exceptions, such as Bernhard of Clairvaux, who was indeed a truly evangelical witness. The services were conducted in Latin. The Bible was a closed book. In accordance with the Catholic doctrine the Word is not a means of grace in the real sense rather it is a source of knowledge and operates on the intellect, producing a faith whose essence is assent. The Church also exercises its influence in addition to the power of the Word. The Catholic Church regards Christianity as a *nova lex*. The Lutheran Reformation set forth the power and efficacy of the Word of God as a means of grace together with the importance of hearing and reading it. It stated clearly that the Holy Spirit is connected with the Word and operates through it. Sharp distinctions as between the Law and the Gospel were set forth, but by reason of divergent definitions there arose a certain amount of confusion as to terminology, giving rise to difficulties in the Antinomian controversy. The Reformed Church does not consider the Word of God as a means of grace in the real sense. In a study of Calvinism we find that the Word of God is efficacious merely upon the elect. The Holy Spirit does not operate through the Word, but rather by the side of it. However, the great significance of the Word of God is emphasized. Of course, in modern times the significance of the Word as a means of grace is minimized by all who accept the modern higher critical views of the Bible. It may nevertheless be said that all the Protestant denominations emphasize the great value of the Scriptures and labor for the spreading of the Bible, but it is the Lutheran Church, as founded upon the truths of the Bible, which especially sets forth the Word of God as a means of grace.

Justin Martyr, Tertullian, and others set forth the great power of the Word of God unto regeneration and sanctification. Clement of Alexandria and Origen speak of the sanctifying power of the Word of God.

Chrysostom and Augustine emphasized the significance of diligently reading the Word of God, the latter comparing the power and efficacy of the Word of God to that of medicine.

Inasmuch as tradition during the Middle Ages was placed on the same plane as the Word of God, with the Church the interpreter of both, there was not a great deal of importance attached to the written Word. It is evident that since the people did not possess the Scriptures in their own language, and since the preaching in the churches was increasingly neglected, the significance of the Word of God was not felt or else it was ignored. Innocent III forbade the reading of the Bible, so that the people became altogether dependent on the scant expositions of the Word given by the priests. The forerunners of the Reformation, however, placed great value on the Word. Wickliffe and others labored for the dissemination of the Word among the people.

Luther laid great stress on the Word of God as a means of grace. He called the Word *vehiculum gratiae.* Zwingli did not consider that God needed any means of grace, but that He operated directly through the Spirit. Melanchthon in his articles of visitation set forth the importance of true penitence. He points out the significance of preaching the whole Gospel and declares in this connection that the Gospel is *concio poenitentiae*. But Melanchthon viewed the Gospel in this instance as well as in the Apology in a broad sense. Really Melanchthon taught the same as the Lutheran Church that the Law is *concio poenitentiae* (*stricte contritionis*) and that the Gospel is *concio plena consolationis*. The confusion in the use of terms gave rise to the Antinomian struggle in Lutheran form. The Augsburg Confession states that *poenitentia* consists of *contritio et fides*. This was a new conception, inasmuch as the Catholic Church taught that *fides* was not a part of *poenitentia*. According to the Lutheran position *poenitentia* was tantamount to *conversio*. On the other hand, the Catholic Church taught that *conversio* was only *contritio*. Agricola gave another answer than the Lutherans to the question: How is contrition produced? He stated that the Gospel is the true *concio poenitentiae*, viewing the Gospel in the ordinary sense, and not in the broad sense, as Melanchthon did. In support of his position he cites the conversion of Saul. He declares that penitence was not to be learnt from the Law of Moses, but from the suffering and death of the Son of God; the Law ought really not to be learnt during any stage of the process of sanctification nor prior to it. *Contritio* prior to faith has no significance for salvation; only the contrition which succeeds faith possesses this significance. This contrition does not consist in sorrow because of any transgression of the Law, but because of sin against Christ. The relationship between the Law and the Gospel was dissolved, the latter being shorn of its peculiar significance and becoming a legal Gospel. Andreas Poach declared that the Law even per se was not normative in relation to the righteousness demanded by God. Even if a person were to fulfill the Law perfectly, the Law nevertheless could not give any promise of salvation. The office of the Law was one of judgment, even with regard to good works, i.e., to damnation. Agricola denied the significance of the Law unto salvation, but acknowledged its significance per se and stated that it was incapable of producing salvation because of sin which prevents men from keeping the Law. Poach said that even if the Fall had not taken place, still the keeping of the Law would not have possessed any significance relative to salvation. Otto von Noruhausen carried Antinomianism to its culmination, stating that it is most profitable for the Christian to know nothing of the Law. Christians are not to be tormented with the Law, whose didactic significance he rejected. Christians are incapable of sinning and are above the Law. He denied that the Gospel demands good works as an evidence of faith. *The Formula of Concord* sets forth the difference between the Law and the Gospel. When *poenitentia* is viewed in its restricted sense, then the Law is *concio poenitentiae*. Only when viewed in its broad sense may the Gospel be included, but in that case the Gospel does not exercise an *opus proprium*, but an *opus alienum*. Properly speaking, therefore, the Gospel should not be called *concio poenitentiae*. The threefold use of the Lawis set forth, in which the *tertius usus legis* is especially emphasized, thereby answering the question as to how the believer can at once be free from the Law, and yet be bound by it. In his work *"Das Gnadenrelch"* of the year 1621, Rathman taught that the Word did not possess any indwelling power, but was efficacious only through the operation of the Holy Spirit. It possessed no power either before or after being used. It was like an ax, which becomes efficacious only in the hands of the wood-chopper. The *Socinians* said that the power and efficacy of the Word was natural. The *Arminians* separated the power of the Spirit from the Word and ascribed the power of the Word of God to authority.

Rationalism set forth merely the natural power and efficacy of the Word. The *Supranaturalists* ascribed the power of the Word to its inspiration and therefore its authority. The mediating theologians did not have a correct conception of the power and efficacy of the Word, and several confused the Law and the Gospel. Nitzsch taught that the Gospel produces true repentance. Of course, the orthodox theologians support the symbolic and old dogmatic position. Gez. Von Scheele expresses himself as follows: "Inasmuch as the Spirit dwells in the Word, therefore it can illumine, regenerate and sanctify. With regard to the manner in which the Holy Spirit operates through the Word the Lutheran Church does not conceive of this as taking place merely through reflection. Rather the Spirit of God is conceived of as being personally present in the Word. The activity of the Spirit by means of the Word is also of a personal character, otherwise the effects produced upon the individual could not be so perfectly adapted as they are. The one-sided conception of those who overemphasize the real presence of the divine Spirit in the Word, even when it is not used, or where it is not understood by those who hear and read it, has no support in the Confessions of our Church; and yet the Spirit is, so to speak, potentially present in the Word, always ready, as the angel at the pool of Bethesda (who nevertheless descended only at certain times), to heal those who enter into the life-giving waters."[103] Billing sets forth the teachings of the Confessions concerning the Word of God in the following points: "1) The Word of God is a means of grace by which God operates and does all that is necessary for the sanctification and the salvation of the soul of man. Through the same means the Church is built and her life sanctified. 2) The Word operates not only through its logical and moral

[103] *Symbolik*, p. 303.

influence, but through the indwelling presence of Christ and the Holy Spirit, who are given unto the children of men. 3) This is the character of the Word of God as a means of grace, no matter in what form it may be used, whether it be preached or heard, whether it be read or recalled in memory. The question as to whether the Word possesses this power *extra usum* is not discussed in the Confessions."[104] Dr. H. E. Jacobs says: "It must, however, be always borne in mind that the efficacy belongs to the truth conveyed, and not to the words themselves. This truth is just as efficacious, if expressed in other words. More children of God have been converted and been nourished in the divine life by the use of translations, than by that of the original texts of Scripture. — Nor even does the efficacy of the Word depend upon man's faith. Faith is always necessary to the reception of the efficacy, but not to its presence. There is no lack of efficacy in the medicine which is not taken by the patient. If his symptoms grow worse, he could not tell his physician that there was no efficacy in the prescription. All the while that the wheat was covered by the cerements of the mummy with which it was buried, its efficacy was not lost. Thousands of years elapsed, and when placed in relations more favorable to its development, it was proved to have been present. If it had died after a thousand years, and never been placed where it could sprout, this would not have proved any lack of efficacy during that millennium. It is not ground and moisture and sunlight that give the seed its vitality and efficacy. We find these in an inner principle, which, however, requires for its exercise such external conditions. So the efficacy of the Word depends upon the abiding presence of the Spirit within it, as a life-force, which, however, is not operative in the application of redemption and the salvation of men, unless it secure lodgment in man's heart, and be cherished there."[105]

---

[104] Lutherska kyrkans bekännelse, p. 317.

[105] *Elements of Religion*, pp. 151, 154.

§36. The Sacraments.

The Word and the Sacraments are internally related, inasmuch as it is the Word of God that makes the Sacraments means of grace. It is through the connection with the Word of God that the water in Baptism becomes a gracious water of life, while it is the words of the institution that make the bread and the wine vehicles of the sacramental gift of grace in the Holy Supper. An old Latin sentence puts it this way: *"Verbum accedit ad elementum et fit sacramentum."* The Word is *verbum audibile* and the Sacrament is *verbum visibile.*

1. Definition of Sacrament.

A sacrament is *a holy act instituted by God, in which visible and earthly means, through the Word of God, become vehicles of invisible and heavenly gifts of grace, which are imparted to all participants, but whose blessing is dependent on the subjective state of the participants.* Hollazius defines as follows: "A sacrament is a holy and solemn rite, divinely instituted, by which God, through the mediation of human servants, by means of an external and visible element in-connection with the words of the institution, dispenses heavenly gifts to the individuals using the sacrament, in order to offer to all men and to apply and seal to the believers the grace of the Gospel."[106]

Since man possesses not only a spiritual personal life, but, as a physical being, also a natural disposition, there was need of a more palpable presentation of the gifts of salvation than that which occurs in the Word. In the Sacrament, the Lord makes use of visible means as a vehicle of His grace. Absolution may also be considered especially as an applicable and cognizable means, but the visible element is nevertheless wanting.

The Sacraments are necessary because the Lord has instituted them and through them dispenses special gifts. Of course, they are not necessary in the absolute sense, but they are *ordinata* in a relative sense. If any distinction were to be drawn between the Sacraments, then Baptism must

---

[106] *Exam. Theol. Acroam.* Pars III, §1, Cap. III.

be considered more necessary than the Lord's Supper, because it is the Sacrament of regeneration. Both are, however, necessary and have their special purpose.

The Sacraments are distinguished by the following characteristics: 1) the visible elements which God has ordained; 2) the divine command to use these elements in accordance with the institution; 3) the divine words and promises which set forth that the visible elements are vehicles of special gifts; 4) the Sacraments must be rightly administered and used in accordance with the Word of God.

2. The **Forma Et Materia** *of the Sacraments.*

Forma sacramenti consists of the following parts: 1) *consecratio,* which takes place through the reading of the words of the institution, by which the elements are set apart for a holy purpose. This consecration does not involve any special magical power dependent on the character or state of mind of the officiating priest or minister. Nor is there any secret power in the sound of the words, nor in their number. The elements are not transformed, but simply consecrated as vehicles of the gifts of grace. The minister *ecclesiae* consecrates, but the Sacrament is not dependent on his spiritual character or frame of mind; all that is necessary is that he strictly follows the command and institution of Christ; 2) *dispensatio,* since the Sacrament must be dispensed. Baptism would not be a baptism unless someone were baptized; neither would the Lord's Supper be such, save as the elements are distributed. In the Sacrament of the Lord's Supper both elements must be dispensed; 3) *receptio,* inasmuch as the elements must be received.

Materia sacramenti is *res terrestris et res celestis. Res terrestris* in Baptism is pure water. Nothing else can be substituted. *Res terrestris* in the Lord's Supper is bread and real wine of the grape. Neither may there be any substitution in this Sacrament, and both elements must be consecrated, distributed and received. *Res celestis* in each Sacrament is the special gift which the Lord has promised. Opinions are divided with regard to *res celestis* in Baptism but in the Lord's Supper *res celestis* is the real body and blood of Christ and there is no dispute among confessional theologians concerning this matter. Read further on Baptism and the Lord's Supper in the following sections.

3. The Effects of the Sacraments.

As has already been mentioned in the discussion of the means of grace, the Sacraments are not operative *ex opere operato*; their blessed and saving efficacy is conditioned by the faith of the recipient. *Res celestis* is indeed dispensed to all, but it is efficacious unto salvation only to believers. The heavenly element also serves to confirm the believers. The Sacraments likewise have external significance and constitute signs of confession. Their principal effect, however, is spiritual.

When viewed as a *verbum visibile* it might seem as though the effect of the Word and the Sacraments were the same For this reason the Apology says: "*Quare idem est utriusque effectus.*" But the Apology sets this forth from the point of view of the doctrine of justification. Both the Word and the Sacraments work faith and justification. The Lutheran Church must emphasize the importance of the Word as over against the position of the Catholic Church in order that the Word may not be placed in a subordinate position to the Sacraments. On the other hand, the Lutheran Church must likewise stress the significance of the Sacraments as against the position of the Reformed Church and therefore set forth fully the special gifts of grace dispensed in the Sacraments.

4. Notes on the History of Dogma.

The term "sacrament" was variously understood in the early Church. The incarnation, the death of Christ, indeed, Christianity itself, were called sacraments. The word arose from the Vulgate translation of *μυστήριον*. Many of the Church Fathers, although they considered Baptism and the Lord's Supper as the real Sacraments, nevertheless counted many of the sacred acts of the Church as Sacraments. The Catholic doctrine of the Sacraments was established as early as the Polemical period, but was developed more especially during the Scholastic period. The number of the Sacraments was fixed by Otto of Bamberg at seven. Peter Lombard determined their order. The seven Sacraments were the following: Baptism, confirmation, the Lord's Supper, penance, extreme unction, ordination, and marriage. Ordination was regarded as the fundamental Sacrament, and great stress was laid on the intention of the officiating priest. The Protestants decided, in accordance with the Word of God, that the Sacraments are only two. They rejected the Catholic doctrine of the efficacy of the Sacraments *ex opere operato*, also that of intention, etc. But the Lutheran Church, which represents the conservative Reformation, adopted a sound historical view in its doctrine of the Sacraments and was not carried to the extremes that characterized the Reformed Protestantism. The Reformed doctrine of the Sacraments suffers from the same fault as their doctrine of the Word. They retained the shell and threw away the kernel. Within the Reformed Church there are to be found variants of the doctrines of Zwingli and Calvin concerning the Sacraments, some even approaching the Lutheran position, but there is no denomination within the Reformed Church that has adopted the Biblical doctrine which our Church has set forth. Several of the modern Lutheran theologians distinguish between the efficacy of the Sacraments and the Word, stating that the former is efficacious especially in relation to man's human nature, while the Word appeals more directly to his spiritual personality. In the interest of Apologetics many Lutheran theologians have in recent times made powerful contributions in the presentation and defense of the Lutheran doctrine of the Lord's Supper.

Justin Martyr held that there were two Sacraments, which he set forth as the two set ways in which man entered into relationship with God. Tertullian was the first who especially made use of the word Sacrament in regard to Baptism and the Lord's Supper. Cyprian said that the Sacraments, i.e., external signs or means duly consecrated, possess immanent and efficacious powers unto salvation. He emphasized the act of consecration by the ordained minister.

Augustine set forth this dictum: *verbum accedit ad elementum et fit sacramentum*. Although he taught that Baptism and the Lord's Supper were the real Sacraments, still he used the same term for the laying on of hands, ordination, and marriage. Jerome called penance a secondary means of rescue for fallen sinners, which gave rise to the fact that penance was established as a Sacrament. Isidore of Seville made the positive assertion that the Sacraments were efficacious through an indwelling divine power. John of Damascus speaks only of two mysteries or Sacraments, Baptism and the Lord's Supper.

Peter Lombard and others taught that the Sacraments of the New Testament bestow; salvation, which the Sacraments of the Old Testament merely promised, for which reason it is stated that the efficacy of the latter was dependent on the subjective state of the recipient and therefore operated *ex opere operantis,* while the former operated *ex opere operato.* Both Lombard and Alexander of Hales taught that an absolute and conscious intention on the part of the priest was necessary to insure the validity of the Sacrament. Thomas Aquinas stated that neither the officiating priest nor the recipient was allowed to say anything contrary to the intention of the Church. Duns Scotus and Gabriel Biel taught that passivity was all that was necessary for the beneficial effect of the Sacrament, or that its efficacy was not counteracted by any mortal sin. The order of the Sacraments established by Lombard was confirmed at Florens in 1439. As has already been stated, ordination was held to be fundamental in relation to the other Sacraments. The Sacrament of marriage was considered basic for the moral life of the home and the state. Confirmation completed the grace of Baptism. Its principal rite was the anointing and laying on of hands. The Sacrament of extreme unction does not dispense forgiveness for gross or mortal sins, but only for *peccata venialia et reliquiae peccatorum.* Practically speaking, therefore, penance became one of the chief Sacraments. Private confession was first ordered by Leo the Great. In 1215 Innocent III commanded that all members of the Church must make private confession at least once a year. In the penance of the early Church the pedagogical intent was a prominent feature, but in the Catholic Church penance became a system of legal discipline. The ecclesiastical law was tantamount to the civil law in the Church of the

Middle Ages, through the confessional. Directions for the practice of penitential discipline are given in various Penitentials or Confessionals, which, after the pattern of forensic productions, settle the amount of penal exactions for all conceivable sins in proportion to their enormity, the state putting its civil forces at the disposal of the Church to enforce judgment. The object of penance was to cure sin. The effect of the Sacrament of penance was to save souls from hell, but not from temporal punishments and purgatory. The means used in relation to these were the satisfactions. In this connection arose the doctrine of supererogation, together with those of indulgence and masses for the dead. In this way *contritio* came to have a subordinate significance, while the importance of *confessio* and *satisfactio* was greatly stressed. While the doctrine of absolution was set forth theoretically, still in practice the emphasis was laid on *satisfactio*. The Council of Trent and the Roman Catholic catechism make mention of absolution merely in passing. Absolution is looked upon more as an act of church discipline than as an act of grace. Penance was a system of satisfactions for sins committed after Baptism, the satisfactions consisting in deeds and labores. For this reason penance is called not only a plank grasped by a shipwrecked man, but also *laboriosus baptismus*. In this way auricular confession became necessary in order that the priest as a judge might absolve from and impose satisfactions.

The Lutheran Church sets forth absolution as the principal element in confession, which is called *privata absolutio*. Private confession is retained for the sake of absolution and in order to provide an opportunity for instruction. Absolution is not regarded as being distinct from the other means of grace, but is nevertheless a special function of the power of the keys. By this power application of the Gospel is made upon the individual and ought to be accepted in true faith. In his *Large Catechism* Luther calls Baptism *sacramentum poenitentiae*. The forgiveness of sins granted in Baptism remains in force day by day in relation to the penitent as long as they live. Absolution rests on the foundation of Baptism and is an application of the forgiveness of sins conferred in Baptism. The Word of God sets forth the forgiveness of sins in general, but in absolution there is a personal application of this grace of God, which reinstates the believer in the grace of Baptism and therefore becomes a real preparation for the Holy Supper, which confirms the grace of God already received and confers new grace The Reformed Church teaches that private confession is unnecessary, but may be used in case of spiritual need. Absolution comprises the preaching of the Gospel together with church discipline.

As a means of grace absolution is tantamount to the preaching of the Gospel. The specific characteristic of absolution, however, consists in an act of discipline. In this sense the Reformed Church approaches more nearly to the Catholic Church than to the Lutheran. Zwingli viewed the Sacraments as signs. Calvin stated that they were the seals of the grace of God, but he denied that they were vehicles of the gifts of God's grace. The Sacraments do not possess any real objective value. The theory of predestination, of course, exerted its influence on his doctrine of the Sacraments. The *Socinians* view the Sacraments merely as symbols of confession. The *Arminians* held the same view. At most the Sacraments are seals of the grace of God.

The *Rationalists* consider the Sacraments merely as signs and ceremonies. The mediating theologians incline to the Reformed view. Schleiermacher stated that the Sacraments constituted a means whereby Christ continued His high-priestly activity, maintaining and strengthening the living communion between Himself and the Church. Martensen says that Christ was the Redeemer not only of the soul and spirit of man, but also of his body, for which reason He imparts Himself sacramentally not only in a spiritual sense, but also as to His glorified humanity. Ritschlianism values the Sacraments merely from the ethical point of view. Through Baptism we are received into the communion which Christ has established, while the Holy Supper serves to strengthen the memory of the historical Christ, whom we ought ethically to emulate. Thomasius states that the Sacrament makes its appeal to the natural side of man, affecting directly his physico-spiritual nature, while the Word of God is efficacious more particularly in relation to the spiritual side of man and influencing his intellect and will.

§37. Baptism.

Baptism occupies the first place among the Sacraments, because it is the *sacramentum initiationis et regenerationis,* while the Lord's Supper, on the other hand, is called *sacramentum confirmationis.* However, this designation of the Sacrament of the Altar does not set forth its full significance.

Baptism was indeed found before the establishment of the Church. John made use of Baptism as an external point of contact and as a symbol of purification preparatory to the conversion which he had been commissioned to preach. However, Baptism was in fact an idea of Christ and is really a Christian institution. It may be said that the Baptism of John was the connecting link between the Old Testament Sacrament of initiation and the New Testament Baptism of the Spirit and therefore preparatory to the Sacrament which was actually to confer what the Old Testament could merely typify. Christ instituted Baptism in its present form and with its present content and significance.

1. The Definition of Baptism.

Baptism is *a sacred sacramental act, instituted by Christ, in which water, connected with the Word of God, on the basis of the divine promise, becomes a vehicle of a special grace of the Holy Spirit, which effects the forgiveness of sins and regeneration, where there are no subjective hindrances.* Hollazius defines as follows: "Baptism is a sacred and solemn action, divinely instituted, by which sinful men, actually born and living, without distinction of sex or age, are washed in water in the name of the Father, Son, and Holy Ghost, that by washing of water divine grace, promised in the Gospel, may be applied, conferred upon, and sealed to them."[107] Baier defines as follows: "Baptism may be defined as a sacred act, instituted by Christ, by which men are washed with water, without distinction of sex and age, in the name of the Father, Son, and Holy Ghost, and are thus regenerated and renewed,

107

that they may secure eternal life."[108] *Causa efficiens principalis* is Christ, one with the Father and the Spirit. *Causa impulsiva interna* is the divine goodness. *Causa impulsiva externa* is the merit of Christ. *Causa efficiens minus principalis* ordinarily is *minister ecclesiae* or in extreme emergency *laicus aut femina*. With regard to baptism performed by heretics our Dogmaticians say that they are valid if administered according to the institution of Christ. Those persons commit a grave error, however, who seek the services of heretics when an orthodox pastor may be secured.

In this connection we desire to set forth the differences between the Baptism of John and that of Jesus. The Baptism of John constituted the historical background for the Baptism of Jesus and was merged into the latter. In the Baptism of John the subjective element was indeed to be found, but it lacked the objective sacramental power. The Baptism of John was a Baptism in water unto repentance, the Baptism of Christ was a spiritual Baptism unto regeneration. The former was symbolical, the latter was a vehicle of the heavenly gift of grace. When Jesus instituted the New Testament Baptism, the administration of which began on the day of Pentecost, the real birthday of the Church, He merged the Baptism of John into the Christian Baptism and bestowed upon it the fullness of the New Testament content. Compare Matt. 3:11; Luke 3:16; John 1:33; "John answered, saying unto them all, I indeed baptize you with water; but there cometh he that is mightier than I, the latchet of whose shoes I am not worthy to unloose: he shall baptize you in the Holy Spirit;" Acts 11: 16; 19: 4, 5: "John baptized with the baptism of repentance, saying unto the people that they should believe on him that should come after him, that is, on Jesus. And when they heard this, they were baptized into the name of the Lord Jesus."

2. The Necessity of Baptism.

Our Lutheran Church teaches that in order to be saved it is necessary to be born again of water and the Holy Spirit. Compare John 3: 5, together

---

108

with the Augsburg Confession, Art. II and IX. However, the Church teaches that this necessity is absolute in relation to the work of the Spirit, but relative in relation to Baptism. God is not bound in the absolute sense, so that it would be impossible for Him to regenerate without Baptism, but Baptism is necessary for us, inasmuch as God has connected His promise with the Sacrament and has imparted to us no other word or promise upon which we might establish any other doctrine. Regeneration is absolutely necessary for all, concerning which, in connection with Baptism, we read in John 3:5: "Except one be born anew, he cannot see the kingdom of God." Compare Mark 16: 16. It is, therefore, perfectly plain and clear that Baptism is necessary. If God makes justifiable exceptions, these do not justify us in not adhering to the rule. We are safe in following the clear expressions of the Word and in obeying God's commandment. With regard to possible exceptions the Lutheran theologians make the following declaration: *non privatio sed contemtus sacramenti damnat.* The following reasons may therefore be advanced as showing forth the necessity of Baptism: 1) Because Baptism has been instituted by God, for which reason no one can be saved who frivolously neglects or despises the Sacrament; 2) because all men are born with original sin, for which reason all men need the saving grace which is dispensed in Baptism; 3) because Baptism is *sacramentum regenerationis* and that without regeneration no man can be saved; 4) because God has connected the most gracious promises with the sacrament of Baptism, which cannot be replaced by any virtue or merit in us, not even our faith. The necessity of Baptism takes on primary significance in relation to children, inasmuch as they cannot be influenced by means of the Word, but only by *sacramentum regenerationis.* It is necessary for unbaptized adults in reaching the stage of true faith likewise to be baptized, because Baptism completes the new creation, strengthens and seals it with the Holy Spirit of promise. In the case of the person who has fallen away from the grace of Baptism and has again been converted to the Lord there is no necessity of being re-baptized, inasmuch as the baptismal covenant on the Lord's side always stands secure In the case of a person baptized in unbelief and afterwards converted, there is no need of a second Baptism, inasmuch as his first Baptism is perfectly valid, although his subjective state at the time of Baptism made him non-receptive for the regenerating grace of the Sacrament. Compare the case of Simon the sorcerer, Acts 8:9-22. Although it is stated that he believed, still he may have fallen, because his heart was not right before God. But Peter does not speak of the necessity of a new Baptism, but merely admonishes him to repent and pray. If this admonition were heeded, then the validity of the sacramental blessing would still be in force.

3. The Elements of Baptism.

The elements in Baptism, or *materiala baptismi,* are: 1) *materia seu res terrestris,* or pure water, which is not only a suitable subjective symbol and an external token of a spiritual gift, but is also a vehicle of the gift, or the means by which it is imparted; 2) *materia seu res celestis,* which is the Holy Spirit, who is bestowed for the holy purposes of the Sacrament. The normal, but not necessary, result of the impartation of the Spirit is regeneration, depending on the subjective state of the baptized. The impartation of the Spirit in this case is sacramental. For this reason the Dogmaticians speak of *unio sacramentalis* and this is set forth as being *realis et exhibitiva,* which means that the heavenly gift is truly and really present. Dogmaticians entertain divergent views concerning *materia celestis.* Compare the History of Dogma. Some have declared that the gift is comprised of the entire Trinity, but they qualify the statement by adding, *peculialiter et determinative,* the Holy Spirit. The Biblical foundation for this view concerning the entire Trinity is the expression in the words of the institution, viz., that Baptism takes place into the name of the Father, and of the Son, and of the Holy Spirit. The following passages are quoted to prove that the *materia celestis* is the Holy Spirit: "Water and the Spirit" (John 3:5); "The same is he that baptizeth in the Holy Spirit" (John 1:33); "Be baptized, every one of you, in the name of Jesus Christ unto the remission of your sins; and ye shall receive the gift of the Holy Spirit" (Acts 2:38); "For in one Spirit were we all baptized" (1 Cor. 12:13); "The washing of regeneration and renewing of the Holy Spirit" (Titus

3:5). Some have objected, stating that Cornelius, received the Holy Spirit before he was baptized. Cf. Acts 10:47, 48. However, this was part of the extraordinary outpouring of the Spirit that prevailed at the time and in no wise hindered Cornelius from receiving in his Baptism the special gift of the Spirit unto the newness of life which all receive in Baptism. Baptism may therefore be called the Sacrament of the Spirit, because there is a communion of the Spirit, just as in the Lord's Supper there occurs a communion of the body and blood of Christ. Baptism is therefore not only water, but a water of God, as Luther says in his large Catechism, and confers a gift upon all that are baptized, although the sacramental blessing is dependent on the subjective state or condition of the recipient. When this required condition exists or is realized, then the sacramental power and gift is there and the purpose of Baptism is fulfilled.

4. The **Formale** *or* **Modus** *of Baptism.*

Formale baptismi, or the essential form and mode of Baptism, consists in baptizing with water into the name of the Father, and of the Son, and of the Holy Spirit. The words of the institution ought to be read. In comparing Acts 8:16 and 10:48 it would appear that Baptism was administered in the name of Jesus, but these passages do not deal with the mode of Baptism, but merely set forth the purpose of Baptism as a Baptism into Christ. Baptism may be administered either by pouring, sprinkling or immersion, but the Lutheran Church does not make use of the last mentioned method, inasmuch as this would constitute a concession to those who insist on the necessity of immersion. The denominations that maintain that pouring is just as correct a mode of baptizing as immersion stand on secure ground philologically, Biblically and traditionally. The Greek word *βαπτίζω* comes from *βάπτω*, which means not only to dip, to dip in dye, but also to wash, to pump water, to moisten, to besprinkle. These are the translations of *βάπτω* given by distinguished lexicographers. We would cite some Scripture passages where *βάπτω* is used. Compare Lev. 14:4-6. The Septuagint translates the Hebrew word *tabhal* by *βάπτω*. Despite the fact that Fürst translates *tabhal* by bedew, moisten, besprinkle and immerse, still the context in this passage clearly shows that *tabhal* and *βάπτω* could not mean immerse, inasmuch as it would be physically impossible to immerse the bird, the cedar wood, the scarlet, and the hyssop in the blood of a single bird. In Daniel 5:21 we read of Nebuchadnezzar that his body was wet with the dew of heaven. Here *βάπτω* is used and refers to the dew of heaven and not to any immersion. Luther translates *βάπτω* in Rev. 19:13 with sprinkle. This translation corresponds to the Syrian, Ethiopian and other translations together with that of Origen. This passage refers to Isa. 63:2, 3, and for this reason we cannot possibly think of immersion. *βαπτίζω* is likewise translated by distinguished lexicographers not only dip and immerse, but also wash, pour out upon, besprinkle, etc. An investigation of the passages in which *βαπτίζω* occurs in the Septuagint will plainly show that it may be translated to wash, to pour out upon. Compare 2 Kings 5:14 and Isa. 21:4. Most convincing, however, is the use of *βαπτίζω* in the New Testament. *βαπτίζω* occurs about seventy-five times, and in many of these passages reference is made to the washing and cleansing prescribed by the Law of Moses. Compare the following Scripture passages: "When they come from the market-place, except they bathe themselves, they eat not; and many other things there are, which they have received to hold, washings of cups, and pots, and brasen vessels" (Mark 7:4); "Now there were six waterpots of stone set there after the Jews' manner of purifying, containing two or three firkins apiece" (John 2:6). The letter to the Hebrews (Heb. 9:10) calls these divers washings *βαπτισμοί* This proves that baptize and immerse are not identical in meaning. In John 3:25 reference is made to a questioning that arose with regard to purifying, while the whole context of the passage refers to Baptism. Also compare John 1:19-25, and especially the words, "Why then baptizest thou, if thou art not the Christ, neither Elijah, neither the prophet? John answered them, saying, I baptize in water." Did the question concern immersion and was it foretold that both the forerunner and Christ Himself were to baptize by means of immersion? Read Mal. 3:1-3: "He will purify the sons of Levi, and refine them as gold and silver." Baptism was therefore regarded as a cleansing, a purification. Furthermore, it is not certain that baptism in water is the same as immersion in water. Did not John say that he baptized with water, but that Christ would baptize with the Holy Spirit? This Baptism occurred for the first time on the day of Pentecost. Peter says of this Baptism that it consisted in the pouring out of the Holy Spirit. Compare Acts 2:17, 18; 10:44; Titus 3:6. This Baptism with the Spirit bears testimony in favor of pouring and not immersion. Even John 3:23 does not constitute a signal proof for immersion, inasmuch as *ὕδατα πολλά* means many streams, and in any case the original text does not necessarily prove that "much water" implies that the water was as deep as was required for immersion. If John had wished to baptize in deep water he might indeed have continued to baptize in Jordan, but many proofs can be cited to demonstrate that he also baptized by means of pouring. The coming up out of the water does not necessarily mean that immersion had taken place, since they might just as well have stood in the water during the process of pouring and still come up out of the water at the conclusion of the act. The first act of Christian Baptism in the real sense was performed on the first Christian day of Pentecost when 3,000 persons were baptized. It is hardly possible that all these were baptized by immersion. This could not have taken place either in Bethesda, Siloam or the Kidron. In consideration of the circumstances in the case it is hardly possible to conceive of the Apostles arranging for great receptacles to immerse so large a number. The Ethiopian eunuch was very certainly baptized by means of pouring, since competent judges, such as Eusebius, have proved that there was not sufficient water for immersion in the place where the baptism occurred. The coming up out of the water does not prove that the eunuch had been under the water, since Philip also came up out of the water. Compare Acts 9:17-19 concerning the Baptism of Paul. In 1 Cor. 10:1, 2 it is stated that the Israelites were all baptized in the cloud and in the sea, but a careful examination of the passage will show that the Baptism did not take place by means of immersion, but by sprinkling from the cloud and the sea, while the Egyptians were swallowed up by the waters that were closed on them and were drowned. Compare 1 Peter 3:20, where it is stated that eight souls were saved through water, but who would say that they were immersed? Neither Rom. 6:4 nor Col. 2:12 constitutes a proof for immersion, inasmuch as these passages set forth the significance of Baptism and do not determine its method. From the passages quoted together with others it is plainly evident that the meaning of *βαπτίζω* is not limited to dip or immerse, but that the verb also means to pour out upon, to wash, to besprinkle, et cetera. Inasmuch, therefore, as *βαπτίζω* possesses a special significance, which is nevertheless not limited, therefore the Lutheran Church acknowledges all three modes of Baptism. In this as in many other instances, however, she takes a mediating position and most generally uses the mode of pouring in the administration of the Sacrament of Baptism.

5. The Subjects of Baptism.

Finis cui et subjectum baptismi, or the subjects of Baptism, are not only adults, but also children. There is no argument with regard to the Baptism of proselytes, which takes place after the candidates have been properly instructed and have made their confession. Our specific interest at this time is centered about the Baptism of infants. The position of the Lutheran Church and others that children ought to be baptized is justified by the words of the institution of Baptism, which do not make mention of grown persons any more than of children, but include both in the command: "Make disciples of all nations" (Matt. 28:19). The word *μαθητεύσατε* implies that the work of the Gospel in general and does not therefore describe an antecedent and completed condition for Baptism. Disciples are made through Baptism and instruction. No one is a true disciple who is not baptized. It is indeed significant that in the words of the institution baptize is first mentioned, followed by teaching, which fits perfectly the condition of the child. For this reason it always has been and is now the general practice to baptize children. Most Christians acknowledge infant Baptism. If children were to be excluded from the New Covenant, how inferior this would be to the Old, where they were taken up into communion with the Theocracy at the age of eight days? Paul sets forth the relationship between the Sacraments of the Old and the New Covenant in the following passage:

"In whom ye were also circumcised with a circumcision not made with hands, in the putting off of the body of flesh, in the circumcision of Christ; having been buried with him in baptism" (Col. 2:11, 12). When the Lord through circumcision received the small children into the Covenant of the Law without their own choice or assent, or faith, how can we conceive of the children of the Covenant of Grace enjoying fewer privileges. Indeed their privileges are greater. The Lord Jesus, the Founder of the Church and the Friend of the children, has clearly set forth the position of the children in the kingdom of God. Compare Mark 10:14 and 15. In the latter verse we read: "Verily I say unto you, Whosoever shall not receive the kingdom of God as a little child, he shall in no wise enter therein." Inasmuch as children are set forth as examples in regard to the proper reception of the kingdom, ought they not to be considered as proper subjects for Baptism as adults? If the kingdom is theirs, ought they not have the privilege of entering in through the door of Baptism in order that they may actually belong to the kingdom? The Lord desires that the children should come to Him, and the Sacrament of Baptism is the only way by which they may come and receive the blessing. Normally there is but one way or order of salvation, for which reason Christ has not instituted Baptism for adults and another way of salvation for children. As a rule the following words apply to everybody: "He that believeth and is baptized shall be saved" (Mark 16:16) and also: "Except one be born of water and the Spirit, he cannot enter into the kingdom of God" (John 3:5).

No one can enter into heaven that has not been regenerated. The children must therefore be born again in order to be saved. Inasmuch as the infant is a child of nature and cannot understand the Word, therefore the Sacrament of Baptism is the only revealed means by which children can be made partakers of the grace of salvation.. The ordinary objection has always been that children cannot believe and that Baptism does not work faith. But if the Holy Spirit is unable to effect saving faith in the children, then the only conclusion is that the baptized children must be accounted unbelievers and subject to condemnation, inasmuch as it is impossible for unbelievers to enter into the kingdom of Heaven. Therefore faith must be effected if children are to be saved. We are familiar with the inconsistent position of the Baptists that the children are incapable of faith and still are saved without faith. To be sure, the infant stands in a relation to the saving grace of the Spirit different from that of the adult, inasmuch as there is wanting in the child active and conscious resistance to the operations of the Spirit. The child is in a state of passivity which makes possible the successful work of the Spirit. Through Baptism the grace of God is bestowed upon the child and effects a *fides directa,* which is a saving faith. There are many degrees of faith. This *fides directa* is not a finished or mature faith like *fides reflexa,* but as the beginnings of the fully mature man are found in the child, so is also faith in its embryo stage. The child is a real child, although not self-conscious; the faith of the child is a true faith, although it is not conscious of its faith, nor of the conception of faith. Faith is the work of the Spirit, both as *directa* and *reflexa.* Even in the adult, faith in its embryo state is like unto a tender shoot and a *fides directa,* which afterwards develops and becomes *reflexa.* As the children grow in years, so they develop in understanding and appropriate ever-increasingly the gifts of God, provided they remain faithful to their baptismal covenant. In this process the Word of God must be used, and instruction given. The Church must provide for the instruction of the baptized children. An analogy to the faith of the child has been sought in the relationship that subsists between the children and their parents. The child stretches forth its hands to its mother, and yet the action may be wholly unreflected. In the same way the child is drawn to the Lord when He approaches it in the grace of Baptism. The degree or state of faith in the child is therefore not a conclusive argument against infant Baptism. Furthermore, it is not faith that makes Baptism a means of grace. As we have seen, it has happened in the Baptism of proselytes that unbelievers have been baptized, but the Baptism has nevertheless possessed its significance and become a blessing to them in their conversion. But the children are passive, and the Lord works in them faith, which is receptive. Viewed from the standpoint of receptivity, faith may be found even in a state of unconsciousness. Just as children may be the possessors of enormous wealth, their parents bestowing great gifts upon them, which for the time being they are unable to appreciate, so God is able to dispense His gracious gifts to the children. With regard to the divine operations in infant children, yea, while yet in the womb, compare Jer. 1:15 and Luke 1:15. The latter passage reads: "He shall be filled with the Holy Spirit, even from his mother's womb." Would it not seem possible for the same Lord to bestow His Spirit upon the infant children through Baptism? We may be certain that He can. The Lord has bestowed His Holy Spirit upon those that have been baptized in infancy and thereby confirmed their Baptism. To be sure, the Bible does not expressly mention infant Baptism, but children are not excluded in the passages which relate to Baptism. Compare Eph. 5:25, 26. In the membership of the Church the children are included, but if they were not baptized they would not belong to the Church. It is also stated that whole families were baptized, which constitutes a proof that the Apostles also baptized children, since it is hardly to be assumed that all these families were childless. The following are specially mentioned: Cornelius and his household in Acts 10:47; Lydia and her household in Acts 16:15; the jailor at Philippi with all his house in Acts 16:33; Crispus with all his house in Acts 18:8; the household of Stephanas in 1 Cor. 1:16; the house of Onesiphorus in 2 Tim. 4:19; the households of Aristobulus and Narcissus in Rom. 16:10, 11. If we confine ourselves to the first five of these passages it is altogether evident that the children also were baptized. *Oikos*, translated "house" or "household," is an expression which implies that there were children in the family and not only servants.

6. The Effect and Purpose of Baptism.

Effectus seu finis proximus baptismi is regeneration and renovation. Of course, regeneration presupposes justification. We need hardly remark that the effect of Baptism does not take place *ex opere operato*, i.e., independent of the subjective state of the baptized. However, Baptism is always a means of grace, so that the Holy Spirit is imparted unto regeneration, which takes place when the proper subjective conditions are present. Regeneration takes place always in infant Baptism, but in the Baptism administered to a proselyte or an adult it may happen by reason of the lack of faith on the part of the recipient that regeneration does not take place, but when faith is present or is brought about later, then Baptism is efficacious unto regeneration. With the subjective presuppositions at hand, regeneration becomes the immediate effect of the administration of Baptism, which is indeed the normal effect of this Sacrament of regeneration. In the absence of the subjective prerequisites regeneration does not take place, but a sacramental connection is nevertheless established. God has a grip, so to speak, upon the baptized, as Gisle Johnson says. In the case of an adult the subjective prerequisites may be present before Baptism, indeed, some time before, but normally regeneration is made complete through the administration of the Sacrament, which is a washing of regeneration. Compare Titus 3:5; Heb. 10:22. Regeneration is effected through the Holy Spirit by means of Baptism and the Word in indissoluble connection. Cf. Eph. 5:26: "That he might sanctify it, having cleansed it by the washing of water with the word." Such passages as 1 Peter 1:23; James 1:18; 1 John 2:29 do not militate against the doctrine that regeneration is effected through the cooperation of Baptism and the Word, inasmuch as the Word of God must be interpreted according to the analogy of faith. If regeneration is effected independently of Baptism, this must be considered as God's own exception to the rule, when persons through no fault of their own are deprived of the Sacrament. We are not to be concerned with the exceptions; it is our duty to follow the rule. In the case of infant Baptism the Word is present in the words of the institution, while in the Baptism of adults the Word has been instrumental in preparing the candidate for the administration of the Sacrament, and in their Baptism the Word is connected with water. As the baptized children grow up they are to be instructed in the Word. Because of the fact that in the processes of conversion and regeneration in adults the Word of God works a self-conscious choice, therefore it has been customary for some theologians to call infant regeneration the basic, principal, and potential regeneration. And this is true when we consider the development of the spiritual life, but it is not to be construed to mean that a real regeneration has not taken place. In Baptism a new birth occurs. A spiritual child is born into the world of the Spirit, which shall grow up and mature, subject to the conditions of this earthly life, until it shall please the Lord to remove such a person to the life which is eternal. The normal effect of Baptism, therefore, is regeneration. This necessarily implies that Baptism works forgiveness of sins. Baptism removes the guilt of original sin. The *materiale* of sin, or the evil desire, to be sure, remains, but with this difference, that the Holy Spirit begins the work of counteracting this desire. The blessed effects of Baptism are to be seen in the whole nature of man, both material and spiritual. It affects the whole course of life. Luther says: "Baptism worketh forgiveness of sins, delivers from death and the devil, and confers everlasting salvation on all who believe as the Word and promise of God declare." This is particularly evident when we reflect on the new relationship of the baptized person with God, who becomes his true Father, Christ his personal Saviour and Brother, and the Holy Spirit his Comforter and Sanctifier.

The following passages may be cited and considered: "And Peter said unto them, Repent ye, and be baptized every one of you in the name of Jesus Christ unto the remission of your sins; and ye shall receive the gift of the Holy Spirit. For to you is the promise, and to your children" (Acts 2:38, 39). This proves that Baptism effects regeneration, since he that has received the forgiveness of sins must also be called a child of God. Compare once more John 3:5 and Titus 3:4, 6. The Baptists say that the expression "by water" means spiritual life. But this is plainly a misinterpretation of Scripture. There is much in the third chapter of John which proves that the subject of Baptism was being discussed. Nicodemus was familiar with the work of John the Baptist. The whole context proves that the "water" refers to Baptism. If water is used figuratively in this connection, then Spirit must also be so used, and no one maintains the latter. There is no reason for asserting the former. Cf. 1 John 5:6-8. Even there Spirit and water are distinguished, so that the Spirit is the Holy Spirit, and water is not used figuratively. In Titus we read of the "washing of regeneration" instead of water, and in the place of Spirit we read Holy Spirit and the renewing of the Holy Spirit. "Enter into the kingdom" is replaced with, "He saved us." Christ and Paul, therefore, clearly taught that Baptism effects regeneration. In Gal. 3:27 we read: "For as many of you as were baptized into Christ did put on Christ." Compare also Acts 22:16; Col. 2:11, 12 and 1 Peter 3:20, 21. This last-named passage reads as follows: "Wherein few, that is, eight souls, were saved through water: which also after a true likeness doth now save you, even baptism." Concerning the significance of Baptism read Rom. 6:3, 4. This includes new life, a new creation, and new conduct. This significance of Baptism presupposes that it is the Sacrament of regeneration. If the baptized person remains in the grace of Baptism, or, having fallen from the grace of Baptism, again returns to the Lord through conversion and afterwards abides faithfully by the Word of God unto the end, he shall become the object of the final purpose of Baptism. *Finis seu, effectus ultimus* is the eternal salvation of the baptized.

7. Notes on the History of Dogma.

The early Church set forth Baptism not only as a symbol, but as a means of grace unto regeneration and salvation. The validity of infant Baptism was attested as an apostolic tradition. The principle of freedom ruled in regard to the mode of administering the Sacrament. Immersion was not used because of its necessity, but as a more complete expression of the idea of baptismal purification. The sick were baptized by means of pouring or sprinkling. When this method was called in question and persons so baptized were called *clinici*, then Cyprian defended this mode of Baptism. In one form or another, however, the usual method of administering Baptism was by immersion. This immersion, however, did not always take place in the ordinary manner, but in many cases the candidate for Baptism stood in the water, while the water was poured over him. The Greek Catholic Church still retains immersion, although the degrees of immersion may vary. Pouring is, however, permissible in cases of necessity, as when there is a scarcity of water and especially in *periculo mortis*. In the Roman Church immersion continued to be used, but Thomas Aquinas permitted *perfusio* or pouring, upon the head. The Council of Ravenna in 1311 expressly permitted a choice as between *immersio et perfusio*. The Church of the Middle Ages acknowledged Baptism as a means of grace. In conformity with the creational theory of the origin of the soul and the doctrine of sin it was taught that original sin was totally eradicated through Baptism and a new character *indelebilis* was imparted. It was taught that *sacramentum poenitentiae* secured deliverance from sins committed after Baptism. Penance was considered to be a *secunda tabula salutis* for such as had fallen from Baptism as out of the ship of salvation. The Lutheran Church set forth Baptism as a means of grace and emphasized its necessity and effect as the Sacrament of regeneration. Stress was laid on the subjective state as being of prime importance in receiving the sacramental blessing. Infant Baptism was sanctioned and the three modes of the administration of the Sacrament were acknowledged, although pouring was the method generally used. The Reformed Church viewed Baptism either as a symbol of purification or of church membership or as an earnest of regeneration through the Spirit, but Baptism was not considered as a real means of grace. The Arminians said that the necessity of Baptism was dependent on the command of Christ. Baptism is merely a symbolic action. Infant Baptism was acknowledged, but it was not considered necessary. Rationalism and the philosophical schools of thought, of course, minimized the significance of Baptism and at most viewed the Sacrament as an attractive ceremony. The views of the mediating theologians correspond closely to those of the Reformed Church. The denominations of the latter church support either the Zwinglian or the Calvinistic positions, with the exception of the Baptists and others, who are the modern Anabaptists. The orthodox theologians have contended for the conservative positions and in general have combatted the exclusive standpoint of the Baptists. Some theologians have especially emphasized the influence of Baptism on man's human nature. They have stressed the distinction between regeneration in infant Baptism and in adults, characterizing the former as substantial and objective, the latter subjective and personal. Below are set forth more detailed notes on the doctrine of Baptism.

Barnabas sets forth the symbolic significance of the water as well as of the cross and states that those who arise out of the water have received the fruits of the Spirit. Hermas says that the forgiveness of sins is the fruit of Baptism. The patriarchs were baptized in the world of the Spirit. Ignatius stated that the Holy Spirit was imparted in Baptism. In the *Didache* (*Διδαχή*) or the *Teaching of the Twelve Apostles* (chapter seven), immersion as well as pouring are acknowledged as proper modes of Baptism. Inasmuch as the *Didache* dates from the first century the significance of its testimony concerning the mode of Baptism is very great. Justin Martyr speaks of the forgiveness of sins, purification and regeneration in Baptism and calls the Sacrament *φωτισμός*. He says that he was personally acquainted with Christians sixty and seventy years old who had become disciples of Jesus in childhood. He expresses himself as follows: "We admonish those who are convinced and believe that what is taught among us is true and who promise to live in accordance therewith, in the first place to fast and pray and implore God for the forgiveness of their sins, while we fast and pray with them. Afterwards we lead them to some place where there is water and there they are regenerated by the same method that was used in our regeneration." Irenaeus was the disciple of Polycarp and Polycarp was the disciple of John. Irenaeus, instructed by Polycarp, expresses himself as follows: "He (Christ) came to save all through Himself; all, I say, who through Him are born again unto the Lord, infants, small children, boys and girls and adults. For this reason He passed through every age of man, becoming an infant for infants," etc. Inasmuch as the word regenerate was used for baptize in the same sense as we use christen, therefore it is evident that infant children were baptized. Clement of Alexandria said that Baptism confers the forgiveness of sins, sonship, and immortality. Tertullian said that the Spirit sanctifies the water. In this water we are regenerated. He opposed infant Baptism for the reason that this Sacrament effects the forgiveness of all sins committed prior to Baptism, wherefore he considered it profitable to postpone its administration. His opposition proves that infant Baptism was in use. The manner in which he uses the word baptism precludes the sense of immersion. Pouring seems to have been the mode in vogue at the time. Cyprian calls Baptism the second birth, producing a new creature. In the Sacrament forgiveness is conferred for sins previously committed. He considered that children should be baptized as early as possible and called a council of African bishops which confirmed the validity of infant Baptism. He defended pouring as a mode of Baptism. Origen taught that Baptism confers the forgiveness of sins and the Holy Spirit and that it constitutes the potent beginning of the new life. He testifies that the Church from the time of the Apostles had received the command to baptize children. Origen was born in 185. His father, grandfather and great-grandfather were Christians. It may also be stated that he used the word baptism in the sense of pouring.

Cyril of Jerusalem says that Baptism confers the Holy Spirit, the forgiveness of sins and victory over death. Basil said that in Baptism that which is mortal is swallowed up in immortality. Gregory of Nyssa speaks of the sick being baptized by means of pouring or sprinkling. Augustine acknowledged infant Baptism and taught that the faith of the Church takes the place of the child's faith. Baptism works the forgiveness of sins and regeneration. In the case of apostasy followed by conversion, Baptism is again efficacious.

Peter Lombard said that the effect of Baptism consisted in a renewal of mind. Adults receive in Baptism the forgiveness of sins together with *gratia operans et cooperans*, but children receive only the forgiveness of original sin. Later on, however, or in 1311, it was declared that children also receive the *gratia* above referred to. Thomas Aquinas taught that a *character indelebilis* was imparted in Baptism. Not only was the guilt of original sin removed, but the sin itself was eradicated so that the evil desires remaining in the heart are not sin but only *fomes peccati*. The *Thomists* seem to have taught that there was spiritual power in the water independent of the Word connected therewith. Duns Scotus taught that in Baptism sin was not washed away through the water and the Word, but through the will of God. God, therefore, operated apart from Baptism.

While the Roman Church taught that Baptism eradicated original sin through the impartation of a new *character indelebilis,* still the blessing of Baptism was nevertheless modified by this additional teaching that the Sacrament was efficacious in case the baptized did not interpose any obstacle (*non ponit obicem*) to nullify the effect of Baptism. This came only to mean, however, that the baptized was not to be guilty of any mortal sin.

Luther, as we know, has clearly and completely set forth the doctrine of Baptism. He has expressed many beautiful thoughts on this Sacrament, but his explanation of the essence and significance of Baptism as contained in his catechisms can hardly be excelled. Some have asserted that Luther was an immersionist by reason of his utterances concerning Baptism in a sermon in 1519. His statements have indeed been colored, although it is true that he did then prefer immersion. We ought to remember, however, that this utterance occurred before he made a thorough study of the subject and ten years before the publication of his catechisms. It is evident that Luther in 1519 believed that *βαπτισμός* and *Taufe* meant immersion in accordance with their etymology, but not in actual practice. Many proofs could be advanced to show that Luther considered that *βαπτισμός* as to its actual use meant cleansing or purifying independent of the method. His translation of the Roman ritual, his translation of the Bible, his own ritual for Baptism, which prescribes only pouring, together with many other utterances which sanction pouring prove that he was not a Baptist as to the method of administering the Sacrament. In the *Schwabach Articles* of 1529 he wrote that we baptize with water (*mit Wasser*) and in this connection uses *begiessen,* to pour. There are some who would prove by means of a letter written in 1530 in answer to a question concerning the Baptism of a Jewish girl that Luther favored immersion as the only method of Baptism. The misunderstanding concerning the advice of Luther depended on an incorrect translation, but in the original Latin text we find that Luther preferred pouring, but allows both methods in accordance with the Latin ritual. He says: "It would therefore satisfy me (*mihi placeret*) if water were modestly poured on her (*verecunde perfunderetur*), or if she sits in water which reaches to her neck, that her head be immersed with a threefold submersion (*caput ejus trina immersione immergeretur*)." This does not prove that Luther was a Baptist, but merely that he took the liberal position of our Church with regard to the mode and that he preferred pouring. The Augsburg Confession in articles II and X expresses clearly the Lutheran position concerning the necessity and significance of Baptism. It teaches that original sin is real sin and condemns all who are not regenerated through Baptism and the Holy Ghost. Baptism offers and confers the grace of God. It acknowledges infant Baptism. The Apology expresses especially the Lutheran doctrine of the efficacy of Baptism in relation to sin. All the Confessional writings set forth Baptism as a means of grace. Baptism is also called *sacramentum poenitentiae*, signifying that Baptism always retains its power, always extends its comfort to those that return to the grace of Baptism. The teaching of Jerome is therefore rejected, since the ship of Baptism is not destroyed, but through sin we fall out of the ship. It is also pointed out that we may reenter the ship. Zwingli considered Baptism as a symbolical act through which man became obligated to purification symbolized by the water at Baptism. Calvin viewed Baptism as an earnest of the forgiveness of sins and regeneration, but Baptism is not a vehicle for the impartation of the Spirit. Regeneration is brought about independently of Baptism. The *Calvinists* teach concerning Baptism that it is one of the Sacraments of the New Covenant in which the forgiveness of sins and regeneration are sealed upon the elect who are received into the family of God through the blood of Christ and the Holy Ghost. The efficacy of Baptism is therefore dependent on election. The *Anabaptists* deny the essence of Baptism as a means of grace. It was the symbol of obedience and therefore necessary in that sense. Infant Baptism was rejected, since innocent children have no need of Baptism, are incapable of believing, and can receive no spiritual benefit through earthly means. The *Socinians* accepted merely the Baptism of proselytes and even this was a matter of indifference. Infant Baptism was rejected or at least its significance was minimized. Baptism "was not the Sacrament of regeneration. The *Arminians* taught that Baptism implies merely an external acknowledgment of a covenant through which the baptized confess their faith and receive the witness of the grace of God. The old Dogmaticians spoke of a double *materia* in Baptism. Beza set forth that the blood of Christ was a part of the substance of Baptism. With regard to *materia celestis* some declared with Luther that *res celestis* was the Word or the name of God. Gerhard, Calovius and Hollazius took the position that the *res celestis* was the entire Trinity, but especially the Holy Ghost. Hutterus said that it was the blood of Christ, while Dannhauer declared that it was the Holy Spirit. The old Dogmaticians also held divergent views concerning the salvation of unbaptized children. Some expressed hope especially for the children who were born within the fold of the Church. Others would not express an opinion. To the latter belonged Gerhard.

Schleiermacher looked upon Baptism as a means of reception into the communion of the Church, through which also the individual entered into communion with Christ. Infant Baptism is a perfect baptism only as it is made complete through instruction and confession. Among the theologians who emphasize the influence of Baptism even upon the physical nature of man we would mention Thomasius, who says that the Word appeals to man as a self-conscious person, while Baptism affects particularly man's nature as such, the Spirit reaching down to the depths of his nature and influencing both his physical and spiritual powers. Martensen says that infant Baptism effects a substantial but not a personal regeneration which can be brought about only in adults. Granfelt says that infant Baptism is the Sacrament of objective regeneration and requires a subjective content. This is supplied in confirmation, which constitutes on the part of the grown child the confirmation of the covenant with God entered into at Baptism. In this confirmation, when true and sincere, is to be found the earnest of personal regeneration accomplished. S. L. Bring says that as the Spirit of God in the beginning of creation moved upon the face of the waters, so in Baptism the Spirit hovers over the personal and human nature of the baptized in order that through the consecrated water of the Sacrament a new creature may be brought about. Through Baptism man is surrounded with a holy and spiritual atmosphere, which, like the atmosphere in the natural world, becomes the element in which we live spiritually. He declares that infant Baptism is the normal Baptism. There is to be found in the child even prior to Baptism an embryonic, yearning faith, but through Baptism there is brought about a receptive and apprehensive faith. The child apprehends the grace of God as a child is able to apprehend. Infant faith is also faith. Gisle Johnson says that *res celestis* is the Holy Spirit. Baptism is an act which *realiter* and *effective* mediates the impartation of the Holy Spirit to the sinner, which means that regeneration is effected, provided the immanent regenerating power of Baptism is not hindered from producing its normal effect. Man may render null and void the effect of Baptism, but not its efficacious power. He also says that Baptism possesses this power by reason of its organic connection and co-operation with the Word. He further states that regeneration is possible through the Word alone only in case the subjective presuppositions are at hand and that for one reason or another the Sacrament cannot be administered.

§38. The Lord's Supper.

The Lord's Supper was instituted at a Passover feast when Christ and His disciples for the last time celebrated this Old Testament feast. The bread that was broken was the bread of the Passover, while the cup that was used contained the wine of the feast. The Lord's Supper became a new Passover supper. The antitype took the place of the type. Christ became the true paschal Lamb. His body and His blood corresponded to the flesh and blood of the lamb. If the true paschal Lamb were not present in the Holy Supper, if His body and blood were not really imparted in the Sacrament, then the substance of the Lord's Supper would be more of a shadow than the shadow itself, the antitype would have less significance than the type, and the Passover feast of the Jews would be more real than the Christian Sacrament of the Altar. The Lord's Supper is a Sacrament in the full sense of the Word, while the Passover feast of the Jews was a Sacrament only in a symbolic sense. It was merely a shadowy outline which was filled in with its proper content in the Lord's Supper. The doctrine of the Lord's Supper belongs to the deepest mysteries of faith and leads us into a holy place with sacred memories, where religion as a bond of communion with God becomes more real and palpable, yet mysterious, where the religious sense of devotion is intensified, and where our communion with Christ, with the saints, and with the real and future world of the Spirit becomes ever increasingly a living experience in our lives.

1. Definition of the Lord's Supper.

The Lord's Supper is *a sacred and solemn sacramental act in which, on the basis of the words of the institution and the promises connected therewith, the earthly elements, the bread and the wine, become vehicles for the importation of the true body and blood of Christ to all communicants, the effects differing in accordance with their subjective state.* Hollazius defines this Sacrament as follows: "*Eucharistia* is the sacred and solemn action, instituted by Christ, through which the true and substantial body of Christ by means of consecrated bread and His true and substantial blood by means of consecrated wine are given to the Christian communicants to eat and drink and both of them to be received an eaten and drank in a supernatural manner in commemoration of the death of Jesus and in confirmation of the grace of the Gospel."[109] *Causa efficiens principalis* is Christ, who instituted the Lord's Supper. *Causa impulsiva interna* is the goodness and love of Christ. *Causa impulsiva externa* is the merit of Christ, His suffering and death. *Causa instrumentalis* is the *minister ecclesiae.*

2. The Form of the Lord's Supper.

The *forma* of the Lord's Supper consists of the words of the institution, the distribution and the reception in accordance with the institution. The words of the institution do not possess magical power so as to transform the elements, as the Catholic Church teaches, neither are they a mere

[109] *Exam. Theol. Acroam.* Pars III, §2, Cap. V, p. 579.

repetition of the historical words of Christ, but through them the elements are set apart and consecrated so as to become the vehicles of the body and blood of Christ. The *forma* comprises three parts: 1) *consecratio*, through which the bread and wine are set apart and consecrated as means for the sacramental action of the Lord; 2) *distributio*, or the distribution of the elements thus set apart and consecrated; 3) *communio seu sumtio*, or the reception. The sacramental union, or *unio sacramentalis*, takes place in the distribution and the reception of the elements in accordance with the institution of Christ. On the other hand, the Catholic Church teaches that this sacramental union is effected during the reading of the words of the institution, the officiating priest producing transubstantiation, all of which takes place independent of the distribution and the reception. The Lutheran Church says that the sacramental action must be complete and that the body and the blood of Christ are present in the use. When, therefore, the sacramental action comprises the three parts of the *forma* of the Lord's Supper, then we say that the body and the blood of Christ are really present in *coena Domini*. In case the elements are not distributed and received, then there is no Sacrament.

3. The Elements of the Lord's Supper.

Materia terrestris is the bread and wine. The bread may be leavened or unleavened. The wine must be the fermented juice of the grape, but may be diluted with water, if necessary. The breaking of bread is not necessary in the sacramental action. Christ did not break the bread in order to symbolize His death or the breaking of His body. Assuming that the text of 1 Cor. 11:24 in accordance with the *textus receptus* is correct, still the words, "which is broken for you," must be harmonized with Luke 22:19, where we read, "given for you," and also with Matt. 26:22 and Mark 14:22, where nothing is said about the breaking of the body. On good ground the best critical texts have elided *κλώμενον* from 1 Cor. 11:24. If the breaking of the bread had been symbolical of the body of Christ, then we should have expected Him also to pour out the wine as being symbolical of the shedding of His blood. From the Scriptures we learn, however, that He simply took the cup and bade al! the disciples drink of it.

Materia celestis is the true body and blood of Christ. The specific gifts of the Lord's Supper, therefore, consists in the partaking of the true body and blood of Christ in a manner in which we cannot otherwise receive them. The whole Christ is present in the Lord's Supper, but the sacramental union has reference only to His body and blood which are imparted in, with and under the bread and wine and are received orally. The whole Christ is, however, received spiritually, so that there is a sacramental eating and a spiritual eating. The latter occurs, so to speak, with the mouth of faith in the reading and the hearing of the Word of God as well as in the Lord's Supper. Only those communicants who are worthy, however, eat spiritually and receive the promise, while all the communicants eat and drink in a sacramental sense. Quenstedt says in this connection: "It is one thing that the whole Christ is present in the Holy Supper, and another that the whole Christ or the celestial object is united with the element of bread and wine, and thus also the whole is sacramentally eaten. The former we affirm, the latter we deny. For we say that the body of Christ only is united with the bread, and the blood with the wine, but that the whole Christ is received spiritually by the mouth of faith." Chemnitz speaks of a threefold manducation in the Lord's Supper: 1) *manducatio panis*, which is physical; 2) *manducatio corporis Christi*, which is a *manducatio oralis* and a sacramental eating; 3) *manducatio spiritualis*, which takes place through faith.

4. Further Definition and Explanation of the Doctrine.

The doctrine of the Lord's Supper may be determined in a negative and a positive manner. The negative and positive terms supplement each other. The negative terms form a framework about the positive terms in such a way as to cause them to appear in a clearer light. In spite of all explanations, however, the mystery of the doctrine of the Lord's Supper remains a mystery of faith, and still the terms that are here used serve to reveal much of the profound and glorious content of the Sacrament.

The negative terms, or that which we do not teach, but reject, are contained principally in the following doctrines: 1) transubstantiation. This doctrine, held by the Catholic Church, implies a transformation of the elements in the Sacrament. The Lutheran Church teaches that the elements are not changed as to their substance, but become vehicles of the heavenly gifts. The term transubstantiation was not officially used before 1215. The doctrine means that at the consecrating words by the priest the substance of bread and wine ceases to be and is changed into another substance, namely, the body, blood, soul, and divinity of Jesus Christ, the body and blood of our Lord only looking like bread and wine, tasting as bread and wine, but really there is no bread or wine. In the Roman Catholic celebration thus two miracles occur: The bread and wine are transubstantiated into the body and blood of Christ, and these celestial elements retain the accidents and properties of the earthly elements. The Roman Church believes that "this" refers only to the bread, etc., and not to the complex and, therefore, says: This (bread) is my body, etc., and draws the conclusion: The bread is changed into the body and the wine into the blood; 2) consubstantiation, which implies that a conjunction or union or mixture of the elements takes place in a local and physical sense. This expression is not found in the Confessions, and all theologians of the Lutheran Church reject it. On the contrary, there are many theologians both within and outside the Lutheran Church who have clearly testified that this doctrine is un-Lutheran. Among these may be mentioned Brentz, Chemnitz, Gerhard, Baier, Mosheim, Bucer, Perrone, and Mohler. Even the philosopher Leibnitz bears testimony to the fact that our Church rejects the doctrine of consubstantiation; 3) impanation, or that the body and the blood of Christ are supposed to be found locally in the bread and the wine (invination). Our Church naturally rejects impanation and invination as well as consubstantiation; 4) subpanation, or that the body of Christ in a physical and local manner is present under or beneath the bread; 5) the theory of *unio personalis*, or that the union as between the elements is supposed to be like the personal union in the God-man; 6) the symbolical or significative theory held by Zwingli. According to Zwingli and his adherents among the Reformed sects the Lord's Supper is only a memorial festival. May we never forget the great historical incident at Marburg, when Luther wrote on the table: "This is my body." These words stand as an impregnable fact against Rationalism, Fanaticism and all sectarian views which deny the plain teaching of the words of the institution of the Sacramental Supper; 7) the dynamic theory, or that the substantial presence is merely dynamic, which theory is characteristic of Calvinism. That which is peculiarly characteristic in the Sacrament is lost in accordance with the dynamic theory because of the fact that the sacramental eating is like the daily eating of the body and blood of Christ in the reading of the Word and differs from it only as to manner and in the use of earthly and symbolical elements which together with the solemnity of the celebration of the Sacrament affect the emotions. According to the Bible and the Lutheran Church the bread and wine are the vehicles of the true body and blood of Christ, but according to Calvin the Holy Ghost and a Christian's faith are the vehicles, not of the real body and blood, but only conveying the power immanent in the body and blood of Christ in heaven. According to Paul it is a communion of the real body and blood. According to Calvin the body and blood of Christ are absent.

The positive terms and content of the Lutheran doctrine may be presented in the following propositions: 1) The Lord's Supper is a Sacrament; 2) it is a real supper; 3) it is a covenant act; 4) the sacramental objects are the true body and blood of Christ; 5) the sacramental objects are really present in the Holy Supper; 6) the bread and wine are vehicles of the celestial elements; 7) the celestial elements are received by all the communicants; 8) the means by which the elements are received is called *manducatio oralis*. A fuller development of the content of these propositions follows.

1) *The Lord's Supper is a Sacrament.* The Lord's Supper has been called not only *sacramentum confirmationis* but also *sacramentum nutritionis*. In the very concept of a Sacrament lies the thought that something is imparted in, with and under the visible elements. We meet a real analogy of this relationship in the tree of life in Paradise. Many of the Church Fathers referred to this analogy. Among modern theologians we quote

the following from Krauth: "The great loss of Paradise Lost was that of the Sacrament of Life, of that food, in, with, and under which was given immortality, so objectively, positively, and really that even fallen man would have been made deathless by it. The great gain of Paradise Regained is that of the Sacrament of Life. The cross is the center of Paradise Regained, as the tree of life was the center of the first Paradise. — In the Garden of Eden was a moral miniature of the universe; and with the act of eating were associated the two great realms of the natural and the supernatural; and with this was connected the idea of the one as a means of entering the other. There were natural trees with purely natural properties. But there was also the natural terminating in the supernatural. There were two trees, striking their roots into the same soil, lifting their branches into the same air—natural trees—but bearing, by heaven's ordinance, in, with, and under their fruitage, supernatural properties. One was the sacramental tree of good. We call it the sacramental tree, because it did not merely symbolize life, or signify it; but, by God's appointment, so gave life—in, with, and under its fruit—that to receive its fruit was to receive life. With this tree of life was found the tree which was the sacrament of judgment and of death. — By an eating, whose organs were natural, but whose relations were supernatural, man fell and died."[110] All of this may serve as an analogy to the Lord's Supper. There we find bread, the natural food of mankind. But the bread serves as a means to produce life through the body of Christ. In the Lord's Supper there is also to be found an element of judgment, inasmuch as every unworthy communicant brings damnation upon himself.

2) *The Lord's Supper is a real supper.* At a meal the guests are not served with symbols, signs, etc., but with real food. When the Lord prepared a special supper, the Holy Supper, this would indeed lose its real significance, provided only a little bread and wine were served. But if someone should say with regard to the bread and wine that were served by the host that they were merely symbols of the bread and wine, certainly such an assertion

---

[110] Krauth, *Conservative Reformation*, pp. 586, 587.

would be considered senseless. At the Holy Supper we are the guests of the Lord and He is the Host who says: "Take, eat; this is my body." As He gives the cup He says: "Drink ye all of it; for this is my blood." In the face of these declarations, can we say that the Host, who is the everlasting Truth, does not mean what He says? Indeed not, since in such case Christ would be inferior to an ordinary host. The Lord surely gives what He claims to offer. The bread and cup are the vehicles of the food and drink offered, namely, the body and blood of the Lord, just as a plate and a cup are vehicles. If He therefore offers us His body to eat and His blood to drink, we may feel assured that He imparts His body and blood. Still this Sacrament is a Holy Supper in commemoration of His death and promises, although the significant element in the Lord's Supper is its sacramental character.

3) *The Lord's Supper constitutes a covenant action.* In the words of the institution the Lord says: "This is my blood of the covenant." A covenant is not based on symbols, signs or similitudes, but must have a real foundation and a real content. There may indeed be signs of a covenant, but they constitute the formal side of the contract, the material content is mainly to be considered. In the drawing of a covenant and the specifying of conditions there are no symbols used, the language employed must be clear and literal in its meaning, because it is the written word which decides all action. The content of a covenant must be just as clearly and precisely stated as a last will and testament. Indeed, we may say that the Lord's Supper is a testament in which the Lord before His death expresses His will and bestows upon His own both Himself and all that He possesses. This is the New Testament and the New Covenant. The New Covenant is sealed with the blood of Jesus, wherefore we may be assured that the content is real.

4) *The body and blood of Christ are the sacramental objects.* On carefully considering the words of the institution we shall find that the Lutheran position is the correct one. Let us first examine the meaning of *τοῦτο*, or this. Does *τοῦτο* mean this bread? In Greek there is no agreement between *τοῦτο* and *ἄρτος*, inasmuch as the former is of the neuter gender, while the

latter is masculine, the rule being that a demonstrative pronoun must agree in gender with the noun it modifies. There have been many prominent theologians representing different tendencies who have declared that *τοῦτ* does not refer to *ἄρτος* (or *ἄρτον* in accordance with the context). Among these may be mentioned Gerhard, Quenstedt, Bengel, Maldonatus, Lange, Stier, Alford, Schaff and Krauth. It is further to be noted in opposition to *τοῦτο ἄρτος* that the word *ἄρτος* is not used by the Lord Himself, it simply occurs in the story of Matthew. Neither is it possible to combine *τοῦτο* with *σῶμα* in this connection, since that would produce an identical proposition as follows: This body is my body. We find, therefore, that *τοῦτο* refers to the entire complex and must be understood as a synecdoche. When Jesus said: "Take, eat; this is my body," He meant: This which I offer to you to take and eat is my body. This argument destroys the foundation of the theory of transubstantiation which is held by the Catholic Church, since the bread is not the body of Christ. Rightly understood, however, we may properly say that the sacramental bread is the body of Christ. These expressions have been used by the early Church Fathers and also by Luther. Luther made use of the expression in order to emphasize the reality of the bread in his controversy with the Catholics. He also made use of it against Carlstadt, who excluded the bread from the complex subject in the words of the institution. For this reason the *Formula of Concord* makes use of the following terms: "That the bread does not signify the absent body of Christ and the wine the absent blood of Christ, but that on account of the sacramental union the bread and the wine are truly the body and blood of Christ."[111] Let it not be understood, however, that Luther and others intended to say that *τοῦτο* referred only to *ἄρτος*. The argument concerning *τοῦτο* holds in relation to all the parallel passages that bear on this subject. Compare Matt. 26:26; Mark 14:22; Luke 22:19; 1 Cor. 11:24; Matt. 26:28; Mark 14:24; Luke 22:20; 1 Cor. 11:25. In objecting to this doctrine some theologians have made use of Luke 22:20. In answer we would say that there is no real parallel, inasmuch as the subject in the

[111] Epitome VII: 2.

passage referred to is: "This cup," while the predicate is not the blood of Christ but "The new covenant in my blood." The same reasoning holds with regard to 1 Cor. 10:16, where "bread" is the subject, but where the body of Christ is not the predicate, but "A communion of the body of Christ."

It is necessary for us also to examine the grammatical significance of the copula ἐστίν or "is" in the words of the institution. Zwingli and those like-minded with him have translated this word with signifies, symbolizes, etc. But "is" means "is" and cannot mean anything else. There is no translation of acknowledged worth which translates ἐστίν in the words of the institution with "signifies" or "symbolizes." There is no impartial dictionary which gives "signifies" as a translation of ἐστίν. In making a comprehensive study of the passages where the cupola is used we shall find that that verb must have its literal meaning. If this verb were to be translated with signifies or symbolizes, then the sense of the Word of God would be changed wherever this copula is used. When our Lord says that He is the true vine, we should read: I am a symbol of the true vine. God is a Spirit would be translated: God is a symbol of a Spirit, etc. The copula must be understood in a literal sense even in a metaphor. For example, in Luke 8:11 we read: "The seed is the word of God." The seed is literally the Word of God. But the seed is not seed in a literal sense, since in that case it could not be the Word of God; the reference is to the seed of the Gospel. Hence in expounding the meaning of the copula "is" in accordance with its literal sense we must say that the words of Jesus, "This is my body," really mean that it is His body. There is no foundation for the Zwinglian theory. If there were a simile or metaphor in the sentence it should be found in the word "body." The question then arises as to whether the real body of Christ is to be understood in a literal sense. If the body that was given for us was the body of Christ in a true sense, then it follows that the body which is given in the Lord's Supper must also be the true body of Christ. The words of the institution make this perfectly clear. Inasmuch as it was the true body of Jesus Christ which was given for us, therefore we must understand the word "body" literally. The words of the institution are not a metaphor. For the same reason also it is His true blood that is imparted in the Sacrament, inasmuch as it was His true blood that was shed for us. It has been alleged that the Lutheran Church interprets the first part of the words of the institution literally, while she interprets the latter part concerning the cup figuratively. But this is not the case, for the word cup means not only cup in a literal sense but by metonymy also that which is contained in the cup. This agrees also with the words of the institution when Jesus took the cup and said: "Drink ye all of it."[112]

The words of the institution, therefore, make it perfectly clear that the sacramental objects in the Lord's Supper are the body and blood of Christ. When theologians make use of different expressions, such as natural body and glorified body, we must still bear in mind that the body is the same,viz., the body which suffered on the cross and was given for our sake. The characterizations "true" and "natural" as applied to the body of Christ have reference to its essence, while "glorified" has reference to its state or *conditio*. The body did not become another body through glorification. After the glorification of the body of Christ, however, those divine attributes which were imparted at the incarnation remain in continual operation.

Inasmuch as there are two sacramental objects we must exercise care lest in our conception we dissolve the union between the body and blood of Christ. Christ is a living personality whose body and blood are imparted in a sacramental way. The Christ who is present in the Holy Supper was dead, but lives throughout all eternity. At the same time it is necessary to observe the twofold manner in which the sacramental gifts of grace are imparted, inasmuch as the Lord's Supper is both a *κοινωνία τοῦ αἵματος* and a *κοινωνία τοῦ σώματος*.

5) *The sacramental objects are really present in the Lord's Supper.* The tenth article of the Augsburg Confession expresses this presence as *vere adsint* or, in German, wahrhaftiglich gegenwärtig sei. The Apology adds

[112] As collateral reading study Krauth's *Conservative Ref.*, pp. 692—707.

et substantialiter.[113] The possibility of the real presence of the body and blood of Christ in the Lord's Supper is scientifically proven through the doctrine concerning *communicatio idiomatum.* A clear light is shed on the real presence of Christ in the Holy Supper by a careful consideration of *genus majesticum.* By reason of the fact that the human nature of Christ was made partaker of the divine attributes, therefore Christ as to His entire person, including also His human nature, is omnipresent in a divine manner. However, the human nature has not lost its attributes, for which reason the body of Christ, and therefore in a sense Christ Himself, is definitively present in heaven and in this sense shall remain there until, in accordance with His promise, He shall again return. Our Church has never denied the reality of the ascension. It has, furthermore, never taught that Christ is locally present on the earth or in the Lord's Supper. Neither has our Church taught that Christ has two bodies, one absent and the other present, nor that the body of Christ is omnipresent in an extensive sense. But on the ground of *unio personalis* and *communio naturarum* she teaches that the human nature of Christ is absent in one mode but present in another mode. In one sense Christ has left us, while in another He is present with us always, even unto the end of the world. He has ascended into heaven, and yet He fills all space. The fullness of the Godhead dwells in Him bodily, and just as the divine nature is present on earth and everywhere without departing from the heavenly abode, so the human nature is likewise present everywhere through the divine nature. The presence is substantial and yet not local. By reason of the essential attributes of the two natures these two modes of being present are equally real and substantial, inasmuch as the person of Christ cannot be divided nor His natures separated from each other. What Christ is in accordance with the one nature He is also in accordance with the other. The presence of the human nature on the earth through the divine nature, with which it constitutes one person, is just as real as its presence in heaven on account of its own attributes. We may speak of the divine presence as

[113] Müller, *Symb. Bücher,* 164, 54.

being substantial or phenomenal and operative. The substantial may exist without the phenomenal, but not the latter without the former. Krauth says: "God's substantial presence is alike everywhere. But His phenomenal presence varies in degree. 'Our Father who art in Heaven' marks His purest phenomenal presence, as making that home to which our hearts aspire. As there is phenomenal presence, so there is phenomenal absence; hence, God Himself is frequently represented in Scripture as withdrawing Himself, and as absent, though, in His essence, He neither is, nor can be, absent from any part of the Universe. The absence of God is, so to speak, a relative absence, a phenomenal absence; the tokens of providence and grace by which this presence was actualized, not only to faith, but even to experience, are withdrawn. So the natural phenomenal tokens of the presence of the undivided Christ are withdrawn, yet He is still present substantially, and as thus present is operative in the supernatural phenomena of His grace."[114] By reason of the ubiquitous presence of Christ He may also be specially present for a specific purpose. The substantial presence becomes specifically operative through means. In the Lord's Supper the substantial presence becomes operative graciously in a sacramental way. The specific gift of sacramental impartation, or the body and blood of Christ, is bestowed upon all the communicants in the Lord's Supper, but the whole Christ is present in the Sacrament and is received spiritually through faith. The question here merely concerns the sacramental presence. In the Lord's Supper there is no question of His glorified presence, nor of His hypostatical presence, nor yet of His merely spiritual presence, and still less of His apprehensive presence, the question is as to whether the true body and blood of Christ are present in such mode as to their actual substance that they are really imparted in, with, and under the bread and wine. The Lutheran Church teaches that the body and blood of Christ are really present, not in a physical, local and circumscriptive sense, but in a supernatural, illocal, and definitely sacramental mode. With regard to the objection that the ubiquity of Christ

[114] *Conservative Reformation*, p. 813.

as to His entire person militates against a special and real presence of His body and blood in the Lord's Supper, Hollazius says: "There is no contradiction in maintaining that He is omnipresent, and nevertheless is presented to a particular person by a special kind of presence. For thus we read that the omnipresent Holy Spirit descended on Christ in the form of a dove, was communicated to the apostles under the form of fiery tongues, and dwells truly and by His gracious presence in the bodies of the godly. Although, therefore, a general omnipresence is communicated to the assumed flesh of Christ by reason of the personal union, yet that does not prevent or destroy a special and sacramental presence of the body of Christ."[115]

The objection has been made that the communication of the body and blood of Christ at the institution of the Lord's Supper was different from that which now occurs, since Christ ascended into heaven. The objection implies that Christ could not communicate His true body and blood while He Himself sat or lay at the table at the Paschal feast. But the communication was the same and the mode the same as now occurs. It was the same body and the same blood. The possibility of the first communication is explained in the same way as all subsequent communications, viz., through *genus majesticum*. At the institution of the Lord's Supper, Christ, also in accordance with His human nature, used the divine attributes which had been communicated to this nature in the incarnation. That which occurred then, seemingly so wonderful and incomprehensible, was no more miraculous and supernatural than what occurs now. Whether Christ is phenomenally near or far away at the Lord's Supper, this neither increases nor diminishes His substantial presence or His definitely sacramental presence. Our material sense cannot decide this. There is much in the material world which cannot be perceived by our material senses; why should there not be possible a supernatural presence without our senses perceiving it? There are many thinkers embracing the theories of the idealistic philosophy who

[115] *Exam. Theol. Acroam.* Pars III, §2, Cap. V, Qu. XII, p. 605.

acknowledge in philosophy what they reject in religion. The questions at issue may not be identical, but they nevertheless present phases that in some respects are analogous. Men are ready to accept the dogmatic assertions of philosophy, but with regard to the Christian doctrines they demand observation and experiment.

There have been some misconceptions concerning the presence of Christ as being Capernaitic* (the physical mode of eating and drinking).[116] But even nature teaches us that the same substance under different conditions may possess different attributes. For example, we may consider the different states in which we find water, whether as plain water, ice or steam, or we may think of its component elements, such as the oxygen and the hydrogen, still it is the same water. The body of Christ was of the same substance after His resurrection as before, but possessed of pneumatic attributes. The divine power can perform wonders in the natural world, and what shall we say of the supernatural world? Science with all its discoveries is still in many cases stumbling at letters; it finds it difficult to place them together to form words and still more difficult to formulate the words into sentences. New discoveries are being made continually. Our knowledge of the ether, which pervades all things, sheds a new light on many things that formerly were enigmatical. We must, however, remember that the omnipresence of God as well as the sacramental presence of Christ can never be explained in a natural way, but we must believe the Word of Almighty God. There is no satisfactory and complete analogy. Luther speaks of the substance of the bread and the wine being permeated with the substance of the body and blood of Christ as the iron is permeated with heat in the forge or as the crystal is bathed with light in being held up to the sun. The whole substance of the sunlight is in the crystal and yet it is not localized in the ordinary way. In

---

[116] "Capernaitic mode" was the false conception of spiritual eating and drinking by some persons in Capernaum. They thought that Christ meant the eating and drinking of natural flesh and blood. Compare John 6:52. In the Supper the body and blood, unlike the bread and wine, are not subject to mastication, etc., although we teach *manducatio oralis*. Compare 8) *Manducatio oralis*.

the same way the whole substance of the body of Christ permeates the bread and the whole substance of the blood of Christ permeates the wine. On the basis of God's Word, however, we are certain that the body and blood of Christ are present in the Lord's Supper.

6) *The bread and wine are vehicles of the heavenly elements.* The tenth article of the Augsburg Confession makes use of the words, "*unter der Gestalt des Brots und Weins.*" The Formula of Concord uses the word *species.*[117] *Species* corresponds to *Gestalt.* The tenth article of the Augsburg Confession sets forth that the earthly elements are bread and wine in a real sense and not their accidents. Both of the elements are equally emphasized, for which reason the Confessions reject the Catholic doctrine of de *concomitantia.* Inasmuch as each element is the special vehicle of its own gift, therefore both of the elements must be used. The bread is the bearer of the body of Christ and not the blood, while the wine is the bearer of the blood of Christ and not the body. The Lutheran doctrine corresponds to the words of Paul in 1 Cor. 10:16: "The cup of blessing which we bless, is it not a communion of the blood of Christ? The bread which we break, is it not a communion of the body of Christ?" In this passage both of the elements are mentioned. That which serves as a means of communication cannot be identical with that which is communicated. This passage, therefore, militates against the doctrine of transubstantiation. It likewise makes untenable the position of the Calvinists concerning the Lord's Supper. According to this latter theory the Holy Ghost communicates the body and the blood of Christ, but in accordance with Paul the bread and the wine are the vehicles of the heavenly elements. Calvin says that faith is the means of mediation and that only the believers receive the heavenly elements. In consequence the unbelievers receive only the bread and wine. But Paul says expressly that there are some who eat and drink unto themselves judgment, not discerning the body of Christ. In accordance with Calvin the Lord's Supper is a communion of power which proceeds from Christ, while in accordance with Paul it is a communion of the body

[117] Müller, *Symb. Bücher*, p. 674. 126.

and blood of Christ.

Objections have been made to the use of the expression "in, with and under" the bread and wine. The Lutheran Church, by this expression, simply intends to set forth that the sacramental bread and wine are the vehicles of the body and blood of Christ. Our Church does not lay special emphasis on any one word of this expression but equal emphasis on all. The Formula of Concord explains the use of the expression "in, with and under" as being negative terms in relation to the Catholic and the Reformed positions, but also as positive terms as setting forth the union of the earthly and the heavenly elements.[118] Inasmuch as there is a sacramental union, the body and the blood of Christ are not communicated by the side of or independent of the bread and the wine, but "in, with and under" the bread and wine.

7) The heavenly elements are received by all the communicants. The Augsburg Confession uses the expression *distribuantur vescentibus*, while the Formula of Concord expressly sets forth the doctrine of *communio impiorum*. It is not the faith of men that makes the Word of God a means of grace, nor the Sacraments means of grace and Sacraments. When the Word of God is preached and read it becomes to some the savor from death unto death, to others the savor from life unto life. The sick and the well may eat of the same wholesome food, but to the former it may act as poison, while the latter are nourished and strengthened by it. A lump of gold or a precious diamond may come into the possession of a person who does not appreciate their value, and yet their value remains the same. There were many who came in contact with our Lord when He was on the earth, but all did not experience the effects of His healing and gracious power. The same holds true with regard to the Lord's Supper. Compare 1 Cor. 11:27-30: "Wherefore whosoever shall eat the bread or drink the cup of the Lord in an unworthy manner, shall be guilty of the body and the blood of the Lord. But let a man prove himself, and so let him eat of the bread, and drink of the cup. For he that eateth and drinketh, eateth

[118] Müller, *Symb. Bücher*, p. 654, 35-40.

and drinketh judgment unto himself, if he discern not the body. For this cause many among you are weak and sickly, and not a few sleep." This passage proves conclusively that those who participate unworthily in the Lord's Supper nevertheless receive the body and blood of Christ. The question has been raised as to whether Judas was present at the Lord's Supper and received the elements. Matthew and Mark tell of how Jesus sat at meat with the twelve disciples, but say nothing of His departure. In the beginning of his gospel Luke states that he has made an accurate investigation of all things from the first and that he purposed to write an orderly narrative. According to him, immediately after the Lord's Supper Jesus said: "But behold, the hand of him that betrayeth me is with me on the table" (Luke 22:21). The Gospel of John contains no account of the Lord's Supper, for which reason the statement in John 13:30 cannot be considered decisive in the determination of the presence or the absence of Judas at the Supper itself. Hence special importance attaches to the narratives of the Synoptics. It would therefore seem to be almost certain that Judas was a communicant at the first Supper of the Lord. In any case the doctrine of the Confession is in accord with the Word of God.

8) *Manducatio oralis.* The Formula of Concord makes use of this expression. Just as the reception of the Word of God is mediated through the ear and the eye, so it is necessary that the Lord's Supper be mediated in some manner. The only possible way is by means of *manducatio oralis,* since the elements must necessarily be taken through the mouth. The bread and the wine are received by the mouth immediately and naturally; the body and the blood of Christ are received mediately and supernaturally. The eating is spiritual in opposition to the Capernaitic theory of manducation; but it is likewise real in opposition to the purely spiritual theory of manducation as held in the Reformed doctrine of the Lord's Supper.

5. The Effect and Object of the Lord's Supper.

The Sacrament of Baptism is called *sacramentum regenerationis* and the Sacrament of the Lord's Supper is called *sacramentum confirmationis et nutritionis*. In this latter term is expressed the general purpose of the Lord's Supper. The finis et effectus of this Sacrament are divided and defined as follows: 1) *finis et effectus principalis*: a) the confirmation of the Gospel promises concerning the forgiveness of sins and the strengthening of faith; b) communion with Christ, spiritual nourishment unto life everlasting and the confirmation of the hope of a blessed resurrection. There are some theologians who declare that the effect is twofold, inasmuch as there is a twofold *κοινωνία*. In this respect the feast of the Passover is supposed to have been a type. The blood of the sacrificial lamb meant atonement, while the eating of the flesh, according to Kurtz, on account of the atonement meant the closest communion with Jehovah, a sharing, so to speak, of one's house and board with God. In the Lord's Supper it is expressly stated: "This is my blood of the covenant, which is poured out for many unto remission of sins." Inasmuch as the wine, which is the symbol of refreshing, as a vehicle communicates the blood of Christ, therefore the believer receives an earnest of the forgiveness of his sins. In the forgiveness of sins through the atoning blood faith finds its hypostasis and sure foundation. The bread, which is the symbol of nutrition, as a vehicle communicates the body of Christ, through which the believer is spiritually nourished unto everlasting life; 2) *finis minus principalis*: a) the commemoration of the death of Jesus in meditation and testimony (Luke 22:19; 1 Cor. 11:25, 26); b) the strengthening of the bond of union among the believers. Cf. 1 Cor. 10:17: "Seeing that we, who are many, are one bread, one body: for we all partake of the one bread"; c) the hopeful assurance of the perfect communion with the Lord Jesus in His kingdom, since the Lord's Supper is not simply a feast of remembrance but also of promise. Cf. Luke 22:15-20; 3) *finis ultimus* is the eternal salvation of the communicants.

The effects and the design of the Lord's Supper are fulfilled if the Sacrament is participated in worthily and the communicant remains faithful even unto the end. All the communicants receive the body and blood of Christ, but only the believers, whether their faith be weak or strong, enjoy the blessed effects of the Lord's Supper. It is also true that the believers may under the varying circumstances of life be more or less receptive to the effects of the Sacrament. It may also happen that a believer may not prove equally worthy at all times. Possibly the chastisement that is described in 1 Cor. 11:30 is sometimes visited upon careless and weak Christians because of the fact that they are forgetful as to their conduct in the house of the Lord and in the holy of holies. The judgments of the Lord may differ as to degree, but they are not judgments unto damnation. Compare 1 Cor. 11:32: "But when we are judged, we are chastened of the Lord, that we may not be condemned with the world." It is vitally important to be guided by the judgments of the Lord that a worse thing may not happen to us. On the other hand, the communicant who is dishonest, unrepentant, faithless, and therefore really unworthy, shall be guilty of the body and the blood of the Lord. If he persist in his impenitence his *κρίμα* (judgment) shall become a *κατάκριμα* (condemnation). The believers are always worthy, because they embrace the merit of Christ, and even where there are shortcomings and imperfections in their daily walk and conversation, still they do not receive the Sacrament unto condemnation. It is only the unbelievers who are unworthy in the real sense. When Luther in his Small Catechism sets forth faith as the condition of true worthiness and as constituting the proper preparation for the Holy Supper, he does not thereby determine the degree of faith, but merely its necessity. The spiritual eating as set forth in John 6:53-58 is regularly a prerequisite for a worthy participation in the Lord's Supper. But faith has many degrees. The Formula of Concord, Epitome VII, Affirmative 9, says in this connection: "We believe, teach and confess that no true believer, as long as he retain living faith, however weak he may be, receives the Holy Supper to his judgment, which was instituted especially for Christians weak in faith, and yet penitent, for the consolation and strengthening of their weak faith."[119]t

6. Notes on the History of Dogma.

---

[119] Müller, *Symb. Bücher*, p. 541, 19.

During the first or the Apologetic period the Church Fathers in general held realistic views and taught that both the earthly and heavenly elements were communicated and received in the Lord's Supper. From the time of Cyprian the Holy Supper came to be looked upon as a sacrifice which the priest offered. With a few exceptions the Church Fathers during the Polemical period also adopted a realistic view of the Lord's Supper. They did not support the theory of transubstantiation, although their expressions might be so interpreted. The Lord's Supper was compared to the incarnation of Christ, but their views concerning the relationship of the natures of the Lord prove that the comparison was used as an analogy of the realistic theory. They also taught that the unworthy communicants receive the body and blood of Christ. The effects of the Lord's Supper are both spiritual and bodily. There were several who taught that the Lord's Supper was a repetition of the sacrifice of Christ on the cross. During the Scholastic period the doctrine of the Roman Church was more definitely developed. After the time of Paschasius Radbertus the theory of transubstantiation became generally adopted, although there were many opponents to the theory. The doctrine was further developed by Hildebert of Tours and Lanfrank. After the Lateran Council in 1215 the doctrine of transubstantiation received general and official acknowledgment and sanction. It was customary, in support of the position of the Catholic Church in withholding the cup from the laity, to set forth the doctrine of de *concomitantia*, or that the whole Christ is present in the bread and the wine. The argument was urged that in a body flesh and blood are never separated from each other. Inasmuch as the Lord's Supper constituted a renewed sacrifice of Christ, therefore the doctrine of the sacrifice of the mass together with its consequences was developed. The Protestants rejected these views, but while the so-called ultra-Protestants went to extremes in different directions, the Lutheran Reformation took a conservative position which brought about a return to the doctrine of the early Church such as it was set forth during the Apostolic and the Apologetic periods. Luther presented his doctrine of the Lord's Supper in his work *Das grosse Bekentniss vom Abendmal*, in his catechisms, etc. Zwingli set forth the symbolic theory and Calvin the dynamic theory. Melanchthon's doctrine differed from that of Luther, although possibly in his heart he supported the Lutheran position. In accordance with Melanchthon and Calvin the bread and the wine are not vehicles of the heavenly elements. Melanchthon's position exerted its influence on the Crypto-Calvinists, who made use of expressions as found in his writings, such as "in the act of the administration of the Lord's Supper," "in connection with" or "cum." The Crypto-Calvinists rejected the doctrine of a substantial presence and a real eating and drinking of the body and the blood of Christ, while they asserted that Christ was present merely *spiritualiter per fidem*. The Formula of Concord set forth the Lutheran position against the Sacramentarians. The Arminians, Socinians, and others in the main adopted the Zwinglian symbolic view. The Socinians prepared the way for the Rationalists, who laid stress simply on the beauty of the Sacrament as a ceremonial in remembrance of the Lord. The Supranaturalists taught merely the operative presence of Christ and laid stress on His moral influence. The mediating theologians adopted the doctrines of the Reformed Church in various forms. Several of the more recent theologians set forth the effect of the Lord's Supper on man's human nature. All the leading views on the Lord's Supper have their supporters in our own day. However, there has not been any new development of the dogma, although important contributions have been made in an endeavor to render more clear the content of the Sacrament, while all acknowledge that the Lord's Supper is indeed a mystery of faith.

Ignatius held a realistic view of the Lord's Supper. He writes to Smyrna: "They (*docetae*) abstain from the Eucharist and prayer because they do not confess that the Holy Supper is the flesh of our Saviour, Jesus Christ, which suffered for our sins." To Philadelphia he writes: "Hasten ye then to partake of the Eucharist, for there is the one flesh of our Lord Jesus Christ and one cup for the uniting of His blood." He writes to Ephesus: "The breaking of one bread which is the medicine of immortality, the antidote that we should not die, but live in Jesus Christ forever." Justin Martyr sets forth that the body and the blood of Christ are the sacramental objects and that they stand in such relation to the bread and the wine that the reception of the earthly elements implies also the communication of the body and the blood of Christ. Irenaeus taught that there is a *copraesentia* between the two elements and that the earthly elements are the means by which the heavenly elements are mediated. The effect is supernatural and extends both to the soul and the body. He sets forth the importance of the consecration. Tebtullian is held to lean toward a symbolic interpretation of the Sacrament, but it is not very evident, because he refers to Jer. 11:19 in the Septuagint, where the Jews say: "Come, let us put wood upon his bread."[120] He states that this passage undoubtedly has reference to the body of Christ, inasmuch as God reveals this in the Gospels where the bread is called His body. Tertullian says that the tree is the cross and the bread the body of Christ. He sets forth that Christ explained this mystery in the Lord's Supper. The bread of the prophet is identified as the bread of the Sacrament. Since the one is His true body, i.e., Christ's, so is also the other. Cyprian was the first to set forth the Lord's Supper as a sacrifice in the real sense. At that time it was customary in the Communion prayers to pray for the Christians who were dead, and in this manner the way was prepared for the masses for the dead. Origen looked upon the Supper as a symbolic act.

Eusebius of Caesarea, Basil, and Gregory oNazianzus favored the spiritualistic or figurative view of the Lord's Supper. Gregory of Nyssa says that the bread and the wine are transformed into the body and the blood of Christ, but he regards the transformation as being analogous to the incarnation of Christ. Cyril of Jerusalem compares the transformation in the Lord's Supper to the changing of the water to wine at Cana. He does not have in mind the change implied in transubstantiation. Ambrose also speaks of a change, saying: "When we receive the bread and the cup we receive and partake of the body of Christ." He also sets forth the significance of the consecration and how the Word of God produces the Sacrament. Chrysostom, who held a realistic view of the Sacrament,

---

[120] Adv. Marcion, III, XIX.

says: "That which is in the cup is the same as that which flowed from His side, and of this we become partakers." Augustine taught that the Lord's Supper consists of two species, the one visible, the other invisible, as the person of Christ consists of God and man. He also speaks of the Sacrament from the symbolic viewpoint, although he did not consider it simply as a memorial. Theodoret pointed out that Judas also received the body and the blood of Christ. He advocated in a modified form the theory of consubstantiation to be apprehended by faith. Leo the Great speaks of *manducatio oralis*. Gelasius and Gregory the Great advocated the doctrine of a transformation. John of Damascus taught as follows: "As the body is united with the Logos, so we are united with Him (Christ) through the bread. The Lord's Supper is a real communion because through the same we commune with Christ and become partakers of His body."

Paschasius Radbertus taught that the bread and the wine are transformed and simply appear to be bread and wine. An absorption takes place which obliterates the substance of the earthly elements. The transformation involves a potential creation. However, he denied an oral eating and drinking in the sense that the body of Christ was masticated with the teeth. His theory of transformation contains nevertheless an inconsistency, inasmuch as he declares that the unbelievers receive only bread and wine. Ratramnus taught that the bread and the wine are only in a figurative sense the body and the blood of Christ. Rabanus Maurus and Scotus Erigena held the same view. Berengar also combatted the position of Paschasius and adopted a figurative interpretation. Hildebert of Tours used the term transubstantiation. Lanfbank developed the doctrine of transubstantiation, set forth the whole presence of Christ and taught that the unbelievers become partakers of the body and blood of Christ. Guitmund taught that the whole body of Christ is present in the host and in every part of it. Ansei.m supported the doctrine of transubstantiation together with the view that the whole Christ is imparted in all places wheresoever the Lord's Supper is celebrated. The whole Christ, both as to His divine and human nature, is present in both elements. Peter Lombard taught the same and considered that only bread was necessary in the celebration of the Sacrament. Innocent III sanctioned the doctrine of transubstantiation in 1215. Thomas Aquinas taught that transubstantiation was effected by means of a special inherent power in the consecration. That the bread and the wine retained their accidental properties was dependent on the power of God. The body of Christ is to be found in every small particle of the bread. He also speaks of a sacrifice that is offered by the priest. Occam taught that the body of Christ is to be found in the host in a definitive and not in a circumscriptive sense. Gabriel Biel stated that transubstantiation took place by reason of the divine power which was imparted to the words of institution at the time of the institution of the Lord's Supper. He also said that a succession takes place in the Sacrament, the substance of the bread and the wine being succeeded by the body and blood of Christ. The *Roman Catholic* doctrine of the Lord's Supper contains, therefore, the following points: 1) *transubstantiatio,* or that through the consecration the substance of the bread and the wine is transformed into the substance of the body and the blood of Christ, so that it is not necessary for Christ to descend to the earth. The accidents of the bread and the wine remain, however, and this is regarded as a special miracle; 2) *de concomitantia.* This doctrine implies that the whole Christ is present in both the bread and the wine, so that each element is both the body and blood of Christ; 3) *communio sub una specie,* or that the cup is withheld from the laity. The officiating priest drinks of the cup, but when he himself communes, he receives only the bread. Only the cardinals receive both elements, when the Pope himself officiates on Holy Thursday; 4) the Lord's Supper as a *sacrificium,* or the repetition of the sacrifice of Christ; 5) the adoration of the host; 6) the effect of the Lord's Supper produced *ex opere operato.* Its celebration is considered a meritorious deed; 7) faith is not sufficient for a suitable preparation for the Lord's Supper; good works are likewise necessary.

Luther wrote several works on the Lord's Supper, but his doctrine of the Sacrament appears for the first time in a more developed form in the year 1528, in the work entitled, "*Das grosse Bekentniss vom Abendmahl,*" in which he sets forth the doctrine of the omnipresence of God and Christ.

He also stated that the "right hand" of God is everywhere, that the Word of God is firm and certain and that there are many modes in which God may be present. He defines the difference between the circumscriptive, the definitive, and the repletive presence. The definitive presence is the spiritual mode in which God is present in the Lord's Supper. He rejects the theories of impanation and consubstantiation and calls the union of the elements sacramental. He regards the use of the word "this" in the words of the institution as being a synecdoche. He taught that all the communicants receive the body and the blood of Christ. For further reference see his catechisms. Zwingli considered the Lord's Supper as a memorial and as a feast of confession and thanksgiving. The word "is" in the words of the institution is equivalent to "signifies" or "symbolizes." Zwingli declares that he became convinced that such was the case through a revelation or a dream concerning the meaning of Ex. 12:11, which reads: "It is Jehovah's passover." The subject "it" in this passage refers to the lamb, while the verb "is" is equivalent to "symbolizes." But the verb is not expressed in the original text, but has to be supplied, and in such case cannot have the meaning that Zwingli ascribes to it. Furthermore, the subject "it" in this passage denotes the whole complex action and not merely the lamb. Oecolampadius accepted the symbolical view of the Sacrament and interpreted the word body by metonymy as a sign of the body. Calvin says that the bread and wine in the Sacrament are assurances that the Lord imparts still greater gifts through the bread and wine. There is a potency that proceeds from the glorified body of Christ. The body of Christ cannot actually be present in the Lord's Supper. The impartation of the power of Christ is mediated through the Holy Spirit. On the human side the reception of the divine gift of the Sacrament is mediated through faith. The unbelievers receive only bread and wine. Melanchthon taught that the body and the blood of Christ are presented with the bread and wine. In the Variata we read: "Concerning the Lord's Supper we teach that with the bread and wine the body and blood of Christ are truly presented (*exhibeantur*) to those that participate in the Lord's Supper." He rejected the Lutheran expressions *vere adsint et distribuantur*.

He declared that Christ was present in the sacramental action, and made use of the word *cum* as signifying the connection between the elements, but the bread and wine are not vehicles of the heavenly elements. The most important thing in the Lord's Supper is the living communion with Christ. Schwenkfeld reversed the order in the words of the institution, making the subject the predicate, and vice versa, the sentence reading, "My body is this." John Scaliger taught that even before the distribution, and therefore independent of the distribution, the body and blood of Christ afe united with the bread and the wine through the consecration. The Formula of Concord confirms the expressions of the other Confessions and clearly sets forth the real and substantial presence together with its corollaries, *manducatlo oralis* and *communio impiorum*. *In*, *cum*, and *sub* are employed for the purpose of saying that the earthly elements are real vehicles of the heavenly elements, as well as for combatting the Catholic doctrine of transubstantiation on the one hand, and the spiritualizing tendencies of the Reformed Church on the other. The doctrine of the Lord's Supper is made clear through the doctrine of the person of Christ. It is stated that the body and blood are in *coena Domini*, but the use is emphasized. For further reference, see the Formula of Concord, chapter VII, both the affirmative and negative declarations. The *Socinians* deal with the Lord's Supper as a memorial. The subject "this" in the words of the institution refers to the breaking of the bread and the pouring of the wine. The Arminians taught the same with regard to the significance of the Lord's Supper as a memorial and a confession. The soul is nourished spiritually by the body and blood of Christ.

The *Rationalists* deny the real presence of Christ. At the first Supper the disciples could not indeed believe that the body and blood of Christ were imparted. The doctrine of the Lord's Supper which is taught in the orthodox Church has come about through the dreams of the Scholastics. The *Supernaturalists* departed from the Lutheran doctrine of the Lord's Supper and reduced the presence of Christ to a general and operative presence, just as the sun produces its effects upon us without being near us. Kant believed that the object of the Lord's Supper was to unite mankind into a mundane ethical society, thereby awakening the spirit of brotherly love among men. Schleiermacher emphasized the living communion with Christ, which communion was strengthened through the Lord's Supper as against the baleful influences of the world. Kahnis did not support the strictly Lutheran position on the Lord's Supper. At the same time he rejected the Zwinglian interpretation of the verb "is" in the words of the institution. He says that the bread and the wine are not simply symbols but media, by means of which through the Holy Spirit we appropriate unto ourselves the glorified humanity of Christ, but not that we immediately eat and drink the body and blood of Christ. The body of Christ communicated in the Supper is eucharistic. The eating and drinking are spiritual. He endeavors to combine the views of Luther, Zwingli, and Calvin. Martensen says that the whole Christ and the power of His resurrection are to be found in the two earthly elements. The Lord's Supper is not simply a memorial, nor yet an earnest and assurance, but it is a true union with Christ which is the principle of the marriage between the Spirit and nature. The nourishment provided in the Lord's Supper also exercises its influence on the future resurrection body. Thomasius sets forth the effect of the Lord's Supper both in a bodily and spiritual sense. Since, in accordance with 1 Cor. 11:28-32 (especially v. 30), the unworthy participation in the Lord's Supper brought about such judgments as bodily sickness and even death, therefore a worthy participation must bring God's blessing and exercise a wholesome influence upon the whole man. Schartau says in relation to a worthy participation in the Lord's Supper that all that is necessary for the seeker after salvation is to have experienced the first enlightenment of the Holy Spirit, which implies a desire to hear and read the Word of God together with an initial faith and desire to participate in the Holy Supper. Billing distinguishes between the spiritual and the sacramental eating in the Lord's Supper and declares that the former is necessary in order that we may receive the Sacrament worthily and enjoy its benefits. He states that the spiritual eating is necessary, not because this mode of eating constitutes the Holy Supper a Sacrament, but in order that the Sacrament may prove a blessing to the communicant.

That which makes a man worthy in his participation of the Lord's Supper is faith and nothing but faith. He adds that the degree of faith, whether it be weak or strong, does not constitute a criterion of worthiness, inasmuch as it is not the quality or the degree of faith which renders a communicant worthy; rather that which makes worthy is to be found in the merit of Christ, which is appropriated by faith, by the strong faith no more than by the weak faith. Bring says that in the Lord's Supper are communicated the same body and blood as constituted the human or bodily side of the person of Christ while He sojourned here upon earth, but in the condition of a glorified body and a glorified blood. The fact that the body and blood are glorified marks them off as being permeated with spirit, life, and light, without lacking any essential thing which belongs to any bodily substance. The union of the elements, although not hypostatic, may nevertheless be compared to the union which is effected between the divine and human natures of Christ. As they are received the body and the blood of Christ are indissolubly and inseparably, yet without mixture or transformation, united with the bread and wine. With regard to the purpose of the Sacrament he states that not only are spiritual-bodily gifts imparted, but through their mediation spiritual-bodily effects are also produced. In like manner as the atoning work of Christ and the Holy Spirit's work of sanctification embrace the whole of man, so the gifts which are communicated in the Lord's Supper affect not only the soul, but also the body. The new life produced in Baptism, both the spiritual and the bodily, is nourished and strengthened. The Lord's Supper likewise produces its effect on the seed of life which in the resurrection unites the old body with the new. Bring does not assert that this can be proved, but he gives it as his dogmatic opinion. With regard to the spiritual effect of the Lord's Supper in strengthening the spiritual relationship with Christ he says that as the branch continuously receives new life from the vine, thereby becoming more powerfully attached to and imbedded in the vine, so the believer's union with Christ is strengthened and the new life grows in breadth and length and depth and height. He holds forth faith as the condition of enjoying the blessing of the Lord's Supper, but remarks that faith may be only longing and hungering.

§39. The Office of the Ministry.

The Lord has not only given to the Church the Word of God and the Sacraments, but He has also provided for their administration and therefore established the office of the ministry. The ministry is therefore not a human institution, nor is it a provision made by the Church by reason of the requirements of the situation. The ministry arose with the Church and the Church with the ministry, but the ministry is not extraneous to the Church and independent of it, rather it is found within the Church and belongs to it. The existence of the ministry is, however, not dependent on any decision of the Church; it is a permanent institution in the same sense as the Church itself. While therefore the Church as the subject of the ministry is the medium through which the perpetuity of the ministry is mediated, still the ministry forms such an integral part of the life of the Church that a normal Church cannot be found without the office of the ministry.

1. Definition of the Ministry.

The Ministry is *that office instituted by the Lord to which He has entrusted the administration of the means of grace, in which office, through the mediation of the Church by means of ordination, suitable, and educated men are placed who shall devote all their powers to the upbuilding of the Church and to the glory of God.* Baier defines the office of the ministry as follows: "*Ministerium ecclesiasticum* is the public office instituted by God in which certain persons, legally called and ordained, teach the Word of God, administer the Sacraments, remit and retain sins, care for and arrange for other matters in the work of the Church, unto the conversion, sanctification and eternal salvation of men."[121] *Causa efficiens principalis* is the Triune

---

[121] *Comp. Theol. Posit.* Pars III, Cap. xiv, §15.

God and especially Christ. *Causa minus principalis* is the Church of Christ.

2. The Call To The Ministry.

1) *Necessitas vocationis.* The 14th article of the Augsburg Confession contains the following declaration with regard to the necessity of the call: "Of Ecclesiastical Order, they teach, that no one should publicly teach in the Church or administer the Sacraments, unless he be regularly called." In the administration of the office of the ministry it is not sufficient to belong to the universal priesthood of believers, although no one should be called to the ministry who is not a spiritual priest. All Christians, men and women, old or young, are spiritual priests, but they do not therefore possess the right to administer the means of grace, even if they have an inner call. The inner call must be confirmed by a regular external call. No one can call himself. The call is *necessitas absoluta* and therefore essential in the exercise of the office of the ministry.

2) *Attributa vocations*: a) *interna et externa*; b) *immediata et mediata*. God has called immediately and can do so. However, this immediate call belongs to extraordinary epochs and has reference to the performance of special tasks, as when the Lord called prophets, apostles, and evangelists, but there is no example of the Lord calling a man immediately to the ordinary office of the ministry. As a rule, therefore, the call is *externa et mediata*. The Church is the medium through which the call is extended. Individual members cannot extend a call, except in extraordinary cases, which very seldom occur; and where they do occur, the sanction of the Church must be secured as soon as circumstances permit. The exceptions form no precedent. Hollazius says: "We must distinguish between the right to call ministers and the exercise of the right.[122] The right to call belongs to the whole Church, and all its ranks and members. But the exercise of the right varies, according to the diverse agreement and custom of the particular Church."

3) *Partes vocationis*: a) *electio*, or the choosing of such as have the

[122] *Exam. Theol. Acroam.* Pars IV, Cap. II, Qu. 7, p. 864.

necessary qualifications, so that through studies and a proper training they may be prepared for a possible call to the office of the ministry; b) *vocatio specialis*, or the external call from a congregation or authorized Church body; c) *ordinatio*, through which the call is confirmed by the whole Church of God, thereby making certain the fact that the candidate is truly *rite vocatus*.

Compare the following Scripture passages: Acts 1:15, 24; 13:3; Rom. 10:15; Acts 14:23; Eph. 4:11, 12; 1 Tim. 3:1-7; 4:14; 2 Tim. 2:2; Titus 1:5. These passages set forth clearly that there prevailed a fixed order in the Church from the beginning. The incumbents of the office of the ministry were called to this service after necessary examination, while the office was entrusted to them in a formal way which we call ordination. Even the seven deacons were inducted into their office (Acts 6:6). In accordance, therefore, with the Word of God and the fourteenth article of the Augsburg Confession those that publicly teach and preach are to be *rite vocati*. With reference to the use of the so-called lay preaching it is necessary for the Church as the subject of the ministry to arrange for such activities. The Schmalkald Articles state that laymen may be used in *casu necessitatis*.

3. More Precise Definition of Ordination.

1) Gerhard defines ordination as follows: "*Ordinatio* is a public and solemn declaration or attestation, through which the ministry of the Church is committed to a suitable person called thereto by the Church, to which he is consecrated by prayer and the laying on of hands, rendered more certain of his lawful call, and publicly, in the sight of the entire Church, solemnly and seriously admonished concerning his duty." Ordination does not induct the ordained pastor into an *ordo* with a character *indelebilis*, but constitutes the official confirmation of the call and sets the ordained apart as a minister *ecclesiae*.

2) *Necessitas ordinationis* is relative, but ordination is not a matter of indifference, inasmuch as it is based on Biblical ground. Of course, it is also based on the symbols of the Church. In these the conception

of ordination is modified by the conception of the ministry, while the conception of the latter is in turn dependent on the conception of the Church. The fifth article of the Augsburg Confession sets forth the divine origin of the ministry and the functions necessary for the obtaining of faith, while the fourteenth article states expressly that the holders of the office of the ministry must be *rite vocati.* A comparison of articles VII and XV will show that the Confession is conservative with regard to ritus, but also truly liberal. The conservatism of the Confession makes clearly manifest the fact that our Church earnestly desired to retain the usages of the Apostolic Church. Compare article XIII (7) 3, 11, 12, where ordination by means of the imposition of hands is in a certain sense looked upon as a Sacrament.

3) The different parts of the act of ordination: a) confession; b) the making of vows; c) consecration through the Word of God and prayer, or *Einsegnung,* as the German theologians express it. Of course, this is not consecration and sanctification in the ordinary sense. Spiritual sanctification is a prerequisite, inasmuch as only a spiritual priest is to be ordained as a *minister ecclesiae.* The consecration has reference to the setting apart for the work of the ministry. The Word and promises of God occupy a central place in ordination and really are constituent elements in the ordination. The ordination prayer establishes the connection between the Word of God and the laying on of hands; d) the imposition of hands after the official commitment of the office of the ministry. The ordained servant of God is set apart through this symbolical act for the service of the Lord, while the content of the Word of God and prayer is applied upon him.

4) The *χάρισμα* of ordination. We may say that this is a special divine gift or blessing to be used in the discharge of the office of the ministry. This gift or blessing must be conserved through the study of the Word and prayer. It is vitally important continuously to *ἀναζωπυρεῖν τὸ χάρισμα.*

In 1 Tim. 4:14 we read: "Neglect not the gift that is in thee, which was given thee by prophecy, with the laying on of the hands of the presbytery." The Word of God contains many promises which apply to ministers. We should study those passages. All these promises belong to the "prophecy." The Lord endows every pastor with some gift. Ministers should "stir up the gift of God" (2 Tim. 1:6). The prayer at ordination was not in vain, but ministers should take care of its blessing. The office committed to a pastor is also a gift and the highest calling on earth. "Be diligent in these things; give thyself wholly to them," etc. (1 Tim. 4:15, 16.

Hollazius says that in the first place ordination is a public declaration and a solemn confirmation of the fact that the candidate for ordination is legally called. Through ordination, however, he is placed not only before the entire congregation but also before the sight of God and set apart from all earthly business and ordained as a servant of God. The commitment of the office stands in the closest relationship with the imposition of hands, which is a sign of the divine blessing for the special task.

4. *Potestas Ministerii Ecclesiastici.*

Dogmaticians present the following points as constituting the content of this *potestas*: 1) *publice docendi*, or the public teaching; 2) *sacramenta ordinarie administrandi*, or the administration of the Sacraments; 3) *munus remittendi et retinendi peccata*, or the power of the keys. The first two points constitute *potestas ordinis*, and the third point is called *potestas jurisdictionis seu clavium*. In a certain sense we may say that the *potestas clavium* belongs to the *potestas ordinis*, but not from the standpoint of church polity. In the last instance, as in case of appeal, the *potestas jurisdictionis* belongs to the common or general Church council, whatever it may be in different Churches.

With regard to the potestas clavium the following is quoted from Hollazius: "The power which ministers of the Church have to remit sins is not absolute (*αὐτοκρατική*), or principal and independent (which belongs to God alone, against whom alone sin is committed), but ministerial and delegated (*διακονική*), by which to contrite and penitent sinners they remit all sins without any reservation of guilt or punishment, not only by way of signification and declaration, but also effectually and really, yet ὀ*ργανικως* (instrumentally)."[123]

5. The Object of the Ministry.

Finis ministerii ecclesiastici is divided as follows: 1) *finis proximus,* which is the reconciliation of men with God through faith in Christ with all that is connected therewith; 2) *finis ultimus,* or the eternal salvation of men to the glory of God. The fifth article of the Augsburg Confession sets forth *finis proximus,* inasmuch as it is there stated that the office of the ministry is instituted in order that men may obtain faith. The words read as follows: "That we may obtain this faith, the office of teaching the Gospel and administering the Sacraments was instituted. For through the Word and the Sacraments as through instruments, the Holy Ghost is given, who worketh faith." Of course, *finis ultimus* is also connected herewith, inasmuch as the servants of the Lord not only labor that men may obtain faith, but also that their souls may be preserved in faith unto the end and that they might gain the final object of their faith or eternal salvation. Compare 2 Cor. 5:20; 11:2; 12:15; Gal. 4:19; Eph. 4:11-16; 1 Tim. 4:16.

6. Notes on the History of Dogma.

The Apostolic Church did not lack an ordered ministry, although many of the members were possessed of special charismatic gifts. In conjunction with the congregations the Apostles appointed elders in the Churches who were the pastors. In accordance with the usage of the Jewish language the pastors were called elders or presbyters, and in accordance with the usage of the Greek they were called bishops. After the death of the Apostles it happened, according to natural development, that certain presbyters occupied more prominent positions than others. In many congregations there were several presbyters, wherefore naturally one of them would become the leader as a *primus inter pares.* Titus as an evangelist had the oversight of several congregations, and by reason of this fact we

[123] *Exam. Theol. Acroam.* Pars IV, Cap. II, Qu. 20, p. 878.

possess the Biblical example of a sort of superintendency, which indeed may also be found in the general oversight exercised by the Apostles themselves. On this account it became customary more and more for the bishops or presbyters in the cities and prominent mission stations to become the leaders at the pastoral conferences. It did not take long before they also were charged with the oversight of congregations in the smaller neighboring provinces, in consequence of which the office of the metropolitan soon came to be established, followed in due course of time by the episcopacy in perfect hierarchical form. While, on the one hand, the Word of God presents the office of the presbyter as being identical with that of the bishop, the historical development, on the other hand, very soon tended toward the view that the bishop was the superior of the presbyter *jure divino* and not simply *jure humano*. Distinctions in rank became the order of the day. The episcopal structure of Cyprian lacked a capstone which was nevertheless soon supplied in the Roman primate. The Roman Catholic Church regards the office of the ministry from the point of view of the Old Testament, viz., as a *sacerdotium*. Vast importance is attached to the apostolic succession mediated through the episcopal ordination. The priests are mediators between God and men. The Protestants set forth the universal priesthood of believers. The Lutheran Church made proper distinctions between the office of the ministry and the universal priesthood and was careful not to emphasize either to the detriment of the other. The Ultra-Protestants and fanatics did not regard the office of the ministry properly, owing to their false conclusions drawn from the doctrine of the universal priesthood. The call was an inner rather than an external call and was brought about through the immediate inspiration of the Holy Spirit. The position of the Lutheran Confessions is conservative with regard to the ministry. Since the Reformation there have been various tendencies that have developed with regard to the office of the ministry. Of course, the Roman Catholic Church has been faithful to its fixed opinions. Among the Reformed Protestants there are to be found Romanizing tendencies, but the majority of the denominations lean more decidedly to the "left" than to the "right." The Lutheran Church has also been faithful to its principles, although some of her theologians have inclined more toward high Church tendencies, while others have inclined in the opposite direction. As a rule, however, the office is highly regarded, in accordance with the Word of God, but not more highly than the Scriptures warrant.

Clement of Rome states that the Apostles appointed the elders, but when the congregations had become organized, the appointments were made in conjunction with the latter. Bishop and presbyter were different designations for the same office. Polycarp also testifies that the offices of bishop and presbyter were identical. The *Didache*, or the Teaching of the Twelve Apostles, speaks in the XVth chapter of bishops and deacons. The reference to Phil. 1:1 in this connection shows that the term bishop was used interchangeably with presbyter and therefore was identical with it. Ignatius speaks of the office of bishop in his seven or three letters. The difficulty is, however, that there are extant three editions of his letters, while only one can be authentic, either the lesser Greek edition or the recently discovered Syrian edition. In the latter the references to the episcopal office are lacking, although its principal features may be traced. In his letter to Rome the episcopal office is not mentioned, although Ignatius calls himself the bishop of Syria. The episcopacy, of which he speaks, however, is not the diocesan episcopacy, which arose later, but merely the office of bishop in the congregation. He states that the congregational bishop is the vicar of God and Christ, while the presbyters correspond to the Apostles. He also speaks of the office of the deacon. Justin Martyr does not treat of this subject directly, although in his 65th and 67th apology he makes mention of the fact that in the Lord's Supper the officiating pastor consecrated the elements, which were then distributed by the deacons. From this it is evident that the office of the ministry was not regarded as a sacerdotal office. Irenaeus speaks of the diocesan episcopacy as being a continuation of the apostolic Church and as a vehicle of the Catholic tradition. In his writings, however, there is some confusion as to the use of the terms bishop and presbyter, which proves that the doctrine concerning them was not as yet fixed.

Tertullian shared the same views before he became a Montanist. He clearly distinguishes between bishop and presbyter as well as between *clerici* and *laici*. Cyprian was the typical representative of the high church tendency of the time. He says that the bishop is in the Church and the Church in the bishop, wherefore he who is not with the bishop is not a member of the Church. The bishop is God's representative and the channel which transmits the grace of God. He is appointed by God, is inspired by God, and is responsible to Him. Cyprian sets forth in its main outlines the whole sacerdotal system. In accordance with his conception the implication is that he regarded the priest as a sacrificial priest. Sacerdotalism found a fruitful soil among the heathen Christians, but not among the Jewish Christians, who knew that the Old Testament Levitical service was merely typical and would cease to be when the antitype was revealed. They also knew that the Jewish priesthood did not correspond to the New Testament office of the ministry.

Chrysostom sets forth the identity of bishop and presbyter in the Biblical sense. Jerome also sets forth this identity. He says: "The Apostle clearly shows that presbyter is the same as bishop. It is most clearly proven that bishops and presbyters are identical." With regard to the origin of the episcopacy he states: "When in the course of time a presbyter was elected to preside over others, this was done in order to provide a remedy against schism and in order that each one might not withdraw and surround himself with supporters and thus tear asunder the Church of Christ." He testifies to the fact that the presbyters officiated at the ordination of pastors and were afterwards assisted by the bishops. Augustine says: "There is nothing in this life and especially at this time easier and more delightful and desirable than to hold the office of a bishop, a presbyter, or a deacon, if the calling be administered superficially and to the pleasure of men, but there is nothing more wretched, mournful, and damnable in the sight of God. There is likewise in this life and at this time nothing more difficult, laborious and hazardous than to occupy the office of a bishop, prebyter, or a deacon, and yet in the sight of God there is nothing more blessed, provided the fight is fought in accordance with the Captain's command."[124] He writes to Jerome: "Although the honorable titles, which the practice of the Church has sanctioned, place the office of the bishop above that of the minister, still in many things Augustine is smaller than Jerome." Although Augustine favored the episcopacy, spoke highly of it, and called Rome especially the *sedes apostolica*, still there are to be found expressions in his writings which prove that he did not in the commonly accepted sense support the doctrine of the so-called apostolic succession. Augustine, however, supported, the Catholic doctrine of sacerdotalism and the mediatory office of the priesthood

Peter Lombard presents seven clerical orders: *Ostiarii, lectores, exorcistae, acoluthi, subdiaconi, diaconi, et presbyteri.* Raimund of Sabunde says that those officiating stand in the same relation to the Sacraments as the parents in relation to the birth of their child. They administer the externals in the Sacraments, and God imparts the inner gifts of grace, just as the parents are responsible for the material body, while God creates the soul. Thomas Aquinas sets forth the great significance of ordination in relation to the other Sacraments. He states that while in the other Sacraments the effect is dependent *quod divinam virtutem et significat et continet,* in this Sacrament the effect is dependent on the person who performs the act of ordination.

In accordance with his view it is the act of ordination which is material in constituting the rest. Through ordination an indelible character is imprinted. The Council of Trent confirmed the doctrine as it had been developed. The Council decided that the orders were seven in number. It decided, further, that the number of the Sacraments was seven, that the bishops were superior to the priests, that the priests at their ordination receive the Holy Ghost through the mediation of the bishops, that those who have been ordained can never become laymen, that the hierarchy was established through divine institution, etc. The Council declared anathema upon all who taught otherwise.

Luther laid emphasis on the universal priesthood of believers, but not

---

[124] *Epist. XXI ad Valerium.*

to such an extent as to detract from the office of the ministry. He declares plainly that this latter office is an institution of God and that men are called to this office through the mediation of the Church. Luther also stated that whosoever did not possess the regular call of the Church but boasted of an extraordinary call, which he cannot prove by signs and wonders, shall be Judged as a hedge-preacher. The congregation or the Church must call in accordance with the established order. Calvin took the position that not only was the office of the ministry as instituted by God necessary, but also the presbytery. His views gave rise to the Presbyterian and aristocratic form of Church government. But the Scriptures do not speak of lay elders, but only of ordained presbyters. The *Anabaptists* rejected not only the office of the ministry, but also the office of teaching in the real sense, and together with other fanatics they overemphasized the inner call without taking the external call into consideration. The *Pietists,* such as Spener laid stress on the universal priesthood of believers, but also acknowledged the office of the ministry, stating that no one ought to assume this office without being called.

The Reformed State Church of England, or the Anglican Church, and the Episcopalian Church in general, is characterized by its high church tendencies, and indeed in some quarters by its Catholizing tendencies. William Laud was one of the most noted of the high church representatives in England and has been called the English Cyprian. He maintained that the apostolic succession was a necessity and that it constituted, as it were, the channel through which all the divine grace was communicated to men. He stated that only an episcopal church which possessed the apostolic succession could rightly interpret the Word of God. Episcopal ordination was likewise necessary to make valid the office of the ministry. This high church tendency has been represented in modern times by Puseyism. — There are, however, many evidences to prove that ministers have served in the Episcopal Church who have not received episcopal ordination. Neither has it been conclusively proved that the Episcopal Church possesses an unbroken apostolic succession in relation to the office of the ministry or the episcopacy. — In Germany there have been many tendencies, but the teaching of the symbols concerning the ministry have been normative. Höfling states that the Church is the subject of the ministry, and sets forth a position leaning somewhat toward a low church conception, in common with Thomasius, Harnack, and others. Löhe represents a high church tendency and takes the position that the Church is the object of the ministry. The ministry is an order which is self-perpetuating. Vilmar sets forth the sacramental character of ordination. Kliefoth stresses the institution of the ministry by God before the establishment of the Church. The congregation of believers is the sacrificial people of God ordained through the sacrifice of devotion. Their whole life is a sacrifice of praise and thanksgiving. Out of the ministerial activity of the congregation proceeds the diaconate, which is to be distinguished from the ministry and is the second office in the Church of Christ. There is also a third office in the Church, which is distinguished from both the ministry and the diaconate, viz., the Church Council. Kliefoth lays special stress on the ministry. The means of grace and the ministry are given to the whole Church, but only the incumbents of the ministry possess the right to administer the means of grace. He especially emphasizes the fact that the Sacraments are to be administered through the established ministry. Most of the leading theologians of the State Church of Sweden take a conservative position with regard to the office of the ministry. U. L. Ullman sets forth the significance of the ecclesiastical administration of the means of grace. He proves that the individual does not, either of his own accord or as prompted by the suggestion or command of other individuals, possess the right to administer the means of grace. The Church is not made up of a disorderly conglomeration of individuals, but is rather an organism with organized community life. After stating that the ministry through ordination in orderly fashion is committed by the Church to suitable persons, Ullman sets forth the significance of ordination and states that the imposition of hands is not merely a symbolical action, but also implies the communication of power. The Word of God concerning the office of the ministry, and therefore the ministry itself, its promises and gracious gifts, are really bestowed upon the candidate for ordination by means of the imposition of hands, together with the accompanying prayers of the congregation. Thus the candidate becomes the recipient of gifts necessary in the discharge of his ministry, provided he does not render himself unreceptlve to these gifts through willful obstinacy. He further states that the objective significance of ordination is to be sought in the right which the ordained minister has received to administer the means of grace. The subjective significance depends upon the Word of God and prayer, which must produce some effect. The effect is, however, not produced *ex opere operato*, but depends upon the candidate's subjective state, as to whether or not he embraces and abides by the promises of God in connection with the grace bestowed on the Gospel ministry.

In the Lutheran Church in the United States there has been waged a controversy concerning the office of the ministry between the Missouri and the Iowa Synods. Walther and the *Missouri Synod* support a doctrine which is congregationalistic in the extreme. In accordance with this view the ministry is conferred upon the individual members as constituting the universal priesthood of believers, who limit the exercise of their prerogatives for the sake of order. The *Missouri Synod* holds that the local congregation of believers has the right to call and appoint ministers, the congregation being the original possessor of all church power by the institution of God. Ordination is not a divine ordinance, but an apostolic-ecclesiastical institution. The *Iowa Synod* denies the correctness of this position and declares that the ministry has always been the possession of the Church taken as a totality. This Synod holds that the Church possesses the office in and with the means of grace, not in the spiritual priesthood and in the state of its true members. The *Augustana Synod*, which has been acknowledged by the Archbishop of Uppsala, bishops and the leading representatives of the Swedish mother Church as being the daughter Church in the United States, takes a true, Lutheran and confessional position in relation to this doctrine. While the form of Church government is not episcopal, by reason of peculiar circumstances and conditions that have prevailed since the establishment of the Synod, still the office of the ministry and established order are held in high esteem. The *Augustana Synod* may be said to be neither high church nor low church in its conception of the ministry, but churchly. The *Augustana Synod* in its Constitution says that the Synod shall consist of all pastors and congregations regularly connected with the same, and that the delegates to the synodical conventions shall consist of an equal number of pastors and laymen. Hasselquist supported the conservative viewpoint, swerving neither to the right nor the left, but highly regarding the office of the ministry given by God for the service of the Church.

Krauth says: "Many embarrassing circumstances prevented the Lutheran Church from developing her life as perfectly in her church constitution as in her doctrine and worship. The idea of the universal priesthood of all believers at once overthrew the doctrine of a distinction of essence between clergy and laity. The ministry is not an order, but it is a divinely appointed office to which men must be rightly called. No imparity exists by divine right; an hierarchical organization is unchristian, but a gradation (bishops, superintendents, provosts) may be observed, as a thing of human right only. Government by consistories has been very general. In Denmark, Evangelical bishops took the place of the Roman Catholic prelates who were deposed. In Sweden the bishops embraced the Reformation, and thus secured in that country an "apostolic succession" in the high church sense; though, on the principle of the Lutheran Church, alike where she has as where she has not such a succession, it is not regarded as essential even to the order of the Church. The ultimate source of power is in the congregations, that is, in the pastor and other officers and the people of the single communions."[125] Krauth represented the mediating views of the Lutheran Church. He was neither high-church nor low church. He guarded the rights of both ministers and people. He did not place the source of the ministerial office in the local congregation or limit its authority to the local church. He traced the ministry as to source to the universal Church, in which both the congregation and the

---

[125] Krauth's *Conserv. Ref.*, pp. 152, 153.

ministry take part in the call. Although he did not look upon ordination as absolutely necessary, he did not regard ordination as only a confirmation of the call from the local church, but as the final act in a process by which the ministry concurred in the call. He also held that ordination could not or should not be dispensed with and that only ordained ministers should ordain ministers.[126]

---

[126] A Synopsis of Krauth's Manuscript lectures on art. 5 of the Augsburg Confession and on Ordination may be read in "The Doctrine of the Ministry" by Weidner, pages 88-93 and 107-110, respectively.

7

Eschatology

Eschatology treats of the doctrine of death, the intermediate state, the last times, the return of Christ, the resurrection, the judgment, the consummation, and the two states of eternity.

Christianity is the only true teleological religion. The heathen religions do not possess any real eschatology nor any comprehensive conception of the progress of the world toward the final consummation of all things. Heathenism turns a retrospective eye upon the golden age of the past, but the future is wrapped in shadowy mysticism with only a vagrant ray of hope here and there to lighten up the somber darkness. Heathen speculation has not grasped the meaning of God's eternal plan and purpose. It is the special divine revelation that alone sheds a flood of light upon the end of time and opens up the gates of eternity to our wondering and expectant gaze, so that in some measure we are enabled to understand the import of the final consummation. The Christian religion is not only the religion of faith and love, it is also the religion of hope and life. That which is central and characteristic in the eschatology of the Christian religion is the second advent of Christ. The culture of our present day civilization dreams of a Utopia to be attained by means of human labor and invention, education and general cultural advancement. But Christianity reveals the necessity of divine intervention. Only Christ is able to produce seasons of refreshing. His first advent became the turning point in time toward the goal of salvation; His second advent shall mark the end of the days of man and shall usher in the great consummation in the day of the Son of God. Then the Church will have completed its mission. Ecclesiology and eschatology stand, therefore, in the closest relation to each other. Eschatology begins with the doctrine of death, inasmuch as the Church will be perfected through death and the final transformation, while it closes with the doctrine of the resurrection, the new creation and life everlasting.

§40. Death and the Intermediate State.

Death is a word which inspires both fear and joyous expectancy. To the unbeliever death stalks about as the king of terror and fear, while to the believer it comes softly as a messenger from the heavenly home. Death is, nevertheless, a frightful discord which would never have occurred had not sin entered the world. Even experienced Christians are at times subject to feelings of dejection in contemplating the journey down through the valley of the shadow of death. Paul gives expression to an emotion of this sort in 2 Cor. 5:4, when he speaks of his desire to be clothed upon, in order that what is mortal might be swallowed up of life. In the eighth verse, however, he gives expression to his great willingness to be absent from the body and to be at home with the Lord. The Christians rejoice because the hope of blessed immortality lightens the pathway that leads down through the valley of death and because of their assurance that in the intermediate state they are to be with the Lord. Our condition in the intermediate state will depend on our spiritual state in this life. The intermediate state is not to be considered as a school of probation.

1. Death.

Mors corporalis, or death, *is the unnatural separation of the bodily and spiritual natures of man. Through death the soul is deprived of its material substratum and organ and yet the human and personal characteristics persist in the soul.* In the separation the soul and spirit remain inseparable, inasmuch as they together constitute the same spiritual nature, viewed only from different aspects. But inasmuch as the body is the organ of man's spiritual nature, and inasmuch, furthermore, as man would not be complete without possessing both body and soul or spirit, therefore we may not consider the body as an unessential thing or as a burden to the spiritual nature. We are compelled to reject the Deistic theory, which considers the body and soul as antagonistic to each other, the body being the prison of the soul, from which the soul is released in death. We also reject the Pantheistic theory, which identifies the soul with the body, the death of the latter implying likewise the death of the former. The expression, to kill the soul, occurs indeed in Scripture (*ψυχὴν ἀποκτεῖναι*, Mark 3:4; cf. Job 36:14; Numbers 23:10), but the death of the soul simply means that it is dead in relation to this world. The soul or the spirit per se cannot die. Compare Matt. 10:28, where it is stated that men are indeed able to kill the body, but they are not able to kill the soul.

In death the soul passes out from the body. Compare Gen. 35:18. This departure does not always take place without a struggle, even though the faithful often yearn for the time of their deliverance and entrance into the realms of glory. Compare 1 Kings 17:17 ff., also Isa. 38:12 ff. It must be a peculiar feeling to be "unclothed" and enter into a complete spiritual existence. And still to the Christian, when death comes, it is experienced as and likened to a sweet sleep; in the real sense he shall not taste of death. Death has been called the brother of sleep, for which reason it is said of deceased Christians that they sleep in Jesus.

In the spiritual sense, however, those who have died in Christ do not sleep. Death becomes an epoch-making experience in their existence, inasmuch as they are born into a new world, into the land of the living. While for the time being they have been deprived of their earthly tabernacle, which was not adapted for the present stage of their existence, still at the same time they have been liberated from the body of sin and death. The death of the Christian is not, however, to be thought of negatively only, it must also be considered from the positive point of view, inasmuch as the end of the Christian's earthly life means that the last fight has been fought and a glorious victory won.

2. Immortality.

The soul is immortal, although not in the same sense as God is immortal. The immortality of the soul is clearly taught in the Holy Scriptures. The following passages may be observed: "The breath of life—a living soul" (Gen. 2:7); "Let your heart live forever" (Ps. 22:26); "God is not the God of the dead, but of the living" (Matt. 22:32; Mark 12:26, 27; Luke 20:36-38); "Have eternal life" (John 3:15, 16); "Shall live forever" (John 6:58); "Though he die, yet shall he live" (John 11:25); "To the spirits of just men made perfect" (Heb. 12:23); "I saw the souls of them that had been slain for the Word of God" (Rev. 6:9). We also quote the remarkable passage by Paul in Phil. 1:21-23: "For to me to live is Christ, and to die is gain. But if to live in the flesh, if this shall bring fruit from my work, then what I shall choose I know not. But I am in a strait betwixt the two, having the desire to depart and be with Christ; for it is very far better." Between eighteen and nineteen centuries have passed since Paul penned these words. Only the Lord knows when the trumpet of resurrection will sound. Is it likely that the energetic mind of Paul would have preferred to die, if death had meant a long period of unconsciousness and inactivity? No, No! With the spirits made perfect and living in Paradise Paul since he died has been as active as he was in the body, but in a different way. Death as a sleep refers only to the body and the activities in this temporal life. The passages which speak of eternal punishment and eternal life likewise imply that man is immortal. Many such passages could be cited.

Among other proofs the following may be mentioned: 1) The metaphysical proof, which is based on the immateriality of the soul; 2) the theological proof, which sets forth that in accordance with His love, faithfulness and other attributes God does not desire to annihilate man; 3) the teleological proof, which sets forth the inadequacy of this earthly life fully to develop and exercise the capacities of man; 4) the moral proof, which sets forth that there must be a future life where the virtuous receive their reward and the ungodly are punished; 5) the historical proof or the universal conviction concerning, and faith in, the immortality of the soul.[127]

3. The Intermediate State.

The intermediate state is the abode and condition of the dead between death and judgment. The Scriptures make mention of two abodes in the intermediate state, the one of the wicked, the other of the blessed. The unbelievers are in Hades and the believers are in heaven or Paradise.

1) Hades: a) Hades is not identical with the grave or *kebher*. Sheol or Hades is not used in the same sense as *kebher*. This last expression is used to designate a special place, such as graves in Egypt (Ex. 14:11). A burial place can be bought and sold (Gen. 23: 4-20). Dead bodies are buried in graves by the living (Gen. 50:13). For further study see Sheol in Deut. 32: 22; also Ezek. 32: 21. Hades and the grave are clearly distinguished from each other. Compare Gen. 37:35: "I will go down to Sheol to my son mourning." The 33d verse, however, tells us that Jacob had the impression that Joseph had been devoured and not buried. — Hades was used in contradistinction to heaven, wherefore the reference is not to the grave. Compare Job 11:8. Hades is used synonymously with two other expressions which do not have reference to the grave, viz., *bor* and *eretz tachtith*. With regard to the first expression, compare Ps. 30:4, and with regard to the latter, compare Ezek. 31:14, 16, 18. Those that dwell in Hades are in a conscious state, which is not said of those in *kebher*. Read Isa. 14: 4-17, the tenth verse of which reads as follows: "All they shall answer and say unto thee, Art thou also become weak as we? art thou become like unto us?" The New Testament does not make use of *ᾅδης* in the sense of the grave. Examine Luke 16:23 and Acts 2:27-31. Hades is used eleven times in the New Testament, if 1 Cor. 15:55 is counted, and in none of these passages would grave properly answer as a translation, b) In the New Testament, Hades means the abode of the unbelievers during

---

[127] For further proofs, compare the arguments in the author's *Apologetics*, pp. 177-182.

the intermediate state and is therefore not identical with hell after the judgment.[128] There are many who hold the view that Sheol was divided into two parts, one for the unbelievers, the other for the blessed, which was the same as Abraham's bosom. This view is based upon the fact that the believers in the Old Testament speak of going down and not ascending to heaven. The patriarch Jacob said: "I will go down to Sheol to my son mourning" (Gen. 37:35). The story of Dives and Lazarus is also used as a proof. It is stated that the rich man was in Hades. Of Lazarus it is not said that he was in Hades, but that the rich man saw Abraham afar off, and Lazarus in his bosom. It is stated that the rich man spoke to Abraham, who also replied, among other things, that there was a great gulf fixed between the abodes of the blessed and the damned. In the New Testament we do not read that the faithful at death descend into Hades. It may be true that in the Old Testament Sheol had two divisions but it is evident that in the New Testament Hades is not the abode of the blessed during the intermediate state.[129] Therefore Hades is the abode of the unbelievers until the day of judgment, when the damned shall be cast into *γέεννα* or the real hell . c) Hell is called Gehenna. It has also other names. In the Old Testament hell is called Abaddon, which is translated *ἀπωλεια* in the Greek. In the New Testament the expression, "the lake of fire and brimstone," is used. In the Old Testament the terms Abaddon and Hades were used to distinguish different places, wherefore they were not identical. Compare Job 26:6: "Sheol is naked before God, and Abaddon hath no covering"; also compare Proverbs 15:11; 27:30. In Rev. 20:14 we read that Hades was cast into the lake of fire, for which reason it cannot be identical with

[128]Ἅιδης occurs in the following places: Matt. 11:23; 16:18; Luke 10:15; 16:23; Acts 2:27, 31 (1 Cor. 15:55); Rev. 1:18; 6; 8; 20:13, 14.

[129]Acts 2:27, 31 has been cited to prove that Hades also included Paradise, at least till the resurrection and ascension of Christ. Without expressing a decisive opinion in this matter, still it is certain that after the ascension Hades has reference only to the state and the abode of the unbelievers in the intermediate state. On the day of judgment Hades will be cast into hell or the burning lake. On the other hand. Paradise is described as being in an upward direction or in heaven. Compare 2 Cor. 12:4.

Gehenna, d) The abode of the evil spirits is called ἀβυσσος, the abyss, or Tartaros. With reference to the first expression, read Luke 8:31: "And they entreated him that he would not command them to depart into the abyss." Compare also Rev. 9:1, 2, where the expression, "the pit of the abyss," is used. Read 2 Peter 2:4: "For if God spared not angels when they sinned, but cast them down,to hell." Read also Rev. 20:1. On the day of judgment the evil spirits will be cast into the lake of fire and brimstone, which is the same as Gehenna. Compare Rev. 20:10; Matt. 5: 22; 18: 9, etc.

2) *Paradise*. The abode of the blessed during the intermediate state is called Paradise. Compare Luke 23:43; 2 Cor. 12:4; Rev. 2:7. The first of these passages in the light of the others proves that Paradise is not in Hades. Christ has ascended into heaven, and with Him are the dead who have died in the Lord. Compare John 14:2, 3; Phil. 1:23: "Be with Christ." Also 2 Cor. 5:8: "At home with the Lord."

3) *The Nature of the Intermediate State*: a) The souls of the believers are carried by angels immediately after their separation from the body to the Paradise of God. This journey is of short duration, inasmuch as Jesus said to the penitent thief: "To-day shalt thou be with me in Paradise." The unbelievers enter into Hades. The Bible does not state that they were conveyed thither by evil spirits. Read Luke 16:22, 23 concerning the rich man: "The rich man also died, and was buried. And in Hades he lifted up his eyes, being in torments"; Acts 1:25, where it is stated concerning Judas: "That he might go to his own place." b) The soul is not deprived of its spiritual faculties through death; rather its spiritual and true nature then comes into its own. The intellect, will, emotions, memory, etc., do not lose their activity, but become more intensively active, broader and more comprehensive in their scope. The spiritual tendency of the soul also remains unchanged, c) Corresponding to the spiritual relationship of the soul, its condition in the intermediate state is either that of the blessed awaiting the day of final redemption, or that of the unbelievers who in torment await with terror the day of final judgment and damnation. But Paradise and Hades are not simply states of soul, they are also places of abode, indicated by the Greek expression *τού*, "a where," although their

geographical location is, of course, unrevealed. The location of Paradise, with the testimony of Scripture, is upward in the third heaven, while the direction of Hades is downward in the nethermost parts of the earth. Paradise and the third heaven are very probably not so far distant in the universe as many might feel disposed to believe. When we consider the vast astronomical distances between the planets and the remotest stars, it is very probable that heaven is not to be found beyond the stellar universe, but rather within the bounds of creation and possibly in the very center of the universe. Evidently an angel is not divinely omnipresent, but requires time to journey from heaven to earth. It may be altogether possible for an angel to move more swiftly than light, and still time is required for his movements. Compare Daniel 9:21-23. Gabriel left heaven, it seems, when Daniel began to pray, but reached Daniel before his prayer was ended. This would seem conclusive evidence that heaven is not without the bounds of creation, if Gabriel started from the throne of God. The angel received the commandment to go to Daniel at the beginning of the prayer. In coming to Daniel the angel covered a long distance, as it is stated: "Being caused to fly swiftly." Compare Luke 23:43; 2 Cor. 12: 2-4.
d) The souls do not sleep in the intermediate state, for which reason we reject the doctrine of Psychopannychism. When the dead are said to sleep the reference is to the state of the body in death, which seems to be as one asleep, but this does not imply that the souls sleep spiritually. The souls of the dead are completely conscious and awake as to their spiritual nature, although they rest from their earthly labors and enjoy comfort. We read in Rev. 14:13: "That they may rest from their labors." This passage does not, however, imply complete idleness. The Lord clearly intimates that both the unbelievers and the believers are conscious in the intermediate state. Compare Luke 16:23-31; 23:43. These passages also prove that the dead recognize each other. The occurrences on the Mount of Transfiguration also prove that the intermediate state does not imply idleness or sleep. It is not probable that Paul, if he had conceived of the intermediate state as implying a condition of unconsciousness, would have longed for it and counted it as a great gain. He states clearly that death is the same as

taking our departure from this world to be with Christ. Compare also Isa. 14:4-17; "He is not the God of the dead, but of the living: for all live unto him" (Luke 20:38); "To the spirits of just men made perfect" (Heb. 12:23) ; Rev. 6:9-11. This last passage, especially, reveals the inhabitants of heaven as being perfectly conscious sympathetic and filled with yearning expectancy, e) Although in relation to the new life of the resurrection the state of the soul in the world of the spirit may be said to be *γυμνὸν εἶναι*, and although the spirits do not possess material bodies nor any investiture, still there is a recognizable appearance corresponding to the human form which constitutes an expression of the individual personality. Compare Isa. 14:9, 10; Ezek. 31:15-18; Matt. 17:3; Luke 9: 30, 31; Rev. 6:11. While the souls do not possess bodies, still they are able to see, speak, hear, feel, etc. Paul took for granted that a disembodied spirit could see and hear. Compare 2 Cor. 12:2-4. It is the soul that sees by means of the eye, hears by means of the ear, etc. The soul possesses faculties which it cannot use here. He who created the eye, the ear, etc., has undoubtedly endowed the soul with faculties of sight, hearing, speech, etc., independent of a material body, f) Inasmuch as the souls, therefore, are possessed of consciousness and the faculties of sight; hearing, feeling, memory, etc., it follows that knowledge must increase and a development in that sense take place, but in the intermediate state there must be precluded any thought of continued purification or any progress in sanctification. — The doctrine of purgatory is not to be found in the Bible. Both the Greek and Roman Catholic Churches teach Purgatory. The difference is only in the kind of suffering. The Roman Church speaks of a purifying fire, but the Greek Church only mentions tribulation. According to the teachings of these churches Christ by His atonement did not bring a full pardon for all sins, but He prepared the way for salvation by the means and methods stated in the Bible and revealed through the Holy Spirit. Penitence and penance are necessary. If the penances are not fully done in this life, punishments follow in Purgatory by purifying fires. The Council of Trent in its Catechism teaches thus: "There is a purgatorial fire, where the souls of the righteous are purified by a temporary punishment, that entrance may be given them into their eternal home, where nothing that is defiled can have a place." Very few persons escape Purgatory, because even the very best Christians fail in their penances and neglect the full requirements of satisfaction. Those in Purgatory are relieved by prayers of the pious fellow Christians on earth and also by alms and masses. — The Roman Catholics support their views by the following Bible passages: 2 Macc. 2:43-46, holding it to be inspired; Matt. 5:25; 12:32; 1 Cor. 3:11-15; 15:29; Rev. 21:27. But it is very evident that none of these passages prove the existence of a purgatory. It does not correspond to the life in Paradise. The souls of the blessed are liberated at death from all imperfections and sins. Hades cannot be a purgatory. The Scriptures make mention of only two states in the world of the spirit, wherefore it is impossible to assume a third state or abode. Neither is there to be found in the Scriptures any ground for the doctrine that the souls of men may be converted in Hades and finally transferred to heaven in the judgment. If there were freedom of choice in the intermediate state there might be a possibility of the blessed falling anew into sin. The souls that have come to Hades will remain there until, on the day of judgment, they will be removed to Gehenna, while the souls that have been borne by the angels to Paradise will remain there in their state of blessedness until the resurrection, when they will be received into the kingdom prepared for them from the foundation of the world. The proponents of the doctrine of probation after death most generally make use of speculative arguments. However, they also base their arguments on Scripture. They refer especially to 1 Peter 3:19, 20 and 4:6. The first of these passages, however, does not necessarily imply the preaching of the Gospel, and nothing is said of a continuation of the preaching. There is nothing in the Scriptures to support the position that Christ continues the work of preaching to the souls in Hades, nor that He sends either angels or the disembodied souls of the blessed to perform that work. The latter passage, if connected with the former, cannot be said to prove anything. Considered alone it does not constitute a secure foundation for the doctrine of probation of souls in Hades and their final translation to the Paradise of God. The evangelical preaching spoken of in 1 Peter 4:6 may mean that the dead heard the Gospel while they were living, inasmuch as verse 5 states that the dead are to be judged, which cannot mean that they are to be judged as dead, but judgment is to take place after the resurrection, when they will be alive. If the fifth verse sets forth the judgment of the dead after their resurrection, then the sixth verse may logically be considered to imply the preaching of the Gospel to the dead while they were yet alive on the earth. This exegesis may seem forced, and yet it is evident that the doctrine of probation after death must require more secure foundation than this uncertain passage. It is a rule of Hermeneutics that clear passages must explain uncertain and mysterious passages and not vice versa. In the light of the analogy of faith there is no hope of conversion after death. The judgment will depend on the state and manner in which men lived in this life, which Paul also states in 2 Cor. 5:10: "For we must all be made manifest before the judgment seat of Christ; that each one may receive the things done in the body, according to what he hath done, whether it be good or bad." If 1 Peter 4:6 refers to the preaching of the Gospel to the dead in the world of the spirit, still it is not certain that the ungodly in Hades are meant. Besides, neither the content nor the object of this preaching is made clearly evident. Compare Christology, §19, II, 2, 1). The views of the old Church Fathers are preferable to the modern views of preaching in Hades. Christ in relating the experience of Dives in Hades does not refer to any revival preaching in Hades. The rich man had no hope. If he had had any knowledge of preaching the Gospel in the kingdom of the dead, he had not petitioned Abraham to send Lazarus to his five brethren in his father's house to testify unto them, "lest they also come into this place of torment." The request of the rich man was refused. The rich man knew that once in Hades, there was no escape. If there had been a chance to be saved in Hades and transferred to Abraham's bosom, the rich man had not made his request. And Abraham did not relate that missionaries were sent to the place of torment. On the contrary, Abraham said that there was a great gulf fixed between the two places, hence no one could pass from the one place to the other.

Some people insist that there must be some chance for neglected human beings, even in Christian lands, who die like heathen. We only know what Paul says in regard to those without excuse, but he does not draw the conclusion in relation to possible cases of excuse. Nor does he discuss directly the condition of children who die unbaptized or as heathen. We know that except a man be born anew, he cannot see the kingdom of God. God is not bound absolutely by the means. Christians, therefore, have the hope that the Holy Spirit has made provision for such children, as new birth is necessary and Christ died for them.

With regard to the heathen who have never heard the Gospel it may be stated that the Word of God reveals nothing as to whether or not an opportunity will be given them after death to embrace the Gospel. All speculation along this line is fruitless. The Word of God clearly states that this present life is the time of probation. "Behold, now is the acceptable time; behold, now is the day of salvation" (2 Cor. 6:2); "It is appointed unto men once to die, and after this cometh the judgment" (Heb. 9:27). With regard to those that have not had the privilege of a special revelation, read Rom. 1: 18-20; 2:12. Inasmuch, therefore, as God has not revealed anything directly with regard to the heathen, we ought not to speculate about it, but entrust that matter to the Lord Himself, while we prayerfully labor for the propagation of the Gospel among all the nations in the world. It is clear that the heathen, whether in Christian countries or elsewhere, cannot be saved by good works human wisdom and self-atonement. There may be people outside the pale of Christianity who confess their sins and desire forgiveness, but do not know the way. But however God solves the problem, there is no foundation for the doctrine of probation in Hades. We are bound by God's revelation, must use the means of grace and do all we can to promote missionary activities. Compare Matt. 28:19; Rom. 10:11-14; 2:9-16. g) The relation of the dead to this world. They remember their former life and think of their dear ones. Love is stronger than death. Naturally the blessed in the Lord are vitally interested in the struggles and the triumphs of the Church, while they long for the time of the end and the consummation. Through the angels they learn of much and rejoice over the salvation of souls. Study Luke 15:7; Rev. 6:9-11. See also Luke 9:30 and 31, where we are told that Moses appeared with Jesus in glory and conversed about the latter's death. It is difficult to determine whether or not Heb. 12:1 refers to this question. The twenty-second and the twenty-third verses of the same chapter, however, contain certain evidences of the close spiritual relationship of the Church Triumphant with the Church Militant. Jesus Christ is the common head of both the Church Triumphant and the Church Militant and is present in both. However, this close spiritual relationship does not imply that the dead visit the earth. There need be no doubt that it would be possible for them to do so with divine permission, but it is not probable that the dead depart from their abodes. The instances of Moses and Samuel as well as those who arose at the resurrection of Christ might be cited in support of the possibility of such returns of the dead to this world, but this does not prove that such visits are common. Luke 16:17-31 would seem to prove that the ungodly are unable to reveal themselves upon the earth. This question takes on peculiar significance polemically in relation to the tenets of Spiritualism. It is the Lord alone who possesses the keys to the realms of death and Hades.

4. Notes on the History of Dogma.

Most of the early Church Fathers taught that the soul is immortal by nature. Generally speaking, they accepted the doctrine of the intermediate state. There were many who believed that before the death of Christ the souls of all the dead entered into Hades, although to different parts of it, but that Christ at the time of His descent into Hades liberated the believers of the Old Covenant and brought them with Him to heaven. During the Polemical period it was generally believed and taught that after the death of Christ the believers immediately after death enter into Paradise. The doctrine of probation after death was generally rejected. At the close of the Polemical period, through the influence of Augustine and Gregory, the doctrine of purgatory made its appearance in definite form, which was further developed during the Middle Ages and came to include the doctrine of deliverance from purgatory. It was taught that there were five abodes for the souls of the dead, viz.. hell in the real sense, heaven, *limbus infantum, limbus patrum* for the faithful in the Old Testament, and purgatory. The unbaptized children in *limbus infantum* do not suffer the pains of hell, but they experience the loss of the heavenly bliss. The Protestants rejected the doctrine of purgatory. They also rejected the doctrine of psychopannychism, or of sleep during the intermediate state, which was advocated by the Anabaptists. Calvin wrote a refutation of the psychopannychism of the Anabaptists. Luther expressed himself at times somewhat in favor of a sleep of the soul, although he did not teach that the soul was unconscious in the intermediate state, but that the souls of the blessed rested in God and were filled with ecstatic joy and expectancy. The early Dogmaticians rejected the doctrine of the sleep of the soul. They all set forth clearly the immortality of the soul. Generally speaking, the immortality of the soul is accepted by the Socinians, the Rationalists and philosophers, while, of course, the Materialists reject this doctrine in common with all consistent Pantheists. The Supranaturalists generally advocate the doctrine of probation after death. Some also held the doctrine of an intermediate corporeity in the spirit world. The orthodox Lutheran theologians teach that the eternal state of man is determined on this side of the grave, although there are some who entertain the hope that earnest seekers after salvation among the heathen, who have not had the privilege of hearing the Gospel, may after death be afforded an opportunity of learning to know the Saviour of the world. Conservative theologians, however, do not care to express themselves dogmatically on a subject concerning which the Scriptures contain no direct revelation.

Justin Martyr set forth that the believers are not subject to death by reason of their participation in the absolute life. The duration of the period of the punishment of the ungodly depends on the will of God. Irenaeus says that the soul is immortal by reason of its simplicity and indivisibility, and that the souls of the blessed are in Paradise in disembodied state, but with human form, awaiting the resurrection. Tatian declares that the soul dies with the body, provided it knows not the truth, but that it also is resurrected with the body at the judgment and that it is punished with immortality. The souls of believers remain alive throughout the intermediate state. Tertullian teaches the immortality of the soul and rejects the doctrine of psychopannychism. The prayers of the living contribute to the comfort of the dead. Clement of Alexandria speaks of a purification that takes place in the intermediate state by means of a purifying fire which permeates the soul. Origen bases the immortality of the soul on its knowledge of God. After death the soul receives a sublime body which in form is like the earthly body. The pure souls are carried upward, but the unclean souls hover about the grave. Before the descent of Christ in Hades all the believers were brought to Abraham's bosom, but afterwards they have entered directly into the Paradise of heaven.

Gregory of Nazianzus supported the doctrine of the supplication of the saints. In the form of prayer he speaks to the dead, as to his sister and to Basil. He speaks of a purifying fire in connection with the judgment of the world. Gregory of Nyssa says that the invisibility and supersensuous nature of the soul are proofs of its immortality. He believed in the supplication of the saints and also that the dead can intercede for the living. He himself at one time prayed to Theodorus for his assistance. Chrysostom also supported the doctrine of the supplication of the saints and believed that their intercessions were efficacious. Augustine was the first to place the process of purification in the intermediate state. He denied that the souls have bodies in the intermediate state. Gregory the Great supported the doctrine of *ignis purgatorius* in the intermediate state for minor sins and that the sacrifice of the mass can liberate souls from purgatory.

Thomas Aquinas taught that the soul is immortal, and sought to prove it by the innate thought and desire for immortality in the intellect. However, he distinguished between *anima sensitiva* and *intellectiva*, declaring that *anima intellectiva* was immortal. He taught with regard to purgatory that neither the ungodly nor the very pious saints enter into this state. The doctrine concerning the efficacy of the mass in behalf of the souls in purgatory was confirmed at the Council of Lyons in 1279 and at the

Council of Florence in 1439. At the latter Council it was determined that if the penitent died before satisfactions had been completed he would be purified from the contagion of sin through the pains of purgatory. But these pains are reduced and liberation secured by means of the intercessory prayers, masses, alms and other good deeds of the faithful. The Council of Trent confirmed the same doctrine. Bellarmin declares that the pains of purgatory are more severe than any earthly suffering.

Luther rejected the doctrine of purgatory, but does not dwell at any length on the intermediate state. He also rejected the doctrine of a moral development during the intermediate state. With regard to such as had never heard the Gospel here on earth Luther states that the Lord is able to grant them faith after death, but that it cannot be proved that He does so. The early Dogmaticians, of course, rejected the doctrine of purgatory together with the Catholic views with regard to the distinctive places of abode of the souls of the dead and accepted only two places, caelum et infernum. Calixtus said that the intermediate state implied neither blessedness nor the opposite. The Socinians declared that the immortality of the soul was a gift of the Lord, since by nature souls are mortal. Faustus Socinus said that the soul dies with the body and that both are raised up on the last day.

Leibnitz and Wolff supported the doctrine of the immortality of the soul. Kant likewise supported the theory of immortality, stating that the harmony of moral requirement and happiness cannot be attained in this life, wherefore in accordance with the category of the practical reason there must be a life after this. Swedenborg said that man possesses a finer bodily organism beneath the external material body and that the finer body persists after the death of the latter. The conditions after death are connected with and resemble the conditions in this present life. At death man enters the world of the spirit, where in accordance with his state of soul he is prepared either for heaven or hell. There is no opportunity afforded in the intermediate state for conversion. Only the discords in man's nature are there harmonized. Hell does not imply perpetual punishment. The wretched have periods of refreshing. However, every transgression is followed by terrible sufferings. Heaven is a blessed state in which every one finds suitable employment. The blessed are made more and more perfect. Reinhard maintained that the soul by reason of the great violence of death sinks into a state of unconsciousness for a protracted period. Schleiermacher rejected the retributory as well as the intellectual proofs of the immortality of the soul and stated that the best proof was faith in the unchangeableness of the divine union with the manhood of Christ, for when Christ declares Himself immortal, it has reference to us likewise. The Christian soul is not after death all at once liberated from sin, but only gradually through continued development. Strauss said that on the other side of the grave is to be found the last enemy for speculative criticism to overcome. Martensen supported a theory of corporeity and purgation in the intermediate state. Thomasius rejected these theories and declared that the union with Christ supplied the temporary loss of a bodily organ. Kahnis held that purification and development take place in the intermediate state. Björling entertained the hope that the heathens who had obeyed the natural revelation and become conscious of the need of the forgiveness of sin and reconciliation would be afforded an opportunity to learn of Christ after death. But those heathens who had hardened their hearts against the voice of conscience would have no desire to be instructed and therefore be unable to receive any knowledge of Christ. Some theologians hold the view that heathens, who die repenting and asking God or the gods to save them, will receive instruction in regard to salvation by Christ immediately after death, but not in Hades, because once in Hades, there is no hope. Granfelt supported the doctrine of the inward purification of the soul in the intermediate state. He also maintained that conversion could take place in Hades. In Hades salvation is preached to such as have not heard the Gospel on the earth. Among such he not only counts the heathens but also such persons in Christendom who have been reared as heathens or who have not had favorable opportunities for repentance. Frank states that there is no message of salvation implied in the preaching in Hades spoken of in 1 Peter 4:6. He does not base any hope for the salvation of the heathens on

Rom. 2:14-16 and 27. He does not deny that such Scripture passages as John 3:16; 10:16; 11:52; Acts 10:35; Rom. 2:16; 1 Tim. 2:4; 2 Peter 3:9; 1 John 2:2 contain intimations of the divine plans of salvation in relation to this matter, but in common with other conservative theologians he does not believe that they contain sufficiently clear statements on which to base a dogmatic assertion. He entertains the hope that God will not reject any man simply of his natural state and is willing to abide the fulfillment of Isa. 25:7. This hope he bases on the fact that it is unbelief that condemns a man. Of course, he acknowledges that original sin, per se, is damnatory. But he has no desire to speak dogmatically about such heathens as have not had the opportunity on earth of accepting the grace of salvation through faith.

§41. The Last Times.

In like manner as the earthly life of the individual terminates in a last day, preceded by a period marked with its special characteristics, so the end of the present world aeon will precede the critical beginning of the new and eternal aeon in which the estate of man will depend on the relationships sustained during the period of grace. In a certain sense the whole of the New Testament period constitutes the last times, but, strictly speaking, the last times are the period which immediately precedes the second advent of Christ. The last day may be considered the very last day of the present aeon or the final day of judgment, but it may also be considered as a period of judgment. Compare 2 Peter 3:8; 2 Tim. 3:1; Rev. 1:10; 10:6, 7. The last times have their special characteristics, which, at least by the children of God, may be studied and interpreted, and while the day of the Lord will come unexpectedly to many, it will not come as a thief in the night to Christians who watch and pray. Compare Dan. 12:4; Matt. 24:33; 1 Thess. 5:1-5. While, on the one hand, during the last times Christianity will be spread over the whole earth more generally than ever, still the forces of Antichrist will likewise develop and culminate during that period in their final manifestation of temporal power. This will constitute one of the most clearly apparent signs of the approaching end of the present aeon, but there will also be other signs to show how far advanced are the hands on the great clock of time.

1. The General Spread of Christianity.

In one of the last utterances of our Lord He commanded the disciples to go into all the world and make disciples of all nations. In one of His eschatological addresses Jesus says: "And this gospel shall be preached in the whole world for a testimony unto all the nations; and then shall the end come" (Matt. 24:14). In Mark 13:10 we read: "The gospel must first be preached unto all the nations." It is evident that these passages do not imply that all men are to be converted. The Church of Christ is an *ecclesia* and shall so remain. The great question involved is as to whether or not all nations shall nominally accept Christianity before the return of the Lord. The passages cited do not necessarily imply such a conclusion. The Gospel of the kingdom will be preached in all the world for a testimony unto them, but the prophecies contained in these passages do not state that the whole world and all the nations shall belong to the Christian Church before Christ's second coming. Paul, the Apostle to the heathen nations, did not entertain the view concerning the evangelization of the whole world which is now very generally implied in the expression that the Gospel is to be preached among all nations. Compare Col. 1:23, where he states that even in his time the Gospel had already been preached in the whole creation under the heavens. These words of Paul are peculiarly illuminating in relation to the solution of this problem. The fact that the Gospel is to be preached as a testimony is to be emphasized. This does not mean that all nations are to embrace Christianity. We know even now that where the sun of Christianity formerly shone in all its midday brilliance, the crescent now sheds its dubious light. The work of missions has made wonderful progress and the teachings of Christianity are disseminated among all peoples. But in comparing Rev. 9:20 we find that as far down in time as the sixth trumpet there will be idolatry upon the earth. With regard to the conditions which will obtain at the time of Christ's second coming, note the following: "When the Son of man cometh, shall he find faith on earth?" (Luke 18:8). By this we do not mean to deny that missionary endeavors have been crowned with great success, but simply state that at the time of our Lord's advent all nations will not have accepted Christ. Our missionary duty remains quite as compelling in the face of these facts, inasmuch as it is incumbent on us to obey the commands of our Lord to labor for the ingathering of all the nations into the fold of the Church. The Scriptures speak of the times of the Gentiles and of the fullness of the Gentiles, expressions which imply that all nations have their periods of divine visitation and that our Lord shall from all the peoples of the earth gather those that He foresees shall believe and therefore belong to the true *ecclesia*.[130] In relation to the Jews, all nations are called Gentiles. Even during the time of the Gentiles many Jews will be saved, but in accordance with the prophecies of the Scriptures the Jews will in the last times more generally than ever before embrace Christianity. In Romans 11:25 we read these especially important words: "For I would not, brethren, have you ignorant of this mystery, lest ye be wise in your conceits, that a hardening in part hath befallen Israel, until the fullness of the Gentiles be come in; and so all Israel shall be saved." These last words do not mean that all Jews will be saved, and very probably they do not mean that they will even nominally become Christian, but they do mean that the Jewish nation will finally assume an attitude toward Christ

[130]The Times of the Gentiles are counted as covering the times of Israelitish and especially Jewish oppression by the world powers. The Babylonian captivity marks the real beginning and the Roman captivity intensifies the oppression, because with the destruction of Jerusalem, A.D. 70, the dispersion of the Jews among all nations became a fact and was realized more and more. The Times of the Gentiles began with Nebuchadnezzar and the Babylonian empire and have continued through the Medo-Persian, the Greek-Macedonian and the Roman empires. The last revelation of the Roman power will be during the full manifestation of the ten kingdoms, the little horn or rather the two beasts. Compare Dan. 7, 8, 11 and Rev. 13. A great sign of the approach of the end of the Times of the Gentiles is the downfall of the Turkish power. The occupancy of Palestine by a Christian power as a result of the World War was a remarkable fulfillment of prophecy.

and His Church different from that which now obtains. With regard to the receiving of the Jews, Paul writes in Romans 11:15 as follows: "For if the casting away of them is the reconciling of the world, what shall the receiving of them be, but life from the dead?" But this expression does not constitute a conclusive proof that the Jewish nation as such will become a Christian nation before the second advent of the Lord. There are many passages in Scripture which seem literally to mean that the Jewish people will finally return to their own country and possess it. There are very distinct evidences of this return in our day. All the Jews did not return to Palestine after the Babylonian captivity. The conditions will be the same at the end of the so-called Roman captivity. More Jews have returned to Palestine during the nineteenth and twentieth centuries than returned to the Holy Land after the Babylonian captivity. For further reference concerning the return of Israel, read Deut. 30:3, 4; Isa. 11:11, 12; Ezek. 36:4-38; 39:23-28; Dan. 12:7; Zech. 12:10-14; Acts 15:15-17.

2. Antichristianity.

Christianity had hardly gained a foothold in the Roman Empire before violent opposition was encountered. The Church was made the object of such frightful persecutions and had experienced such a fearful tribulation that many believed that Antichrist had already come. Many have maintained that Nero was the Antichrist. By reason of the visions of Daniel concerning the little horn and the vision of John concerning the beast there was good ground for the assumption that the Antichrist was either a political power or personality, such as the emperor of the world empire. However, when Christianity became the religion of the State, this view lost its force, although there were many pious and thoughtful souls who viewed with sorrow the Antichristian tendencies within the Church. We ought to bear in mind, however, that even during the Apologetical period the view was prevalent that Antichrist was an individual who would appear shortly before the advent of Christ. This view was supported by Justin Martyr, Irenaeus and others of their day, and later by Chrysostom, Jerome, and Augustine. During the seventh and especially during the eighth century as well as during the Middle Ages the assumption prevailed that Mohammedanism was Antichrist. But even during this time there were some who believed that Antichrist would be a person who would appear at the end of the world. Joachim of Floris said that Antichrist would be a *universalis pontifex* and therefore concluded that some pope would appear as Antichrist. It is generally believed that Amalrik of Bena was the first to teach clearly that the Roman Hierarchy was the Antichrist, in which view the Waldensians and the Hussites concurred, holding that the papacy was Antichrist. In the Schmalcald Articles it is stated that the Pope is Antichrist. The specific reference is as follows: *"Haec doctrina praeclare ostendit papam esse ipsum verum antichristum."*[131] The Apology states that the Papacy is a part of the kingdom of Antichrist.[132] Luther said that the Pope was Antichrist, but he also said that the Turk was the little horn.[133] The old Dogmaticians called the papacy the occidental Antichrist and Mohammedanism and the Turkish power the oriental. However, they stated that the doctrine of the Antichrist is *non fundamentalis*.

The historical school of prophecy takes the position that the Papacy is Antichrist. The reasons advanced, among others, are the following: The Papal Church represents the apostasy described in 2 Thess. 2:3; the sale of indulgences in the Roman Church; the desire of the Papacy for temporal power; forbidding the laity to read the Word of God; the sacerdotal and hierarchical system within the Roman Church; Jesuitism, the Inquisition, the power of the Popes, the dogma of infallibility, the adoration of the saints, the worship of images and relics, supposed miracles, etc. On mature consideration it cannot be denied that the reasons adduced in support of the contention are potent. Furthermore, we do not know what forces may be concealed in the Roman Church which may develop into even more Antichristian tendencies and finally culminate into Antichrist himself. There is nothing in the Confessions which militates against the

---

[131] Müller, *Symb. Bücher*, p. 308, 10.

[132] Müller, *Symb. Bücher*, p. 209, 18.

[133] Köstlin. *Theology of Luther*, Book 4, chapter IX.

position that Antichrist will appear in personal form. The quotation from the Schmalcald Articles states that the Pope is truly the Antichrist. Even if the expression Pope is interpreted to mean the Papacy, still the system must have a personal head. The expression in the Apology that the Papacy is a part of the kingdom of Antichrist would indicate that this kingdom embraces more than the Roman Catholic Church. In studying closely 2 Thess. 2:3-10, we find first the expression *ἀποστασία* and then ὁ *ἀνθωπός τῆς ἀνομίας* or ὁ *ἀνομός*. The first expression may signify false Christianity in general and the Papacy in particular, while the latter expressions, the "man of sin" and the "lawless one," refer to the culmination of Antichrist in a personal head as a representative of the Antichristian political and ecclesiastical development. Philippi, who represents the old dogmatic conservative view, says: "No Lutheran can or may doubt that the Papacy is Antichristian, even if he cannot consider it the final form and culmination of Antichrist." There are many Lutheran theologians who hold the view that the fully developed form of Antichrist will be consummated in an individual so that a personal Antichrist will appear before the second coming of Christ. They believe that this personal Antichrist will have been. preceded by many types, such as Antiochus Ephiphanes, Mohammedanism and the Papacy. John speaks af many antichrists: "And as ye have heard that antichrist cometh, even now have there arisen many antichrists; whereby we know that it is the last hour" (1 John 2:18); "This is the antichrist, even he that denieth the Father and the Son" (1 John 2:22); "Every spirit that confesseth not Jesus is not of God: and this is the spirit of the antichrist, whereof ye have heard that it cometh; and even now it is in the world already" (1 John 4:3). We have already stated that Luther interpreted the little horn of Daniel to be the Turk. He, therefore, did not refer it to the Papacy. Rev. 13 speaks of two beasts. Some commentators have supported the view that the beast which John saw coming up out of the earth more particularly represents Antichrist in personal form while the beast that he saw coming up out of the sea represents the position of the historical school with relation to Antichrist. Philippi says that the first beast represents the worldly side of

Antichrist, while the second beast represents the spiritual and religious side.[134] He declares that the second beast is the Papacy considered as a heretical Church. Frank says that the Roman caricature of Christianity will always constitute an essential element in the presentation of the final Antichrist, which he considered personal.[135]

We here set forth a number of Biblical expressions which would seem to indicate that the present form of Antichristianity will in its final development appear in a more personal form. It is clearly evident that the little horn in Daniel must be an Antichristian prince who represents the world power as opposed to Christianity. Compare Daniel 7:23-27; 8: 23-25; 11:36-45. The words of our Lord in John 5:43 also seem to indicate that Antichrist will appear in personal form. The Lord says: "I am come in my Father's name, and ye receive me not: if another shall come in his own name, him ye will receive." It is not unbelievable, rather it is very probable, that Satan will finally find a personal servant who will be willing to serve and worship him. As a recompense such a person will receive the kingdom of the world. Compare Matt. 4:9. Christ has prophesied that in the last times false Christs and false prophets will arise. Compare Matt. 24:23, 24. Not only the Jews but also others expect a Messiah. The dragon, the father of lies, will send forth the son of perdition and together with him another beast who will finally appear as a great wonder-working false prophet. These three will constitute a diabolical trinity. With regard to the coming of the "lawless one" Paul says in 2 Thess. 2:9: "Whose coming is according to the working of Satan with all power and signs and lying wonders." Cf. Rev. 13:2. With regard to the "lawless one" it is stated in 2 Thess. 2:8, "whom the Lord Jesus shall slay with the breath of his mouth, and bring him to nought by the manifestation of his coming." Comparing this passage with Rev. 19:20 we find that these passages seem to confirm the view that an individual person is referred to, indeed, that the final appearance of the beast will be personal, inasmuch as the first beast and

---

[134] *Kirchliche Glaubenslehre,* VI. pp.171, 172.

[135] *System der Christliche Wahrheit,* zweite Aufl., zweite Hälfte, p. 470.

the false prophet are both to be taken and cast alive into the lake of fire that burneth with brimstone. Compare also Daniel 7:26; 8:25; 11:45. Study the presentation of the beast in Rev. 13 and compare it with Rev. 17:3-13. Generally speaking, the first beast is a symbolical presentation of world power revealed in its fully developed form, for which reason the ten horns are mentioned first. The seven heads, of which it is said that five are fallen, are taken to mean seven successive powers among the kingdoms of the world. The first that had already fallen were Egypt, Assyria, Babylon, Persia and Greece. In Rev. 13:2 the leopard is mentioned as referring to the Greek or Macedonian power, the bear to the Medo-Persian power, and the lion to the Babylonian power. The sixth power is the Roman. Daniel makes mention of only four powers, the fourth being the Roman power. According to Daniel the ten horns or ten kings and kingdoms arise out of the Roman power and afterwards the little horn which was to overcome three horns or kings and kingdoms. A close study of Daniel 8:9 will show that the little horn is to arise out of that portion of the Roman power which formerly belonged to the Greek or Macedonian power. It is therefore especially noteworthy that we read in Rev. 13:2: "And the beast which I saw was like unto a leopard." With regard to the seventh head we read in Rev. 17:10: "When he cometh, he must continue a little while." This must refer to a new form of the Roman power, but this power would not long endure.[136] The seventh head cannot be the Papacy, inasmuch as it has already existed a long time and still possesses great power. However, the Roman Church stands in close relationship with the Roman world power. Many Bible commentators consider that the great harlot represents all false religions and especially the false Church which is enthroned in the spiritual Babylon or Rome. According to Rev. 17:3 the great harlot was seen sitting upon the scarlet-colored beast. The beast is one of the seven, and yet he is the eighth. Compare Rev. 17:11, 12:

[136] Many exegetes say that the seventh head is the Napoleonic empire. Auberlin holds that it is the Germano-Slavic. The geographic position and the short existence of both favor one of these views. The Napoleonic and German empires did not last long. The eighth, which is also one of the seven, is then the next head.

"And the beast that was, and is not, is himself also an eighth, and is of the seven; and he goeth into perdition. And the ten horns that thou sawest are ten kings, who have received no kingdom as yet; but they receive authority as kings, with the beast, for one hour." The final form of the world power will therefore consist in a confederation of ten kings and kingdoms. All of these kings have one mind, and they give their power and authority unto the beast. In this way the beast makes his appearance as a world prince. The first beast has been supported during the course of historical development by the second beast. Compare Rev. 13:11-17. When the first beast has developed to such an extent that the son of perdition makes his appearance upon the scene of world action, then he will be powerfully supported by the great false prophet. Although it is true that the second beast is represented in every false system of religion, still the content of Rev. 13:11-17 proves that only an individual person will answer fully the prophetical description of the second beast. The time set for the activity of the beast would likewise seem to prove that the final form of the Antichristian power is to be personal. Compare Rev. 13:5: "And there was given to him authority to continue forty and two months," which corresponds to the 1260 days or three and a half years. The historical school says that the 1260 days are 1260 years, but by reason of the description of the same time in terms of months the indication would seem to be that the time ought to be interpreted literally, although it is possible that in a symbolical and historical sense the days may also represent years, as in a grand rehearsal reaching its climax in a literal fulfillment of so many days. In the latter case the time indicated would have reference to the most important period in the history of Antichristianity, the occidental as well as the oriental.[137]

* * *

Although, strictly speaking, it does not come within the province of

---

137

Dogmatics to set forth the various chronological calculations of the different schools of prophetic thought and interpretation, still for the sake of completeness it is necessary to set forth by way of illustration the following brief summary of chronological data especially as used in the historical school. We hasten to remark, however, that calculations of this sort are only of comparative value, inasmuch as the study of chronology in connection with prophecy is encumbered with difficulties that the fulfillment of prophecy alone can solve. The historical school generally interprets a day to mean a year. A "time" is 360 years. Therefore it is assumed that 1260, 1290, 1335 and 2300 days mean so many years, either solar or lunar years. For instance, in Rev. 10, which is taken to have reference to the Reformation, it is stated in verse 6 that there shall be delay (time) no longer. This is interpreted to mean that hardly a "time" shall elapse between some important year connected with the Reformation and the events that shall transpire before the judgment period. Manifestly such calculations are uncertain. But some of them are interesting. Adding "a time" (360 years) to 1510, when Luther, on Pilate's staircase in Rome, was reminded of the words, "The just shall live by faith," we come to 1870, when the Pope lost his temporal power. All the leading dates in the Reformation era have led to or may lead to important events in modern times by similar calculations. In the same manner it is stated that the times of the Gentiles are equal to seven "times" or 2520 years.

The main Scripture passage cited is Lev. 26. There is no unanimity in determining the *terminus a quo*, but Nebuchadnezzar's vision of the image is taken to be a description of the times of the Gentiles, which becomes the determining factor in fixing the *terminus a quo*. The times of the Gentiles as to *terminus a quo* is usually counted from some important date in the reign of Nebuchadnezzar. If we add 2520 years to the earliest year of this king, we reach 1914, the beginning of the late World War. This year became a link in the chain binding the prophecies together to show the approach of a new Jewish era or history. Nebuchadnezzar ascended the throne the year 604-3. Add the 2520 years and we reach the year 1917, when Jerusalem was delivered to the English. We come to the same year, if we count from 622, the beginning of the Hegira period or starting point of the Mohammedan calendar and use the lunar scale. It was a great blow to the Turkish power when Jerusalem was captured or occupied by the English in December, 1917. The 2300 days in Daniel 8:14 mean as many years and the starting point is taken to be either the seventh or the twentieth year of the reign of Artaxerxes Longimanus. At the conclusion of this period (1844-1856), the Turkish power would begin to wane and correspondingly brighten the prospects of the Jews to reoccupy the Promised Land. And it is a fact that the Turkish power began to go to pieces in that decennary.

The Historical school of prophecy claims that the 30 and 45 days in Dan. 12:11, 12 added as years to the 1260 days or years makes a difference of 75 years, which makes 1335 days or years. If the 75 years are added to the decennary 1844-1856, we reach first 1918-1919, when Palestine in fact was taken from the Turks, and later we also reach the period of more and more Christian and Jewish occupancy of Palestine. If the 2520 years are counted from the capture of Zedekiah and the burning of the temple in the year B. C. 587, the time is so much more extended to remove hindrances standing in the way of the return of the Jews. Independent of the calculations of the length of the Times of the Gentiles, these times will end and the Gentiles cease to tread down Jerusalem, when the Lord interferes and overcomes the enemies of the Jewish people. The present events and attempts to settle the Jews in Palestine are signs of the times which should be carefully studied.

We would especially call attention to the calculation of the historical school in regard to the duration of the reigning power of Antichrist. It is assumed that the power of the occidental as well as the oriental Antichrists would last from 1260 to 1335 years. Compare Dan. 12 and Rev. 13. The historical school says 42 months, 1260 days and the expressions "time," "times," and "half a time" correspond to 1260 years Inasmuch as the Roman world power delayed (2 Thess. 2:6) the establishment of the Papacy, therefore the Antichristian period of the Papacy is counted either from the fall of Rome or from the. time that the Pope received temporal power or was recognized by Justinian and Phocas as the head of the Christian Church (between the years 533 and 607 or 610). The power of Mohammedanism is counted from some important year in the life of Mohammed or from the year of the conquest of Jerusalem by the Saracens and the building of the Mosque of Omar on the temple area in Jerusalem. The Mosque of Omar is supposed to be the abomination of desolation. Sometimes the time of the oriental Antichrist is reckoned in lunar years. The 1260 lunar years correspond to 1222 solar years and 1290 lunar years to 1250 solar years. There are many striking results which can be obtained by means of calculations from different starting points in Roman and Mohammedan history. Let us mention one example. From the death of Phocas in 610 to 1870 is just 1260 years. The Pope lost his temporal power in 1870, but he still possesses great political power indirectly. The historical school, however, points out the extension of 30 and 45 years beyond the 1260 years spoken of in Daniel 12. We ought to state that not all adherents of the historical school follow these calculations. Without going into further detail, we desire to express the assumption that if the 1260 days do not represent a round number symbolically, then they represent so many days literally.

On account of the seventy weeks in Dan. 9, being year-weeks, it is possible or even probable that the days in Daniel mean years. Dan. 12:6, 7 seems to favor the year-day theory, but verses 8-12. speaking of "the issue of these things," uphold the literal day theory. The Revelation of John treats principally of the issue or the so-called last times. The thousand years could not mean so many days. The usage of days and months favors the literal day theory. In Rev. 13 the 1260 days correspond to 42 months, which strengthens the literal interpretation. The latter interpretation is further strengthened in Rev. 11, where the two witnesses are mentioned, and these must be real persons. The days in verses 3, 9, and 11 must be literal days. The 1260 days mark the culmination in the development of the Antichristian power as well as the period of great tribulation. We would not deny that the above-mentioned calculations may have their significance in typifying on a great scale that which at the end of this age will appear in more concentrated and limited form. The Lord says: "And except those days had been shortened, no flesh would have been saved: but for the elect's sake those days shall be shortened" (Matt. 24:22).

It behooves us to exercise the greatest care in the interpretation of the data of prophecy which indeed are not given to us in order to satisfy our human curiosity, but for the comfort and the guidance of the Christian Church and especially of such Christians as are alive during those critical periods. In the time of fulfillment the mysterious will become clear and the numbers also will assist men in watching the signs of the time.

3. *The Signs of the Last Times.*

Signa temporis sive diei novissimi are, among others: 1) *Remota,* among which may be mentioned: a) the continued victory of truth and the judgments of history; compare Rev. 6:2, which deals with the first seal; Isa. 26:9; Ps. 64:7-9; 110:1-3; b) wars and rumors of wars; compare Rev. 6:4, which deals with the second seal; Matt. 24:6; Mark 13:7; Luke 21:9; c) famine; compare Rev. 6:5, 6, where the third seal is described; Matt. 24:7; Mark 13:8; Luke 21:11; d) pestilence and other misfortunes; compare Rev. 6:8, where the fourth seal is described; Matt. 24:7; Mark 13:8; Luke 21:11; e) persecutions; Rev. 6:9, containing a description of the fifth seal; Matt. 24:8, 9; Mark 13:9; Luke 21:12. These signs continue throughout a protracted period, while the sufferings which are portrayed vary as to degree. It is also evident that these signs may occur successively or simultaneously. We may therefore say that these signs are of a more general nature and do not constitute a clear indication of the near approach of the last day. For this reason our Lord warns His disciples, saying: "Take heed that ye be not led astray: for many shall come in my name, saying, I am he; and, The time is at hand: go ye not after them. And when ye shall hear of wars and tumults, be not terrified: for these things must needs come to pass first; but the end is not immediately" (Luke 21:8, 9).

2) *Propinqua,* among which may be counted the following: a) the apostasy (*ἀποστασία,* mentioned especially in 2 Thess. 2:3), which shall continue a

long time and ripen toward the end. In a certain sense the "falling away" began early in the history of the Church. Compare Acts 20:29, 30; 1 John 2:18, 19; 4:3. But the true Church of Christ continues nevertheless in spite of the apostasy and continues to win great victories. This was very clearly seen during the Reformation period. However, the old apostasy has not ceased, and new apostasies have taken place. "And many false prophets shall arise, and shall lead many astray" (Matt. 24:11); b) increasing unbelief, the old heathenism appearing in new forms; "For the time will come when they will not endure the sound doctrine; but having itching ears, will heap to themselves teachers after their own lusts; and will turn away their ears from the truth, and turn aside unto fables" (2 Tim. 4:3, 4); c) great increase of spiritual knowledge (Daniel 12:4) and the rapid growth of the sciences; d) general feeling of security and self-confidence by reason of wonderful human progress. Compare Isa. 47:7; Rev. 18:7; 2 Peter 3:4; e) watchful and prayerful waiting on the part of the Christians for the coming of the Lord. Compare Luke 12:36; 1 Thess. 5:4-6.

3) *Propinquiora*, among which we wish to point out the following: a) Spiritualism, or the doctrine of evil spirits (*προσέχοντης πνεύμασιν πλάνοις καὶ διδασκαλίαις δαιμονίων*, 1 Tim. 4:1); b) difficult social problems. Compare 2 Tim. 3:1-4; c) political signs, causing grave anxiety by reason of great disturbances, which occur toward the close of the present world dominion before the beast has made his appearance in fully developed form. Compare Daniel 2: 41—43; 7:7; 8: 9; d) the spirit of indifference in the Christian Church, the Laodicean period. Compare Rev. 3:15-17; Matt. 25:5; Luke 17:26-29; e) the increasing power of lawlessness. Compare Matt. 24:12; f) the beginning of the end of the dispersion of the children of Israel, accompanied by signs which will mark the close of the times of the Gentiles. Compare Daniel 12:7; Luke 21:24. Some of the Bible statements refer to the restoration from Babel, others speak plainly of a restoration from all parts of the earth. "And it shall come to pass in that day, that the Lord will set his hand again the second time to recover the remnant of his people. . .and from the islands of the sea. And he will set up an ensign for the nations, and will assemble the outcasts of Israel

and gather together the dispersed of Judah from the four corners of the earth" (Isa. 11:11, 12). There are many passages which plainly prove that there will be a more national return to the Holy Land than the present immigration. And yet the returning Jews from Babylon numbered only about fifty thousand. The Christian occupancy of Palestine will further Jewish immigration and colonization. The second restoration will also include Israelites of the ten tribes. All these things may seem impossible, but God will accomplish it when the time is ripe. The first return of a greater number by various influences does not imply a conversion to Christianity. On account of Mohammedan resistance to the colonization of Jews and rebuilding of the temple and also by political hindrances, there may be a delay in forming a Jewish state. This may finally lead to the "firm covenant" spoken of in Dan. 9:27. If the "little horn" or the "prince that shall come," see verses 26, 27, promises the Jews an independent state, they may accept him as a Messiah. Christ said: "I am come in my Father's name, and ye receive me not; if another shall come in his own name, him ye will receive" (John 5:43). The forming of such a state under a false Messiah is not the restoration promised by God. The real restoration will come later after the great tribulation;[138] g) calamitous visitations, such as the continually recurring *signa remota*, which become increasingly apparent and significant. Earthquakes, storms, disasters, pestilence, famine, wars and rumors of wars and similar plagues will take place here and there in the world and will increase in frequency. But in spite of these visitations everything will be as usual. The work of the Church will continue. The

---

[138]The restoration promised in the prophets is often referred to. "In that day Jehovah made a covenant with Abram, saying, Unto thy seed have I given this land, from the river of Egypt unto the great river, the river Euphrates" (Gen. 15:18). In regard to the future of Israel, read Deut. 30-33; Hosea 14; Isaiah 11:11, 12; such a passage cannot be spiritualized; Jeremiah 30:2, 3; 31:10, 33, 34, referring to their national conversion; Zech. 12:10-13:1; this passage in Zechariah does not only speak of an outpouring of the Spirit upon the house of David and the inhabitants of Jerusalem, but brings before us, how Jehovah speaks of Himself as pierced. The Jews will then know whom they crucified, and then follows the national mourning. The last chapter of Zechariah presents the nation as delivered and restored. In the New Testament prophecies Luke 1:30-33 is usually spiritualized in regard to the last three 'snails,' but there are many exegetes who hold that these three 'shalls' must be literally fulfilled, just as the four preceding. Not all of these interpreters hold the view that the Lord will occupy an earthly throne, but that the Lord will rule from the heavenly Jerusalem, "coming down out of heaven from God," and rule over the house of Jacob as David's son. This would not come in conflict with the universal kingship of the Lord, and does not prevent the prominence of the old Jerusalem in a theocratic kingdom during a possible millennial age. And the King of kings can appear in Jerusalem and other places. The second advent of the Lord does not mean a short stay and then another ascension and withdrawal. If the Lord visits different parts of His kingdom and His throne is in the Jerusalem from above, there is no real absence of the King and no cessation of the second advent. He will never more leave the saints. There are many passages in regard to the restoration and the kingdom of God during the transition period and the full establishment of the eternal kingdom. Such passages belong to exegesis and not to Dogmatics. Among such passages we only call attention to a few. such as Amos 9:11-15; Isaiah 2:2-4; Jer. 33:14-18; in the study of the 18th verse we should follow the law of Hermeneutics, that the clear passages must explain the dark and mysterious and not the reverse. When the Jews accept Christianity, they will not continue to offer burnt offerings for sin. The epistle to the Hebrews and the whole New Testament proves it. There are also similar problems of exegesis in regard to Ezekiel's new temple. As there cannot be any contradictions in the Bible, all problems will be solved. The following passages may also be specially interesting in exegetical research: Ezekiel 44:1-3; 45:7; compare Isaiah 32:1, 2; Zech. 14:9-21.

times will become better and worse. The children of this world will not understand the signs of the times and will explain them in the natural way. With regard to many the saying of Scripture will find application: "And they repented not of their murders, nor of their sorceries, nor of their fornication, nor of their thefts" (Rev. 9:21); compare Rev. 8 and 9 with regard to the six trumpets, which may be reckoned as *signa propinquiora*. It may be said with regard to the time characterized by these signs: "But all these things are the beginning of travail" (Matt. 24:8).

4) *Proximo*, are the signs which occur immediately before the revelation or epiphany of Christ. We would point out the following: a) the preaching of the Gospel in the whole world for a testimony unto all the nations. Compare Matt. 24:14; Mark 13:10; b) the culminating activity of the beast and his last personal manifestation. Compare Dan. 2:44; 7:24-26; 8:23-26; 11:31-45; 2 Thess. 2:8, 9; Rev. 13; 17:11-13; c) the abomination of desolation. The golden image of Nebuchadnezzar (Daniel 3) is a type of the abomination of desolation. Daniel 9:27 makes mention of this abomination. Literally translated the words read: "Upon the wing of abominations, the desolator." The desolator or the so-called little horn or the beast is borne, as it were, upon the wing of abominations into power. These abominations may include all the evil powers and influences which labor together in the final development and expression of Antichristianity. The abomination of desolation, spoken of as standing in the holy place, has reference to the image of the beast set forth in Rev. 13:14, 15; compare

Daniel 3:1-15; 9:27; 11:31; 12:11; Matt. 24:15;[139] d) the great tribulation. Compare Daniel 11: 41; 12: 1; Matt. 24: 15—22; Mark 13: 19, 20; Rev. 7: 14; 13: 16, 17. This tribulation is the greatest of all tribulations and the last great tribulation. The time of this tribulation is limited and in its severest form it will very probably not last more than three and a half years. However, this question cannot be dogmatically determined. There are different opinions with regard to prophetic chronology. The Scriptures have the following to say with regard to the limitation of time in relation

[139] In order to understand better the development leading to the abomination of desolation, remember the covenant (Dan. 9:27) which will be made by the false Messiah with the returned Jews. Correct exegesis is here very important. The best modern exegetes hold that "the anointed one, the prince" in the 25th verse is not the same as the prince in the latter part of the 26th verse, which prince will be the little horn or the Antichrist. The anointed one in the 25th verse and in the beginning of the 26th verse is Christ or the true Messiah. From a certain decree issued to rebuild Jerusalem during the rule of Artaxerxes 483 years should elapse until Christ. Some claim that the anointing refers to the Baptism of Christ, and others say it refers to the entrance of Christ into Jerusalem on Palm Sunday. In either case it is a remarkable fulfillment of prophecy. Many commentators hold that the 70th year-week should be continuous with the 69. It seems to them that the 490 years should run without any break. But a closer study of the text and facts proves that there is a break. It is stated that after the 483 years the Messiah shall be cut off, which means His death on the cross. Then it is further stated that the City and the temple shall be destroyed by the people of the prince that shall come. We know that the Romans destroyed the City and the temple in the year 70, and the text states that wars, etc., shall continue unto the end. Nothing continuous with the 69th year-week or immediately following the cutting off of Christ is mentioned. Christ did not make a covenant for seven years and after three and a half years cause the sacrifice, etc., to cease. Some of the exegetes claim that the *terminus ad quem* was the Baptism of Christ and that after three and a half years He died, when sacrifices ceased to have a meaning. But then we have nothing to mark the end of the firm covenant of seven years. This proves that the 483 years are not followed by the seven years, but there is a break which will continue until the actual beginning of the seven last years of the Times of the Gentiles from which 490 years were apportioned off to relate what would refer to the Jewish people and the Holy City and besides concerns all the children of God. What should be accomplished in these years reaches to the end of the present age or time. During this unreckoned time from the end of the 69th year-week the Church is fulfilling its mission, the Gospel is preached for a testimony unto all the nations and the fullness of the Gentiles is gathered in. At the correct time the 70th year-week shall begin.

to the great tribulation: "And except those days had been shortened, no flesh would have been saved: but for the elect's sake those days shall be shortened" (Matt. 24:22). Important events take place in connection with the great tribulation, such as the appearance of the two witnesses, their death in Jerusalem (Rev. 11:8), together with their ascension into heaven. The seven bowls of wrath poured out upon the adherents of the beast belong to this period, as well as the judgment of the great harlot or the fall

---

Who will confirm the seven-year covenant? Dan. 9:27 answers the question. The prince that shall come from the people that destroyed the Holy City and temple. He will, therefore, come from the territory of the Roman empire and be a Roman. This verse in Dan. 9 does not say from what part of the Roman world. The last manifestation of the Roman empire will be the Ten Kingdom Confederacy. When the little horn arises and conquers three of the former horns, this little horn does not remain little, but soon develops into a world emperor or "the prince that shall come." In the middle of the year-week this world-emperor or the political Antichrist will cancel all his promises and become the beast, as pictured in Daniel and Revelation. During the first three and a half years the Jews will enjoy religious liberty. During that time the Jews will begin rebuilding their temple and sacrifices will be offered. But "in the midst of the week he shall cause the sacrifice and oblation to cease." In the meantime the second beast or the false prophet appears and commands that an image of the first beast be erected and worshipped. This will be the concrete expression of the abomination of desolation. Antiochus Epiphanes and his abomination of desolation were only types of the political Antichrist and the abomination of desolation in the last times. The views of the so-called higher critics cannot be correct, since Christ refers to Daniel and places the abomination in the future. The destruction of Jerusalem and the burning of the temple can only be a type. Titus cannot be considered as the Antichrist, and he tried to save the temple. Notice also that verse 14 in Matt. 24 describes the Gospel period. And then follows the description of the last times.

of Babylon, etc.[140] During this period the sixth and seven seals are also broken and their prophecies consummated. Compare Rev. 11:3-14; 16:1-16; 17:16-18; 18:2-8; e) Har-Magedon and the great battle at Jerusalem in connection with the second advent. In Rev. 16:13-16 we read that from the Dragon, the Antichrist and the False Prophet (second beast or the religious Antichrist) went forth three unclean spirits or demons, working signs, which go forth unto the kings of the whole earth to gather them together unto the great war of the great day of God, the Almighty. And they were gathered together into the place called Har-Magedon. Compare Rev. 16:13-16. The Megiddo or Esdraelon plain has been one of the great battlefields of the nations. When the nations of the world will send armies to Palestine, some fighting against the two Antichrists and most of them fighting on the side of the world emperor or political Antichrist and the False Prophet, we can understand why the battlefield will extend from

---

[140] During the first centuries of the Christian era the City of Rome was often designated by the symbolical name Babylon. Tradition cannot in every instance be rejected. Irenaeus was a disciple of Polycarp, who was the disciple of St. John, and he says that the Great Babylon spoken of in Revelation meant Rome. In his Fifth Book against Heresies, chapter 26, he calls Rome by the symbolical name of Babylon. He evidently had been informed by Polycarp what John meant by Babylon. Tertulllan says, "Babylon is a figure of the Roman City, mighty, proud of its sway and fiercely persecuting the saints" (Lib. adv. Jud.). Jerome and Eusebius held the same opinion. Roman Catholics like Bellarmin and Bossuet admitted that Rome was meant, but not Papal Rome. The Historical School of Prophecy holds that Babylon is Papal Rome, although some adherents of this school think that Constantinople will materialize as Babylon of the last days. Many Futurists hold that it means Rome as revived Pagan during the two Beasts (Rev. 13), when Antichristianity attains to its climax. It is interesting to note that the coins and medals of old Rome in many cases bear the figure of a woman sitting on seven hills, and she is styled "The mistress of the world." If Rome in the last period before the second advent should become the Great Babylon as Capital of the last phase of Antichristianity, it does not prevent other cities from being included in the Confederacy of evil. We must also consider that the symbolical name also implies that Babylon is a harlot and mother of the harlots and the abominations of earth which brings into review false religions, persecutions of every description and counter-persecutions, but the 17th chapter of Revelation pictures the climax as it appears shortly before Christ's return to judgment and the historical background.

Har-Magedon to Bozrah, a distance of 1600 stadia. Rev. 14:20. Cf. Isa. 63:1-6. Although some exegetes have referred this to Calvary or the atonement, it is evident that this text is a prophecy which will be fulfilled at the second advent. It pictures one of the awful scenes of "the great and dreadful day of the Lord." Josephus relates that when the Romans destroyed Jerusalem so great was the bloodshed that the whole city ran with blood to such a degree that fires in furnaces were quenched by it. The Bible does not overdraw the picture of the bloodshed on the battlefield from Har-Magedon to Bozrah. Compare also Isa. 34:1-8; Ps. 2:1-5; Ezek. 38:14-23; Joel 2:1, 2; 3:1, 2; Zech. 12:2, 3; "And it shall come to pass in that day, that I will seek to destroy all the nations that come against Jerusalem" (v. 9); read carefully Zech. 14:1-5, which describes the last battle at Jerusalem in connection with the second coming; cf. Joel 3:12. Read carefully Matt. 24:16-31; Mark 13:14-27, which refer to the second advent period; Luke 21:20-24 refers to the destruction of Jerusalem in the year 70; read also Rev. 19:11-21. As all nations more or less will be represented by armies, it is interesting to study Ezekiel, 38th and 39th chapters. Some exegetes hold the view that Gog is identical with "the little horn" or the political Antichrist, and others that he is the king of the North, mentioned in Daniel, but if neither view is correct, it is clear that he is an ally with the political Antichrist and the False Prophet at the battles on the old Esdraelon plain and at Jerusalem, as it is stated that in the latter days he shall come against Israel (Ezek. 38:16). He is called Gog of Magog, prince of Rosh (perhaps Russia), Meshech (Moscow) and Tubal (perhaps Tobolsk). Gomer in the sixth verse covered Germany and Austria of our day. Persia, Cush and Put are also mentioned. According to Rev. 16:12, "the kings of the sunrising" shall also take part, i.e., the rulers east of Euphrates; f) a great earthquake and terrifying signs in the heavens. Many earthquakes will have preceded, and one is especially mentioned in Rev. 11:13, but this earthquake will be the greatest. "And there was a great earthquake, such as was not since there were men upon the earth, so great an earthquake, so mighty. And the great city was divided into three parts, and the cities of the nations fell" (Rev. 16:18, 19); "And there was a great earthquake; and the sun became black as sackcloth of hair, and the whole moon became as blood; and the stars of heaven fell unto the earth" (Rev. 6:12, 13). These signs occur not long after, and very probably immediately after, the great tribulation and at the time of our Lord's coming on the clouds of heaven with power and great glory. The following Scripture passages prove that these signs are the last and decisive signs before the second advent period of Christ: "But immediately after the tribulation of those days the sun shall be darkened, and the moon shall not give her light, and the stars shall fall from heaven, and the powers of the heavens shall be shaken: and then shall appear the sign of the Son of man in heaven: and then shall all the tribes of the earth mourn, and they shall see the Son of man coming on the clouds of heaven with power and great glory" (Matt. 24:29, 30); "But in those days, after that tribulation, the sun shall be darkened, and the moon shall not give her light, and the stars shall be falling from heaven, and the powers that are in the heavens shall be shaken" (Mark 13:24, 25). Compare Luke 21:25-28; Rev. 10:5-7.

Many earnest Christians, in studying the signs of the times and longing for the return of the Lord, inquire if there are no means of calculation as to the period in which we live. The New Testament does not contain such a clear prophecy in regard to the time of the second advent as the seventy weeks in Dan. 9 point out the time of the first advent. Although only God knows the exact time, year, and date of the return of Christ, there are prophecies describing clear signs from which we may conclude in what period we live. Among such prophecies in the Old Testament we call attention to Dan. 2, which has been called the Almanac of prophecy. Nebuchadnezzar had a dream vision which Daniel revealed and interpreted to the king. Daniel regarded the dream as a communication from God. The great image which the king had seen in the dream was a revelation concerning the destiny of several world dominions in their historical development to the end of the present world and a description of the kingdom of God which will supercede the great world empires. In studying the meaning of the prophecy, great emperors and empires pass in review, from Nebuchadnezzar and Babylon to the last form of the Roman empire during the ten kings' confederacy. We see in this review the kingdoms of gold, silver, brass, iron and the mixed kingdom of clay and iron. Then follows the eternal kingdom, presented as a stone kingdom for reasons that are plain. It is clear to all Bible students that the great four, Babylon, Medo-Persia, the Greek-Macedonian and the old Roman empires, have passed. The iron legs of the figure have stretched through many centuries, and everything proves that we have reached the feet, yea, the middle of the feet, and that the next formation is the confederacy of the ten kingdoms, when according to the figure we have come to the toes. When we consider the league of nations and the association of nations, it is evident that the confederacy of the ten kingdoms or the revival of the Roman empire will follow at the mature time in the future. If we consider the present state of society and especially the political upheaval in Europe and in the near East, it is also clear that we have entered the period "of miry clay and iron" or the last period before the judgment era. Only God knows the length of the period. Consider also that we, according to the seven church periods, have come to the Laodicean period of lukewarmness, disorder and worldly domineering. Whether we follow the Historical School of prophetical interpretation or the Futurist method, we know what periods are passed and where we are, according to Daniel and other prophecies in their clear statements. If the day of the Lord will come to unbelievers "as a thief in the night," it is also true what Paul says in 1 Thess. 5:4: "But ye, brethren, are not in darkness, that that day should overtake you as a thief."

Gerhard presents four reasons why Christ foretold the signs of the end of the world:[141] 1) as a proof of love (*ut essent sui erga nos amoris demonstrativa*); 2) as a means of expelling security (securitas expulsiva); 3) as an antidote against exaggerated anxiety or curiosity (*περιεργίας alexipharmaca*). On the one hand he warns men against false security and on the other against immoderate curiosity. The Lord has not revealed the day nor the hour of His coming. It is certain that we are to die, but we

[141] *Loci Theologici,* Tomus Nonus, Cap. VII, XIX, 274, etc.

do not know the day of our death. In the same manner it is certain that the day of the Lord will come, but we cannot tell when. He refers us to Matt. 24:44; Luke 12:46; 1 Thess. 5:3; 4) as a remedy for pusillanimity (*μικροψυχίας remedia*). Christ says: "But when these things begin to come to pass, look up, and lift up your heads; because your redemption draweth nigh" (Luke 21:28).

§42. The Second Coming of Christ.

During the Old Testament dispensation the faithful looked with longing expectancy for the time when the sun of righteousness would arise with healing in his wings and spread the light of heaven in the world of darkness. That time came, and the star of Bethlehem appeared glimmering in the heavens, and the Light of the world shone upon the earth. This light has not been extinguished, although the Lord is not now visibly present upon the earth. And yet while the New Testament possesses the light of day in comparison with the Old Testament, still the believers expect a still more glorious day when the Lord shall come again. In this respect the believers of the New Testament resemble the faithful Israelites of the Old Testament, inasmuch as both look for the Christ. In His first advent the Lord came in the fullness of time, and when the predetermined time of His second advent shall arrive, He will come again. The first advent throws light upon the second advent, and the latter completes the former. There are many prophecies in the Old Testament which have reference to the second advent, although the prophets did not seem to understand that the Messiah would appear twice upon the earth. Not even John the Baptist had a clear conception of the two advents. His twofold prophetic testimony concerning Christ resembled the prophecies of the predecessors, and he was himself astonished that the work of the Messiah was that of a Saviour alone and not also that of a Judge. But Christ came the first time as a Saviour, and the second time He shall come again as a Judge and Redeemer. The Scriptures set forth much in connection with the advent of our Lord, but the full import and significance of it will be made perfectly clear only by the coming of the great day itself. And yet, although the cloak of mystery conceals much and renders many problems in eschatology difficult of solution, still the doctrine of the second coming of Christ is very precious and of great worth, because upon it rests the hope of the Church that the kingdom of God shall enter upon its state of perfection in the new heaven and upon the new earth.

1. Definition of the Second Advent.

The Second Advent of Christ is the act of Christ, the God-man, when in accordance with His promise He shall come on the clouds of heaven with power and great glory for the purpose of redeeming His own, completing His work and judging the world according to His eternal purpose, to the honor of God and the joy of the blessed in the eternal kingdom. The first advent of Christ was characterized by the work of atonement and in principle the redemption, the second advent will be characterized by the practical works of redemption when the Lord shall also sit in righteous judgment upon all men. He is the Lion that is of the tribe of Judah, the Lamb that hath overcome (Rev. 5), He is the Redeemer who is worthy to open the book, and to loose the seals thereof. And when the seals have been broken, then shall great voices sound forth in the seventh trumpet in heaven and say, "The kingdom of the world is become the kingdom of our Lord, and of his Christ; and he shall reign for ever and ever" (Rev. 11:15). Compare Rev. 19:6, 11-16.

2. The Attributes Of The Second Advent.

Adventus Christi, which includes both *παρουσία* and *επιφάνεια* ἡ *ἀποχάλυψις*, is more precisely defined by the following attributes: 1) *personalis*, or personal, which term is used against such as say that the advent takes place when men die or that it takes place spiritually in the dispensations of Providence; 2) *certus*, or certain. In the Old Testament there are many prophecies concerning the advent that are expressed in such language that only the second advent can be referred to. In the New Testament there are many clear and precise promises and prophecies in relation to the second advent of Christ. About one-thirtieth of the content of the New Testament relates to eschatology. There is sure ground for the doctrine of the personal advent of Christ in the Word of God; 3) *visibilis*, or visible. We direct attention to the following Scripture passages: "For as the lightning cometh forth from the east, and is seen even unto the west; so shall be the coming of the Son of man" (Matt. 24:27); "And they shall see the Son of man coming on the clouds of heaven" (Matt. 24:30); "Henceforth ye shall see the Son of man sitting at the right hand of Power, and coming on the clouds of heaven" (Matt. 26:64). These last words were uttered under oath before the high priest. Compare Rev. 1:7. The Greek expressions, such as *επιφάνεια*, indicate that the advent will be visible. This is not disproved even if it can be proved that the epiphany will be preceded by a *παρουσία* when the marriage supper of the Lamb (Rev. 19:7-9) is to be celebrated, as some commentators assert. The Scriptures are very clear in making the second coming of our. Lord an *adventus visibilis*; 4) *gloriosus*, or glorious. In the nature of the case the second coming will be glorious and majestic. Compare Luke 21:27; Matt. 25:31; 5) *terribilis*, or terrible, for the unbelievers. Compare Rev. 6:15-17; 6) *exoptatus*, or greatly longed for, by the believers. The epistles of Paul speak more frequently of the coming of Christ than of death and of the blessed intermediate state. The advent of Christ is the hope of the saints. Even the blessed dead long for it (Rev. 6:10, 11); 7) *beatificus*. The faithful who have passed away are indeed blessed in the intermediate state, but their salvation will be completed when Christ returns again. To those that are alive at the second coming of the Lord and who are members of the true Church the second advent will be blessed (*beatificus*) in a double sense, inasmuch as they escape the experience of death and instead will be changed and caught up in the clouds to meet the Lord in the air. Compare 2 Cor. 5:2; 1 Thess. 4:17.

At the ascension of Christ into heaven not all prophecies relating to the advent were fulfilled, which proves that He will come again, when the remaining prophecies will be fulfilled. Although the prophecies in regard to the personal second coming are plain, there are many skeptics who either doubt the second advent or claim that the event took place at the destruction of Jerusalem, and there are others who say that Christ comes to each believer at death. The last view does not explain the personal return of Christ, when He will be seen by all living and resurrected in the judgment period. The second coming will be just as real, personal and visible as the first advent. Some cannot comprehend the seeing of Christ with mortal eyes. They forget that Christ was seen by the disciples in His resurrection body. Christ did not receive another body at the ascension. And He will return in the same body as He ascended. The appearance in glory is not another body, but only another condition of the same body. Even in the state of humiliation His body was glorified at the transfiguration.

In order to assist in removing some misunderstandings, where there are seeming contradictions, we call attention to some passages that have troubled Bible readers. One of these passages is Matt. 16: 27, 28. In regard to the statement in verse 27, we will find by comparing the parallels in Mark and Luke that there is no attempt to give a chronological order of events. Verse 27 is simply an argument used by Matthew. He wrote his gospel primarily to convince the Jews that Jesus was the Christ. His object was not to present Eschatology in perfect chronology. The key to a correct understanding lies often in considering if the parallels are true as to a given passage or false in that respect. The kingdom of God has two phases, just as the first and second advent are two phases of the advent. The Old Testament speaks of the advent, but fulfillment proves that the advent is divided in two. When Christ stood before Pilate (John 18:36, 37) He spoke of the kingdom in its first phase and, therefore, the kingdom of another world and a kingdom of truth. When Jesus stood before the high priest, He swore that He was the Christ, the Son of God, and said: "Henceforth ye shall see the Son of man sitting at the right hand of Power, and coming on the clouds of heaven." By this saying He referred to His glorious visible return and the kingdom in its second phase. This declaration of Christ on oath was not fulfilled at the destruction of Jerusalem, A. D. 70, and it has not been fulfilled yet. Christ has not returned. The second coming belongs to the future. The kingdom, therefore, having two phases, does Matt. 16:28 refer to the first phase or to the last? Plainly to the first phase, if we follow the law of true parallels. Otherwise Christ had returned during the first century, because some of those listening should not taste of death, "till they see the Son of man coming in his kingdom." This problem will be solved by the true parallels and by necessary common sense in interpretation. Compare Mark 9:1 as a parallel: "Till they see the kingdom of God come with power." Some of those disciples who were listening saw the kingdom of God in power at the transfiguration of Christ, at the entrance of Christ into Jerusalem on Palm Sunday, at His resurrection and ascension, at Pentecost and in the victories of Christianity in the Roman empire. If the second advent took place at the destruction of Jerusalem, a great part of the New Testament becomes meaningless. Let us also notice the meaning of Matt. 24:34: "This generation shall not pass away, till all these things be accomplished." It is claimed that generation only means an ordinary lifetime, and, therefore, everything must have been fulfilled at the destruction of Jerusalem. Prominent scholars claim that the Greek word for generation also means race or nation. Christ may, therefore, have used the word in the sense "race or nation" and probably did. No one can contradict the fact that the Jews exist as an exclusive race and without a national home keep intact as a nation. Even if we should forego the legitimate translation and meaning of the word, we must carefully note the time connection of the passage. It is evident that Christ spoke as by anticipation describing the time of fulfillment. He transplants the hearers to the time when these things take place and means that the generation then living would not pass away before all was fulfilled. Some have translated: "That generation (then living) will not pass away." In either case there will be no contradiction. — Matt. 10:23 will be clear by studying the context and by following the same principle as in the interpretation of Matt. 16:28. — Rev. 1:1 and 3 and also 22:20 contain prophetic expressions which do not necessarily imply the human way of counting. Compare 2 Peter 3:8 and context. Note "speedily" in Luke 18:7, 8. There would be no conflict with the prophetical formula in

Rev. 1 and 22, if we would interpret the phrases to mean that the events would "shortly come to pass" or would soon begin to be fulfilled, one after the other, although the content, humanly speaking, would require a long time to develop. If we consider the seven churches in their prophetic meaning, the statements in the Revelation began to materialize quickly in the historical development, although the Book of Revelation principally pictures the period of the second advent and the climax of the historical development.

In regard to the certainty of the future second advent the promises are many and clear. While on earth, Christ gave many and plain promises as to His visible and glorious return. Besides, Christ declared on oath, as already mentioned, that He shall return on the clouds of heaven. When He had just ascended visibly, the two heavenly messengers said: "Ye men of Galilee, why stand ye looking into heaven? this Jesus, who was received from you into heaven, shall so come in like manner as ye beheld him going into heaven." This passage, Acts 1:11, cannot be twisted to disprove the visible return of Christ by claiming that the rendering "in like manner" is a wrong translation. The deniers of a future visible return contend that the Greek words should be translated as in Matt. 23:37; Acts 7:28; 2 Tim. 3:8. If "in like manner" is excluded and the translation would be rendered "shall come as," the text would support the view that Christ shall return visibly and personally as He ascended. Compare the Greek original. The best scholars have translated "shall so come in like manner as." The analogy of faith and true parallels of ideas prove plainly that Christ shall return visibly and as He ascended. We might quote Zech. 14:4, but it is not necessary. The passage is interesting as describing locality in a detailed manner, proving that it is not a figurative passage. Another clear passage is Acts 3:29, 21: "That he may send the Christ who hath been appointed for you, even Jesus, whom the heavens must receive until the times of restoration of all things." The times of refreshing and restoration have not yet come. The whole statement proves that Jesus Christ shall return personally. Study also the following passages: 1 Thess. 1:10 and 3:13, "to wait for his Son from heaven" and "at the coming of our Lord Jesus with all his saints"; 1 Cor. 15:51, 52 (the revealed mystery); 1 Thess. 4:13-17; 2 Thess. 2, relating how "the lawless one" shall be slain by the Lord Jesus at His manifestation; 1 Thess. 4:16: "The Lord himself shall descend from heaven, with a shout, with the voice of an archangel, and with the trump of God: and the dead in Christ shall rise first." This has not yet occurred. All these passages and many more prove the certainty of Christ's personal and visible return. If Christ does not return, the book of Revelation would be a New Testament apocrypha and not "an apocalypsis." But as the book of Revelation is the Apocalypse of Jesus Christ at His second advent, this whole book becomes the climax in the arguments for the visible, personal and glorious return of Christ as Redeemer.

3. The Effects of the Second Advent.

In connection with the second advent of Christ there will take place the resurrection, first of the dead in Christ who shall rise first, accompanied by the transformation of the believers in Christ who are then alive; the meeting of the true Church with the Lord in the air; the marriage of the Lamb; the various acts of judgment; the end of the present world aeon and the beginning of the eternal kingdom. — We quote the following passages to prove that the transformation of the believers takes place in connection with the resurrection of the dead: "Behold, I tell you a mystery: We all shall not sleep, but we shall all be changed, in a moment, in the twinkling of an eye, at the last trump: for the trumpet shall sound, and the dead shall be raised incorruptible, and we shall be changed" (1 Cor. 15:51, 52). Compare 1 Thess. 4:15; also 2 Cor. 5:2-4, where the change is spoken of as being "clothed upon." This transformation or being "clothed upon" is called *ἐπενδύσασθαι* (2 Cor. 5:2-4), to die or be "unclothed" is called *ἐκδύσασθαι*, while to arise or "being clothed" is called *ἐνδύσασθαι*. The Scripture passages which especially set forth the meeting of the true Church with the Lord in the air are the following: Luke 17:34-37; 1 Thess. 4:17; Rev. 12:5. With regard to the marriage of the Lamb, read Matt. 25:1-13; 2 Cor. 11:2; Eph. 5:32, and with regard to the marriage supper, read Rev. 19:7-9. Among the acts of judgment connected with the second coming of the Lord may be mentioned the war of the great day of God, the Almighty (Rev. 16:14). According to Rev. 16:16 it would seem as if this struggle were to be fought in the plain of Esdraelon, the battlefield of Jewish history, or Har-Magedon. Compare also Zech. 14:1-7, 12-15, which proves that the struggle is to take place likewise at Jerusalem. During this struggle the judgment of the two beasts takes place. Compare Rev. 19:19-21. With regard to this struggle the Lord has issued warning words to those that live in Judea. Compare Matt. 24:15-28. While these warning words, in accordance with Luke 20:20-24, may have had reference to the destruction of Jerusalem under Titus, still the judgment on Jerusalem was merely the type of a still greater destruction and tribulation. In accordance with Matthew and Mark these warnings would seem to have reference to the time of our Lord's second coming. Compare §41, 3, e. With regard to the judgment in the specific sense together with the end of the world, note the special paragraphs which treat of them.

The most difficult problem which eschatology is called upon to solve is the question as to whether the eternal kingdom is to be preceded by or begun with a preparatory aeon or period, which is called the millennium. There are some who have believed that the millennium would precede the second coming of Christ, and this view is called Postmillennialism, while others state that the millennium will begin immediately after the coming of the Lord, and this view is called Premillennialism. The adherents of gross Chiliasm conceive of the millennium as being an earthly carnal kingdom of glory and happiness, as though the kingdom of God were of this world. The Augsburg Confession in its XVII Article has the following to say about this theory and the Chiliastic view of the Anabaptists: "*Damnant et alios, qui nunc spargunt iudaicas opiniones, quod ante resurrectionem mortuorum pii regnum mundi occupaturi sint, ubique oppressis impiis.*"[142] Translated, this reads: "They also condemn others who spread Jewish opinions, that before the resurrection of the dead the

[142] Müller, *Symb. Bücher*, p. 63.

godly shall occupy the kingdom of the world, the wicked being everywhere suppressed." Melanchthon declares in Variata that the Anabaptists are referred to. The Confessions have not otherwise given expression to any Views on the millennium. But this expression of the Augsburg Confession makes clear the position of the Lutheran Church in rejecting gross Chiliasm together with the view that the millennium would take place before the resurrection of the dead and therefore before the second advent of Christ. Although Lutheran theologians have rejected the theory of the millennium in the sense referred to in the Confession, still they have endeavored to explain the significance of the so-called millennium. It is clearly evident that Rev. 20 cannot be wholly ignored. Some of the Lutheran Dogmaticians, such as Gerhard, have placed the millennium in the past. Others interpret the thousand years and in general the contents of Rev. 20 in a figurative and symbolic sense. Among the recent theologians opinions are divided. And yet even among confessional theologians there are some who interpret Rev. 20 literally. Among such theologians may be mentioned Frank.[143] If the millennium is not to be conceived of as an expression of the world conquest of the Christian Church during the New Testament period, and if a closer study of Rev. 20 leads to the conclusion that its contents must in the main be literally interpreted, the theory of Premillennialism is thereby strengthened. While Lutheran Dogmatics does not express decisive views on this question and while the Confessions have said nothing more than what is expressed in the quotation from the Augsburg Confession, still the following reasons may be presented as arguments against the view that the millennium will precede the second coming of Christ: 1) Neither Christ nor His Apostles have spoken of a millennium as preceding the second advent of Christ. 2) If the Apostles thought of a millennium, it was in accordance with premillennarian views, inasmuch as their hope was connected with the return of Christ. Their description of the last times is not postmillennial. 3) The general presentation in the New Testament concerning the position

[143] *System der Christliche Wahrheit*, II, 471.

of the Church during the present dispensation does not accord with the view that the millennium will occur before the second advent of our Lord. 4) The reiterated warnings of our Lord to watch and wait for His coming prove conclusively that the millennium would not precede His coming, since in that case there would have been no need of watching, inasmuch as the disciples would know that at least a thousand years must pass by before the Lord would come again. 5) The coming of our Lord is constantly set forth as the blessed hope of the Christians. 6) The doctrine of Antichrist and the great tribulation before the coming of the Lord militates against the doctrine of a preceding millennium. 7) The only chapter in the Bible which expressly presents the millennium places this period after events which specifically are connected with the second coming of the Lord. 8) The general view in the Apostolic Church was premillenarian. *If*, therefore, the millennium is to follow the second coming of our Lord, in accordance with a literal interpretation of Rev. .20, it is also evident that Rev. 19:11-16 together with other passages in the same book refer to Christ's personal and visible advent. 2 Thess. 2:8 (compare 2 Thess. 1:5-10) presents the epiphany of the Lord as preceding the judgment of the "lawless one." Rev. 19:20 speaks of the judgment of the two beasts. After this follow the occurrences set forth in Rev. 20, although the resurrection spoken of in the sixth verse must be conceived of as taking place at the time of the second advent. In case the millennium is thought of as marking the transition to the eternal kingdom, then the period designated by the thousand years must imply a new order of things in the gracious dispensation of the Lord. While it is not possible for us to pass dogmatically on the question of the millennium, still we do not believe that in case of its realization the world would thereby become a paradise, although it is certain that such a period would become comparatively better and happier than all preceding periods. And yet it must be remembered that the kingdom of God will still be in the world, although not of the world. Even during a period of that sort the believers will not conquer the whole world, since the wicked are still in the world and toward the close of the period, we are told, Satan will deceive many.

However, the truths of Christianity will become dominant and by reason of the government of Christ and the Church of the firstborn the kingdom will be a kingdom of righteousness and justice. Although the kind of government is not described in detail, still we direct attention to the fact that the rule of the believers with Christ is not only said to be *βασιλεύσουσιν* (Rev. 20:6), but also as *ποιμανεῖ αυτοὺς ἐν ῥάβδῳ σιδηρᾷ*

(Rev. 2:27; 19:15). This government will, therefore, be one of love, but also of strict shepherdizing, so that externally, at least, the nations will be compelled to obey the principles of the Christocracy. In this sense the millennium will be a judgment period or a judgment day, although it will continue to be a period of grace. In this connection we may mention that some commentators have interpreted the thousand years as being the days of the Son of man during the period of the Second Coming, referring to 2 Peter 3:8, "One day is with the Lord as a thousand years, and a thousand years as one day." To the millennial government the objection has been raised that the peculiar situation would arise that glorified men with spiritual bodies would associate with the inhabitants of the earth. The adherents of Premillennialism answer that the Logos led the Children of Israel in the wilderness, and they point out the repeated theophanies in the Old Testament, the appearance of Moses and Elias on the Mount of Transfiguration and the appearance of our Lord between His resurrection and ascension. The visible appearance and association of glorified saints with men on earth would be like Christ's appearances between His resurrection and ascension. But with Christ the saints would rule from the New Jerusalem in the sky. The following Scripture passages are taken to refer to the millennium: Isa. 32:1; 33:20-24; 62:1-7; 65:19-25; Daniel 7:13, 14, 27; Zech. 8:20-23; 14:16-21; Matt. 26:29; Luke 22:29, 30; Acts 3:20, 21. However, the kingdom of God will not cease after the thousand years, whatever be its form and activity during that time, inasmuch as the kingdom is an eternal kingdom. Compare Isa. 66:22; Daniel 2:44; 7:14; Rev. 11:15; 21:1; 22:5. The manner in which the transition to the eternal kingdom of glory is to be effected is not as important as the eternal existence of the kingdom. The prelude to a musical composition is beautiful and important as preparing the way for the composition, but the composition itself is of prime importance. While we may not succeed in fixing definitely the doctrine of the millennium, still it is certain that Christ shall come again and with Him the kingdom of God.

4. Notes on the History of Dogma.

The oldest Church Fathers accepted the doctrine of the millennium and Premillennialism. But Chiliasm lost its hold as the persecutions ceased and Christianity became the state religion. Augustine rejected Chiliasm and declared that the Church was the promised kingdom. During the Catholic Scholastic period there were not many who looked for a millennium, inasmuch as the triumphant Catholic Church answered to all expectations in that direction. The Reformers thought that the end of the world was near at hand, for which reason they did not accept the theory of a millennium before the second coming of Christ, unless it be in the sense that the whole of the New Testament period was such a millennium. The Augsburg Confession rejected or condemned the fanaticism of the Anabaptists. The old Dogmaticians placed the millennium in the past and stated in general that all the final eschatological occurrences will take place at one time and that the eternal kingdom of glory will begin without any transition period. The eschatological question has become the subject of much careful investigation in modern times, but there is no unanimity in positions taken. The Würtemberg School, and especially Bengel, aroused great interest in the study of prophecy, and particularly in Chiliasm. This theory has gained many adherents in the Reformed Church, and certain sects have indeed arisen which have especially supported this doctrine. In the Lutheran Church there are many who accept a millennium, but not a few stand by the old dogmatic view, while others feel that they cannot take a definite position on the question. There are three schools that have especially made their influence felt in eschatological questions in modern times, namely, the Preterist, the Historical, and the Futurist schools of interpretation. The Preterists take the position that the greater part of the prophecies of Revelations were fulfilled during the first centuries, that Nero was Antichrist, and that the millennial kingdom is the kingdom of grace on earth between the first and second advents of Christ. The Historical school states that the events of history are foretold in the prophetical writings. The Papacy is regarded as the occidental Antichrist, while Mohammedanism is regarded as the oriental Antichrist. The events of history are symbolized by the prophetical seals, trumpets, bowls, etc. Among the interpreters of the Historical school are to be found premillennians and postmillennians. The premillennians teach that Christ comes before the thousand years, and the postmillennians that He comes after the thousand years. Others of this school place the millennium in the past or else declare it to be the victories of the Christian Church during the New Testament period, while the majority expect a future millennium. The Futurists take the position that the majority of the prophecies in the Book of Revelation are to find their fulfillment in the future, that Antichrist is to come and that he will be destroyed at the second coming of Christ, that Satan is to be bound and that the millennium will begin after the first resurrection, etc. But som Futurists are postmillennians. It may be stated finally that there are some theologians who have adopted both the historical and futurist methods of interpretation and declare that the development of history typifies the literal fulfillment of prophecy.

Lately a new prophetical school has been formed which has won many adherents. This may be called the Historico-Futurist school. According to Biblical Hermeneutics, only one meaning can be correct. In the Old Testament the advent of the Messiah was not presented as two advents, but the New Testament in describing the first advent promises a second advent of Christ, when the remaining prophecies will be fulfilled. It is only two phases of the advent and there is, therefore, no double meaning. What refers to the first phase has only one meaning, and the case is the same in the second phase. Therefore, when prophecies are fulfilled in past and present history, the same prophecies cannot have a future fulfillment. If the millennium has been fulfilled in the past or is now realized, a new millennium of the same kind cannot be expected.

The New Testament_speaks of the thousand years only in one chapter. The thousand years are either past, present or future. A future event may have types and there may be historical foundations which develop into a climax, but there is only one real fulfillment. The prophecies in the Book of Revelation cannot have two meanings, but there may be historical foundations and developments leading to a climax which is the fulfillment. According to the Historico-Futurist school the prophesied future event may have historical developments leading to the time of the actual fulfillment. The Book of Revelations contains three main divisions, the last beginning with the fourth chapter. If the last main division describes the last phase of the actual fulfillment, we still find that the historical background and development is more or less pictured. In some chapters of the prophetical books we are reminded of the recapitulation principle of Biblical Hermeneutics.

Barnabas, Papias, and Hermas accepted the doctrine of a millennium. Justin Martyr says that Christ shall reign in the restored Jerusalem that together with the saints Christ would reign a thousand years after the power of Antichrist had been destroyed. He found the days of creation typical days, each one meaning a thousand years. He says that Matt. 19:29 and 26:29 refer to the millennium. Tertullian also accepted the theory of the millennium. Origen rejected the doctrine of Chiliasm.

Lactantius believed in the millennium. He declared that the world in its present form would continue 6,000 years, but that the seventh millennium would be a sabbath. Naturally Chiliasm became discredited more and more as the Church won recognition by the State through Constantine. Augustine rejected the traditional doctrine of the millennium. He probably was the first to present the Preterist theory of interpretation, containing the following points: That Satan was bound at the first advent of Christ; by the first resurrection is meant the spiritual resurrection from spiritual death; the thousand years are the kingdom of grace upon the earth; at the end of this time Satan will be loosed again, persecutions will take place under Antichrist, after which will follow the second coming of Christ, the resurrection, the judgment and the new world order. According to another view of the Preterist school, Nero was the Antichrist.

The theologians did not greatly occupy themselves with investigations concerning the millennium during the Scholastic period. About the year 1000 there were many who expected the coming of *dies irae* and the end of the world. The historical method of interpretation made its appearance in the eleventh century and the Book of Revelation was viewed as an historical compendium. There were many devoted believers who began to fear that the Papacy was Antichrist.

Luther believed that the second advent of the Lord was at hand. He counted the millennium from the time of the first advent of Christ as well as from the writing of the Book of Revelation. Gog and Magog are the Turks. At the time of Luther there were no conservative theologians who expected a period of triumph for the Church before the second coming of Christ. The Futurist theory of interpretation, which was accepted in the ancient Church, came to life again toward the close of the sixteenth century. The Jesuits Ribera and Alcazar accepted this theory for reasons that are apparent. Gerhard said that the period of a thousand years began with Constantine, at which time Satan was bound. The millennial period closed during the fifteenth century. Grotius taught that heathen Rome was Antichrist and that the millennium began with Constantine and closed when the Turks captured Constantinople. Spener hoped for better times in the future and was supposed to favor a refined form of Chiliasm. Whitby presented the theory of Postmlllennialism, which sets forth a spiritual millennium before the advent of Christ. Antichrist will come before the millennium and Christ at its close. Bengel made peculiar calculations. He assumed that Satan would be bound a thousand years and that these thousand years would precede the thousand years in which the saints would reign. He therefore extended the millennium to two thousand years and believed that it would begin in 1836. But Bengel himself said that if the year 1836 passed without any special change, then there must be some radical fault with his calculations.

Auberlen accepted the doctrine of a millennium, although he seems to interpret the question of time symbolically. He says that Rev. 20 is not the only place which deals with this subject. Hengstenberg taught that the millennium began with Charlemagne. Elliot and Gaussen supported the doctrine of a millennium. Von Hofmann taught that a millennium would come when the glorified Church would not only reign over the nations of the earth but also dwell there, so that there would be found on the earth a contrast between the glorified and the unglorified human and natural life. Philippi viewed the time limit as the expression of a protracted period which began with the victory of Christianity over heathenism, when the Church of Christ became dominant. Frank discusses at the close of his Dogmatics the goal of a humanity consecrated to God. The final goal is prepared through the general preaching of the Gospel, the conversion of Israel, the appearance of Antichrist and his judgment, the second coming of Christ, the first resurrection and the millennium. He therefore supports the doctrine of a future millennium which will be the Church's period of triumph. This kingdom will begin with the second advent of Christ. Luthardt accepts the doctrine of a coming millennium and adopts the premillennian view. Among Swedish theologians who accept the doctrine of a future millennium and have adopted premillennian views may be mentioned Bring, who in his Dogmatics expresses himself as follows: "The Book of Revelation is the capstone or the chief corner stone, as Genesis is the foundation stone in the great temple building of the Holy Scriptures. But in Revelation there is also a foundation stone which is to be found in the doctrine of the kingdom of Christ and the victory of the saints on the earth together with the binding of Satan for a thousand years. Without this victory the history of the Christian Church would lack, the relative denouement which is required in the very conception of the kingdom. Attempts have been made to escape the doctrine of the future millennium contained in the Book of Revelation by placing it in the past. Some have begun this kingdom with Constantine, as the old Lutheran Dogmaticians do, counting their terminus ad quem the establishment of the Turkish empire, when the devil was loosed, or else from the time of Charlemagne. But in any case the description contained in the Apocalypse of John cannot be conceived of as corresponding to the world situation during the periods above mentioned, provided one does not idealize the world situations and at the same time discredit the ideal conditions set forth by the prophet as being descriptive of the glory of the millennial kingdom. So far as Chlliasm is concerned and the condemnatory expressions of the Augsburg Confession in connection therewith, we would state that these words of condemnation are directed against the carnal conception of the millennium as held by the Anabaptists and their still more carnal attempts to realize this kingdom." Bring believes that Antichrist will finally appear in personal form and that he will be destroyed at the second coming of Christ. He interprets the first resurrection in a literal sense. With regard to the government during the millennium he says: "The heavenly Church together with the resurrected believers will rule with Christ from heaven and not on the earth. In order that the latter might be realized there would be necessary a new earth and not only, as might be expected during a millennium, a partly glorified earth. A glorified heavenly Church in the midst of ordinary men with flesh and blood would certainly appear extraordinary and magical. It is sufficient that the heavenly Church stands in such close and living relationship with the Church on earth during the millennial period that great heavenly powers are imparted to the latter." Myrberg also sets forth a millennium, but the time limit he interprets symbolically as meaning a protracted son of time when Satan will be bound. To be sure there will be sin, but it will have lost its force and will not appear as a world power. The kingdom of Christ will be dominant. Many more quotations could be made, but it is not necessary. Opinions are divided, but the majority who expect a coming millennium reject the theory of gross Chiliasm. There are some who prefer the theory of the old Dogmaticians who believed that the millennium to a greater or less degree corresponds with the present period, which began either with the establishment of the Christian Church or with the overcoming of heathenism by the Church in the fourth century, but they do not desire to deny the possible truth of the futuristic and premillennian theories of interpretation. There are others who decidedly reject millennialism in every form and especially the Futurist view.[144]

In regard to the second advent many modern theologians make a distinction between two stages (*παρουσία* and *επιφάνεια*), the former called Rapture and the second Epiphany. According to these theologians the Rapture preceded by a division in the first resurrection would occur before the great tribulation. Some Lutheran exegetes hold this view. Among them may be mentioned Seiss. He holds that the "Elders" in chapter four in Revelation are those who were in the first Rapture at the second advent. We quote from his Lectures on the Apocalypse: "They were saints from earth, for they sing of being redeemed by Christ's blood 'out of every kindred, and tongue, and tribe, and people.' They are in resurrection life, for they are enthroned and crowned; and no saints are crowned till 'the resurrection of the just.' — They are already in heaven, before ever a seal is broken, a trumpet sounded, or a bowl of wrath emptied." Seiss belonged to the Futurist school of prophecy. We also quote the following from Seiss: "It is thus clear and manifest, even to the extent of demonstration itself, that the first resurrection is not one summary event, but is made up of various resurrections and translations at. different times, beginning with the resurrection of Christ, who is the head and front of 'the resurrection of the just,' and receiving its last additions somewhere about the final overthrow of the Beast and his armies." The upholders of the Rapture theory base their belief on Rev. 4 and 5; Luke 21:28: "When these

[144] Many modern theologians hold that the millennium or thousand years covers the same period which is called the Day of Jehovah. This day of the Lord begins with the second advent period and continues until the appearance of the new earth and the new heavens. It is clear that the day of the Lord cannot be an ordinary day. The days of the Son of man at the first advent lasted nearly thirty-four years. The second advent period may last longer. If such be the case, it will be easier to harmonize many passages, such as 2 Peter 3: 10. When Peter says that a thousand years are to the Lord as a day, it is plain that the burning of the earth and heavens does not necessarily mean a renovation of the earth and heavens at the beginning of the day of the Lord, and the fire may occur both at the beginning and close of the thousand years. In Obadiah 15 we read: "For the day of Jehovah is near upon all nations." In Joel we read five times of the day of Jehovah. Compare Hosea 11th chapter; Isaiah 2:12-21; 13:9-13, and study especially "Isaiah's Apocalypse," chapters 24-27; Zephaniah 1:14-18, etc.

things *begin*—your redemption draweth nigh"; Rom. 8:23; John 14:2, 3; Matt. 24:27, 28 (note that the tribulation follows); 1 Thess. 4:13-17; Luke 21:36, 36, the last verse reading, "But watch ye at every season, making supplication, that ye may prevail to escape all these things that shall come to pass, and to stand before the Son of man"; Rev. 3:10; all passages relating to watching are also used, because watching is necessary, as the Lord may come sooner than expected; if signs would be very plain, like the great tribulation, then people would calculate; "Watch therefore: for ye know not on what day your Lord cometh" (Matt. 24:42); compare the preceding context and verse 44: "Therefore be ye also ready; for in an hour that ye think not the Son of man cometh." H. Grattan Guinness, who belonged to the Historical school of prophecy, and who was a prominent student of prophecy, does not favor the distinction of Rapture and Revelation with such a chronological calculation as the Futurists hold, but he teaches that the Rapture takes place first and the Epiphany follows, without speculating in regard to the length of time between the two events. In referring to Rev. 19, describing the Epiphany, he says: "He who had previously come for His people now comes with them; not that there are two future comings of Christ, but only one. That coming, however, has not only two aspects, but two stages." Guinness believed that the Papacy is the Western Antichrist and Mohammedanism the Eastern, and that we live near the judgment period. He also says: "While, therefore, we see no authority for making chronological distinctions between separate stages of the one advent, we see, on the other hand, abundant reason in Scripture to believe that the millennial reign of Christ will not be fully established in a day or year. It must be remembered that He comes, not peacefully to ascend a vacant and waiting throne, welcomed by a willing people, but to dispossess a mighty usurper and to overthrow a great rebellion, to right the accumulated wrong of ages." Fjellstedt in Sweden has exercised a great influence in shaping eschatologlcal thought according to the grammatical, literal understanding of the text, when such exegesis was possible. He entertained the belief in a millennium, but not in the sense that Christ will rule from David's throne in the earthly Jerusalem. He believed that there will be a first resurrection before the millennium, but favored no speculations in regard to the length of time between two stages in the second advent.

§43. The Resurrection.

The doctrine of the resurrection is most closely related to Christianity. The resurrection of our bodies, or the resurrection of the dead, is based upon the resurrection of Christ. We may say that our resurrection is founded potentially in the resurrection of Christ. He was the first to arise from the dead with a pneumatic glorified body, for which reason He is called the firstfruits of them that are asleep. When He shall come again out of the land of the living, then will break the dawn of the everlasting day, then the great Easter morning will come and the Christian hope will be realized. Man is a spiritual and material entity. The body, which is an integral part of man, must arise, which means that the whole person will arise. In the resurrection man appears in his fully developed form. The intermediate state does not bring with it the fully developed forms either of death or life. When the resurrection has taken place, then will follow either the second death or eternal life. All men will arise, but the resurrection to the fullness of everlasting life is the resurrection which all true believers long and strive for. We may be absolutely certain that even the spirits of just men made perfect long for the day of Christ and the resurrection of life.

1. The Definition of the Resurrection.

Hollazius defines as follows:* "the Resurrection of the dead *is the work of the Triune God through which all the dead will at the right time receive the same bodies which they had in life, awakened from the dead and reunited with their souls, unto the full participation of eternal salvation or condemnation, and* *unto the manifestation of the divine justice, both remunerative and punitive."*[145] Hollazius also defines *resuscitatio*, which stands in relation to *resurrectio* as *causa* to *effectus*.

With regard to the active causes the old Dogmaticians say: 1) *causa efficiens principalis* is the Triune God and especially Christ, the God-man; 2) *causa impulsiva interna* is the divine justice, *justitia remuneratoria* with regard to the godly and *vindicativa* with regard to the ungodly; 3) *causa impulsiva externa* is, in relation to the godly, the merit of Christ as accepted through faith, and in relation to the ungodly, impenitence. Compare the following Scripture passages: "Knowing that he that raised up the Lord Jesus, shall raise up us also with Jesus" (2 Cor. 4:14; cf. John 5:21); "The dead shall hear the voice of the Son of God" (John 5:25, 28); "I will raise him up at the last day" (John 6:54); "But if the Spirit of him that raised up Jesus from the dead dwelleth in you, he that raised up Christ Jesus from the dead shall give life also to your mortal bodies through his Spirit that dwelleth in you" (Rom. 8:11). Compare Luther's explanation of the third article of the Creed.

2. Further Definition of the Resurrection.

Subjectum quod resurrectionis, i.e., the subjects of the act of the resurrection, are all men. Compare John 5:28, 29. The resurrection may then be divided into the resurrection of the righteous and of the unrighteous. The resurrection of the righteous takes place first. Jesus speaks of the resurrection of the believers as follows: "But they that are accounted worthy to attain to that world and the resurrection from the dead" (Luke 20:35). The Greek words for the resurrection from the dead are: *τῆς ἀνάστεως τῆς ἐκ νεκῶν*. Paul also strove to attain unto this resurrection from the dead — *εἰς τὴν ἐξανάστασιν τὴν ἐκ νεκῶν* (Phil. 3:11). Compare the following passages: "But each in his own order: Christ the firstfruits; then

[145] Hollazius: "Resurrectio mortuorum est opus Dei Triunius, quo defuncti homines omnes eadem numero corpora, quae in hac vita habuerunt, e morte excitata, et cum animabus suis redunita recipient, ad plenam beatitudinis aut damnationis aeternae participationem, et ad manifestationem justitiae divinae remuneratoriae et vindicativae."

they that are Christ's, at his coming" (1 Cor. 15:23);[146] "The dead shall be raised incorruptible, and we shall be changed" (1 Cor. 15:52); "The dead in Christ shall rise first" (1 Thess. 4:16) ; "Blessed, and holy is he that hath part in the first resurrection" (Rev. 20:6). Without dogmatically determining the lapse of time between the first and second resurrection, it is evident that the believers arise first at the coming of the Lord and that the faithful believers who are living upon the earth are thereafter changed, before the remaining dead are raised up. This is the Biblical sequence as to the resurrection, and the lapse of time, even though it be of but short duration, between the resurrection and transformation of the believers and the resurrection of the unbelievers implies judgment for the latter. The resurrection of the unbelievers is called the resurrection of judgment (John 5:29).

It is interesting to observe that Paul received a special revelation in regard to the immediate events at the return of the Lord. In 1 Thess. 4:15 we read the following clear statement: "For this we say unto you by the word of the Lord, that we that are alive, that are left unto the coming of the Lord, shall in no wise precede them that are fallen asleep. For the Lord himself shall descend from heaven, with a shout, with the voice of

---

[146] When it is stated that Christ is the firstfruits of them that are asleep, that is, that He was the first to arise from the dead with a pneumatic body, we must bear in mind that others also arose immediately after His resurrection. They could not arise first, inasmuch as Christ was the firstfruits, although their graves were probably opened at the death of Christ. Compare Matt. 27:52, 53. It is not probable that these saints arose with their earthly bodies and afterwards died again, but they arose as the saints shall arise at the second advent of our Lord. Nohrborg says in his sermon for the 26th Sunday after Trinity that those who came out of their graves at the resurrection of Christ are excepted from the last resurrection, inasmuch as they probably ascended to heaven with the Lord at His ascension and now stand with glorified bodies before the throne of the Lamb in heaven.— There is a possibility that these resurrected saints are the same persons as those who in Rev. 4:4 are called the twenty-four elders. The number is not hereby fixed, but they are called elders because they were the first to arise from the dead after Christ. The resurrection from the dead is called a regeneration. The twenty-four elders represent the church of the firstborn. Since then no one has arisen. Compare 1 Cor. 15:23: "Then they that are Christ's at his coming."

the archangel, and with the trump of God; and the dead in Christ shall rise first; then we that are alive, that are left, shall together with them be caught up in the clouds, to meet the Lord in the air; and so shall we ever be with the Lord." Compare 1 Cor. 15:51, 52: "Behold, I tell you a mystery: We all shall not sleep, but we shall all be changed in a moment, in the twinkling of an eye, at the last trump." Compare also Luke 17:34, 35: "In that night there shall be two men on one bed; the one shall be taken, and the other shall be left. There shall be two women grinding together; the one shall be taken, and the other shall be left." It is not stated what will immediately befall those that are left. But it is clearly related what will befall those that are raised from the dead and those living who are changed. Both parties are caught up in the clouds to meet the Lord in the air to be ever with Him. They do not return to the earth, but are with the Lord in the events that will follow on the great day of the Lord. This day is not an ordinary day in length. The expression *first* resurrection in contradistinction to the *second* occurs only in Rev. 20. But 1 Thess. 4:16; 1 Cor. 15:23 and the expressions "from the dead" prove plainly that there is to be a first resurrection at Christ's return. According to the literal, grammatical exegesis of Rev. 20:4-6, John saw different orders of those raised from the dead, namely, thrones and they that sat upon them, martyrs who had been beheaded and "such as worshipped not the beast," etc. The first resurrection includes, if we compare also other passages, all saints who have lived before the second advent. The first division mentioned in Rev. 20:4 does not refer to martyrs only, but to all saints, whether martyrs or not, who belong to the first resurrection and translation. We should also notice carefully that the souls in Rev. 6:9-11 especially, the two witnesses in Rev. 11:11, the manchild (ἄρσεν, neuter gender) in Rev. 12:5 possibly, Rev. 14:1-5 describing the 144,000, and the second and third division in Rev. 20:4 (compare Rev. 7:9-17) refer to the sufferers and martyrs during the great tribulation in the time of the two beasts. The passages in the Gospels, in the Acts of the Apostles and in the Epistles speak of the resurrection from the dead of all believers generally and the translation of them and the living at the second advent. These passages also declare that the unbelievers shall rise. In reference to the children of God it is stated, "each in his own order," but in regard to the unbelievers no such statement is made. Only in Rev. 20:5 we read: "The rest of the dead lived not until the thousand years should be finished." If interpreters have many opinions in reference to the exegesis of Rev. 20, all orthodox exegetes teach a general resurrection on the great day of the Lord. This statement does not preclude that the believers arise first, as previously explained.

Subjectum quo is the body. In the Apostles' Creed the term *carnis* is used in Latin and *σάρκος* in Greek, but, of course, they both refer to the resurrection of the whole man. both body and soul. The reasons that the expressions *credo carnis resurrectionem* or *πιστεύω σάρκος ἀνάστασιν* were used, was because the Church Fathers desired thereby to emphasize the reality and the identity of the body. If there were no such identity, then we could not speak of the resurrection of the body. This identity does not, however, imply that all the atoms, molecules and material elements of the former earthly body are to be reproduced. Even during our earthly life there are constant changes taking place in our bodies, and yet our identity is preserved. The resurrection is called a regeneration. Human life is produced from a protoplasmic cell. While this natural process will not explain the mode in which our identity is preserved in the resurrection body, still it shows how identity may be preserved through change. In this connection we call to mind the figure of Paul when he speaks of the grain of wheat that falls into the ground only to die in order to become quickened and produce new life and a new body. Compare 1 Cor. 15:35-38. The resurrection body is therefore in a sense the same body with its identity preserved, but at the same time it is a new body, a pneumatic and heavenly body. With regard to the process by which the old body is raised up again into the new resurrection body we must reject the theory of John Scotus Erigena, who propounded the following doctrine: *Anima corpus suum creat*. The soul does not create the new body. Even though it might be acknowledged that the new body is to a certain extent the consummated product of the potential principle indwelling in the spiritual man by reason of the living communion with Christ, still this does not prove that the new resurrection body is produced by evolution from within. The natural body is produced from the embryo in a certain sense, but this does not fully explain its existence. We must remember that the natural body is dependent on its environment. The new, spiritual, resurrected body is likewise dependent on its environment. There is therefore both an internal and an external principle. But throughout all these processes it is God that is active, and the action becomes supernatural not only from within, but also from without and from above. Although the resurrection is a supernatural act, it does not imply an origination from nothing. When there is to be a resurrection of the body, there must be a connecting link between the old and the new body. But this connecting link cannot be a material cell, but the spiritual principle behind it. In Anthropology we have been taught that behind the nucleus in the *ovum* is the indestructible invisible principle which is a real entity. In death this invisible principle, which also had a physical spiritual potency, will not be annihilated, but may be the connecting link between the former body as to identity and the new spiritual body in the resurrection. This seems to be much more plausible when we consider that the soul, being immortal, in Christian experience does not even taste death. Besides, all men existed in Adam as spiritual principles, sinned and died in Adam. Whereas men are intrinsically immortal as to their souls, and their physical nature belonged to their existence in Adam as invisible principles just as much as their souls, so that man in his entirety has both body and soul, the resurrection of the body is a necessity. The entire human being will therefore experience the conditions in the eternal state. To God no one is actually dead, but all live to Him. Christ stated this clearly to the Sadducees, when they disputed with Him about the resurrection.[147] We would call attention to the following passages: "When Christ, who is our life, shall be manifested, then shall ye also with him be manifested in glory" (Col. 3:4); "He that eateth my flesh and drinketh my blood hath eternal life; and I will raise

---

[147] Compare Lindberg, *Apologetics*, pp. 184-188.

him up at the last day" (John 6:54); "Who shall fashion anew the body of our humiliation, that it may be conformed to the body of his glory, according to the working whereby he is able even to subject all things to himself" (Phil. 3:21). The bodies of the ungodly are also produced by God according to their nature and made conformable to their environment.

The following attributes are ascribed to the resurrection body of the believer: 1) *spirituale,* which does not mean, however, that the body is exclusively spiritual. Those who are resurrected are not spirits, but possess pneumatic bodies which have spiritual properties and are no longer subject to the wants and conditions of the natural body. Compare the following passages: "It is raised a spiritual body" (1 Cor. 15:44); "Meats for the belly, and the belly for meats: but God shall bring to nought both it and them" (1 Cor. 6:13). This last passage does not, however, prove that the saints in glory do not eat and drink. Compare Luke 24:42, 43; 22:16; Matt. 26:29. Christ ate after His resurrection, although He had a spiritual body, but this fact does not prove that He needs food; only that He can partake of food, when He so desires. The saints raised from the dead or translated while living are also able to eat and drink, but they do not need sustenance to live. Christ intimates quite plainly the possibility of the use of food in His Father's kingdom. We quote what He said at the first Holy Communion: "But I say unto you, I shall not drink henceforth of this fruit of the vine, until that day when I drink it new with you in my Father's kingdom." Some interpreters explain this saying figuratively. But such exposition is against all laws of grammar. There are other passages proving the possibility of the use of food for enjoyment. Though there be heavenly food for enjoyment, the spiritual experience of the heavenly life and joy is the most important. "Eat and drink at my table in my kingdom" (Luke 22:30); "And they shall come from the east and west, and from the north and south and shall sit down in the kingdom of God" (13:29); 2) *ἰσάγγελον,* "They are as angels in heaven" (Matt. 22:30); 3) *gloriosum*; cf. Dan. 12:3; Matt. 13:43; 1 Cor. 15:41; Phil. 3:21; 4) *incorruptible*; cf. Luke 20:36; 1 Cor. 15:42, 53; 5) *ἐπουράνιον*; "Are sons of God" (Luke 20:36); "As is the heavenly, such are they also that are heavenly. And as we have borne the image of the earthy, we shall also bear the image of the heavenly" (1 Cor. 15:48, 49).

The bodies of the ungodly are also spiritual and indestructible, but their appearance is dishonorable, corresponding to their inner nature. Their resurrection is a resurrection unto judgment. They can suffer and will suffer and become like unto the evil angels, and they shall be sent to the place prepared for the devil and his angels. Compare the following passages: "Vessels of wrath" (Rom. 9:22); "Another unto dishonor" (Rom. 9:21); "Some unto dishonor" (2 Tim. 2:20); "They that have done evil, unto the resurrection of judgment" (John 5:29). The Scriptures do not speak as much about the resurrection of the ungodly as of the godly. It is stated that they shall arise, but the character of their bodies is not definitely described. The resurrection of the ungodly is the dark side of the general resurrection.

3. The Object of the Resurrection.

Finis resurrectionis is twofold: 1) *finis proximus* in relation to the blessed is the full realization of divine glory, and in relation to the ungodly it is the whole import of condemnation; 2) *finis ultimus* is the glory of the divine righteousness and justice.

Inasmuch as man is a material and spiritual entity, therefore the conditions in the intermediate state, i.e., the comfort of Paradise and the torment of Hades, cannot correspond to the object of God's love and justice in relation to man. The saints are indeed called in Hebrews 12:23 the spirits of just men made perfect, and still they long for the resurrection. Through the resurrection they become alive again in the full sense of the word in relation to the normal state of human existence and activity. During the intermediate state there is life, to be sure, but in a sense limited by the lack of a bodily organ, especially in comparison with the external and active life that is begun with the resurrection and continued throughout eternity in the kingdom of glory. As a complete person man has lived, labored, and sown in this world of trial, for which reason it is but natural that man should also live, labor, and reap in the new world, which will be the external form of the eternal kingdom of God. The ungodly have also sown unto the flesh, wherefore they shall also of the flesh reap corruption in the eternal kingdom of death.

4. Notes on the History of Dogma.

During the Apologetical period the teaching of the Bible with regard to the resurrection was accepted with childlike faith and hope. The resurrection of the dead was indeed one of the great thoughts of Christianity. It was taught that the resurrection body would be identical with the earthly body, but in new form. Some of the old fathers believed that the first resurrection would take place at the beginning of the millennium and the general resurrection at the end of that period. There was no special development of the doctrine of the resurrection during the next two periods, although attempts were made to prove satisfactorily the possibility and necessity of the resurrection. The old Lutheran Dogmaticians taught that the resurrection consisted *formaliter* in the reproduction of the former body. They distinguished between the quickening and the resurrection. There has been no new dogmatic development during modern times. There are some who have adopted the position of the old Dogmaticians, while others have reverted to the views of the early Church.

Clement of Rome sets forth night and day together with the fable of Phoenix as analogies of the resurrection. Justin Martyr speaks of two resurrections, one before, the other after the millennium. He believed that in eternity we will possess the same body with all its members and that the sex difference will continue. Irenaeus said that the resurrection is a less wonderful miracle than the creation. He believed that the same substance would arise and that the general resurrection would take place after the millennium. Tertullian taught that the believers would arise at the beginning of the millennium, but not all at one time, since some would by reason of shortcomings be compelled to remain some time in the spiritual world. Origen adopted the view that the new body would develop out of the basic material of the old body. There would not be new material in the new body, merely a new form.

Lactantius set forth two resurrections and stated that the bodies of the believers would become more psychic at the beginning of the millennium, but at the end of that period more pneumatic or like that of the angels. Ambrose proves the necessity of the resurrection by reason of the fact that the body has participated in good as well as evil deeds. He sets forth natural proofs, but lays the greatest stress on the fact that there had been resurrections already, such as the resurrection of Christ and those who arose with Him. Gregory of Nyssa believed the resurrection necessary because the original condition of man would thereby be restored. Augustine taught that the same body will arise, although it will be a pneumatic body. The sex difference will continue. The children will arise with the size and form of body that they would have possessed in case they had lived.

Peter Lombard said that the bodies would arise with the form that they possessed at thirty years of age. Thomas Aquinas taught that the resurrected are like men and women in their youth. The sex difference continues, but there are no fleshly lusts. The new bodies will be beautiful, glorious, and brilliant. The bodies of the ungodly will possess an unsightly and offensive appearance. The resurrection body can be touched as the body of Christ and is partly dependent on time and space, but the resurrected are able to move from one place to another with great swiftness.

Luther liked especially the figure used by Paul in comparing the transformation of the body to the growth of the grain of wheat. The resurrection body of the blessed will be beautiful, healthy, and strong. After the resurrection we shall be able to move from one place to another with the swiftness of thought. Sex differences will continue, just as different seed grains retain their own nature. Selnecker took a peculiar view of the resurrection. He referred to Matt. 27:52 and taught that the first resurrection took place at the resurrection of the Lord and that such resurrections take place continuously from time to time throughout the whole of the New Testament dispensation. Calovius set forth that the resurrection is not a creation, inasmuch as it does not take place out of nothing; the atoms of the former body are brought to life again.

Martennsen, Thomasius and others set forth the identity of the resurrection body with the earthly body, so that the same individuality appears, although glorified and become like unto Christ. Frank refers to Luke 14:14; Phil. 3:11; 1 Cor. 15:23, 24, and Rev. 20:1-6 as proofs that the first resurrection will precede the general resurrection. The first resurrection is the resurrection of the righteous. He asks if it is necessary to prove that *ἔξησαν* in Rev. 20:4 does not refer to a spiritual but a real resurrection. He presents a similar question with regard to the following words in the fifth verse: *οἱ λοιπὸι τῶν νεκρῶν οὐκ ἔξησαν ἄρχι τελεσθῇ τὰ χίλια ἐτή*. Philippi says that the first resurrection is the translation to the blessed life in heaven which follows after death. The words "and they lived" in Rev. 20:4 he did not consider as implying a bodily resurrection. Alford interprets Rev. 20:4, 5 in a literal sense. He takes the position that if the words, "The rest of the dead lived not until the thousand years should be finished," point to a real resurrection, then the words in the fourth verse, "they lived," must imply a bodily resurrection. If the first resurrection is a spiritual resurrection, then the second resurrection must be spiritual likewise. Brown, on the other hand, argues against the literal interpretation. Among the reasons advanced may be mentioned the following: A first resurrection taking place a thousand years before the general resurrection is mentioned in but one place in the Scriptures. If this first resurrection were a real resurrection, then it would not be necessary to explain that "over these the second death hath no power." No mention is made of any resurrection in verses 7-10, which describe the events that take place immediately after the millennium. The opening of the book of life is equivalent to the revealing of those whose names are written therein, but inasmuch as the revealing of the children of God occurs at their resurrection, therefore the resurrection of the believers must take place simultaneously with the general resurrection. Verse 4 makes mention especially of the martyrs and therefore the bodily resurrection of the righteous cannot be referred to. Among American theologians who take the position that the first resurrection will precede the millennium may be mentioned Seiss. With regard to the martyrs mentioned in verse 4 he states that their resurrection could not have been a spiritual resurrection, because they were already spiritually alive. Their living again signifies that they have regained that which was lost through their martyrdom, for which reason a physical resurrection is implied. He states that the expression ἀνάσταοις is generally used throughout the whole of the New Testament in the sense of bodily resurrection. He also says that the first resurrection does not take place at one time, but consists of several resurrections, which occur at the time of the second advent. All the believers who have died before the coming of Christ have part in the first resurrection. He refers to Rev. 4, which speaks of the elders, the deliverance of a son (ὑιον ἄρσει), spoken of in Rev. 12, etc. Opinions are greatly divided, therefore, on this question. Jacobs says that the bodies of the glorified "are not as ethereal, and unlike those which we have now, as is often supposed. They are not new bodies, but the very same bodies, only endowed, like our Lord's resurrection body, with new properties. It is not necessary to the identity of these bodies with those we now have that the identity of the atoms of matter of which they are composed be maintained. As the body of the aged man is the same as that which he had in his infancy, while all its particles have been repeatedly changed, so with the resurrection body. The requisites of identity in the one case must not be more rigid than in the other. The identity of our bodies in the present state does not lie even in the succession of particles of matter, but in the permanent impress which the soul has made upon the body, so that the body correctly expresses the soul, and continues as its organ. But while this is all that is necessary for the preservation of identity, it is not for us to determine the limits of God's omnipotence in the resurrection, or to say that God will do no more than the very least that is necessary to maintain this identity."[148] Theologians generally express themselves in the same manner with regard to the identity of the body. As has been stated, there has been no real development of the

---

[148] *Elements of Religion*, p. 222.

dogma during recent times.

§44. The Judgment.

The judgment takes place in connection with the resurrection. While the judgment will be preceded by a judgment period, still this period must end in a decisive crisis or final judgment. The history of the world has been called the judgment, and the judgments of the last times will doubtless set forth the truth contained in this often repeated assertion, but the present world's history will at some time, now unknown, be fully written. The last judgment is not to consist in the mediate intervention of the Lord in the affairs of men, but in immediate action when the Lord shall come in a visible manner to judge the living and the dead.

1. Judgment Defined.

The Last Judgment is the act of judgment, both glorious and terrible, in which the Triune God, through the Lord Jesus Christ, the God-man, shall judge all angels and men in accordance with their spiritual state and their deeds, which judgment will bring everlasting salvation and reward to the righteous as well as eternal damnation and punishment to the wicked.

The old Dogmaticians called the judgment that takes place at death and which is decisive with regard to the spiritual state *judicium particulare et occultum*, while they termed the final judgment *universale et manifestum*. The judgment implies in general a confirmation in regard to salvation and damnation, inasmuch as the eternal spiritual state of the angels and the resurrected and transformed saints of God is already decided, while there will be a judgment in a double sense for those still living on the day of judgment, a pronouncement to enter into the kingdom and also rewards or a sentence to hell and consequent retribution. The Christians have already passed out of death into life and will not come into judgment in the ordinary sense, which is clearly proven from the fact that they will have part in the resurrection of the just or in their transformation, while their salvation, already begun, will be confirmed and publicly declared, after which they take possession of the kingdom. In this connection compare the words of our Lord: "Verily, verily, I say unto you, He that heareth my word, and believeth him that sent me, hath eternal life, and cometh not into judgment, but hath passed out of death into life" (John 5:24). But even if the state of the resurrected and transformed is decided and the judgment becomes a confirmation, still in another sense all will come into judgment. The last judgment will be a judgment of works. Paul says: "For we must all be made manifest before the judgment-seat of Christ; that each one may receive the things done in the body, according to what he hath done, whether it be good or bad" (2 Cor. 5:10). In this respect the judgment is of great significance also for the Christians, determining, as it does, their position in heaven. While the Christians are saved by grace alone and cannot glory in having done more than was their duty to do, still the Lord will not forget any good deed done in faith, but will on the day of judgment dispense a just reward. The ungodly will also be dealt with according to their works. We would call attention to the following illuminating passages of Scripture: "Verily I say unto you, that ye who have followed me, in the regeneration when the Son of man shall sit on the throne of his glory, ye also shall sit upon twelve thrones, judging the twelve tribes of Israel" (Matt. 19:28); "He shall receive a hundredfold, and shall inherit eternal life" (Matt. 19:29); "Well done, thou good servant: because thou wast found faithful in a very little, have thou authority over ten cities" (Luke 19:17 ff.); "If any man's work abide which he built thereon, he shall receive a reward. But if any man's work shall be burned, he shall suffer loss: but he himself be saved; yet so as through fire" (1 Cor. 3:14, 15); "In due season we shall reap, if we faint not" (Gal. 6:9); "For he that doeth wrong shall receive again for the wrong that he hath done: and there is no respect for persons" (Col. 3:25); "God is not unrighteous to forget your work" (Heb. 6:10); "Behold, I come quickly; and my reward is with me, to render to each man according as his work is" (Rev. 22:12) ; compare also Matt. 10:42; 25:14-30; Rom. 2:9, 10; 2 Tim. 1:18, and especially the two main Scripture passages on the judgment in Matt. 25:31-46 and Rev.

20:12.

Considering the Bible passages quoted, it is evident that the last judgment contains several acts and may be distributed during a judgment period. God does not need to hurry. All men shall be judged. As the angels also shall be judged, it must be a special act, and whatever may be the order in time, the judgment of angels will not precede the judgment of men, at least not the judgment of saints as to their rewards, because the saints will participate in the judgment of the angels. The saints who are raised and the living translated with them to meet the Lord in the air will not be judged as to salvation, but according to the previously quoted passages they shall be judged according to their works in order to receive by the grace of God their due rewards. Compare the following Bible passages: 2 Cor. 5:10; Matt. 19:28, 29; Luke 19:13-19, where we read concerning the faithful use of the talents and the rewards in ruling over five and ten cities; 1 Cor. 3:14, 19, which plainly teaches rewards according to material of building, whether gold, silver, etc.; Rev. 22:12, "Behold, I come quickly; and my reward is with me, to render to each man according as his work is," etc. There is also a judgment of the living, the living nations. At every morning service we confess that Christ shall come again to judge the living and the dead. Many commentators hold that Matt. 25:31-46 describes principally the judgment of the living. There are evidently three parties, those on the right side, those on the left, and "these my brethren" nearer the judgment throne which may be those who belonged to the first resurrection and translation. During the great tribulation especially there will be many instances of showing such love and neglect of it as Christ relates in this narrative of the judgment of the living nations, although such tests of Christian character have been made and repeated throughout the existence of the Church. To the judgment of the living belong also many other events related in the prophecies, as, Rev. 19:11-21. If there be a millennium, these judgments will be premillennial, or going before. This is clear from Rev. 11:15-19, because it is the time of the seventh angel, when he shall sound his trumpet. Read especially the 18th verse. According to the literal, grammatical sense of Rev. 20:11-15, there will be a judgment of the dead before Him who shall sit upon the white throne. The dead here are, in the first instance, those who in the 5th verse are mentioned as "the rest of the dead." There must also be included all those who died during the thousand years, among them both saints and sinners, while "the rest of the dead" in the 5th verse refer only to the wicked. In regard to the last judgment before the white throne we quote Rev. 20:12, 13 and 15: "And I saw the dead, the great and the small, standing before the throne; and books were opened: and another book was opened, which is the book of life: and the dead were judged out of the things which were written in the books according to their works. And the sea gave up the dead that were in it; and death and Hades gave up the dead that were in them: and they were judged every man according to their works. And if any was not found written in the book of life, he was cast into the lake of fire." The dead from Hades were already condemned, their judgment was merely confirmed and their punishments were determined according to what was written in the books. We remember that Hades is the intermediate state of unbelievers or the wicked between death and the last judgment. The persons who were written in the book of life entered the kingdom of God and they stood before the white throne only to receive their rewards.

In the 14th verse of the same chapter it is stated that at the last judgment death and Hades will be cast into the lake of fire. The last enemy, death, is then conquered, and Hades as an intermediate place and state is no longer needed. The inhabitants of Hades have been sentenced to Gehenna or the lake of fire. In verses 7-10 the last act of the devil or Satan is described, before he is sentenced to Gehenna, and it is stated: "where are also the Beast and the False Prophet; and they shall be tormented day and night for ever and ever."

2. The Factors in the Judgment.

1) The subject of the judgment, i.e., the one who executes judgment, is the Triune God through the Lord Jesus Christ. Compare John 5:22, 27; Acts 17:31; Rom. 2:2-11; Heb. 12:23. But Baier points out that Christ

has *assessores* and *ministri* (assistants and servants at court), which are the saints and the good angels.[149] Compare the following passages: "Know ye not that the saints shall judge the world? Know ye not that we shall judge angels?" (1 Cor. 6:2, 3); "And all the angels with him" (Matt. 25:31); "Behold, the Lord came with ten thousand of his holy ones" (Jude 14). The fact that the saints are to be judged in a certain sense proves that the judgment consists of several acts. How the saints are to participate in the judgment is not revealed in Scripture. Baier says that the saints are to be testes et comprobatores and refers to Matt. 19:28; Luke 22:30; 1 Thess. 4:14 and Rev. 19. However, their participation in the judgment would seem to imply greater activity.

2) The object of the judgment, or *subjectum quod,* are all men and angels. The Lord shall judge all men, both the living and the dead. There is a judgment pronounced on the living, in that the believers at the coming of the Lord are transformed or clothed upon and caught up in the clouds to meet the Lord in the air, while the others are left behind. Compare 1 Cor. 15:51, 52; 1 Thess. 4:17; Luke 17:34-36. It is also a judgment of the dead who are not immediately raised up at the coming of the Lord, inasmuch as the resurrection of the righteous will precede the resurrection of the ungodly. The angels will also be judged, but very probably only the evil angels, since a judgment upon the good angels would simply imply the bestowal of rewards and different places of honor in the kingdom of glory. However, the Scriptures say nothing about this. It is not an easy matter to explain the content of 1 Cor. 6:3, already quoted: "Know ye not that we shall judge angels?" If this passage concerns the evil angels, then it is perfectly clear. The evil angels are kept in everlasting bonds under darkness unto the judgment of the great day (Jude 6).

3) The *modus* of the judgment. With regard to the mode in which the judgment is to be carried out the old Dogmaticians have set forth the following: a) *Praeparatio,* which consists in the preparatory acts of judgment and the gathering before the judgment seat. Many of the events

---

[149] Comp., Part I, Cap. X, §VIII.

spoken of in Revelation belong to this preparation. The gathering is described in Matt. 24:31; 25:32; Mark 13:27; 1 Thess. 4:16, 17; Rev. 20:12, 13. b) *Administratio,* which consists in the investigation, when the accounting shall be made and all things revealed. Of course, the method of procedure is not the same as before an earthly judgment seat, since the Judge is none other than God, who knows the hearts of all men, together with the history of all nations and individuals. In some way the deeds of all shall be brought before the judgment seat. Paul says: "For we shall all stand before the judgment-seat of God. So then each one of us shall give account of himself to God" (Rom. 14:10 and 12; cf. 2 Cor. 5:10).[150] In Matt. 25: 31—46 the investigation is detailed and the deeds of all men revealed. When Rev. 20: 12 speaks of the opening of the books and the judgment according to the works recorded in them, this is not to be understood merely as a figurative expression, because even if on the great day of judgment there may be no ordinary books opened, still there will be something corresponding. The thoughts, words and deeds of all men are recorded in a way that corresponds to the conditions of the spiritual world. When we contemplate the many inventions by means of which the spoken word of man can be preserved for generations to come, then we can understand how God can preserve all the data necessary for the judgment. God needs no record books for Himself, inasmuch as He is omniscient, but since He works through means it may be possible for the sake of His creatures that He uses such means as otherwise would be unnecessary. It is not probable that the sins and shortcomings of the righteous will be recounted in the judgment, although possibly everything may be vividly called to mind. This remembrance is, however, not to be construed as a new judgment, since they have been justified and have washed their robes and made them white in the blood of the Lamb. There are many passages which indicate that the good deeds of the righteous will be revealed, and when the believers examine themselves in the light of that revelation they will be enabled better to understand the greatness of God's

[150]Notice that the noun *βῆμα* is used both in Rom. 14 and 2 Cor. 5.

grace and holy love together with their own unworthiness and the eternal blessedness of their salvation. The deeds of the ungodly will also be made known both to themselves individually and publicly, the latter in so far as it is necessary to set forth the righteous judgment of the Lord. God will not simply leave them to condemnation, He will also punish them in accordance with their deeds, c) *Promulgatio sententiae,* or the promulgation of the sentence. This will be equivalent to a *confirmatio* for the resurrected souls and in a sense also for the transformed, inasmuch as the judgment corresponds to their former state, but the judgment will also be a *judicium retributionis.* The Scriptures do not make specific mention of the character of the different rewards and punishments, but we can be assured that God will deal justly. The states of eternal salvation and damnation for the godly and the ungodly are set forth so clearly in Scripture that it is unnecessary for us to speculate on the details of the rewards and the punishments.

4) The day of judgment. Opinions are divided with regard to the duration of the judgment, but it is evident that one day will be the last day and one judgment the final judgment. Whether the judgment will be carried out during the course of an ordinary day or take longer, it is difficult to determine in an absolute sense. The ordinary interpretation combines the day of the Lord and the day of judgment. But if one of these two expressions refer to a period, the second has the same meaning. The theologians who accept the doctrine of a millennium after the second advent say that there will be judgments both before and after this period, indeed some declare that the whole period constitutes the day of the Lord. According to these theologians the final judgment will take place after the millennium. Bring, a Swedish theologian, says: "The final judgment combined with the resurrection of the dead and the separation of the blessed from the damned cannot take place before the tares and the wheat that grow on the great field of the kingdom of God, viz., the world, have grown to maturity. As would appear from various prophecies, this final harvest will be preceded by a relative victory in the kingdom of God on earth, growing out of frightful struggles between the powers of darkness

and light."[151] Other theologians, who hold this view, take the position that a judgment will take place at the coming of the Lord, when the faithful will be judged as well as those then living, while the judgment after the millennium will be a judgment of the ungodly, who will then be raised up, and, of course, upon all who have lived during that period. We have set forth this view in the interest of completeness. Whatever may be the course of events in the days of prophetical fulfillment, the day of judgment will come at the appointed time. Paul says: "He hath appointed a day in which he will judge the world in righteousness" (Acts 17:31).

There are many references in the Bible to the day of Jehovah, which is the great day, when He shall be revealed on earth. During nearly 1900 years there has not occurred any visible appearance of the absent Lord. The Church of God is waiting for the Redeemer, who will also be the judge of the world. But during these years of expectancy, silence reigns. We experience the spiritual presence of God and angels and see their presence in the effects of their influence, and we realize God's active nearness and work in us through the means of grace. In the Lord's Supper we partake of the body and blood of our Saviour. According to 1 Cor. 11:26 this Sacrament is celebrated not only as a remembrance of the Lord, but also to remind us of His return. The signs are many that the second coming is not very far distant. Lukewarm Christians and the worldly people dread the day of the Lord. But the Bible chapters and verses relating to the event are so clear that there is no denying the explicit statements concerning the second advent and the judgment day. We have already quoted the leading passages in section 42. Compare also the note to History of Dogma in the same section. The Old Testament is full of passages referring to the great day of Jehovah. We cannot quote the many passages; if so, we should begin with Numbers 24:17, concerning the "Scepter out of Israel," or Deut. 32, which Delitzsch calls "a key to all prophecy." Study all the prophets and even the five books of the Psalms. Joel describes the day of Jehovah five times. Read the vivid description or portraiture in 3:17-16 and compare

---

[151] *Den kristliga trosläran*, II. §182.

all the parallel ideas of the other prophets. Read comparatively Isaiah 63:1-6; Zech. 1-8; Rev. 14:17-20 and 19:11-21. Studying all the events that are scheduled to take place on the Lord's day, it is evident that the day of Jehovah is not a day of twenty-four hours. "For a thousand years in thy sight are but as yesterday, when it is past, and as a watch in the night" (Ps. 90:4). The period or aeon in which we live is also called man's day, and it has lasted thousands of years. Compare also John 5:25, where this age is called an hour, and that hour still continues. At the second advent the day of man ends and the Lord's day begins. The events on the Lord's day are partly described in Rev. 4-21. Although the Lord's day is a judgment day (1 Thess. 5:2, 3) and a rule with a rod of iron, we should not forget that it is also a day of consolation and restoration (Acts 3:19-21), nor fail to notice the expression, "seasons of refreshing from the presence of the Lord" and "the times of restoration." These seasons and times imply a period and not an ordinary day. When the Lord returns to realize the practical redemption and to judge the world, the work of restoration, judging and ruling will not be executed in haste, but in a manner which will convince every being, angelic and human, that God's mercy and justice are immutable and in every detail correct.

3. The Object of the Judgment.

Baier says that *finis judicii extremi* is the honor of the divine wisdom, power, goodness and retributive righteousness.[152] The day of judgment will prove that the divine government was all-wise, that God's power was almighty, that His goodness surpasses the thought of man and that He judges justly. The righteousness and justice of God in all His ways will appear in the history of the world, of the Church, and of every individual. — The day of judgment will also mark the end of the present world order, and the kingdom of God will be revealed as an eternal kingdom of glory, forever separated from the kingdom of evil. "Glory and power belong to our God: for true and righteous are his judgments!" (Rev. 19:1, 2).

---

[152] Comp. Theol., I, Cap. X, §XVII.

§45. The End of the World.

When the final judgment has taken place, then the present world both as *κόσμος* and *ἀιών* in its present form will be destroyed and succeeded by new cosmic conditions and by the aeon of aeons or *ἀιών τῶν ἀιώνων*. The earth and the heavens will be so completely changed by the fires of destruction and purification that they will appear as a new earth and a new heaven. The end of the world is therefore also the beginning of the world. This will be a new genesis, a new paradise, and an eternal heaven.

1. The Destruction of the World.

In the Scriptures there are three words rendered by "world," viz., *γῆ*, earth, *κόσμος*, external order, harmony, form, etc., but not substance, and *ἀιῶν*, meaning world-age, a protracted period and also eternity. The word *ἀιῶν* is the expression most generally used in the Scriptures to indicate the end of the world. When it is stated in Matt. 24:35 that "heaven and earth shall pass away," the Greek verb *παρέρχομαι* is used. This verb means to go past, to pass by, to pass from one place to another, as a ship sailing from one port to another. It never implies annihilation. The idea which it conveys is a passing by, a change, a transformation. In this passage the verb means that great changes will be wrought and an entire transformation, but does not imply total destruction and annihilation. A comparative study of 2 Peter 3:5, 6 will shed light on the subject. The latter verse reads: "By which means the world that then was, being overflowed with water, perished." There the strong expression *ἀπώλετο* is used, but the earth was not destroyed in the sense that it was annihilated, but the whole human race perished save those in the ark. Another analogy may be pointed out in the expressions which are used in relation to the renewal of man, e.g., as in the Scripture passage: "The old things are passed away; behold, they are become new" (2 Cor. 5:17). In this process man is not annihilated, he is thoroughly changed. The transformation in creation spoken of in Matt. 19:28 is called the regeneration (*παλιγγενεσία*). Compare 2 Peter 3:10 and 12: "The heavens shall pass away with a great noise, and the elements shall be dissolved with fervent heat, and the earth and the works that are therein shall be burned up." In this verse the verbs παρέρχομαι and λύω are used. The latter verb means to loose, to dissolve, etc. Compare its use in relation to Lazarus in John 11:44. Also compare Rom. 8:20-22. Also in this connection we may cite Eccles. 1:4: "The earth abideth forever." The conclusion is, therefore, that a thorough purification and transformation shall take place in the earth through fire. An analogy may be found in the relation between the old body of man and the resurrection body. It is a new body and yet it is the old by reason of the identity between them. The earth and the heavens shall perish through fire, which means a transformation and not a total annihilation.

2. The Restoration of All Things.

As a man through the regeneration will be restored to his original state, which will be reached through the resurrection and the transformation, so there will be a restoration in creation. "For the creation was subjected to vanity, not of its own will, but by reason of him who subjected it, in hope that the creation itself also shall be delivered from the bondage of corruption into the liberty of the glory of the children of God" (Rom. g: 20, 21). Compare Rev. 21: 1, where we read of a new heaven and a new earth as a result of the transformation through fire. The times of the restoration shall begin with the second coming of our Lord. Compare the following: "And that he may send the Christ who hath been appointed for you, even Jesus: whom the heaven must receive until the times of the restoration of all things, whereof God spake by the mouth of his holy prophets" (Acts 3: 20, 21). Note especially that "times" is used. This restoration does not, however, imply that all men are to be saved, inasmuch as in the world of liberty the principles of freedom are in effect. The ungodly have of their own free will and determination rejected the way of salvation. Therefore, Gehenna will remain, but Gehenna and its inhabitants will not serve as a disturbing factor in the new world. The universe is large and Gehenna will be located in a detached place. Even in the intermediate state there was a great gulf fixed between the blessed and the ungodly in Hades, and it is therefore probable that the gulf will be still greater in the eternal state. The restoration merely implies that God will complete His plan of salvation in relation to those who will constitute the new humanity. The new earth will be a paradise and the heavens will be more brilliant than ever. The New Jerusalem will come down out of the heaven from God and be located somewhere near the earth (Rev. 21:10). The throne of God and of the Lamb will be therein, and from there God will rule the entire kingdom of glory with its many mansions (Rev. 22:3-6).

3. Notes on the History of Dogma.

During the first period the position was taken that the world was to be purified and transformed through fire. Generally it was taught, therefore, that the earth and the heavens were not to be totally destroyed in the world conflagration. The same moderate view was held during the Reformation period. However, the old Dogmaticians took the position that the end of the world meant a total annihilation. The newer Dogmaticians indeed teach the dissolution of the world through fire, but do not understand by this an annihilation of the very substance, but merely such a thorough transformation as is necessary for the new creation.

Justin Martyr speaks of a destruction through fire. Irenaeus taught that the world would be changed as to its form, but the material substance would remain. Tertullian also supported the theory of transformation. Clement of Alexandria held the same view. Cyprian considered that the world would finally grow old and perish in the seventh millennium. Origen said that the world conflagration would not destroy but merely cleanse the substance of the created world. However, he taught the restoration of all things in the sense that all men and even Satan would finally be saved.

Lactantius states that the world would be transformed after the millennium. Augustine says that the world conflagration would not destroy the material substance, but merely the form of the elements. During the conflagration the righteous will be preserved in the higher regions or else they will be like unto the three men in the fiery furnace.

No real development in the dogma took place during the Catholic Scholastic period. It was generally taught that the world would be destroyed and renewed through fire.

Luther said the heavens and the earth would be changed as a garment is cleansed. The world would then take on a festive garb and be glorified in correspondence with the glorified bodies of the redeemed. Gerhard says that the world would be destroyed *non per renovationem ac qualitatum immutationem, sed per substantialem abolitionem*. Quenstedt says expressly that the world conflagration does not imply a change, but an annihilation. Baier sets forth that the substance will be totally destroyed. Hollazius defines as follows: "The end of the world is the act of the Triune God, through which by means of fire He will destroy and annihilate the whole fabric of heaven and earth together with all created things with the exception of intelligent creatures, to the honor of His truth, power and Justice, and to the redemption of the elect."

Thomasius teaches that the world shall be dissolved by the fire of judgment as to its elements and transformed into a new world where the new humanity will dwell. Seiss states that the destruction of the world merely implies a transformation through fire and not a total annihilation, and that the new earth must therefore be identical with the present earth. In accordance with Eccles. 1:4, he emphasizes the fact that the earth will abide forever. He also calls attention to the promise of God to Noah as contained in Gen. 8:21, 22. Among other arguments he uses the following: The fact that the earth and the heaven fled away from the face of Him who sat upon the great white throne (Rev. 20:11) does not imply that the material world disappeared entirely, inasmuch as later John saw that the sea gave up its dead, etc. Seiss also presents an unusual view in stating that the earth shall be inhabited by men just as now, and does not therefore teach that the resurrected and transformed shall dwell upon the new earth. The latter will dwell in heaven and in the new Jerusalem and from there rule over the earth and the heavens. He quotes Eph. 3:21; Joel 3:20; Ezek. 37:25 ff.; Isa. 65:17-25 and Rev. 21:24. However, he does not explain how men are to be preserved during the world conflagration. Other

American theologians also declare that the end of the world does not imply a total annihilation.[153] This view seems to be the position adopted by the majority of theologians both in the Lutheran and the Reformed Churches. — With regard to the doctrine of the restoration of all things (*χρόνων ἀποκαταστάσεως πάντων*) in the wrong sense it may be stated that this view has found defenders at the close of the Protestant Scholastic period and also during the modern period. We would mention Petersen, Hahn, Oetinger, and especially Schleiermacher. But confessional theologians in general have taken the correct position on this doctrine, setting forth how the wrong view lacks Scriptural foundation and a reasonable basis, provided the principle of freedom is to be maintained and the demands of divine justice are to be satisfied. If compassion would wish that antinomy could cease, we may be assured that God has a deeper sympathy than the most tender human heart. When God is absolute love, most gracious, merciful and just, we should be satisfied with the explicit statements in the Bible and not criticize the divine mercy and justice. God's government is all-wise.

§46. Eternal Damnation.

The final judgment is accompanied by an eternal separation of the good from the evil, which is indeed a comforting thought, but at the same time it implies that the men who have rejected the means of salvation will forever be cast together with the evil spirits into Gehenna, the place prepared for the devil and his angels. This is a terrifying thought and a fearful reality. The necessity of such a state of damnation is to be explained by the autonomy of the relative personality in the light of the righteousness of the absolute personality. When God created man in His image and endowed him with self-consciousness and self-determination there was indeed a certain risk that man might fall,—this God could not avoid. But

[153]Jacobs, *Elements of Religion*, p. 223. Weidner, *N. T. Theology*. Vol. I, pp. 236-238.

man cannot justly regret the autonomy which freedom provides, inasmuch as the creation of the personality carried with it inestimable privileges for time and eternity, if man would but permit his power of self-determination to be moved by the will of God. God has done everything that can be done to prepare the way to eternal salvation. Some have objected and stated that by reason of His foreknowledge in relation to every individual God ought to interfere and prevent the birth of every person of whom He knew that they would reject the means of salvation. But how can we speak of foreknowing the state and conditions of men who have never existed? This objection, furthermore, presupposes a determinism and an arbitrariness in the divine essence which do not correspond to God's holy love and wisdom. If there had been any possibility of preventing eternal damnation, the great God of love would certainly have interfered. Apart from the laws which rule in the realm of personality, it is impossible for God in His almightiness to do anything which would militate against His righteousness.

1. Eternal Death.

Eternal Death is *the everlasting separation from God together with the loss of eternal life, but implies an etettial existence and suffering as a punishment for sin and especially unbelief.*

The following proofs are presented to show that the sufferings are eternal: 1)The clear teachings of Scripture. It is unnecessary to recount the passages which relate to this matter. However, it may be pointed out that Christ Himself has repeatedly spoken of Gehenna and the eternal duration of the suffering of the damned. Since we believe that the canonical Scriptures are inspired, the evidence is quite sufficient; 2) the punitive righteousness of God cannot be appeased in any other way than the Scriptures set forth, and the way of salvation was open during the period of grace; 3) sin was committed against the loving God, whose goodness man despised by rejecting the means of salvation; 4) inasmuch as man continued in the evil of his heart under the best influences during the period of grace, it is evident that with the conditions surrounding him in

Gehenna there will be no hope of salvation; 5) because no new valid and just test or trial can be conducted either in Hades or in Gehenna, since the proper conditions are not there to be found; 6) the same expressions are used for eternity both in relation to salvation and damnation. If the former is eternal, so must the latter be; 7) the vicarious atonement of Christ, when He suffered the essence of the eternal punishments of Gehenna in dereliction on the cross, proved that those who die in unbelief shall suffer the eternal punishments, because in case the sufferings in hell were limited to a certain time, an aeon or several aeons, there had been no necessity for Christ to experience the pangs of hell to cover the eternal sufferings of mankind. If the wicked are sentenced only like prisoners in this world and given some years of suffering in a penitentiary, then the great suffering of Jesus Christ would be inexplicable.

The proofs are strengthened by reason of the significance of the Greek expressions *αἰών* and *αἰώνιος*. The word is derived from ἀεί and ὤν, always existing. The Latin *aevum* comes from attic. From *aevum* is derived *aeviternus* and by *synchope aeternus*. According to Aristotle, *αἰών* means an eternal or never-ending existence. The word is sometimes used in other senses, but this is its real meaning. The Septuagint makes use of *αἰών* and *αἰώνιος* as a translation of the Hebrew *olam*. Gesenius says that *olam* means eternity and that its full meaning is evident in such passages as describe the nature and existence of God. In the New Testament the word *αἰών* occurs over a hundred times. In the majority of cases where it occurs it is used with the preposition εἰς to mean eternity. The plural form has the same significance. When *αἰών* is used to designate this world the demonstrative pronoun *οὗτος* or the preposition ἐν is used in connection with the singular instead of the plural number of the noun. Compare the following passages where *αἰών* is used in relation to the everlasting punishments: 2 Peter 2:17; Jude 13; Rev. 14:11; 19:3; 20:10. *Αἰώνιος* occurs about seventy times and means never-ceasing, everlasting existence. With regard to the eternal punishments, compare the following Scripture passages: Matt. 18:8; 25:41; 25:46; Mark 3:29; 2 Thess. 1:9; Heb. 6:2; Jude 7. Note especially these words of the Lord: "And these shall go away into eternal punishment (εἰς κόλασιν αἰώνιον), but the righteous into eternal life (εἰς ζωὴν αἰώνιον)" (Matt. 25:46). Matt. 12:32 also proves that the punishment is eternal: "It shall not be forgiven him, neither in this world, nor in that which is to come (οὗτος ἐν οὔτε ἐν τούτῳ τῶ αἰῶνι οὔτε ἐν τῷ μέλλοντι)."

Gehenna, the place where the eternal punishment is to be endured, is mentioned twelve times in the New Testament.[154] It is especially noteworthy that Christ Himself uses it eleven times. It is self-evident that Christ would not have used the expression and the severe utterances concerning eternal punishments, if Gehenna were not a reality, to which place Satan, the devils and the wicked would be finally sentenced. Christ as Son of God knew the truth as to the future world. He died to save all who would believe in Him. When we consider His intense love and His earnest warnings, it is an awful satanic delusion by which many are led astray to disbelieve the plain teachings of the Word of God.

2. The Character of the Eternal Punishments.

Poenas damnatorum are divided as follows: 1) *privativae*: a) the loss of the beatific vision of God; Matt. 22:13; 25:41; b) separation from the society of the good; Matt. 8:12; 25:46; c) exclusion from the heavenly light and rest; Matt. 25:30; 2 Thess. 1:6, 8, 9; d) the loss of all sympathy; Isa. 66:24; Luke 16:24, 25; e) without any hope of deliverance and therefore despair; Luke 16:25, 26; Mark 9:48; 2) *positivae*: A) *internae*: a) the indescribable anguish of soul; Mark 9:44, 46, 48; b) the damned will acknowledge with their intellect the justice of the divine judgment and yet in their heart burn with hatred toward God; Luke 16:25; 2 Thess. 1:6; Matt. 25:24; B) *externae*, which nevertheless imply internal sufferings; a) association with evil and tormenting spirits; Matt. 25:41; b) association with the damned; Rev. 21:8; c) a most foul dwelling place; Matt. 25:30; Mark 9:43, 47; d) a fire that is never quenched, which burns, but does not consume; Rev. 14:10, 11; 20:15. If the fire is not material in the temporal sense,

---

[154] *Γέενα* occurs in the following passages: Matt. 5:29, 30; 10:28; 23:15, 33; Mark 9:43, 45; Luke 12:5; Matt. 5:22; 18:9; Mark 9:47; James 3:6.

still there is a real correspondence. There was no other word in human language which could express the matter. The bodies will be pneumatic and the fire will correspond in nature. This fire may, however, be real in a deeper sense than we put into the expression. What we call the spiritual world possesses greater reality than the so-called material world. The pneumatic bodies cannot perish as the present material bodies. With regard to the fire it is stated that it will not be quenched. Inasmuch as it is not only the soul which is cast into Gehenna, but also the body, so the eternal punishments involve sufferings not only for the soul, but also for the body. Compare Matt. 5:29, 30; 10:28; Mark 9:47, 48.

3. Notes on the History of Dogma.

During the first period, except for Origen, it was taught that the punishments of Gehenna were eternal. During the following period it was likewise taught that the punishments were eternal, although there were some who taught differently, such as Gregory of Nyssa, who held the view of Origen, and Arnobius, who taught that the ungodly were annihilated after terrible sufferings. The Scholastics held the doctrine of eternal punishments, but John Scotus Erigena accepted the doctrine of Origen with regard to the final restoration of all things. The Reformers taught that the punishments are eternal. The seventeenth article of the Augsburg Confession sets forth that Christ will on the last day condemn the ungodly and the devils to be tormented without end. The doctrine of the Anabaptists was condemned. These taught that there would be an end of the punishments of the condemned men and devils. All confessional theologians embrace the doctrine of eternal punishments. In modern times the opinions are divided. Schleiermacher and others reject the doctrine of eternal punishments in Gehenna. There are even sects, such as the Universalists, who believe and confess that all men will finally be saved. The fact that prominent men in different denominations have defended the doctrine of at least an extension of the period of grace after death, while some have expressed the hope that the dualism of eternity might finally be dissolved, has led to a more thorough investigation of the meaning of the words *αἰών* and *αἰώνιος*. Indeed the question has been discussed in its entirety. The result has been the confirmation of the truth of the old orthodox position.

Clement of Rome taught that there is no room for repentance after death. He also taught that the punishments of Gehenna are eternal. Barnabas set forth the doctrine of eternal death. Ignatius wrote to the Ephesians that whoever destroyed faith by false teaching would be subject to the punishments of unquenchable fire. Justin Martyr declared with great emphasis that the ungodly would be punished continuously and be subjected to eternal torments. Tatian also said that the punishments are eternal. Irenaeus also emphasized the teaching that the sufferings of Gehenna are eternal, and declared that those persons are without understanding who set forth the divine goodness but forget the judgment. Tertullian describes the suffering as aeternae poenae in an eternal fire, which burns the damned but does not consume them. Origen acknowledged that the Scriptures speak of eternal punishment, and believed that God permitted the presentation of such a doctrine in order to terrify men and keep them from sin, but he rejected the doctrine of eternal punishment. He also stated that all are not punished alike and that the aim and purpose of the punishments was repentance. He entertained the hope that even Satan would finally be saved.

Lactantius states that the ungodly after the millennium will be raised up unto everlasting suffering, that their bodies will not be destroyed, being unlike their former earthly bodies, and that they, therefore, will continue in anguish and fire throughout eternity. Athanasius declared that there was no hope for the ungodly and that they would be consigned to the same fire as the devil and his angels. Chrysostom states that there will be no end to the sufferings of Gehenna. Jerome calls the sufferings *aeterna tormenta* and says that those who once enter the place of torment will never be released. Augustine speaks of perpetua mors and states that there will be no end of the sufferings of the damned; but he leaves the question undecided as to whether the fire and the worm refer to spiritual or physical torments.

John Scotus Erigena stated that the state of the damned is one of repentance, but speaks of an eternal consciousness of sin, although he taught that all men would finally be saved. Thomas Aquinas believed that the fire was material. Inasmuch as man had sinned against an eternal God, therefore the punishment would be eternal. The intensive character of the punishment is transformed into an extensive punishment.

Luther taught clearly that the punishment of the ungodly is eternal. He says that the condemned will die eternally (*ewiglich sterben*) together with the devil and his angels. Farrar in England has misinterpreted Luther's view. The famous letter of Luther used by Farrar deals with the question as to whether anyone who dies without faith can be saved and contains nothing concerning the cessation of the eternal punishments. He deals with the prospects of those who in this life never had an opportunity of acquiring faith and sets forth God's power to provide such opportunity, but he does not say that God does so (*aber class er es thut, kann man nich beweisen*). The old Dogmaticians, of course, taught that the punishments are eternal. Gerhard and Quenstedt said that the fire was immaterial and that the torments would be in accordance with the character of the sins. Hollazius stated that the fire was immaterial and that there were degrees of suffering. *Poena damni* is alike for all, but *poena sensus* depends upon the number and character of the sins.

Schleiermacher does not accept the doctrine of eternal punishments, holding that as the damned became accustomed to the torments the poignancy of torture would be reduced or cease. He held further that pangs of conscience must imply reformation, and that the bliss of the redeemed would be disturbed by the sufferings of the damned. He supports the doctrine of the restoration of all things and therefore also the view that all men will finally be saved. In recent times the doctrine of annihilation has again made its appearance in theology. Some accept a modified view of the doctrine, stating that the ungodly suffer after death, but that finally the fire of suffering destroys the sinner so that he no longer exists. Some Adventists believe that the ungodly are annihilated, while others state that they never arise but remain forever in the sleep of death. 'The so-called Evangelical Adventists teach that the ungodly arise and that they are condemned unto everlasting torment. Ballou, who is called the father of Universalism (although Relly and Murray were the original founders), taught that there will be no suffering in the life after this. They reject the doctrine of eternal punishments. Maurice in England also rejected this doctrine. Farrar sets forth the hope of the possibility of repentance after death. He does not assume the doctrinal position of the Universalists dogmatically, but he rejects the doctrine of annihilation, conditional immortality and purgatory. However, he makes violent attacks on the orthodox position, rejects the doctrine of eternal suffering and in fact accepts the universalist position. There have also in recent times arisen powerful defenders of the orthodox view. Such lexicographers and exegetes as Gesenius, Cremer, Meyer, Alford, Ellicott and others state clearly that the doctrine of eternal punishments is based upon the evident teaching of the Word of God. Many opinions could be cited. Among theologians in Sweden, M. Johansson has clearly proven that *αἰώνιος* means eternity in its fullest sense. Just as surely as the blessedness of the faithful is unlimited as to time, so surely is the condemnation of the ungodly unlimited and eternal.

§47. Eternal Salvation.

The Paradise of God that was lost has been regained, the gates of the New Jerusalem are open to the children of God, and the way has been prepared to the tree of life at the river of water of life. Joyfully we turn our eyes from the outer darkness to the eternal world of light and to the many mansions of our Father in heaven. In eternity there is but one place of darkness, although it has many inhabitants, while the number of the mansions of light is greater than we know. Heaven is the common name of the mansions of the blessed. Of course, there is a heaven where God is enthroned and a great city of God to which the blessed have access. The kingdom of God is a great kingdom, the kingdom of eternal life. Human words fall far short of describing the glory of the life which is everlasting. The definitions and terms used in Dogmatics do not suffice, but constitute an earnest attempt to set forth the final goal to be realized in the eternal kingdom of God.

1. Eternal Life.

Eternal Life is *the life lived in communion with God, finally realized not only in an internal but also in an external sense in the greatest and most perfect fullness of life, which the children of God enjoy eternally after having received their glorified bodies either through resurrection or translation in the great regeneration and thereby admitted to the land of the living, where they shall behold and serve God eternally.*

The eternal life of the Christian begins in the kingdom of grace through regeneration. The Christians therefore possess eternal life now, but this new life grows and develops gradually during our earthly life and in the departure at death (*ἀναλύσις*) is transferred to the Paradise of God, but reaches its full fruition only in the resurrection. Compare John 17:3; 11:25; Phil. 1:23; 2 Tim. 4:6; Col. 3:3, 4. Life in its fullest sense is enjoyed only in the blessedness of eternity, inasmuch as man will then be restored to himself as originally planned. There, perfect harmony will rule internally and externally, because the image of God will then be perfectly restored.

The old Dogmaticians, such as Quenstedt and others, state that all the redeemed will possess and enjoy the fullness of life and eternal salvation and that the difference between the saints will be *non essentialis, sed accidentalis*. There will be simply differences in God's gracious rewards in accordance with His righteous judgment. Quenstedt says that there will be a difference in relation to the external glory and position (*sessio*) in the kingdom. Compare Daniel 12:2; Matt. 25:21; 1 Cor. 3:14; 15:41, 42.

2. The Blessings of Everlasting Salvation.

The attributes of everlasting salvation are divided as follows: 1) *privativa*: a) deliverance from sin and its consequences; Eph. 5:27; Rev. 19:8; 21:4; b) deliverance from the fear of death, for death is no more; Isa. 25:8; Hosea

13:14; 1 Cor. 15:26; Rev. 21:4; c) the absence of the imperfections and distressing experiences of life; Rev. 7:16,17; 1 Cor. 6:13; 15:43; Rev. 21:4; 2) *positiva*: A) *interna*: a) the perfect enlightenment of the intellect; 1 Cor. 13:9, 10; b) complete rectitude of the will; Eph. 4:24; 5:27; c) the sense of security in all eternity; John 16:22; Rom. 8:38, 39; d) a spiritual body with heavenly properties, which is in *ubi definitive,* but can move swiftly from place to place, a body not subject to suffering, beautiful and indestructible; Matt. 22:30; 13:43; Luke 20:36; 1 Cor. 15:44, 47; Phil. 3:21; B) *externa*: a) association with the Triune God; John 12:26; 14:3; 17:24; 1 Thess. 4:17; Rev. 21:3; b) association with the blessed, both known and at present unknown; Matt. 8:11; Luke 13:29; Heb. 12:23; c) association with angels; Heb. 12:22; d) a most glorious abode; John 14:2, 3; Heb. 11:16; Rev. 21:27; e) an occupation corresponding to the state of eternal glory; Rev. 3:11, 12; 3:21; 22:3-6.

Viewed even from the negative or the privative standpoint, eternal salvation is a most inexpressibly blessed state. The hope of complete deliverance from sin and all its consequences is sufficient to fill our hearts with the greatest joy. When, in addition, we contemplate the positive blessings, then the heavenly glory indeed surpasses all human thought. We are not now capable of comprehending the joy of life such as it will be experienced in a spiritually and physically sound organism in the midst of an environment of perfect glory and with a suitable occupation. Man would not be happy without some occupation. Therefore in eternity he will honor God, serve Him in accordance with His commands, varied with the constantly changing joys of association with the inhabitants of heaven, while he is privileged to contemplate with perfect vision and understanding the miracles of God in all the wide universe. The Scriptures do not mention specifically in what the occupation of the saints in glory will consist, but state that they will glorify and serve God and also that they will rule with Him. There is, however, no detailed explanation given of the character of this rule in eternity.

Exegetes who hold that humanity will continue to be propagated on the new earth believe that the saints shall rule on the new earth. But it is a speculation based on the repeopling of the earth after the flood and also upon Rev. 22:2, where it is stated in regard to the tree of life: "And the leaves of the tree were for the healing of the nations." In such a case Paradise would be restored on the new earth, and the people on earth would in due times be changed and translated to heaven. Others hold the view that the redeemed will live on the new earth. But then the question arises: Who will be the subjects, if all the saints belong to the royal priesthood? Another question would be presented, whether the new earth as a dwelling place of all the saved would be larger than the present. It is stated in Rev. 21:1: "And the sea is no more." The renewed earth will probably have the same size as the old, but, if there be no oceans, the habitable earth will be larger. But would the new earth be sufficiently large as a dwelling place for all the saved? If the saints shall rule over the angelic host in the many worlds of the universe, there will be ample room, but the old home, the new earth, rich in memories, will often be visited by the saints who are rulers in other spheres of the universal kingdom. The saints are kings and the Lord is King of kings. While the full character of the reign is not revealed in detail, it is clearly stated that the ruling saints "shall reign for ever and ever."

The highest degree of blessedness consists in the communion and association with God and in the fulfilling of His will. We must nevertheless count as one of the most blessed experiences in heaven the association with those that were near and dear to us on earth, provided they are saved, and also with all who are of the household of God and the communion of saints. It is not necessary to prove that those who knew each other in the Church militant will recognize each other in the Church triumphant; this lies in the nature of the case. It would almost seem that we shall also know saints with whom we were unacquainted on the earth, perhaps through spiritual intuition. In comparing Matt. 17:3 we find that the disciples recognized Moses and Elias. When the rich man in Hades lifted up his eyes he recognized Abraham afar off in Paradise. It is evident that at least relatives and friends will know each other in heaven. Compare Matt. 8: 11. Also the following: "They may receive you into the eternal tabernacles—*εἰς τὰς αἰώνιος σκηνάς*" (Luke 16:9). But in John 14:2 the mansions in heaven are called *μοναί* or permanent and solid buildings. We cannot now tell where these heavenly mansions are or will be located. According to the promise of the Lord we expect new heavens. There is nothing to be gained by speculating in a matter that is beyond our power of comprehension and discovery, as has been done, for instance, in the conjecture that Paradise is located on the star Alcyone in the Pleiades. We have made mention of the fact that the Paradise of God is located in the third heaven, in accordance with the words of Paul in Cor. 12:2-4. In accordance with Rev. 21:1, 2, however, the capital city of the new kingdom, the New Jerusalem, will be located not far from the new earth, while the kingdom of heaven will include all the glorious mansions in all the universe of God.

Although we cannot geographically locate Paradise, where the blessed now dwell during the intermediate state, it cannot be a place outside of the visible universe, considering that man, created in the image of God, lives on earth and that the Son of God lived here and shall return when the appointed time comes. Still the heavenly land may be far away according to human calculations. "Thine eyes shall see the king in his beauty: they shall behold a land that reacheth afar" (in Hebrew, the land of far distance), Isaiah 33:17. We can never measure the length of these distances. No telescope has as yet discovered all the stellar worlds, and probably never will. But it is interesting to study the distance to the nearest stars, which proves that there are immense spaces between the solar systems. Alpha Centauri is as far as now known the nearest star to us. As it is not easy to calculate the distance in miles or to make it clear to our understanding, if we say nearly twenty-five million millions of miles, astronomers use another unit in dealing with the distance of the so-called fixed stars, namely, the light year. If light travels about 185,000 miles a second, a ray of light from Alpha Centauri would not reach the earth in less than four years and three months. Then think of the distance from the next nearest, such as 61 Cygni, Sirius and *μ* Cassiopeiae. And then speculate or try to calculate the distance to Orion, Polaris, Pleiades and stars in the Milky Way. The stars are to us innumerable. Herschel examined only one 250th part of the sky. In his telescope (magnifying power 120) he estimated that in one field he had seen 116,000 stars. And at another occasion he calculated that 258,000 stars had passed in forty-one minutes. Astronomers have estimated by the use of the best reflectors that twenty millions of stars or more have passed in review. We may be assured that the many solar systems, which roll and shine in the empyrean, are not wasting their light upon empty space. There are plenty of homes in the stellar universe for the great orders of angels: thrones, dominions, principalities and powers. And there are and will be many grand mansions in the great heaven for the children of God or the kings of and from earth. When the present universe is so grand and magnificent, who can describe the new or renewed heaven? No pen can portray the vistas of glory that shall open before the saints when they take possession of the kingdom. This heavenly kingdom shall cover the whole universe with the exception of Gehenna. We have already mentioned that the capital shall be the New Jerusalem. This capital of the kingdom of God is described in Rev. 21-22:1-5. This is the City for which Abraham looked, the City whose maker and builder is God. It is the City spoken of in Heb. 11:16; 12:22; 13:14. This City is coming down from heaven to the vicinity of earth and is called, in Gal. 4:26, Jerusalem which is above. When it is stated that the nations on earth shall walk by its light, it is evident that the City is over them. This is one of the reasons why many commentators hold the view that mankind shall continue to be propagated on earth. But it is also possible that saved nations may live on the new earth or that the saints may often visit the earth. The saints of God will also visit the New Jerusalem, and many may have their abode in the capital, attending to such duties as God has commanded them to perform. The New Jerusalem will be the great place of assembly. Although the New Jerusalem is a vast city, all the saved will not constantly live in the capital of the immense kingdom of God. If the faithful saints shall be kings and rule in different parts of the kingdom, this throws light on the statement that the kings of the earth shall bring their glory into the New Jerusalem. It is also stated:

"And the gates thereof shall in no wise be shut by day" (for there shall be no night there), Rev. 21:25. There may be night on earth and in other parts of the universe. The sun, moon and stars will shine. But the new earth will also have light from the New Jerusalem. The nearness of the glory of God shall be as the brightest sun. The new heaven with its solar systems and stars will shine more brilliantly than the old. And in the City of God there is no need of a sun. The New Jerusalem is a large city, when we consider that the length, the breadth and height thereof are equal, twelve thousand furlongs. If the height is 1500 miles, and if the main avenues were a mile above each other, the magnitude would be stupendous. Notice that the wall is 144 cubits "according to the measure of a man, that is, of an angel." Think of the City towering high above the great wall! And look at the foundations, the gates and the wall with the precious stones in different brilliant colors! No human pen can describe heaven. "Things which eye saw not, and ear heard not, and which entered not into the heart of man, whatsoever things God prepared for them that love him" (1 Cor. 2:9).

Inasmuch as finis *beatitudinis humanae,* to use once more an old dogmatic expression, is the honor of the divine goodness, wisdom, fidelity and power, so shall the glorious praise of the multitudes of the redeemed sound before the throne of God and the Lamb: "Unto him that sitteth on the throne, and unto the Lamb, be the blessing, and the honor, and the glory, and the dominion, for ever and ever!" (Rev. 5:13).

Made in the USA
Las Vegas, NV
11 January 2022